D0522469

COPINGER AND SKONE JAMES

on

COPYRIGHT

SECOND CUMULATIVE SUPPLEMENT
to the FIFTEENTH EDITION

00211257

AUSTRALIA
Law Book Co.
Sydney

CANADA and USA
Carswell
Toronto

HONG KONG
Sweet & Maxwell Asia

NEW ZEALAND
Brookers
Wellington

SINGAPORE and MALAYSIA
Sweet & Maxwell Asia
Singapore and Kuala Lumpur

COPINGER AND SKONE JAMES

on

COPYRIGHT

SECOND CUMULATIVE SUPPLEMENT
to the FIFTEENTH EDITION

BY

GILLIAN DAVIES, D.L., Ph.D.
Barrister

GWILYM HARBOTTLE, B.A. (Oxon)
Barrister

THOMSON

™

SWEET & MAXWELL

2007

First edition by W.A. Copinger 1870
Second edition by W.A. Copinger 1881
Third edition by W.A. Copinger 1893
Fourth edition by J.M. Easton 1904
Fifth edition by J.M. Easton 1915
Sixth edition by F.E. Skone James 1927
Seventh edition by F.E. Skone James 1936
Eighth edition by F.E. Skone James 1948
Ninth edition by F.E. & E.P. Skone James 1958
Tenth edition by E.P. Skone James 1965
Eleventh edition by E.P. Skone James 1971
Second imprint by E.P. Skone James 1977
Twelfth edition by E.P. Skone James, John F. Mummery
    and J.E. Rayner James 1980
Thirteenth edition by E.P. Skone James, John F. Mummery,
    J.E. Rayner James and K. M. Garnett 1991
Fourteenth edition by K.M. Garnett, J.E. Rayner James
    and G. Davies 1999
Fifteenth edition by K.M. Garnett, G. Davies and G. Harbottle 2005

Published in 2007 by Sweet & Maxwell Limited
of 100 Avenue Road,
London, NW3 3PF
(www.sweetandmaxwell.co.uk)
Typeset by Sweet & Maxwell's electronic publishing system
Printed and Bound in Great Britain by Athenaeum Press Ltd, Tyne & Wear

No natural forests were destroyed to make this product,
only farmed timber was used and replanted

A CIP catalogue record for this book is available from the British Library

ISBN 978-1-847-03265-2

HOW TO USE THIS SUPPLEMENT

This is the Second Cumulative Supplement to the Fifteenth Edition of *Copinger and Skone James on Copyright*, and has been compiled according to the structure of the main work.

Together with the main Table of Contents, each Chapter has its own mini table of contents which is identical to that preceding the corresponding Chapter of the Main Work. Where a heading in these tables of contents has been marked with the symbol ■, this indicates that there is relevant information in the Supplement to which you should refer.

Within each chapter, updating information is referenced to the relevant paragraph in the main work. New paragraphs which have been introduced in this Supplement have been identified as, *e.g.* 1—30A. Likewise new footnotes which have been introduced in this Supplement have been identified as, *e.g.* 8a. This enables references contained within these paragraphs to be identified in the tables included in this Supplement.

The table of contents for Volume 2 material has been referenced to the relevant section (of the Main Work) and page (of this Supplement).

FOREWORD

In the year since the publication of the first supplement to *Copinger and Skone James on Copyright* developments in the law have continued apace, while policy initiatives, both domestic and European, have continued to proliferate.

This second supplement covers all relevant new international and European developments, including the important cases of *Rafael Hoteles*, *Laserdisken* and *Microsoft* in the CFI. We also deal with significant domestic cases such as *Nova v Mazooma* and *Baigent v Random House* in the Court of Appeal, and the *Peer* litigation. At the same time, the sections on individual industries have been fully updated, in the case of the Music Industry by Allen Dixon, whom we are delighted to welcome on board.

We are equally delighted that Hui Ling McCarthy has been able to take over the Taxation Chapter.

As before, we would like to express our gratitude to Kevin Garnett QC for his assistance as Consulting Editor and to all the Assistant and Specialist Editors named at the front of this volume. We also thank those at Hogarth Chambers who provided valuable assistance with particular Chapters: Nicholas Saunders (Chapter 18), Alexander Learmonth (Chapters 20 and 21) and Victoria Jones (Chapter 28).

Thanks are also due to Christian Zimmerman, Legal and Enforcement Officer, Design and Artists Copyright Society Ltd and Henry Nampandu, PhD student, Centre for Commercial Law Studies, Queen Mary, University of London, for their extensive research. We would also like to thank everyone at Hogarth Chambers for their help and encouragement, especially the clerks and our third six month pupil, Tom St Quintin. Finally we thank the team at Sweet and Maxwell for all their help, support and patience, particularly in dealing with material based on developments which took place after the copy date.

As usual, comments from readers are always very welcome. Please feel free to contact us by email to barristers@hogarthchambers.com (with the word *Copinger* in the subject heading) or by post to Hogarth Chambers, 5 New Square, Lincoln's Inn, London WC2A 3RJ.

Together with the fifteenth edition, this Supplement is available online at Westlaw UK as part of the specific practice area "Westlaw Intellectual Property" service.

We have endeavoured to state the law as of July 31, 2007, but later developments have been incorporated where possible.

Gillian Davies
Gwilym Harbottle

CONTENTS

TABLE OF CASES

References are to paragraph numbers.

TABLE OF STATUTES

References are to paragraph numbers.

TABLE OF STATUTORY INSTRUMENTS

References are to paragraph numbers.

TABLE OF TREATIES

References are to paragraph numbers.

TABLE OF CONVENTIONS

References are to paragraph numbers.

TABLE OF AGREEMENTS

References are to paragraph numbers.

TABLE OF EUROPEAN COMMUNITY LEGISLATION

References are to paragraph numbers.

TABLE OF INTERNATIONAL LEGISLATION

References are to paragraph numbers.

CHAPTER ONE

INTRODUCTION—CLASSIFICATION AND SCOPE OF THE PROTECTION OF COPYRIGHT, RELATED RIGHTS AND DESIGN RIGHTS

NOTE 2. **Delete** and **substitute:** In 2003, the creative industries that are   **1–02**
substantially dependent on copyright represented a major part of the UK
economy, generating 7.8 per cent of Gross Value Added, which is expected to
rise to 10 per cent of the economy in the near future. These industries employed
up to 1.15 million people in 2004 and have grown in the last five years at about
twice the rate of the rest of the economy.[1]

1. CLASSIFICATION OF THE RIGHTS DEALT WITH IN THIS WORK

A. COPYRIGHT GENERALLY

The 1988 Act. Third sentence. **Delete** and **substitute:** A number of other specific   **1–03**
rights provided for by special legislation outside the 1988 Act and having a connection with copyright, such as the Public Lending Right (PLR) and the new
Artist's Resale Right (*Droit de Suite*) are also dealt with.

---

[1] House of Commons Culture, Media and Sport Committee, "New Media and the Creative
Industries", Fifth Report of Session 2006/7 (HC 509–1), May 16, 2006.

B. SUBJECT-MATTER OF THIS WORK

(iv) Rights in performances

Add new paragraph:

(aa) Performers' moral rights

1–14   The WIPO Performers and Phonograms Convention (WPPT) 1996, to which the United Kingdom is a signatory, is the first international treaty to include provisions relating to moral rights for performers. The Treaty requires two moral rights to be afforded to performers, the right to claim to be identified as the performer of a performance (the right to be identified or the right of paternity) and the right to object to any distortion, mutilation or other modification of his performance that would be prejudicial to his reputation (the right to object to derogatory treatment, often referred to as the right of integrity).[2] The Performances (Moral Rights, etc.) Regulations 2006[3] has implemented these provisions in the UK in relation to any type of live performances and to sound recordings of any type of performance, regardless of whether that is made directly from the live performance or indirectly. These new rights are described also in Chapter 12, below.

(v) Design right in original designs

1–16   **Delete and substitute:** Unregistered forms of protection for industrial designs include design right, unregistered European Community design and copyright. A design is, in broad terms, the plan or scheme for the appearance of an article (or a part of an article). It is concerned with what an article looks like or is intended to look like. It is not concerned with how an article performs its function, which is the concern of patent law. Industrial design covers a wide range of activity. An unregistered industrial design may be protected against acts of copying under the following bases: design right, introduced by the 1988 Act; unregistered European Community design under the Community Design Regulation 6/2002 and copyright. These rights are described in Chapter 13, below.

(vi) Miscellaneous other specific rights

Add new paragraph:

(i) Artist's Resale Right.

1–24A   A new intellectual property right, the artist's resale right, previously unknown to the law of the United Kingdom, has been created by The Artist's Resale Right Regulations 2006, which entered into force on February 14, 2006.[4] The new right was introduced in implementation of the European Directive on the resale right for the benefit of the author of an original work of art.[5] Artist's resale right consists in the entitlement of artists to receive a royalty on the resale of their works, provided that an art market professional is involved in that sale and the sale price is above a specified minimum threshold. The minimum threshold established by the Regulations is the equivalent of EUR 1000, and the royalty set

---

[2] WPPT, Art. 5.

[3] SI 2006/18.

[4] SI 2006/346.

[5] Directive 2001/84/EC of the European Parliament and of the Council, dated September 27, 2001.

is four per cent of the sale price. For the time being, the royalty is payable on the sale of works by living artists only. The right lasts for as long as the copyright in the work subsists, which is normally for 70 years after the death of the artist. The right is inalienable. The right is described in a new Chapter 19A, below.

C. INTELLECTUAL PROPERTY RIGHTS NOT DEALT WITH IN THIS WORK

(i) Registered designs

Delete and **substitute:** Design right in original designs, referred to in para. 1–16   **1–25** above, is to be distinguished from the protection conferred on registered designs under the Registered Designs Act 1949, as amended by the Registered Design Regulations 2001, which were introduced in implementation of the EC Directive on the Legal Protection of Designs 1998. A detailed discussion of the law of registered designs is outside the scope of this work but Chapter 13 contains an outline of the relevant law.

(ii) Patents for invention

First paragraph. Fifth sentence. **Delete** and **substitute:** Thus, applicants for   **1–26** patents in the United Kingdom may apply for a national patent at the United Kingdom Patent Office and/or for a European patent at the European Patent Office, designating whichever of the currently 32 Member States of the EPC in which protection is sought, including the United Kingdom, if desired.

Second paragraph. Fifth sentence to end. **Delete** and **substitute:** The European Union, seeking to clarify the issue, in 2004 reached political agreement on a common position on a proposal for a Directive on the patentability of computer implemented inventions, stipulating that for a computer-implemented invention to be patentable it must meet the other requirements of patentability, namely, industrial applicability, novelty and inventive step. However, in July 2005, the European Parliament rejected the Council common position and the legislative procedure was closed. The proposed Directive would have confirmed the present position under the EPC. Meanwhile, the European Patent Office continues its existing practice.

NOTE 20. Second sentence. **Delete** and **substitute:** As of July 31, 2007, the EPO had the following 32 Contracting States: Austria, Belgium, Bulgaria, Cyprus, Czech Republic, Denmark, Estonia, Finland, France, Germany, Greece, Hungary, Iceland, Ireland, Italy, Latvia, Liechtenstein, Lithuania, Luxembourg, Malta, Monaco, Netherlands, Poland, Portugal, Romania, Slovakia, Slovenia, Spain, Sweden, Switzerland, Turkey and the United Kingdom. Norway is expected to become the 33rd Contracting State on January 1, 2008.

(v) Plant Varieties Act 1997

Add: The Patents and Plant Variety Rights (Compulsory Licensing) Regulations   **1–29** 2002, which came into force on March 1, 2002, established a new regulatory framework for compulsory licences and cross-licences between holders of patents and plant breeders' rights. The Regulations implemented in the United Kingdom the provisions of European Directive 98/44/EC on the legal protection of bio-technological inventions[6]; the Directive provides for compulsory licensing of plant breeders' rights and patent rights in circumstances where the existence of one right hinders the acquisition or exploitation of the other right.

---

[6] Art.12.

(vi) Protection of the Olympic and Paralympic Symbols

1–30 First, second and third sentences. **Delete** and **substitute:** The Olympic Symbol, etc. (Protection) Act 1995,[7] as amended by the London Olympic Games and Paralympic Games Act 2006, which entered into force on March 30, 2006, establish the Olympics and Paralympics association rights. The 1995 Act as amended confers exclusive rights in relation to the use of the Olympic symbol, the Olympic motto and certain words associated with the Olympic Games, such as Olympic, Olympiad and Olympian. The right is infringed by any person who, in the course of trade, uses a representation of the Olympic symbol, the Olympic motto or a protected word, or a word so similar to a protected word as to be likely to create in the public mind an association with the Olympic Games or the Olympic movement. The Act provides for certain permitted acts in relation to the right as well as for civil remedies and criminal sanctions in relation to infringement of the right. The 2006 Act creates the same rights, etc. in relation to the Paralympic symbol and motto and certain protected words such as Paralympiad, Paralympian and Paralympic. The Act also makes provision in connection with the Olympic Games and Paralympic Games that are to take place in London in the year 2012.

NOTE 32. **Delete** and **substitute:** The Treaty was open for signature at Nairobi until December 31, 1982, and at Geneva until June 30, 1983. As of July 31, 2006, the Treaty had 46 Member States (for up-to-date status see the WIPO website at *www.wipo.int*).

2. SCOPE OF SUCH RIGHTS GENERALLY

D. TERRITORIALITY AND ENFORCEMENT OF RIGHTS

1–36 **Enforcement.** NOTE 36. **Add:** The OECD estimated in a recent study ("The Economic Impact of Counterfeiting and Piracy", OECD document 2007) that the value of international trade in counterfeit and pirated products could have been up to USD 200 billion in 2005.

E. INTERNATIONAL STANDARDS FOR THE PROTECTION OF COPYRIGHT AND RELATED RIGHTS

(iii) Regional and bilateral treaties

1–40 **Regional treaties.** Second paragraph. **Delete** and **substitute:** There are also a number of Conventions concerned with the protection of copyright and related rights adopted under the auspices of the Council of Europe between 1958 and 2003, which are dealt with at para.24–166 *et seq.*, below.

3. GENERAL SCHEME OF PROTECTION

1–42 **Approaching a copyright problem.** Third paragraph, point 3(a). First sentence. **Delete** and **substitute:** Who was the first owner of the copyright in question (*cf.* Chapter 5.1)?

---

[7] The Olympic Symbol, etc. (Protection) Act 1995 (c.32), brought into force by SI 1995/2472, September 20, 1995.

CHAPTER TWO

NATURE AND HISTORY OF COPYRIGHT

Contents   Para.

1. NATURE OF COPYRIGHT

Ownership of copyright. NOTE 33. **Add:** The new artist's resale right is also   **2–03**
inalienable.

No copyright in ideas. Add: A recent case in this area is the *Da Vinci Code*   **2–06**
case.[1] The claimants asserted that the novel *The Da Vinci Code* was a non-textual
infringement of the copyright in their book *The Holy Blood and the Holy Grail*,
which was presented as a book of non-fiction. They alleged that their book
contained a "central theme" of 15 interconnected points and that this theme had
been infringed. The trial judge held that there was no infringement, finding that
there was actually no central theme to *HBHG* and that the alleged theme of the
claimants was a construct for the litigation.

An appeal against the decision was dismissed.[2] The appeal court agreed with
the trial judge's finding that what the defendant had taken from HBHG amounted
to generalised propositions, at too high a level of abstraction to qualify for copyright protection, because it was not the product of the application of skill and labour by the authors of HBHG in the creation of their literary work. It lay on the
wrong side of the line between ideas and their expression. The court also endorsed
the judge's finding that the central theme was not a theme of HBHG at all, but
rather was no more than a selection of features of HBHG collated for forensic
purposes.

2. HISTORY OF COPYRIGHT

Developments. Add new paragraph: Since the main work was published in 2005,   **2–39**
the 1988 Act has been further amended by Regulation in order to transpose further EC Directives into the law of the United Kingdom. The regulations include:
the Performances (Moral Rights, etc.) Regulations 2006,[3] which entered into
force on February 1, 2006; the Artist's Resale Right Regulations 2006,[4] which
entered into force on February 14, 2006; and the Intellectual Property (Enforcement, etc.) Regulations 2006,[5] which entered into force on April 29, 2006.

The Future. Second paragraph. First two sentences. **Delete** and **substitute:** The   **2–40**
EC harmonisation programme is likely to continue. In October 2005, the Com-

---

[1] *Baigent and Leigh v The Random House Group Limited* [2006] EWHC 719 (Ch).
[2] [2007] EWCA Civ 247.
[3] SI 2006/18.
[4] SI 2006/346.
[5] SI 2006/1028.

mission adopted a recommendation on management of online rights in musical works.[6] The recommendation puts forward measures for improving the EU-wide licensing of copyright for online services. It may be that the recommendation will be followed in due course by a Directive if insufficient progress is made.[7]

Add: The first stage in codifying the *acquis communautaire* was reached in December 2006, when the Rental and Related Rights Directive 92/100/EEC and the Term Directive 93/98/EEC were both repealed and replaced by new codified texts, which take account of amendments made to the two Directives by subsequent EC legislation, such as, for example, the Information Society Directive 2001/29/EC. These new Directives are codifying measures only.[8]

In the past year, the European Commission has published two major studies. The first, published in November 2006, examined the *aquis communautaire* with a view to consolidating it and filling in gaps and inconsistencies in the current legislation.[9] The second, published in February 2007, examined the implementation and effect of the Information Society Directive 2001/29/EC in Member States' laws in the light of the development of the digital market.[10] Both these reports make recommendations for amendments to the *acquis communautaire*. It is to be expected, therefore, that there will be further consultation and that new proposals for legislation to amend the existing Directives and for further harmonisation will be put forward by the Commission in due course.

Meanwhile much attention has been paid in the past year to the intellectual property regime in the United Kingdom. Three major reports affecting copyright and related rights have been published since the first supplement to the 15th Edition of this work was published in late 2006. The conclusions of these reports will influence future UK legislation and the position of the United Kingdom in future discussions on new harmonisation measures within the European Community. These three reports are the following: (1) The Gowers Review of Intellectual Property (the Gowers Review) , published in December 2006; (2) The Review of the Copyright Tribunal, published by the UK Intellectual Property Office in May 2007; and (3) The Report of the House of Commons Culture, Media and Sport Committee, entitled "New Media and the Creative Industries" (HC 509–1, Fifth Report of Session 2006–07).

The Gowers Review was set up by the Government to establish whether the intellectual property system in the UK was "fit for purpose in an era of globalization, digitization and increasing economic specialization". It concluded that the system was not in need of a radical overhaul but suggested that there was room for reform in a number of areas, including some concerning copyright. The specific suggestions and proposals are referred to in this supplement in the context of their subject-matter. Not all the recommendations are within the purview of the UK Government, being subject to EU legislation, but the recommendations are timely in view of the European Commission's own review of the *acquis communautaire*.

The Review of the Copyright Tribunal examines the subject of copyright and the role of the collecting societies. The Review's recommendations are discussed

---

[6] Commission Recommendation of May 18, 2005, on collective cross-border management of copyright and related rights for legitimate online music services (2005/737/EC).

[7] Commission Press Release, IP/05/1261, October 12, 2005.

[8] New Directives 2006/115/EC and 2006/116/EC dated December 27, 2006, see paras 25–52 and 25–62, below.

[9] B. Hugenholtz *et al.*, "The Recasting of Copyright and Related Rights for the Knowledge Economy", Institute for Information Law, University of Amsterdam, November 2006.

[10] L. Guibault and G. Westkamp *et al.*, "Study on the Implementation and Effect in Member States' Laws of Directive 2001/29/EC", Institute for Information Law, University of Amsterdam, in co-operation with the Queen Mary Intellectual Property Research Centre, University of London, February 2007.

in Chapter 28, below, and make some far-reaching proposals for organisational reform of the Copyright Tribunal and its procedures.

The House of Commons report considers the impact on the creative industries of recent and future developments in digital convergence and media technology and the effect on these industries of piracy and counterfeiting as well as unauthorised dissemination of creative content. It considered also the question where the balance should lie between the rights of creators and the expectations of consumers. The report concluded by addressing a series of recommendations to Government, some of which would require amendments to the law of copyright and related rights.

Further legislative initiatives may be foreseen, therefore, to adapt the present law of copyright in the United Kingdom and at the level of the European Union.

CHAPTER THREE

REQUIREMENTS FOR COPYRIGHT PROTECTION

2. SUBJECT MATTER OF PROTECTION

A. Introduction: copyright works

3–06   **What amounts to a "work"?** NOTE 32. *Brighton v Jones* is now reported at [2004] E.M.L.R. 26 and [2005] F.S.R. 16. *Taylor v Rive Droite Music Ltd* went to appeal, but not on this point: [2005] EWCA Civ 300; [2006] E.M.L.R. 4. **Add** at end: *IPC Media Ltd v Highbury-Leisure Publishing Ltd* [2004] EWHC 2985 (Ch); [2005] F.S.R. 20, para.5.

NOTE 34. **Add** at end: In *Coffey v Warner/Chappell Music Ltd* [2005] EWHC 449 (Ch); [2005] F.S.R. 34; [2005] E.C.D.R. 21; [2006] E.M.L.R. 2, para.12,

Blackburne J. accepted that as a general proposition circumstances may exist which justify regarding a constituent part of a larger entity as in itself a copyright work, but stated that that could only be where the part in question could fairly be regarded as so separable from the material with which it was collocated as itself to constitute a copyright work.

NOTE 35. **Add** at end: See also *IPC Media Ltd v Highbury-Leisure Publishing Ltd* [2004] EWHC 2985 (Ch); [2005] F.S.R. 20 at para.23 and *Coffey v Warner/ Chappell Music Ltd* [2005] EWHC 449 (Ch); [2005] F.S.R. 34; [2005] E.C.D.R. 21; [2006] E.M.L.R. 2 at paras 8 to 10.

B. LITERARY WORKS

(ii) Literary works in general

Protected subject matter. NOTE 58. *R Griggs Group Ltd v Evans* is now reported at [2004] F.S.R. 31. The decision has been upheld on appeal: [2005] EWCA Civ 11; [2005] F.S.R. 31; [2005] E.C.D.R. 30. **Add** at end of Note: In *Navitaire Inc v easyJet Airline Co Ltd* [2004] EWHC 1725 (Ch); [2006] R.P.C. 3 at para.80, Pumfrey J. held that it was clear that single words in isolation were not to be considered as literary works.   **3–13**

Add at end of paragraph: In *Navitaire Inc v easyJet Airline Co Ltd* [2004] EWHC 1725 (Ch); [2006] R.P.C. 3 at paragraph 79, Pumfrey J. noted that the definition of literary work in the 1988 Act was new and stated: "When one considers the modern definition (anything written spoken or sung which is not a dramatic or musical work ...) it becomes essential to eschew any attempt at further definition".

"Literary" work. NOTE 73. **Add:** In *Navitaire Inc v easyJet Airline Co Ltd* [2004] EWHC 1725 (Ch); [2006] R.P.C. 3 at para.80, Pumfrey J. doubted the present utility of the dictum from *Hollinrake v Truswell*, which he described as being "from a different world", given that the definition of a literary work now embraces tables and compilations, computer programs, preparatory design material for computer programs and databases. He went on to say, however, that although to concentrate on the word "literary" may mislead, it must not be ignored: "In the end, the question is merely whether a written artefact is to be accorded the status of a copyright work having regard to the kind of skill and labour expended, the nature of copyright protection and its underlying policy. It is not sufficient to say that the purpose of the act is to protect original skill and labour: there was plenty of that in *Exxon*. Nor is it of much weight that other forms of protection may be available."   **3–15**

NOTE 76. For the position as to simple computer commands, see para.3–28, below.

NOTE 89. **Add:** *Cembrit Blunn Ltd v Apex Roofing Services LLP* [2007] EWHC 111 (Ch) at [241].

Names and titles as literary works. NOTE 12. *R Griggs Group Ltd v Evans* is now reported at [2004] F.S.R. 31.   **3–16**

Add at end of sixth sentence: In *Animated Music Ltd's Trade Mark* [2004] E.C.D.R. 27 (Trade Mark Registry), the title *Nellie the Elephant* was held not to be protected.

NOTE 16. **Add:** See also *University of Waikato v Benchmarking Services Ltd* [2004] NZCA 90.

Copyright in ideas. NOTE 27. See also *London General Holdings Ltd v USP Plc* [2005] EWCA Civ 931; [2006] F.S.R. 6, paras 29 and 44.   **3–18**

(iii) Tables, compilations and databases

3–22   **Databases: statutory definition.** NOTE 51. *Fixtures Marketing v OPAP* is reported at [2005] 1 C.M.L.R. 16; [2005] E.C.D.R. 3. *BHB v William Hill* is reported at [2005] R.P.C. 35; [2005] E.C.D.R. 28.

    Add: In an *obiter* passage in *Navitaire Inc v easyJet Airline Co Ltd* [2004] EWHC 1725 (Ch); [2006] R.P.C. 3 at paragraph 274, Pumfrey J. suggested that schemas or material which were entered into database programs in order to change the structure of the database by adding or subtracting fields or adding or removing datasets were protected (if at all) as computer programs, not databases. The Judge also expressed the view that it was difficult to see how the metadata defining the fields and datasets or the tables, rows or columns fell within the definition of "database" in section 3A of the 1988 Act, if only because they were not a collection of data. The Judge stated that he could not help but feel that section 3A was directed to the contents of the database. He noted that Recital 15 of the Database Directive stated that the criteria for copyright protection of databases should be "defined [sc. confined?] to the fact" that the selection or arrangement of the contents of the database was the author's own intellectual criterion; and that such protection should cover the structure of the database (see para.3–146 of the Main Work, where this is discussed in detail). However, he stated that in the case of an electronic database there was no compelling need to view the programs or scripts creating the database as part of the database even though they define its arrangement or structure. In any event, he said, they acquire copyright even if no database is ever generated from them. The Judge's inclination was to say that this was because they were computer programs.

3–23   **Table or compilation. Add:** In *Navitaire Inc v easyJet Airline Co Ltd* [2004] EWHC 1725 (Ch); [2006] R.P.C. 3 it was argued that a collection of commands for the operation of a computer program was protected as a compilation. The Judge rejected this argument. His main reason was that the commands amounted to a computer language (see below, para.3–28). However, he also held that there was no compilation of commands, only an "accretion". The collection of command names and syntax was never designed as such. It did not have an author. It did not have joint authors since it was perfectly possible to distinguish the contributions of the various authors. The only influence that one command or set of commands had on the others was that it was necessary that they should all have different names. The Judge gave permission to appeal on this point (*Navitaire Inc v easyJet Airline Co Ltd (No.2)* [2005] EWHC 0282 (Ch); [2006] R.P.C. 4, paragraph 139(iv)). The appeal has since been compromised.

3–24   **Compilations of literary and artistic works.** NOTES 55 and 56. The *Panini* case is reported at [2004] 1 W.L.R. 1147; [2004] F.S.R. 1; [2003] E.C.D.R. 36.

3–25   **Tables and compilations other than databases. Add:** In *Navitaire Inc v easyJet Airline Co Ltd* [2004] EWHC 1725 (Ch); [2006] R.P.C. 3 at paragraph 96, Pumfrey J. held that "VTO100" screens, which displayed only printable characters in 80 single-character columns and 24 rows, some of which could be seen in the code, were properly to be viewed as tables. However, they were not protected because they were "ideas which underlie … interfaces" in the sense used in Art.1(2) of the Software Directive, providing the static framework for the display of the dynamic data which it was the task of the software to produce.

(iv) Computer programs and preparatory design material for a computer program

3–27   **History of protection of computer programs. Add** at end: In *Nova Productions*

Ltd v Mazooma Games Ltd [2007] EWCA Civ 219; [2007] R.P.C. 25; [2007] E.M.L.R. 14; [2007] E.C.D.R. 6 it was common ground that those parts of the 1988 Act relating to copyright in computer programs must be interpreted in accordance with the Directive [27].

What is a computer program? NOTE 24. **Add:** In *Navitaire Inc v easyJet Airline Co Ltd* [2004] EWHC 1725 (Ch); [2006] R.P.C. 3 at para.88, Pumfrey J. held that computer languages were excluded from copyright protection, although the point could not be said to be entirely clear and would have to be referred to the Court of Justice (para.88).

3–28

NOTE 25. **Add:** See *Navitaire Inc v easyJet Airline Co Ltd* [2004] EWHC 1725 (Ch); [2006] R.P.C. 3 at para.88.

NOTE 27. **Add:** See also *Telephonic Communicators International Pty Ltd v Motor Solutions Australia Pty Ltd* (2004) 62 I.P.R. 323 (Fed Ct of Aus).

NOTE 31. **Delete** and **substitute:** In *Navitaire Inc v easyJet Airline Co Ltd* [2004] EWHC 1725 (Ch); [2006] R.P.C. 3 at para.80, Pumfrey J. held that copyright could not subsist in individual command words and letters used in a computer program.

The Judge also held that so-called "complex commands" were not protected either. Such "complex commands" consisted of a command letter or word together with data, for example the text "A13JUNLTNAMS", which if followed by pressing the return key would require the computer to display available seats on June 13 between Luton and Amsterdam. The claim failed amongst other things because complex commands were only recorded in the sense that it was possible to analyse the code to ascertain that a machine operating according to that code would "recognise" the command as requiring that display. As the Judge put it: "this "syntax" is recorded without being stated. The reason it is recorded rather than stated is that the reader, in effect, has to turn him- or herself into a machine in order to work out what the machine will recognise when operating according to this program" (para.83). Accordingly, the alleged work was not recorded in the manner contemplated by s.3(2). The Judge gave permission to appeal on this point (*Navitaire Inc v easyJet Airline Co Ltd (No.2)* [2005] EWHC 0282 (Ch); [2006] R.P.C. 4, para.139(iii)). The appeal has since been compromised.

The Judge went on to note that the fact that the complex commands were not recorded was purely a result of the way the claimant's program had been written. The same result could have been achieved by recording the command names and their syntax expressly and using a program known as a parser generator to construct a parser that recognised such commands accompanied by arguments according to such a syntax. The commands and their syntax would then be recognisable as such in the source code of the parser generator. In that case, the copyright owner would be able to point to a written work describing exactly how the alleged infringer's program parsed the code and the consequences would be "very different".

The Judge went on to conclude (*obiter*) that on this hypothetical state of things the claimant would still not have succeeded. It was not possible to infringe the copyright in the source code for a parser or a parser generator by observing the behaviour of the final program and constructing another program to do the same thing (at para.86—see also para.7–48, below). The complex commands amounted to a "defined user command interface" and the principles underlying that interface amounted to an ad hoc computer language in which copyright did not subsist (paras 88 and 89). The Judge gave permission to appeal on this point (*Navitaire Inc v easyJet Airline Co Ltd (No.2)* [2005] EWHC 0282 (Ch); [2006] R.P.C. 4, para.139(iii)). The appeal has since been compromised.

The Judge went on to hold that the same applied to the collection of commands considered as a compilation: they were a computer language, not a program, and therefore not entitled to copyright (para.92). This finding was not *obiter*. It is not clear how the Judge felt able to reach this conclusion without a reference to the Court of Justice to clarify his doubt as to the extent to which computer languages were in fact excluded from the scope of copyright protection. For the Judge's alternative findings on the compilation point, see above, para.3–23.

NOTE 32. **Add:** In *Navitaire Inc v easyJet Airline Co Ltd* [2004] EWHC 1725 (Ch); [2006] R.P.C. 3 at para.96, Pumfrey J. held that "VTO100" screens, which displayed only printable characters in 80 single-character columns and 24 rows, some of which could be seen in the code, were properly to be viewed as tables. However, they were not protected because they were "ideas which underlie ... interfaces" in the sense used in Art.1(2) of the Software Directive, providing the static framework for the display of the dynamic data which it was the task of the software to produce.

NOTE 34. **Add:** See *Nova Productions Limited v Mazooma Games Limited* [2006] EWHC 24 (Ch); [2006] R.P.C. 14; [2006] E.M.L.R. 14, discussed in para.3–56, below. This decision was upheld on appeal: *Nova Productions Ltd v Mazooma Games Ltd* [2007] EWCA Civ 219; [2007] R.P.C. 25; [2007] E.M.L.R. 14; [2007] E.C.D.R. 6.

3–29 **Preparatory design material for a computer programs.** NOTE 37. **Add** at end: In *Nova Productions Ltd v Mazooma Games Ltd* [2007] EWCA Civ 219; [2007] R.P.C. 25; [2007] E.M.L.R. 14; [2007] E.C.D.R. 6 at [28], Jacob L.J. criticised this mode of implementing the Directive: "The EU legislation appears to contemplate just one copyright in a computer program, not two, one in the preparatory work and the other in the program itself. I do not think anything turns on the difference here. But one can think of cases where it might. Suppose for example different authors for the program and its preparatory material. When does the copyright expire—on different dates depending on the death of the respective author? Or suppose different dealings in the 'two' copyrights—is that possible given that the Directive supposes only one copyright?"

C. DRAMATIC WORKS

(ii) Under the 1988 Act

3–35 **Meaning of "dramatic work".** NOTE 62. **Add:** See *Nova Productions Limited v Mazooma Games Limited* [2006] EWHC 24 (Ch); [2006] R.P.C. 14; [2006] E.M.L.R. 14, para.118.

Add at end of paragraph: In *Nova Productions Limited v Mazooma Games Limited* [2006] EWHC 24 (Ch); [2006] R.P.C. 14; [2006] E.M.L.R. 14, it was held that the "visual experience generated by" coin-operated computer games based on the theme of pool was not capable of amounting to a dramatic work. The game was not intended to be or capable of being performed in front of an audience. Although the game had a set of rules, the sequence of images presented on screen depended very much on the way the game was played. Thus, there was insufficient unity in the game for it to be capable of performance (para.116). In any event, the particulars of similarity relied on in support of the claim for infringement were analogous to those relied on in the *Green* case: they were not capable of performance; they did not have sufficient certainty, being drawn at a very high level of generality; they were simply aspects of the game (para.117).

The conclusion that the games were not protected as dramatic works was not challenged on appeal: [2007] EWCA Civ 219; [2007] R.P.C. 25; [2007] E.M.L.R. 14; [2007] E.C.D.R. 6 at [3].

Elements or features of a dramatic work. NOTE 87. **Add:** As to literary 3–41
characters, see Klement, "Copyright Protection of Unauthorised Sequels under
the Copyright, Designs and Patents Act 1988" [2007] 1 Ent. L.R. 13 and Mc-
Cutcheon, "Property in Literary Characters: Protection under Australian Copyright Law" [2007] 4 E.I.P.R. 140.

NOTE 89. **Add:** In Italy it has been held that a football match is not protected
as an original work: *Re Sky Srl's application for an emergency order* [2006]
E.C.D.R. 27 at [20].

Television show formats. Add at end: The Australian case of *Nine Films &* 3–42
Television Pty Ltd v Ninox Television Ltd [2005] FCA 1404; (2005) 67 IPR 46,
concerned allegations of infringement of copyright in the format of a home reno-
vation reality TV series. The format was claimed to consist of a number of elements, in two categories, "Events and characters" and "Emotional elements".
The first category contained the following elements: sponsor friendly; two
couples; selection by public application; attempt to out-renovate each other; strict
budget to work to; one room completed per episode; time frames strictly enforced;
completely renovate and decorate; two old relocatable houses; houses same size;
house same value; helped by team of experts; houses auctioned in finale; winner
keeps house; second place winner keeps $20,000. In the second category were
the following: pressure dealing with mess, budgets, builders; impact on relation-
ships; tears, tantrums, trying to finish on time; human drama, anger, sadness, joy,
betrayal, triumph, despair; builders do structural work when contestants at work
during week; couples work on decorating outside business hours [28]. It seems
highly unlikely that this would have been enough to attract copyright protection
as a matter of English law, but it does not appear that subsistence was in dispute
[34].

The judgment is not easy to follow. The Judge began by holding that the allegedly infringing series was the product of independent creation [70]. However, he
went on to consider whether there had been reproduction of a substantial part,
concluding that simply by reason of the fact that there were large elements of un-
scripted dialogue and interaction within the overall framework of the programs,
there could not be any substantial reproduction [74]. He went on to say that the
various pleaded elements "as portrayed in the productions of the two programmes" were "not at the necessary level of detail and did not bear any sufficient resemblance in mood, tone, portrayal, structure, visual and aural impact,
or by way of general impression from content" [75]. Finally, he went on to hold
that none of the pleaded elements or no significant number of them were actually
present in the allegedly infringing production or format [91].

See Klement, "Protecting Television Show Formats under Copyright Law:
New Developments in Common Law and Civil Law Countries" [2007] 2 E.I.P.R.
52.

D. MUSICAL WORKS

(ii) Under the 1988 Act

Statutory definition: musical work. Delete the fourth to seventh sentences 3–46
(from "It is suggested that ..." to "... appreciated by the human ear") and NOTES
6 to 8 and **substitute:** *Hyperion Records Ltd v Sawkins* [2005] EWCA Civ 565;
[2005] 1 W.L.R. 3281; [2005] R.P.C 32 (on appeal from *Sawkins v Hyperion Records Ltd* [2004] EWHC 1530 (Ch); [2005] R.P.C. 4; [2004] E.M.L.R. 27; [2005]
E.C.D.R. 10) concerned the question whether the claimant was entitled to copyright in his creation of modern performing editions of musical works by the
seventeenth and eighteenth century French composer Lalande.

At paragraph 53, Mummery L.J., with whom Mance L.J. and Jacob L.J. appear to have agreed (see paras 71 and 72), stated:

"In the absence of a special statutory definition of music, ordinary usage assists: as indicated in the dictionaries, the essence of music is combining sounds for listening to. Music is not the same as mere noise. The sound of music is intended to produce effects of some kind on the listener's emotions and intellect. The sounds may be produced by an organised performance on instruments played from a musical score, though that is not essential for the existence of the music or of copyright in it. Music must be distinguished from the fact and form of its fixation as a record of a musical composition. The score is the traditional and convenient form of fixation of the music and conforms to the requirement that a copyright work must be recorded in some material form. But the fixation in the written score or on a record is not in itself the music in which copyright subsists. There is no reason why, for example, a recording of a person's spontaneous singing, whistling or humming or of improvisations of sounds by a group of people with or without musical instruments should not be regarded as 'music' for copyright purposes."

Mummery L.J. went on to say that in music copyright the sounds are more important than the notes, as is evidenced by the fact that it is possible to infringe a musical work without taking the actual notes (para.54, applying *Austin v Columbia Gramophone Co* [1917–23] Mac.C.C. 398).

Finally on this point, he said that in principle, there was no reason for regarding the actual notes of music as the only matter covered by musical copyright, any more than, in the case of a dramatic work, only the words to be spoken by the actors are covered by dramatic copyright (para.55). Accordingly, it was wrong in principle to single out the notes as uniquely significant for copyright purposes and to proceed to deny copyright to the other elements that make some contribution to the sound of the music when performed, such as performing indications, tempo and performance practice indicators, if they are the product of a person's effort, skill and time, bearing in mind the relatively modest level of the threshold for a work to qualify for protection (para.56).

Mummery L.J. upheld the first instance decision that copyright subsisted in the claimant's work on the basis that he had:

- Selected which manuscript to use;
- Transcribed the manuscripts into modern notation, making them playable or more easily playable;
- Corrected errors;
- Inserted material from other sources;
- Included the "figured bass" (notation which provides guidance to the player of the bass-line above the continuous bass); and
- Inserted "advisory" or courtesy indications, such as tempo and ornamentation (see paras 42 and 43).

Jacob L.J. upheld the decision on the basis that in relation to the piece in respect of which the claimant had made the fewest interventions:

"Dr Sawkins started by choosing which original manuscript(s) to use (actually he used mainly 2 out of 4, using one to correct ambiguities in the other), he checked every note and supplied 27 'corrections' (*i.e.* his personal evaluation as to what note Lalande really intended), supplied many suggestions for the figured bass, and put the whole into modern notation. This was not mere servile copying. It had the practical value (unchallenged) of making the work playable. He re-created Lalande's work using a considerable amount of personal judgment. His re-creative work was such as to create something really new using his own original (not merely copied) work." (para.86).

Mance L.J. agreed with both judgments (para.71).

On the decision on appeal, see Robinson, "Hyperion Records Ltd v Dr Lionel Sawkins: It's Like That And That's The Way It Is" [2005] 7 Ent. L.R. 190. On the first instance decision, see Jones, "Musical Works: Out with the Old and In with the New?" [2005] 4 Ent. L.R. 89.

In the earlier first instance decision of *Coffey v Warner/Chappell Music Ltd* [2005] EWHC 449 (Ch); [2005] F.S.R. 34; [2005] E.C.D.R. 21; [2006] E.M.L.R. 2, copyright was claimed in a song entitled *Forever After* which was stated to be "... an original musical work comprising the combination of vocal expression, pitch contour and syncopation of or around the words 'does it really matter'." It was contended that the words "does it really matter" were repeated throughout the song and comprised its lyrical hook. In further information, the claimant stated that by "vocal expression" she meant timbre; by pitch contour she meant "the general shape of the pitches" rather than the notes themselves; and by "syncopation of or around the words 'does it really matter'" she meant the "unnatural metrical stress" given to the syllables of those four words "in terms of their placement within the two bars [in which they are sung] and the unusual rhythmic and durational stress in terms of their elongated durations".

Blackburne J. doubted whether these features were capable of attracting copyright protection because they were interpretation or performance characteristics rather than matters of composition (para.6). Although the precise nature of the claimant's case in *Coffey* is not easy to understand from the report, it seems that if he had had the benefit of the Court of Appeal's decision in *Hyperion Records Ltd v Sawkins* the Judge might well have taken a different view at least in relation to the "syncopation" of or around the words "does it really matter". In the event, the claim was struck out not on this ground but because rather than relying on the whole of her work and contending that the defendant's work was a copy of a substantial part of it, the claimant was seeking to rely only on certain elements of her work and thus to improve her position on the "substantial part" issue (para.9, applying *IPC Media Ltd v Highbury-Leisure Publishing Ltd* [2004] EWHC 2985 (Ch); [2005] F.S.R. 20 at para.8). See Jones, "What Constitutes a Copyright Work—Does it Really Matter?" [2005] 5 Ent. L.R. 129.

NOTE 10. *Hayes v Phonogram Ltd* is now reported at [2003] E.C.D.R. 11.

Add at end: See Saw, "Protecting the Sound of Silence in 4'33": A Timely Revisit of Basic Principles in Copyright Law" [2005] 12 E.I.P.R. 467.

E. ARTISTIC WORKS

(iii) Graphic works

Statutory definition: graphic work. Add at end of first sub-paragraph: All these things are static. Accordingly, a series of still images which provides the illusion of movement, whether created by drawing for a cartoon film or by a computer, is not protected as a separate artistic work in addition to the individual images: *Nova Productions Ltd v Mazooma Games Ltd* [2007] EWCA Civ 219; [2007] R.P.C. 25; [2007] E.M.L.R. 14; [2007] E.C.D.R. 6 at [16].   **3–55**

NOTE 46. **Add:** The law has developed differently in New Zealand: see *ABB Ltd v New Zealand Insulators Ltd* [2006] NZHC 1072 at [176].

NOTE 53. *Gabrin v Universal Music Operations Ltd* is now reported at [2004] E.C.D.R. 4.

3–56   **Examples of graphic works.** NOTE 66. *R Griggs Group Ltd v Evans* is now reported at [2004] F.S.R. 31 (on appeal but not on this point: [2005] EWCA Civ 11; [2005] F.S.R. 31; [2005] E.C.D.R. 30). **Add:** See also *Australian Chinese Newspapers Pty Ltd v Melbourne Chinese Press Pty Ltd* [2003] F.C.A. 878 (on appeal *Melbourne Chinese Press Pty Ltd v Australian Chinese Newspapers Pty Ltd* (2004) 63 I.P.R. 38), in which it was conceded that a logo consisting of three characters in a particular calligraphic style used for a newspaper masthead was a copyright work.

NOTE 67. **Add:** *Henkel KgaA v Holdfast New Zealand Ltd* [2006] NZSC 102; (2006) 70 IPR 624; [2007] 1 N.Z.L.R. 336 at [36], [47] (design drawing for packaging comprising a combination of "common form" elements of a glue bottle affixed to a card of a dominant blue primary colour with pictures of two uses and a list of applications; but note that in England the claim would have probably fallen foul of s.51 of the 1988 Act).

Add: In *Navitaire Inc v easyJet Airline Co Ltd* [2004] EWHC 1725 (Ch); [2006] R.P.C. 3 at paragraph 97, Pumfrey J. held that Microsoft Windows GUI screens, which had been drawn by selecting from a palette of available objects things such as command buttons, toggle buttons, checkboxes, scrolling lists and so on and moving them around on a form until a satisfactory layout had been achieved, were artistic works. It did not matter that they were recorded only in the complex code which displayed them. It seems that the contrary was not seriously argued (see para.74). The icons which appeared on the screens were also protected as artistic works "albeit minor" (para.99).

The Judge gave permission to appeal on the question whether the screens were sufficiently original to amount to copyright works and also as to whether a substantial part had been taken (*Navitaire Inc v easyJet Airline Co Ltd (No.2)* [2005] EWHC 0282 (Ch); [2006] R.P.C. 4, para.139(v)). The appeal has since been compromised.

In *Nova Productions Limited v Mazooma Games Limited* [2006] EWHC 24 (Ch); [2006] R.P.C. 14; [2006] E.M.L.R. 14, Kitchen J. emphasised that the definition of "graphic work" in subs.4(2) is inclusive (para.100). He held (albeit on the basis of an apparent concession) that the following were graphic works:

- Bitmap (digital image) files created using computer tools such as the mouse and on-screen tools such as notional brushes and pencils and the screen colour palette. As the Judge said, these files create a visual effect which is very similar to a painting or drawing (para.101).
- Composite frames generated by the computer program using the bitmap files. The case concerned coin operated computer games based on the theme of pool. The computer program built up composite images by combining individual bitmap images, for example of the table, the cue and the balls (para.104).

This was common ground on appeal: [2007] EWCA Civ 219 [12].

(viii) Works of artistic craftsmanship

3–69   **Examples: copyright conferred.** The High Court of Australia has now pronounced on *Swarbrick v Burge: Burge v Swarbrick* [2007] HCA 17. To some extent the decision turned on the terms of and background to the then Australian exception to copyright protection in respect of artistic works which have been industrially applied, which differed significantly from section 52 of the CDPA 1988. However, the Court considered the English authorities in some detail. Two aspects of its decision are of particular note. First, after considering at length an article by Professor Dennicola (Applied Art and Industrial Design: A Suggested

Approach to Copyright in Useful Articles (1982–83) 67 Minnesota Law Review 707) together with certain dicta of Lord Simon in *Hensher*, the Court concluded that it would be unwise to seek to define the term "work of artistic craftsmanship" but went on: "determining whether a work is a work of artistic craftsmanship does not turn on assessing the beauty or aesthetic appeal of work or on assessing any harmony between its visual appeal and its utility. The determination turns on assessing the extent to which the particular work's artistic expression, in its form, is unconstrained by functional considerations" [83]. Accordingly, the more constrained the designer is by functional considerations, the less likely the work is to be a work of artistic craftsmanship. It is a matter of degree [84]. Second, the Court held that although evidence from the designer as to his intention is admissible, such evidence needs to treated with caution [65] and should be tested against the contemporary documents [69]. On the facts, the yacht plug did not qualify as a work of artistic craftsmanship because matters of visual and aesthetic appeal had been subordinated to achievement of the purely functional aspects required for a successfully marketed "sports boat" and thus for the commercial objective in view [73].

Examples: copyright denied. NOTE 82. **Add:** See Thompson and Wilkinson   **3–70**
"Not Such a Crafty Corkscrew?" [2004] 12 E.I.P.R. 548.

H. BROADCASTS

(i) History of protection

(e) *European Directives*

NOTE 54. **Add** at end: This Directive and its amendments have now been codified   **3–89**
as Directive 2006/115/EC: [2006] O.J. L376/28. The new Directive took effect on January 16, 2007: Art.15.

NOTE 57. Arts 6–9 of the Rental and Related Rights Directive are now Arts 7–10 of Directive 2006/115/EC.

NOTE 58. Arts 6(2) and (3) of the Rental and Related Rights Directive are now Arts 7(2) and (3) of Directive 2006/115/EC.

I. TYPOGRAPHICAL ARRANGEMENTS OF PUBLISHED EDITIONS

Background to protection for typographical arrangements. NOTE 95. Art.4 of   **3–102**
the Term Directive is now Art.4 of Directive 2006/116/EC.

3. FIXATION

A. FIXATION IN GENERAL

Introduction. NOTE 12. **Add:** See also *IPC Media Limited v Highbury-Leisure*   **3–105**
Publishing Limited [2004] EWHC 2985 (Ch); [2005] F.S.R. 20 at paras 7 and 8, and *Baigent v The Random House Group Limited* [2006] EWHC 719 (Ch); [2006] E.M.L.R. 16 at para.156, citing the need for certainty as a reason for the absence of copyright protection for ideas at a high level of abstraction: "if what is asserted to be infringed is so general that it cannot be certain that would lead to a conclusion that it is [at] such a level of abstraction that no protection should be afforded to it". This statement was not the subject of comment in the Court of Appeal: [2007] EWCA Civ 247; [2007] R.P.C. 25; [2007] E.M.L.R. 14; [2007] E.C.D.R. 6.

B. LITERARY, DRAMATIC AND MUSICAL WORKS

3–119   **Fixation of artistic works.** NOTE 41. **Add:** See *ABB Ltd v New Zealand Insulators Ltd* [2006] NZHC 1072 at [158]: the mere specification of a colour to be used in manufacturing a label is not protected in the absence of any drawing, graphic design or other object that could be said to be the original example of the labelling concept.

4. ORIGINALITY

A. LITERARY, DRAMATIC, MUSICAL AND ARTISTIC WORKS

(i) Introduction

3–124   **History of requirement of originality.** NOTE 59. **Add:** In *Hyperion Records Ltd v Sawkins* [2005] EWCA Civ 565; [2005] 1 W.L.R. 3281; [2005] R.P.C. 32, Mummery L.J. stated (at para.33) that *Walter v. Lane* remained good law, citing the *Express Newspapers* case. Jacob L.J. noted (at para.79) that the Court of Appeal had not been presented with a full frontal attack on *Walter v Lane*. He accepted that it was "highly probable" that *Walter v Lane* was still good law and went on to express the view that the reasoning in the *Sands McDougall* case adopted in the *Express Newspapers* case was "right". Mance L.J. (at para.71) agreed with both judgments. See also Gravells, "Authorship and Originality: the Persistent Influence of *Walter v Lane*" [2007] I.P.Q. 267, arguing that reliance in the present day on *Walter v Lane* is "at best inappropriate and at worst misconceived".

3–126   **EC Directives.** NOTE 71. The Term Directive and its amendments have now been codified in Directive 2006/116/EC [2006] O.J. L372/12. The new Directive took effect on January 16, 2007: Art.13.

     NOTES 72 and 73. Art.6 of the Term Directive is now Art.6 of Directive 2006/116/EC.

(ii) Principles of originality

3–128   **Nature of skill or labour required.** Second sentence. In *Hyperion Records Ltd v Sawkins* [2005] EWCA Civ 565; [2005] 1 W.L.R. 3281; [2005] R.P.C. 32, Jacob L.J. (with whom Mance L.J. agreed) suggested that in certain circumstances a "mere copyist" might obtain copyright in his copy. See below, paragraph 3–131.

     NOTE 83. **Add:** In *Hyperion Records Ltd v Sawkins* [2005] EWCA Civ 565; [2005] 1 W.L.R. 3281; [2005] R.P.C. 32, Mummery L.J. stated (at para.31) that a work need only be "original" in the limited sense that the author originated it by his efforts rather than "slavishly" copying it from the work produced by the efforts of another person; while Jacob L.J. stated (at para.85) the question in terms of whether the claimant's work went beyond mere "servile copying". Mance L.J. (at para.71) agreed with both judgments.

(iii) Non-derivative works

3–129   NOTES 98 and 7. *R Griggs Group Ltd v Evans* is now reported at [2004] F.S.R. 31 (on appeal, but not on this point: [2005] EWCA Civ 11; [2005] F.S.R. 31; [2005] E.C.D.R 30).

     NOTE 9. *Guild v Navabi* is now reported as *Guild v Eskandar Ltd* at [2003] F.S.R. 3.

(iii) Derivative works

Mere copy. The statement in the text that the exercise of skill, labour and judgment merely in the process of copying cannot confer originality is based on *obiter* dicta of Lord Oliver in *Interlego A.G. v Tyco Industries Inc* [1989] A.C. 217. These dicta must now be read subject to the contrary observations of Jacob L.J. (with which Mance L.J. agreed) in *Sawkins v Hyperion Records Ltd* [2005] EWCA Civ 565; [2005] 1 W.L.R. 3281; [2005] R.P.C. 32 at para.83:

> "... the true position is that one has to consider the extent to which the 'copyist' is a mere copyist—merely performing an easy mechanical function. The more that is so the less is his contribution likely to be taken as 'original'. Prof. Jane Ginsberg, (The Concept of Authorship in Comparative Copyright Law, *http://ssrn.com.abstract_id=368481*) puts it this way:
>
> > 'Reproductions requiring great talent and technical skill may qualify as protectable works of authorship, even if they are copies of pre-existing works. This would be the case for photographic and other high quality replicas of works of art'.
>
> In the end the question is one of degree—how much skill, labour and judgment in the making of the copy is that of the creator of that copy? Both individual creative input and sweat of brow may be involved and will be factors in the overall evaluation."

Mummery L.J., with whom Mance L.J. also agreed, said this at paragraph 31: "A work need only be 'original' in the limited sense that the author originated it by his efforts rather than *slavishly* copying it from the work produced by the efforts of another person" (emphasis added).

The decisions on the facts in the *Interlego* and *Reject Shop* cases are entirely consistent with the observations of Jacob L.J. The former concerned a process of tracing akin to photocopying while the latter concerned a photocopy enlargement. See the analysis of *Interlego* in the design right case of *Dyson Limited v Qualtex (UK) Limited* [2006] EWCA Civ 166; [2006] R.P.C. 31, paragraphs 86 to 88.

In *Vitof Ltd v Altoft* [2006] EWHC 1678 (Ch) at paragraph 143, the Judge (Richard Arnold QC) accepted a submission that computer code, 10 per cent of which was either different from or a modified version of part of a previous version, was original since it had not been slavishly copied.

Other use of existing subject-matter. NOTE 30. **Add** at end: and *Henkel KgaA v Holdfast New Zealand Ltd* [2006] NZSC 102; (2006) 70 IPR 624; [2007] 1 N.Z.L.R. 336 at [47] (design drawing showing a combination of "common form" elements of a glue bottle affixed to a card of a dominant blue primary colour with pictures of two uses and a list of applications; but note that in England the claim would have probably fallen foul of s.51 of the 1988 Act).

Successive versions. NOTE 34. **Add** at end: *IPC Media Ltd v Highbury-Leisure Publishing Ltd* [2004] EWHC 2985 (Ch); [2005] F.S.R. 20 at para.5.

New arrangement or adaptation of music. NOTES 64 and 65. **Add:** The decision in *Sawkins v Hyperion Records Ltd* was upheld by the Court of Appeal: *Hyperion Records Ltd v Sawkins* [2005] EWCA Civ 565; [2005] 1 W.L.R. 3281; [2005] R.P.C. 32. See paras 32 to 36, 71 and 77 to 86. On the first instance decision, see Groves, "Better Than It Sounds: Originality of Musical Works" [2005] 1 Ent. L.R. 20.

NOTE 67. **Add:** In *Hyperion Records Ltd v Sawkins* [2005] EWCA Civ 565; [2005] 1 W.L.R. 3281; [2005] R.P.C. 32 at para.84, on the basis that *Walter v Lane* was probably still good law, Jacob L.J. stated that a transcription of a musi-

3–131

3–132

3–134

3–137

cal work would be original, citing the example of the 14-year-old Mozart's transcription of Allegri's unpublished *Miserere* after he had heard it at a performance in the Vatican.

(iv) Photographs and films as dramatic works.

3–142   **Photographs present their own problems in relation to originality.** NOTE 78. **Add:** See now Art.6 of Directive 2006/116/EC, the codified version of the Term Directive and its amendments.

   Add: In *Hyperion Records Ltd v Sawkins* [2005] EWCA Civ 565; [2005] 1 W.L.R. 3281; [2005] R.P.C. 32, Jacob L.J. (with whom Mance L.J. agreed) stated (at para.83) that in his view "as a generality" the comment from Lord Oliver's speech in *Interlego* which is reproduced in the text to paragraph 3–142 of the Main Work was inconsistent with *Walter v Lane*. See further, paragraph 3–131, above.

(vi) Compilations, tables and databases

3–145   **The "old" originality requirement.** NOTE 27. **Add:** A similar case is *TS & B Retail Systems Pty Ltd v 3Fold Resources Pty Ltd (No 3)* [2007] FCA 151.

3–146   **The "new" originality requirement for databases. Add** at end: In *Pennwell Publishing (UK) Ltd v Ornstein* [2007] EWHC 1570 (QB) at [107(f)] the Judge stated (*obiter*) that he was far from persuaded that the exercise of assembling a list of the details of 1650 contacts which was maintained Outlook system and in an Excel spreadsheet met the standard of originality required for copyright protection. It is suggested that the Judge was entirely correct not to be so persuaded.

(vii) Computer generated works

3–147   **Add:** In *Nova Productions Limited v Mazooma Games Limited* [2006] EWHC 24 (Ch); [2006] R.P.C. 14; [2006] E.M.L.R. 14, it was held that in so far as composite frames for use in a coin-operated computer game were computer-generated works, their author was the individual who had devised the appearance of the various elements of the game and the rules and logic by which each frame was created and he wrote the relevant computer program (para.105). The fact that this was done in his capacity as director of a company appears to have been regarded as irrelevant. This issue did not arise on appeal: [2007] EWCA Civ 219 [12].

5. QUALIFYING CONDITIONS

C. EXISTING WORKS

3–188   **Foreign existing works.** NOTE 10. Second sentence. **Delete** and **substitute:** See now the Copyright and Performances (Application to Other Countries) Order 2007 (SI 2007/273), below at **C1**.

   NOTE 11. **Delete** and **substitute:** See para.7(1) and (2) of the 1979 Order and now Art.7 of the Copyright and Performances (Application to Other Countries) Order 2007 (SI 2007/273), below at **C1**.

6. FOREIGN WORKS

A. Protection of works of foreign origin: application of Act

(i) General

(c) *Position under the 1956 Act*

Unrepeated provisions of 1957 Order   3–211
  (c) As to revocation of previous Orders
  (ii) Taiwan. Note 56. **Delete** and **substitute:** Currently by the Copyright and
Performances (Application to Other Countries) Order 2007 (SI 2007/273). See
below at **C1.**

(iii) Singapore Note 61. **Delete** and **substitute:** Currently by the Copyright and   3–212
Performances (Application to Other Countries) Order 2007 (SI 2007/273). See
below at **C1.**

(iv) Indonesia Note 63. **Delete** and **substitute:** Currently by the Copyright and   3–213
Performances (Application to Other Countries) Order 2007 (SI 2007/273). See
below at **C1.**

(d) *Position under the 1988 Act*

Order in Council under section 159 of the 1988 Act   3–219
  (a) Generally. Add: Since the publication of the Main Work, three further
Orders in Council have been made under section 159: the Copyright and Perfor-
mances (Application to Other Countries) Order 2005 (SI 2005/852) ("the 2005
Order"), the Copyright and Performances (Application to Other Countries) Order
2006 (SI 2006/316) ("the 2006 Order") and the Copyright and Performances
(Application to Other Countries) Order 2007 (SI 2007/273) ("the 2007 Order").
With effect from April 6, 2007, the 2007 Order (by Art.1(3)) revokes the 2006
Order which itself revoked the 2005 Order. Each Order was made under sections
159 and 208 CDPA 1988 and section 2(2) of the European Communities Act
1972 (c.68).
  The basic structure of all the Orders made under section 159 prior to 2005 was
to apply relevant parts of sections 153 to 156 of the 1988 Act to individuals or
companies connected to, works first published in and (as the case might be)
broadcasts made from specified countries as they applied to individuals or
companies connected to, works first published in or (as the case might be)
broadcasts made from the United Kingdom. The Orders then went on to provide
that where copyright subsisted in a work as a result, the whole of Part I of the
1988 Act applied in relation to that work. See paragraphs 3–221 to 3–223 of the
Main Work. They then set out certain exceptions based on the absence of reciprocal protection in relation to certain types of work.
  By contrast, the 2007 Order, like the 2005 and 2006 Orders, simply applies all
relevant provisions of Part I of the 1988 Act in relation to specified countries "so
that" those provisions apply in relation to individuals or companies connected to,
works first published in and (as the case may be) broadcasts made from such
countries as they apply to individuals or companies connected to, works first
published in or (as the case may be) broadcasts made from the United Kingdom:
see *e.g.* article 2(1) of 2007 Order. This structure reverts to that adopted in the

Orders made under the 1956 Act (see *e.g.* the Copyright (International Conventions) Order 1979 (SI 1979/1715)). It is not thought that there is any substantive difference between the two approaches. In the discussion which follows, the term "relevant connection" is used to mean a connection between a particular work and a particular country of the type referred to in one of sections 153 to 156 of the 1988 Act.

There are other changes too.

First, like the 2005 and 2006 Orders, the 2007 Order does not contain any equivalent to article 6 of the earlier Orders, which provided that nothing in the 1999 Order was to be taken to derogate from paragraph 35 of Schedule 1 to the 1988 Act, which provided that every work in which copyright subsisted under the 1956 Act immediately before commencement of the 1988 Act was deemed to qualify for protection under the 1988 Act. Paragraph 35 is however referred to in the Explanatory Note to the 2007 Order, which also reminds the reader that the effect of section 153(3) of the 1988 Act is that the Order does not affect works in which copyright already subsists. Evidently it is no longer thought necessary to make express reference to paragraph 35 in the text of the Order.

Second, the saving provisions in Article 7 of the earlier Orders are not repeated in the same form. Article 7 provided for circumstances where expenditure or liability was or had been incurred in connection with, for the purpose of or with a view to doing an act which at the time was not a restricted act. If copyright subsequently subsisted in the work in question by reason of the Order, the doing or continued doing of that act thereafter was deemed not to be a restricted act unless compensation was paid.

Article 7 of the 2005, 2006 and 2007 Orders begins with the concept of an "excluded act", which is defined (in Art.7(1)) as an act in respect of which two requirements are satisfied at a time when the act neither infringed nor was restricted by copyright or moral rights. The requirements are first, that a person (called in the Orders "A") must have incurred expenditure or liability in connection with the act; and secondly, that that person must have either begun in good faith to do that act or to have made in good faith effective and serious preparations to do the act.

Article 7(2) provides that where a person (called in the Orders "B") acquires copyright or moral rights in the work pursuant to the Order in question, A has the right to continue to do the excluded act or to do the excluded act (as the case may be) even though the excluded act infringes or is restricted by the copyright or the moral rights.

Article 7(3) provides that where B or his exclusive licensee pays reasonable compensation to A, Article (2) no longer applies and accordingly the act becomes an infringement.

Article 7(4) provides that where B offers to pay compensation to A but they cannot agree on the amount, either may refer the matter to arbitration.

It will be noted that the 2005, 2006 and 2007 Orders use the words "pursuant to this Order". It appears to follow that where a person in the position of B acquired copyright pursuant to an earlier Order the relevant saving provision is that contained in the earlier Order.

Despite the change in terminology, there only appears to be one substantive difference between the new and old saving provisions. This is the introduction of a requirement that the doing of the act or (as the case may be) the making of the preparations for the act should have been in good faith. Presumably this new requirement is intended to cover the possibility that a person might have incurred the expenditure or liability and commenced the act or preparations for it with notice that a particular country had become a party to a relevant convention but that the Government had not yet made provision for this by the making of an Order listing that country. It is not clear what degree of notice will be considered sufficient to deprive a person of good faith.

(c) Literary, dramatic, musical and artistic works, films and the typographical arrangements of published editions. Delete text of paragraph and **substitute:** Article 2(1) of the 2007 Order provides that all the provisions of Part I of the 1988 Act, insofar as they relate to literary, dramatic, musical and artistic works, films and the typographical arrangement of published editions, apply in relation to the countries listed in the second column of the table set out in the Schedule to the Order so that those provisions apply: **3–221**

   (a) in relation to persons who are citizens or subjects of, or are domiciled or resident in, those countries as they apply to persons who are British citizens or are domiciled or resident in the United Kingdom,

   (b) in relation to bodies incorporated under the laws of those countries as they apply in relation to bodies incorporated under the law of a part of the United Kingdom, and

   (c) in relation to works first published in those countries as they apply in relation to works first published in the United Kingdom.

As before, section 155(3) of the Act provides that for these purposes publication in one country is not to be regarded as other than first publication by reason of simultaneous publication elsewhere and for this purpose publication elsewhere within the 30 previous days is to be treated as simultaneous.

Article 2(2) of the 2007 Order provides that where a literary, musical or artistic work was first published before June 1, 1957 (the date of commencement of the 1956 Act) it shall not qualify for copyright protection by reason of section 154 of the 1988 Act (qualification by author). This reproduces Article 2(2)(a)(i) of the 1999 Order. Otherwise, however, the complex limitations in Article 2(2) and (3) of the 1999 Order no longer apply.

Each of the countries listed in the second column of the table qualifies for inclusion on one or more of the following bases: it is a party to the Berne Convention, the Universal Copyright Convention or the TRIPs agreement; it is a Member State of the European Community or the European Free Trade Agreement; or it is otherwise considered to give adequate protection under its law: see the Explanatory Note.

(d) Sound recordings. Delete text of paragraph and **substitute:** Article 3(1) of the 2007 Order provides that with certain exceptions all the provisions of Part I of the 1988 Act, insofar as they relate to sound recordings, apply in relation to the countries listed in the third column of the table set out in the Schedule to the Order so that those provisions apply: **3–222**

   (a) in relation to persons who are citizens or subjects of, or are domiciled or resident in, those countries as they apply to persons who are British citizens or are domiciled or resident in the United Kingdom,

   (b) in relation to bodies incorporated under the laws of those countries as they apply in relation to bodies incorporated under the law of a part of the United Kingdom, and

   (c) in relation to works first published in those countries as they apply in relation to works first published in the United Kingdom.

Article 3(2) in effect lays out three separate regimes. The first applies to countries whose entry in the third column of the table includes an asterisk, that is countries which are parties to the Rome Convention (see paras 24–88 to 24–108 of the Main Work) or are Member States of the European Community or the European Free Trade Agreement or otherwise give adequate protection under their laws: see the Explanatory Note. All the provisions of Part I of the 1988 Act so far as applicable to sound recordings apply in relation to these countries.

The second regime applies to countries listed in the third column of the table and marked with a hash (#). This regime applies to countries which are parties to the WIPO Performances and Phonograms Treaty (see paras 24–119 to 24–134 of the Main Work) but not to the Rome Convention. The United Kingdom has not ratified the WIPO Performances and Phonograms Treaty, but has agreed to do so together with the European Community and with the other Member States in accordance with Council Decision 2000/278/EC [2001] O.J. L89/6 (see the Main Work, Vol. 2 at I1). Protection is therefore accorded to Contracting Parties in anticipation of ratification on the basis that upon ratification those countries will provide protection under their laws: see the Explanatory Note. All the provisions of Part I so far as applicable to sound recordings apply to these countries except sections 18A (infringement by rental and lending to the public) insofar as it applies to lending, 19 (infringement by playing in public), 20 (infringement by communication to the public) so far as it concerns broadcasting, 26 (secondary infringement by provision of apparatus for infringing performance, etc.), 107(2A) (criminal liability for communicating to the public) so far as it concerns broadcasting and 107(3) (criminal liability for playing in public).

The third regime applies to all other countries listed in the table. All the provisions of Part I so far as applicable to sound recordings apply to these countries except sections 18A (insofar as it applies to lending), 19, 20, 26, 107(2A) and 107(3).

3–223   **(e) "Broadcasts". Delete** text of paragraph and **substitute:** The concept of a "cable programme" no longer features in the 1988 Act (see para.3–82 of the Main Work). However, for the purposes of the 2007 Order a distinction is drawn between wireless and non-wireless broadcasts. Article 4 deals with wireless broadcasts and Article 5 deals with other broadcasts.

As to wireless broadcasts, Article 4(1) provides that with certain exceptions and subject to certain provisos, all the provisions of Part I of the 1988 Act, insofar as they relate to wireless broadcasts, apply in relation to the countries listed in the fourth column of the table set out in the Schedule to the Order so that those provisions apply:

(a) in relation to persons who are citizens or subjects of, or are domiciled or resident in, those countries as they apply to persons who are British citizens or are domiciled or resident in the United Kingdom,
(b) in relation to bodies incorporated under the laws of those countries as they apply in relation to bodies incorporated under the law of a part of the United Kingdom, and
(c) in relation to broadcasts made from those countries as they apply in relation to broadcasts made from the United Kingdom.

The effect of Articles 4(1) and 4(2) is that where a country's entry in the fourth column of the table does not include an asterisk, the protection granted to broadcasts connected with it is not limited in extent (see below, however, for duration). These countries are parties to the Rome Convention (see paras 24–88 to 24–108 of the Main Work), Member States of the European Community or the European Free Trade Agreement or otherwise give adequate protection under their laws: see the Explanatory Note.

Where, however, a country's entry includes an asterisk, the following provisions of Part I do not apply: sections 18A (infringement by rental and lending to the public), 19 (infringement by showing or playing in public), but only insofar as it relates to broadcasts other than television broadcasts, 20 (infringement by communication to the public), except in relation to broadcasting by wireless telegraphy, 26 (secondary infringement by provision of apparatus for infringing performance, etc.) but only insofar as it relates to broadcasts other than television broadcasts and 107(2A) (criminal liability for communicating to the public) except in relation to broadcasting by wireless telegraphy. The asterisked countries are parties to the TRIPs agreement (see the Main Work paras 24–135 to 24–153) but not to the Rome Convention. By reason of paragraph 9(a) of Schedule 1 to the Act, protection never extends to such broadcasts made before June 1, 1957: see the Explanatory Note.

The effect of Article 4(3) and 4(4) is that the provisions of Part I of the 1988 Act do not apply in relation to wireless broadcasts made before the date which is specified against each country's entry in the fourth column of the table set out in the Schedule. Paragraph 9(b) of Schedule 1 to the 1988 Act provides that no copyright subsists in a broadcast made before the commencement of the Copyright Act 1956 on June 1, 1957. Accordingly, that is the earliest date which may be so specified. The other date which is frequently specified is January 1, 1996, the date on which the TRIPs agreement took effect (see paras 24–135 and 24–153 of the Main Work).

Article 4(5) provides that for the purposes of section 14(5) of the 1988 Act (which concerns the term of copyright in repeat broadcasts) any wireless broadcast which does not qualify for copyright protection shall be disregarded.

(f) "Cable programmes". Delete heading and text of paragraph and **substitute: Non-wireless broadcasts.** Article 5 of the 2007 Order provides that all the provisions of Part I of the 1988 Act insofar as they relate to non-wireless broadcasts, apply in relation to the countries indicated in the fifth column of the table set out in the Schedule so that those provisions apply: **3–224**

(a) in relation to persons who are citizens or subjects of, or are domiciled or resident in, those countries as they apply to persons who are British citizens or are domiciled or resident in the United Kingdom,

(b) in relation to bodies incorporated under the laws of those countries as they apply in relation to bodies incorporated under the law of a part of the United Kingdom, and

(c) in relation to broadcasts made from those countries as they apply in relation to broadcasts made from the United Kingdom.

The countries in the fifth column are Member States of the European Community or the European Free Trade Agreement or otherwise considered to give adequate protection under their laws. The effect of paragraph 9(b) of Schedule 1 to the 1988 Act is that protection does not extend to such broadcasts made before January 1, 1985. See the Explanatory Note to the Order.

B. PROTECTION OF WORKS ORIGINATING IN THE BRITISH COMMONWEALTH: EXTENSION OF ACT

(iv) Position under the 1988 Act

Extension of the 1988 Act to other countries. NOTE 5. **Add:** Although provision has been made in the past for the extension with modifications of provisions of Part I of the 1988 Act to Gibraltar (see most recently the Copyright (Gibraltar) **3–250**

Order 2005 (SI 2005/853)), such provision has now been revoked (by the Copyright (Gibraltar) Revocation Order 2006 (SI 2006/1039)). Works and performances originating in Gibraltar are now governed by the Copyright and Performances (Application to Other Countries) Order 2007 (SI 2007/273).

3–257   **Dependent Territories**

(iii) Isle of Man. Add: However, that Order (the Copyright (Application to the Isle of Man) Order 1992 (SI 1992/1313)) was revoked with effect from May 1, 2005 by Article 8(a) of the Copyright and Performances (Application to Other Countries) Order 2005 (SI 2005/852) ("the 2005 Order"). The 2005 Order has since been revoked, as has its replacement, the Copyright and Performances (Application to Other Countries) Order 2006 (SI 2006/316). The position in respect of works originating in the Isle of Man is now governed by the terms of the Copyright and Performances (Application to Other Countries) Order 2007 (SI 2007/273), as to which see, generally, paragraph 3–219, above.

NOTE 35. SI 1989/1292 was partially revoked by the Registered Designs (Isle of Man) Order 2001 (SI 2001/3678) with effect from December 9, 2001.

7. WORKS DENIED PROTECTION

3–260   **Copyright is a creature of statute.** NOTES 51, 55, 56. *Ashdown v Telegraph Group Ltd* is now reported at [2002] Ch. 149; [2002] R.P.C. 5; [2001] E.M.L.R. 44 and [2003] E.C.D.R. 32.

3–263   **Works infringing other works.** NOTE 73. **Add:** In *Vitof Ltd v Altoft* [2006] EWHC 1678 (Ch) at para.147.

3–264   **Copyright and freedom of expression.** NOTES 77 and 78. *Ashdown v Telegraph Group Ltd* is now reported at [2002] Ch. 149; [2002] R.P.C. 5; [2001] E.M.L.R. 44 and [2003] E.C.D.R. 32.

CHAPTER FOUR

AUTHORSHIP OF COPYRIGHT WORKS

1. INTRODUCTION

Add: Likewise, the artist's resale right, newly introduced into the law of the   **4–01**
United Kingdom, is not assignable and may not be waived.[1]

Conflict with civil law systems of copyright. Tenth sentence. **Delete** and **substi-**   **4–03**
tute: A further economic right of authors, which was formerly alien to the common law system is the artist's resale right, known as the "*droit de suite*". The
right has recently been introduced into the law of the United Kingdom in order to
bring the law into conformity with an EC Directive on the subject.[2] The right
gives authors of certain works a right to a continuing interest on successive sales
of their work.

NOTE 12. **Delete** and **substitute:** See The Artist's Resale Right Regulations
2006 (SI 2006/346) and Ch.19A, below. See also para.24–44, below, for a commentary on the artist's resale right provisions of the Berne Convention (Art.
14*ter*) and para.25–72, below, for a commentary on the EC Resale Right Directive (2001/84/EC), the implementation of which introduced the right into the law
of the United Kingdom.

---

[1] The Artist's Resale Right Regulations 2006 (SI 2006/346), regs 7(1) and 8(1). As to the transfer
   of the resale right on death, see reg.9. As to the artist's resale right generally, see Ch.19A, below.
[2] Directive 2001/84/EC on the Resale Right for the Benefit of the Author of an Original Work of
   Art, of October 13, 2001.

2. LITERARY, DRAMATIC, MUSICAL AND ARTISTIC WORKS

4–10   NOTE 35. **Add:** The Artist's Resale Right Regulations 2006 (SI 2006/346) also defines the author, in relation to a work, as the person who creates it (reg.2).

4–17   **Computer-Generated Works.** NOTE 62. **Add:** See *Nova Productions Limited v Mazooma Games Limited* ([2006] EWHC 24 (Ch) affirmed on appeal [2007] EWCA Civ 219). The case concerned two actions for copyright infringement of arcade video games and raised the question of authorship of computer-generated works. Kitchin J. held that:

> "Insofar as each composite frame is a computer-generated work then the arrangements necessary for the creation of the work were undertaken by Mr. Jones because he devised the appearance of the various elements of the game and the rules and logic by which each frame is generated and he wrote the relevant computer program. In these circumstances, I am satisfied that Mr. Jones is the person by whom the arrangements necessary for the creation of the works were undertaken and therefore is deemed to be the author by virtue of s. 9(3). ...Before leaving this topic there is one further complexity I must consider and that is the effect of player input...The player is not, however, an author of any of the artistic works created in the successive frame images. His input is not artistic in nature and he has contributed no skill or labour of an artistic kind. Nor has he undertaken any of the arrangements necessary for the creation of the frame images. All he has done is to play the game."

For a comment on the case, see S. Miles and E. Stokes, "Nova Productions Ltd. v Mazooma Games", ENT.L.R. [2006] 181.

C. MUSICAL WORKS

4–28   First sentence. **Add:** In a recent case, *Fisher v Brooker* ([2006] EWHC 3239 (Ch)), a claimant who had contributed the independently composed organ part of a song was granted a declaration that he was a co-author of the work and a joint owner of the musical work. The organ solo was sufficiently different from [the rest of the composition] to qualify in law, by a wide margin, as an original contribution to the work.

Add at end: This situation was illustrated by the case of *Hyperion Records Ltd. v Sawkins* [2005] EWCA Civ 565 where a musicologist created modern performing editions of certain out-of-copyright works. His authorship of and copyright in the editions was confirmed on appeal because his work showed the necessary level of effort, skill and time.

3. JOINT AUTHORSHIP: LITERARY, DRAMATIC, MUSICAL AND ARTISTIC WORKS

4–38   **Importance of distinction between joint authors and co-authors.** NOTE 49A. See on this issue L. Zemer, "Contribution and collaboration in joint authorship: too many misconceptions", J.I.P.L. & R. 2006, 1(4) 283.

4–39   **Definition.** NOTE 57. See also T. Lauterbach, "Joint Authorship in a Copyright Work Revisited" [2005] E.I.P.R. 119.

4–41   **All collaborators must be "authors".** **Add:** In a recent example, B collaborated with M to amend the lyrics of a rap song written by M to give them an authentic rap feel, resulting in an adaptation which was held to be both significant and original in the copyright sense; B was a joint author and thus a joint owner of the rights in the song.[3]

Contributions distinct. NOTE 90. See also *Fisher v Brooker* [2006] EWHC 3239 (Ch).   **4–44**

4. SOUND RECORDINGS, FILMS, BROADCASTS AND TYPOGRAPHICAL ARRANGEMENTS

Introduction. Last sentence. **Delete** and **substitute:** Consistently with this approach, "authors" of these categories of works are not generally granted moral rights in respect of these works. There are two exceptions to this: the director of a copyright film, since the passing of the 1988 Act; and the performer in the case of broadcast performances and sound recordings, since the entry into force on February 1, 2006, of The Performances (Moral Rights, etc.) Regulations 2006.[4]   **4–47**

B. FILMS

Regime 1

Producer. NOTE 35. **Add:** *Seven Network Operations v TCN Channel Nine Pty Ltd* [2005] FCAFC 144; (2005) 66 IPR 101, concerned a television documentary about a group of schoolboys on an expedition. The idea of the film was that of a youth worker who arranged and organised funding for the expedition, including the travel and accommodation costs of the freelance camera operator and sound recordist. A television company supplied a "script" consisting of the kinds of things to be filmed, paid the remuneration of the camera operator and sound recordist and supplied film equipment. The camera operator and sound recordist decided on what scenes and sequences would be filmed but took into account suggestions from the youth worker and others. In financial terms the youth worker's contribution was much greater than that of the television company. The Judge found that the youth worker and television companies jointly were "the person by whom the arrangements necessary for the making of the film were undertaken" and accordingly under Australian law (which was equivalent to the United Kingdom's Regime 2) were joint first owners of the copyright in the film. On appeal, Lindgren J. agreed with this conclusion [15]; Finkelstein J. expressed the view that it was "probably incorrect" but had not been challenged on appeal [89]. Edmonds J. took the view that the film had been made as a joint venture; accordingly, the film company and the youth worker were "multiple owners": the film company took rights to broadcast the film while the youth worker took all other rights [117].   **4–59**

G. TYPOGRAPHICAL ARRANGEMENTS

This heading has now been renumbered to be: F. TYPOGRAPHICAL ARRANGEMENTS.   **4–77**

---

[3] *Brown v Mcasso Music Production Ltd.*, (PCC) Patents County Court [2006] E.M.L.R. 3.
[4] See Ch.11, below.

CHAPTER FIVE

THE CHAIN OF TITLE

1. THE FIRST OWNER OF COPYRIGHT

B. LITERARY, DRAMATIC, MUSICAL AND ARTISTIC WORKS

(ii) Works of employees

5–08   **Introduction.** NOTE 14. **Add:** For the choice of law issues which may arise, see Torremans, "Authorship, Ownership of Rights and Works Created by Employees: Which Law Applies" [2005] 6 E.I.P.R. 220.

Was the author employed under a "contract of service"? NOTES 24 and 27.   **5–12**
Ultraframe (UK) Ltd v Fielding [2003] EWCA Civ 1805 is now reported at
[2004] R.P.C. 24 and [2004] E.C.D.R. 34.

No contact of service. **Add:**   **5–14**

  (i) A performer under an agreement with a management company pursuant
      to which the latter agreed "to render its services ... to use its best endeav-
      ours in the promotion and furtherance of the career and interest of the
      Performer" in return for a percentage of the performer's income while the
      performer agreed to render to the management company his exclusive ser-
      vices for a term. The agreement was a management agreement. In addi-
      tion, it had nothing to do with vesting copyright in the management
      company. *Experience Hendrix LLC v Purple Haze Records Ltd* [2007]
      EWCA Civ 501 at [68–9].

Owner-directors of companies. NOTE 56. *Ultraframe (UK) Ltd v Fielding*   **5–16**
[2003] EWCA Civ 1805 is now reported at [2004] R.P.C. 24 and [2004] E.C.D.R.
34.

Scope of employment. A contract of employment often evolves in the course of   **5–19**
time so that it may be unsafe to have regard only to the terms contained in an
initial written contract of employment: see *Liffe Administration and Management
v Pinkava* [2007] EWCA Civ 217; [2007] R.P.C. 30 at [56], [58].

Work done outside course of employment: "Moonlighting". NOTE 66. *Service*   **5–21**
Corp International PLC v Channel Four Television Corp is also reported at
[1999] E.M.L.R. 83.

(iv) Commissioned artistic works

The 1956 Act. NOTE 34. *Ultraframe (UK) Ltd v Fielding* [2003] EWCA Civ   **5–34**
1805 is now reported at [2004] R.P.C. 24 and [2004] E.C.D.R. 34.
    NOTE 48. *Gabrin v Universal Music Operations Ltd* is now reported at [2004]
E.C.D.R. 4.
    NOTE 52. *Ultraframe (UK) Ltd v Fielding* [2003] EWCA Civ 1805 is now
reported at [2004] R.P.C. 24 and [2004] E.C.D.R. 34. *Gabrin v Universal Music
Operations Ltd* is now reported at [2004] E.C.D.R. 4.

C. SOUND RECORDINGS AND FILMS

(i) Sound recordings

The 1988 Act. NOTE 90. The Rental and Related Rights Directive and its amend-   **5–41**
ments have now been codified as Directive 2006/115/EC: [2006] O.J. L376/28.

(ii) Films

(a) *Regime 1*

Films made on or after July 1, 1994. NOTE 4. Art.13(4) of the Rental Directive   **5–48**
is now Art.11(4) of Directive 2006/115/EC.
    NOTE 5. The Rental Directive and its amendments have now been codified as
Directive 2006/115/EC: [2006] O.J. L376/28.

5–49   **Transitional.** NOTE 9. **Delete:** 9/100. **Substitute:** 92/100. **Delete:** lead. **Substitute:** led. **Add:** The Rental Directive and its amendments have now been codified as Directive 2006/115/EC: [2006] O.J. L376/28.

F. TYPOGRAPHICAL ARRANGEMENTS

5–61   This heading has now been renumbered to be: E. TYPOGRAPHICAL ARRANGEMENTS.

2. TRANSMISSION OF TITLE

B. TRANSFER OF LEGAL TITLE BY ASSIGNMENT

(i) General

5–81   **Transitional.** NOTE 11. *Novello & Co Ltd v Keith Prowse Music Publishing Co Ltd* is now reported at [2004] E.M.L.R. 16 and [2004] R.P.C. 48. The decision of Patten J. was upheld on appeal: [2005] E.M.L.R. 21; [2005] R.P.C. 23.

(iii) Partial assignments

(b) *Presumption of transfer of rental right*

5–103   **Presumption of transfer of rental in case of film production agreement.** NOTE 86. The Rental Directive and its amendments have now been codified as Directive 2006/115/EC: [2006] O.J. L376/28.

        NOTE 94. Art.2(5) of the Rental Directive is now Art.3(4) of Directive 2006/115/EC.

        NOTE 97. Art.2(5) of the Rental Directive is now Art.3(4) of Directive 2006/115/EC.

(v) Limitations on the right to assign

(a) *Right to equitable remuneration where rental right transferred*

5–111   NOTE 41. The Directive on Rental and Lending Rights and its amendments have now been codified as Directive 2006/115/EC: [2006] O.J. L376/28.

        NOTE 44. **Add:** See now Art.5 of Directive 2006/115/EC.

        Last but one line. **Delete:** s.146 of the Law of Property Act 1925. **Substitute:** s.136 of the Law of Property Act 1925.

        NOTE 49. The reference to Snell, *Principles of Equity* should now be to *Snell's Equity* (31st ed.), para.3–12 *et seq.*

(b) *Reversionary rights under the 1988 Act*

5–112   NOTE 52. *Novello & Co Ltd v Keith Prowse Music Publishing Co Ltd* is now reported at [2004] E.M.L.R. 16 and [2004] R.P.C. 48. **Add** at end of first sentence: and see paras 22 to 24 of the judgment of Lloyd J. in the Court of Appeal: *Novello & Co Ltd v Keith Prowse Music Publishing Co Ltd* [2005] E.M.L.R. 21; [2005] R.P.C. 23.

5–113A   **Further points.** NOTES 63 and 64. *Novello & Co Ltd v Keith Prowse Music Publishing Co Ltd* is now reported at [2004] E.M.L.R. 16 and [2004] R.P.C. 48. **Add:** See also paragraph 10 of the judgment of Lloyd J. on appeal: [2005] E.M.L.R. 21; [2005] R.P.C. 23. In *Redwood Music Ltd v B. Feldman & Co Ltd*

[1979] R.P.C. 1 it was held that the term "legal personal representatives" included executors named in the will of a person who died domiciled abroad even if they had not proved the will in England and Wales. In *Peer International Corporation v Termidor Music Publishers Ltd* [2006] EWHC 2883 (Ch); [2007] E.C.D.R. 1, Lindsay J. stated that the reasoning in Redwood was "not above doubt" [68], particularly insofar as the Judge (Robert Goff J.) had relied by analogy on the provisions of section 19 of the Revenue Act 1889 [70]. Lindsay J. said that his preferred construction of the term "legal personal representatives" would be "those obtaining an English grant", but that if that were wrong the term certainly did not extend to "heirs, next-of-kin, devisees, legatees or creditors in respect of whom no grant or order of any Court, English or foreign, has been made as to title to or as to the vesting of the deceased's personal property." [72]. Clearly, the decision in *Redwood v Feldman* is inconsistent with Lindsay J.'s "preferred construction". Presumably, however, that decision is reconcilable with Lindsay J.'s alternative construction because the claimants in Redwood claimed through named executors as opposed to heirs etc. (it is however noteworthy that Lindsay J. took the view that there might well have been a United States grant [67]). On the facts of *Peer*, the authors had died intestate and there had been no English grant. Accordingly, there were no "legal personal representatives" and the reversionary rights vested in the Public Trustee [71].

NOTE 66. First sentence. *Novello & Co Ltd v Keith Prowse Music Publishing Co Ltd* is now reported at [2004] E.M.L.R. 16 and [2004] R.P.C. 48. The decision of Patten J. has been upheld on appeal: see [2005] E.M.L.R. 21; [2005] R.P.C. 23. **Add** at end: and para.24 of the judgment on appeal of Lloyd J.

NOTE 80. *Novello & Co Ltd v Keith Prowse Music Publishing Co Ltd* is now reported at [2004] E.M.L.R. 16 and [2004] R.P.C. 48. The decision of Patten J. has been upheld on appeal: see [2005] E.M.L.R. 21; [2005] R.P.C. 23.

C. TRANSMISSION BY TESTAMENTARY DISPOSITION AND OPERATION OF LAW

NOTE 2. *Peer International Corp v Termidor Music Publishers Ltd* is now reported at [2004] Ch. 212; [2004] R.P.C. 23; [2003] E.M.L.R. 34.   **5–121**

(i) Death

In whom vested on death. NOTE 13. *Gabrin v Universal Music Operations Ltd* is now reported at [2004] E.C.D.R. 4.   **5–123**

NOTE 11. **Add:** In *Peer International Corporation v Termidor Music Publishers Ltd* [2006] EWHC 2883 (Ch); [2007] E.C.D.R. 1, Lindsay J. appeared to reject an argument that although there was no grant of letters of administration, a claimant which had obtained assignments from all those entitled on intestacy could sue for declaratory relief on the basis that it had a better title than anyone else in equity [80]. The claimant's application to be appointed administrator of the copyrights or for an accountant to be so appointed also failed on the facts [85, 86].

Death of person with foreign domicile. NOTE 15. *Peer International Corp v Termidor Music Publishers Ltd* is now reported at [2004] R.P.C. 22; [2003] E.C.D.R. 22; [2003] E.M.L.R. 19.   **5–124**

NOTES 16 and 17. In *Peer International Corporation v Termidor Music Publishers Ltd* [2006] EWHC 2883 (Ch), the question arose as to the correctness of the statement in *Redwood Music Ltd v B. Feldman & Co Ltd* that "English copyright which forms part of the estate of a testator who dies domiciled abroad can vest in the executors appointed in his will, without any Grant of Probate or

Letters of Administration in this country". It was common ground that this statement was *obiter* [64]. Lindsay J. stated that the reasoning in Redwood was "not above doubt" [68], particularly insofar as the Judge (Robert Goff J.) had relied by analogy on the provisions of s.19 of the Revenue Act 1889 [70]. In the event, however, Lindsay J. was able to distinguish Redwood on the basis that the deceased in *Peer* had all died intestate [71].

3. RIGHTS IN EXTENDED AND REVIVED TERMS OF COPYRIGHT

B. RIGHTS IN THE EXTENDED TERM OF COPYRIGHT IN SOUND RECORDINGS UNDER THE INFORMATION SOCIETY DIRECTIVE

(i) Introduction

5–142 Article 3(2) of the Term Directive (as amended) is now Article 3(2) of Directive 2006/116/EC.

4. JOINT AUTHORS AND JOINT OWNERS

5–165 **Joint authors as first owners of copyright.** NOTE 40. **Add:** *Fisher v Brooker* [2006] EWHC 3239 (Ch); [2007] F.S.R. 12; [2007] E.M.L.R. 9 at [96], awarding a 40 per cent share [98].

5. EQUITABLE OWNERSHIP

A. CREATION OF AN EQUITABLE TITLE

(i) Equitable title arising on creation of a work

5–173 **Equitable title by virtue of contract.** NOTE 56. *Peer International Corp v Editora Musical de Cuba* [2002] EWHC 2675 (Ch) is now reported as *Peer International Corp v Termidor Music Publishers Ltd* at [2004] R.P.C. 22; [2003] E.C.D.R. 22; [2003] E.M.L.R. 19. The decision on appeal is reported at [2004] Ch. 212; [2004] R.P.C. 23; [2003] E.M.L.R. 34.

NOTE 59. The decision in *R Griggs Group Ltd v Evans* [2004] F.S.R. 31 was upheld on appeal [2005] EWCA Civ 11; [2005] F.S.R. 31; [2005] E.C.D.R. 30.

5–174 **Commissioned works.** NOTE 73. In *R Griggs Group Ltd v Evans* [2005] EWCA Civ 11; [2005] F.S.R. 31; [2005] E.C.D.R. 30 at para.14, the summary of the law on this topic in *Ray v Classic FM* was described by the Court of Appeal as "masterful".

NOTES 77 and 77. The decision in *R Griggs Group Ltd v Evans* [2004] F.S.R. 31 was upheld on appeal: [2005] EWCA Civ 11; [2005] F.S.R. 31; [2005] E.C.D.R. 30. The defendant had been commissioned to produce a logo. Although the claimant had intended to use the logo for all purposes throughout the world, the defendant had been told (and believed) that it would only be used on point of sale material in the United Kingdom. On appeal the argument that it was only necessary to imply a licence to use the logo on point of sale material in the United Kingdom was dismissed as "fantastic": if an officious bystander had asked at the time of the contract whether the rights were to be so limited, both parties would have replied "of course not". The defendant had no further interest in the work (para.19). The fact that the defendant had been paid the proper rate for the use of the logo for all purposes throughout the world disposed of any argument that he needed to retain the copyright in order to call for payment for such further use (para.21). The Court of Appeal went on to observe that questions of further use often caused problems in relation to commissioned works and that it was always better if provision was made for payment for such use in the contract. A right to further payment for unforeseen or undisclosed further use might be implied in some cases. In others, the author might indeed retain copyright and actually be able to prevent such further use. Everything depended on the circumstances (para.21). On the first instance decision, see Baines, "Copyright in Commissioned Works: A Cause for Uncertainty" [2005] 3 E.I.P.R. 122. On the decision on appeal, see Groves, "Copyright in Commissioned Work: Court of Appeal Put the Boot In" [2005] 3 Ent. L.R. 56.

In *Wrenn v Landamore* [2007] EWHC 1833 (Ch), the defendant had been engaged by the claimant to write software for use in interfaces between car radios and third party audio equipment. A royalty had been agreed. It was held to be sufficient to imply an exclusive licence. Such a licence would be sufficient to enable the claimant to market interfaces embodying the software. An outright assignment might give the defendant no rights in the event of non-payment of royalties, whereas a licence could be terminated on an accepted repudiation [37]. It was necessary for the licence to extend to the source code both so as to enable source code to be compiled into object code in the manufacture of interfaces but also to enable the software to be developed by others as the defendant appeared to have envisaged might happen [38]. The source code included a so-called "emulation layer", which had been written by the defendant prior to his involvement with the claimant. It was contended on behalf of the defendant that the licence should exclude the source code or alternatively that it should exclude the emulation layer. This argument was rejected but the grounds for rejecting the alternative argument are not easy to understand [42].

NOTE 80. However, it by no means follows that whenever the commissioner has some right in respect of a contribution of a different nature to the overall project, he will obtain exclusive rights to everything produced within that project. It all depends on the circumstances: *Clearsprings Management Ltd v BusinessLinx Ltd* [2005] EWHC 1487 (Ch) at para.37.

NOTE 81. However, where the maker's contribution to the work of such a team is distinct and it is clear that the parties would have intended the maker to be free to use it or would have been indifferent to such use, an assignment is both unnecessary and unworkable: *Clearsprings Management Ltd v BusinessLinx Ltd* [2005] EWHC 1487 (Ch) at para.36. The case concerned computer software. Both parties contemplated that the maker would re-use the code created for the project in question. The court implied a non-exclusive licence together with a restriction on the maker using information about the commissioner's operating procedures for purposes other than those of the commissioner.

Company directors and other fiduciaries. NOTE 87. *Ultraframe (UK) Ltd v Fielding* [2003] EWCA Civ 1805 is now reported at [2004] R.P.C. 24 and [2004] E.C.D.R. 34.

5–176

NOTE 88. **Add:** See also *Vitof Ltd v Altoft* [2006] EWHC 1678 (Ch) at paras 144 to 147, citing with apparent approval all but the last sentence of this paragraph in the Main Work, together with *Charly Acquisitions Ltd v Immediate Records Inc* (Pumfrey J., February 7, 2002) at paras 78 to 79 and the trade mark case of *Ball v The Eden Project Ltd* [2002] F.S.R. 43. The Judge also held (at paras 148 to 149), following the *A-One* case, that the copyright in source code created in contemplation of the incorporation of a company and for its benefit was held on trust for the company.

NOTES 89, 91, 92. *Ultraframe (UK) Ltd v Fielding* [2003] EWCA Civ 1805 is now reported at [2004] R.P.C. 24 and [2004] E.C.D.R. 34.

NOTE 93. *Service Corp International v Channel Four Television Corp* is reported at [1999] E.M.L.R. 83.

5–177 **Partners. Add** at end: Similar considerations apply to performers' property rights: see *Bourne v Davis* [2006] EWHC 1567 (Ch) at [25]. In that case it was held that if the performers' property rights of a particular partner were indeed partnership assets, the assignment by that partner of his rights to a third party would not be void. It might affect the process of accounting between the co-partners but the co-partners would have no right to require the third party to reassign the rights [29].

(ii) Equitable title arising subsequent to creation of work

5–179 **Agreement to assign.** NOTE 2. *Peer International Corp v Editora Musical de Cuba* [2002] EWHC 2675 (Ch) is now reported as *Peer International Corp v Termidor Music Publishers Ltd* at [2004] R.P.C. 22; [2003] E.C.D.R. 22; [2003] E.M.L.R. 19.

C. INCIDENTS OF EQUITABLE OWNERSHIP

5–187 **Rights as against legal owner.** NOTE 23. *R Griggs Group Ltd v Evans* is now reported at [2004] F.S.R. 31 (on appeal [2005] EWCA Civ 11; [2005] F.S.R. 31; [2005] E.C.D.R. 30). *R Griggs Group Ltd v Evans (No.2)* is reported at [2005] Ch. 153; [2004] F.S.R. 48.

NOTE 24. **Add:** In *Vitof Ltd v Altoft* [2006] EWHC 1678 (Ch) at para.174 it was definitively held that a bare legal title is no defence to an infringement claim by the beneficial owner.

5–188 **Rights as between equitable owners.** NOTE 25. The reference to Snell should now be to *Snell's Equity* (31st ed.), para.4–51 *et seq.*

6. MORTGAGES AND CHARGES

5–191 **Mortgages.** NOTE 28. The reference to Snell should now be to *Snell's Equity* (31st ed.), para.35–16.

5–193 **Charges.** NOTE 39. The reference to Snell should now be to *Snell's Equity* (31st ed.), para.34–03.

7. LICENCES AND RELATED ISSUES

A. INTRODUCTION

5–194 NOTE 42. *Frisby v B.B.C.* is reported at [1967] Ch. 932.

NOTE 46. **Add** at end of first sentence: A statutory exclusive licence is, however a "right over property" and thus a "non-cash asset" for the purposes of s.320 of the Companies Act 1985: *Ultraframe (UK) Ltd v Fielding (No.2)* [2005] EWHC 1638 (Ch); [2006] F.S.R. 17 (design right).

Transitional. NOTE 54. *Novello & Co Ltd v Keith Prowse Music Publishing Co*   **5–198**
Ltd is now reported at [2004] E.M.L.R. 16 and [2004] R.P.C. 48. The decision of
Patten J. was upheld on appeal: see [2005] E.M.L.R. 21; [2005] R.P.C. 23.

B. ASSIGNMENT OR LICENCE?

Principles of construction. NOTE 74. *R Griggs Group Ltd v Evans* is now   **5–202**
reported at [2004] F.S.R. 31. The decision was upheld on appeal: [2005] EWCA
Civ 11; [2005] F.S.R. 31; [2005] E.C.D.R. 30.

C. EXCLUSIVE LICENCES

(ii) Statutory exclusive licences

Transitional. NOTE 9. *Novello & Co Ltd v Keith Prowse Music Publishing Co*   **5–208**
Ltd is now reported at [2004] E.M.L.R. 16 and [2004] R.P.C. 48. The decision of
Patten J. was upheld on appeal: see [2005] E.M.L.R. 21; [2005] R.P.C. 23.

E. IMPLIED AND INFORMAL LICENCES

Implied licences. NOTE 33. *Brighton v Jones* is now reported at [2004] E.M.L.R.   **5–213**
26; [2005] F.S.R. 16. In *Barrett v Universal-Island Records Ltd* [2006] EWHC
1009 (Ch), the Barretts participated in the recording of songs, knowing that the
recordings were to be delivered to a record company for inclusion in an album
for distribution to the public. They left it to Bob Marley to make whatever business arrangements he thought fit with the record company. At the time the recordings were made, the means of reproduction were vinyl records and cassettes. It
was held (*obiter*) that if the Barretts had owned any copyright in the songs, any
implied licence would have extended not only to the making of such records and
cassettes but also to the making of CDs and DVDs, which the Judge described as
"a more technologically advanced means of reproducing the same work in essentially the same form" (para.360). The Judge's decision on this point was
influenced by the fact that the contracts under which the recordings were
delivered specifically contemplated reproduction by means other than vinyl records and cassettes, including audio-visual means (albeit the Barretts were not
parties to them). The Judge went on to hold that it would not have been necessary
to imply an *exclusive* licence: if the Barretts had wanted to license others to
perform any songs in which they had copyright or to perform them themselves,
they should have been free to do so. The Judge accepted that since neither of the
Barretts knew that they were entitled to any copyright, there could be no intention to create legal relations and accordingly that any licence was not contractual
(para.362).

In *Independiente Ltd v Music Trading On-Line (HK) Ltd* [2007] EWHC 533
(Ch); [2007] F.S.R. 21, the Judge appeared on one reading of paragraph [21] of
his judgment to assimilate the test for whether a licence had been granted by a
copyright owner to import goods to the test for whether a trade mark proprietor
had consented to the placing of an article on the market in the EEA for the
purposes of considering an exhaustion defence. It is suggested that the two tests
are not necessarily the same.

Effect of estoppel and acquiescence. NOTE 38. **Add:** *Fisher v Brooker* [2006]   **5–216**
EWHC 3239(Ch); [2007] F.S.R. 12; [2007] E.M.L.R. 9, emphasising at [81] that
if estoppel is found the court has then to go on to consider how to give effect to
that equity, often by balancing the expectation or assumption generated by the
estoppel against the degree of detriment suffered on the faith of the conduct which

has given rise to the expectation or assumption. *Brighton v Jones* is now reported at [2004] E.M.L.R. 26; [2005] F.S.R. 16.

F. CONSTRUCTION AND TERMS OF LICENCES

5–225   **New technologies.** NOTE 2. See, however, *Barrett v Universal-Island Records Ltd* [2006] EWHC 1009 (Ch), above, para.5–213.

5–226   **Effect of non-compliance with licence terms. Add** at end: In *Leofelis SA v Lonsdale Sports Ltd* [2007] EWHC 451 (Ch) at [56] it was held that there is no principled distinction between the circumstances of landlord and a tenant and those of the licensor of a trade mark and his licensee. Accordingly, prima facie the licensee should be entitled to rely on the acceptance of royalties as a clear indication that the licensor was confirming the continuation in force of the licence.

5–227   **Revocation and termination.** NOTE 19. *Godfrey v Lees* should be compared with *Fisher v Brooker* [2006] EWHC 3239 (Ch); [2007] F.S.R. 12; [2007] E.M.L.R. 9, in which no such estoppel was established. Such an estoppel may, depending on the facts, be terminable on reasonable notice: see *Barrett v Universal-Island Records Ltd* [2006] EWHC 1009 (Ch), para.363.

    Add at end: The revocation of a licence will not affect contracts or arrangements entered into prior to the revocation: *Barrett v Universal-Island Records Ltd* [2006] EWHC 1009 (Ch), para.366, following *Brighton v Jones* [2004] EWHC 1157 (Ch); [2004] E.M.L.R. 26; [2005] F.S.R. 16.

G. ARCHITECTS' PLANS AND WORKS OF ARCHITECTURE

5–229   **Examples.** NOTE 28. **Add:** See also *Parramatta Design & Developments Pty Ltd v Concrete Pty Ltd* [2005] FCAFC 138: where an architect had gratuitously provided plans to a joint venture in order to keep the venture going, obtain planning permission and see the development constructed by the joint venture partners, it was held that the implied licence did not extend to a purchaser of the site.

5–230   **Current RIBA conditions.** Third line. **Delete:** 1992. **Substitute:** 1992, with amendments.

    Delete third, fourth and fifth sentences and NOTES 44 to 47. **Substitute:** They provide that the client may reproduce the plans for purposes related to the project on the site or part of the site to which they relate. Those purposes expressly include the operation, maintenance, repair, reinstatement, alteration, extension, promotion, leasing and sale of the building. This licence is subject to numerous qualifications, including the following. First, the design may not be used for any extension of the project or any other project unless a licence fee is specified in the agreement. Second, if the use occurs between the last provision by the architect of services and practical completion, the client must (a) if the architect has not completed detailed proposals under Work Stage D obtain the architect's consent (not to be unreasonably withheld) and/or (b) pay a reasonable licence fee if none is specified in the agreement. Third, the architect can suspend the licence on seven days' notice if the client is in default of payment of any fees or other amounts due. Use of the licence "may be resumed" on receipt of the outstanding amounts.

    Add at end: The trap was effective in the Scottish case of *Dorrans v The Shand Partnership* [2004] E.C.D.R. 21, which concerned a version of the RIBA Conditions which contained provisions (a), (b) and (c) set out in paragraph 5–230 of the Main Work. The benefit of the agreement was stated not to be assignable without the architect's consent. The architect produced plans for a potential developer of a site in support of a planning application. Planning permission was granted but the purchase fell through. It was held that given the prohibition on assignment there was no basis for construing the expression "the Client" as extending to future proprietors of the property, nor was there room for an implied term to that effect.

CHAPTER SIX

DURATION OF COPYRIGHT

2. THE HISTORY OF THE DEVELOPMENT OF THE TERM OF COPYRIGHT PROTECTION

6–02   **What is a fair term for copyright?** NOTE 11. **Add:** Directive 93/98/EEC has been repealed and replaced by Directive 2006/116/EC, without prejudice to the obligations of the Member States relating to the time-limits for transposition into national law of the Directives, and their application. Directive 2006/116/EC is a consolidating measure, taking into account amendments to the Term Directive made by the Information Society Directive (Directive 2002/29/EC), and has not made any substantive changes to the law. However, it should be noted that the numbering of the recitals and articles of the two directives differ somewhat, References in this supplement are to the new codified directive unless otherwise indicated.

6–05A   **Revision to Berne Convention: Stockholm and Paris Acts.** Last sentence. **Delete**, and **substitute:** As regards photographic works, the Stockholm Act introduced a minimum term of 25 years from the making of such work, which was retained in the Paris Act.[1] However, the World Copyright Treaty (WCT) 1996 provides that, in respect of photographic works, the Contracting Parties shall not apply the provisions of Article 7(4) of the Berne Convention.[2] Article 7(4) of the Berne Convention provides:

> "It shall be a matter for legislation in the countries of the Union to determine the term of protection of photographic works and that of works of applied art in so far as they are protected as artistic works; however, this term shall last at least until the end of a period of twenty-five years from the making of such a work."

The result is that parties to the WCT are obliged to protect photographs as artistic works for the life of the author and fifty years after his death in accordance with Article 7(1) of the Paris Act of the Berne Convention.

The Rome Convention. Second sentence. **Delete**, and **substitute:** This Convention is based on the principle of according national treatment to the works originating in other Contracting States; however, as regards the term of protection of its beneficiaries, performers, producers of phonograms and broadcasting organisations, it stipulates a minimum period of 20 years computed from the end of the year in which: **6–06**

(a) the fixation was made—for phonograms and for performances incorporated therein;
(b) the performance took place—for performances not incorporated in phonograms;
(c) the broadcast took place—for broadcasts.

The TRIPs Agreement and the WPPT. Under the Agreement on Trade-Related Aspects of Intellectual Property, 1994 (the TRIPs Agreement),[3] the term of protection accorded to performers and producers of phonograms shall last at least until the end of a period of 50 years computed from the end of the calendar year in which the fixation was made or the performance took place. Broadcasts benefit from a minimum term of 20 years from the end of the calendar year in which the broadcast took place.[4] The WIPO Performances and Phonograms Treaty, 1996, (WPPT),[5] provides also for a minimum of 50 years for performers and producers of phonograms. For performances, the term is computed, as under the TRIPs Agreement, from the end of the year in which the performance was fixed in a phonogram; for producers, the period is calculated from the end of the year in which the phonogram was published, or failing such publication within 50 years from fixation of the phonogram, 50 years from the end of the year in which the fixation was made.[6]   **6–06A**

European harmonisation of the term of protection. Last sentence. **Delete** and **substitute:** This led to the adoption by the Council of the European Communities, on October 29, 1993, of Directive 93/98 harmonising the term of protection of copyright and certain related rights, which has recently been repealed and replaced by a codifying Directive 2000/116/EC.[7] These Directives are collectively referred to hereafter as "the Term Directive".   **6–08**

---

[1] Art.7(4) in each Act.
[2] WCT, Art.9.
[3] See Ch.24, para.24–135 *et seq.,* below.
[4] TRIPs Agreement, Art.14(5).
[5] See Ch.24, para.24–119 *et seq.,* below.
[6] WPPT, Art.17.
[7] [2006] O.J. L372.

NOTE 44. **Add:** Directive 93/98/EEC has been repealed and replaced by Directive 2006/116/EC, without prejudice to the obligations of the Member States relating to the time-limits for transposition into national law of the Directives, and their application. Directive 2006/116/EC is a consolidating measure, taking into account amendments to the Term Directive made by the Information Society Directive (Directive 2002/29/EC), and has not made any substantive changes to the law. However, it should be noted that the numbering of the recitals and articles of the new Directive differ slightly from that of Directive 93/98/EC, as some provisions as to entry into force , etc. had become obsolete. References in this supplement are to the new codified Directive 2006/116/EC, unless otherwise indicated.

NOTE 46. **Delete** and **substitute:** Term Directive, Art.10(2) and Art.13(1) of Directive 93/98/EC; as also is the term provided for in (2).

NOTE 53. **Delete** and **substitute:** Term Directive, recital (10).

NOTE 54. **Delete** and **substitute:** Term Directive, recitals (3) and (12).

NOTE 55. **Delete** and **substitute:** Term Directive, Art.10(2) and Art.13(1) of Directive 93/98/EEC.

NOTE 61. **Delete** and **substitute:** Directive 93/98/EEC, recital (25).

NOTE 62. **Delete** and **substitute:** Term Directive, recital (25).

6–10   **Further international harmonisation of the term of protection.** NOTE 71. **Delete** and **substitute:** Term Directive, recital (21) and Art.7.

3. THE PRESENT POSITION UNDER THE 1988 ACT AS AMENDED

6–11   **Implementation of the Term Directive in the United Kingdom.** NOTE 74. **Delete** and **substitute:** Art.13(1) of Directive 93/98/EEC.

6–15   **Existing works in the public domain in the United Kingdom but protected in another EEA state on July 1, 1995.** NOTE 99. **Delete** and **substitute:** Term Directive, Art.10(2) and Art.13(1) of Directive 93/98/EEC.

6–19   **Country of origin: other works.** NOTE 26. **Delete** and **substitute:** See CDPA 1988, s.13A(4) and 14(3).

4. THE EFFECT OF TRANSITIONAL PROVISIONS ON THE TERM OF EXISTING WORKS

C. THE 1956 ACT

6–37   **Transitional provisions. Add:** In *Novello & Co Ltd v Keith Prowse Music Publishing Co Ltd*,[8] the Court of Appeal held that the transitional provisions of the 1956 Act, in particular, Schedule 7, paragraph 28(3), applied only to assignments which had come into effect in accordance with Schedule 7, paragraph 28(1), namely, before the commencement of the 1956 Act. The effect of paragraph 28(3) was to preserve the effect of the previous law in relation to things done under the previous law and in particular it preserved the provisions of the proviso to section 5(2) of the 1911 Act. There was nothing in paragraph 28(3) for it to apply prospectively and accordingly it did not relate to assignments which had come into effect after the commencement of the 1956 Act.

---

[8] [2004] EWCA Civ 1776.

D. THE 1988 ACT

Transitional provisions. Add: The Gowers Review of Intellectual Property of   **6–44**
December 2006, recommended *inter alia* that policy makers should adopt the
principle that the term and scope of protection for IP rights should not be altered
retrospectively in the future.[9]

6. SOUND RECORDINGS

A. SOUND RECORDINGS MADE ON OR AFTER JANUARY 1, 1996

Limit imposed on term. NOTE 91. **Add:** However, on January 1, 2005, sound   **6–58**
recordings published on or before December 31, 1954, fell into the public domain,
making available for exploitation many famous and still successful recordings
without the payment of royalties. This led to calls from the recording industry
and performers to prolong the period of protection afforded to them to 70 years or
more. In May 2007, support for an increase in the term of protection to at least 70
years came from the House of Commons Culture, Media and Sport Committee in
its report entitled "New Media and the Creative Industries".[10] The issue is currently under consideration by the European Commission. However, the Gowers
Review of Intellectual Property of December 2006 recommended against requesting the European Union to consider such an extension[11] and the Department of
Culture, Media and Sport announced on July 27, 2007, that it would not support
extending the term of protection of either producers of sound recordings or
performers.

Works of non-EEA origin. NOTE 95. **Delete** and **substitute:** That is the date the   **6–59**
original Term Directive 93/98/EC was adopted.

7. FILMS

A. FILMS MADE ON OR AFTER JANUARY 1, 1996

General Position. Second sentence. **Delete**, and **substitute:** Previously, films   **6–67**
were treated in the United Kingdom as original works in accordance with Article
14*bis*(1) of the Berne Convention, which provides that a cinematographic work
shall be protected as an original work and that the owner of copyright in a
cinematographic work shall enjoy the same rights as the author of an original
work. The Berne Convention provides also that ownership of copyright in a
cinematographic work shall be a matter for legislation in the country where
protection is claimed.[12] The United Kingdom recognised the film producer as the
author of the film and protected films for 50 years from the end of the year in
which it was made,[13] thus affording films a regime of protection similar to that of
phonograms. At the international level, however, films remain protected under
the Berne Convention as cinematographic works, whereas phonograms are
subject to the related rights regime of the Rome Convention.

---

[9] Recommendation 4.
[10] Fifth Report of Session 2006–2007, HC 509–1, dated May 1, 2007, Recommendation 28.
[11] Recommendation 3.
[12] Art.14 *bis*(2)(a).
[13] But see para.6–71, below.

11. ABANDONMENT OF COPYRIGHT

6–85   Second paragraph. Fourth sentence. **Delete**, and **substitute:** The view expressed
by Whitford J. has not subsequently been endorsed in the courts of England and
Wales.[14] However, Aldous J., in *Merrell Dow Pharmaceuticals Inc. and Another
v N.H. Norton & Co. Ltd*,[15] pointed out that Whitford J.'s statement of the law
was made without the benefit of considering *Werner Motors Ltd. v A.W. Gamage
Ltd.*[16] In the latter case, the Court of Appeal had held that there was no basis for
putting an applicant to an election between a patent for an article and registration
of a design for the shape of a similar article. Aldous J. stated, further, that since
1982, a considerable body of judicial opinion had pointed out the difficulty of ac-
cepting Whitford J.'s statement as the law. It should be noted, however, that the
cases referred to were decided in various other jurisdictions.[17]

---

[14] The point was treated as arguable by Slade J. in *General Electric Co v Turbine Blading Ltd.*
[1980] F.S.R. 510, on an application in a copyright action for discovery of patent drawings, and
Falconer J. distinguished *Catnic (Catnic Components Ltd v Hill and Smith* [1978] F.S.R. 405) on
its facts, without deciding its correctness on this point in *Gardex Ltd v Serata Ltd* [1986] R.P.C.
623. See also Whitford J. in *Rose Plastics GmbH v William Beckett & Co (Plastics) Ltd* [1989]
F.S.R. 113 at 123–4.

[15] [1994] R.P.C. 1.

[16] (1904) 21 R.P.C. 621.

[17] *House of Spring Gardens Ltd v Point Blank Ltd.* [1983] F.S.R. 213 at 269 (High Court of Ireland,
affirmed on appeal: [1985] F.S.R. 327); *Ogden Industries Pty Ltd v Kis (Australia) Ltd* [1983]
F.S.R. 619 (Supreme Court of New South Wales); *Wham-O Manufacturing Co v Lincoln
Industries ltd* [1982] R.P.C. 281 at 297 (High Court of New Zealand); and, in particular, *Inter-
lego AG v Tyco Industries Inc* [1987] F.S.R. 409, where the point was fully discussed at 455
(Court of Appeal of Hong Kong).

CHAPTER SEVEN

THE RIGHTS OF A COPYRIGHT OWNER: PRIMARY INFRINGEMENT

Contents

2. THE REPRODUCTION RIGHT

A. INTRODUCTION

European Directives. NOTE 33. **Add:** The Rental and Related Rights Directive 7–10 and its amendments have now been codified as Directive 2006/115/EC: [2006] O.J. L376/28.

Idea versus expression. NOTE 49. **Add** at end of first sentence: *IPC Media Ltd v* 7–13 *Highbury-Leisure Publishing Ltd* [2004] EWHC 2985 (Ch); [2005] F.S.R. 20 at para.14; *Hyperion Records Ltd v Sawkins* [2005] EWCA Civ 565; [2005] 1 W.L.R. 3281; [2005] R.P.C. 32, *per* Mummery L.J. (with whom Mance L.J. agreed) at para.29: "copyright can be used to prevent copying of a substantial part of the relevant form of expression, but it does not prevent use of the information, thoughts or emotions expressed in the copyright work."

Proof of copying. NOTE 86. **Add:** See also *Nova Productions Limited v Ma-* 7–17 *zooma Games Limited* [2006] EWHC 24 (Ch); [2006] R.P.C. 14; [2006] E.M.L.R. 14 at para.123. This issue did not arise on appeal: [2007] EWCA Civ 219; [2007] R.P.C. 25; [2007] E.M.L.R. 14; [2007] E.C.D.R. 6.

NOTE 88. **Add** at end: See also *Baigent v The Random House Group Ltd* [2007] EWCA Civ 247; [2007] F.S.R. 24 at [4], [122].

NOTE 89. **Add:** See also *EPI Environment Technologies Inc v Symphony Plastic Technologies plc* [2006] EWCA Civ 3; [2006] 1 W.L.R. 495 (note).

NOTE 96. **Add** at end: For the importance of not being misled by "similarity by excision", see *IPC Media Ltd v Highbury-Leisure Publishing Ltd* [2004] EWHC 2985 (Ch); [2005] F.S.R. 20 at para.8: "In copyright cases, chipping away and ignoring all the bits which are undoubtedly not copied may result in the creation of an illusion of copying in what is left. This is a particular risk during a trial. Inevitably the court will be invited by the claimant to concentrate on the respects in which his work and the alleged infringements are similar. But with sufficient concentration one may lose sight of the differences. They may be just as important in deciding whether copying has taken place." See on this case Theobald, "Looking for Inspiration in Homestyle Magazines" [2005] 4 Ent. L.R. 92.

7–18   **The role of expert witnesses.** For a music copying case in which (exceptionally) no expert evidence was called, see *Barrett v Universal-Island Records Ltd* [2006] EWHC 1009 (Ch). One issue was as to whether the addition of an "instrumental bridge" to an existing work was sufficient to give rise to a new copyright work. The Judge was asked to listen to both works and then reach a view without the assistance of expert evidence. The Judge held that in principle this was "not the way to proceed" (para.355) and stated that in the absence of expert evidence he was unable to reach any conclusion about whether the bridge was an original composition, a question of interpretation or performance or part of an overall arrangement of the song as a whole (para.356). For the importance of expert evidence in cases involving allegations of copying the lyrics of rap compositions, see *Confetti Records v Warner Music UK Ltd* [2003] EWHC 1274; [2003] E.M.L.R. 35 at paragraph 154 and *Brown v Mcasso Music Production Ltd* [2005] EWCC 1 (Cpwt); [2005] F.S.R. 40; [2006] E.M.L.R. 3 at paragraph 10.5. See Hughes, "Rapper's Delight?" [2006] 3 Ent.. L.R. 98.

NOTE 11. **Add:** See also *IPC Media Ltd v Highbury-Leisure Publishing Ltd* [2004] EWHC 2985 (Ch); [2005] F.S.R. 20 at paras 40 and 43.

NOTE 14. *IPC Media Ltd v Highbury-Leisure Publishing Ltd* is reported at [2005] F.S.R. 20.

NOTE 15. **Add:** See also *IPC Media Ltd v Highbury-Leisure Publishing Ltd* [2004] EWHC 2985 (Ch); [2005] F.S.R. 20 at paras 40 to 42.

7–19   **Transient and incidental copying: copying by electronic means.** NOTE 18. **Add:** For an example of the application of this principle to reproduction on a computer screen, see *UEFA v Briscomb* [2006] EWHC 1628 (Ch).

In *Woolworths Ltd v Olson* [2004] NSWSC 849; (2004) 63 IPR 258, an employee attached copyright works to emails and sent them from his work address to his wife's home email address where they "arrived" in her inbox on their home computer. Before the emails were opened, the computer was seized under an Anton Piller order and the emails deleted by the claimants. It was held that the act of sending the emails caused a reproduction of the copyright works on the defendant's email server which remained in existence until such time as they were deleted. As a matter of Australian law there had been a reproduction of the works in a material form by their reproduction in a digital form of storage from which they were capable of further reproduction by the act of downloading [330]. Although the Australian test is different, the result would be the same in the United Kingdom.

7–20   **Works in digital form.** NOTE 23. *Sony Computer Entertainment v Owen* is reported as *Kabushi Kaisha Sony Computer Entertainment Inc v Owen* [2002] E.M.L.R. 34; [2002] E.C.D.R. 27.

B. Substantial part

Substantial part: the test. Add: In *Baigent v The Random House Group Ltd* **7–25**
[2007] EWCA Civ 247; [2007] F.S.R. 24 at [144], Mummery L.J., with whom
Rix L.J. agreed, expressed the view that there was no real point in seeking to
define the term "substantial part": "That sort of question is only a path to a dictio-
nary and to the dubious substitution or addition of other words which do not help
to answer the crucial question of fact".

Substantial part: a question of mixed fact and law. NOTE 73. **Add:** For a **7–27**
recent example, see *HRH The Prince of Wales v Associated Newspapers Ltd*
[2006] EWHC 522 (Ch); [2006] E.C.D.R. 20 at para.160. This part of the decision at first instance was not challenged on appeal: [2006] EWCA Civ 1776;
[2007] 3 W.L.R. 222; [2007] 2 All E.R. 139 at [76].

Sub-paragraph (f). First sentence. In *Baigent v The Random House Group Ltd*
[2007] EWCA Civ 247; [2007] F.S.R. 24, at [131], [132], Mummery L.J., with
whom Rix L.J. agreed, emphasised that it is wrong to dissect the claimant's work:
"On the issue of subsistence it is wrong to divide up the whole copyright work
into parts and to destroy the copyright in the whole work by concluding that there
is no copyright in the individual segments. Similarly, on the issue of infringement, it is wrong to take the parts of the original copyright work that have been
copied in the alleged infringing work, to isolate them from the whole original
copyright work and then to conclude that 'a substantial part' of the original copyright work has not been copied because there was no copyright in the copied
parts on their own."

NOTE 83. **Add:** See *Nova Productions Limited v Mazooma Games Limited*
[2006] EWHC 24 (Ch); [2006] R.P.C. 14; [2006] E.M.L.R. 14 at para.125; on
appeal [2007] EWCA Civ 219; [2007] R.P.C. 25; [2007] E.M.L.R. 14; [2007]
E.C.D.R. 6.

NOTE 85. **Add** at end: See also *Coffey v Warner/Chappell Music Ltd* [2005]
EWHC 449 (Ch); [2005] F.S.R. 34; [2005] E.C.D.R. 21; [2006] E.M.L.R. 2 at
paras 8 to 10.

NOTE 87. At end of first sentence, **add:** See also *Nova Productions Limited v
Mazooma Games Limited* [2006] EWHC 24 (Ch); [2006] R.P.C. 14; [2006]
E.M.L.R. 14 at para.124; on appeal [2007] EWCA Civ 219; [2007] R.P.C. 25;
[2007] E.M.L.R. 14; [2007] E.C.D.R. 6.

NOTE 90. **Add** at end: In *Nova Productions Ltd v Mazooma Games Ltd* [2007]
EWCA Civ 219; [2007] R.P.C. 25; [2007] E.M.L.R. 14; [2007] E.C.D.R. 6, it
was held that Lord Scott's observation was confined to the facts of the case and
did not lay down any general principle [26].

NOTE 98. **Add:** See also *Nova Productions Limited v Mazooma Games Limited*
[2006] EWHC 24 (Ch); [2006] R.P.C. 14; [2006] E.M.L.R. 14 at para.122; on
appeal [2007] EWCA Civ 219; [2007] R.P.C. 25; [2007] E.M.L.R. 14; [2007]
E.C.D.R. 6.

NOTE 99. In *Baigent v The Random House Group Limited* [2006] EWHC 719
(Ch); [2006] E.M.L.R. 16 at paras 174 to 176, the Judge stated that where a book
was intended to be read as "a factual historical event" (sic) and the defendant accepts it as fact and does no more than repeat certain of those facts, the claimant
cannot complain if the defendant has contrived a novel based on those facts unless the result amounts to an appropriation of the claimant's literary labours. In
other words, the facts are not protected but the way they are put together may be.

Other considerations. Sub-paragraph (a). **Add:** In *Baigent v The Random House* **7–28**
Group Ltd [2007] EWCA Civ 247; [2007] F.S.R. 24 at [97], Lloyd L.J., with
whom Rix L.J. and Mummery L.J. agreed, described the maxim "what is worth
copying is worth protecting" as a misleading rhetorical device.

Sub-paragraph (d). **Add:** In *Baigent v The Random House Group Ltd* [2007]

EWCA Civ 247; [2007] F.S.R. 24 at [97], Lloyd L.J., with whom Rix L.J. and Mummery L.J. agreed, said that *animus furandi* is a red herring in modern English copyright law, and that it should not be invoked in future.

NOTE 18. **Add:** In *Henkel KgaA v Holdfast New Zealand Ltd* [2006] NZSC 102; (2006) 70 IPR 624; [2007] 1 N.Z.L.R. 336 at [48] the Supreme Court of New Zealand stated that if the defendant's work was of sufficient originality to amount to a copyright work, there would have been no infringement. This approach does not accord with English law.

C. LITERARY, DRAMATIC, MUSICAL AND ARTISTIC WORKS

(i) Literary works

(a) *Introduction*

7–34   **Defendant's work must represent claimant's.** NOTE 49. *Lambretta Clothing Co Ltd v Teddy Smith (UK) Ltd* [2003] EWHC 1204 (Ch) is reported at [2003] R.P.C. 41.

(b) *Substantial part: general considerations*

7–36   **Non-literal or non-textual copying.** NOTE 57. **Add:** *Baigent v The Random House Group Limited* [2006] EWHC 719 (Ch); [2006] E.M.L.R. 16, concerned a claim that the "central theme" of a work of "historical conjecture" had been taken. The theme relied on by the claimants consisted of a series of 15 "points" arranged in chronological order. The points included the idea that Jesus married and had children (points 2 and 3) and that in the fifth century Jesus's descendants intermarried with the royal line of the Franks to produce the Merovingian dynasty (point 7). Although 10 or 11 of these points were found in the defendant's work (paras 275 to 292), the claim failed: the "central theme" was not actually the central theme of the claimants' work (para.250); if it had been, it was merely the expression of a number of facts and ideas at a very general level (para.259); the arrangement of the alleged facts in chronological order was not significant— it was too general and at too low a level of "extraction" (*sic*) (para.261); in any event, that chronological order was not actually reproduced in the claimants' or the defendant's work (paras 262 and 264).

This decision was upheld on appeal: [2007] EWCA Civ 247; [2007] F.S.R. 24. Accordingly to Lloyd L.J., with whom Rix L.J. and Mummery L.J. agreed, the Judge had been entitled to find that what had been taken by the defendant amounted to generalised propositions, at too high a level of abstraction to qualify for copyright protection, because it was not the product of the application of skill and labour by the claimants in the creation of their literary work. It lay on the wrong side of the line between ideas and their expression. The Judge had also been entitled to find that the claim as pleaded depended on showing that the "central theme" was indeed a central theme of the claimants' work, sufficient to qualify as a substantial part of the work, albeit as a combination of features obtained by abstraction, and that this assertion by the claimants was not justified. See at [99], [100].

It should also be noted that Mummery L.J. (at [138]), with whose judgment Rix L.J. agreed, criticised the characterisation of the 15 "points" as a "central theme": "In ordinary usage a "theme" of a literary work simply describes what it is about in general terms. I would not normally regard a list of individual assertions of actual or virtual history (such as that the Roman Empire under Constantine adopted Pauline Christianity as officially sanctioned religion or as to the creation of the Knights Templar as an arm of the Priory of Sion) as themes or as theme points".

At [140–142] Mummery L.J. criticised the use of "loose non-statutory terminology" such as "textual" copying as misleading, giving the example of the reproduction of an original anthology of out of copyright poetry in which the text would be copied but the infringement would lie in the selection and arrangement of the poems.

On the question of substantial part, Mummery L.J. expressed the view that there was no point seeking to define further the term "substantial part" [144] but went on to say that the decided cases help in identifying the relevant necessary and sufficient conditions for substantiality [145]. Thus, it is not necessary for the actual language of the copyright work to be copied or even for similar words to be used, tracking the language of the copyright work like a translation. It is sufficient to establish that there has been substantial copying of the original collection, selection, arrangement, and structure of literary material, even of material that is not in itself the subject of copyright [145]. It is not, however, sufficient for the alleged infringing work simply to replicate or use items of information, facts, ideas, theories, arguments, themes and so on derived from the original copyright work [146]. No clear principle can be laid down on how or where to draw the line between the legitimate use of the ideas expressed and the unlawful copying of their expression [147].

As to the facts of the case, Mummery L.J. stated that the individual elements of the claimants' work which appeared in the defendant's work were not of a sufficiently developed character to amount to a substantial part. They were too generalised. They were an assortment of items of historical fact and information, virtual history, events, incidents, theories, arguments and propositions. There were no detailed similarities of language or "architectural" similarities in the detailed treatment or development of the collection or arrangement of incidents, situations, characters and narrative, such as was normally found in cases of infringement of literary or dramatic copyright. The 11 aspects of the Central Theme in the defendant's work were differently expressed, collected, selected, arranged and narrated [154]. The use of items of information, fact and so on derived from assembled research material was not, in itself, "a substantial part" of the claimants' work simply because it had taken time skill and effort to carry out the necessary research [155]. Copyright existed in the claimants' work by reason of the skill and labour expended by them in the original composition and production of it and the original manner or form of expression of the results of their research. Original expression includes not only the language in which the work is composed but also the original selection, arrangement and compilation of the raw research material. It does not, however, extend to clothing information, facts, ideas, theories and themes with exclusive property rights, so as to enable a claimant to monopolise historical research or knowledge and prevent the legitimate use of historical and biographical material, theories propounded, general arguments deployed, or general hypotheses suggested (whether they are sound or not) or general themes written about [156].

NOTE 58. *Brighton v Jones* is now reported at [2004] E.M.L.R. 26; [2005] F.S.R. 16. For a discussion of the authorities on the copying of literary features of fictional characters, see McGee and Scanlan, "Copyright in Character, Intellectual Property Rights and the Internet" Parts I [2005] 8 Ent. L.R. 209 and II [2006] 1 Ent. L.R. 15.

(c) *Compilations, databases and other works of reference*

Examples.   7–45

(h) *Historical Works*. See also *Baigent v The Random House Group Limited* [2006] EWHC 719 (Ch); [2006] E.M.L.R. 16 on appeal [2007] EWCA Civ 247; [2007] F.S.R. 24, discussed above, paragraph 7–36.

7–47   **Rearrangement or scrambling of compilations.** NOTE 38. **Add:** See also *Robertson v The Thomson Corporation* (2004) 243 D.L.R. (4th) 257 (C.A. Ontario): the reproduction of the contents of a newspaper in an online database was not an infringement of the compilation copyright.

(d) *Computer programs*

7–48   NOTE 42. **Delete** and **substitute:** The Directive defines the restricted acts by reference to reproduction "in any form, in part or in whole". By contrast, the 1988 Act defines the restricted acts in respect of all works including computer programs by reference to "the work as a whole or any substantial part of it". There is no significance in this: the Directive's meaning must be limited to reproduction of a substantial part. Otherwise it would require the copying of insubstantial parts to be an infringement, which would be absurd. See *Nova Productions Ltd v Mazooma Games Ltd* [2007] EWCA Civ 219; [2007] R.P.C. 25; [2007] E.M.L.R. 14; [2007] E.C.D.R. 6 at [29].

NOTE 50. *Navitaire Inc v easyJet Airline Company* [2004] EWHC 1725 (Ch) concerned a claim to copyright in the software for an airline booking system. The defendant had commissioned a system which was substantially indistinguishable from the claimant's system in respect of its user interface, that is, the appearance which the running software presented to the user. Thus, the defendant's system acted on identical or very similar inputs to those of the claimant's system and produced very similar results. However, the defendant and its software developer never had access to the source code of the claimant's system and accordingly the source codes were quite different.

The claimant contended that this taking of its "business logic" was analogous to the taking of the plot of a novel or play. The defendant contended that this was an attempt to claim copyright in the functional idea of the program rather than the expression of that idea in the software.

Pumfrey J. rejected the "plot" analogy, for a number of reasons. First, two completely different computer programs can produce a result which is identical not only at some level of abstraction, but at any level of abstraction. This is so even if the author of one had no access at all to the other but only to its results. Second, it is wrong to say that a computer program has a "plot": rather it amounts to a set of instructions. There is no theme, there are no events and there is no narrative flow. It is merely a series of pre-defined operations intended to achieve a desired result in response to the requests of the customer (para.125).

Pumfrey J. went on to consider an analogy. If a chef develops a recipe for a pudding, that will be a literary work. If a competitor, after much culinary labour, but without using the original recipe, succeeds in emulating the result and records his recipe, the resulting record will not be an infringement of the original recipe even though the end result, the plot and purpose of both (the pudding) is the same (para.127).

The Judge concluded that the "business function" embodied in the program was not relevant skill and labour of the kind protected by copyright (para.129). He stated that he reached this conclusion without regret: if the policy of the Software Directive was to exclude both computer languages and the underlying ideas of the interfaces from protection, then it should not be possible to circumvent those exclusions by seeking to identify some overall function which it was the sole purpose of the interface to invoke and relying on that instead (para.130).

The Judge gave permission to appeal on this point (*Navitaire Inc v easyJet Airline Co Ltd (No.2)* [2005] EWHC 0282 (Ch); [2006] R.P.C. 4 at para.139(i)). The appeal has since been compromised.

This part of the *Navitaire* decision was applied in *Nova Productions Limited v Mazooma Games Limited* [2006] EWHC 24 (Ch): see paras 134, 248 and 253. On appeal (*Nova Productions Ltd v Mazooma Games Ltd* [2007] EWCA Civ 219; [2007] R.P.C. 25; [2007] E.M.L.R. 14; [2007] E.C.D.R. 6), it was held that this part of the *Navitaire* decision was right: "merely making a program which will emulate another but which in no way involves copying the program code or any of the program's graphics is legitimate" [52]. In the *Nova* appeal the contrary argument proceeded as follows: copyright in computer programs extends to copyright in preparatory design work for computer programs; copyright extends to such material even to the extent that it consists of ideas as to what the program should do; accordingly, if the defendant's program does what is set out in the preparatory design material, it infringes [49]. The Court of Appeal rejected the argument. The Directive expressly extends protection to preparatory design material but it does not provide that protection extends to ideas contained in such material. The reason such express provision was made is not that it was intended that protection should extend beyond the literary expression of such material to the ideas contained in it but because not all Member States necessarily provided such protection [51].

See Stokes, "The Development of UK Software Copyright Law: From John Richardson Computers to Navitaire" [2005] C.T.L.R. 129.

Ideas only? Nova Productions Ltd v Mazooma Games Ltd ([2006] EWHC 24   **7–50** (Ch); [2006] R.P.C. 14; [2006] E.M.L.R. 14; on appeal [2007] EWCA Civ 219; [2007] R.P.C. 25; [2007] E.M.L.R. 14; [2007] E.C.D.R. 6) concerned an allegation of infringement of the copyright in a program for a computer game based on the theme of pool and in design notes for that program. There was no allegation that the code had been copied and the claimant primarily relied on the alleged copying of certain visual features of its game. The Judge held that some of these features, such as the idea of synchronising a pulsing cue with a pulsing power meter, had been copied, but that there was no infringement. One aspect of the Judge's reasoning was that the features which had been taken were "cast at such a level of abstraction" and "so general" that they were incapable of amounting to a substantial part of the claimant's program. "They are ideas which have little to do with the skill and effort expended by the programmer and do not constitute the form of expression of the literary works relied upon": [2006] EWHC 24 (Ch); [2006] R.P.C. 14; [2006] E.M.L.R. 14 at [247].

The Court of Appeal upheld this decision. Jacob L.J. emphasised the following points. First, Article 1.2 of and Recitals (13) and (15) to the Directive make abundantly clear that the "idea/expression" dichotomy applies to copyright in computer software [31]. Second, for these purposes, applying *Designers Guild*, ideas are not protected if they have nothing to do with the nature of the work (for these purposes, the nature of the work is a computer program having all the necessary coding to function) [35]. Accordingly, the exclusion of "ideas" extends to mere ideas as to what the program should do [35] and is not limited to ideas which "underlie an element of the program" (as to which, see Recital (13) of the Directive) [36]. Third, these propositions are reinforced by the fact that even though the Directive predates TRIPS, it is to be construed in accordance with TRIPS (applying Case C–89/99 *Schieving-Nijstad v Groeneveld* [2001] E.C.R. I–5851; [2001] 3 C.M.L.R. 44; [2002] F.S.R. 22; [2002] E.T.M.R. 4). Article 9.2 of TRIPS positively provides that "copyright protection shall extend to expressions and not to ideas". This is a positive rule as to the point beyond which copyright protection may not go. To protect by copyright mere ideas as such would contravene TRIPS [38].

For other aspects of this decision, see paragraph 7–48 of this supplement.

(ii) Dramatic works

7–52   NOTE 71. *Brighton v Jones* is now reported at [2004] E.M.L.R. 26; [2005] F.S.R. 16.

(iii) Musical works

7–53   NOTE 90. **Add:** This decision ([2005] R.P.C. 4; [2004] E.M.L.R. 27; [2005] E.C.D.R. 10) has been upheld by the Court of Appeal: *Hyperion Records Ltd v Sawkins* [2005] EWCA Civ 565; [2005] 1 W.L.R. 3281; [2005] R.P.C. 32.

(iv) Artistic works

7–55   **Reproduction: general principles.** NOTE 99. **Add:** See also *Australian Chinese Newspapers Pty Ltd v Melbourne Chinese Press Pty Ltd* [2003] F.C.A. 878 (upheld on appeal *Melbourne Chinese Press Pty Ltd v Australian Chinese Newspapers Pty Ltd* (2004) 63 I.P.R. 38): copyright in a logo consisting of three characters in a particular calligraphic style was infringed by making a similar version using a computer typesetting program.

F. BROADCASTS

7–72   **Add:** In an Australian case it has been held that no special rules apply to the question whether a substantial part of a broadcast has been taken: *TCN Channel Nine Pty Ltd v Network Ten Pty Ltd* [2005] FCAFC 53; (2005) 65 IPR 571.

3. THE ISSUE OF COPIES TO THE PUBLIC: THE DISTRIBUTION RIGHT

7–78   **EC Directives.** NOTE 36. **Add:** The Rental and Related Rights Directive and its amendments have now been codified as Directive 2006/115/EC: [2006] O.J. L376/28. Art.9 of the original Directive is now Art.9 of Directive 2006/115.

7–80   **Issue to the public: meaning.** NOTE 51. **Add** at end: The Rental and Related Rights Directive and its amendments have now been codified as Directive 2006/115/EC: [2006] O.J. L376/28.

NOTE 59. *The Football Association Premier League Ltd v Panini UK Ltd* is now reported at [2004] 1 W.L.R. 1147; [2004] F.S.R. 1; [2003] E.C.D.R. 36.

KK Sony Entertainment v Pacific Game Technology (Holding) Ltd [2006] EWHC 2509 (Ch) concerned the sale by a Hong Kong company via a website of an article to a UK consumer who paid by credit card. The sale was alleged (amongst other things) to amount to an issue of the article to the public in the UK. The Judge, applying the trade mark case of *Euromarket Designs Inc v Peters* [2001] F.S.R. 20; [2000] E.T.M.R. 1025, treated the matter as a question of whether the website would convey to a reasonable consumer an offer for sale within the UK (or the EEA) [23]. On the facts, the Defendants' website did do that and accordingly there was issue to the public in the UK even though the property in the goods passed in Hong Kong [25]. The Judge made the point that if it were otherwise, intellectual property rights in the EEA could be avoided merely by setting up a website outside the EEA crafted to sell within it [27].

In *Independiente Ltd v Music Trading On-Line (HK) Ltd* [2007] EWHC 533 (Ch); [2007] F.S.R. 21, CDs were ordered online by consumers in the UK from a company based in Hong Kong which despatched them directly to the consumers using the Hong Kong and UK postal services. It was common ground that property passed before the CDs were delivered to the Hong Kong postal services. It was also common ground that a copy is "issued to the public" when it is "delivered" to a member of the public [42]. The defendant contended that delivery took place when the CDs were delivered to the Hong Kong postal authorities and accordingly that the person responsible for putting them into circulation was the purchaser. In response the claimant relied on the law of sale of goods. Under section 32(1) of the Sale of Goods Act 1979, where the seller is authorised or required to send the goods to the buyer, delivery to the carrier is presumed to be delivery of the goods to the buyer. However, in the case of sales of goods to a buyer who "deals as consumer" this rule is disapplied (by s.32(4)) so that the goods remain at the seller's risk during transit. Accordingly, the claimant contended and the Judge held, it was the supplier which delivered the CDs to the consumer and was liable for having issued them to the public. As in the *KK Sony* case the defendant's website was clearly intended to have effect in the UK to attract consumers. The Judge said that this strengthened his view, but that his conclusion would have been the same even if the site had not been so intended [51].

There is a clear tension between the approaches in these two cases. Since the defendants in the *KK Sony* case did not attend the hearing and the *KK Sony* decision was cited in the *Independiente* case, the latter is more authoritative. However, it sits uneasily with the House of Lords decision in *Sabaf SpA v MFI Furniture Centres Ltd* [2004] UKHL 45; [2005] R.P.C. 10 (see para.8–14 of this supplement) in which the question of who was responsible for an importation was determined without regard to the technicalities of the contract of sale (although the contractual position was referred to). It is suggested that in such cases what is required is the application of a broad common sense view rather than a descent into the technicalities of the law of sale of goods which was developed for the purpose of regulating the legal position between buyer and seller rather than that between right holder and alleged infringer.

4. THE RENTAL AND LENDING RIGHTS

Background. NOTE 63. **Add** at end: The Rental and Related Rights Directive   7–81
and its amendments have now been codified as Directive 2006/115/EC: [2006]
O.J. L376/28.

Applicable works. NOTE 69. **Add** at end: See now Directive 2006/115, Art.3(2).   7–83
  NOTE 71. **Add** at end: See now Directive 2006/115, Art.3(2).
  NOTE 72. **Delete** "of Directive 92/100,".

Rental right. NOTE 77. Art.1.2 of Directive 92/100 is now Art.2(1) of Directive   7–84
2006/15.

The lending right. NOTE 81. **Add** at end: See now Directive 2006/115, Art.2(1).   7–85
  NOTE 82. Recital (13) of Directive 92/100 is now Recital (10) of Directive
2006/115.
  NOTE 83. Recital (14) of Directive 92/100 is now Recital (11) of Directive
2006/115.

Excluded acts. NOTES 85, 87 and 88. Recital (13) of Directive 92/100 is now Re-   7–87
cital (10) of Directive 2006/115.

5. PERFORMANCE, SHOWING OR PLAYING OF A WORK IN PUBLIC: THE PUBLIC PERFORMANCE RIGHT

7–96   **"In public". Add** at end: In *Brown v. Mcasso Music Production Ltd* [2005] EWCC 1 (Cpwt); [2005] F.S.R. 40; [2006] E.M.L.R. 3, a "showreel" including an infringing copy of a musical work had been archived to a sub-site within the defendant's website, described by the Judge as "a sort of electronic waste basket—or at any rate a locked cupboard", with a view to disposing of it because it was no longer considered to be useful, current publicity. However, it could be accessed by members of the public, if only by someone with considerable competence with computers. The Judge held (para.50, *obiter*) that the availability of the material was not a performance of the work in public.

7–96A   **Hotel bedrooms etc.** NOTE 57. **Add:** In Case C–306/05, *Sociedad General de Autores y Editores de España (SGAE) v Rafael Hoteles SL* [2007] Bus. L.R. 521; [2007] E.C.D.R. 2, the ECJ held that the re-broadcasting by a hotel proprietor of works included in television programmes to individual guests' rooms constituted a communication to the public.

6. THE COMMUNICATION TO THE PUBLIC RIGHT

(c) *European Directives*

7–102   **The Rental and Related Rights Directive.** NOTE 69. **Add:** The Rental and Related Rights Directive and its amendments have now been codified as Directive 2006/115/EC: [2006] O.J. L376/28. Art.8(2) of Directive 92/100 is now Art.8(2) of Directive 2006/115.

(e) *Broadcasting*

7–111   **Where does the act of broadcasting take place?** NOTE 96. **Add:** In Case C–28/04, *Lagardère Active Broadcast v Société pour la perception de la rémunération équitable (SPRE)* [2005] 3 C.M.L.R. 48; [2006] E.C.D.R. 1, signals were transmitted from France to a satellite and thence to repeater stations in France, which transmitted the signals to parts of France on FM, and also to a transmitter in Germany, which transmitted them to other parts of France on long wave. In the event of malfunction of the satellite, the signals were transmitted to the German transmitter by a digital audio terrestrial circuit. An issue arose as to whether the broadcaster was obliged to pay one or two licence fees in respect of the German transmissions. The broadcaster contended that only one set was payable, since Art.1(2)(b) of Directive 93/83 provides that communication to the public by satellite occurs solely in the Member State where the programme-carrying signals are introduced into the chain of communication. However, the Court of Justice held that the satellite was not a "satellite" within Art.1(1) of the Satellite and Cable Directive. First, it did not operate on frequency bands which were reserved for the broadcast of signals for the reception to the public. Second, although it operated on frequency bands which were reserved for closed, point-to-point communication, the circumstances in which reception took place were not comparable to those applicable in the case of frequency bands reserved for the broadcast of signals for the reception of the public (the signals emanating from the satellite were encoded and could only be received by professional equipment). Third, the signals were not intended for reception by the public within the meaning of Art.1(2)(a). Fourth, there was no uninterrupted chain of communication leading to the satellite and down towards the earth as required by Art.1(2)(a). Finally, the fact that the satellite could be replaced by a digital audio circuit in the event of malfunction and the Directive would immediately cease to apply meant that the application of the Directive for which the broadcaster contended would be dependent on the vagaries of satellite operations and thus fraught with uncertainty.

Re-broadcasts. Add: In Case C–306/05, *Sociedad General de Autores y Editores de España (SGAE) v Rafael Hoteles SL* [2007] Bus. L.R. 521; [2007] E.C.D.R. 2, the ECJ held that the re-broadcasting by a hotel proprietor of works included in television programmes to individual guests' rooms constituted a communication to the public.   **7–113**

(f) Making the work available on demand

What constitutes the act of making a work available and who is liable? See, however, *Polydor Ltd v Brown* [2005] EWHC 3191 (Ch), in which it was held that connecting a computer to the Internet, where the computer is running peer-to-peer software, and where music files containing copies of copyright works are placed in a shared directory amounts to communication to the public of those works by the person in control of the computer ("the uploader"): paragraph 7.   **7–115**

For a general discussion of the liability of search engines and data aggregators, see Allgrove and Ganley, "Search Engines, Data Aggregators and UK Copyright Law: A Proposal" [2007] 6 E.I.P.R. 227.

When does the act of making available occur? In *Polydor Ltd v Brown* [2005] EWHC 3191 (Ch), the Judge apparently did not consider it necessary that there should have been an actual transmission. Case C–306/05, *Sociedad General de Autores y Editores de Espana v Rafael Hoteles SA* [2007] Bus. L.R. 521; [2007] E.C.D.R. 2, is to the same effect. The case concerned the provision by cable of television programmes to hotel bedrooms. The ECJ held that while the mere provision of physical facilities (in this case television sets) did not as such constitute an act of communication to the public, the installation of such facilities might make public access to broadcast works technically possible [46]. For there to be a communication to the public it was sufficient that the work was made available in such a way that the public might access it. Accordingly, it was not decisive that customers who had not switched on the television had not actually had access to the works [43].   **7–116**

Where does the act of making available take place? NOTE 8. The reference to Directive 93/98 should be to the Information Society Directive (Dir. 2001/29).   **7–117**

8. AUTHORISATION

Meaning of "authorise". NOTE 55. *CCH Canadian Ltd v Law Society of Upper Canada* is reported at [2004] F.S.R. 44.   **7–132**

Examples of "authorisation". NOTE 92. *CCH Canadian Ltd v Law Society of Upper Canada* is reported at [2004] F.S.R. 44.   **7–133**

CHAPTER EIGHT

SECONDARY INFRINGEMENT OF COPYRIGHT

Contents

2. DEALINGS IN INFRINGING COPIES

B. INFRINGING COPY

8–03   *R. v M and others* [2007] EWCA Crim 218 concerned the meaning of the word "article" in section 57 of the Terrorism Act 2000. For these purposes, "article" was defined (in s.121) to include "substance and any other thing". Section 58 of the Terrorism Act 2000 created different offences in relation to "a document or record". The Court of Appeal appears to have been of the view that in the absence of section 58 the word "article" would have included such items as computer hard drives (including one on a Bradford University computer), CDs and DVDs, a USB storage device and a video recording [32], [36]: "There is no practical difference between a book which a person can read (perhaps with help) and a CD which can be read by inserting it into a computer. To submit that the CD is not an article because it can only be read with a computer seems to us far-fetched."

8–06   **The European Communities Act 1972.** NOTE 24. **Add:** Thus, it is not open to Member States to provide that the distribution right in respect of the original or copies of a work is exhausted where the first sale or other transfer of ownership is made by the holder of that right or with his consent outside the Community: Case C–479/04, *Laserdisken ApS v Kulturministeriet* [2007] 1 C.M.L.R. 6; [2006] E.C.D.R. 30.

NOTE 26. **Add:** The Rental and Related Rights Directive and its amendments have now been codified as Directive 2006/115/EC: [2006] O.J. L376/28.

Add at end: In *Independiente Ltd v Music Trading On-Line (HK) Ltd* [2007] EWHC 533 (Ch); [2007] F.S.R. 21, the Judge appeared on one reading of para. [21] of his judgment to assimilate the test for whether an article has been placed on the market in the EEA with the consent of the copyright owner with that applicable in the field of trade marks. This is plainly right: see *Mastercigars Direct Ltd v Hunters & Frankau Ltd* [2007] EWCA Civ 176; [2007] R.P.C. 24; [2007] E.T.M.R. 44 (now the leading trade mark case on this point in this jurisdiction) at [14]. In the latter case, the Court of Appeal accepted certain propositions [16, 17] which can be adapted to the copyright field as follows:

(1) For there to be consent such consent must relate to each individual item of the product in respect of which exhaustion of rights is pleaded.

(2) Consent to the marketing of goods within the EEA may be implied where it is to be inferred from facts and circumstances which unequivocally demonstrate that the copyright owner has renounced his right to oppose placing of the goods on the market within the EEA.

(3) Implied consent cannot be inferred from:

   (a) the fact that the copyright owner has not communicated his opposition to marketing within the EEA to all subsequent purchasers of goods placed on the market outside the EEA; or

   (b) the fact that the goods carry no warning of a prohibition on their being placed on the market within the EEA; or

   (c) the fact that the copyright owner has transferred the ownership of the goods without imposing a contractual reservation and that, according to the law governing the contract, the rights transferred include, in the absence of such a reservation, an unlimited right of resale or at least a right to market the goods within the EEA.

(4) The onus lies on the defendant to prove consent express or implied.

E. PARTICULAR ACTS

Importation. Add: In the patent case of *Sabaf SpA v MFI Furniture Centres Ltd*   **8–14**
[2004] UKHL 45; [2005] R.P.C. 10, the Italian manufacturer of infringing goods sold them to an English company and arranged their transport to England on behalf of the English company, which reimbursed the cost of doing so. Property passed in Italy. As a matter of the law of international carriage of goods by road, the contract of carriage was presumed to have been made on behalf of the consignee and owner of the goods. On this basis, the manufacturer was not the importer. However, according to the House of Lords, it was not necessary to resort to the technicalities of the contract of sale. The manufacturer was not the importer because whoever had contracted with the carrier, the English company was the importer [41]. It might have been liable for the importation as a joint tortfeasor but no such contention was made [40].

4. PERMITTING OR ENABLING PUBLIC PERFORMANCE

Permission. NOTE 99. See also *ACUM (Society of Authors and Composers) v*   **8–18**
R.K. Orel Events Ltd (Civil Case 7779/03, Haifa Magistrates Court) [2004] Ent. L.R. N–67, which is to the same effect.

CHAPTER NINE

PERMITTED ACTS

Contents   *Para.*

1. GENERAL INTRODUCTION

First sentence. Delete and substitute: Chapter III, Part I, of the 1988 Act, containing some 69 sections, permits certain acts which would otherwise amount to copyright infringement.   **9–01**

The Berne Convention, and the "3-step" test. NOTE 9. **Delete and substitute:** For examples of cases which are generally considered to fall within this permitted exception, see S. Ricketson and J.C. Ginsburg, *International Copyright and Neighbouring Rights, The Berne Convention and Beyond* (2nd ed., Oxford University Press, 2006), para.13.31 *et seq.*   **9–02**

The WIPO Copyright Treaty and the WIPO Performances and Phonograms Treaty. The WCT provides for limitations and exceptions to the rights granted   **9–04A**

provided that they comply with the three-step test.[1] The WPPT permits the same kinds of limitations or exceptions with regard to the protection of performers and producers of phonograms as they provide for, in their national legislation, in connection with the protection of copyright in literary and artistic works, provided also that they are in conformity with the 3-step test.[2]

9–05   **European Directives.** NOTE 14. **Add:** See, however, with respect to the law of the European Community, para.25–105 of this Supplement, below.

9–06   **The Information Society Directive.** NOTE 32. **Delete** and **substitute:** Harmonisation to this degree has never been attempted by the signatories to the Berne Convention (see generally, S. Ricketson and J.C. Ginsburg, *International Copyright and Neighbouring Rights, The Berne Convention and Beyond* (2nd ed., Oxford University Press, 2006), or the Rome Convention, and it must be also doubted whether the workings of the Internal Market were in the past affected in any substantial way by the patchwork of exceptions which existed within the Community. Of course, the effects in the future in a digital environment are more uncertain.

NOTE 34. **Add:** Thus, the UK may not introduce any new exception. However, this has not deterred the Gowers Review of Intellectual Property (HM Treasury Report, December 2006) from recommending to the European Union (Recommendation 11) that the Information Society Directive 2001/29/EC be amended to allow for an exception for what it describes as "creative, transformative or derivative works", within the parameters of the Berne Convention "3-step test" (see para.9–02 above). The Review considers that transforming works can create "huge value and spur on innovations". It cites as an example of such a transforming work a composition derived from the practice of "sampling" recordings of other musical works and performances, which is currently likely to infringe. The Review further proposes that the EU should amend Directive 2001/29/EC to include a commercial "orphan works" exception. By "orphan work" is meant a work whose owner cannot be identified by someone else who wishes to use the work. It is proposed that any such exception should permit the use of genuine orphan works, provided the user has performed a reasonable search and, where possible, gives attribution (Recommendation 13).

3. GENERAL PROVISIONS

A. THE MAKING OF TEMPORARY COPIES

9–15   **Introduction: The Information Society Directive.** Second sentence. **Delete** and **substitute:** The requirement applies to all forms of subject-matter with which the Directive is concerned, but not to computer programs or databases.[3]

9–17   **Transmissions in networks.** Eighth sentence. **Delete** and **substitute:** The fact that an infringement of copyright has been committed by the sender, or will be

---

[1] WCT, Art.10.

[2] WPPT, Art.16.

[3] See Information Society Directive (2001/29), Art.1(2). Works of these types are subject to the provisions of Arts 5 and 6 of the Software Directive and Art.5 of the Database Directive respectively, which provide their own code of exceptions. Art.5(1) of the Software Directive in particular provides that temporary acts of reproduction of a computer program shall not require authorisation by the rightholder where they are necessary for the use of the computer program by the lawful acquirer in accordance with its intended purpose. The exceptions permitted in the case of computer programs are dealt with by ss.50A–50C and s.50D of the 1988 Act respectively.

committed by the recipient of the transmission, does not affect the intermediary's exemption from liability, even if he knows or has reason to believe that an infringement is taking place.

4. THE FAIR DEALING PROVISIONS

A. OVERVIEW

The Berne Convention NOTE 20. Second sentence. **Delete** and **substitute:** See S. Ricketson and J.C. Ginsburg, *International Copyright and Neighbouring Rights, The Berne Convention and Beyond* (2nd ed, Oxford University Press, 2006), paras 13–39 to 13–43.

9–20

NOTE 21. **Delete** and **substitute:** As to the doubtful nature of the exception, see S. Ricketson and J.C. Ginsburg, *International Copyright and Neighbouring Rights, The Berne Convention and Beyond* (2nd ed, Oxford University Press, 2006), paras 8–104 to 8–106.

The Human Rights Act. NOTE 24. **Add:** But see *HRH Prince of Wales v Associated Newspapers Ltd.* ([2006] EWHC 522 (Ch)). The case related to an application by the Prince of Wales (W) for summary judgment against a newspaper publishing company (N) for reproducing without consent private journals obtained illegally via a breach of confidence. It was held that when balancing W's right to privacy under the Human Rights Act 1998, Sch., Pt I, art.8, against N' s right to freedom of expression under art.10 of the 1998 Act, it was impossible to say that N's disclosures from a particular journal's contents were necessary in a democratic society for the protection of the rights and freedoms of others, and that W's entitlement to confidentiality in respect of that journal should be overridden. The extracts quoted from the journal formed a substantial part, both qualitatively and quantitatively, of the whole, and there was no real prospect that the defence of fair dealing under s.30(2) of the 1988 Act would succeed. An appeal against the decision was dismissed ([2006] EWCA Civ 1776). The Court of Appeal held that N's publication of the information did not in the circumstances constitute fair dealing for the purposes of reporting current events; nor did N have any defence of fair dealing for the purposes of criticism or review.

9–22

B. NON-COMMERCIAL RESEARCH AND PRIVATE STUDY

(i) Introduction.

Second sentence. **Delete** and **substitute:** By granting a limited right to copy articles and small sections of other works, these groups are repeatedly able to consult sources to which they may not have ready access, provided that the copying remains within the bounds of what is fair (see para.9–53, below).

9–25

Add: In this connection, it should be noted that the Gowers Review of Intellectual Property (HM Treasury, December 2006) has recommended that the fair dealing exceptions permitting private copying for the purposes of research for a non-commercial purpose should be extended to cover all forms of content, including for the first time sound recordings and films. The recommendation relates to the copying, not the distribution of media (Recommendation 9).

(ii) Non-commercial research

The 1988 Act, as amended. Fourth sentence. **Delete** and **substitute:** As it happens, the Whitford Committee had recommended that commercial research

9–27

should be excluded from the scope of fair dealing[4] but this did not survive lobbying from British industry.[5]

9–29 **Sufficient acknowledgement.** Fifth sentence. **Add:** NOTE 52A. In *Fraser-Woodward v BBC* ([2005] EWHC 472), it was held that sufficient acknowledgement of the author did not require express identification. All that was required was that there was an identification and it was a question of fact whether there was or not.

(iii) Private study

Add new paragraph:

9–31A The Gowers Review of Intellectual Property (HM Treasury, December 2006) has recommended (Recommendation 8) that a limited private copying exception should be introduced in the UK by 2008 to permit format shifting (*i.e.* transferring a work from CD to an MP3 player or from a video tape to DVD) for works published after the date that the law comes into effect. It proposes that there should be no accompanying compensation, although it is questionable whether this would be in conformity with Article 5(2)(b) of the Information Society Directive 2001/29/EC.

C. CRITICISM OR REVIEW

9–39 **Criticism or review "of a work".** NOTE 83. **Add:** In *Fraser-Woodward Ltd v BBC* ([2005] EWHC 472) the criticism and/or review was of two things, of the photographs themselves and the philosophy behind them. It was held that the ideas or philosophy underlying a certain style of journalism could be subject to criticism which fell within s.30 of the CDPA 1988 and the use of the photographs was held to amount to fair dealing under s.30(1) of the CDPA 1988.

Add new paragraph:

9–41A **Caricature, parody or pastiche.** The Gowers Review of Intellectual Property (HM Treasury, December 2006), noting that the Information Society Directive 2001/29/EC specifically allows for an exception for "caricature, parody or pastiche", recommends that such an exception to copyright be created by 2008 (Recommendation 12). The rationale for the proposal is that an exception to cover parody in the UK would reduce transaction costs across Europe and create value.

9–43 **Sufficient acknowledgement.** NOTE 98. **Delete** and **substitute:** See para.9–22, above.
NOTE 2. **Delete** and **substitute:** See para.9–29, above.

---

[4] That this was the committee's view is evident from paras 676–677. Also see *Hansard*, HL Vol.491, col.93.
[5] See *Hansard*, HL Vol.493, cols 1153–1157. Reliance was placed on the transaction cost argument, that is to say, that any revenue raised from licensing agreements would be swallowed up by the costs of administrating such agreements (see *Hansard*, HL Vol.491, cols 92–94). It is instructive to contrast the position in the United States, where the ready availability of licenses has meant that the reproduction of single copies of articles for commercial research purposes does not amount to fair use (*American Geophysical Union v Texaco Inc.* 60 F.3d 913 (2d Cir. 1994)).

E. THE CONCEPT OF FAIRNESS

Relevant considerations. NOTE 43. **Add:** See also *Fraser-Woodward Ltd v BBC*   **9–55**
([2005] EWHC 472) where Mann J. set out the basic principles on which fair
dealing are to be assessed. First, regard should be had to the motives of the user;
second, fair dealing is a matter of impression; third, the amount of the work used
is relevant and excessive use could render the use unfair; fourth, the court can
have regard to the purpose of the use made, *i.e.* is it a genuine piece of criticism
or review, or something else? In addition, as regards substantiality, particular
care should be taken with photographs; lastly, the "3-step" test of the Berne
Convention should be respected. *Cf.* T. Theobald, "Copyright Infringement or is
it Just Fair Dealing"[2005] Ent. L.R. 16(6), 153–156.

NOTE 59. **Add:** *Fraser-Woodward Ltd v BBC* [2005] EWHC 472.

NOTE 73. **Add:** *Fraser-Woodward Ltd v BBC* [2005] EWHC 472.

F. GENERAL PROVISIONS: INCIDENTAL INCLUSION OF COPYRIGHT MATERIALS

Incidental. Sixth sentence. **Delete** and **substitute:** But that does not mean that its   **9–59**
inclusion either is, or is not, incidental.

5. VISUAL IMPAIRMENT

(i) The core provisions

Introduction. NOTE 87. **Add:** For a critique of the Act, see K. Garnett, "The   **9–63**
Copyright (Visually Impaired Persons) Act 2002" [2003] E.I.P.R. 25(11), 522–
527. See also D. Bradshaw, "Making Books and Other Copyright Works Accessible, without Infringement, to the Visually Impaired: A Review of the Practical
Operation of the Applicable, and Recently-Enacted, UK Legislation" I.P.Q. 2005,
4, 335–360.

6. EDUCATION

D. RECORDING OF BROADCASTS

Add new paragraph:

The Gowers Review of Intellectual Property (HM Treasury, December 2006)   **9–97A**
recommends that section 35 CDPA 1988 should be amended because at present it
does not extend to situations where students are not on the premises of the
educational establishment. It has recommended, therefore (Recommendation 2),
that copyright should not be infringed where a copy of a broadcast (for example,
a television programme) is communicated to distance learning students who are
not located within the educational establishment. In order to ensure that access to
such material should not be generally available to the public, it is proposed that
such students will need to access the material securely via a virtual learning
environment (VLE).[6]

---

[6] A VLA is a software system designed to facilitate the task of teachers in the management of
educational courses for their students.

E. REPROGRAPHIC COPYING

Add new paragraph:

9–98A   The Gowers Review of Intellectual Property (HM Treasury, December 2006) recommends that section 36 CDPA 1988 should also be extended to permit passages from works to be made available to students by email or VLE without infringing copyright, provided that no licensing scheme is in place for their use (*i.e.* s.36(3) should apply also to the extended exception) (Recommendation 2).

7. LIBRARIES AND ARCHIVES

E. SUPPLY OF COPIES TO OTHER LIBRARIES

9–109   Lines 17 and 24. In each case, **delete:** "a sum not less than" and **substitute:** "a sum equivalent to but not exceeding".

NOTES 57 and 58. In each case **delete:** "SI 1996/2967" and **substitute** "SI 1989/1212".

F. REPLACEMENT COPIES OF WORKS

9–110   NOTE 61. **Delete:** SI 1996/2967. **Substitute:** SI 1989/1212.

NOTE 62. **Delete:** SI 1996/2967. **Substitute:** SI 1989/1212. **Delete:** a sum not less than. **Substitute:** a sum equivalent to but not exceeding.

Add new paragraph:

9–110A   The Gowers Review of Intellectual Property (HM Treasury, December 2006) recommends that section 42 CDPA 1988 should be amended by 2008 to permit libraries to copy all classes of work (including sound recordings, television programmes and films, which were previously excluded from the exception) in permanent collections for archival purposes and to allow further copies to be made from the archived copy to mitigate against subsequent wear and tear (Recommendation 10a). Furthermore, the Review proposes a further amendment to section 42 by 2008 to enable libraries to format shift archival copies to ensure records do not become obsolete (Recommendation 10b).

G. COPYING OF UNPUBLISHED WORKS

9–111   **Introduction.** Third sub-paragraph. **Delete:** made on or after August 1, 1989. **Substitute:** whether made before or after August 1, 1989.

9–113   Paragraph heading. **Delete: Works made on or after August 1, 1989. Substitute: Copying by librarians or archivists.**

Delete first sentence and NOTE 75.

Second sentence. **Delete:** As to such works, the. **Substitute:** The.

NOTE 76. **Delete:** SI 1996/2967. **Substitute:** SI 1989/1212.

Add at end of second sentence: This exception applies to works whether they were made before or after August 1, 1989.

Note 77. **Delete:** SI 1996/2967, reg.7 **Substitute:** SI 2003/2498, reg.14.

8. PUBLIC ADMINISTRATION

A. PARLIAMENTARY AND JUDICIAL PROCEEDINGS

NOTE 21. **Add:** See also *Vitof Ltd. v Altoft* [2006] EWHC 1678.   **9–126**

E. PUBLIC RECORDS

First sentence. **Delete** and **substitute:** Public records within the meaning of the   **9–130**
Public Records Act 1958, The Public Records (Scotland) Act 1937, or the Public
Records Act (Northern Ireland) 1923, or in Welsh public records (as defined in
the Government of Wales Act 2006), which are open to public inspection, may
be copied, and a copy may be supplied to any person, provided this is done by or
with the authority of an officer appointed under one of those Acts.

NOTE 49. **Delete** and **substitute:** CDPA 1988, s.49 as amended by the Government of Wales Act 2006 (c.32), Sch.10, para.24.

9. COMPUTER PROGRAMS

B. DECOMPILATION

Rationale. The Court of First Instance considered the meaning of "interoperabil-   **9–134**
ity" in Case T–201 *Microsoft v Commission*. See paragraph 25–50A of this
Supplement.

10. DATABASES

Acts permitted in relation to databases. NOTE 97. **Add:** See *Navitaire Inc v*   **9–139**
Easy Jet Airline Co Ltd (No. 3) [2004] EWHC 1725.

11. DESIGNS

A. DESIGN DOCUMENTS AND MODELS

NOTE 10. **Add:** See *Ultra Marketing (UK) Ltd. V Universal Components Ltd*   **9–142**
[2004] EWHC 468 (Ch).

NOTE 11. **Add:** See *Lambretta Clothing Co Ltd v Teddy Smith (UK) Ltd* [2004]
EWCA Civ 886.

NOTE 21. **Add:** See also *Dyson Ltd. v Qualtex (UK) Ltd.* [2006] EWCA Civ
166, para.76 *et seq.* on the meaning of the term "surface decoration".

CHAPTER TEN

CROWN, PARLIAMENTARY AND OTHER RIGHTS

Contents

1. CROWN RIGHTS

C. STATUTORY CROWN COPYRIGHT

(i) The position under the 1988 Act

(a) *Background*

10–11   **The policy of the 1988 Act.** NOTE 45. Guidance Note 5 is now on the Office of Public Sector Information ("OPSI") website (*www.opsi.gov.uk*). It was further revised on May 9, 2005.

(b) *Works made on or after August 1, 1989*

10–12   **Subsistence and ownership.** NOTE 46. The phrase "officer and servant of the Crown" in s.163(1) means someone engaged in the service of the executive branch of the Government. The Prince of Wales is not such a person: *HRH The Prince of Wales v Associated Newspapers Ltd* [2006] EWHC 522 (Ch); [2006] E.C.D.R. 20 at [153]. This part of the decision was not challenged on appeal: [2006] EWCA Civ 1776; [2007] 3 W.L.R. 222; [2007] 2 All E.R. 139 at [75].

With effect from May 3, 2007, the expression "the Crown" now also includes the Crown in right of the Welsh Assembly Government: see para.29(2) of Sch.10 to the Government of Wales Act 2006.

The list of bodies considered by HMSO to have Crown status is now issued by OPSI's Information Team. It also includes a list of bodies which do not have Crown status but are often erroneously thought to do so. See *www.opsi.gov.uk/advice/crown-copyright/uk-crown-bodies.htm*.

NOTE 47. Subs.163(1A) has now been repealed with effect from May 3, 2007: see para.26(2) of Sch.10 to the Government of Wales Act 2006. Copyright in works of the Welsh National Assembly is now a form of parliamentary copyright like the copyright in the works of the Scottish parliament and the Northern Ireland assembly. See para.10–73 of this supplement.

Application of Part I of the 1988 Act to Crown copyright. NOTE 59. Guidance   **10–15**
Note 3 is now on the OPSI website. It was further revised on May 9, 2005. Paragraph 11 now reads (so far as relevant): "The fair dealing provisions of the Copyright, Designs and Patents Act 1988 which cover copying for the purposes of research and private study, criticism, review and news reporting and incidental inclusion of copyright material apply equally to Crown Material as to other copyright protected works."

(d) *Acts and Measures*

Acts and Measures passed on or after August 1, 1989. Add at end of fourth   **10–19**
sentence: Since May 3, 2007, Her Majesty has been entitled to the copyright in Acts and Measures of the National Assembly for Wales: see paragraph 27 of the Government of Wales Act 2006, amending section 164 of the 1988 Act.

Fifth sentence. **Add** at end: or, in the case of a Measure of the National Assembly for Wales, until the end of the period of 50 years from the end of the calendar year in which the Measure was approved by Her Majesty in Council.

(iii) Enforcement and management of Crown Copyright: the present position

Administration. Delete and **substitute:** HMSO is now part of the Office of Pub-   **10–27**
lic Sector Information ("OPSI"), which in turn is part of the Cabinet Office reporting structure. The respective roles of HMSO and OPSI are explained on the OPSI website, in particular at *www.opsi.gov.uk/about/team-information/index.htm*. In short, OPSI "operates as the principal focal point for public sector information in the UK. It is at the heart of information policy, setting standards, providing a practical framework of best practice for advising on and encouraging the re-use of PSI." HMSO "with its core activities of management of Crown copyright and database rights, publication of legislation and provision of official publishing guidance continues to operate from within OPSI".

At present at least, the Director of OPSI is also the Controller of HMSO, a position which she holds by letters patent from the Queen. She also holds the offices of Queen's Printer of Acts of Parliament and Government Printer for Northern Ireland (reporting to United Kingdom Ministers); and of Queen's Printer for Scotland (reporting to Scottish Ministers).

OPSI's Information Policy Team (also sometimes described as the Licensing Team) manages and licenses Crown Copyright material on behalf of the Controller of HMSO and Parliamentary material on behalf of the Speaker of the House of Commons and the Clerk of the Parliaments. The team defines policy and provides advice and guidance on copyright matters. See *www.opsi.gov.uk/about/team-information/information-policy.htm*.

Guidance on the policy arrangements on the licensing of Government information could formerly be found at *www.opsi.gov.uk/advice/crown-copyright/copyright-guidance/policy-arrangements-on-the-licensing-of-government-information.htm* (hereafter *"Policy Arrangements"*). According to this guidance, the activities of departments in managing their information can be categorised under six broad headings, as follows:

1. **Freedom of information**: the provision of information in response to requests from individuals. See *Policy Arrangements*, paragraphs 3.1, 5

and 6. This is governed by the Freedom of Information Act 2000 (c.36) and similar legislation. The supply of information does not include permission to re-use it.

2. **Government publishing**: the official publication of government information. See *Policy Arrangements*, paragraphs 3.2 and 7–10. All Government departments have a responsibility for communicating policy and information. They can do this under a central delegation from the Controller, either by publishing the information themselves (including on their websites) or by contracting others to do so (in some instances under central contracts managed by HMSO). However, there are restrictions. Private sector publishers must not be granted exclusive publishing rights other than in the official edition because this effectively prevents others from re-using the material. Such publishers must not be granted the right to license the re-use of Crown copyright material except in the context of end-user licensing of electronic products and services. Standard publishing clauses have been made available: see the OPSI website. When publishing material, departments are obliged to make every effort to ensure that appropriate notices and acknowledgments are included in their publications. See Guidance Notes 12 (official publications) and 13 (websites), reproduced on the OPSI website.

3. **Bibliographic Information, Information Asset Register and Publication Schemes**: telling the public what information is held. See *Policy Arrangements*, paragraphs 3.3 and 12–16. A complete bibliographic record of United Kingdom Official Publications is maintained on behalf of the government by The Stationery Office Limited ("TSO"). See Guidance Note 17 (revised May 9, 2005): Maintaining the Bibliography of Official Publications, *www.opsi.gov.uk*. In addition, each department is obliged to maintain a catalogue of unpublished information resources which can be searched online, known as an Information Asset Register. See Guidance Note 18 (revised May 9, 2004): Information Asset Register and Freedom of Information—a co-ordinated response to information access: *www.opsi.gov.uk*. Finally, each department is obliged to establish a publication scheme, specifying the classes of information it publishes or intends to publish, how the information is or is intended to be published and whether there is any charge for it: see, generally, Guidance Note 18, above.

4. **Licensing the re-use of government information**: See *Policy Arrangements*, paragraphs 3.4 and 17–31. This is the responsibility of the Controller of HMSO. However, there is a general delegation of this responsibility to departments (see above, "Government publishing"). In addition, delegations are issued in the following specified circumstances: where a department wishes to license re-use of photographs, films and other visual material from an archive it maintains; where a department wishes to authorise the re-use of its departmental logo (provided that it does not involve the reproduction of the Royal Arms); in some cases of licensing of computer software and programs; and where the copyright element of material is subsidiary to a range of other forms of intellectual property such as patents, inventions and designs. In addition, most government trading funds have been granted delegations of authority by the Controller to license the re-use of the material that they originate. See *Policy Arrangements*, paragraphs 26–31. HMSO's position in relation to such licensing is considered in detail in the Main Work, paragraphs 10–29 to 10–50.

5. **Data supply in agreed formats**: See *Policy Arrangements*, paragraphs 3.5 and 37. Where users need information in a particular format, departments may charge them for its conversion.

6. **Re-use of Crown Copyright material by departments**: In contractual matters, the Crown is regarded as a single legal entity. Accordingly, a department does not require a formal licence to re-use copyright material originated by another part of government. However, formal guidance must be followed: see *Policy Arrangements*, paragraphs 3.6 and 41–46.

Enforcement and management policy. NOTE 42. *A Citizens Guide: Access to* **10–28** *Unpublished Documents* is now at *europa.eu.int/comm/secretariat_general/sgc/ citguide/docs/en.pdf*. For an analysis of the relationship between Regulation 1049/2001 and Regulation 45/2001 on the protection of individuals with regard to the processing of personal data by the Community institutions and bodies and on the free movement of such data ([2001] O.J. L 8/1, January 12, 2001), see the European Data Protection Supervisor's Background Paper *Public access to documents and data protection* (July 2005), which can be found at *www.edps.eu.int/ publications/policy_papers/Public_access_data_protection_EN.pdf*. On Regulation 1049/2001, see De Leeuw, Common Market Law Review [2005] 42(1) 261. Court of First Instance cases on Regulation 1049/2001 include Case T–84/03 *Turco v Council* [2005] O.J. C 31/20; Case T–168/02 *IFAW Internationaler Tierschutz-Fonds GmbH v Commission* [2005] O.J. C 31/19; Case T–2/03 *Verein für Konsumenteninformation v Commission* [2005] O.J. C 155/14; Case T–187/03 *Scippacercola v Commission* [2005] O.J. C 143/32; and Case T–264/04 *Worldwide Fund for Nature European Policy Programme v The Council*.

The *IFAW* decision is under appeal: Case C–64/05P. See the Advocate-General's Opinion of July 18, 2007.

Second sub-paragraph. **Delete** from "In order to enable members of the public to locate such information ..." to "unless an exemption from disclosure applies".

Typographical arrangements. NOTE 59. Guidance Note 1 is now on the OPSI **10–29** website. It was further revised on May 9, 2005 but without materially altering the position as stated in the Main Work: see *www.opsi.gov.uk*

NOTE 60. Guidance Note 6 is now on the OPSI website. It was further revised on May 9, 2005 but without materially altering the position as stated in the Main Work: see *www.opsi.gov.uk*.

NOTE 61. Guidance Note 9 is now on the OPSI website. It was further revised on May 9, 2005 but without materially altering the position as stated in the Main Work: see *www.opsi.gov.uk*.

NOTE 71. **Delete:** HMSO Guidance Note 6, para.14. **Substitute:** Guidance Note 6, para.13(a). **Delete:** HMSO Guidance Note 6, para.15. **Substitute:** Guidance Note 6, para.13(b).

Unpublished public records: background. NOTE 72. **Delete:** the Government **10–32** of Wales Act 1998 (c.38). **Substitute:** the Government of Wales Act 2006.

Unpublished public records: scope of the waiver. NOTE 75. Guidance Note 3 **10–33** is now on the OPSI website. It was further revised on May 9, 2005 but without materially altering the position as stated in the Main Work except as set out below: see *www.opsi.gov.uk*.

NOTE 77. No doubt the Guidance Note will shortly be amended to update the reference to the Government of Wales Act 1998 to the Government of Wales Act 2006.

Add after footnote indicator 80: The waiver is limited to the text of the material and does not extend to the reproduction of images, including copies of documents: see Guidance Note 3, para.5.

10–35   **Court forms: background to and scope of the waiver.** NOTE 89. Guidance Note 4 is now on the OPSI website. It was further revised on August 2, 2007 but without materially altering the position as stated in the Main Work except as set out below: see *www.opsi.gov.uk.*

NOTE 95. **Delete:** the Ministry of Justice. **Substitute:** the Department for Constitutional Affairs. The address and telephone number are the same.

10–37   Sub-heading. **Delete: Birth, death and marriage certificates. Substitute: Birth, death, marriage and civil partnership certificates and marriage registers.**

NOTE 98. Guidance Note 7 (revised May 9, 2005) is now entitled Copying of Birth, Death, Marriage and Civil Partnership Certificates and Marriage Registers and is on the OPSI website: *www.opsi.gov.uk.* The guidance also applies to extracts in Scotland. The material changes are outlined below.

Line 2. **Add** after "marriage": "civil partnership".

Sentence starting "Any number of certificates". **Delete:** provided they are not purchased for the purposes of issuing copies to the public. **Substitute:** but they may not be copied except for limited purposes.

Add at end: The form of marriage registers is also Crown copyright. The limited class of persons who have the power to issue marriage certificates also have the power to issue certified copies of such certificates and to copy the marriage registers: see Guidance Note 7, paragraph 5.

10–38   Sub-heading. **Delete: Birth, death and marriage certificates. Substitute: Birth, death, marriage and civil partnership certificates and marriage registers.**

Add after sub-heading: "It is assumed (although the revised text of the Guidance Note does not make this clear) that what follows applies both to certificates and to the content of marriage registers".

10–39   **National Curriculum and similar material: background. Add** at end of first sentence: "The DfES also has responsibility for the implementation of the National Literacy and the National Numeracy Strategies in England."

NOTE 4. Guidance Note 8 was revised on January 16, 2006 and is on the OPSI website: *www.opsi.gov.uk.* Delete "paras 1 to 7" and substitute "paras 1 to 4 and 7".

NOTE 5. Guidance Note 10 was revised on May 9, 2005 and is on the OPSI website *www.opsi.gov.uk.* The material changes are outlined below. Delete "paras 1 to 6" and substitute "paras 1 to 3 and 6".

10–40   **National Curriculum and similar material which may be reproduced freely subject to conditions.** NOTE 9. **Delete:** para.12. **Substitute:** para.11.

After footnote indicator 9, **delete:** and.

After "the Attainment Targets" **add:** ; the Schemes of Work and the National Curriculum Vocabularies. The Schemes of Work are the guidelines produced by the QCA which help schools implement the Programmes of Study. The National Curriculum Vocabularies are the Standard Terms (that is "the compilation and organisation of subject-specific and cross curricular terms within their cosmetic headings hierarchy produced by QCA") and the QCA's classification using the Standard Terms of the Programmes of Study, Schemes of Work, the National Literacy and Numeracy Documents and the Key Stage 3 Strategies. The Schemes of Work and the National Curriculum Vocabularies are licensed by the QCA, which retains copyright in them: see Guidance Note 10, paragraph 11.

National Curriculum and Literacy and Numeracy Strategy Material may be   **10–41**
reproduced under license. NOTE 11. At start of italicised section **add:** (c).
  NOTE 18. **Delete:** para.13. **Substitute:** para.12.
  NOTE 20. **Delete:** para.13. **Substitute:** para.12.
  NOTE 21. **Delete:** para.12. **Substitute:** para.14.
  NOTE 22. **Delete:** para.15. **Substitute:** para.14.

Government Press Notices for England, Northern Ireland and Wales; Press   **10–42**
Notices issued by the Scottish Administration. NOTE 25. Guidance Note 9 was
revised on May 9, 2005 and is on the OPSI website: *www.opsi.gov.uk*.
  NOTE 27. **Delete:** *ibid*. **Substitute:** Guidance Note 9, para.7; Queen's Printer
for Scotland Guidance Note 2 para.6. The list of Crown bodies is now on the
OPSI website.

The Record of Proceedings of the National Assembly of Wales. NOTE 30.   **10–43**
Guidance Note 15 was revised on May 9, 2005 and is on the OPSI website:
www.opsi.gov.uk. **Delete:** para.8. **Substitute:** para.1.
  Add after "as follows:": reproduction must be from the Official Record; material must be reproduced accurately; selective quotations must be stated to be
such; care should be taken to ensure that the most recent version of the Official
Record is used; where the Assembly member spoke in Welsh, the Welsh text
must be reproduced, with the English translation being optional; translations into
languages other than English or Welsh should be made faithfully and by a
competent translator;.
  Delete: where the copy is being published, circulated or issued to others,.
  NOTE 31. **Delete:** paras 10 to 16. **Substitute:** paras 9 to 16.
  Add at end: In addition, a complimentary copy or subscription (with supporting end-user licence, where appropriate) of each commercially published product
which features the Record must be sent to the Assembly: Guidance Note 15,
paragraph 9(g).

Value added material. NOTE 33. **Delete** text of note and **substitute:** *Policy Ar-*   **10–44**
rangements (see para.10–27, above), para.22.
  NOTE 34. **Delete** text of note and **substitute**: *Policy Arrangements*, para.23.
  Lines 14 and 21. **Delete:** core information. **Substitute:** core material.
  NOTE 35. **Delete** and **substitute:** *Policy Arrangements*, para. 19.
  NOTE 36. **Delete** and **substitute:** See the OPSI publication: *Examples of Value-
Added Material* on the OPSI website.

Value added material: licensing policy and prices. NOTE 37. *Charging for*   **10–45**
value-added material is now on the OPSI website.
  NOTE 38. **Delete** and **substitute:** An electronic application form, a standard
form licence and information about charges can be found on the OPSI website.
  NOTE 41. **Delete:** para. 10. **Substitute:** para.11.

Other material: the Core Licence. The Core Licence is now called the PSI   **10–46**
licence. For the licence terms and how to apply, see *www.opsi.gov.uk*.
  NOTE 46. **Delete:** the Vehicle Inspectorate. **Substitute:** the Vehicle and Operator Services Agency.
  NOTE 50. The list of material in respect of which departmental approval is
required is now at *www.opsi.gov.uk/click-use/core-licence-information/out-of-
scope.htm#dept*.

Core Licence: procedure. NOTE 68. The registration form is now on the OPSI   **10–48**
website.

10–49   **Articles written by Ministers and civil servants.** NOTE 75. **Delete** and **substitute:** Guidance—Publication of Articles written by Ministers and Civil Servants in Journals and Conference Proceedings (May 14, 2005): see the OPSI website.

10–50   **The British passport.** NOTE 78. Guidance Note 20 was revised on January 2007. There are significant revisions.

10–51   **The future: the Directive on the reuse of public sector information. Delete** first and last sentences and NOTE 86.

Add at end: The Directive has now been implemented in the United Kingdom with effect from July 1, 2005 by the Re-use of Public Sector Information Regulations 2005 (SI 2005/1515) ("the Regulations"). According to the Explanatory Memorandum "The general approach has been to copy out the Directive although in some places provisions have been drafted to use more usual UK legislative language and to tie in with existing definitions": paragraph 4.1.

10–53   **No effect on intellectual property rights.** In accordance with the Directive, the Regulations do not impose any obligation to permit re-use. Rather, regulation 7(1) simply states: "A public sector body may permit re-use". Article 1(2)(b) is implemented by regulation 5(1)(b), which provides that the Regulations do not apply to a document where a third party owns "relevant intellectual property rights" in the document: regulation 5(2). The term "relevant intellectual property rights" means copyright, database right, publication right and rights in performances: see regulation 2.

10–54   **"Public sector body" and "body governed by public law".** In accordance with the Directive, the Regulations apply to a "public sector body". Regulation 3(1)(a) to (v) contains a list of specific persons and bodies which are defined as public sector bodies for these purposes. They include Ministers of the Crown, government departments, the Houses of Commons and Lords, local authorities and similar bodies. In addition, the term "public sector body" includes bodies satisfying the definition in the Directive of "a body governed by public law": see regulation 3(1)(w).

10–55   **"Document".** Regulation 2 defines "document" in substantially the same terms as Article 2(3) of the Directive. In accordance with Recital 9, computer programs are expressly excluded from the definition. The text of Recital 7 is not incorporated into the definition.

10–56   **Documents to which the Directive does not apply.** The exclusions of categories of document from the ambit of the Directive which are provided for in Article 1(2) of the Directive are implemented as follows.

Article (2)(a), which excludes documents the supply of which is an activity falling outside the scope of the public task of the public sector body concerned, is substantially reproduced in regulation 5(1)(a). There is no attempt to implement the definition of "public task" in Article 1(2)(a), presumably on the basis that it was thought unnecessary to do so. No doubt in cases of difficulty the terms of Article 1(2)(a) of and Recital 9 to the Directive (see NOTE 7 in the Main Work) can be taken account of.

The Article 1(2)(b) exclusion (third party intellectual property rights) is dealt with above.

Article 1(2)(c) provides that the Directive does not apply to documents which are excluded from access by virtue of access regimes in the Member States. According to the Explanatory Memorandum (para.3.2), this has been taken to mean that the Directive is inapplicable to documents which are not accessible under specific statutory provision, in particular the Freedom of Information Act 2000 and similar legislation. This created a difficulty because these measures exempt from access documents which are reasonably accessible to the applicant otherwise than under their terms. Thus, the effect of a literal implementation of Article 1(2)(c) would be to exclude from the ambit of the implementing Regulations a vast number of documents, including, for example, all documents which are publicly available on public authorities' websites. According to the Explanatory Memorandum: "This is unacceptable in policy terms and if implemented would render this instrument largely redundant".

According to the Explanatory Memorandum, a further difficulty arose because the request for re-use will not necessarily be to the person "holding" the document for the purposes of the Freedom of Information Act. The Directive only applies to documents which are already accessible. Accordingly, a request to re-use a document which is not already accessible necessarily entails a Freedom of Information request. Where the body that receives the re-use request also "holds" the document for the purposes of the Freedom of Information Act, this does not present a problem. However, this will not always be the case. The Explanatory Memorandum cites the example of HMSO. It states that requests for re-use of Crown copyright documents will be made to HMSO (this is not something which is provided for in the Regulations, which in fact apply to documents "held by a public sector body": reg.4(1), but is presumably the inevitable consequence of the fact that re-use is likely to require a copyright licence and HMSO is responsible for the management of Crown copyright: see above, para.10–27). However, HMSO will be unlikely to actually hold the document. Such a request would place HMSO in the impossible position of having to adjudicate on the Freedom of Information request without actually having the document or being in receipt of a valid Freedom of Information request. According to the Explanatory Memorandum, such adjudications would not be subject to the jurisdiction of the Information Commissioner. Moreover, the implementation of such a system would arguably amount to a change in the national rules for access to documents, something which the Directive is not intended to require (see Recital 9).

To deal with these problems, regulation 5(2) provides that the Regulations apply to a document if it (a) has been identified by the public sector body as being available for re-use; (b) has been provided to the applicant; or (c) is accessible by means other than making a request for it within the meaning of the Data Protection Act 1998, the Freedom of Information Acts or the Environmental Information Regulations.

The practical result is intended to be as follows. If the request for re-use is made to the body which also "holds" the document for Freedom of Information purposes, the request will be treated as a Freedom of Information request as well. If the document is one to which the Freedom of Information Act applies, then it will be provided to the applicant and it will fall within the scope of the Regulations (reg.5(2)(b)). If the document is only excluded from the Freedom of Information Act because it is reasonably accessible, it will also come within the scope of the Regulations (reg.5(2)(c)).

If, however, the request is made to a body which does not "hold" the document for Freedom of Information purposes, the Regulations will not apply to it. The applicant will have first to identify the body which holds the document for Freedom of Information purposes and make an application for access. If that application succeeds, the applicant will then have to make a fresh request for re-use to the body with the power to grant re-use.

The authors of the Explanatory Memorandum recognise that regulation 5(2) involves a "divergence from the approach of the Directive", but consider that in practice its policy intention will still be achieved.

The exclusions in Article 1(2)(d), (e) and (f) in respect of documents held by broadcasters, education and research establishments and cultural establishments are substantially reproduced in regulation 5(3).

As has already been stated, in accordance with Recital 9, the definition in regulation 2 of "document" expressly excludes computer programs.

The exclusion of documents "covered by industrial property rights" which is referred to in Recital 22 but not in the body of the Directive is not covered in the Regulations. The purpose and meaning of this exclusion is far from clear. It has presumably been decided that the Regulations should apply to such documents. Since the Directive is only intended to impose a minimum set of rules, this is permissible.

10–57   **"Reuse".** The definition of "re-use" in Article 2(4) contains a positive and a negative element. The positive element (use of documents held by public sector bodies for commercial or non-commercial purposes other than the initial purpose within the public task for which they were produced) is implemented effectively verbatim in regulation 4(1). The only change is to delete the unnecessary words "commercial or non-commercial". The negative element of Article 2(4) provides: "Exchange of documents between public sector bodies purely in pursuit of their public tasks does not constitute re-use". In the Regulations, this element has been implemented by regulation 4(2)(a) and (b). Regulation 4(2)(a) provides that re-use shall not include "the transfer for use of a document *within* a public sector body for the purposes of carrying out its own public task" (italics added). According to the Transposition Note, this is considered to be an elaboration on Article 2(4): "it seemed illogical that the transfer of documents between PSBs would not constitute re-use but those transferred for use within a PSB would". It is not clear why this elaboration was thought necessary given that transfer within a public sector body will presumably be for "the initial purpose within the public task for which the documents were produced". Regulation 4(2)(b) provides that the transfer from one public sector body to another for the purpose of either body carrying out its public task shall not constitute re-use.

10–58   **Other limitations.** NOTE 18. For "Art.1(2)(3)" read "Art.1(3)".

NOTE 19. For "Art.1(2)(4)" read "Art.1(4)".

NOTE 20. For "Art. 1(2)(5)" read "Art.1(5)".

Add: The "particular interest" exception in Article 1(3) is implemented in regulation 5(5) which states that the Regulations do not apply where a person is under a legal obligation to prove an interest in order to gain access to documents. It was thought unnecessary to make express provision to implement Article 1(4) (Directive without prejudice to data protection legislation) and 1(5) (Directive applicable only so far as compatible with international agreements on intellectual property): see the Transposition Note.

10–59   **General principle.** The first sentence of Article 3 is implemented by regulation 7, which provides that a public sector body may permit re-use and that where it does so, it shall do so in accordance with regulations 11 to 16. The second sentence of Article 3 is implemented by regulation 11(2) which provides that where possible and appropriate a public sector body shall make a document available for re-use by electronic means.

10–60   **Processing of requests for reuse.** These provisions are implemented as follows. Regulation 10 provides that where possible and appropriate, a public sector body shall ensure that the procedure for processing a request for re-use is capable of being carried out by electronic means. Regulation 8(1) provides that in general a public sector body shall respond to a request for re-use (that is, refuse it, make the document available or offer re-use on conditions—see regulation 8(4)) promptly and in any event before the end of the 20th working day beginning with the day after receipt. Regulation 8(2) provides that where the documents are extensive in quantity or the request raises complex issues, this time period may be extended by the public sector body for a reasonable time. Regulation 8(3) provides that where time is extended in this way, the public sector body must notify the applicant in writing that no decision on re-use has yet been reached and of an estimated date by which it expects to respond to the request. Such notification must be given before the end of the 20th working day following receipt.

The obligation to respond to a request laid down by regulation 8(1) does not apply in a case where the Regulations do not apply to the document by reason of the exceptions laid down in regulation 5(3), that is where it is held by a broadcaster, education or research establishment or a cultural establishment: regulation 9(2). In such cases, in accordance with Article 4(5) of the Directive, there is not even an obligation to acknowledge receipt of the request.

Refusals and appeals. These provisions are implemented as follows. Regulation **10–61** 9(1) provides that in general, where a public sector body refuses a request, it must notify the applicant in writing of the reason for refusal. The notice must contain a reference to the means of redress available to the applicant: regulation 9(3). Naturally, these provisions do not apply where the document is held by a broadcaster, education or research establishment or a cultural establishment: regulation 9(2). Regulation 9(4) provides that where the reason for the refusal is that a third party owns relevant intellectual property rights in the document (reg.5(1)(b)), the regulation 9(1) notification must identify, where known, the name of the person who owns the relevant rights or the person from whom the public sector body obtained the document. Regulation 9(4) goes beyond the terms of Article 4(3), which only obliges the public sector body to identify the right-holder or alternatively the licensor from whom it has obtained the material.

The means of redress are provided for by regulations 17 to 21. It should be noted at the outset that in accordance with Article 7 of the Directive, complaints procedures may not be limited to refusals to supply documents but must extend to all the public sector body's "actions under these Regulations" and must apply where a person "believes that a public sector body has failed to comply with any requirement of these Regulations". In summary, the first port of call is the public sector body's internal complaints procedure. If that does not resolve the problem, the complaint may be referred further. If the original request was to OPSI, HMSO or the Queen's Printer for Scotland (for these bodies, see para.10–27 of this Supplement), the complaint is considered by the Advisory Panel on Public Sector Information ("the Advisory Panel"). If, on the other hand, the initial request was made to any other public sector body, there is a two-stage process. The complaint may first be referred to OPSI. A complainant who is dissatisfied by OPSI's decision may ask the Advisory Panel to review it. No express provision is made for challenging decisions of the Advisory Panel, but it is thought that these may be amenable to judicial review.

Regulation 17(1) requires public sector bodies to establish internal complaints procedures for determining complaints arising under the Regulations. Regulation 17(2) provides that where a person believes that a public sector body has failed to comply with any requirement of the Regulations, he may complain in writing in accordance with the body's internal complaints procedure. Regulation 17(3) provides that any complaint must be determined within a reasonable time and thereafter the body must notify the complainant without delay. The notification must be in writing and must give reasons: regulation 17(4).

Regulation 18 provides for further redress where the public sector body has failed to deal with a complaint within a reasonable time or the regulation 17 procedure has been exhausted. Where the original request was made to OPSI, HMSO or the Office of the Queen's Printer for Scotland (for these bodies see para.10–27 of this Supplement), the complainant may refer the complaint to the Advisory Panel on Public Sector Information ("the Advisory Panel"): regulation 18(3), (4). The Advisory Panel is a Non-Departmental Public Body, established on April 14, 2003 by Douglas Alexander, Minister of State at the Cabinet Office. Where the original request was made to any other body, the complaint may be referred to OPSI: regulation 18(1). Any complaint so referred must be in writing, state the nature of the complaint and include a copy of the written notification under regulation 17(3) where one exists: regulation 18(2).

OPSI is obliged to publish procedures for considering complaints referred to it under regulation 18(1) and to consider such complaints in accordance with such procedures: regulation 19(1), (2). OPSI is obliged to give a written notification to the complainant of "its recommendation": regulation 19(3), (4). A complainant who is dissatisfied with such a recommendation may request the Advisory Panel to review it: regulation 20(1). Any such request must be in writing, must state the reason for the request for the review and must include a copy of any written notifications under regulation 17(3) or 19(3). OPSI's complaints procedure is at *www.opsi.gov.uk/about/contact-us/complaints/complaints-procedure.htm*.

The Advisory Panel is obliged to publish procedures for considering complaints referred to it under reg.18(3) and for conducting reviews under regulation 20(1) and to deal with such complaints and reviews in accordance with those procedures: regulation 21(1), (2). Again, it is obliged to give a written notification to the complainant of "its recommendation": regulation 21(3), (4). The Advisory Panel's complaints procedure is at *www.appsi.gov.uk/complaints-resolution/psi-complaints-procedure.doc*.

10–62   Conditions for reuse. Article 5 of the Directive is implemented in substantially identical terms by regulation 11 ("Format of documents"). Challenges to a public sector body's actions under regulation 11 would no doubt be capable of being the subject of a complaint under regulations 17 to 21.

10–63   Charges. Article 6 of the Directive (charging) is implemented in this way. Regulation 15(1) permits public sector bodies to charge for re-use. Regulation 15(2) provides that the total income from any charge shall not exceed the sum of (a) the cost of collection, production, reproduction and dissemination of documents; and (b) a reasonable return on investment. Regulation 15(3) provides that any charges for re-use shall, so far as reasonably practicable, be calculated in accordance with the accounting principles applicable to the public sector body from time to time and on the basis of a reasonable estimate of the demand for documents over the appropriate accounting period. Regulation 15(4) prohibits public sector bodies from charging an applicant for the cost of collection, production, reproduction and dissemination of documents if the same applicant has already been charged in respect of the same activities by that body for access under information access legislation. Regulation 15(5) provides that where reasonably practicable standard charges shall be established. Such charges must be published under regulation 16(1)(b). On request from an applicant, public sector bodies must specify the basis on which any standard charge has been calculated or, if there is no standard charge, the factors that will be taken account in calculating the charge: regulation 15(6), (7).

10–64   Licences. Article 8 (Licences) is implemented by regulation 12 ("Conditions").

Regulation 12(1) provides that a public sector body may impose conditions on re-use. Regulation 12(2) provides that such conditions shall not unnecessarily restrict either "the way in which a document may be re-used" or "competition". These provisions implement Article 8(1). Article 8(2) (which requires the provision of standard digital licences for electronic processing) is not specifically implemented in the Regulations but standard electronic licences have been published on the OPSI website.

Practical arrangements. Article 10 (non-discrimination) is implemented without any significant changes by regulation 13. No express provision is made in respect of Recital 19, presumably because this was considered to be unnecessary.   **10–65**

Non-discrimination. Article 11 (prohibition of exclusive arrangements) is implemented by regulation 14. The requirement in Article 11(2) that exclusive arrangements established after the entry into force of the Directive shall be "transparent" and "made public" is implemented by regulation 14(4), which provides that any exclusive arrangement entered into on or after December 31, 2003 shall be published by the public sector body.   **10–66**

2. PARLIAMENTARY RIGHTS

B. PARLIAMENTARY COPYRIGHT

(i) Copyright in works other than Parliamentary Bills

Delete heading and **substitute: Scottish, Welsh and Northern Irish parliamentary copyright.**   **10–73**

Third sentence. **Delete** and **substitute:** By section 157(1), the 1988 Act extends to Wales, Scotland and Northern Ireland.

Add at end: Similar provision has now been made in respect of Wales by the Parliamentary Copyright (National Assembly for Wales) Order 2007 (SI 2007/1116). By Article 1(2), the Order comes into effect immediately after the ordinary election under section 3 of the Government of Wales Act 1998 held in 2007. That election took place on May 3, 2007.

The first owner of Welsh parliamentary copyright is the National Assembly for Wales Commission: Article 2(2).

For the purposes of section 165 as applied to the National Assembly for Wales, works made by or under the direction or control of the Assembly include any work made by a "relevant person" in the course of his duties, and any sound recording, film or live broadcast of the proceedings of the Assembly (including proceedings of a committee or sub-committee of the Assembly). However, a work is not to be regarded as made by or under the direction or control of the Assembly by reason only of its being commissioned by or on behalf of the Assembly. Relevant persons are: the presiding officer and deputy presiding officer of the National Assembly for Wales, the members of the Assembly Commission and the members of the staff of the Assembly: see Article 2(3).

(ii) Copyright in Parliamentary Bills

Delete heading and **substitute: Bills of the Scottish Parliament, Welsh Assembly and Northern Ireland Assembly.**   **10–82**

Add at end: With effect from May 3, 2007, similar provision is made in respect of proposed Measures and Bills of the National Assembly for Wales by the introduction of new sections 166C and 166D of the 1988 Act. Copyright in such proposed Measures and Bills belongs to the National Assembly for Wales Commission: section 166C(1) and section 166D(1).

(iii) Position of the Houses of Parliament and the Scottish and Northern Irish Assemblies

10–83 **Ownership and legal proceedings. Add** at end: Welsh parliamentary copyright is owned by the National Assembly for Wales Commission: CDPA 1988, sections 166C and 166D.

(iv) Enforcement of parliamentary copyright

10–86 **Administration.** NOTE 42. HMSO document ref. CO(P)48/1022 was further revised on May 9, 2005. It is now entitled *Guidance for Publishers* and can be found at *www.opsi.gov.uk/advice/crown-copyright/copyright-guidance/ guidance-for-publishers.doc*. The reference to para.3.2 remains correct.

Delete third sentence (starting "The day to day administration") and NOTE 43. **Substitute:** The day-to-day administration of this material is carried out by OPSI's Information Policy Team which reports to the Controller of HMSO: *Guidance for Publishers*, paragraph 3.2.

NOTES 44 to 46. In each case, **delete:** *Dear Publisher Letter* and **substitute:** *Guidance for Publishers*.

10–87 **Policy of the Licensing Division.** NOTES 48 and 50. In each case, **delete:** *Dear Publisher Letter* and **substitute:** *Guidance for Publishers*.

10–88 **United Kingdom Parliamentary Bills and Explanatory Notes.** NOTE 53. Guidance Note 14 was further revised on May 9, 2005 and can now be found at *www.opsi.gov.uk/advice/crown-copyright/copyright-guidance/reproduction-of- bills-and-explanatory-notes.htm*.

10–89 **Reproduction other than photocopying: general.** NOTES 64 to 71. In each case, **delete:** *Dear Publisher Letter* and **substitute:** *Guidance for Publishers*.

10–90 **Reproduction other than photocopying: works which may be freely reproduced.** NOTES 72 and 73. In each case, **delete:** *Dear Publisher Letter* and **substitute:** *Guidance for Publishers*. The Annexes to *Guidance for Publishers* are evidently intended to contain tables as before, but (at least at *www.opsi.gov.uk/ advice/crown-copyright/copyright-guidance/guidance-for-publishers.doc*) their content has been reproduced without boxes making it difficult to follow.

10–91 **Reproduction other than photocopying: Select Committee Reports.** NOTES 75 to 80. In each case, **delete:** *Dear Publisher Letter* and **substitute:** *Guidance for Publishers*.

10–92 **Reproduction other than photocopying: other categories of material.** NOTES 81 to 93. In each case, **delete:** *Dear Publisher Letter* and **substitute:** *Guidance for Publishers*.

10–93 **Photocopying of parliamentary copyright material.** NOTE 94. The *Dear Librarian Letter* was further revised on May 9, 2005 and is now entitled *Guidance for Librarians*. It can be found at *www.opsi.gov.uk/advice/crown-copyright/ copyright-guidance/guidance-for-librarians.doc*.

NOTES 95 to 99. In each case, **delete:** *Dear Librarian Letter* and **substitute:** *Guidance for Librarians*.

CHAPTER ELEVEN

MORAL RIGHTS

1. INTRODUCTION

Droit moral. NOTE 1. **Add:** See also S. Ricketson and J.C. Ginsburg, *Interna-*   **11–01**
tional Copyright and Neighbouring Rights, The Berne Convention and Beyond,
(2nd. ed., Oxford University Press, 2006), para.10.01 *et seq.* and E. Adeney, The
Moral Rights of Authors and Performers—An International and Comparative
Analysis, (Oxford University Press, 2006).

NOTE 2. **Delete** and **substitute:** In *International Copyright and Neighbouring
Rights, The Berne Convention and Beyond* (2nd ed., Oxford University Press,
2006), para.10.01 *et seq.*, Ricketson and Ginsburg note that the adjective "moral"
has no precise English equivalent in this context, although the words "spiritual",
"non-economic" and "personal" convey something of the intended meaning.

EC Commission proposals. Add at the beginning: The Commission has kept   **11–07**
under review the question whether there is a need for harmonization of moral

rights within the European Union. The report of an independent study commissioned by the European Commission concerning moral rights in the context of the exploitation of works through digital technology published in 2000 concluded that there was no need for such harmonisation.[1]

11–08 **WIPO Performances and Phonograms Treaty.** Last sentence. **Delete** and **substitute:** These provisions of the WPPT have been implemented by the Performances (Moral Rights, etc.) Regulations 2006,[2] which entered into force on February 1, 2006, and introduced moral rights for performers into the law of the United Kingdom. These rights are described in this Supplement at Chapter 12, below.

2. THE RIGHT TO BE IDENTIFIED AS AUTHOR OR DIRECTOR

B. THE CIRCUMSTANCES IN WHICH THE RIGHT EXISTS

(ii) Musical works

11–13 First paragraph, point (2). **Add:** See *Sawkins v Hyperion Records Ltd*[3] where the Court of Appeal held that the effort, skill and time expended by the author of performing editions of musical works in the public domain were sufficient to satisfy the requirement that the performing editions should be "original" musical works in the copyright sense and that failure to identify the author of these editions as such on CDs issued to the public was an infringement of the right to be known as the author of one's work and in breach of section 77.

D. THE FORM OF IDENTIFICATION

11–18 NOTE 88. **Add:** The decision was affirmed by the Court of Appeal in *Sawkins v Hyperion Records Ltd.* [2005] EWCA Civ 565, paras 66–69.

NOTE 89. **Add:** The decision was affirmed by the Court of Appeal in *Sawkins v Hyperion Records Ltd.* [2005] EWCA Civ 565, para. 67.

NOTE 90. **Add:** The decision was affirmed by the Court of Appeal in *Sawkins v. Hyperion Records Ltd.* [2005] EWCA Civ 565.

E. ASSERTION OF THE RIGHT

11–19 Second sentence. **Add:** NOTE 90A. See *Christoffer v Poseidon Film Distributors Ltd.* [2000] E.C.D.R. 487, where C had not asserted himself as the author of relevant scripts under s.78 of the Act and therefore PFD were not at fault for failing to identify him in the credits.

3. THE RIGHT TO OBJECT TO DEROGATORY TREATMENT OF A WORK

A. DEROGATORY TREATMENT

11–37 **Treatment.** NOTE 71. **Add:** For a discussion of the role of moral rights in the

---

[1] M. Salokannel and A. Strowel with the collaboration of E. Derclaye, Final Report Study Contract No. ETD/99/B5-3000/E 28.
[2] SI 2006/18.
[3] [2005] EWCA Civ 565.

protection of images, see S. Teilmann, "Framing the Law: the Right of Integrity in Britain" [2005] E.I.P.R. 27(1), 19–24.

Prejudicial to honour or reputation. Fifth sentence. "Honour", which is as- **11–40** sociated with both reputation and good name, is more a matter of respect for a person and his position.

Add: NOTE 89A. As regards the concept of "honour" when considering the test for breach of the right of integrity, see E. Adeney, "The moral right of integrity: the past and future of 'honour'" I.P.Q. 2005, 2, 111–134.

NOTE 89. See S. Ricketson and J.C. Ginsburg, *International Copyright and Neighbouring Rights, The Berne Convention and Beyond* (2nd ed., Oxford University Press, 2006), para.10–07.

NOTE 90. See S. Ricketson and J.C. Ginsburg, *International Copyright and Neighbouring Rights, The Berne Convention and Beyond* (2nd ed., Oxford University Press, 2006), para.10–09.

Destruction. Add: However, in *Sehgal v the Union of India*,[4] the argument that, **11–42** where a work is destroyed there is no prejudice to the author's reputation, since it no longer exists and cannot therefore be viewed by anyone, was rejected. It was held that, on the contrary, the destruction of a work of art was an extreme form of mutilation and by reducing the volume of the author's creative corpus it affected his reputation prejudicially. In the case in question, the work was a famous bronze mural sculpture, commissioned by the Indian government from an internationally renowned sculptor, but some years later taken down, stored and badly damaged.

5. RIGHT TO PRIVACY OF CERTAIN PHOTOGRAPHS AND FILMS

Private and domestic purposes. Add: NOTE 78A. *Mahmood v. Galloway* [2006] **11–59** EWHC 1286, where the Court, refusing an application for the continuation of an interim injunction, held that neither of two photographs had been taken for a private or domestic purpose.

8. REMEDIES FOR INFRINGEMENT OF MORAL RIGHTS

NOTE 28. **Add:** An interesting discussion of the difficulty of enforcing moral **11–71** rights in the digital environment, including the potential effect of choice of law on Internet disputes, is to be found in C. Waelde and L. de Souza, "Moral Rights and the Internet: Squaring the Circle" [2002] I.P.Q. 3, 265–288.

9. SUPPLEMENTARY PROVISIONS

A. CONSENT AND WAIVER OF RIGHTS

Waiver. NOTE 39. **Add:** For an example of a case where the exercise of the right **11–76** of integrity was held to have been waived, see decision of the Athens Court of First Instance: *Architecture Studio and Architectes Associés Pour l'Environnement v Organisation of Labour Housing* [2002] E.C.D.R. 36.

---

[4] HC (Ind) [2005] F.S.R. 39.

CHAPTER TWELVE

RIGHTS IN PERFORMANCES

1. INTRODUCTION

A. HISTORICAL

12–01   **Nature of performers' rights.** Third paragraph, last two sentences. **Delete** and **substitute:** Subsequently, the Act has had to be amended on a number of occasions to comply with EC Directives and to meet other international obligations.[1]

---

[1] See para. 12–04, below. On the evolution of performers' rights in the UK, see R. Arnold, *Performers' Rights* (3rd ed., Sweet and Maxwell, 2004), Ch.1.

The 1988 Act. Last three sentences. **Delete** and **substitute:** However, in 1992   **12–04**
the Rental and Related Rights Directive[2] required that performers should be afforded certain transferable property rights. As a result, in 1996 considerable additions and changes were made to the scheme of protection under the 1988 Act in
order to implement such legislation in the United Kingdom and to meet other
international obligations.[3] The result was the creation of a two-tier system of
protection; the original rights of the 1988 Act, which granted performers certain
non-property rights, and new performers' property rights. Although these new
rights were not described as copyright, in effect a new copyright was conferred
on performers. Yet further changes were required in 2003 on implementation of
the Information Society Directive.[4] Finally, regulations were introduced in February 2006[5] to provide moral rights for performers in fulfillment of the United
Kingdom's obligations under the WIPO Performances and Phonograms Treaty,
1996, (the WPPT).[6] These are all discussed in further detail below.

C. THE INTERNATIONAL PERSPECTIVE

(ii) European Community Legislation

The Rental and Related Rights Directive. NOTE 27. **Delete** and **substitute:**   **12–13**
Directive 2006/115/EC ([2006] O.J. L376 (codified version)), repealing and
replacing Council Directive 92/100 on rental right and lending right and on
certain rights related to copyright in the field of intellectual property [1992] O.J.
L346/61.

NOTE 28. **Delete** and **substitute:** Art.7(1).

NOTE 30. **Delete** and **substitute:** Art.9(1).

NOTE 31. **Delete** and **substitute:** Art.3(1)(b).

NOTE 34. **Delete** and **substitute:** As far as the reproduction right is concerned,
the original provision of Directive 92/100/EEC has been repealed and replaced
by Art.2(b) of the Information Society Directive; as regards the other rights, see
Arts 3(3) and 9(4) of the codified Directive 2006/115/EC.

NOTE 36. **Delete** and **substitute:** Art.5, which applies also to authors. See
para.12–19 *et seq.*, below.

The Term Directive. NOTE 39. **Delete** and **substitute:** Directive 2006/116/EC   **12–15**
([2006] O.J. L372 (codified version)), repealing and replacing Council Directive
93/98 harmonising the term of protection of copyright and certain related rights
[1993] O.J. L290/69.

---

[2] Directive 2006/115/EC [2006] O.J. L376 (codified version), which repealed and replaced Council
Directive 92/100/EEC; see further at paras 12–13 and 25–52 of the Main Work.

[3] See para.12–10 *et seq.*, of the Main Work.

[4] Directive 2001/29/EC of the European Parliament and of the Council, see further at paras 12–16
and 25–79 *et seq.*

[5] The Performances (Moral Rights, etc.) Regulations 2006.

[6] See para.12–106 *et seq.*, and paras 12–18 and 24–119 of the Main Work.

2. THE SUBSTANTIVE RIGHTS

A. Implementation of Directives and overview

12–19   **Amendments to the 1988 Act.** First three sentences. **Delete** and **substitute:** The United Kingdom's obligations under the Rome Convention were fully addressed by the 1988 Act. However, the various Community measures referred to above necessitated significant additions and amendments to the Act. Moreover, the introduction of moral rights for the benefit of performers into the law of the United Kingdom was necessary to permit the United Kingdom to ratify the WIPO Performers and Phonograms Treaty, 1996.[7] Changes were effected by means of four statutory instruments[8]: the Duration of Copyright and Rights in Performances Regulations 1995,[9] the Copyright and Related Rights Regulations 1996,[10] the Copyright and Related Rights Regulations 2003[11] and the Performances (Moral Rights, etc.) Regulations 2006.[12] The latter Regulations came into force on February 1, 2006, and in addition to creating two new rights for performers, the right to be identified as the performer and the right to object to derogatory treatment (so-called moral rights), the Regulations divide up Part II of the 1988 Act into four chapters and make a number of minor amendments. The four new chapters of Part II are the following: Chapter 1 entitled "Introductory" includes sections 180–181, which give an overview of the various rights granted in Part II, as amended; Chapter 2 entitled "Economic Rights" includes sections 182–205B; Chapter 3 entitled "Moral Rights" includes sections 205C–205N (moral rights); and Chapter 4 entitled "Qualification for protection, extent and interpretation" includes sections 206–212.

12–20   **Present Rights.** First sentence. **Delete** and **substitute:** The new rights required by the Rental and Related Rights Directive and the Performances (Moral Rights, etc.) Regulations were added to the existing scheme, leaving the original rights in place, subject in the case of the latter Regulations to the rearrangement of Part II of the Act into four chapters.

> (ii) *Further rights granted on amendment of the 1988 Act*
> *Performers' property rights.* NOTE 63. **Add:** *Barrett v Universal-Island Records Ltd.* where it was held that the rights conferred on a performer by the 1988 Act were rights to authorise or prohibit an act and were sufficiently different rights from those conferred by s.182 of the Act as to amount to new rights.
> **Add:** *Performers' moral rights.* The Performances (Moral Rights, etc) Regulations 2006[13] have introduced a new Chapter 3 of Part II of the Act, entitled "Moral Rights". This confers the following moral rights on a

---

[7] Cm.3728.

[8] All three of the Directives relevant to Part II of the 1988 Act were implemented after the dates required by their provisions. The Rental and Related Rights Directive (Dir.92/100) was due to be implemented by July 1, 1994, but was not implemented in the UK until December 1, 1996. The Duration Directive (Dir.93/98) was due to be implemented by July 1, 1995, but was not implemented in the UK until January 1, 1996. The Information Society Directive was due to be implemented by December 2002, but was not implemented in the UK until October 31, 2003. Potential liability under *Francovich v Italy* ([1991] E.C.R. I–5357) and *Brasserie du Pêcheur SA v Germany* ([1996] 1 C.M.L.R. 889) has been limited by the drafting of the transitional provisions, which are generous to users.

[9] SI 1995/3297.

[10] SI 1996/2967.

[11] SI 2003/2498.

[12] SI 2006/18.

[13] SI 2006/18.

performer, the right to be identified and the right to object to derogatory treatment of his performance. The rights are granted in respect to any type of live performances, broadcasts of live performances or performances recorded (fixed) in sound recordings and which are communicated or issued to the public. These rights are conferred by sections 205C to 205N of the Act as amended, and are described in paras 12–106 to 12–119, below.

Add as first sentence: The rights referred to above as performers' non-property rights and performers' property rights are now laid down in Chapter 2 of Part II of the Act entitled "Economic Rights". The new performers' moral rights are contained in Chapter 3 of Part II of the Act, entitled "Moral Rights". **12–21**

Transitional provisions. Add: The moral rights conferred by Chapter 3 of Part II of the Copyright, Designs and Patents Act 1988 (as inserted by the Performances (Moral Rights, etc.) Regulations, 2006) do not apply to any performance that took place before the Regulations came into force on February 1, 2006.[14] **12–22**

B. Protected Performances

(ii) Qualifying performances of performers

NOTE 88. **Add:** In this connection, see *Experience Hendrix LLC v Purple Haze Records Ltd* [2005] EWHC 249 (Ch); *Experience Hendrix LLC v Purple Haze Records Ltd* [2006] EWHC 968 (Ch); *Experience Hendrix LLC v Purple Haze Records Ltd* [2007] EWCA Civ 501. In a series of decisions concerning the same parties concluding with a decision of the Court of Appeal, it has been held that it was accepted that performances given in the UK prior to the commencement of the Act were qualifying performances due to the specifically retrospective nature of the legislation (*cf.* s.180(3) of the 1988 Act). The same retrospective effect should be given also to other qualifying countries; no distinction could be drawn between countries who were qualifying members at the commencement of the Act and those that joined subsequently. Swedish performances were qualifying performances for the purposes of s.181. Individual performers who participated in a group performance enjoyed individual rights under the Act, which proceeded on the basis that each individual performer had the rights conferred by the Act so long as the performance was a qualifying performance or the individual was a qualifying individual. For comments on the case, see P. Groves, "Once you are dead, you are made for life", Ent. L.R. 16(7), 196 and P. Gardiner and N. Newing, "Case Comment" [2007] Ent. L.R. 18(1), 34–35. **12–24**

(iii) Reciprocal protection

NOTE 97. Delete last two sentences. **12–25**

NOTE 1. **Delete** and **substitute:** See The Copyright and Performances (Application to Other Countries) Order (SI 2007/273), which entered into force on April 6, 2007; see Vol.2 at **C1.iv** (as amended in this Supplement). The purpose of the Order is to apply Part I of the Act to works originating from other countries and to confer on certain countries reciprocal protection under Part II of the Act in order to satisfy the United Kingdom's international obligations under the Berne Convention, the Universal Copyright Convention, the Rome Convention, the TRIPs Agreement and arising from its membership of the European Community.

---

[14] *cf.* s.8.

In particular, in relation to performances, the Order satisfies the obligations imposed by the European Union's membership of TRIPs and also the obligations imposed on member States under Council Decision 2000/278/EC relating to the WIPO Performances and Phonograms Treaty (WPPT) 1996. A consolidated list of the protection afforded to other countries is contained in the Order and the designated Convention countries are listed in the Schedule to the Order.

(iv) Territoriality

12–26   Last paragraph, second sentence. **Delete** and **substitute:** A "British ship" means a ship which is a British ship for the purposes of the Merchant Shipping Act 1995 otherwise than by virtue of registration in a country outside the United Kingdom.[15]

C. SUBSISTENCE OF RECORDING RIGHTS

(iii) Qualifying person

12–29   First sentence. **Delete** and **substitute:** A "qualifying individual" means a citizen or a subject of, or an individual resident in, a qualifying country; and a "qualifying person" means a qualifying individual or a body corporate or other body having legal personality which is formed under the law of a part of the United Kingdom or another qualifying country[16] and has in any qualifying country a place of business at which substantial business activity is carried on.[17]

D. DURATION OF RIGHTS

(i) General

12–30   NOTE 20. **Delete** and **substitute:** Directive 2006/116/EC [2006] O.J. L372 (codified version), repealing and replacing Directive 93/98 harmonising the term of protection of copyright and certain related rights.

NOTE 24. **Delete** and **substitute:** Duration Directive 2006/116/EC.

(iii) Transitional provisions

Add new paragraph:

12–37A   **Proposals for the extension of the term of protection of sound recordings.** On January 1, 2005, sound recordings published on or before December 31, 1954, fell into the public domain, making available for exploitation many famous and still successful recordings without the payment of royalties. This led to calls from the recording industry and performers to prolong the period of protection afforded to sound recordings to 70 years or more. In May 2007, support for an increase in the term of protection to at least 70 years came from the House of Commons Culture, Media and Sport Committee in its report entitled "New Media and the Creative Industries" (Fifth Report of Session 2006–2007, HC 509–1, dated May 1, 2007, Recommendation 28 and paras 232–236). The Committee considered this was necessary to provide reasonable certainty that an artist will be able to derive benefit from a recording throughout his or her lifetime; it also

---

[15] s.210(2). The Merchant Shipping Act now in force is that of 1995.
[16] CDPA 1988, s.206 (1). See para.12–24, above. See also Ch.3, above.
[17] CDPA 1988, s.206(1).

considered there was no reason why composers should benefit from a longer term than performers. The issue is currently under consideration by the European Commission and the Committee called on the UK Government to press for the extension. However, the Gowers Review of Intellectual Property of December 2006 recommended against requesting the European Union to consider such an extension on economic grounds; it concluded that there was little evidence that extension would benefit performers, increase the number of works created or made available, or provide incentives for creativity and it noted a potentially negative effect on the balance of trade. Subsequently, however, the Department of Culture, Media and Sport announced on July 27, 2007, that it would not support extending the term of protection of either producers of sound recordings or performers.

3. OWNERS AND TRANSMISSION OF RIGHTS

B. TRANSMISSION

(i) Performers' non-property rights

NOTE 63. **Add:** The Court of Appeal has confirmed that even prior to the enactment of the CDPA 1988 a performer had a civilly enforceable right to protect his economic interests and that right would have devolved on his personal representatives by operation of law. The amended Act did not take away the rights conferred in respect of performers who had died before the Act came into force; see *Experience Hendrix LLC v Purple Haze Records Ltd* [2005] EWHC 249 (Ch); *Experience Hendrix LLC v Purple Haze Records Ltd* [2006] EWHC 968 (Ch) and *Experience Hendrix LLC v Purple Haze Records Ltd* [2007] EWCA Civ 501.   **12–41**

(iii) Performers' property rights

NOTE 69. **Delete** and **substitute:** CDPA 1988, s.191A. Subs.191A(4) provides that where a performer's property rights (or any aspect of them) is owned by more than one person jointly, references in Pt II to the rights owner are to all the owners, so that, in particular, any requirement of the licence of the rights owner requires the licence of all of them. See *Bourne v Davis (t/a Brandon Davis Publishing)* [2006] EWHC1567, where it was held that a member of a group of musicians had individual performer's property rights in their group performances and any infringement of those rights without his consent or the consent of any assignee was prohibited.   **12–43**

Right to equitable remuneration for exploitation of a sound recording. Second sentence. **Delete** and **substitute:** The meaning of "commercially published" is not exactly clear; the Performances (Moral Rights, etc.) Regulations 2006[18] have amended section 182D on this point by the addition of a new subsection 1A, which provides: "In subsection 1, the reference to publication of a sound recording includes making it available to the public by electronic transmission in such a way that members of the public may access it from a place and at a time individually chosen by them".   **12–46**

NOTE 87. First sentence. **Delete** and **substitute:** The Performances (Moral Rights, etc.) Regulations 2006 has inserted a definition of "collecting society" as a new subs.(8) to s.182D. It reads: "In this section "collecting society" means a

---

[18] SI 2006/18.

society or other organisation which has as its main object, or one of its main objects, the exercise of the right to equitable remuneration on behalf of more than one performer". This definition is in line with that contained in s.191G(6).

8. PERFORMERS' MORAL RIGHTS (CPDA PART II, CHAPTER 3)

A. INTRODUCTION

12–106 **The WIPO Performers and Phonograms Convention (WPPT), 1996.** The WPPT, to which the United Kingdom is a signatory, is the first international treaty to include provisions relating to moral rights for performers. The Rome Convention provides limited protection to performers, giving them the possibility of preventing certain acts done without their consent, including the possibility of preventing *inter alia* the broadcasting and the communication to the public of live performances, the fixation by means of sound recordings of live performances and the reproduction of such fixations without their consent.[19] Note that the Convention specifically excludes protection for performances which are incorporated in a visual or audio-visual fixation.[20] The WPPT requires two moral rights to be afforded to performers, the right to claim to be identified as the performer of a performance (the right to be identified or right of paternity) and the right to object to any distortion, mutilation or other modification of his performances that would be prejudicial to his reputation (the right to object to derogatory treatment, often referred to as the right of integrity).[21] In line with the Rome Convention,[22] the WPPT only requires these rights to be granted in respect of live aural performances or performances recorded (fixed) in sound recordings. The term "aural" means the "sound element" of any performance. The Performances (Moral Rights, etc.) Regulations 2006[23] has implemented these provisions of the WPPT in the United Kingdom by means of secondary legislation made under the European Communities Act 1972.[24] In doing so, however, the Government has exceeded its obligations under the WPPT by providing moral rights in relation to any type of live performances and to sound recordings of any type of performance, regardless of whether that is made directly from the live performance or indirectly. However, moral rights have not been introduced in relation to fixations of audiovisual performances.[25]

12–107 **History of Performers' Moral Rights.** The WPPT provisions concerning the moral rights of performers had their origin in a proposal by the International Bureau of WIPO to the first session in 1993 of the Committee of Experts on a possible new instrument on the rights of performers and producers of

---

[19] Art.7.
[20] Art.19; see para.24–97 *et seq.*
[21] WPPT, Art.5.
[22] Art.19.
[23] SI 2006/18.
[24] The WPPT was specified by the European Communities (Definition of Treaties) (WIPO Copyright Treaty and WIPO Performances and Phonograms Treaty) Order 2005 (SI 2005/3431) to be a Community Treaty as defined in s.1(2) of the European Communities Act, 1972.
[25] The following analysis in para.12–107 *et seq.*, of the provisions of the Performances (Moral Rights, etc.) Regulations 2006 (SI 2006/19) takes into account the Regulations themselves and the Patent Office Notice dated December 10, 2004, entitled *Consultation on regulations implementing performers' moral rights in the United Kingdom resulting from the WIPO Performances and Phonograms Treaty (WPPT)*. For a comment on the proposals on which the consultation was based, see R. Sprawson, "Moral Rights in the 21st Century: a Case for Bankruptcy?" [2006] Ent. L.R. 17(2), 58.

phonograms.[26] The proposal responded to the concern that technology has made it possible by means of digital technology to manipulate and alter recordings of performances in ways which could easily be very damaging to a performer. During the preparatory work leading to the Diplomatic Conference in 1996 and the adoption of the WPPT, there was general support for the proposals, which were modeled on Article 6*bis* of the Berne Convention. At the Diplomatic Conference there was a strong body of opinion in favour of the protection of performers' moral rights from European and Latin American delegates, the national laws of many of whom recognised such rights already.[27]

B. Nature of Rights

Right to be identified as performer

Definition of the right. The right to be identified as the performer arises when a   **12–108**
qualifying performance is given live in public or broadcast live or when a sound recording of such a performance is communicated or issued to the public.[28] In this context, communication means communication by electronic transmission.[29] The right applies in relation to the whole or any substantial part of a performance.[30] The right can be satisfied flexibly as follows:

- for live performance, by identification of the performer in a programme accompanying the performance or in some other manner likely to bring his identity to the notice of a person seeing or hearing the performance ;
- in the case of a broadcast performance by identification in a manner likely to bring his identity to the notice of a person seeing or hearing the broadcast;
- in the case of a sound recording communicated to the public by identification in a manner likely to bring his identity to the notice of a person hearing the communication; and
- for copies of a recording of a performance issued to the public to be identified in or on each copy or, if that is not appropriate, in some other manner likely to bring his identity to the notice of a person acquiring a copy.

In all these cases, identification in such other manner as the parties may agree is also permitted.[31]

Group performances. In relation to a performance given by a group, the right to   **12–109**
be identified is not infringed where it is not reasonably practicable for each member of the group to be identified, provided that the group itself is identified. "Group" means two or more performers who have a particular name by which they may be identified collectively. This makes it clear that there is no right for performers to be identified individually where a performance is given by a group.[32]

---

[26] [1993] *Copyright* 142, 148.
[27] S. Ricketson and J.C. Ginsburg, *International Copyright and Neighbouring Rights, the Berne Convention and Beyond* (2nd ed., Oxford University Press, 2006), Vol.II, para.19.52.
[28] CPDA, s.205C (1).
[29] See CPDA, s.20.
[30] CDPA, s.205K (1).
[31] CPDA, s.205C(2).
[32] CPDA, s.205C(3).

12–110　　**Requirement that right be asserted.** The right to be identified must be asserted, in a similar manner to the rights of authors and film directors.[33] The right may be asserted generally, or in relation to any specified act or description of acts by instrument in writing signed by or on behalf of the performer, or on an assignment of a performer's property rights, by including in the instrument effecting the assignment a statement that the performer asserts his right to be identified in relation to the performance. The persons bound by an assertion of the right are anyone to whose notice the assertion is brought and, in relation to an assignment of the performer's property rights, the assignee and anyone claiming through him, whether or not he has notice of the assertion. Any assertion on behalf of a group of performers must be by a person acting on behalf of the group.[34] The requirement that an instrument be signed by a person is also satisfied in the case of a body corporate by signature on behalf of the body or by the affixing of its seal.[35]

12–111　　**Exceptions to the right to be identified.** The right does not apply: where it is not reasonably practicable to identify the performer, or the group; or in relation to any performance given for the purpose of reporting current events or advertising any goods or services. The right is not infringed in the following circumstances: news reporting; incidental inclusion of a performance or recording; things done for the purpose of examination; parliamentary and judicial proceedings; Royal Commissions and statutory inquiries.[36]

Right to object to derogatory treatment of performance (integrity right)

12–112　　**Definition of the right.** The right to object to derogatory treatment of a performance is infringed if:

- the performance is broadcast live, or
- by means of a sound recording the performance is played in public or communicated to the public,

with any distortion, mutilation or other modification that is prejudicial to the reputation of the performer.[37] The right applies in relation to the whole or any part of a performance (it does not have to be a substantial part, as in the case of the right to be identified).[38] The right to object to derogatory treatment applies to all performers individually and so there is no separate provision for groups.

12–113　　**Exceptions to right.** The right is subject to the following exceptions.[39] It does not apply in relation to any performance given for the purposes of reporting current events and is not infringed by modifications made to a performance which are consistent with normal editorial or production practice. Furthermore, the right is not infringed by anything done for the purpose of avoiding the commission of an offence, complying with a duty imposed by or under an enactment, or, in the case of the British Broadcasting Corporation, avoiding the inclusion in a programme broadcast by them of anything which offends against good taste or decency or which is likely to encourage or incite crime or lead to disorder or to be offensive to public feeling. All of these are subject to sufficient disclaimer being provided, *i.e.* a clear and reasonably prominent indication that the modifications did not have the consent of the performer, given at the time of the act and

---

[33] *cf.* CDPA, s.78.
[34] CDPA, s.205D.
[35] CPDA, s.210A(2).
[36] CPDA, s.205E.
[37] CDPA, s.205F.
[38] CDPA, s.205K(2).
[39] CDPA, s.205G.

appearing with the identification of the performer, if any. There are similar provisions regarding authors.[40]

Infringement of right by possessing or dealing with infringing article. Possessing or dealing with a sound recording of a performance with modifications prejudicial to the performer's reputation infringes the performer's integrity right.[41] This follows similar provisions for authors.[42]

12–114

C. SUPPLEMENTARY PROVISIONS

Duration of rights. A performer's moral rights in relation to a performance subsist so long as that performer's economic rights subsist in the performance. "Performer's rights" in this context includes rights of a performer which are vested in a successor of his.[43] This is in conformity with the WPPT requirement that a performer's moral rights should subsist so long as the economic rights subsist in a performance.[44]

12–115

Consent and waiver of rights. It is not an infringement of the performers' moral rights to do any act to which consent has been given by or on behalf of the person entitled to the right. Moreover, any of the rights may be waived.[45] This must be done in writing and signed by or on behalf of the person giving up the right. A waiver may relate to a specific performance, to performances of a specified description or to performances generally, and may relate to existing or future performances, and may be conditional or unconditional and may be expressed to be subject to revocation. If a waiver is made in favour of the owner or prospective owner of a performer's property rights in the performance or performances to which it relates, it shall be presumed to extend to his licensees and successors in title unless a contrary intention is expressed. Finally, it is provided that nothing in the new provisions shall be construed as excluding the operation of the general law of contract or estoppel in relation to an informal waiver or other transaction in relation to either of the performer's moral rights. The requirement that an instrument be signed by a person is also satisfied in the case of a body corporate by signature on behalf of the body or by the affixing of its seal.[46]

12–116

Moral rights not assignable. The rights to be identified and to object to derogatory treatment of a performance are not assignable, like the performers' non-property rights, although all these rights are transmissible on death. The property rights of performers, namely, the reproduction right, distribution right, rental right and lending right, are transmissible by assignment, by testamentary disposition or by operation of law, as personal or moveable property. The personal nature of moral rights, which are attached to the person of the right owner, is the justification for their not being assignable.

12–117

Transmission of moral rights on death. On the death of a person entitled to a moral right, the right passes to such person as he may by testamentary disposition specifically direct; if there is no such direction but the performer's property rights in respect of the performance in question form part of his estate, the right passes

12–118

---

[40] CDPA, s.81.
[41] CDPA, s.205H.
[42] CDPA, s.83.
[43] CDPA, s.205I.
[44] WPPT, Art.5(2).
[45] CDPA, s.205J.
[46] CPDA, s.210A(2).

to the person to whom the property rights pass; if neither of the above is the case, the right is exercisable by his personal representatives. Where a performer's property rights are divided between two or more persons, the right is correspondingly divided. In such a case, the right to object to derogatory treatment of a performance is exercisable by each of them, and is satisfied in relation to any of them, if he consents to the treatment or act in question, and any waiver of the right by one of them does not affect the rights of the others. A consent or waiver previously given or made binds any person to whom a right passes on death. Damages recovered by personal representatives in respect of an infringement after a person's death shall devolve as part of his estate as if the right of action had subsisted and been vested in him immediately before his death.[47]

12–119   **Remedies for infringement of moral rights.** Infringement of moral rights is actionable as a breach of statutory duty owed to the person entitled to the right.[48] Where there is an infringement and a person falsely claiming to act on behalf of a performer consented to the relevant conduct or purported to waive the right, and there would have been no infringement if he had been so acting, that person shall be liable, jointly and severally with any person liable in respect of the infringement, as if he himself had infringed the right.[49] In proceedings for infringement, it shall be a defence to prove that a person claiming to act on behalf of the performer consented to the defendant's conduct or purported to waive the right and that the defendant reasonably believed that the person was acting on behalf of the performer.[50] The court may, if it thinks it is an adequate remedy in the circumstances, grant an injunction on terms prohibiting the doing of any act unless a disclaimer is made, in such terms and in such manner as may be approved by the court, disassociating the performer from the broadcast or sound recording of the performance.[51]

12–120   **Transitional provision.** Moral rights do not apply in relation to any performance that took place before the Performers (Moral Rights, etc.) Regulations 2006[52] entered into force on February 1, 2006

---

[47] CDPA, s.205M.
[48] CDPA, s.205N(1).
[49] CDPA, s.205N(2).
[50] CDPA, s.205N(3).
[51] CDPA, s.205N(4).
[52] SI 2006/18.

CHAPTER THIRTEEN

DESIGN RIGHT, UNREGISTERED COMMUNITY DESIGN AND THE PROTECTION OF WORKS OF INDUSTRIAL APPLICATION

1. THE SCHEME OF PROTECTION

D. HISTORY OF PROTECTION OF INDUSTRIALLY APPLIED WORKS

13–28   **The 1986 White Paper.** NOTE 99. **Add:** In *Dyson Ltd v Qualtex (UK) Ltd* [2006] EWCA Civ 166; [2006] R.P.C. 31, the Court of Appeal endorsed the Judge's view that the White Paper clearly rejected both the notion that spare parts should be exempted from any protection regime and the notion that they should be subject to some special regime. They were to be dealt with like all other functional articles.

13–29   **Copyright Designs and Patents Act 1988. Add:** In *Dyson Ltd v Qualtex (UK) Ltd* [2006] EWCA Civ 166; [2006] R.P.C. 31 at [11], the Court of Appeal rejected submissions that the design right provisions of the 1988 Act ought to be construed "with some sort of clear purpose in mind", concluding in relation to spare parts: "Here on the one hand Parliament refused to create a general spare parts exception, and on the other hand clearly did not intend that OEMs should have absolute control over the manufacture of spares. A compromise (some might say fudge) in the form of the language actually chosen in the Act was what was done. We must construe it as it would be read by a reasonable reader. Here that means taking the language as it stands."

3. DESIGN RIGHT: SUBJECT MATTER OF PROTECTION

A. DEFINITION OF DESIGN

The "design". NOTES 54 and 55. *A Fulton & Co Ltd v Totes Isotoner (UK) Ltd* is **13–45** reported at [2004] R.P.C. 16.

NOTE 58. **Add:** See also *Ultraframe (UK) Ltd v Eurocell Building Plastics Ltd* [2005] EWCA Civ 761; [2005] R.P.C. 36.

Add: There is no reason in principle why a simple geometric shape such as a sphere or a spiral or combination of spirals may not be a "design": *Sales v Stromberg* [2005] EWHC 1624 (Ch); [2006] F.S.R. 7.

No requirement of aesthetic merit or eye appeal. NOTE 62. *A Fulton & Co Ltd* **13–46** *v Totes Isotoner (UK) Ltd* is reported at [2004] R.P.C. 16. For the position in relation to community designs, see para.13–200 of this Supplement.

Any aspect. NOTE 64. *A Fulton & Co Ltd v Totes Isotoner (UK) Ltd* is reported **13–47** at [2004] R.P.C. 16. **Add:** See also *Dyson Ltd v Qualtex (UK) Ltd* [2006] EWCA Civ 166; [2006] R.P.C. 31 at [22]–[26]: protection extends to a "mere twiddle" provided it is discernible or recognisable even if considered as part of the whole article it is visually insignificant.

Shape or configuration. NOTES 68 and 69. *Lambretta Clothing Co Ltd v Teddy* **13–48** *Smith (UK) Ltd* is reported at [2005] R.P.C. 6.

NOTE 70. *Lambretta Clothing Co Ltd v Teddy Smith (UK) Ltd* is reported at [2005] R.P.C. 6. **Add:** See also *Vitof Ltd v Altoft* [2006] EWHC 1678 (Ch) in which designs for the positioning of components, the printed copper connecting layers and the holes in the board were held to be protected.

NOTE 73. *Lambretta Clothing Co Ltd v Teddy Smith (UK) Ltd* is reported at [2005] R.P.C. 6.

B. EXCLUDED DESIGNS

(i) A method or principle of construction

NOTE 91. **Add:** See also *Landor & Hawa International Ltd v Azure Designs Ltd* **13–55** [2006] EWCA Civ 1285; [2007] F.S.R. 9 at [13] and [14], approving this sentence of the Main Work and adopting a passage from Russell-Clarke, *Copyright in Industrial Designs*, which includes the following: "The real meaning is this: that no design shall be construed so widely as to give its proprietor a monopoly in a method or principle of construction. What he gets is a monopoly for one particular individual and specific appearance. If it is possible to get several different appearances, which all embody the general features which he claims, then those features are too general and amount to a method or principle of construction." *Bailey v Haynes* [2006] EWPCC 5; [2007] F.S.R. 10 at paras 51 to 62, is to the same effect. For the purposes of considering whether the design claimed is excluded on these grounds, the notional addressee of the design document is a person familiar with the subject matter of the drawing (as is the case for infringement); and descriptive material referring to part or parts of the drawing may be taken into account: *Landor*, para.15.

(ii) The "must fit" and "must match" exclusions

13–56 NOTE 1. *Ultraframe (UK) Ltd v Eurocell Building Plastics Ltd* is reported at [2005] R.P.C. 7.

Add at end: Whilst the scope of the "must fit" and "must match" exclusions is significant, it should not be overplayed. As Jacob L.J. has commented, the exclusions "do not give a *carte blanche* for pattern spares. Those who wish to make spares during the period of design right must design their own spares and cannot just copy every detail of the [original equipment manufacturer's] part. To be on the safe side they will have to make them different as far as possible—for trying to navigate by the chart provided by this crude statute (*i.e.* the 1988 Act) is a risky business." *Dyson Ltd v Qualtex (UK) Ltd* [2006] EWCA Civ 166; [2006] R.P.C. 31 at [126].

It should be noted that the terms "must fit" and "must match", whilst convenient, are not terms used in the 1988 Act. It is, therefore, important to look at the actual wording of the relevant statutory provisions. See *Dyson Ltd v Qualtex (UK) Ltd* [2006] EWCA Civ 166; [2006] R.P.C. 31 at [27].

(iii) The "must fit" exclusion

13–58 **The relationship between the two articles.** NOTE 4. **Add:** Not all design features that allow an interface with parts of the human body will be excluded. See para.13–61 of this Supplement. The term "article" includes a carpet or a floor: *Dyson Ltd v Qualtex (UK) Ltd* [2006] EWCA Civ 166; [2006] R.P.C. 31, paras 42 and 43.

NOTE 5. **Add** at end: In *Ultraframe (UK) Ltd v Eurocell Building Plastics Ltd* [2005] EWCA Civ 761; [2005] R.P.C. 36, the Court of Appeal left the question unresolved.

13–59 **So that either article may perform its function. Add** at end: Fourthly, the exclusion may apply even though the articles in question were designed at different times. See *Dyson Ltd v Qualtex (UK) Ltd* [2006] EWCA Civ 166; [2006] R.P.C. 31 at [46]. Fifthly, it is important to bear in mind that, for the exclusion to apply, the design feature in question need not be the actual interface feature (*i.e.* the feature that actually performs the interface with the other article). Instead, it must be a feature that "*enables*" the interface "*so that either article can perform its function*". Thus, where a vacuum cleaner handle which doubled as a cleaning hose was designed with bleed holes, the exclusion was found to apply. The bleed holes allowed air to pass into the hose even if the hose was pushed hard up against the carpet or floor being cleaned. Accordingly, they were design features which enabled the handle to be placed against a flat surface so as better to perform its function as a cleaning hose. See *Dyson Ltd v Qualtex (UK) Ltd* [2006] EWCA Civ 166; [2006] R.P.C. 31, [40]–[43]. Although this qualitative approach suggests that the exclusion may be of wide application, a design is likely to have other features that are protected. The position of a spare parts manufacturer is, therefore, a risky one (see para.13–56 of this Supplement). Sixthly, the fact that one working part of an article is designed so that it does not interfere with the working of another part of that article (or another article) does not mean that the space between the parts is a feature that enables function. *Dyson Ltd v Qualtex (UK) Ltd* [2006] EWCA Civ 166; [2006] R.P.C. 31 at [38] and [47].

NOTE 5. **Add:** The first instance decision in *Ultraframe (UK) Ltd v Eurocell* is reported at [2005] R.P.C. 7. The Court of Appeal left the point open on the basis that any decision would be *obiter* and that cases where the point arose were likely to be rare because it was difficult to imagine cases where an overall design of an assembly of parts (*e.g.* a car) would not be the subject of design right whilst the component parts were. See [2005] R.P.C. 36 at [69].

NOTE 6. **Add:** That the exclusion can operate where the design feature in question allows an article to perform its function more efficiently is also clear from *Dyson Ltd v Qualtex (UK) Ltd* [2006] EWCA Civ 166; [2006] R.P.C. 31 at [43].

NOTE 8. **Add:** See the trial judge's propositions quoted by the Court of Appeal in *Dyson Ltd v Qualtex (UK) Ltd* [2006] EWCA Civ 166; [2006] R.P.C. 31 at [28].

NOTE 9. The first instance decision in *Ultraframe (UK) Ltd v Eurocell* is reported at [2005] R.P.C. 7. The point was not argued on appeal [2005] R.P.C. 36.

Examples. NOTE 15. The first instance decision in *Ultraframe (UK) Ltd v Eurocell* is reported at [2005] R.P.C. 7. The point was not argued on appeal [2005] R.P.C. 36.   **13–60**

Add at end of Example (6) (**Plates**): This seems to be why the design of the handle of, say, a teapot, does not fall within the exclusion even though it must interface with the hand of a person holding it. See the concession by counsel referred to in *Dyson Ltd v Qualtex (UK) Ltd* [2006] EWCA Civ 166; [2006] R.P.C. 31 at [28]. See also the discussion in *Dyson* at [52].   **13–61**

(iv) The "must match" exclusion

Dependent upon the appearance of another article. Add: In *Dyson Ltd v Qualtex (UK) Ltd* [2006] EWCA Civ 166; [2006] R.P.C. 31 at [64] Jacob L.J. stated as follows: **13–64**

> "One has to approach the provision [s.213(3)(b)(ii)] bearing in mind that Parliament did not intend to exclude all spare parts, or even all externally visible portions of spare parts, …. 'Dependency' must be viewed practically. In some cases the answer is obvious—the paradigm example being body parts of cars. In others it may be necessary to examine the position more carefully. But unless the spare parts dealer can show that as a practical matter there is a real need to copy a feature of shape or configuration because of some design consideration of the whole article, he is not within the exclusion. It is not enough to assert that the public 'prefers' an exact copy for it will always do so …. The more there is design freedom the less is there room for the exclusion. In the end it is a question of degree—the sort of thing where a judge is called upon to make a value judgment." He went on to approve (at para.68) as "essentially the right test" the test adopted by Mr Julian Jeffs Q.C. in the *Ford* case: whether "substitutions can be made without radically affecting the appearance or identity of the vehicle".

(v) Surface decoration

NOTES 35 and 38. *Lambretta Clothing Co Ltd v Teddy Smith (UK) Ltd* is reported at [2005] R.P.C. 6. In *Dyson Ltd v Qualtex (UK) Ltd* [2006] EWCA Civ 166; [2006] R.P.C. 31 at [76], Jacob L.J. commented that *Lambretta* was "an   **13–66** exceptional case" where what was sought to be protected fell between copyright protection and design right protection and had neither. See para.13–288 of this Supplement.

Add: In *Dyson Ltd v Qualtex (UK) Ltd* [2006] EWCA Civ 166; [2006] R.P.C. 31 at [73]–[84], Jacob L.J. stated that the word "surface" limits the exclusion to what can fairly be described as a decorated surface. Thus, although the concept of surface decoration is not limited to the decoration of a previously unpainted surface, there was nothing wrong with a test that required that the article could notionally be perceived as one with a surface provided with decoration. He went on to hold that surface decoration might be either two- or three-dimensional (citing the *Mark Wilkinson* case) but that not everything provided on a surface amounts to surface decoration—it is a question of degree. He went on to hold that surface features which have "significant function" cannot be surface decoration, although trivial additional function (such as the covering over of cracks effected by the beading in the *Mark Wilkinson* case) might not matter.

4. CONDITIONS FOR SUBSISTENCE

B. ORIGINALITY

13–71   **Originality and commonplace tests relate to *the design* relied on.Add** after second sentence: In *Dyson Ltd v Qualtex (UK) Ltd* [2006] EWCA Civ 166; [2000] R.P.C. 31, Jacob L.J. stated that technically originality should be considered in relation to each and every aspect of a design in suit, but he saw no reason why a judge should not take a short cut by considering whether the design of the whole of an article was original first. Then, unless there was a special point about a particular aspect, each and every aspect would be original too.

NOTE 52. **Add:** See also *Ultraframe (UK) Ltd v Eurocell Building Plastics Ltd* [2005] EWCA Civ 761; [2005] R.P.C. 36.

NOTE 53. **Add:** In *Dyson Ltd v Qualtex (UK) Ltd* [2006] EWCA Civ 166; [2006] R.P.C. 31 at [96], Jacob L.J. stated that merely adding an old thing on to something else, even if the latter is new, is not sufficient in itself to create an original new design.

Delete last sentence and **substitute:** It has been argued that because it is the design that is tested, one must look at the whole design including "must fit" and "must match" features.

NOTE 54. *Ultraframe (UK) Ltd v Eurocell Building Plastics Ltd* is reported at [2005] R.P.C. 7.

Add: But see *Dyson Ltd v Qualtex (UK) Ltd* [2006] EWCA Civ 166; [2006] R.P.C. 31 at [91], where, when assessing originality, attention was focussed on the design features that were not excluded as "must fit".

13–72   **Originality in the copyright sense.** NOTE 59. *Guild v Eskandar* is reported at [2003] F.S.R. 3.

NOTE 62. *Lambretta Clothing Co Ltd v Teddy Smith (UK) Ltd* is reported at [2005] R.P.C. 6.

Add: See also *Dyson Ltd v Qualtex (UK) Ltd* [2006] EWCA Civ 166; [2006] R.P.C. 31 paras 85 to 90.

13–73   **Commonplace in the design field at the time of its creation.** NOTE 61. **Add:** See also *Dyson Ltd v Qualtex (UK) Ltd* [2006] EWCA Civ 166; [2006] R.P.C. 31 at [109], where the court commented that the claimant's redesign "was no trivial operation—there was nothing trite about it."

Note 62. *Lambretta Clothing Co Ltd v Teddy Smith (UK) Ltd* is reported at [2005] R.P.C. 6.

Design field. Note 68. Delete text of note and **substitute:** [2005] R.P.C. 6 at [43]–[47]. *Lambretta* was followed in *Ultraframe (UK) Ltd v Eurocell Building Plastics Ltd* [2005] R.P.C. 36.   **13–74**

Commonplace. Note 74. The first instance decision in *Ultraframe (UK) Ltd v Eurocell* is reported at [2005] R.P.C. 7. The point was not argued on appeal ([2005] R.P.C. 36).   **13–75**

Note 76. *Lambretta Clothing Co Ltd v Teddy Smith (UK) Ltd* is reported at [2005] R.P.C. 6.

Add: In *Ultraframe (UK) Ltd v Eurocell Building Plastics Ltd* [2005] EWCA Civ 761; [2005] R.P.C. 36, Jacob L.J., with whom the other members of the Court agreed on this point, stated (at para.60) that that which is commonplace in a design field will be ready to hand, not matter that has to be hunted for and found at the last minute.

C. Recorded in a design document or article made

Design document. Add: In *Sales v Stromberg* [2005] EWHC 1624 (Ch); [2006] F.S.R. 7, the apparent lack of artistic merit in the design drawings was held to be irrelevant because there had been no difficulty in making a prototype to the design.   **13–79**

E Qualifying conditions

(iii) Design created in the course of employment

Note 17. *Intercase UK Ltd v Time Computers Ltd* is reported at [2004] E.C.D.R. 8.   **13–88**

5. DURATION

Articles made to the design made available to the public. Delete last sentence and Note 50 and **substitute:** In *Dyson Ltd v Qualtex (UK) Ltd* [2006] EWCA Civ 166; [2006] R.P.C. 31 at [118] to [119] the Court of Appeal upheld the Judge's decision that the natural meaning of the expression "made available" connotes something that is actually in existence; and accordingly that articles are "made available" for these purposes when the public can get them rather than when they are offered for sale or advance orders are taken for them.   **13–103**

6. TITLE TO AND DEALINGS WITH DESIGN RIGHT

B. First owner of design right

Commissioner as first owner. Add: In *Vitof Ltd v Altoft* [2006] EWHC 1678 (Ch), it was held arguable that section 215(2) should be construed as being subject to the words "absent any agreement to the contrary". The Judge went on to emphasise that section 215(2) only regulates the legal ownership and accordingly that if there was a contrary agreement, equitable title could lie elsewhere.   **13–108**

F. Licences of right

Terms of a licence of right. Note 24. Add: In *NIC Instruments Ltd's Licence of*   **13–126**

Right (Design Right) Application [2005] R.P.C. 1 at para.18, the Comptroller adopted the willing licensor and licensee approach, rejecting submissions that the correct approach was that which would be adopted by a court assessing damages. He also held that the licence fee should not reflect any adverse effect on the right owner's business arising from the sale by the applicant of articles made to the design.

NOTE 27. **Add:** See also *NIC Instruments Ltd's Licence of Right (Design Right) Application* [2005] R.P.C. 1 at para.48.

Add at end: In *NIC Instruments Ltd's Licence of Right (Design Right) Application* [2005] R.P.C. 1 a number of issues arose as to the terms of the licence. The Comptroller held that the licence may include a provision which requires the applicant to mark goods as his rather than those of the design right owner. However, such a provision was refused on the facts (see paras 50 to 53). The Comptroller also refused to include a warranty as to title in the licence, but was content to adopt the design right owner's concession that the licence should contain a recital that the design right owner had represented that it owned the design right (para.56). The Comptroller also refused to include a provision for termination for breach on the part of the licensee on the grounds that such a provision was pointless when the licensee could apply for and obtain a new licence immediately following the termination. He held that the licensor's remedy for breach was an action for what was in effect a breach of contract (para.59). Finally, the Comptroller refused a provision for an annual audit on the grounds that the cost would be out all proportion to the sums involved and ordered interest on late payments at 2.5 per cent above base (para.60).

13–127   **The licence fee.** NOTE 31. **Add:** See also *NIC Instruments Ltd's Licence of Right (Design Right) Application* [2005] R.P.C. 1 at para 42.

NOTE 33. **Add:** See also *NIC Instruments Ltd's Licence of Right (Design Right) Application* [2005] R.P.C. 1 at para.18.

NOTE 40. **Add:** See also *NIC Instruments Ltd's Licence of Right (Design Right) Application* [2005] R.P.C. 1. On the facts, the Comptroller allowed the applicant half its normal overhead rate in calculating the available profits (para.38).

NOTE 42. **Add:** The same percentage split was applied in *NIC Instruments Ltd's Licence of Right (Design Right) Application* [2005] R.P.C. 1 (para.40).

Add: In *NIC Instruments Ltd's Licence of Right (Design Right) Application* [2005] R.P.C. 1, the applicant sold the articles made to the design as components of a kit. On the evidence the vast majority of its sales of these kits would not have been made if the articles had not been included. The Comptroller held that a willing licensor and licensee would have taken this into account in one of two ways. They could have based the royalty rate on the value of the kit, but if so they would have discounted it to reflect the fact that the kit contained other components on which the applicant would expect to make a reasonable margin. Alternatively, they could have based the rate on the components alone but would have increased it to take account of the fact that the components were allowing a higher-value product to be sold. The Comptroller concluded that the actual royalty would end up the same and that the question whether the royalty should be based on the kit or the components was therefore more one of convenience than of fundamental principle (para.23). He decided to calculate the royalty as a percentage of the price of the kits (para.24).

In this case, the applicant sold the articles through middlemen whereas the design right owner sold them through its own distribution network. The question arose as to whether the royalty should be based on the price at which the applicant sold the articles to the middlemen (which would only take account of the profit made by the applicant) or at the price paid by the end-user (which would take account of the profit made by the middlemen as well). The Comptroller held that a willing licensor and willing licensee would have taken some but not full account of the additional profit of the middlemen; accordingly a "half way house" was appropriate (para.31).

7. THE RIGHTS OF THE DESIGN RIGHT OWNER AND INFRINGEMENT

B. EXCLUSIVE RIGHTS AND PRIMARY INFRINGEMENTS

(i) Making articles to the design

Infringement by making articles exactly or substantially to the design. NOTE   **13–149**
19. *Lambretta Clothing Co Ltd v Teddy Smith (UK) Ltd* is reported at [2005] R.P.C. 6.

A. Fulton v Totes Isotoner. NOTE 44. *A Fulton & Co Ltd v Totes Isotoner (UK)*   **13–154**
Ltd is reported at [2004] R.P.C. 16.

8. EXCEPTIONS TO RIGHTS

B. PARALLEL COPYRIGHT PROTECTION—SECTIONS 236 AND 51

Examples. NOTE 79. *Lambretta Clothing Co Ltd v Teddy Smith (UK) Ltd* is   **13–167**
reported at [2005] R.P.C. 6.

9. PARTIES TO ACTION AND REMEDIES FOR INFRINGEMENT

C. REMEDIES

Damages. NOTES 92 and 93. *Badge Sales v PMS International Group Ltd* [2004]   **13–172**
EWHC 3382 (Ch) is reported at [2006] F.S.R. 1. In that case it was also held that the standard of proof is the balance of probabilities and the test is objective.

Effect of undertaking by defendant to take a licence of right. Add at end: An   **13–176**
undertaking may be given even though the design right has expired by the time it is offered: *Ultraframe (UK) Ltd v Eurocell Building Plastics Ltd* [2005] EWCA Civ 761; [2005] R.P.C. 36.

Privilege for professional designs representatives. Regulation 4 of the Com-   **13–178A**
munity Design Regulations 2005 (SI 2005/2339) provides with effect from October 1, 2005 a special privilege from disclosure in legal proceedings of communications as to any matter relating to the protection of any design. The privilege extends to any such communication in two alternative circumstances (reg.4(2)). The first is if it passed between a person and his "professional designs representative", defined by regulation 4(3) as a person who is on the special list of professional representatives for design matters referred to in Article 78 of the Community Design Regulation. (as to which see the Main Work, Vol.2, p.594.). In this case, the communication is privileged in the same way as a communication between a person and his solicitor. The effect of this is to place persons who

are entitled to represent clients in design matters at OHIM but are not patent agents on the same footing as patent agents (communications with whom are already privileged under CDPA 1988, s.220). The second set of circumstances in which the privilege applies is where the communication was made for the purposes of obtaining information which a person is seeking for the purpose of instructing his professional designs representative or in response to a request for such information. Where the privilege applies, the communication is privileged in the same way as a communication for the purposes of obtaining or in response to a request for information which a person is seeking for the purposes of instructing his solicitor.

10. THREATS

13–184 **Person issuing threats.** NOTE 39. **Add:** In *Reckitt Benkiser UK v Home Pairfum Ltd* [2004] EWHC Pat 302; [2004] F.S.R. 37 the court refused permission to join a firm of solicitors as defendants to a threats action because one of the reasons for the joinder was to make the solicitors and their relationship with the claimant uncomfortable. The claim would therefore be an abuse of process.

12. UNREGISTERED COMMUNITY DESIGNS

A. INTRODUCTION

13–197 **Add:** As the Regulation applies across the Community, it is desirable that there be some degree of consistency of interpretation across all member states. For these purposes, decisions of the Office for Harmonisation of the Internal Market (OHIM) and of the courts of other Member States provide useful guidance—see *Procter & Gamble Co v Reckitt Benckiser (UK) Ltd* [2006] EWHC 3154; [2007] F.S.R. 13 at [24].

B. DEFINITION OF A COMMUNITY DESIGN

13–200 **Definition of a design.** NOTE 78. *Lambretta Clothing Co Ltd v Teddy Smith (UK) Ltd* is reported at [2005] R.P.C. 6.

NOTE 79. **Add:** A claimant may choose whether or not to rely on his designs for the colour or colours of a product. If he wishes to do so, his job in establishing the individual character of his design may be easier (see the two *Bumag v Procter & Gamble* decisions given by OHIM on May 15, 2006—ICD 1741 and 1CD 1758) but the scope of his protection is narrowed.

For the significance of colour in relation to registered community designs, see paragraph 13–260 of this Supplement.

Add: An interesting question that arises is whether an internal design feature can be protected as a community design. In this regard, it has been held by the District Administrative Court in Warsaw ([2007] E.D.C.R. 3) that the definition of a design in the European Directive 98/71 (the same as that in the Regulation) is concerned only with features that can be visually perceived and would not, therefore, extend to the internal features of an ice cream. There is considerable force in this conclusion. In the case of complex products, component parts that are not visible during normal use are deprived of protection by Article 4(2) which provides that such features are not novel and have no individual character (see para.13–206). It would seem strange to deprive these features of protection whilst allowing protection for the internal features of non-complex products. In this respect, the protection offered by community design may be narrower than that under UK design right where, (as set out in para.13–46), it has been suggested that UK design right can apply to design features that are not usually visible.

Product. NOTE 82. **Add:** Commentary on the different purposes behind trade   **13–201**
mark protection and designs protection was given by Jacob L.J. in *The Procter &*
Gamble Company v Reckitt Benckiser (UK) Ltd [2007] EWCA Civ 936 at [27]
and [28].

C. REQUIREMENTS OF NOVELTY AND INDIVIDUAL CHARACTER

Requirement that a design be new and have individual character. Add at   **13–202**
end: In *Bailey v Haynes* [2006] EWPCC 5; [2007] F.S.R. 10, at para.54 H.H.J.
Fysh Q.C. held that the onus was on the person seeking to challenge the subsistence of the Community Design to prove that it was not new and did not have
original character. The learned Judge did not refer in this context to Article 85(2)
of the Designs Regulation, which provides that the Community Design Court
shall treat the Community design as valid if the right holder produces proof that
the conditions laid down in Article 11 have been met and indicates what constitutes the original character of his Community design. There are separate tests for
novelty and for individual character. It is, therefore, possible that a design will
pass the first test but fail the second. See *Procter & Gamble Co v Reckitt Benck-*
iser (UK) Ltd [2006] EWHC 3154; [2007] F.S.R. 13 at [25].

Meaning of individual character. Add: The meaning of "individual character"   **13–204**
was considered by the Court of Appeal in *The Procter & Gamble Company v*
Reckitt Benckiser (UK) Ltd [2007] EWCA Civ 936 (a case concerning a registered
community design). The following points of importance arise.

The informed user—In *Procter & Gamble*, Jacob L.J. pointed out that the
"informed user" is not a designer nor is he the same as the "average consumer"
known to trade mark law ([16], [24]). Instead, he is a user—but a user who must
be taken to be aware of other similar designs which form part of the "design
corpus" and who will, therefore, be reasonably discriminatory ([17], [23]). He
should be "able to appreciate enough detail to decide whether a design creates an
overall impression which has individual character" ([23]). He is also taken to
know where shapes are, to some extent, required to be the way they are by reason
of function. Thus, in *Procter & Gamble*, the informed user would take into account the fact that there were design constraints arising from the fact that the
spray canisters in question had to be "grippable so that the index finger could pull
the trigger, the trigger had to be shaped to fit the finger and had to have sufficient
space behind it for it to be pulled" ([29]). An informed user is, in effect, alert to
design issues and "fairly familiar" with them ([28], [35(ii)]). It seems clear,
therefore, that the informed user is someone who would approach the task of
determining individual character with some degree of method and with more ri-
gour than would an ordinary consumer.

Overall impression—*Procter & Gamble* also provides important guidance as
to the "overall impression" test. To have individual character, the overall impression which a design produces on the informed user must *clearly* differ from the
overall impression produced by other designs in the design corpus. In this regard,
although the word "clearly" does not appear in Art.6(2) of the Regulation, it does
appear in Recital (14) and is "plainly … relevant" to the issue whether a design
qualifies for protection (Jacob L.J. at [18]). It is, therefore, read into Art.6(2). In
this regard, there is a significant difference between the "overall impression" test
in the context of the protection of a design (Art.6(2)) and the "overall impression" test in the context of the infringement of a design (Art. 10(2), as to which
see para.13–232 of the Main Work and of this Supplement). In the latter context,

the word "clearly" is not read into Art.10(2). The reason for this distinction is (see Jacob L.J. at [19]) that "Different policies are involved. It is one thing to restrict the grant of a monopoly right to designs which are shown 'clearly' to differ from the existing design corpus. That makes sense—you need clear blue water between the registered design and the 'prior art', otherwise there is a real risk that design monopolies will or may interfere with routine, ordinary, minor everyday design modifications—what patent lawyers call 'mere workshop modifications'. But no such policy applies to the scope of protection. It is sufficient to avoid infringement if the accused product is of a design which produces a 'different overall impression'. There is no policy requirement that the difference be 'clear'. If a design differs, that is enough—an informed user can discriminate."

In applying the overall impression test, what matters is what strikes the mind of the informed user looking at the relevant design *as a design* (Jacob L.J. at [25] to [27]). Further, it is what strikes the mind *when* carefully viewing the design. The possibility of imperfect recollection (*i.e.* that which sticks in the mind *after* looking) has only a limited part to play (Jacob L.J. at [25] and [35(v)]).

Design Freedom—in assessing whether the overall impression produced by a design differs from other designs in the context of both individual character and in the context of infringement, the informed user must have regard to "the degree of design freedom of the designer in developing the design" (see Arts.6(2) and 10(2)). Jacob L.J. commented (at [30]) that "smaller differences will be enough to create a different overall impression where freedom of design is limited" and he agreed (at [31]) with the approach of Lewison J. at first instance who had rejected the suggestion that the designer's own internal constraints (*e.g.* his financial or production resources) were relevant when considering the issue of design freedom and who had concluded that "the test must be an objective one which applies to all designers" ([2006] EWHC 3154; [2007] F.S.R. 13 at [43]).

What is to be compared?—As mentioned above (and at para.13–232 of the Main Work), the question of the overall impression produced on the informed user arises not only when testing for individual character but also when testing for infringement. Both require the court to conduct a comparison of impressions produced on an informed user. The question remains, however, what it is that is being compared. In comparing designs in the context of infringement in *Procter & Gamble*, Lewison J. (at first instance) rejected the argument that the comparison should be between the claimant's design and the whole of the allegedly infringing product and found, instead that it was between the claimant's design and the corresponding part of the defendant's design (see [2006] EWHC 3154; [2007] F.S.R. 13 at [44]–[49]). One must, in effect, compare like with like. As that case was a registered design case, the claimant's design was the design as registered. This emphasises the importance of defining the design to be protected with care. As Lewison J commented (at [48]), if the claimant's design is defined too generally, it may be invalidated by other designs in the design corpus. If, however, it is defined too narrowly, it may not have been infringed.

Clearly, the same approach will apply in unregistered community design cases where the comparison will be between the design as identified by the claimant in its pleadings and the corresponding part of the defendant's design.

It would seem that the same approach should also apply in determining whether the claimant's design has individual character for the purpose of seeing whether that design is entitled to protection. If so, then the comparison in such a case would be between that design on the one hand and the corresponding parts of the designs in the design corpus on the other.

Design corpus—the meaning of the words "existing design corpus" in Recital (14) was not considered by the Court of Appeal in *Procter & Gamble*. However, Lewison J. at first instance ([2006] EWHC 3154; [2007] F.S.R. 13) commented first, that the design corpus is the "existing" design corpus not the whole history of product development and secondly, that the word "corpus" is indicative of the general body of design rather than each and every example of it.

In *Arrmet, S.R.L.'s Design* [2004] E.C.D.R. 24 (OHIM) it was held that the informed user is familiar with the basic features of the product in question and with the prior art known in the normal course of business to the circles specialised in the sector concerned (paras 16 and 18). In taking into consideration the limitations to the freedom of the designer the informed user will "weigh the various features consequently" and in particular will pay more attention to similarities of non-necessary features and dissimilarities of necessary ones (para.17). In considering whether the design in question produces a different overall impression on the informed user to that produced by an earlier design, the designs must be compared both on their various features taken individually and "on the weight of the various features according to their influence on the overall impression" (para.19). When assessing the overall impression, the informed user will focus his or her attention mainly on the features which are essential or characteristic of the product in question, at least where (as was the case) those features are the ones with the largest surface area and "the most important visibility" (para.22). Where the most important visual parts of the design do not give a different overall impression and the other parts of the design are not sufficiently different in appearance or importance to change the impression given by the main elements, then the overall impression produced by the Community design is not different from that produced by the prior design (para.26).

The relevant passage from the judgment of H.H.J. Fysh Q.C. in *Woodhouse* was quoted with apparent approval in *The Procter & Gamble Company v Reckitt Benckiser (UK) Ltd* [2007] EWCA Civ 936 at [32].

In the registered designs case of *Woodhouse UK Plc v Architectural Lighting Systems* [2005] EWPCC (Des) 25; [2006] R.P.C. 1, H.H.J. Fysh stated (*obiter*) that the informed user must be a regular user of articles of the sort which is the subject of the design. He could thus be a consumer or buyer or be otherwise familiar with the subject matter, for example through use at work. He is not a manufacturer, nor is he simply an average consumer. The concept imports the notion of "what's about in the market?" and "what has been about in the recent past?". It does not require an archival mind or more than average memory but does demand some awareness of product trend and availability and some knowledge of basic technical considerations (if any). However, since the territory is designs and not patents, what matters most is the appearance of things; accordingly, focus on eye-appeal is more pertinent than familiarity with the underlying operational or manufacturing technology (if any).

In *Bailey v Haynes* [2006] EWPCC 5; [2007] F.S.R. 10, H.H.J. Fysh Q.C. stated at paragraph 55 that when the court is considering novelty and individual character the enquiry focuses on those having a practical interest in the use to which the product incorporating the design is to be put.

Made available to the public. The view expressed in the Main Work as to the **13–205** meaning of the phrase "the sector concerned" seems to be supported by the decision in *Green Lane Products Ltd v PMS International Group Ltd* [2007] EWHC 1712 where Lewison J. held that, for the purposes of Article 7 of Council Regulation 6/2002, the "sector concerned" was the sector that consists of or includes the sector of the alleged prior art.

Whilst Lewison J. also accepted a submission that, in principle, the persons who were in the circles specialising in that sector would comprise all individuals who conduct trade in relation to products in that sector (including those who design, make, advertise, distribute and sell such products in the course of trade), he also commented that in some cases, the circles would be more restricted than that.

Add: In *Mafin SpA's Design* [2005] E.C.D.R. 29 (OHIM) it was held that a design which had been published as an application for a three-dimensional trade mark had been made available to the public. In *Thane International Group's application* [2006] E.C.D.R. 8 (Landsgericht Frankfurt am Main) it was held that prior publication of a design in the United States meant that it had been made available to the public for these purposes.

D. OTHER EXCLUSIONS FROM PROTECTION

(i) Designs dictated by their technical function.

13–208   It has now been held that the narrower construction of Article 8(1) is the correct one—see *Landor & Hawa International Ltd v Azure Designs Ltd* [2006] EWCA Civ 1285; [2007] F.S.R. 9 where reference was made to this paragraph of the Main Work. *Bailey v Haynes* [2006] EWPCC 5; [2007] F.S.R. 10 is to the same effect. Whilst this seems to be what was intended by Article 8(1), it does severely limit the scope of the exclusion. Indeed, it has been commented that "it is not easy to think of concrete examples where this exclusion would apply. A table tennis ball must be a sphere, perhaps"—see *Procter & Gamble Co v. Reckitt Benckiser (UK) Ltd.* [2006] EWHC 3154; [2007] F.S.R. 13 at [28].

E. GROUNDS FOR INVALIDITY

13–214   **Grounds of invalidity.** NOTE 9. **Add:** For an example of this provision in operation, see *Zellweger Analytic's Design* [2006] E.C.D.R. 17.

Sub-paragraph (f) **Delete:** authorised. **Substitute:** unauthorised.

F. DURATION

13–216   **Date when design made available to the public. Add:** For the meaning of "the sector concerned", see paragraph 13–205 of this Supplement and *Green Lane Products Ltd v PMS International Group Ltd* [2007] EWHC 1712.

I. RIGHTS CONFERRED BY A COMMUNITY DESIGN AND INFRINGEMENT

13–231   **Rights conferred by a Community design.** NOTE 22. **Add:** Consistently with this, it has been commented that the design of an aerosol can, in principle, be infringed by, say, a vase. See *Procter & Gamble Co v Reckitt Benckiser (UK) Ltd.* [2006] EWHC 3154; [2007] F.S.R. 13 at [27].

13–232   **Scope of protection. Add:** Guidance as to the scope of protection for community designs was provided by the Court of Appeal in *The Procter & Gamble Co v Reckitt Benckiser (UK) Ltd* [2007] EWCA Civ 936. Jacob L.J. commented (at [34]) that the test whether the accused design creates a different overall impression on the informed user is "inherently rather imprecise" as it needs to cover not only exact imitations but also things which come too close. For this reason it leaves a considerable margin for the judgment of the trial judge just as the "substantial part" test does in copyright cases. He left open whether the sort of margin was the same in both types of case.

Jacob L.J. also made a number of general observations as to the test for infringement (see [35]). These were, in summary:

(1) The accused product will infringe if its design does not produce a different

overall impression on the informed user. As has already been seen, the word "clearly" is not read into this test (see para.13–204 of this Supplement). Thus, to defeat a claim of infringement, a defendant need not show that the accused design produces a *clearly* different overall impression. It is enough that it produces a different overall impression.

(2) The informed user is fairly familiar with design issues. (For more on the identity and characteristics of the informed user, see para. 13–204 of this Supplement.)

(3) If the protected design is markedly different to the general design corpus, its overall impression would be more significant and the room for differences which do *not* create a substantially different overall impression will be greater. In effect, the scope of protection for such a design is greater. In this regard, the informed user is taken to be aware of the existing design corpus (see [17]).

(4) Despite this, the test remains "is the overall impression different"? It is not sufficient to ask whether the accused product is closer to the protected design than to the general design corpus.

(5) The comparison between the protected design and the accused design is conducted with a reasonable degree of care. As pointed out in paragraph 13-204 of this Supplement, the possibility of imperfect recollection plays only a limited role.

(6) The court must identify the overall impression of the protected design with care. It may be helpful to use pictures as part of the identification.

(7) The court must descend to the level of generality that the notional informed user would use. On the facts of *Procter & Gamble*, it would be too general to say that the overall impression was of a canister fitter with a trigger device on the top.

(8) The court must then identify the overall impression of the accused product.

(9) Finally, the court must ask whether the two overall impressions are different. This, Jacob L.J. stated, is "almost the equivalent to asking whether they are the same—the difference is nuanced, probably, involving a question of onus and no more".

As regards the significance of the scope of design freedom available in respect of the design and what it is that is compared when testing for infringement, see paragraph 13–204 of this Supplement. For the significance of colour, see paragraph 13–260 of this Supplement.

J. PERMITTED ACTS

Government use. Add: Article 23 of the Regulation has been implemented with effect from October 1, 2005 by regulation 5 of and the Schedule to the Community Design Regulations 2005 (SI 2005/2339) which make provision for Crown use of Community designs (both unregistered and registered). In general, the provisions are substantially identical to those in respect of unregistered United Kingdom design right, as to which see paragraph 13–131 *et seq.* of the Main Work. However, in view of the terms of Article 23, the definition of "services of the Crown" is different. For the purposes of unregistered United Kingdom design right, the following are "services of the Crown": the defence of the realm; foreign defence purposes; and health service purposes (see para.13–132 of the Main Work). For the purposes of Community designs, "services of the Crown" are limited to those which are necessary for essential defence and security needs. Not surprisingly, there is no attempt to define the expression "essential defence or security needs".

13–238

L. JURISDICTION AND REMEDIES

13–245   **Community design courts.** NOTE 30. **Delete** and **substitute:** These are as follows. In England and Wales, the High Court and any county court designated as a Patents County Court under section 287(1) of the CDPA 1988 and (for the purposes of hearing appeals from judgments of the courts so designated) the Court of Appeal; in Scotland, the Court of Session (at first instance and also for appeals); and in Northern Ireland, the High Court and (for appeals) the Court of Appeal. See the Community Designs (Designation of Community Design Courts) Regulations 2005 (SI 2005/696).

13–248   **Remedies. Add:** Express national provision has now been made for remedies for the infringement of Community designs by Regulations 1A to 1D of the Community Design Regulations 2005 (SI 2005/2339) which were inserted by paragraph 9 of Schedule 3 to the Intellectual Property (Enforcement etc.) Regulations 2006 (SI 2006/1028) with effect from April 29, 2006. The new provisions are expressed to be without prejudice to the court's duties under Article 89(1)(a) to (c) to make orders for injunctions, delivery up and seizure of infringing materials and implements used to make them. They mirror certain existing provisions in relation to unregistered United Kingdom design right. Accordingly, regulation 1A(2), in substantially identical terms to section 229(2) of the 1988 Act (as to which see para.13–171 of the Main Work), provides that in proceedings for infringement of a Community design all such relief by way of damages, injunctions, accounts or otherwise is available to the holder of the Community design as is available in respect of the infringement of any other property right. Regulations 1B and 1C make provision for delivery up and disposal orders in substantially the same terms as sections 230 and 231 of the 1988 Act (see paras 13–177 and 13–178 of the Main Work) and for these purposes the definition of "infringing article" (in reg.1D) is substantially the same as that contained in section 228 (see para.13–158 of the Main Work). It should be noted that there is no equivalent to section 233 of the 1988 Act, which provides partial defences for "innocent" infringers.

13–250A   **Privilege for professional designs representatives.** See paragraph 13–178A, above.

M. THREATS

13–250B   **Background.** Provisions making groundless threats to sue for infringement actionable have been part of United Kingdom registered design and patent law for many years and were introduced for United Kingdom unregistered design right by section 253 of the CDPA 1988: see paragraph 13–179 *et seq.* of the Main Work. Similar provision has now been made in relation to Community designs.

13–250C   **The threats.** Regulation 2(1) of the Community Design Regulations 2005 (SI 2005/2339) provides with effect from October 1, 2005 that where any person (whether entitled to or interested in a Community design or not) by circulars, advertisements or otherwise threatens any other person with proceedings for infringement of a Community design, any person aggrieved thereby may bring an action against him. The words "by circulars, advertisements or otherwise" do not appear in section 253 of the 1988 Act and are borrowed from section 70 of the Patents Act 1977 and section 26 of the Registered Designs Act 1949. They have been widely construed; in particular it has been held that the words "or otherwise" are not to be construed ejusdem generis with the words "circulars, advertisements": see *Speedcranes Ltd v Thomson* [1978] R.P.C. 221. As is the case for United Kingdom unregistered design right, mere notification that a design is a Community design does not constitute a threat (reg.2(6)) and there is no liability for threats to bring proceedings for an infringement alleged to consist in the making or importing of anything (reg.2(5)). For the rationale behind the latter provision, see paragraph 13–182 of the Main Work.

Person aggrieved. It is anticipated that this term will be interpreted in the same as for unregistered United Kingdom design right, as to which see paragraph 13–183 of the Main Work. **13–250D**

The defence. Regulation 2(4) provides that where the defendant proves that the acts in respect of which the proceedings were threatened constitute or (if done) would constitute an infringement of an unregistered Community design right, the claimant shall not be entitled to relief. Regulation 2(3) provides that where the defendant proves that the acts constitute or would constitute an infringement of a registered Community design, the claimant will only be entitled to relief if he shows that the registration was invalid. In each case the onus is on the defendant. It seems that either defence is available irrespective of whether the threat concerns a registered or an unregistered Community design. **13–250E**

Remedies. The remedies available are a declaration, an injunction and damages: reg.2(2). See paragraph 13–186 of the Main Work. **13–250F**

13. REGISTERED DESIGNS AND REGISTERED COMMUNITY DESIGNS

A. INTRODUCTION

Add: The international protection of registered designs will become simpler as from January 1, 2008 when the European Community's accession to the Geneva Act of the Hague Agreement becomes effective. The European Community's instrument of accession was deposited with the Director General of WIPO on September 24, 2007. The current membership of the Geneva Act can be found on the WIPO website: *www.wipo.int.* **13–251**

NOTE 41. **Add:** See also Izquierdo Peris, "Registered Community Design: First Two-Year Balance from an Insider's Perspective" [2006] E.I.P.R. 146.

Background. Add: The Registered Designs Act 1949 has now been further amended by two statutory instruments. **13–252**

The first set of amendments are effected by regulation 2(1) of and Schedule 1 to the Intellectual Property (Enforcement, etc.) Regulations 2006 (SI 2006/1028) with effect from April 29, 2006. There are three major changes, none of which are material to the outline account of registered United Kingdom designs which is given in the Main Work. First, a new section (15A) provides that like registered designs (as to which there is no change), applications for registered designs are now items of personal property. According to paragraphs 7.5 and 7.6 of the Explanatory Memorandum, this resolves an uncertainty arising from the fact that Article 34(1) of the Community Designs Regulation provides that an application for a registered Community design "as an object of property" is to be dealt with "as a national design right" in accordance with Article 27. Secondly, the concept of a statutory exclusive licensee with a right to sue for infringement has been introduced into the field of registered designs by new sections 15C and 24F. The absence of such provision was anomalous: see the Government's transposition note. Thirdly, the statutory remedies for infringement are brought into line with those for infringement of other intellectual property rights. Thus it is provided that in an action for infringement of a United Kingdom registered design, all such relief by way of damages, injunctions, accounts or otherwise is available to the registered proprietor as is available in respect of the infringement of any other property right (s.24A); and there is a statutory scheme for delivery up and disposal of infringing articles (ss.24C to 24E). These four new sections have been introduced in order to ensure "transparency of implementation" of the Enforcement Directive: see the transposition note. Section 9 (which concerned exemptions from liability to financial remedies in the case of "innocent" infringers) has been repealed and re-enacted as section 4B.

The second set of amendments are effected by the Regulatory Reform (Registered Designs) Order 2006 (SI 2006/1974) with effect from October 1, 2006. None of these amendments affect the outline account of registered UK designs which is given in the Main Work.

13–253   **Transitional provisions for the 1949 Act. Add:** An attack on the validity of the transitional provisions in regulation 12 failed in *Oakley Inc v Animal Ltd* [2005] EWCA Civ 1191; [2006] Ch. 337.

B. THE NEW LAW

13–255   **Definition of design. Add:** Although the definition of a design is the same as for unregistered community designs, the monopolistic protection provided by registration cannot extend beyond the design depicted in the application for registration: see *Procter & Gamble Co v Reckitt Benckiser (UK) Ltd.* [2006] EWHC 3154; [2007] F.S.R. 13 at [27].

For the significance of colour, see paragraph 13–260 of this Supplement.

13–259   **Ownership.** NOTE 58. **Add:** "Claiming to be the proprietor" for these purposes means rightfully claiming to be the proprietor. Save for commissioned works, the proprietor of a new design is its author. See *Woodhouse UK Plc v Architectural Lighting Systems* [2006] R.P.C. 1 at [25].

13–260   **Monopoly rights conferred by registration, infringement and permitted acts.** As has been mentioned (see para.13–255 of this Supplement), the protection conferred by registration will depend on what was depicted in the application for registration. If only a part of an article was depicted, that part alone will be protected. However, although an applicant is required to identify the products to which his design will be applied, the scope of protection is not limited to such products (see Art.36(6) of the Regulation). Instead, as has been seen (see para.13–231 of the Main Work), it extends to any product. A defendant who has made a different product may, therefore, infringe, unless he can show that his design would create a different overall impression on the informed user (see para.13–232 of the Main Work).

With regard to the protection of colour as part of a design, Lewison J. commented at first instance in *Procter & Gamble* [2006] EWHC 3154; [2007] F.S.R. 13 at [29] that if an applicant wishes to have protection for his design of colours, those colours must be depicted. This is clearly correct. However, Lewison J. went on to comment that in the case of a monochrome line drawing, what is protected is likely to be the shape or contours of the product and that colours will not be protected if they are not depicted. In this regard, it is important to bear in mind that registration of a design depicted in black and white provides protection for the depicted shape and configuration whatever the colour used. Thus, a defendant (as was the case in the *Procter & Gamble* case itself) cannot rely on the different overall impression created by its use of colours in relation to its product. Of course, for the same reason, it may be more difficult to establish the validity of a design depicted in black and white than one depicting colours (see the two *Bumag v Procter & Gamble* decisions given by OHIM on 15 May 2006—ICD 1741 and 1CD 1758).

C. THE OLD LAW

Exclusion of designs for articles of primarily literary character. NOTE 85.   **13–269**
The Registered Designs Rules 1995 are revoked, subject to transitional provisions, with effect from October 1, 2006: see the Registered Designs Rules 2006 (SI 2006/1975).

15. COPYRIGHT WORKS OF INDUSTRIAL APPLICATION MADE ON OR AFTER AUGUST 1, 1989

B. SECTION 51

No correlation between the operation of section 51 and the availability of   **13–281**
design right protection. NOTE 16. *Lambretta Clothing Co Ltd v Teddy Smith (UK) Ltd* is reported at [2005] R.P.C. 6.

Recording or embodying a design. NOTES 29 and 30. *Lambretta Clothing Co*   **13–287**
Ltd v Teddy Smith (UK) Ltd is reported at [2005] R.P.C. 6.
    NOTE 31. **Add:** In *The Flashing Badge Company Ltd v Groves* [2007] EWHC 1372, the claimant relied on the copyright in design drawings of badges. Insofar as the drawings recorded the shape of the badges, s.51 applied because the drawing was a design for something that was not in itself an artistic work. However, insofar as the drawings recorded the surface decoration for such badges, s.51 did not operate.

Lambretta Clothing Co Ltd Teddy Smith (UK) Ltd. NOTE 32. **Add:** [2005]   **13–288**
R.P.C. 6.
    NOTE 33. **Add:** In *Dyson Ltd v Qualtex (UK) Ltd* [2006] EWCA Civ 166, Jacob L.J. analysed *Lambretta* as an exceptional case where "the shape of the article was unoriginal and so not within UDR and the colourways had no independent notional existence from the article and were not surface decoration", stating that such cases would be rare. That *Lambretta* was an exceptional case is also clear from the decision of Rimer J. in *The Flashing Badge Company Ltd v Groves* [2007] EWHC 1372. Although the designs of the surface decoration of the badges had to follow the design of the shape of the badges, they were not designs that could only exist as part of the shape of the badges. They could be applied to any other substrate. Section 51 did not, therefore, operate to exclude copyright protection from the design of that surface decoration.

A design *for* anything other than an artistic work. NOTE 39. The appeal deci-   **13–289**
sion in *Guild v Eskandar* is reported at [2003] F.S.R. 3.

SEMICONDUCTOR TOPOGRAPHIES

2. PROTECTION OF SEMICONDUCTOR TOPOGRAPHIES

B. SUBSISTENCE OF DESIGN RIGHT

14–09   **Qualifying person. Delete** the whole paragraph and NOTES 25 TO 34 and **substitute:** With effect from August 1, 2006, the definition of a "qualifying person" is the same as for design right except that the definition of "qualifying country" is different (see below). See the amendments to the Design Right (Semiconductor Topographies) Regulations 1989 (SI 1989/1100) effected by the Design Right (Semiconductor Topographies) (Amendment) Regulations 2006 (SI 2006/1833) which came into force on August 1, 2006.

Accordingly, pursuant to CDPA 1988, section 217, the following are qualifying persons in relation to semiconductor topographies:

(a) A qualifying individual, meaning a citizen or subject of or an individual habitually resident in a qualifying country: CDPA 1988, section 217(1). For the term "qualifying country", see below. For the the terms "citizen or subject of" and "habitually resident", see paragraph 13–97 of the Main Work.

(b) A body corporate or other body having legal personality which (i) is formed under the law of a part of the United Kingdom or of another qualifying country and (ii) has in any qualifying country a place of business at whichsubstantial business activity is carried on: CDPA 1988, section 217(1). For the term "qualifying country", see below. For the other terms in this definition, see paragraph 13–98 of the Main Work.

(c) The Crown and the government of any other qualifying country: CDPA 1988, section 217(2).

The term "qualifying country" now means the United Kingdom, another Member State of the European Community, the Isle of Man, Gibraltar, the Channel Islands, any colony and any country listed in the Schedule to the 1989 Regulations as substituted by SI 2006/1833: see regulation 4(2) of SI 2006/1833. The object of the 2006 Regulations was to give effect to the Council Decision of

December 22, 1994 on the extension of the legal protection of topographies of semiconductor products to persons from a member of the World Trade Organization (94/824/EC; [1994] O.J. L 349/210). Accordingly, the Schedule to the 1989 Regulations has been substituted by a list of parties to the Agreement establishing the World Trade Organisation (other than Member States who are already within the definition of "qualifying country"). For the previous Schedule, see Vol.2 of the Main Work at **B9.i**.

CHAPTER FIFTEEN

CIRCUMVENTION OF PROTECTION MEASURES AND RIGHTS MANAGEMENT INFORMATION

1. INTRODUCTION

15–01   **Protection measures. Add:** For recent accounts of the technology and attempts to circumvent it, see Koempel, "Digital Rights Management" [2005] C.T.L.R. 239; Akester, "Digital Rights Management in the 21st Century" [2006] 3 E.I.P.R. 159; Stromdale, "The Problems with DRM" [2006] 1 Ent. L.R. 1; Stromdale, "Public and Private Sectors Focus on DRM and Copy Protection" [2006] 3 Ent. L.R. 101; and Fox, "Another Nail in the Coffin for Copy-protection Technologies? Sony BMG's XCP and MediaMax Debacle" [2006] 7 Ent.L.R. 214. For a Canadian perspective, see Sookman, "TPMs and Copyright Protection" [2005] C.T.L.R. 143.

As to the future, see, generally, the following:

- the Communication from the Commission to the Council, the European Parliament and the European Economic and Social Committee on the Management of Copyright and Related Rights in the Internal Market (COM/2004/0261 final), *europa.eu.int/eur-lex/lex/LexUriServ/site/en/com/2004/com2004_0261en01.pdf*, especially at paragraph 1.2.5;
- the Final Report of the Commission's High Level Group on Digital Rights Management, March-July 2004, *europa.eu.int/information_society/eeurope/2005/all_about/digital_rights_man/doc/040709_hlg_drm_final_report.doc*, which concentrates on interoperability, the relation between digital rights management and private copying levies and the use of digital rights management systems to encourage consumers to migrate from illegal to legal file-sharing services;
- the report of the OECD's Working Party on the Information Economy entitled *Digital Broadband Content: Music*, DSTI/ICCP/IE(2004)12/FINAL, December 13, 2005, *www.oecd.org/dataoecd/13/2/34995041.pdf*, especially at pages 92–93;
- the Article 29 Data Protection Working Party's *Working document on data protection issues related to intellectual property rights*, January 18,

2005, *europa.eu.int/comm/justice_home/fsj/privacy/docs/wpdocs/2005/
wp104_en.pdf*, especially at pages 2–3; and
- *Automated Rights Management Systems and Copyright Limitations and
Exceptions*, a report dated April 27, 2006 by Nic Garnett for WIPO's
Standing Committee on Copyright and Related Rights.

2. PROTECTION MEASURES: HISTORY OF PROTECTION

The Software Directive and the 1992 amendment. NOTES 7 and 8. *Kabushiki* 15–04
Kaisha Sony Computer Entertainment Inc v Ball is now reported at [2005] F.S.R.
9; [2004] E.C.D.R. 33.

The WIPO Copyright Treaty and the WIPO Performances and Phonograms 15–05
Treaty. Add: See, generally, Barczewski, "International Framework for Legal
Protection of Digital Rights Management Systems" [2005] E.I.P.R. 165.

The Information Society Directive. Add: See, generally, Barczewski, "Interna- 15–06
tional Framework for Legal Protection of Digital Rights Management Systems"
[2005] E.I.P.R. 165.

3. PROTECTION MEASURES: COMPUTER PROGRAMS

"Technical device". NOTE 34. *Kabushi Kaisha Sony Computer Entertainment* 15–08
Inc v Owen is reported at [2002] E.M.L.R. 34; [2002] E.C.D.R. 27. *Kabushiki
Kaisha Sony Computer Entertainment Inc v Ball* is now reported at [2005] F.S.R.
9; [2004] E.C.D.R. 33.

    Add: See MacCulloch, "Game Over: The Region Lock in Video Games"
[2005] 5 E.I.P.R. 176.

    NOTE 36. *Kabushiki Kaisha Sony Computer Entertainment Inc v Ball* is now
reported at [2005] F.S.R. 9; [2004] E.C.D.R. 33.

Making or dealing with means. NOTES 46 and 49. *Kabushiki Kaisha Sony Com-* 15–10
puter Entertainment Inc v Ball is now reported at [2005] F.S.R. 9; [2004]
E.C.D.R. 33.

    NOTE 48. *Kabushi Kaisha Sony Computer Entertainment Inc v Owen* is
reported at [2002] E.M.L.R. 34; [2002] E.C.D.R. 27.

"Unauthorised". NOTE 55. *Kabushiki Kaisha Sony Computer Entertainment Inc* 15–12
v Ball is now reported at [2005] F.S.R. 9; [2004] E.C.D.R. 33.

4. PROTECTION MEASURES: WORKS OTHER THAN
COMPUTER PROGRAMS

A. CIVIL REMEDIES

"Technological measures". NOTES 85, 86 and 88. *Kabushiki Kaisha Sony Com-* 15–18
puter Entertainment Inc v Ball is now reported at [2005] F.S.R. 9; [2004]
E.C.D.R. 33.

Examples of technological measures. NOTE 95. **Add:** See also Stromdale, "The 15–20
Problems with DRM" [2006] Ent. L.R. 1.

    NOTE 96. *Kabushi Kaisha Sony Computer Entertainment Inc v Owen* is
reported at [2002] E.M.L.R. 34; [2002] E.C.D.R. 27.

NOTES 97 and 99. *Kabushiki Kaisha Sony Computer Entertainment Inc v Ball* is now reported at [2005] F.S.R. 9; [2004] E.C.D.R. 33.

Add at end of seventeenth sentence: In Norway attempts were made to prosecute a teenager for alleged offences committed while developing and publishing DeCSS. His acquittal was upheld on appeal: *Public Prosecutor v Johansen* [2004] E.C.D.R 17 (Borgarting Appellate Court).

NOTE 9. **Add:** On appeal, however, (*Stevens v Kabushiki Kaisha Sony Computer Entertainment* [2005] HCA 58; see also Ciro and Fox, "Competition v Copyright Protection in the Digital Age" [2006] 6 E.I.P.R. 329) it was held that Sony's measures did not amount to technological protection measures as defined in s.10(1) of the Australian Copyright Act. The definition refers to "a device or product, or a component incorporated into a process, that is designed, in the ordinary course of its operation, to prevent or inhibit the infringement of copyright in a work". It was held not to be sufficient that the measures generally discouraged the making of infringing copies as a prelude to playing them on PlayStation consoles. In addition, as a matter of Australian law, the copying which occurred when the game was loaded into the console's RAM did not amount to an infringement. This authority is of little relevance in England given that such use is likely to infringe unless it is a permitted act: see *Kabushiki Kaisha Sony Computer Entertainment Inc v Ball* [2004] EWHC 1738; [2005] F.S.R. 9; [2004] E.C.D.R. 33, at [13]–[17], but note that the point was conceded in part.

Add: Other types of protection measures which have been the subject of litigation in other jurisdictions include: a user identity and password granted to secure access to internet services (*IMS Inquiry Management Systems Ltd v. Berkshire Information Inc* 307 F. Supp. 2d 521—this was held to be an effective technological protection measure, but not to have been circumvented by the improper use of someone else's validly issued user identity and password to gain access; see also *Egilman v Keller & Heckman LLP* 401 F. Supp. 2d 105); and a "secret handshake" which enabled the server run by the provider of a 24-hour online gaming service for purchasers of games software on CD to check the authenticity of the purchaser's product code (*Davidson & Associates, Inc v Internet Gateway* 334 F. Supp. 2d 1164, affirmed in *Davidson & Associates v Jung* 422 F. 3d 630).

15–24   Devices and services: acts attracting liability. NOTE 23. *Kabushiki Kaisha Sony Computer Entertainment Inc v Ball* is now reported at [2005] F.S.R. 9; [2004] E.C.D.R. 33.

15–25   Devices and services: conditions for liability. NOTES 28 and 29. *Kabushiki Kaisha Sony Computer Entertainment Inc v Ball* is now reported at [2005] F.S.R. 9; [2004] E.C.D.R. 33.

C. REMEDY WHERE MEASURES PREVENT PERMITTED ACTS

15–33   Introduction. NOTE 69. **Add:** See Dusollier, "Technology as an Imperative for Regulating Copyright: from the Public Exploitation to the Private Use of the Work" [2005] 6 E.I.P.R. 201; Barczewski, "International Framework for Legal Protection of Digital Rights Management Systems" [2005] 5 E.I.P.R. 165; and Akester, "Digital Rights Management in the 21st Century" [2006] E.I.P.R. 159, pointing out that difficulties may arise because Art.6(4) does not apply to anti-circumvention devices themselves and considering the implications for freedom of speech. See also *Automated Rights Management Systems and Copyright Limitations and Exceptions*, a report dated April 27, 2006 by Nic Garnett for WIPO's Standing Committee on Copyright and Related Rights, concentrating on visually impaired persons and distance education.

5. RIGHTS MANAGEMENT INFORMATION

"Rights management information". Add at end: In the United States case of **15–42** *The IQ Group Ltd v Wiesner Publishing LLC* 409 F. Supp. 2d 587 (US DC NJ January 10, 2006), the question arose as to whether a logo and a hyperlink which appeared on copies of emails advertising insurance services to agents amounted to "copyright management information" for the purposes of 17 U.S.C. § 1202. The hyperlink directed the user to a page of the alleged copyright owner's website which (it claimed) contained copyright notices. It was held that since the logo was a service mark, to allow it protection as copyright management information would impermissibly blur the distinction between copyright and trade mark law. It was further held that neither the logo nor the hyperlink amounted to copyright management information since on its true construction 17 U.S.C. § 1202 only protected information which functioned as a component of an automated copyright protection or management system. This decision was not followed in *McClatchey v The Associated Press* 2007 W.L. 776103 (US DC W.D. Pa March 9, 2007). The claimant claimed that using a computer she had made a print of a photograph taken by her. On the print appeared the title, her name and a copyright notice. A photograph of the print was taken by a photographer employed by the defendant news agency, and the claimant claimed that the defendant then cropped the title, her name and the copyright notice and replaced them with other material before distributing the revised version. On the defendant's summary judgment application the court held that 17 U.S.S. § 1202 protects information which is not in digital form.

The rights. Line 16. **Delete:** 296ZD. **Substitute:** 296ZG. **15–45**

CHAPTER SIXTEEN

FRAUDULENT RECEPTION OF TRANSMISSIONS

Contents

2. POSITION UNDER THE 1988 ACT

B. Offence of fraudulently receiving programmes

16–07 **Offence under section 297. Add:** In *Gannon v FACT* (Bolton Crown Court, March 24, 2006, H.H. Judge Warnock and Justices) the defendant publican, using a decoder and enabling card, had received by satellite a signal from a Greek television broadcast which enabled him to present in his public house a live (but for a two-second time delay) broadcast of a Premiership football match during the so-called "closed" period on Saturday afternoons when no such live transmissions are permitted by the Football Association Premier League. The signal had originated in the United Kingdom and then went "by way of multipoint transmission to the subsequent broadcasters out of the jurisdiction".

The court held that the Prosecution had not proved its case under section 297(1). The court's primary ground was that it was not satisfied on the facts that the defendant was dishonest in the *Ghosh* sense. However, the court went on to "indicate" that it was not satisfied that the signal which emanated from the United Kingdom was a "broadcast" or "broadcasting service" (it will be noted that s.297 only applies to broadcasting services provided from a place in the United Kingdom). Two reasons were given: first, the court was not satisfied that the signal was uninterrupted from its point of origin to the defendant's public house; secondly, it was not satisfied that what was received at the defendant's public house was not a retransmission from Greece and therefore not a "broadcast". In addition, insofar as it was relevant, the court was not satisfied that there had been an "unlawful use of and interference with" the intellectual property rights in the broadcast (it is not clear why this was thought to be relevant: s.297 does not require the prosecution to prove that the rights in the broadcast have been infringed). Finally, the court was not satisfied that there was any intent to avoid payment of any "charge". The rights to this "live" broadcast were not for sale and accordingly there was no or no sufficient evidence of any actual charge. There is anecdotal evidence of a number of other acquittals on similar grounds but also of one conviction (*R. v Murphy*) which has been upheld by Portsmouth Crown Court.

It is suggested (depending on the facts) that the use of section 297A of the 1988 Act may be more appropriate in such cases (see para.16–09 *et seq*. of the Main Work).

C. OFFENCES RELATING TO UNAUTHORISED DECODERS

"Information society service": the basic definition. Third sentence. **Delete:**   **16–11**
(provided in each case a fee is charged). **Add** at end of third sentence: In *Bunt v Tilley* [2006] EWHC 407; [2006] E.M.L.R. 18, Eady J. held (*obiter*) that the provision of Internet access by an Internet service provider (ISP) amounted to the provision of an information society service. He appeared to accept that a service would be "for remuneration" provided the ISP obtained remuneration from some source, for example from advertising or commission on telephone charges. It is not clear from the judgment whether the ISPs in question charged a fee for their services.

"At the individual request of a recipient of services". NOTE 46. In Case C–89/   **16–14**
04, *Mediakabel BV v Commissariaat voor de Media* the ECJ held that the definition of television broadcasting in Art.1(a) was independent of the E-Commerce Directive. Accordingly, it was not defined by opposition to the concept of "information society service" and therefore did not necessarily cover services which were not covered by that concept. The case concerned a pay-per-view service offered as an adjunct to a monthly television subscription service which was accessed using a decoder and smartcard. The pay-per-view service enabled subscribers to order films using their remote control or telephone. After identifying himself by a personal identification code and paying by automatic debit, the subscriber received an individual key which allowed him to view one or more of 60 films on offer each month, at times indicated on the television screen or in the programme guide. The list of films was determined by the service provider; the selection of films was offered to all subscribers on the same terms; the films were accessible at the broadcast times determined by the provider; and the individual key allowing access to the films was only a means of decoding images the signals of which were sent simultaneously to all subscribers. The Court held that a service would be a television broadcasting service within Art.1(b) if it consisted of the initial transmission of television programmes intended for reception by the public, that is an indeterminate number of potential television viewers to whom the same images were transmitted simultaneously. The manner in which the images were transmitted was not a determining factor in that assessment. The service fell within this definition of television broadcasting service. In addition, the Court held that the service was not "commanded individually by an isolated recipient who had free choice of programmes in an interactive setting" and accordingly constituted a "near-video on-demand" service provided on a "point to multipoint" basis. Such services are specifically referred to in Annex V as being excluded from the definition of "information society service".

D. APPARATUS, ETC. FOR UNAUTHORISED RECEPTION OF TRANSMISSIONS

Section 298: persons entitled to rights and remedies. Add before last sentence: **16–22**
Another case which was decided under the pre-2000 wording of section 298 was *The Football Association Premier League v Vision On (Midlands) Limited* (Jacob J., July 5, 1999). The facts were that the claimant caused to be transmitted by satellite encrypted copies of broadcasts of its football matches to a Norwegian broadcaster which decoded them, added Norwegian language commentary and captions, re-encrypted the resulting version and broadcast it by satellite in

Norway for reception by subscribers with the appropriate smartcards. Jacob J. held (at an uncontested trial) that the claimant fell within one or other of the categories in section 298(1) and probably the first. He went on to hold that it did not matter who was responsible for the encryption in Norway or that the Norwegian transmissions were different. Accordingly the defendants, who sold "pirate" smartcards which enabled people in the United Kingdom to view the matches during the "blocked" period on Saturday afternoons (as to which, see para.29–242 of the Main Work), were liable under section 298.

16–23   **Section 298: persons against whom relief is available.** NOTE 71. **Add:** See also *The Football Association Premier League v Vision On (Midlands) Limited* (Jacob J., July 5, 1999): "It is sufficient that the person who receives is not authorised to receive in the sense that the person who sent out the programme or transmission did not want them to receive."

CHAPTER SEVENTEEN

PUBLICATION RIGHT

2. BACKGROUND

First sentence and NOTE 4. The Term Directive and its amendments have been   **17–02**
codified in a new Directive (2006/116/EC) on the term of copyright and certain
related rights [2006] O.J. L372/12. The new Directive took effect on January 16,
2007: see Article 15. Article 4 of the Term Directive is now Article 4 of Directive
2006/116/EC.

3. WHEN THE PUBLICATION RIGHT IS AVAILABLE

A. PUBLISH

NOTE 8. Article 4 of the Term Directive is now Article 4 of Directive 2006/116/   **17–04**
EC.

B. RELEVANT WORKS

Exclusions. Article 4 of the Term Directive is now Article 4 of Directive 2006/   **17–06**
116/EC.

C. THE REQUIREMENT THAT THE WORK BE PREVIOUSLY UNPUBLISHED

Place of first publication. NOTE 23. The Term Directive and its amendments   **17–10**
have been codified in a new Directive (2006/116/EC). That phrase in question
appears in Art.4.

Unauthorised publication where copyright subsists. NOTE 31. Art.4 of the   **17–14**
Term Directive is now Art.4 of Directive 2006/116/EC.

First publication in another EEA State. NOTE 34. Art.4 of the Term Directive   **17–17**
is now Art.4 of Directive 2006/116/EC.

D. THE REQUIREMENT OF EXPIRY OF COPYRIGHT

17–19 **Works in which copyright has never subsisted.** NOTE 37. The Term Directive and its amendments have been codified in a new Directive (2006/116/EC).

17–35 **Additional consequences.** NOTE 83. Recital (2) of the Term Directive is now Recital (3) of Directive 2006/116/EC.

E. QUALIFICATION

17–36 Articles 1 and 3 of the Term Directive are now Articles 1 and 3 of Directive 2006/116/EC.

NOTE 87. Art.7 of the Term Directive is now Art.7 of Directive 2006/116/EC.

5. THE NATURE OF THE RIGHT

17–40 **Civil remedies. Delete** last sentence and **substitute:** The presumptions contained in sections 104 to 106 of the 1988 Act (as to which see paras 22–21—22–220 of the Main Work) do not apply: see the Copyright and Related Rights Regulations 1996, regulation 17(2)(b). However, with effect from April 29, 2006, a new presumption applies where civil proceedings are brought for infringement of publication right in a work. The new regulation 17A of the Copyright and Related Rights Regulations 1996 (SI 1996/2967) inserted with effect from April 29, 2006 by the Intellectual Property (Enforcement etc.) Regulations 2006 (SI 2006/1028) provides that where copies of the work as issued to the public bear a statement that a named person was the owner of publication right in the work at the date of issue of the copies, that statement shall be admissible as evidence of the fact stated and shall be presumed to be correct until the contrary is proved. Like the presumptions in sections 104 to 106 of the 1988 Act, the presumption does not apply in criminal proceedings for an offence, but does apply in proceedings in the criminal courts for delivery up under CDPA 1988 section 108 (as applied to publication right by regulation 17): see regulation 17B.

17–44 **Duration.** NOTE 3. Arts 4 and 8 of the Term Directive are now Arts 4 and 8 of Directive 2006/116/EC.

CHAPTER EIGHTEEN

DATABASE RIGHT

1. INTRODUCTION

Background. NOTE 12. **Add:** Following the reference in this case to the   **18–02**
European Court of Justice, the Court of Appeal issued a further decision on appeal: [2005] EWCA Civ 863; [2005] R.P.C. 35.

3. THE SUI GENERIS DATABASE RIGHT

Database right. Add after fifth subparagraph: The substantial investment   **18–04**
requirement has been considered by the Dutch Appeal Court in the case of *Ned-*
erlandse Vereniging van Makelaars in Onroerende Goederen en Vastgoed-
deskundigen NVM v Zoekallehuizen.nl, unreported 4 July 2006, noted at [2007]
E.I.P.R. N73–4. In this case an assertion that *sui generis* rights existed in an
estate agent's property database failed.

Add after eighth subparagraph: The findings of the European Court of Justice
in the *British Horseracing Board* case were subsequently considered by the Court
of Appeal. The British Horseracing Board submitted that the European Court had
proceeded on a misunderstanding of the facts concerning the investment that had
been made in the database and detailed a series of seven steps that led to the
database being created. Jacob L.J. held that the European Court did not
misunderstand the primary facts, nor indulge in an illegitimate fact-finding
exercise. The principal flaw in the British Horseracing Board's submissions was
held to be that the Court of Justice had implicitly rejected an approach permitting
a deconstruction of the database—it focussed solely on the final database that
was eventually published. Consequently, when the question was asked whether
the British Horseracing Board published database was one consisting of "existing
independent materials" the answer was held to be no. The British Horseracing
Board database contained unique information—the official list of runners and rid-
ers—but the nature of the information changed as a result of the British Horseracing Board's imprimatur and it thus became something different from a mere
database of existing material. The European Court had concluded that the "…
investment in the selection, for the purpose of organising horse racing, of the
horses admitted to run in the race concerned relates to the creation of the data
which make up the lists for those races which appear in the BHB database." In
considering this sentence, Jacob and Pill L.JJ. in the Court of Appeal noted that
"selection might, out of context, be taken to denote something like a creative
choice but in context it clearly does not have that meaning." This finding is supported by the French version of the European Court's judgment (the court's work-

ing language) which employs the term *determination* which does not imply a requirement for creativity.

NOTES 26, 30, 31, 33 to 37, 39 and 40. **Add:** *British Horseracing Board Ltd v William Hill Organisation Ltd* is now reported at [2005] E.C.D.R. 1; [2005] R.P.C 13. The Fixtures Marketing cases are now reported as follows: *Fixtures Marketing v Oy Veikkaus AB* at [2005] E.C.D.R. 2, *Fixtures Marketing v Organismos Prognostikon Agonon Podosfairou (OPAP)* at [2005] 1 C.M.L.R. 16 and [2005] E.C.D.R. 3 and *Fixtures Marketing Ltd v Svenska SpelAB* at [2005] E.C.D.R. 4.

NOTE 41. **Delete** last two sentences. **Substitute:** The Court of Appeal in British *Horseracing Board v William Hill Organisation Ltd* [2005] EWCA Civ 863; [2005] R.P.C. 35 nevertheless upheld the findings of the ECJ in the face of submissions on the basis of the Arsenal case.

NOTES 42 to 46. **Add:** *British Horseracing Board Ltd v William Hill Organisation Ltd* is now reported at [2005] E.C.D.R. 1; [2005] R.P.C. 13. The *Fixtures Marketing* cases are now reported as follows: *Fixtures Marketing v Oy Veikkaus AB* at [2005] E.C.D.R. 2, *Fixtures Marketing v Organismos Prognostikon Agonon Podosfairou (OPAP)* at [2005] 1 C.M.L.R. 16 and [2005] E.C.D.R. 3 and *Fixtures Marketing Ltd v Svenska SpelAB* at [2005] E.C.D.R. 4.

18–05 **Definition of database.** NOTES 58 to 67. *Fixtures Marketing v Organismos Prognostikon Agonon Podosfairou (OPAP)* is now reported at [2005] 1 C.M.L.R. 16 and [2005] E.C.D.R. 3.

18–07 **First ownership. Add** after first paragraph: These ownership provisions were considered in *Pennwell Publishing (UK) Limited v Onstein* [2007] EWHC 1570 (QB). The case concerned a departing employee from Pennwell who had added his various non-work related contact details to the Microsoft Outlook email system maintained by his employer. The key question was whether the relevant database was prepared in the course of employment. The court held that where an address list is maintained on Outlook or a similar program which is part of an employer's email system, the rights in question will usually belong to the employer regardless of whether it also contains personal contacts of the employee.

18–10 **Infringement.** NOTE 87. **Add:** See also *Nederlandse Vereniging van Makelaars in Onroerende Goederen en Vastgoeddeskundigen NVM v Zoekallehuizen.nl*, unreported, Arnheim Appeal Court, July 4, 2006 noted at E.I.P.R. 2007, 29(5), N73–4.

NOTE 88. **Add:** See also *Re Musical Hits Database*, Bundesgerichtshof (Germany), decision of July 21, 2005 [2006] E.C.C. 31.

18–11 **Extraction and re-utilisation.** NOTES 90 to 99, 2 and 4 to 8: **Add:** *British Horseracing Board Ltd v William Hill Organisation Ltd* is now reported at [2005] E.C.D.R. 1; [2005] R.P.C. 13.

NOTE 95. **Add:** See also *Finn No AS v Supersok AS* [2007] E.C.D.R. 12, which concerned the repeated consultation of estate agent databases.

18–12 **Substantiality.** NOTES 10 to 17: **Add:** *British Horseracing Board Ltd v William Hill Organisation Ltd* is now reported at [2005] E.C.D.R. 1; [2005] R.P.C. 13.

CHAPTER NINETEEN

PUBLIC LENDING RIGHT

1. PUBLIC LENDING RIGHT ACT 1979

The right to control lending. NOTE 3. The Rental Rights Directive and its   **19–02**
amendments have now been codified as Directive 2006/115/EC: [2006] O.J.
L376/28.

Line 2. The reference to Article 1 of the Rental Rights Directive should now be
to Article 1 of Directive 2006/115/EC.

Line 4. The reference to Article 5 of the Rental Rights Directive should now be
to Article 6 of Directive 2006/115/EC.

Penultimate line. The reference to Article 5.1 of the Rental Rights Directive
should now be to Article 6(1) of Directive 2006/115/EC.

2. THE SCHEME

History of the Scheme. First Sentence. **Add:** Recent amendments which have   **19–08**
been made to the Scheme are set out at **B3.ii** below.

ARTIST'S RESALE RIGHT

Contents

1. INTRODUCTION

19A–01 **Artist's resale right.** On February 14, 2006, an entirely new and controversial intellectual property right, the Artist's Resale Right, was introduced into the law of the United Kingdom when "The Artist's Resale Right Regulations 2006"[1] entered into force, giving British artists the right to receive a royalty on the resale of their works. The Regulations implemented the much-debated EC Directive on the resale right for the benefit of the author of an original work of art, which came into force on October 13, 2001, after 10 years of negotiation, hereafter the EC Directive.[2] The United Kingdom had strongly opposed the EC Directive and voted against it on the ground that it posed risks to the UK art market, the largest in the European Union. The artist's resale right is a Continental import more commonly known as the "*droit de suite*", the expression used in France, where the right was first introduced in 1920. The Regulations also amount to the implementation by the United Kingdom of the option to introduce such a right given by Article 14*ter* of the Berne Convention for the Protection of Literary and Artistic Works (Paris Act 1971, hereafter the Berne Convention). The new intellectual property right "artist's resale right" is to be enjoyed by the creator of a work of art (and that artist's successors in title) for as long as copyright continues to subsist in the work, which is normally for 70 years after the death of the artist. The right consists in the entitlement to claim a royalty on the resale of the work following its first transfer by the artist. The amount of the royalty is calculated on the basis of the sale price and not on any increase in the value of the work.

19A–02 **History of the artist's resale right.** The origin of the *droit de suite* is to be found in legislation adopted in France in 1920.[3] The concept of the right for visual artists had been first promoted by Albert Vaunois in an article in the *Chronique de*

---

[1] SI 2006/346. For a commentary on the law and practice of this new right, see S. Stokes, *Artists' Resale Right (Droit de suite)*, 2006, Institute of Art and Law Ltd, Leicester.
[2] Directive 2001/84/EC of the European Parliament and of the Council ([2001] O.J. L272/32). See also para.25–72 *et seq.*, below.
[3] Law of May 20, 1920.

Paris in 1893,[4] which resulted in a successful campaign for legislation on the subject in France. The idea behind the right is to look after the interests of artists and other creators of artistic works. It is a well-known feature of the art market, past and present, that artists at an early stage of their career may be obliged to sell work cheaply to earn a living. Thereafter, the work may be resold a number of times, passing through different hands and in the process the work may increase considerably in value, benefiting the successive owners of the work, as well as dealers and the art market. The only person who fails to benefit in such a scenario is the original artist who created the work and to whose talent and growing fame increases in value are largely attributable. The resale right aims to redress this imbalance by allowing the artist to follow (hence the expression *droit de suite*, or right to follow) the fortunes of his work and to participate in the profit made from the increase in value each time the work changes hands. The justification for the right, according to the EC Directive, is "to ensure that authors of graphic and plastic works of art share in the economic success of their original works of art. It helps to redress the balance between the economic situation of authors of graphic and plastic works of art and that of other creators who benefit from successive exploitations of their works".[5]

Artist's Resale Right in the Berne Convention. The example of the new French law on *droit de suite* was followed by Belgium in 1921; subsequently, these two countries, supported by the ALAI (*Association littéraire et artistique internationale*), an international association representing the interests of authors, raised the issue at the Revision Conference for the Berne Convention, which took place in Rome in 1928. The Rome Conference adopted the following "voeu" (or resolution) on the subject:

19A–03

> "The Conference expresses the desire that those countries of the Union which have not yet adopted legislative provisions guaranteeing to the benefit of artists an inalienable right to a share in the proceeds of successive public sales of their original works should take into account the possibility of considering such provisions".[6]

The United Kingdom, together with a number of other countries, abstained from the vote.

However, the example set by France and Belgium gradually attracted support and after the Second World War the number of States recognising resale right grew steadily. Thus, at the Brussels Revision Conference in 1948, the principle of the *droit de suite* was introduced into the Berne Convention, thereby gaining acceptance as the subject-matter of copyright protection as opposed to that of related rights. Since a number of delegations, including that of the United Kingdom, still raised objections to the inclusion of the right in the Berne Convention, it was made optional, so that Union members were not obliged to introduce it, and subject to material reciprocity.

Article 14*ter* of the present text of the Berne Convention is substantially the same as the original text and reads as follows[7]:

"Article 14ter, paragraph (1). Scope of the right

The author, or after his death the persons or institutions authorized by national

---

[4] *Chronique de Paris*, February 25, 1893.

[5] Directive, Recital 3.

[6] *Actes de la Conférence de Rome* 1928, 283.

[7] Originally it was Art.14 *bis* and very minor amendments were made at the Paris Revision Conference in 1971, the word "transfer" being substituted for "disposal" in para.(1) and "extent" for "degree" in para.(2).

legislation, shall, with respect to original works of art and original manuscripts of writers and composers, enjoy the inalienable right to an interest in any sale of the work subsequent to the first transfer by the author of the work.

Article 14ter, paragraph (2). Applicable Law

The protection provided by the preceding paragraph may be claimed in a country of the Union only if legislation in the country to which the author belongs so permits, and to the extent permitted by the country where this protection is claimed.

Article 14ter, paragraph (3). Procedure

The procedure for collection and the amounts shall be matters for determination by national legislation."

It should be noted that Article 14*ter* covers not only works of art but also original manuscripts of authors and composers. However, this option has not been taken up in either the EC Directive or in the UK 2006 Regulations. The right does not apply to works of architecture or to applied art. The right is not assignable; this is to prevent the artist, in order to make a living, being forced to part with it. But it is transmissible on death. The right is optional in that Union members are not obliged to introduce it and it can only be claimed in a Union country if, and to the extent that, it forms part of the law there. Thus, contrary to the general principle of national treatment on which the Berne Convention is based, this right is subject to material reciprocity and can only be claimed by a national of a country which grants the right in another country which also grants the right and to the extent of the protection granted in the latter country.[8]

19A–04   **The position of the United Kingdom.** As discussed above, the United Kingdom opposed the inclusion of the resale right in the Berne Convention and was instrumental in ensuring that the right was made optional and not obligatory. It was also opposed to the EC Directive. The reason for this long-standing opposition was simply that successive UK governments did not believe the introduction of the right was in the national interest. At present, the United Kingdom has the largest art market within the European Union and a pre-eminent position in the international art market. It has always been the Government's position that the introduction of the resale right into the United Kingdom would pose the risk of sales being diverted from the United Kingdom to countries which do not apply a resale right, thus putting the London art market at a competitive disadvantage compared to its main competitors in the art trade, primarily Switzerland (Geneva) and the United States of America (New York).

Following the adoption of the EC Directive, the UK Government accepted its obligation to legislate on resale right but approached the task of implementing the EC Directive with a view to minimising the risk of sales being diverted from the United Kingdom, while taking account of the needs of artists.

"The Directive is largely prescriptive although there are a number of options

---

[8] See further on Art.14 *ter* C. Masouyé, *Guide to the Berne Convention* (WIPO Geneva, 1978), and S. Ricketson and J.C. Ginsburg, *International Copyright and Neighbouring Rights, The Berne Convention and Beyond*, (2nd ed., Oxford University Press, 2006), para.11–53 *et seq*. There is extensive literature on resale right; the following references give a general overview on its origins and status under the Berne Convention and in a few major countries: F. Hepp, "Royalties from Works of the Fine Arts: Origin of the concept of *droit de suite* in Copyright Law" (1959) 6 Bull Cop Soc USA 91; R. Plaisant, " *Droit de suite*" [1969] *Copyright* 157; E. Ulmer, "The *'Droit de Suite'* in International Copyright Law" (1975) 6 IIC 12; W. Nordemann, "The ' *Droit de Suite*' in Art.14 *ter* of the Berne Convention and in the Copyright Law of the Federal Republic of Germany" [1977] *Copyright* 337; US Copyright Office, *Droit de suite: The Artist's Resale Royalty* (1992 report), summarised at 16 *Columbia—VLA Journal of Law & the Arts* 318 (1992); K. Graddy and S. Szymanski, "Scoping Study: Artist's Resale Right" (report prepared by the Intellectual Property Institute on behalf of the UK Patent office, October 2005, Ref. CT/CONS/016); P. Valentin " *Droit de suite*" [2006] E.I.P.R. 28(5), 268.

available to Member States. As made clear in consultations with interest groups both before and after adoption of the Directive, it has always been the Government's intention to minimize the diversion of trade and to allow the gradual adaptation of the art market in the United Kingdom to this new right".[9]

The Government also took the view that a number of the requirements within the EC Directive itself, namely the sliding scale of royalties and the cap on any one royalty payment, in themselves will provide significant protection to the UK art market.

At the time of the adoption of the 2006 Regulations, the Government announced that "the regulations ensure a just reward for living British artists' creativity while protecting the valuable UK art market...The balanced Government approach will benefit struggling artists without placing a heavy administrative burden on the art market and will minimize the risk that sales would be driven offshore."[10]

The fears of the UK Government that the new artists' resale right might have a negative impact on the UK art market have not been realised so far. Since the implementation of the Regulations, the art market has continued to prosper with record prices being achieved for works by contemporary artists and there has been no indication that sales are being diverted from the UK.

2. THE SUBSTANTIVE RIGHT

Artist's Resale Right. The Artist's Resale Right Regulations 2006[11] create a new intellectual property right (resale right) to be enjoyed by the author of a work in which copyright subsists. The right entitles the author to claim a royalty on any sale of his work which is a resale subsequent to the first transfer of ownership by the author (resale royalty) for as long as copyright continues to subsist in the work.[12] The author, in relation to a work, means the person who creates it (and that artist's successors in title).[13] The amount of the royalty is based on the sale price, *i.e.* the price obtained for the sale, net of the tax payable on the sale, and converted into euro at the European Central Bank reference rate prevailing at the contract date (for the calculation of the resale royalty, see Regulations, Sch.I, and para.19A–17, below).[14]

19A–05

The following analysis takes into account the Regulations themselves and the explanatory memorandum to the Regulations prepared by the Department of Trade and Industry and laid before Parliament on December 14, 2005, as well as the consultation documents published by the UK Patent Office.

Resale. The resale right applies to a royalty on any sale of the work which is a resale subsequent to the first transfer of ownership by the author ("resale royalty"[15]). Regulation 12 defines when a sale is to be regarded as a resale, thereby attracting the obligation to pay resale royalty. The sale of a work may be regarded as a resale notwithstanding that the first transfer of ownership was not made for a monetary (or any) consideration. Thus, a resale following a gift by the artist would also qualify.

19A–06

---

[9] *Patent Office Regulatory Impact Assessment*, February 14, 2006, para.2.4.
[10] DTI Press Release, February 14, 2006.
[11] SI 2006/346.
[12] reg.3 (1) and (2).
[13] regs 3(2) and 9.
[14] reg.3(4).
[15] reg.3(1).

However, the sale of a work may be regarded as a resale only if the following conditions are met:

    (a) the buyer or the seller, or (where the sale takes place through an agent) the agent of the buyer or the seller, is acting in the course of a business of dealing in works of art; and

    (b) the sale price is not less than 1,000 euro.

Thus, an art-market professional must be involved in the sale, either as principal or agent, and a minimum price threshold of 1,000 euro is imposed. In setting this threshold, the Government took into account that 88 per cent of works by living artists sold in the United Kingdom in the 1,000–3,000 euro price range in 2003–2004 were by British artists. Another concern was that a higher threshold could have excluded some forms of art, such as photographs, from benefitting from the right.

Furthermore, there is an exemption for certain sales where the work was recently acquired from the artist, namely, where:

    (a) the seller previously acquired the work directly from the author less than three years before the sale; and

    (b) the sale price does not exceed 10,000 euro.

This provision aims to encourage galleries to support new talent by buying works, secure in the knowledge that, if a work is sold relatively quickly, and for less than 10,000 euros, no further payment will be due to the artist.

3. WORKS COVERED

19A–07   **Definition of works.** The Regulations define the works of art covered by them as meaning any work of graphic or plastic art such as a picture, a collage, a painting, a drawing, an engraving, a print, a lithograph, a sculpture, a tapestry, a ceramic, an item of glassware or a photograph. A copy of a work is not to be regarded as a work unless the copy is one of a limited number which have been made by the author or under his authority.[16] This definition follows closely that of the EC Directive.[17] It should be noted, however, that the definition is not exhaustive, due to the inclusion of the words "such as". Accordingly, the sale, for example, of original pieces of jewellery and furniture is not necessarily excluded from the scope of the resale right.

4. OWNERSHIP AND TRANSMISSION OF RIGHTS

19A–08   **The owner of the right.** The resale right vests in the individual artist who creates the work and is the author thereof.[18] The right is personal to the author and is inalienable, which means that it may neither be assigned nor waived.[19] The right may be transferred only in limited circumstances. "Transfer of ownership by the author" includes, in particular; (a) transmission of the work from the author by testamentary disposition, or in accordance with the rules of intestate succession; (b) disposal of the work by the author's personal representatives for the purpose of the administration of his estate; and (c) disposal of the work by an official

---

[16] reg.4 (1) and (2).
[17] Art.2(1)
[18] reg.3(1).
[19] reg.7(1).

receiver or a trustee in bankruptcy, for the purpose of the realisation of the author's estate.[20]

Joint authorship. Regulation 5 makes provision for works which are the joint product of two or more artists. In the case of a work of joint authorship, the resale right belongs to the authors as owners in common and the right is held in equal shares or in such other shares as may be agreed. Any such agreement must be in writing signed by or on behalf of each party to the agreement. A work of joint authorship means a work created by two or more authors.   **19A–09**

Proof of authorship. Regulation 6 lays down a rebuttable presumption that a signatory of the work is its creator. Thus, where a name purporting to be that of the author appeared on the work when it was made, the person whose name appeared, shall, unless the contrary is proved, be presumed to be the author of the work. The same applies, in the case of a work alleged to be a work of joint authorship, in relation to each person alleged to be one of the authors.   **19A–10**

Inalienability of the right. In conformity with the Berne Convention and the EC Directive, the resale right is not assignable and any charge on a resale right is void.[21] However, the transfer of a resale right where it has been transmitted to a qualifying charitable body is permitted, provided that the transfer is to another such charitable body.[22] A resale right may also be transferred to a trustee for the person who would otherwise be entitled to exercise the right (the beneficiary), or from the trustee to the beneficiary.[23]   **19A–11**

No waiver of the right. Resale right may not be waived and any agreement to share or repay resale royalties is precluded. This, does not, however, prevent a collecting society from collecting resale right royalties on the right holder's behalf in return for a percentage of the royalty.[24]   **19A–12**

Persons entitled on succession. On the death of its holder, a resale right may be transmitted as personal or moveable property by testamentary disposition or in accordance with the rules of intestate succession and it may be further so transmitted by any person into whose hands it passes. It may be so transmitted to a natural person or to a qualifying charitable body. If it is transmitted to more than one person, it shall belong to them as owners in common. It is also made clear that in the absence of any heirs it may pass to the Crown as *bona vacantia* ("ownerless property").[25]   **19A–13**

Qualified persons. Regulation 10 lays down certain nationality requirements for the enjoyment of the resale right. Resale right is a right based on reciprocity and, therefore, may be exercised only by a qualifying individual or body and may only be transmitted by a person who, at the time of his death, is a qualifying individual. A qualifying individual is one who is a national of a State of the European Economic Area (EEA) or of a State according reciprocal protection under the Berne Convention and listed in Schedule 2 of the Regulations. The EC Directive provides the option to additionally confer the right upon artists habitually resi-   **19A–14**

---

[20] reg.3(5)
[21] reg.7(1) and (2).
[22] reg.7(3),(4) and (5).
[23] reg.11.
[24] regs 8 and 14.
[25] reg.9.

dent in the United Kingdom,[26] but this was not taken up by the Government.[27] It follows that an individual who does not satisfy these requirements may nevertheless inherit resale right, but such an individual may not exercise it or further pass it on while the requirements remain unsatisfied. However, there is nothing to prevent a resale right from being exercised after it has been transmitted as *bona vacantia*.

19A–15   **Vesting of right by operation of law.** Resale right may vest by operation of law in a personal representative of a deceased person; or by an official receiver or a trustee in bankruptcy and there is nothing to prevent a resale right from being exercised by any person acting in that capacity.

5. EXERCISE OF THE RIGHT

19A–16   **Liability to pay resale royalty.** Under Regulation 13, a specified art-market professional involved with the sale is made jointly and severally liable with the seller to pay the resale royalty. This was done to simplify and reduce the cost of collecting the payments, since otherwise artists and collecting societies would have been left with the tasks of obtaining details about sellers from the art dealer or gallery, tracking down the seller and extracting payment from him. The art-market professional who is so liable (the so-called relevant person) is the agent of the seller, or where there is no such agent, the agent of the buyer, or (again if there is no such agent) the buyer. Thus, where the agent of the seller is a professional, that agent will be liable; and a buyer who is a professional will be liable only if no professional is involved, whether as an agent of the seller or the buyer. The expression "art-market professional" comes from the EC Directive.[28] It encompasses galleries, auctioneers and generally any dealers in works of art.

19A–17   **Calculation of resale royalty.** The resale royalty payable on the sale of a work shall be the sum of the following amounts, being percentage amounts of consecutive portions of the sale price:

Portion of the sale price	Percentage amount
From 0 to 50,000 euro	4%
From 50,000.01 to 200,000 euro	3%
From 200,000.01 to 350,000 euro	1%
From 350,000.01 to 500,000 euro	0.5%
Exceeding 500,000 euro	0.25%

Thus, as from February 14, 2006, when an artist's work is resold on the UK art market for the equivalent of 1,000 euro or more, he will receive a royalty of four per cent of the sale price. The rates were largely determined by the EC Directive,[29] but, in so far as the Directive allows a choice of percentage for the lowest price band, the lowest figure of four per cent was chosen.

---

[26] Art.7(3).
[27] Countries outside the EEA whose nationals may enjoy resale right are the following: Algeria, Brazil, Bulgaria, Burkina Faso, Chile, Congo, Costa Rica, Croatia, Ecuador, Guinea, Iraq, Ivory Coast, Laos, Madagascar, Mali, Monaco, Morocco, Peru, Philippines, Romania, Russian Federation, Senegal, Serbia and Montenegro, Tunisia, Turkey and Uruguay.
[28] Art.1(2).
[29] Art.4.

However, the total amount of the royalty payable on any sale shall not in any event exceed 12,500 euro.[30]

Collective management. Compulsory collective management is imposed by Regulation 14 so that the resale right may be exercised only through a collecting society. This applies even where the holder of the resale right has not transferred the management of his right to a collecting society. In such case, the collecting society which manages copyright on behalf of artists shall be deemed to be mandated to manage his right. Where there is more than one such collecting society, the right holder may choose which of them to give his mandate to. The Government took the view that compulsory collective management would be the most efficient and reliable method of ensuring artists received their royalties. This will become of even greater importance once the right is applied to the works of deceased artists in due course.[31] Evidence from collecting societies in other countries, which are already managing resale rights, shows that the right can be managed effectively and at reasonable cost even when dealing with small amounts.

19A–18

At present, July 2007, there are two collecting societies in the United Kingdom with the mandate to administer the resale right, namely, the Artists' Collecting Society (ACS), set up with the sole object of collecting resale right royalties and the Design and Artists Copyright Society Ltd. ("DACS"). As mentioned above, if an artist has not mandated any particular society to collect resale royalties on his or her behalf then the collecting society which manages both copyright, in general, for all artists and artists' resale right will be deemed to be mandated. Currently DACS is the only society which meets this criterion. Therefore any artist who has not mandated another society will be deemed to have mandated DACS to collect on their behalf. Following the introduction of the resale right in February 2006, DACS started to distribute royalties to artists as early as July 2006. By July 2007, DACS had collected over £2.5 million in resale royalties and made distributions to over 700 artists.[32]

6. ENFORCEMENT

Right to information. Holders of a resale right are empowered to obtain the information necessary to enable them to enforce their rights. These powers are laid down in Regulation 15 and enable the holder of the right in respect of a sale, or a person acting on his behalf, to have the right to obtain information by making a request from any art-market professional involved in the sale. Such requests must, however, be made within three years of the sale in question.

19A–19

The information that may be so requested is any that may be necessary in order to secure payment of the resale royalty, and, in particular, to ascertain the amount of the royalty that is due and, where the royalty is not paid by the person to whom the request is made, the name and address of any person who is liable. Information supplied is to be treated as confidential.

Sanctions. If the requested information is not supplied within 90 days of the receipt of the request, the person making the request may, in accordance with the

19A–20

---

[30] Artist's Resale Rights Regulations 2006, Sch.1.
[31] See para. 19A–23, below.
[32] Media release, July 6, 2006. For further information about DACS, see its website: *www.dacs.org.uk*. See also para.28–53 of the Main Work and this Supplement. The editors are grateful to Catherine Retter, Artist's Resale Right Manager at DACS, for her assistance in updating this chapter.

rules of the court, apply to the county court for an order requiring the person to whom the request is made to supply the information.[33]

7. TRANSITIONAL PROVISIONS

19A–21   **Date of application.** The Regulations do not apply to sales where the date of the relevant contract for sale preceded the commencement of the Regulations, February 14, 2006. However, they do apply notwithstanding that the work sold was made before that commencement.[34] Resale right will, of course, only exist if the work is still in copyright.[35]

19A–22   **Transitional rules of succession.** Regulation 16(2) deals with the situation where the author of a work (or a person to whom the resale right in that work is deemed to have been transmitted) died before the commencement of the Regulations, and was at his death a qualifying individual. In such circumstances, resale right cannot at the time have been transmitted to the artist's successors under Regulation 9.[36] Accordingly, a rule is provided to determine who should then be regarded as the artist's successors for the purpose of holding resale right. Under this rule, the right is deemed to have passed with copyright in the work, if the copyright formed part of the artist's estate; or failing that, to have passed with the work itself. If the artist owned neither the work nor the copyright in it, or if neither passed to a specific beneficiary, resale right in the work is deemed to have been transmitted to the person(s) beneficially entitled to his residuary estate. The same rule applies where the deemed successor in turn died before the commencement of the Regulations.

Where the deceased author of the work was one of a number of joint authors, the right deemed to have been transmitted by the author under regulation 16 is one of that number of equal shares in the resale right. Where a resale right is deemed to have been transmitted to more than one person, the right shall be deemed to have been transmitted to them in equal shares as owners in common.

19A–23   **Postponement of application to sales of deceased artists.** Regulation 17 lays down that those to whom a resale right is transmitted (or deemed to be transmitted) after the death of the artist, in accordance with the Regulations, may not exercise the right until January 1, 2010. The provision was introduced in the exercise of an option open under the Directive to Member States such as the United Kingdom which did not have resale right at the date of entry into force of the Directive (October 13, 2001).[37] The UK Government declared at the time the Regulations entered into force that it had exercised this option to protect the most valuable sector of the UK art market, which is works by deceased artists. There is provision in the Directive[38] for the delay in the application of the right to this market to be extended to 2012 and the Government has stated that it will seek to extend it indefinitely.[39] The Government justifies the delay by the need to allow sufficient time for the market to make adjustments and to monitor the effect of the new Regulations. However, the United Kingdom will be obliged to put forward a fully reasoned case to the Commission to obtain any such extension.

---

[33] In Scotland, such an application shall be made by way of summary application to the sheriff, and the procedure for breach of an order shall proceed in like manner as for a contempt of court.

[34] reg.16(1).

[35] reg.3(1) and (2).

[36] See para. 19A–13, above.

[37] Directive, Art.8(2).

[38] Art.8(3).

[39] DTI Press release, February 14, 2006.

CHAPTER TWENTY

RIGHTS OF CONFIDENCE

1. INTRODUCTION

A. ELEMENTS OF ACTION FOR BREACH OF CONFIDENCE

NOTE 7: *Campbell v MGN Ltd* is now also reported at [2004] 2 A.C. 457; **20–02**
[2004] 2 All E.R. 995 and [2004] E.M.L.R. 15.

3. CONFIDENTAL INFORMATION

B. FORM OF INFORMATION

NOTE 49: *Campbell v MGN Ltd* is now reported at [2004] 2 A.C. 457; [2004] 2 **20–06**
All E.R. 995; [2004] E.M.L.R. 15. **Add:** *Douglas v Hello! Ltd (No.3)* [2005]
EWCA Civ 595; [2006] Q.B. 125; [2005] All E.R. 128; [2005] E.M.L.R. 28. This

decision was appealed to the House of Lords: *OBG Ltd v Allan* [2007] UKHL 21; [2007] 2 W.L.R. 920; [2007] E.M.L.R. 12. It was there held (by a bare majority) that the confidence extended not just to those photographs taken by the Douglases' official photographer but also to all photographic information of the wedding, and that accordingly the third claimant OK! was entitled to claim damages for breach of that confidence, despite the fact that it had already put its own photographs into the public domain by publishing them.

NOTE 51. **Add:** See also *HRH Prince of Wales v Associated Newspapers Ltd* [2006] EWHC 522; [2006] E.C.D.R. 20 where his Royal Highness's private journals of state functions overseas circulated to no more than 75 friends and relations were held confidential. This decision was upheld on appeal: [2006] EWCA Civ 1776; [2007] 2 All E.R. 139.

NOTE 58. **Add:** *HRH Prince of Wales v Associated Newspapers Ltd* [2006] EWHC 522; [2006] E.C.D.R. 20 upheld on appeal: [2006] EWCA Civ 1776; [2007] 2 All E.R. 139.

F. PERSONAL CONFIDENCES

20–11 NOTE 8. *Campbell v MGN Ltd* is now also reported at [2004] 2 A.C. 457; [2004] 2 All E.R. 995 and [2004] E.M.L.R. 15.

NOTE 10. See also *Ash v McKennitt* [2006] EWCA Civ 1714; [2007] E.M.L.R. 4, where publication of a biography containing personal information not in the public domain was prevented.

Add at end of second sub-paragraph: The publication of the addresses of care homes for disturbed teenagers, including juvenile sex offenders, was restrained in *Green Corns Ltd v Claverley Group Ltd* [2005] EWHC 958; [2005] E.M.L.R. 31.

NOTE 12. **Add:** This decision was upheld in *Douglas v Hello! Ltd (No.3)* [2005] EWCA Civ 595; [2006] Q.B. 125; [2005] All E.R. 128; [2005] E.M.L.R. 28, although not in relation to the right of OK!, who had bought the right to the confidential information from the Douglases; the Court of Appeal decided that they had rights only in respect of the official photographs. This part of the Court of Appeal's decision was reversed on appeal: *OBG Ltd v. Allan* [2007] UKHL 21; [2007] 2 W.L.R. 920; [2007] E.M.L.R. 12 at [113] to [117]. This shows that the law of confidential information relating to personal confidences should be applied in a similar way to that relating to trade secrets.

NOTE 14. **Add:** *HRH Prince of Wales v Associated Newspapers Ltd* [2006] EWHC 522; [2006] E.C.D.R. 20 upheld on appeal: [2006] EWCA Civ 1776; [2007] 2 All E.R. 139.

NOTE 21. **Add:** see also *Douglas v Hello! Ltd (No.3)* [2005] EWCA Civ 595; [2006] Q.B. 125; [2005] All E.R. 128; [2005] E.M.L.R. 28.

20–12 **Add** at end of first sub-paragraph: The fact that a minor is being advised about or being prescribed contraceptives by her doctor was held to be confidential to the minor in *R. (on the application of Axon) v Secretary of State for Health* [2006] EWHC 37; [2006] Q.B. 539; [2006] 2 W.L.R. 1130; [2006] 2 F.L.R. 206; [2006] H.R.L.R. 12.

NOTE 33. The correct citation for *Campbell v MGN Ltd* is now [2004] 2 A.C. 457. The decision is also reported at [2004] 2 All E.R. 995 and [2004] E.M.L.R. 15.

Add at end of second sub-paragraph: However, there is no general rule that an adulterer cannot obtain an injunction to restrain publication of matters relating to his or her adulterous relationship: *CC v AB* [2006] EWHC 3083 (QB); [2007] E.M.L.R. 11.

4. CONFIDENTIAL OBLIGATION

A. INTRODUCTION

NOTE 77. *Campbell v MGN Ltd* is now also reported at [2004] 2 A.C. 457; [2004] **20–15**
2 All E.R. 995 and [2004] E.M.L.R. 15.

C. CONTRACTS OF SERVICE

A list of contacts compiled by a journalist during the course of his employment **20–18**
on his employer's email programme and backed up onto the employer's server
has also been held to be confidential information belonging to the employer,
notwithstanding that they were journalistic contacts: *Pennwell Publishing (UK)
Ltd v Ornstien* [2007] EWHC 1570 (QB).

D. OTHER EXAMPLES OF CONFIDENTIAL RELATIONSHIPS

Add at end of first sub-paragraph: A professional regulatory body may have a **20–19**
confidential relationship with its members, so that information provided to it by a
member under investigation may be confidential, but the body's findings are not:
Deloitte & Touche LLP v Dickson [2005] EWHC 721; [2005] A.C.D. 103.

Benefit of confidence. Add at end: This suggestion that the right to personal **20–20**
confidences cannot be assigned has been disapproved by the decision of a majority in the House of Lords in the *Douglas v Hello!* case (*OBG Ltd v. Allan* [2007]
UKHL 21; [2007] 2 W.L.R. 920; [2007] E.M.L.R. 12 at [117]), where it was held
that the Douglases had assigned to OK! magazine not only the right to publish
the official wedding photographs, but also the benefit of their right to prevent others publishing photographs. OK! was therefore entitled to recover damages from
Hello! even though OK! had already published its own photographs and thereby
put them into the public domain.

5. WRONGFUL USE

Justifiable use and public interest. Add at end: Commonwealth jurisdictions **20–23**
have gone further. In *Nam Tai Electronics Inc v PriceWaterhouseCoopers* [2005]
2 HKLRD, the Defendant was held to be justified in publishing confidential
financial information about a company where that was necessary to show that it
was not guilty of a conflict of interest. The test for justifiable use in the public
interest was set out by the Court of Appeal in *HRH Prince of Wales v Associated
Newspapers Ltd* [2006] EWCA Civ 1776; [2007] 2 All E.R. 139 at [68] as being
"not simply whether the information was a matter of public interest, but whether
in all the circumstances it was in the public interest that the duty of confidence
should be breached and whether, having regard to the nature of the information
and all the relevant circumstances, it is legitimate for the owner of the information to seek to keep it confidential". The public interest in disclosing the diary's
contents did not outweigh the confidentiality therein.

6. REMEDIES

Add at end: It is possible in strong cases to obtain summary judgment for an **20–26**
injunction, as in *HRH Prince of Wales v Associated Newspapers* [2006] EWCA
Civ 1776; [2007] 2 All E.R. 139.

A. INJUNCTION

20–27   NOTE 84. *Cream Holdings Ltd v Banerjee* [2004] UKHL 44 is now reported at [2005] 1 A.C. 253; [2004] 4 All E.R. 617; [2005] E.M.L.R. 1.

Add at end: In an appropriate case it is possible to obtain a "John Doe" injunction, to prevent persons unknown from revealing confidential information: *X & Y v Persons Unknown* [2006] EWHC 2783 (QB); [2007] E.M.L.R. 10; [2007] H.R.L.R. 4. This is a useful tool for claimants where a leak is anticipated but it is not known to which newspaper the source will take his story.

20–28   **Add:** Further guidance on interim injunctive relief was given in *Douglas v Hello! Ltd (No.3)* [2005] EWCA Civ 595; [2006] Q.B. 125; [2005] All E.R. 128; [2005] E.M.L.R. 28, where the Court of Appeal held that the judge at first instance had erred in discharging the interim injunction because he had not given enough weight either to the strength of the Douglases' claim or to the fact that damages would be inadequate both as compensation and deterrent.

B. DAMAGES

20–30   NOTE 5. **Add:** *Douglas v Hello! Ltd (No.3)* [2005] EWCA Civ 595; [2006] Q.B. 125; [2005] All E.R. 128; [2005] E.M.L.R. 28.

20–31   **Add** at end of first sub-paragraph: The Court of Appeal's view in *Douglas v Hello! Ltd* [2005] EWCA Civ 595; [2006] Q.B. 125; [2005] All E.R. 128; [2005] E.M.L.R. 28 that a notional licence fee would be an inappropriate measure of damages in cases of personal confidences appears now to be open to doubt in the light of the more commercial approach adopted by the House of Lords on appeal *OBG Ltd v. Allan* [2007] UKHL 21; [2007] 2 W.L.R. 920; [2007] E.M.L.R. 12.

THE PROTECTION OF GOODWILL

2. THE ELEMENTS OF PASSING OFF

Goodwill. The nature of goodwill as a commodity is nicely illustrated in the case of *I N Newman Ltd v Adlem* [2005] EWCA Civ 741; [2006] F.S.R. 16. Having sold his funeral parlour business "Richard T Adlem"—together with its goodwill—to the claimants, Mr Adlem was not entitled to start a new business under that name even after the expiry of a five-year restrictive covenant. **21–03**

Descriptive name. For example, "Phones4U" for a business or shop selling mobile phones was recently held not to be so descriptive as to prevent goodwill being acquired in it: *Phones4U Ltd v Phone4U.co.uk Internet Ltd* [2006] EWCA Civ 244; [2007] R.P.C. 5. **21–04**

NOTE 34. *Associated Newspapers Ltd v Express Newspapers Ltd* is reported at [2003] F.S.R. 51.

Misrepresentation. The distinction between "mere confusion" (which will not found an action in passing off) and deception, or confusion caused by misrepresentation (which will) was recently elucidated in *Phones4U Ltd v Phone4U.co.uk Internet Ltd* [2006] EWCA Civ 244. Jacob L.J. (with whom the other members of the Court of Appeal agreed) said (at para.19): "A more complete test would be whether what is said to be deception rather than mere confusion is really likely to be damaging to the claimant's goodwill or divert trade from him. I emphasise the word 'really'." He further emphasised that it was not necessary to show that the confusion had actually led to lost sales, as other forms of damage to the claimant's goodwill would suffice. **21–06**

3. CLAIMS BY AUTHORS AND COPYRIGHT OWNERS GENERALLY

21–11   **Claimant's work represented to be another's.** In *Scansafe Ltd v MessageLabs Ltd* [2006] EWHC 2015 (Pat) a reverse passing off claim was held arguable where the defendant had advertised his own product as being Version 2.0 so as falsely to suggest that it had been built on the claimant's existing technology.

4. PROTECTION OF TITLES

A. NEWSPAPERS AND PERIODICALS

21–22   NOTES 8 to 11. *Associated Newspapers Ltd v Express Newspapers Ltd* is reported at [2003] F.S.R. 51.

B. BOOKS

21–24   **Examples of descriptive titles of books.** In *Knight v Beyond Properties Pty Ltd* [2007] EWHC 1251 (Ch), the name "Mythbusters" for a series of children's books about the investigation of extraordinary things (such as dragons) was held to be descriptive in one sense, but not so as to prevent goodwill attaching to it. On the facts, however, the scale of the goodwill established was only trivial. Accordingly, the defendants were not passing off by producing a series of television programmes aimed at adults and investigating "urban myths" under the same name.

D. MUSICAL WORKS

21–31   NOTE 48. The neutral citation for *Byford v Oliver* is [2003] EWHC 295, and it is reported at [2003] F.S.R. 39.

6. GET-UP AND APPEARANCE OF GOODS

21–38   **Get-up of publication.** In *GMG Radio Holdings Ltd v Tokyo Project Ltd* [2005] EWHC 2188 (Ch); [2006] F.S.R. 16; [2006] E.C.D.R. 3, the defendant had used artwork on a CD cover which was similar to the same artist's artwork which had been used by the claimants. The court held that although the claimants had established that there was "an issue to be tried", they would have "considerable difficulty" in establishing their case at trial. An interim injunction was refused on the balance of convenience.

8. WEBSITES AND THE INTERNET

21–48   The scope of passing off by domain names appears to be as flexible as the ingenuity of the information technology world. For example, in *Tesco Stores Ltd v Elogicom Ltd* [2006] EWHC 403 (Ch), it was held to be passing off to register domain names containing the word "Tesco" even where they were automatically linked to Tesco's real website; the purpose of this arrangement was to obtain commission for the referral from Tesco through otherwise legitimate "trade-affiliation" software.

    NOTE 46. The neutral citation for *Musical Fidelity v Vickers* is [2002] EWCA Civ 1989. *Bonnier Media v Smith* is reported at [2002] E.T.M.R. 86. **Add:** It is not necessary to show use of the domain name: *Global Projects Management Ltd v Citigroup Inc* [2005] EWHC 2663; [2006] F.S.R.39.

Chapter Twenty Two

CIVIL REMEDIES

1. OVERVIEW

22–03   **The Enforcement Directive.** The Directive has now been implemented by the Intellectual Property (Enforcement etc.) Regulations 2006 (SI 2006/1028) which came into force on April 29, 2006 ("the Enforcement Regulations"), and by certain changes to the Civil Procedure Rules and Practice Directions: see CPR Update 41, published on April 6, 2006. The changes effected by the implementation of the Enforcement Directive are mentioned below where applicable.

The Government believes that Article 4 of the Directive imposes no obligations on Member States to create any new classes of persons entitled to sue: see the Transposition Note attached to the original consultation on implementation, which can be found on the Patent Office website. Accordingly, it has not extended the categories of persons entitled to sue for infringement of the rights covered by this Chapter.

Two points should, however, be noted. First, the Government has created a new concept of a statutory exclusive licensee in the field of registered designs, which is modelled on that in the copyright and unregistered designs field: see Regulation 2(1) of and Schedule 1, paragraph 2 to the Enforcement Regulations. Second, following the consultation process, the Government announced its intention to permit right holders to empower representative associations to bring infringement proceedings on their behalf. Proposed statutory provisions were presented in the Government's post-consultation report and representations were invited. However, opinion was divided, with some pressing for the provisions to go further and others querying the need for them. Accordingly, the Government has concluded that the issue needs further investigation. On September 26, 2006 it launched a further consultation with a closing date of December 18, 2006. See the Patent Office website.

The Commission has published a list of intellectual property rights to which it believes the Enforcement Directive applies: 2005/295/EC, L94 page 37. The list appears to include all the rights covered in this Chapter.

Community designs. Add: It is now provided that in an action for infringement **22–10** of a Community design, all such relief by way of damages, injunctions, accounts or otherwise is available as is available in respect of the infringement of any other property right: see regulation 1A(2) of the Community Design Regulations 2005 (SI 2005/2339) introduced by regulation 2(3) of and paragraph 9 of Schedule 3 to the Enforcement Regulations with effect from April 29, 2006. In appropriate circumstances, the court may now also make orders for the delivery up and disposal of infringing articles and of things specifically designed or adapted for making infringing articles: see regulations 1B to 1D of those Regulations which have been introduced in the same way.

Database right. With effect from April 29, 2006, the statutory remedy of delivery **22–12** up (see para.22–182 of the Main Work) together with the right to seize infringing copies without the need for a court order (see para.22–46 of the Main Work) apply to database right as they apply to copyright: see regulation 2(3) of and paragraph 6 of Schedule 3 to the Enforcement Regulations.

2. WHO MAY SUE

B. EQUITABLE OWNER

Copyright. NOTE 62. *Music Fidelity Ltd v Vickers* [2002] EWCA Civ 1989 is **22–17** reported at [2003] F.S.R. 50.

NOTE 65. **Add:** In *Vitof Ltd v Altoft* [2006] EWHC 1678 (Ch) at para.174 it was definitively held that a bare legal title is no defence to an infringement claim by the beneficial owner.

E. JOINT OWNERS

Copyright, performers' property rights, design right and database right. In **22–29** *Experience Hendrix LLC v Purple Haze Records Ltd* [2005] EWHC 249 (Ch); [2005] E.M.L.R. 18, the Judge declined to express a view on the question whether one co-owner of a performer's rights may sue in respect of them without joining his co-owners. The Judge noted that "a respectable body of authority" in the field of copyright allowed such an action by a co-owner and stated that it would be surprising if CPR 19.3 had altered this. (CPR 19.3 provides that where a claimant claims to be entitled to a remedy jointly with another person, that person must be joined as a party unless the court otherwise orders). The Judge then stated that sections 191I and 191A(4) of the 1988 Act appeared to contemplate all joint owners being parties to the action (para.23). Section 191I provides that an infringement of a performer's property rights is actionable by "the rights owner". Subsection 191A(4) provides that where a performer's property rights (or any aspect of them) is (sic) owned jointly, references in the Act to the rights owner are to all the owners. The Judge did not say why he thought that sections 191I and 191A(4) were any different to sections 96(1) and 173(3) of the 1988 Act, which are in substantially identical terms. It is suggested that there is no material distinction.

3. RELEVANT DATE OF TITLE

22–31   NOTE 10. **Add:** See also *Hendry v Chartsearch Ltd* [1998] C.L.C. 1382 and *Maridive & Oil Services (SAE) v CAN Insurance Company (Europe) Ltd* [2002] EWCA Civ 369; [2002] 2 Ll. Rep. 9.

4. WHO MAY BE SUED?

A. COPYRIGHT AND DESIGN RIGHT: PRIMARY INFRINGERS

22–32   *Bloomsbury Publishing Group Ltd v News Group Newspapers Ltd* is reported at [2003] 1 W.L.R. 1633; [2003] F.S.R. 45.

D. JOINT TORTFEASORS

22–35   **General.** In *Sabaf SPA v MFI Furniture Centres* [2002] EWCA Civ 976; [2003] R.P.C. 14 at [59], the Court of Appeal stated as follows: "The underlying concept for joint tortfeasance must be that the joint tortfeasor has been so involved in the commission of the tort as to make himself liable for the tort. Unless he has made the infringing act his own, he has not himself committed the tort. That notion seems to us what underlies all the decisions to which we were referred. If there is a common design or concerted action or otherwise a combination to secure the doing of the infringing acts, then each of the combiners has made the act his own and will be liable." Applying that general principle, the Court went on to uphold the Judge's decision that a supplier which merely supplied goods to a purchaser which was free to do what it wanted with them was not a joint tortfeasor even though the supplier knew that the goods would be imported into and sold in the United Kingdom and in supplying the goods facilitated the commission of the tort. The issue was not appealed further: [2004] UKHL 45; [2005] R.P.C. 10 at [39].

NOTES 22 and 24. *MCA Records Inc v Charly Records Ltd* [2001] EWCA Civ 1441 is reported at [2002] F.S.R. 26; [2002] E.M.L.R. 1; [2002] E.C.D.R. 37.

22–38   **Supply of equipment which may be used to infringe. Add:** In *Navitaire Inc v easyJet Airline Co Ltd (No.2)* [2005] EWHC 0282 (Ch); [2006] R.P.C. 4, software had been supplied by a company located outside the jurisdiction to a company within the jurisdiction which then used it. The supplier had consulted closely with the person to whom it was supplied and incorporated what were held to be infringing copies of code and graphic works. The supplier had no say in whether the software was used or not. It was held (at para.99) that the supplier was not jointly liable for the infringing use of the software within the jurisdiction.

22–38A   **Liability in respect of file sharing networks. Delete** last three sentences and **substitute:** Actions in the United States against those who distributed software for such systems failed at first instance (*Metro-Goldwyn-Mayer Studios Inc v Grokster Ltd* 259 F. Supp. 2d 1029 (C.D. Cal. 2003)) and on appeal 380 F. 3d 1154 (9th Cir. 2004). However the Ninth Circuit's decision was overturned by the Supreme Court, which held unanimously that Grokster was not entitled to summary judgment and remanded the case for reconsideration of the plaintiffs' motion for summary judgment: 125 S Ct. 2764 (2005).

The Supreme Court recognised that the case concerned the tension between on the one hand supporting creative pursuits through copyright protection and on the other promoting innovation in new communication technologies by limiting the incidence of liability for copyright infringement: "The administration of copyright law is an exercise in managing the trade-off". The plaintiffs argued that the ease of digital copying was fostering a disdain for copyright protection. The defendants contended that imposing liability could limit further development of beneficial technologies. The Supreme Court stated, however, that the argument for imposing liability was powerful given the number of infringements and the difficulty of enforcement against individual infringers.

According to the Supreme Court, the Ninth Circuit had interpreted the Supreme Court decision in *Sony Corp v Universal City Studios Inc* 464 US 417 (SC 1984) to mean that "whenever a product is capable of substantial lawful use, the producer can never be held contributorily liable … it read the rule as being this broad, even when an actual purpose to cause infringing use is shown by evidence independent of the design and creation of the product, unless the distributors had specific knowledge of infringement at a time at which they contributed to the infringement, and failed to act upon that information".

This view of *Sony* was error, converting the case to one about liability resting on imputed intent to one about liability on any theory. Because *Sony* did not displace other theories of liability, it was therefore unnecessary to revisit it. In particular, where the evidence goes beyond a product's characteristics or the knowledge that it may be put to infringing uses and shows statements or actions directed to promoting infringement, *Sony's* rule will not preclude liability.

The Supreme Court held that the applicable principles were as follows. A person who induces an infringement is contributorily liable for it. One who distributes a device with the object of promoting its use to infringe copyright, as shown by clear expression or other affirmative steps taken to foster infringement, is liable for the resulting acts of infringement by third parties. Mere knowledge of potential or actual infringing uses is not enough. Nor are ordinary acts incidental to product distribution (technical support, product updates). The inducement rule premises liability on purposeful, culpable expression and conduct.

On the facts, there was clear evidence of unlawful intent: at a time when Napster was under threat in the courts, the defendant had "beamed" advertisements on to the screens of Napster users inviting them to take up the defendant's software by way of replacement; there was no filtering; and revenue depended on advertising which in turn depended on high volume infringing use.

On November 8, 2005, Grokster announced that it was closing down. Other defendants settled, leaving Streamcast Inc the only defendant.

On September 27, 2006, the Plaintiffs obtained summary judgment against Streamcast: *Metro-Goldwyn-Mayer Studios Inc v Grokster Ltd* 454F. Supp. 2d. 966 C.D. Cal., 2006. After rejecting various technical evidential points, the court stated that it was sufficient for the plaintiffs to prove that "Streamcast distributed the product with the intent to encourage infringement". Once that was established there was no need to prove any specific actions beyond product distribution which caused specific acts of infringement.

The court held that evidence of Streamcast's unlawful intent was overwhelming:

- The software was used overwhelmingly for infringement (on the evidence, 97 per cent of the files requested for downloading were infringing or likely to be infringing).
- While Napster was under legal threat, Streamcast marketed its first-generation P2P software (MusicCity) to Napster users as an alternative. As Napster went down, these users were migrated to Morpheus, a second-generation (decentralised) service.
- Streamcast gave users technical assistance for "playback" of copyright content and invited a user to upload copyright content for sharing.
- Streamcast "ensured its technology had infringing capabilities" *i.e.* tested the system by searching for infringing content and blocked the network from various enforcement attempts.

- The business model depended on massive infringing use (revenue depended on advertising and bundling which in turn depended on infringement).
- There was no attempt at or interest in filtering.

See Giblin-Chen, "On Sony, Streamcast, and Smoking Guns" [2007] 6 E.I.P.R. 215.

The point of fundamental importance for the Supreme Court, although not for the Ninth Circuit, was the fact that the distributors of the file sharing software had deliberately encouraged the use of the software for infringing purposes. In *CBS v Amstrad* (n.34 to para.22–38 of the Main Work) it was held that Amstrad would have been liable if they had procured an infringement, by inducement, incitement or persuasion. However, they did not procure an infringement merely by selling a machine which could be used for lawful or unlawful copying. The purchaser made unlawful copies not because he was induced, incited or persuaded to do so by Amstrad but because he chose to do so. Generally, inducement, incitement or persuasion must be by a defendant to an individual infringer and must identifiably procure a particular infringement in order to make the defendant liable. It seems likely that in England and Wales a claimant who was able to prove that a Napster user who had received one of Grokster's advertisements had then downloaded the Grokster software and used it to infringe would be held to satisfy these conditions.

In *Buma/Stemra v KaZaA* [2004] E.C.D.R. 16 the Dutch Supreme Court upheld a decision of the Court of Appeals that distribution of KaZaA file-sharing software, a second-generation type, was lawful. See Akester, "Copyright and the P2P Challenge" [2005] 3 E.I.P.R. 106 at 109–110. However, in *Universal Music Pty v Sharman License Holdings Ltd* [2005] F.C.A. 1242, Wilcox J. held that the suppliers of KaZaA software were liable for authorising users' infringements (see Blakeney, "Peer-to-Peer File Sharing under Assault" [2006] C.T.L.R. 55 and Hyland, "Judicial Pragmatism Prevails in Sharman Ruling" [2006] C.T.L.R. 98). The Australian law of authorising is different to that of England and Wales and accordingly the *Sharman* case cannot be regarded as authoritative here. In any event, at least as far as KaZaA is concerned, the point appears to be academic: on July 27, 2006, KaZaA announced that it was going to become a legal download service.

See also: Nasir, "Taming the Beast of File Sharing—Legal and Technological Solutions to the Problem of Copyright Infringement over the Internet" Part I [2005] 3 Ent. L.R. 50, Part II [2005] 4 Ent. L.R.82 and Part III (entitled "From Scare Tactics to Surcharges and Other Ideas—Potential Solutions to Peer to Peer Copyright Infringement") [2005] 5 Ent. L.R. 105; Giblin-Chen, "Rewinding Sony: An Inducement Theory of Secondary Liability" [2005] 11 E.I.P.R. 428; Hyland, "MGM v Grokster: Has the Copyright Pendulum Started to Swing Towards Copyright Holders?" [2005] C.T.L.R. 232; Ganley, "Surviving Grokster: Innovation and the Future of Peer to Peer" [2006] 1 E.I.P.R. 15; Gillen, "File-Sharing and Individual Civil Liability in the United Kingdom: A Question of Substantial Abuse?" [2006] 1 Ent. L.R. 7; Davies, Pryor and Keane, "Peer-to-Peer Case Developments" [2006] 1 Ent. L.R. 25; Nwogugu, "The Economics of Digital Content and Illegal Online File-Sharing: Some Legal Issues" [2006] C.T.L.R. 5; Akester and Lima, "Copyright and P2P: Law, Economics and Patterns of Evolution" [2006] 11 E.I.P.R. 576; and Daly, "Life after Grokster: Analysis of US and European Approaches to File-sharing" [2007] 8 E.I.P.R. 319.

Add at end: Connecting a computer to the Internet, where the computer is running peer-to-peer software, and where music files containing copies of copyright works are placed in a shared directory, amounts to communication to the public of those works by the person in control of the computer ("the uploader"): *Polydor Ltd v Brown* [2005] EWHC 3191 (Ch) at paragraph 7. According to the Judge, the uploader is also liable for "authorising the performance of the infringement" (*sic*): *ibid.*, paragraph 9. In fact, however, it is a prerequisite of liability for authorisation that the alleged "authoriser" has or purports to have authority (see para.7–132 of the Main Work). Can it really be said that the uploader purports to have authority to grant the downloader the right to carry out the download? It is suggested that the better view depending on the facts is that the uploader will be liable for the downloader's infringement as a joint tortfeasor. See also *Universal Music Australia Pty Ltd v Cooper* [2005] FCA 972, in which it was held that operating a website which contained hyperlinks to remote sites which when clicked caused the automatic unlawful download of mp3s did not amount to communication to the public, nor was the operator a joint tortfeasor with the downloaders; however, he was liable for authorisation under Australian law. On appeal by the defendant, the finding of authorisation was upheld: *Cooper v Universal Music Australia Pty Ltd* [2006] FCAFC 187; (2006) 71 IPR 1. A similar result was reached on different grounds in *Brein v Techno Design Internet Programming B.V.* [2006] E.C.D.R. 21 (Court of Appeal of Amsterdam). For a United States case in which similar issues were raised, see *Perfect 10, Inc. v Amazon.com, Inc.* (USCA 9th Cir., May 16, 2007).

E. Conspiracy

NOTE 43. **Add:** On the mental element for conspiracy, see *Douglas v Hello Ltd* [2005] EWCA Civ 595; [2006] Q.B. 125 and *Green v Skandia Life Assurance Company Ltd* [2006] EWHC 1626 (Ch) and the cases cited therein.   **22–40**

Add at end of fourth sentence: An unlawful act actionable at the suit of the claimant is a necessary ingredient of an unlawful means conspiracy: *Revenue and Customs Commissioners v Total Network SL* [2007] EWCA Civ 39; [2007] 2 W.L.R. 1156.

F. Directors and controlling shareholders of companies

Basis for liability. NOTES 47 to 52. *MCA Records Inc v Charly Records Ltd* [2001] EWCA Civ 1441 is reported at [2002] F.S.R. 26; [2002] E.M.L.R. 1; [2002] E.C.D.R. 37.   **22–41**

NOTE 49. **Add** at end: and *Experience Hendrix LLC v Purple Haze Records Ltd* [2005] EWHC 249 (Ch); [2005] E.M.L.R. 18, a case involving rights in performances, where summary judgment was granted against a director who was alleged to have personally arranged for the making and issuing to the public of infringing material.

NOTE 54. *MCA Records Inc v Charly Records Ltd* [2001] EWCA Civ 1441 is reported at [2002] F.S.R. 26; [2002] E.M.L.R. 1; [2002] E.C.D.R. 37.

G. Vicarious liability

NOTE 58. The reference to *Clerk & Lindsell on Torts* should now be to Ch.6 of the 19th edition. See generally *Majrowski v Guy's and St. Thomas' NHS Trust* [2006] UKHL 34; [2007] 1 A.C. 224.   **22–43**

6. DEFENCES

Add: Recent cases on acquiescence or estoppel in this field include *Dyson Ltd v Qualtex (UK) Ltd* [2004] EWHC 2981 (Ch); [2005] R.P.C. 19 (defence failed) and *Navitaire Inc v easyJet Airline Company* [2004] EWHC 1725 (Ch); [2006]   **22–50**

R.P.C. 3 (see para.148—defence failed because there was no reliance on any representation or on the claimant's failure to take steps to enforce copyright).

B. Ignorance not necessarily a defence

22–60 **Copyright and design right.** NOTE 98. *Sony Music Entertainment (UK) Ltd v Easyinternetcafé Ltd* is reported at [2003] F.S.R. 48; [2003] E.C.D.R. 27.

E. Undertaking to take licence of right

22–79 **Procedure. Add:** In a design right case, an undertaking may be given even though the design right has expired by the time it is offered: *Ultraframe (UK) Ltd v Eurocell Building Plastics Ltd* [2005] EWCA Civ 761; [2005] R.P.C. 36.

F. Innocently acquired illicit recordings and infringing articles

22–81 NOTE 39. **Add:** Because s.233(2) refers to reason to believe and not to the defendant's actual belief, the test is objective: *Badge Sales v PMS International Group Ltd* [2006] F.S.R. 1.

G. Public interest

22–82 **Introduction.** NOTE 41. *Ashdown v Telegraph Group Ltd* is reported at [2002] Ch. 149; [2002] R.P.C. 5; [2001] E.M.L.R. 44; [2002] E.C.D.R. 32. **Add:** In *HRH The Prince of Wales v Associated Newspapers Ltd* [2006] EWHC 522 (Ch); [2006] E.C.D.R. 20, Blackburne J. considered (at para.183) a submission that because the claimant was not motivated by commercial considerations but wished to prevent disclosure of information, the copyright claim was an abuse of process, being a surrogate for a privacy claim which was likely to fail. He considered the dictum of Lightman J. in *Service Corporation International plc v Channel Four Television Corporation* [1999] E.M.L.R. 83 to the effect that if a claim based on some other cause of action was in reality a claim brought to protect reputation and reliance on the other cause of action was merely a device to circumvent the rule against the grant of an interim injunction where the defendant intended to plead justification, then the overriding need to protect freedom of speech required the same rule to be applied. The Judge pointed out that the court would not countenance reliance on copyright to prevent disclosure of wrongdoing of the type suggested by the evidence in the *Service Corporation* case. This was a matter covered by the public interest defence. He went on to say that where there was no public interest defence and the claim was not a disguised claim to protect reputation there was no scope for arguing that the court would only entertain a copyright action if the claimant could demonstrate an intention to publish his work or otherwise exploit it for some commercial purpose: "... copyright is essentially a negative not a positive right ... The right is not conditional ... on an intention to exploit the copyright work commercially. Copyright is a property right. Subject to the 'exceptions, exemptions and defences' provided for in the CDPA, including, residually, any general public interest defence, a copyright owner does not have to justify the assertion of his copyright. ... The fact, if fact it be, that the copyright owner asserts his copyright in a work in order to maintain privacy in the work does not appear to me to be any kind of abuse of his ownership right. The position is no different where the claim is advanced as an alternative or, as it is put, as a fall-back to a claim in privacy". See Mitchell and Boura, "HRH The Prince of Wales v Associated Newspapers Ltd: Copyright versus the Public Interest" [2006] Ent. L.R. 210. This argument (which was described as "novel and interesting") did not arise for decision on the appeal because the Court of Appeal accepted that the claimant had a valid claim based on breach of confidence and interference with his Article 8 rights: [2006] EWCA Civ 1776; [2007] 3 W.L.R. 222; [2007] 2 All E.R. 139 at [84].

For recent general discussions of the defence, see Johnson, "The Public Interest: Is It Still a Defence to Copyright Infringement?" [2005] 1 Ent. L.R. 1 and Sims, "The Public Interest defence in Copyright Law: Myth or Reality" [2006] 6 E.I.P.R. 335.

NOTE 42. *Ashdown v Telegraph Group Ltd* is reported at [2002] Ch. 149; [2002] R.P.C. 5; [2001] E.M.L.R. 44; [2002] E.C.D.R. 32.

Tension between copyright and freedom of expression. NOTE 46. *Ashdown v*   **22–83**
Telegraph Group Ltd is also reported at [2002] R.P.C. 5; [2001] E.M.L.R. 44 and [2002] E.C.D.R. 32.

Add at end of sixth sentence: In *HRH The Prince of Wales v Associated Newspapers Ltd* [2006] EWHC 522 (Ch); [2006] E.C.D.R. 20, Blackburne J. accepted the submission that the public interest must be greater to justify the use of the form of the words appearing in the copyright work than to justify the use of the information contained in the work; and that in the absence of any specific clear public interest consideration over and above those available under the fair dealing defences it would be wholly disproportionate to extinguish the claimant's property rights in this copyright work by reason of the application of the public interest defence (para.180). It is not clear why the Judge considered that a successful public interest defence in one case would necessarily have the effect of extinguishing the copyright. The question did not arise on the appeal: [2006] EWCA Civ 1776; [2007] 3 W.L.R. 222; [2007] 2 All E.R. 139.

Add at end: See also the Dutch case *Church of Spiritual Technology, Religious Technology Center, New Era Publications International APS v Dataweb B.V.* [2004] E.C.D.R. 25 (publication of extracts from texts on the Internet in order to warn people about alleged dangers of Scientology: no copyright infringement).

H. USE IN ELECTRONIC NETWORKS: MERE CONDUIT, CACHING AND
HOSTING

(i) Introduction

Review. On June 8, 2005, the DTI published a Consultation Document on the   **22–90**
Electronic Commerce Directive: the liability of hyperlinkers, location tool services and content aggregators: see *www.dti.gov.uk/files/file13986.pdf*. See Calleja, "Limitations on Liability of Intermediaries—DTI Consultation" [2005] C.T.L.R. 219.

(ii) The defence of more conduit

The operation of the defence. Add: According to evidence accepted (*obiter*) by   **22–95**
Eady J. in *Bunt v Tilley* [2006] EWHC 407; [2006] E.M.L.R. 18, internet service providers (ISPs) normally delete emails automatically on initial transmission to the subscriber. The Judge appeared to accept a submission that an ISP which had done no more than provide Internet access to individuals who had allegedly used such access to post defamatory material on a Usenet message board would be able to rely on the "mere conduit" defence. By contrast, the Judge appeared to accept the suggestion that an ISP which provides web-based email services is unlikely to be considered a mere conduit in relation to the messages because they

are retained on its server until deleted by the recipient. Such an ISP is likely to be held to have "hosted" the messages.

(iii) The defence of caching

22–96 **The defence of caching.** For an account of the process of caching, see *Bunt v Tilley* [2006] EWHC 407; [2006] E.M.L.R. 18. It was conceded that the "caching" defence would not be available where an ISP had hosted the Usenet message board on its servers, stored postings for a few weeks to enable the users to access them and, while not operating the newsgroups, had the ability to remove postings from its news group server (albeit they might still be viewed via other servers).

(iv) Hosting

The defence of hosting

22–104 In *Bunt v Tilley* [2006] EWHC 407; [2006] E.M.L.R. 18, Eady J. appeared to accept (*obiter*) the suggestion that an ISP which provided web-based email services is likely to be held to have "hosted" the messages. In respect of the defendant ISP which had hosted the Usenet message board on its servers, stored postings for a few weeks to enable the users to access them and, while not operating the newsgroups, had the ability to remove postings from its news group server (albeit they might still be viewed via other servers), the Judge held (*obiter*) that the hosting defence was satisfied on the facts because the claimant had no prospect of proving actual knowledge within the meaning of regulation 19(1)(a)(i). In particular, the claimant had failed to comply with the notice provisions of regulation 22.

(v) Injunctions and other provisions

22–107 **Mere conduit, caching and hosting: termination of infringement.** In *Bunt v Tilley* [2006] EWHC 407; [2006] E.M.L.R. 18, Eady J. suggested (*obiter*) that ISPs which had done no more than provide Internet access to individuals who had allegedly used such access to post defamatory material on a Usenet message board would be able to rely on the "mere conduit" defence. He also suggested that the grant of an injunction against such ISPs to restrain the publication of the same or similar words defamatory of the claimant would be "unworkable and disproportionate". The ISPs in question did not host any of the material about which the claimant complained, nor did they have the power to amend or modify any Usenet content. The grant of an injunction in respect of a defendant which had no way of ensuring compliance with its terms would be pointless.

7. REMEDIES AND PROCEDURE

A. JURISDICTION

22–114 **Extent of the 1988 Act may be increased.** NOTE 8. **Add:** Although provision has been made in the past for the extension with modifications of provisions of Part I of the 1988 Act to Gibraltar (see most recently the Copyright (Gibraltar) Order 2005 (SI 2005/853)), such provision has since been revoked (see the Copyright (Gibraltar) Revocation Order 2006 (SI 2006/1039)).

22–116 **Jurisdiction over foreign rights and infringements thereof: general.** NOTE 13. The citation for the Council Regulation should be [2001] O.J. L12/1.

Position under the Judgments Regulation and the Brussels and Lugano   **22–117**
Conventions. Add at end: Under the so-called "Rome II" Regulation (Regulation (EC) No. 864/2007 on the law applicable to non-contractual obligations [2007] O.J. L. 199/40), which comes into force on January 11, 2009, the law applicable to a non-contractual obligation arising from an infringement of an intellectual property right shall be the law of the country for which protection is claimed (Art.8(1)); while in the case of a non-contractual obligation arising from an infringement of a unitary intellectual property right the law applicable shall for any question not governed by the relevant Community instrument, be the law of the country in which the act of infringement was committed: Article 8(2). These provisions may not derogated from by agreement: Article 8(3).

Position in other cases. NOTE 17. The reference to Dicey & Morris should now   **22–118**
be to Rule 24 of the 14th edition.

NOTE 18. The reference to Dicey & Morris should now be to Rule 31 of the 14th edition.

NOTE 20. The reference to Clerk & Lindsell on Torts should now be to para. 7–09 of the 19th edition.

NOTE 23. The reference to Dicey & Morris should now be to Rule 122(3) of the 14th edition.

NOTES 24 and 25. *R Griggs Group Ltd v Evans (No. 2)* is reported at [2005] Ch. 153 and [2004] F.S.R. 48.

The court's *in personam* jurisdiction. NOTE 28. The reference to Dicey & Mor-   **22–119**
ris should now be to Rule 122(3)(a) of the 14th edition.

NOTE 30. **Delete** and **substitute:** See Dicey & Morris, The Conflict of Laws (14th ed.), paras 23–041 to 23–050.

NOTE 31. *R Griggs Group Ltd v Evans (No. 2)* is reported at [2005] Ch. 153 and [2004] F.S.R. 48.

B. INTERIM RELIEF

(i) Injunction

General. Add: The court now has the power in intellectual property proceedings   **22–120**
to make an order under Article 9 of the Enforcement Directive making the continuation of an alleged infringement subject to the lodging of guarantees: see CPR 25.1(p). The purpose of this provision is to implement part of Article 9(1)(a) of the Enforcement Directive (see the Main Work, para.22–03 and Vol.2, H14). Article 9(1)(a) makes clear that the order is intended to be an alternative to the grant of an interim injunction and that the guarantees are intended to ensure that the rightholder is compensated in the event that it emerges at trial that there was in fact an infringement. There is no definition of intellectual property proceedings in CPR 25.1(p). However, the Commission has expressed the view that the Directive covers a wide range of rights, including all the rights covered in this Chapter: see 2005/295/EC, L94 p.37. In general, where damages would be an adequate remedy and the defendant would be in a position to pay them an interim injunction is likely to be refused. It would clearly be open to a claimant to argue in such a case that guarantees should be lodged instead. No doubt a defendant would riposte that guarantees are unnecessary.

Without notice applications. NOTE 35. **Add:** *Mayne Pharma (UK) v Teva UK*   **22–121**
Ltd [2004] EWHC 3248 (Ch); *Cinpres Gas Injection Ltd v Melea Ltd* [2005] EWHC 3180 (Pat).

22–124   *Series 5 Software Ltd v Clarke.* Note 46. **Add:** See also *O2 Ltd v Hutchison 3G UK Ltd* [2004] EWHC 2571 (Ch); [2005] E.T.M.R. 61, where the Judge took account of the weakness of the claim in a trade mark case where the defendant wished to rely on the comparative advertising defence.

22–126   **Where decision will determine the case.** In *Play it Ltd v Digital Bridges Ltd* [2005] EWHC 1001 (Ch), Morritt V.-C. stated that in most cases involving intellectual property not only were damages an inadequate remedy to both sides, but the decision whether or not to grant an injunction was likely to be determinative because there was little incentive to an unsuccessful applicant to continue to trial and little point in an unsuccessful respondent going to trial because of the difficulty, even if he won, of reverting commercially to the position he occupied before the injunction was wrongly granted. For that reason, Morritt V.-C. held that if in such a case the pecuniary remedy of the parties was inadequate to each of them, it was appropriate to consider the strength of their respective cases.

22–128   **Cases involving freedom of expression.** Note 60. *Cream Holdings Ltd v Banerjee* is now reported at [2005] 1 A.C. 253 and [2005] E.M.L.R. 1.

Note 63. The neutral citation for *Greene v Associated Newspapers Ltd* is [2004] EWCA Civ 1462. It is reported at [2005] Q.B. 972 and [2005] E.M.L.R. 10.

22–129   **Section 12 of the Human Rights Act and privacy cases: *A v B*.**

A v B needs to be read in the light of subsequent authorities.

McKennitt v Ash [2006] EWCA Civ 1714; [2007] 3 W.L.R. 194; [2007] E.M.L.R. 4, concerned the publication of a book detailing confidential matter confided to a close personal friend by a folk singer who had jealously guarded her privacy.

The Court of Appeal held at [64] that *A v B* could not be regarded as a binding authority on the content of Articles 8 and 10 because it proceeded on the basis of breach of confidence rather than on the basis of the law as laid down by the House of Lords in *Campbell v MGN Ltd*. It went on to hold that the content of Articles 8 and 10 had to be derived from *Van Hannover v Germany* (2005) 40 EHRR 1 (note, however, that in *Murray v Express Newspapers Plc* [2007] EWHC 1908 (Ch) at [62], Patten J. held that if it comes to a straight choice between *Von Hannover* and *Campbell*, the English courts are obliged to follow *Campbell*).

The Court went on to consider two particular aspects of the guidance given in *A v B* in that light.

As to "shared confidences" (sub-para.(11) in the Main Work) the Court held that where a confidence has been shared only in the sense that one party has admitted another into her confidence, which confidence the confidant knows should be respected, any Article 10 rights of the confidant must yield to the Article 8 rights of the confider [51].

As to "public figures" (sub-para.(12) of the Main Work), the Court stated that the terms of *Von Hannover* were "very far away from the automatic limits placed on the privacy rights of public figures in *A v B*" [64]. The Court noted with apparent approval two qualifications which Lord Phillips made to this part of the judgment in *A v B* in the Court of Appeal in *Campbell v MGN Ltd* [2002] EWCA Civ 1373; [2003] Q.B. 633; [2003] E.M.L.R. 2, at [40]–[41]. The first was that when Lord Woolf referred to the public having a legitimate interest in being told information, even including trivial facts, about a public figure, he was not speaking of private facts that a fair-minded person would consider it offensive to disclose. The second was that the fact that a person had become a so-called "involuntary role model" did not mean that his private life could be laid bare by the media.

The Court also expressed doubts as to Lord Woolf's point that weight must be given to the commercial interest of newspapers in reporting matter that interests the public [66].

On the facts of the case, the claimant was "on one view" an involuntary role model. However, she had made great efforts to protect her privacy and was guilty of no improper conduct. Accordingly the appeal failed.

In *Lord Browne of Madingley v Associated Newspapers Ltd* [2007] EWCA Civ 295; [2007] 3 W.L.R. 289, the Court of Appeal stated (at [23]) that where section 12(3) of the Human Rights Act applies the court should first consider whether article 8 is engaged. It should then consider whether article 10 is engaged and, critically, whether the applicant for relief has shown that he is likely to establish at a trial that publication should not be allowed within the meaning of section 12(3). Neither article has precedence over the other [39].

NOTE 65. *Campbell v MGN Ltd* is now reported at [2004] 2 A.C. 457; [2004] E.M.L.R. 15.

NOTE 66. **Delete:** *Cream Holdings Ltd v Banerjee* [2003] EWCA Civ 103. **Substitute:** *Cream Holdings Ltd v Banerjee* [2004] UKHL 44; [2005] 1 A.C. 253; [2005] E.M.L.R. 1.

NOTE 71. *Campbell v MGN Ltd* is now reported at [2004] 2 A.C. 457; [2004] E.M.L.R. 15. *Archer v Williams* is reported at [2003] E.M.L.R. 38. **Add** at end: on appeal, *Douglas v Hello! Ltd* [2005] EWCA Civ 595; [2006] Q.B. 125; [2005] E.M.L.R. 28 (CA) and [2007] UKHL 21; [2007] 2 W.L.R. 950; [2007] E.M.L.R. 12.

An amended version of the Code of Practice was ratified by the Press Complaints Commission on August 3, 2006. The paragraphs extracted in *A v B* now read as follows (there is little substantive change):

3. *Privacy*. (i) Everyone is entitled to respect for his or her private and family life, home, health and correspondence, including digital communications. Editors will be expected to justify intrusions into any individual's private life without consent. (ii) It is unacceptable to photograph individuals in a private place without their consent. *Note—Private places are public or private property where there is a reasonable expectation of privacy.*

4. *Harassment* ... (ii) [Journalists] must not persist in questioning, telephoning, pursuing or photographing individuals once asked to desist; nor remain on their property when asked to leave and must not follow them.

Public interest. 1. The public interest includes, but is not confined to: (i) Detecting or exposing crime or serious impropriety. (ii) Protecting public health and safety. (iii) Preventing the public from being misled by an action or statement of an individual or organisation.

American Cyanamid: Adequacy of damages. NOTE 74. The reference to "IVS Technologies" should be to "IBS Technologies". *Vollers Corset Co Ltd v Cook* is now reported at [2004] E.C.D.R. 28.   **22–131**

Add: Damages were held to be an adequate remedy in the database case of *Planet Ace Ltd v Hendon Mob*, Evans-Lombe J., February 4, 2005, Lawtel document no. AC9100604.

American Cyanamid: Balance of convenience. NOTE 80. *Vollers Corset Co Ltd v Cook* is now reported at [2004] E.C.D.R. 28.   **22–132**

The time factor. In *Play it Ltd v Digital Bridges Ltd* [2005] EWHC 1001 (Ch) and in *Global Coal Ltd v ICAP Energy Ltd* [2006] EWCA Civ 167, the claimants had discovered the infringements at about the time they commenced and began   **22–135**

proceedings expeditiously. In each case, the status quo was taken to be the period immediately before the commencement of the infringement.

22–137   **Cross-undertaking in damages.** NOTE 9. **Add:** See, however, *R v The Medecines Control Agency, ex p. Smith & Nephew Pharmaceuticals Ltd (Primecrown Limited Intervening)* [1999] R.P.C. 705 at 714, suggesting that the measure of damages based on a notional breach of contract may be too narrow.

Add: The benefit of the cross-undertaking may as a matter of discretion be expressly extended to third parties unconnected with the dispute who may incur expenditure in complying with the order or may otherwise be affected by it. However, in the absence of such express provision, such a third party has no claim in restitution against a claimant who has been enriched at the third party's expense by reason of the existence of the injunction. There is also no basis on which the party who has been "wrongfully" injuncted can claim damages on behalf of such a third party, nor can the benefit of the cross-undertaking be extended to such a third party by an estoppel. See *Smithkline Beecham plc v Apotex Europe Ltd* [2006] EWCA Civ 658.

(ii) Search (formerly Anton Piller) orders

22–141   **Search orders.** NOTE 31. **Delete** and **substitute:** The standard form makes specific reference to the privilege against self-incrimination. Para.8.4 of PD25 formerly stated that since there was no privilege against self-incrimination in Intellectual Property cases (see para.22–147 of the Main Work), any references to incrimination in the order should be removed. In *O Ltd v Z* [2005] EWHC 238 (Ch), a search order complied with this requirement. As the Judge (Lindsay J.) pointed out (at para.7), the Practice Direction failed to recognise that an intellectual property case search order might nonetheless incriminate in ways which are not covered by s.72 of the Supreme Court Act 1981. In that case, the search revealed paedophile pornography of a serious nature. It was held that the defendant had waived his privilege against self-incrimination in respect of this material by failing to claim it before it came into the hands of the computer expert engaged in the search (para.71) and the court gave permission for the material to be handed over to the police (para 81). The Judge went on to suggest (amongst other things) that the standard form of search order should be modified to refer to the privilege against self-incrimination in respect of matters not covered by s.72 (para.88(1)). This has now been done (CPR Update 40, September 29, 2005). Para.7.9 of PD 25 now states that there is no privilege against self-incrimination in certain instances, including in Intellectual Property cases in respect of a "related offence" or for the recovery of a "related penalty" as defined in s.72 (for the meaning of the term "related offence" see para.22–147 of the Main Work). Para.7.9 goes on to point out that the privilege may still be claimed as regards potential criminal proceedings outside those statutory provisions. There is no longer any requirement for the references in the order to incrimination to be removed. See also *C plc v P* [2006] EWHC 1226 (Ch). The facts were similar but the defendant by his solicitor indicated his intention to rely on the privilege against self-incrimination before handing over any material and the material was then retained by the Supervising Solicitor pending the determination of the defendant's right to make that claim. On those facts, the defendant was held not to have waived any privilege: the material had remained in the possession of the court through its officers (para.15). However, the Judge went on to hold that since the coming into force of the Human Rights Act the privilege was limited to "testimonial evidence, oral and written" and accordingly did not apply to the material in question, which was "free standing evidence which was not created by the respondent to the search order under compulsion" (para.82). The claimant was released from its implied undertaking so that the material could be passed to the police (para.83). The defendant's appeal was dismissed but on the basis that the privilege against self-incrimination in civil cases had never extended to "independent" evidence: *C Plc v P* [2007] EWCA Civ 493; [2007] 3 W.L.R. 437.

NOTE 38. *Elvee Ltd v Taylor* is reported at [2002] F.S.R. 48.

(iii) Identity of infringers

General. NOTE 42. *Ashworth Hospital Authority v MGN Ltd* [2002] UKHL 29 is   **22–142** reported at [2002] 1 W.L.R. 2033; [2002] E.M.L.R. 36 and [2003] F.S.R. 17. *Financial Times Ltd v Interbrew SA* [2002] EWCA Civ 274 is reported at [2002] E.M.L.R. 24 and [2002] 2 Ll. Rep. 229.

Conditions. NOTE 48. *Ashworth Hospital Authority v MGN Ltd* [2002] UKHL   **22–143** 29 is reported at [2002] 1 W.L.R. 2033; [2002] E.M.L.R. 36 and [2003] F.S.R. 17. *Financial Times Ltd v Interbrew SA* [2002] EWCA Civ 274 is reported at [2002] E.M.L.R. 24 and [2002] 2 Ll. Rep. 229.

Add: In *Mitsui & Co Ltd v Nexen Petroleum UK Ltd* [2005] EWHC 625 (Ch) at paragraph 24. Lightman J. held that where the respondent is innocent of any participation in the wrongdoing, the remedy is one of last resort, only to be exercised if there is no other practicable means of obtaining the information.

Section 10 of the Contempt of Court Act 1981. NOTES 62 and 64–67. *Ashworth*   **22–146** *Hospital Authority v MGN Ltd* [2002] UKHL 29 is reported at [2002] 1 W.L.R. 2033; [2002] E.M.L.R. 36 and [2003] F.S.R. 17.

NOTE 68. *Merseycare NHS Trust v Ackroyd* [2003] EWCA Civ 663 is reported at [2003] E.M.L.R. 36.

NOTE 69. **Add:** In the event, disclosure was refused at trial: *Mersey Care NHS Trust v Ackroyd* [2006] EWHC QB 107; [2006] E.M.L.R. 12. This decision was upheld on appeal: *Mersey Care NHS Trust v Ackroyd* [2007] EWCA Civ 101; [2007] H.R.L.R. 19.

C. FINAL RELIEF

(i) Declaratory judgment

In *Point Solutions Ltd v Focus Business Solutions Ltd*, Focus had alleged that   **22–149** Point had infringed its copyright in computer software. Point commenced proceedings for a declaration of non-infringement, claiming independent design. Focus did not raise a positive case of copying, simply putting Point to proof of its case. No evidence (expert or otherwise) was adduced as to the software in issue. The claim was dismissed, primarily because the Judge found that Focus had failed to prove independent design, but also because there was no evidence that the allegations had caused damage and because a declaration would prevent Focus from alleging infringement in proceedings where all the evidence was available ([2005] EWHC 3096; [2006] F.S.R. 31). On appeal ([2007] EWCA Civ 14), no criticism was made of the Judge's failure to address copying and her decision as to independent design was upheld. The Court of Appeal also stated (*obiter*) that it was not persuaded that the Judge had been wrong to hold that there was no need for a declaration in the absence of damage but criticised the suggestion that a declaration would shut Focus out of proceedings—Focus had chosen not to adduce further evidence.

On the face of it this is an odd decision: Focus had effectively succeeded in shifting the burden of proof on to Point (the presumption of coping derived from substantial similarity together with access did not apply on the evidence). The

Court of Appeal canvassed two possible approaches a Court might take in such circumstances. First, it might put the party in Focus's position to an election, requiring it either to make a positive case as to infringement or to limit the issue at trial to the question whether an allegation of infringement had been made (described as a "put up or shut up" order) [34]. Alternatively, it was suggested, a Judge should be slow to allow a case to come to trial where the parties had failed to adduce the evidence necessary to resolve the real issue between them [47].

As to the continued need for caution in granting declarations of non-infringement, see *Nokia Corporation v InterDigital Technology Corporation* [2006] EWCA Civ 1618; [2007] F.S.R. 23 at [31].

(ii) Permanent injunction

22–150   **General.** NOTE 86. *Ludlow Music Inc v Williams* is reported at [2002] F.S.R 57 and [2002] E.M.L.R. 29.

NOTE 90. In *Landor and Hawa International Ltd v Azure Designs Ltd* [2006] EWCA Civ 1285; [2007] F.S.R. 9; [2006] E.C.D.R. 31, the defendant disputed the claimant's design rights and indicated that it would counterclaim for threats but gave contractual undertakings. Proceedings were issued claiming an injunction and other relief. The defendant maintained its position but then withdrew its undertakings in terms that made it clear that it intended to infringe. The Court of Appeal upheld the Judge's grant of an injunction but only on the basis that the undertakings had been withdrawn [48]. The defendant argued that no injunction should have been granted because at the date proceedings were issued there was no basis for injunctive relief. This argument was rejected. The Court stated that in general the courts take a pragmatic, case by case approach to the question whether it is appropriate to seek an injunction [50]. In view of the combination of the denials and the threats counterclaim, the claimant had been justified in issuing proceedings for an injunction even though in doing so it took a chance (which paid off) that an injunction would be refused with an appropriate costs order [52]. Moreover, on the defendant's argument, in order to have obtained the injunction to which it was entitled the claimant would have had to incur the extra cost of amending or reissuing new proceedings. This was inconsistent with the overriding objective [53].

22–151   **Damages in lieu.** In *Regan v Paul Properties Ltd* [2006] EWCA Civ 1319; [2007] Ch. 135 at [36], Mummery L.J. (with whom Tuckey L.J. and Wilson L.J. agreed) summarised the effect of Shelfer in the following propositions:

(1) A claimant is prima facie entitled to an injunction against a person committing a wrongful act which invades the claimant's legal right.

(2) The wrongdoer is not entitled to ask the court to sanction his wrongdoing by purchasing the claimant's rights on payment of damages assessed by the court.

(3) The court has jurisdiction to award damages instead of an injunction, but the jurisdiction does not mean that the court is "a tribunal for legalising wrongful acts" by a defendant who is able and willing to pay damages.

(4) The judicial discretion to award damages in lieu should pay attention to well settled principles and should not be exercised to deprive a claimant of his prima facie right except under very exceptional circumstances.

(5) Although it is not possible to specify all the circumstances relevant to the exercise of the discretion or to lay down rules for its exercise, it is relevant to consider the following factors: whether the injury to the claimant's legal rights is small; whether the injury can be estimated in money;

whether it can be adequately compensated by a small money payment; whether it would be oppressive to the defendant to grant an injunction; whether the claimant has shown that he only wants money; whether the conduct of the claimant renders it unjust to give him more than pecuniary relief; and whether there are any other circumstances which justified the refusal of an injunction.

The Court of Appeal went on to hold that there is no burden on the holder of the right in question to persuade the court that he should not be left to a remedy in damages [60].

The observations of Mummery L.J. should be compared with those of Lloyd L.J. (with whom Buxton L.J. and Rix L.J. agreed) in *Jacklin v Chief Constable of West Yorkshire* [2007] EWCA Civ 181 at [48]: "the *Shelfer* principles are only a working rule, although a long hallowed and reliable working rule, but it is clear that the four elements ... are cumulative and that it is necessary for a defendant to satisfy the first three, but that it is by no means sufficient for it to do so. There has to be some additional factor, characterised in *Shelfer* and in *Jaggard v Sawyer* as oppression, to justify withholding the injunctive remedy, which is the claimant's prima facie right as ancillary to his property rights."

NOTE 93. **Add:** In *Navitaire Inc v easyJet Airline Co Ltd (No.2)* [2005] EWHC 0282 (Ch); [2006] R.P.C. 4 at para.104, Pumfrey J. held that the grant of an injunction would be "oppressive" if it would be "grossly disproportionate to the right protected".

Public policy, public interest and privacy cases. NOTE 4. The reference to   **22–154**
Douglas v Hello! Ltd should be to [2003] EWHC 786 (Ch), reported at [2003] 1 All E.R. 1087 and [2003] E.M.L.R. 31. *Archer v Williams* is reported at [2003] E.M.L.R. 38.

Scope of injunction: acts in respect of existing rights. NOTE 12. **Add:** See also   **22–157**
Sun Microsystems Inc v Amtec Computer Corporation Ltd [2006] EWHC 62 (Ch); [2006] F.S.R. 35 (trade marks; injunction limited to parallel imports and including provisions exonerating defendant if it had checked with the claimant first and had no knowledge or belief that it was infringing).

(iv) Damages

General. Regulation 3 of the Enforcement Regulations provides as follows: **22–162**

"(1) Where in an action for infringement of an intellectual property right the defendant knew, or had reasonable grounds to know, that he engaged in infringing activity, the damages awarded to the claimant shall be appropriate to the actual prejudice he suffered as a result of the infringement.

(2) When awarding such damages—

(a) all appropriate aspects shall be taken into account, including in particular—

(i) the negative economic consequences, including any lost profits, which the claimant has suffered, and any unfair profits made by the defendant; and

(ii) elements other than economic factors, including the moral prejudice caused to the claimant by the infringement; or

(b) where appropriate, they may be awarded on the basis of the royalties or fees which would have been due had the defendant obtained a licence.

(3) This regulation does not affect the operation of any enactment or rule of law relating to remedies for the infringement of intellectual property rights except to the extent that it is inconsistent with the provisions of this regulation."

The purpose of regulation 3 is to implement Article 13(1) of the Enforcement Directive, which it reproduces in substantially identical terms. According to the Explanatory Memorandum to the Enforcement Regulations, because Article 13(1) contains a number of terms the meaning of which is unclear, such as "actual prejudice" and "moral prejudice", the Government decided to adopt a "copy out approach". The purpose of regulation 3(3) was "to avoid the implication that Article 13(1) provides a complete code that displaces the national law of damages (in particular any suggestion that it introduces punitive damages)".

Regulation 3(2) involves two alternative measures of damages: the first takes "all appropriate aspects" into account. The second involves the assessment of damages "where appropriate" on the user principle (which is discussed in para. 22–163 of the Main Work). There is no guidance in the Regulation as to where it would be appropriate for damages to be assessed on the alternative basis. However, Recital (24) to the Enforcement Directive suggests that the alternative measure would be appropriate "for example where it would be difficult to determine the amount of actual prejudice suffered". Presumably, the existence of alternative measures of damages would not invalidate a result like that in the *Blayney* case (see para.22–164 of the Main Work) in which in effect the terms of reg.3(2)(a) were applied to some parts of the loss while those of regulation 3(2)(b) were applied to the rest.

Obvious difficulties arise from the phrase "any unfair profits made by the defendant". It is not immediately clear why "unfair profits" should be relevant to an assessment of the "damages" which will be "appropriate" to "the actual prejudice suffered by the claimant" and which, according to Recital (26) to the Directive, are intended to be compensatory. Under the previous law a claimant could recover lost profits on sales made by the defendant which the claimant could show he would have made but for the infringement. However, such loss would seem to be included in the phrase "lost profits which the claimant has suffered". Some have argued that if, despite the fact that the award is intended to be compensatory, this part of regulation 3(2) is in fact directed at the award of an account of profits, the effect of the provision is to eliminate the obligation to elect between damages and an account of profits. However, it seems unlikely that an English court would consider it "appropriate" to take into account both damages and an account of profits: they have always been considered to be alternative remedies (see para.22–161 of the Main Work).

Other difficulties may arise from the term "moral prejudice", which is undefined. However, given the availability depending on the circumstances of aggravated and perhaps additional damages, it is not obvious that it will add a great deal to the existing law.

NOTE 46. *Reed Executive plc v Reed Business Information Ltd* [2004] EWCA Civ 159 is now reported at [2004] 1 W.L.R. 3026 and [2005] F.S.R. 3.

22–163   ***General Tire.*** NOTE 48. **Add:** In *Ultraframe (UK) Ltd v Eurocell Building Plastics Ltd* [2006] EWHC Pat 1344 the defendant had been a distributor of the claimant's products before it began to make and sell its own infringing products instead. The Judge rejected (at para.3) an argument that the claimant was not entitled to recover lost profits on sales which it was able to prove it would have made to the defendant but for the infringement.

Add at end of sixth sentence: The assessment of damages for lost profits should take account of the fact that the lost sales are of "extra production" and that only certain specific extra costs (marginal costs) would have been incurred in making the additional sales. Nevertheless, in practice, costs go up and so it may be appropriate to temper this approach in making the assessment: *Ultraframe (UK) Ltd v Eurocell Building Plastics Ltd* [2006] EWHC Pat 1344 at para.47.

NOTE 52. **Add:** See also *Brown v Mcasso Music Production Ltd* [2005] EWCC Cpwt 1 at para. 66 [2005] F.S.R. 40; [2006] E.M.L.R. 3 (permission to appeal refused: [2005] EWCA Civ 621; [2006] F.S.R. 24) and *London General Holdings Ltd v USP PLC* [2005] EWCA Civ 931; [2006] F.S.R. 6 at para.43.

General Tire **groups not exhaustive. Add** at end of fourth sentence: By the **22–164** same token, if the claimant has been forced to keep down or even reduce its prices as a result of the infringement, any resulting loss of profit is a recoverable head of damage: *Ultraframe (UK) Ltd v Eurocell Building Plastics Ltd* [2005] EWHC 2111 (Ch) at para.9(5); *Ultraframe (UK) Ltd v Eurocell Building Plastics Ltd* [2006] EWHC Pat 1344 at paras 47 and 183–185.

NOTE 59. **Add:** See also *Ultraframe (UK) Ltd v Eurocell Building Plastics Ltd* [2005] EWHC 2111 (Ch) at para.9(6).

NOTE 60. **Delete** second sentence and **substitute:** In *Phonographic Performance Ltd v Reader* [2005] EWHC 416 (Ch); [2005] E.M.L.R. 26; [2005] F.S.R. 42, it was held that the claimant could recover by way of ordinary damages the costs of "policing" an injunction where the breaches of the injunction also amounted to infringements of copyright. In *Aerospace Publishing Ltd v Thames Water Utilities Ltd* [2007] EWCA Civ 3; [2007] Bus. L.R. 726 at [86], the Court of Appeal summarised the authorities as to the recovery of internal staff costs resulting from a tort as follows. First, the fact and extent of the diversion of staff time have to be properly established. Second, the claimant has to establish that the diversion caused significant disruption to its business. Third, even though the claim should strictly be cast in terms of a loss of revenue attributable to the diversion of staff time, in the ordinary case, and unless the defendant can establish the contrary, it is reasonable for the court to infer that if their time had not been diverted, staff would have applied it to activities which would have generated revenue to the claimant in an amount at least equal to the costs of employing them during that time.

NOTE 61. *Reed Executive plc v Reed Business Information Ltd* [2004] EWCA Civ 159 is now reported at [2004] 1 W.L.R. 3026 and [2005] F.S.R. 3.

Add at end of eighth sentence: In *Douglas v Hello! Ltd* [2005] EWCA Civ 595; [2006] Q.B. 125; [2005] E.M.L.R. 28, the Court of Appeal held that it was inappropriate to assess damages for the breach of confidence on the basis of a notional licence fee, for the following reasons. First, the whole basis of the Douglases' complaint was upset and affront at invasion of privacy, for which they had been separately compensated, not the loss of the opportunity to earn money. Second, they would not have agreed to the publication. Third, they had sold the rights to *OK!* and would not have been in a position to grant a licence to *Hello!*. Finally, there were difficulties of assessment. See paras 244 to 248. The issue did not arise on appeal: [2007] UKHL 21; [2007] 2 W.L.R. 950; [2007] E.M.L.R. 12.

Limits on amount of damages. NOTE 67. **Add:** See also *London General Hold-* **22–165** *ings Ltd v USP PLC* [2005] EWCA Civ 931; [2006] F.S.R. 6: no damages where all the loss results from use of the ideas contained in a document rather than any unauthorised deployment of its text. In the Australian case of *Eagle Rock Entertainment Ltd v Caisley* [2005] FCA 1238 the defendant had made infringing master copies and provided them to third parties for manufacture of infringing copies in Brazil and Spain. The acts of making and providing the masters took place in Australia. The court granted damages for the claimant's loss of sales in these countries which (it held) was caused by the infringements in Australia.

22–166　**Practice.** NOTES 69 and 70. *Reed Executive plc v Reed Business Information Ltd* [2004] EWCA Civ 159 is now reported at [2004] 1 W.L.R. 3026 and [2005] F.S.R. 3.

(v) Additional damages

22–168　**General**. The Government is consulting on a proposal to replace the term "additional damages" in the 1988 Act with the term "aggravated and restitutionary damages". The Government believes that this will "assist in clarifying the law". See DCA Consultation Paper 9/07 The Law of Damages [211]. Given that the Court's power to award additional damages permits an "aggravation" of an award on a far wider basis than common law aggravated damages (see para.22–172 of the Main Work), the effect of such a change would be to reduce the scope of damages under section 97(2). Regulation 3 of the Enforcement Regulations (see para.22–162, above) may have a countervailing effect, but that will depend on how regulation 3 is interpreted. The Consultation Paper does not discuss the impact of regulation 3 in this respect.

22–169　**Flagrancy.** NOTE 82. **Add:** *Phonographic Performance Ltd v Reader* [2005] EWHC 416 (Ch); [2005] E.M.L.R. 26; [2005] F.S.R. 42.

Where a defendant's contempt is also an infringement of copyright, the court may well award damages (including additional damages) at the same time as it deals with the contempt. See the *Reader* case. Unless there has been a full trial, the court is likely to impose the summary judgment burden on the claimant in respect of such a damages claim: *Independiente Ltd v Music Trading On-Line (HK) Ltd* [2007] EWHC 533 (Ch) at [38].

22–171　**Can the award include a punitive element?** NOTE 89. **Add:** Put another way, an award of additional damages may contain a punitive element provided its purpose is not solely to punish the defendant: *Phonographic Performance Ltd v Reader* [2005] EWHC 416 (Ch); [2005] E.M.L.R. 26; [2005] F.S.R. 42.

22–172　**Other relevant considerations.** NOTE 6. *Ludlow Music Inc v Williams* is reported at [2002] F.S.R 57 and [2002] E.M.L.R. 29.

22–173　**Quantum.** NOTE 10. *Nottinghamshire Healthcare NHS Trust Ltd v News Group Newspapers Ltd* is reported at [2002] R.P.C. 49 and [2002] E.M.L.R. 33. See also *Phonographic Performance Ltd v Reader* [2005] EWHC 416 (Ch); [2005] E.M.L.R. 26; [2005] F.S.R. 42, another case of a 100 % "mark-up", in which the *Peninsular* case was analysed as one where a "broad brush" approach had been adopted.

NOTE 17. *MCA Records Inc v Charly Records Ltd* [2001] EWCA Civ 1441 is reported at [2002] F.S.R. 26; [2002] E.M.L.R. 1; [2002] E.C.D.R. 37.

(vii) Forfeiture

22–180　**Procedure and decision.** Line 3. **Delete:** Part II of the 1988 Act. **Substitute:** Chapter 2 of Part II of the 1988 Act (that is, the Chapter conferring economic rights in performances).

22–181　**Where more than one person interested.** NOTE 62. **Add** at end: (including that section as applied by regulation 4 of the Community Trade Mark regulations 2006, SI 2006/1027); section 24D of the Registered Designs Act 1949; and regulation 1C of the Community Design Regulations 2005 (SI 2005/2339).

(viii) Delivery up

NOTE 73. **Add:** Similar provision is made in respect of Community designs with effect from April 29, 2006 by reg.1A(2) of the Community Design Regulations 2005 (SI 2005/339), introduced by reg.2(3) of and Sch.3, para.9 to the Enforcement etc. Regulations 2006 (SI 200/1028).   **22–182**

Add: Article 10(2) of the Enforcement Directive provides that the courts shall order the measures of delivery up and destruction to be taken at the infringer's expense unless "particular reasons are invoked for not doing so". The Government has added a new paragraph 29.2 to the Practice Direction to Part 63 of the Civil Procedure Rules which states that where a delivery up or destruction order has been made in an intellectual property case, the defendant will pay the costs of compliance unless the court orders otherwise. According to the Government, this provision was introduced in the interests of clarity and because the Directive stipulates that the Court "shall order". It is difficult to conceive of a situation in which someone other than the defendant would have been ordered to pay the costs of such an exercise prior to the introduction of the new paragraph. Accordingly, it seems unlikely that it will involve any change in practice.

Add new sub-heading and paragraph:

(viii(a)) Publicity orders

Article 15 of the Enforcement Directive (see para.22–03, above) requires Member States to ensure that in proceedings for infringement of an intellectual property right the judicial authorities may order at the request of the rights holder and at the expense of the infringer appropriate measures for the dissemination of the information concerning the decision, including displaying it and publishing it in full or in part. Member States are also given a discretion to provide for other additional publicity measures which are appropriate to the particular circumstances, including prominent advertising. According to Recital (27) the object of this provision is "to act as a supplementary deterrent to future infringers and to contribute to the awareness of the public at large".   **22–182A**

No new legislation has been passed but a new paragraph 29.2 has been added to PD63 as follows: "Where the court finds that an intellectual property right has been infringed, the court may, at the request of the applicant, order appropriate measures for the dissemination and publication of the judgment to be taken at the defendant's expense." In Scotland, by contrast, specific provision has been made: see regulation 5 of the Intellectual Property (Enforcement, etc.) Regulations 2006 (SI 2006/1028).

The discretionary part of Article 15 has not been implemented.

(ix) Points as to costs

Cost of split trials. NOTE 98. **Add:** See also *Shepherds Investments Ltd v Walters* [2007] EWCA Civ 292 (where the authorities are listed) and *Hampshire County Council v Supportways Community Services Ltd* [2006] EWCA Civ 1170: enquiry made conditional on payment of percentage of adverse costs order on trial of liability; incidence of balance to be determined by court making enquiry.   **22–187**

22–188 **Costs of internal experts.** NOTE 1. *Admiral Management Services Ltd v Para Protect Europe Ltd* [2002] EWHC 233 (Ch) is reported at [2002] 1 W.L.R. 2722 and [2002] F.S.R. 59. In *Sisu Capital Fund Ltd v Tucker* [2005] EWHC 2321; [2006] F.S.R. 21, Warren J. held that the defendants could not recover as costs the costs of non-expert work carried out by their employees for the purposes of litigation. See, however, para.22–164, above.

8. PROCEDURAL AND RELATED MATTERS

B. PRE-ACTION CONDUCT

22–192 **General.** See, however, CPR Practice Direction—Competition Law—Claims Relating to the Application of Articles 81 and 82 of the EC Treaty and Chapters I and II of Part I of the Competition Act 1998. Where the claim is for breach of statutory duty (*e.g.* for infringement of moral rights or performers' non-property rights) section 2 of the Competition Act 2006 applies. Thus, an apology or other redress does not of itself amount to an admission of breach of statutory duty.

C. COMMENCEMENT OF PROCEEDINGS

22–207 **The particulars of claim. Add:** In the design right case of *Lambretta Clothing Company Ltd v Teddy Smith (UK) Ltd* [2004] EWCA Civ 886; [2005] R.P.C. 6, Jacob L.J. stated that all points of similarity (whether they form important parts of the work alleged to have been copied, unimportant parts or even something which strictly does not form part of the work sued upon) should be disclosed well in advance of trial, normally in the statements of case but at least in the witness statements. In design right cases it is important that the claimant should identify in the particulars of claim with precision each and every "design" relied on. Well-advised claimants will confine themselves to their best case "designs": *Dyson Ltd v Qualtex (UK) Ltd* [2006] EWCA Civ 166 at para.122.

D. FORM OF DEFENCE

22–208 **Add:** In principle a defendant to a design right claim will plead to each alleged design, raising challenges to originality or alleging commonplace or identifying any of the exclusions which are alleged to apply. It may be possible to limit the issues to sample issues by application even before service of the defence. If not, sample issues should be identified at a case management conference. The samples should be such as will in principle determine the whole case (as in *Sweeney v MacMillan* [2002] R.P.C. 35). Following identification of the sample issues, the parties should produce a sort of Scott schedule identifying each design relied on and the defences relied on in relation to each such design: *Dyson Ltd v Qualtex (UK) Ltd* [2006] EWCA Civ 166 at paras 122–4.

F. PRESUMPTIONS

22–210 **Introduction. Delete** third sentence and **substitute:** The presumptions contained in sections 104 to 106 of the 1988 Act do not apply in proceedings for infringement of publication right: see regulation 17(2)(b) of the Copyright and Related Rights Regulations 1996 (SI 1996/2967). However, with effect from April 29, 2006, there is a new regulation 17A of those Regulations, which was introduced by regulation 2(3) and Schedule 3, para.5 to the Intellectual Property (Enforcement etc.) Regulations 2006 (SI 2006/1028) in order to implement Article 5 of the Enforcement Directive (see para.22–03 and Vol.2, H14 of the Main Work).

Regulation 17A provides that in such proceedings where copies of a work as issued to the public bear a statement that a named person was the owner of publication right in the work at the date of issue of the copies, the statement is to be
admissible as evidence of the fact stated and to be presumed to be correct until
the contrary is proved. This presumption does not apply in criminal proceedings
for an offence but does apply in applications for delivery up in criminal proceedings: see regulation 17B.

After footnote indicator 63 **add:** and, with effect from April 29, 2006, rights in
performances.

Rights in performances. With effect from April 29, 2006, in proceedings with
respect to the rights in a performance, where copies of a recording of the performance as issued to the public bear a statement that a named person was the
performer, the statement is to be admissible as evidence of the fact stated and is
to be presumed to be correct until the contrary is proved. See CDPA 1988, section 197A(1), introduced by regulation 2(2) and 10 of Schedule 2, para.10 to the
Intellectual Property (Enforcement etc.) Regulations 2006 (SI 2006/1028) in order to implement Article 5 of the Enforcement Directive (see para.22–03 and
Vol.2, H14 of the Main Work). This presumption does not apply in criminal
proceedings for an offence but does apply in applications for delivery up in criminal proceedings: see CDPA 1988, section 197A(2). Where the performer is not
the owner of the rights, no presumptions arise. Moreover, there is no presumption
in favour of the holders of recording rights.

22–218A

G. PROOF OF COPYING

Similar fact evidence. NOTE 3. *Mattel Inc v Woolbro (Distributors) Ltd* [2003]
EWHC 2412 (Ch) is reported at [2004] F.S.R. 12. **Add:** In *O'Brien v Chief Constable of South Wales Police* [2005] UKHL 26, the House of Lords held that in a
civil case a court faced with deciding on the admissibility of similar fact evidence
must first decide whether the evidence (if true) would be logically probative or
disprobative of some matter which requires proof in the action. If so, the court
must decide whether the admission of the evidence would accord with the overriding objective of deciding cases justly.

22–222

H. EXPERT EVIDENCE

Copying. NOTE 8. **Add:** *Barrett v Universal-Island Records Ltd* [2006] EWHC
1009 (Ch).

22–223

Design right cases. As to how to avoid expert evidence mushrooming out of
proportion in such cases, see *Dyson Ltd v Qualtex (UK) Ltd* [2006] EWCA Civ
166 at para.125.

22–223A

J. PRODUCTION OF ORIGINAL WORK

NOTE 23. In *ABB Ltd v New Zealand Insulators Ltd* [2006] NZHC 1072 at
[164] it was held that this principle is equally applicable to the loss of the original
drawing when considering whether the creation of a work which was derived
from it had involved sufficient skill and labour to confer protection on the new
work. It is suggested that the same principle would apply in England and Wales.

22–227

CHAPTER TWENTY THREE

CRIMINAL REMEDIES AND CUSTOMS SEIZURE

1. CRIMINAL REMEDIES

A. HISTORICAL INTRODUCTION

23–07 **The policy of the 1988 Act.** NOTE 58. **Delete** second and third sentences and **substitute:** Ss.107A and 198A are now in force with effect from April 6, 2007. See the Criminal Justice and Public Order Act 1994 (Commencement No. 14) Order 2007 (SI 2007/621).

B. CRIMINAL OFFENCES AND PENALTIES

(i) Copyright offences

23–11 **"With a view". Add:** See also *R v Dooley* [2005] EWCA Crim 3093; [2006] 1 C.A.R. 21: a person possesses something "with a view to" X if X is one of his objectives. The case concerned possession of indecent photographs of children but the Court of Appeal expressed itself in general terms.

23–13 **Section 107(2A): communicating to the public.** NOTE 80. In the Hong Kong case of *Hksar v Chan Nai Ming* (TMCC 1268/2005) it was held that the transmission of a film to 30 or 40 downloaders using BitTorrent sofware would have prejudicially affected the owner of the copyright. See Tofalides and Fearn, "BitTorrent Copyright Infringement" [2006] 2 Ent. L.R. 81 and Low, "Tackling Online Copyright Infringers in Hong Kong" [2006] 4 Ent. L.R. 122. The issue of whether the copyright owner had been prejudiced did not arise on the defendant's appeal, which was dismissed: *HKSAR v Chan Nai Ming*, HCMA 1221/2005, Beeson J.

23–16 **Trap purchases.** NOTE 15. *R v Loosely* is reported at [2002] 1 W.L.R. 2060. The reference to *Blackstone's Criminal Practice* should now be to para.F2.17 of the 2006 edition.

23–19 **Sentencing for offences committed after November 20, 2002.** NOTE 37. *R v Passley* is reported at [2004] 1 C.A.R. (S.) 419. Contrast the trade mark case of *R* *v Sheikh*, April 27, 2005: the Court of Appeal upheld a sentence of 12 months' imprisonment for a teacher who was of good character who had pleaded guilty to the wholesale sale of mobile phone accessories including counterfeit covers. The sentence was in the context of a confiscation order of £84,548 and an order that the defendant pay prosecution costs of £25,000. The defendant would have to sell his house to pay these sums. In another trade mark case, *R v Wooldridge* [2006] 1 C.A.R. (S.) 13, the defendant had made, decorated and supplied counterfeit pottery making a profit of £4,000 over a period of 10 months. He was charged with trade mark offences. A sentence of nine months' immediate imprisonment was upheld on the grounds (amongst others) that a sentence for trade mark offences has to contain some element of deterrence especially because such crimes are difficult, time consuming and expensive to detect.

(ii) Offences in relation to rights in performances under the 1988 Act

Offences of making, dealing with and using illicit recordings under section   **23–23**
198 of the 1988 Act. Line 8. **Delete:** Part II of the 1988 Act. **Substitute:** Chapter 2 of Part II of the 1988 Act (that is, the Chapter conferring economic rights in performances).
   NOTE 52. **Delete** first sentence.
   Line 17. **Delete:** Part II of the 1988 Act. **Substitute:** Chapter 2 of Part II of the 1988 Act (that is, the Chapter conferring economic rights in performances).

Comparison with civil provisions. NOTE 76. The reference to *Blackstone's*   **23–24**
Criminal Practice should now be to para.A8.2 of the 2006 edition.

Liability of officers. Line 1. After "section 198", **add:** or section 201.   **23–28**

False representations of authorisation. Line 3. **Delete:** Part II of the 1988 Act.   **23–29**
Substitute: Chapter 2 of Part II of the 1988 Act (that is, the Chapter conferring economic rights in performances).

Defences. Line 3. **Delete:** Part II of the 1988 Act. **Substitute:** Chapter 2 of Part   **23–30**
II of the 1988 Act (that is, the Chapter conferring economic rights in performances).

(iii) Some other relevant offences

Incitement. NOTE 2. The reference to *Blackstone's Criminal Practice* should   **23–32**
now be to para.A6.1 *et seq.* of the 2006 edition.

Theft and deception. NOTE 27. The reference to *Blackstone's Criminal Practice*   **23–36**
should now be to para.B4.39 *et seq.* of the 2006 edition.

C. SOME PROCEDURAL MATTERS

(ii) Enforcement methods

The proposed new sections 107A and 198A. Delete last three sentences exclud-   **23–41**
ing NOTE 44 and **substitute:** Sections 107A and 198A are now in force with effect from April 6, 2007. See the Criminal Justice and Public Order Act 1994 (Commencement No. 14) Order 2007 (SI 2007/621). In very exceptional cases, a local authority's decision to prosecute may be the subject of a judicial review: *R (Butler) v Wychavon District Council* [2006] EWHC 2977 (Admin).
   NOTE 44. *R v Adaway* [2004] EWCA Crim 2831, is reported at (2004) 168 J.P. 645.

23–43 **Private prosecution.** NOTE 55. See *R (Ewing) v Davis* [2007] EWHC 1730 (Admin) for the general proposition that anyone can prosecute an offence under a public general act.

NOTE 57. The reference to *Blackstone's Criminal Practice* should now be to para.D5.4 of the 2006 edition. Where the Crown Prosecution Service has brought and discontinued proceedings in respect of an alleged offence, no special rules apply to the Magistrates' decision whether to issue a summons in respect of the same allegations at the behest of a private prosecutor. By contrast, if a Crown Prosecution Service prosecution is already on foot, the Magistrates should be slow to issue such a summons. See *R (Charlson) v Guildford Magistrates' Court* [2006] EWHC 2318 (Admin); [2006] 1 W.L.R. 3494; (2006) 170 J.P. 739; [2007] R.T.R. 1 at [36].

NOTE 60. *R v Adaway* [2004] EWCA Crim 2831, is reported at (2004) 168 J.P. 645. The reference to *Archbold* should now be to para.4–48 *et seq.* of the 2006 edition.

(iii) Choice of remedy

23–44 **Advantages of criminal proceedings.** NOTE 62. *Nottinghamshire Healthcare NHS Trust Ltd v News Group Newspapers Ltd* is reported at [2002] R.P.C. 49 and [2002] E.M.L.R. 33.

23–45 **Disadvantages of criminal proceedings.** NOTE 68. The reference to *Blackstone's Criminal Practice* should now be to para.E18.1 of the 2006 edition.

NOTES 72 and 77. The references to Appendices 6 and 2 of *Blackstone's Criminal Practice* should now be to the corresponding appendices of the 2006 edition.

(iv) Search warrants under the 1988 Act

23–48 **Effect of warrants.** Sixth sentence and NOTE 97. **Delete** and **substitute:** Warrants issued since January 1, 2006 remain in force for three months from the date of their issue: CDPA 1988, section 109(3)(b) and 200(3)(b) as amended by the Serious and Organised Crime and Police Act 2005 (c.15), Schedule 16, paragraph 6.

(vi) Forfeiture in criminal proceedings

23–51 **General provisions as to forfeiture.** NOTE 17. The reference to *Blackstone's Criminal Practice* should now be to para.E20.2 of the 2006 edition.

(vii) The burden of proof

23–58 **Introduction.** NOTE 37. The reference to *Blackstone's Criminal Practice* should now be to para.F3.17 of the 2006 edition.

NOTE 39. **Add:** See also *DPP v Hay* [2005] EWHC Admin 1395.

NOTE 43 should read: See para.23–63, below.

NOTE 44 should read: See para.23–64, below.

NOTE 45 should read: See para.23–22, above.

CHAPTER TWENTY FOUR

INTERNATIONAL TREATIES

2. THE BERNE CONVENTION AND ITS REVISIONS

A. HISTORY

24–04   **Early treaties.** NOTE 11. **Delete** and **substitute:** S. Ricketson and J.C. Ginsburg, *International Copyright and Neighbouring Rights, The Berne Convention and Beyond* (2nd ed., Oxford University Press, 2006), para.1.29 *et seq.*

NOTE 12. **Delete** and **substitute:** S. Ricketson and J.C. Ginsburg, *International Copyright and Neighbouring Rights, The Berne Convention and Beyond* (2nd ed., Oxford University Press, 2006), para.1.30 *et seq.*

NOTE 15. **Delete** and **substitute:** S. Ricketson and J.C. Ginsburg, *International Copyright and Neighbouring Rights, The Berne Convention and Beyond* (2nd ed., Oxford University Press, 2006), para.1.30 *et seq.*

24–05   **Berne Convention.** NOTE 16. **Delete** and **substitute:** S. Ricketson and J.C. Ginsburg, *International Copyright and Neighbouring Rights, The Berne Convention and Beyond* (2nd ed., Oxford University Press, 2006), para.2.19 *et seq.* and para.2.38 *et seq.*

NOTE 17. **Add:** S. Ricketson and J.C. Ginsburg, *International Copyright and Neighbouring Rights, The Berne Convention and Beyond* (2nd ed., Oxford University Press, 2006).

24–06   **Additional Act of Paris 1896.** NOTE 20. **Delete** and **substitute:** S. Ricketson and J.C. Ginsburg, *International Copyright and Neighbouring Rights, The Berne Convention and Beyond* (2nd ed., Oxford University Press, 2006), paras 3.02 to 3.07 *et seq.*

24–07   **The revised Berne Convention of Berlin 1908.** NOTE 23. **Delete** and **substitute:** S. Ricketson and J.C. Ginsburg, *International Copyright and Neighbouring Rights, The Berne Convention and Beyond* (2nd ed., Oxford University Press, 2006), paras 3.08 to 3.20 *et seq.*

24–08   **Rome and Brussels Acts.** NOTE 28. **Add:** S. Ricketson and J.C. Ginsburg, *International Copyright and Neighbouring Rights, The Berne Convention and Beyond* (2nd ed., Oxford University Press, 2006), paras 3.22 to 3.32.

NOTE 31. **Delete** and **substitute:** S. Ricketson and J.C. Ginsburg, *International Copyright and Neighbouring Rights, The Berne Convention and Beyond* (2nd ed., Oxford University Press, 2006), para.3.33 *et seq.*

NOTE 35. Second sentence. **Delete** and **substitute:** S. Ricketson and J.C. Ginsburg, *International Copyright and Neighbouring Rights, The Berne Convention and Beyond* (2nd ed., Oxford University Press, 2006), para.3.31.

Stockholm Act. NOTE 37. **Add:** See also S. Ricketson and J.C. Ginsburg, *International Copyright and Neighbouring Rights, The Berne Convention and Beyond* (2nd ed., Oxford University Press, 2006), paras 3.49 to 3.67.

24–09

B. SUBSTANTIVE PROVISIONS OF PARIS ACT

The 3-step test of the Berne Convention. NOTE 86. **Add:** But see also: S. Ricketson and J.C. Ginsburg, *International Copyright and Neighbouring Rights, The Berne Convention and Beyond* (2nd ed., Oxford University Press, 2006), para.13.12 *et seq.* See also K.J. Koelman, "Fixing the Three-step Test" [2006] E.I.P.R. 28(8), 407–412.

24–33

"Droit de suite" **(Artist's Resale Right).** Last two sentences. **Delete** and **substitute:** However, the situation has changed following the adoption on September 27, 2001, of the Directive of the European Parliament and of the Council on the resale right for the benefit of the author of an original work of art by the European Parliament and Council of the European Communities after many years of negotiation.[1] According to the Directive, Member States were obliged to bring their domestic laws into conformity by January 1, 2006. Accordingly, the UK Government implemented the Directive by the introduction of The Artist's Resale Right Regulations 2006.[2]

24–44

NOTE 16. **Delete** and **substitute:** The Commission of the European Communities first presented a proposal for a European Parliament and Council Directive on the resale right for the benefit of an original work of art (document COM(96) 97 final) on March 13, 1996. Finally adopted on September 27, 2001, the Directive entered into force on October 13, 2001 ([2001] O.J. L272/32, October 13, 2001). For more information on this Directive see Ch.25, para.25–72 *et seq.,* below, and Appendix H.12, below. For the implementation of the Directive in the UK, see Ch.19A, above.

C. ADMINISTRATIVE PROVISIONS AND FINAL CLAUSES OF PARIS ACT

Administrative provisions and final clauses. NOTE 29. **Add:** See also S. Ricketson and J.C. Ginsburg, *International Copyright and Neighbouring Rights, The Berne Convention and Beyond* (2nd ed., Oxford University Press, 2006), paras 16.12 and 16.49.

24–49

D. STOCKHOLM PROTOCOL REGARDING DEVELOPING COUNTRIES

Protocol. NOTE 33. Add: See also S. Ricketson and J.C. Ginsburg, *International Copyright and Neighbouring Rights, The Berne Convention and Beyond* (2nd ed., Oxford University Press, 2006), para.14.18 *et seq.*

24–50

G. ENTRY INTO FORCE OF PARIS ACT

Ratification or Accession. First paragraph. **Delete** and **substitute**: As of July 31, 2007, the following countries have ratified or acceded to the whole of the Paris Act including the Appendix: Albania, Algeria, Andorra, Antigua and Barbuda,

24–64

---

[1] Directive 2001/84/EC.
[2] SI 2006/346 of February 13, 2006.

Argentina, Armenia, Australia, Austria, Azerbaijan, Bahrain, Bangladesh, Barbados, Belarus, Belgium, Belize, Benin, Bhutan, Bolivia, Bosnia and Herzegovina, Botswana, Brazil, Brunei Darussalam, Bulgaria, Burkina Faso, Cameroon, Canada, Cape Verde, Central African Republic, Chile, China,[3] Colombia, Comoros, Congo, Costa Rica, Côte d'Ivoire, Croatia, Cuba, Cyprus, Czech Republic, Democratic People's Republic of Korea, Democratic Republic of the Congo, Denmark, Djibouti, Dominica, Dominican Republic, Ecuador, Egypt, El Salvador, Equatorial Guinea, Estonia, Finland, France, Gabon, Gambia, Georgia, Germany, Ghana, Greece, Grenada, Guatemala, Guinea, Guinea-Bissau, Guyana, Haiti, Holy See, Honduras, Hungary, Iceland, India, Indonesia, Ireland, Israel, Italy, Jamaica, Japan, Jordan, Kazakhstan, Kenya, Kyrgyzstan, Latvia, Lesotho, Liberia, Libyan Arab Jamahiriya, Liechtenstein, Lithuania, Luxembourg, Malawi, Malaysia, Mali, Mauritania, Mauritius, Mexico, Micronesia (Federated States of), Monaco, Mongolia, Montenegro, Morocco, Namibia, Nepal, Netherlands (for the Kingdom in Europe only), Nicaragua, Niger, Nigeria, Norway, Oman, Panama, Paraguay, Peru, Philippines, Poland, Portugal, Qatar, Republic of Korea, Republic of Moldova, Romania, Russian Federation, Rwanda, Saint Kitts and Nevis, Saint Lucia, Saint Vincent and the Grenadines, Samoa, Saudi Arabia, Senegal, Serbia (Republic of), Singapore, Slovakia (Slovak Republic), Slovenia, Spain, Sri Lanka, Sudan, Suriname, Swaziland, Sweden, Switzerland, Syrian Arab Republic, Tajikistan, Thailand, The former Yugoslav Republic of Macedonia, Togo, Tonga, Trinidad and Tobago, Tunisia, Turkey, Ukraine, United Arab Emirates, United Kingdom (with the Isle of Man), United Republic of Tanzania, United States of America, Uruguay, Uzbekistan, Venezuela (Bolivarian Republic of), Viet Nam and Zambia.

Second paragraph. **Delete** and **substitute**: The following countries have now ratified or acceded to the Paris Act, other than Articles 1 to 21 and the Appendix, by reason of having made a declaration under Article 28(1)(b): Bahamas, Malta, South Africa and Zimbabwe. Articles 22 to 38 of the Paris Act apply also to the Netherlands Antilles and Aruba.

Third paragraph. **Delete** and **substitute**: Algeria, Bahamas, Cuba, Democratic People's Republic of Korea, Egypt, Guatemala, India, Indonesia, Israel, Italy, Jordan, Lesotho, Liberia, Libyan Arab Jamahiriya, Lithuania, Malta, Mauritius, Mongolia, Nepal, Oman, Saint Lucia, South Africa, Thailand, Tunisia, Turkey, United Republic of Tanzania, Venezuela (Bolivarian Republic of) and Viet Nam have made declarations that they do not consider themselves bound by Article 33(1) concerning the settlement of disputes by the International Court of Justice. Bosnia and Herzegovina, Cyprus, Montenegro, Serbia and Slovenia have made reservations concerning the right of translation. Portugal has declared that its ratification shall not apply to Article 14*bis*(2)(c) to the effect that the undertaking by authors to bring contributions to the making of a cinematographic work must be in a written agreement. India has made a declaration under Article 14*bis*(2)(b) (presumption of legitimation for some authors who have brought contributions to the making of the cinematographic work). Algeria, Bahrain, Bangladesh, Cuba, Democratic People's Republic of Korea, Jordan, Mongolia and Singapore availed themselves of one or both of the faculties provided for in Articles II and III of the Appendix until October 10, 2004. Bangladesh, Cuba, Jordan, Mongolia, Oman, Philippines, Samoa, Sri Lanka, Sudan, Syrian Arab Republic, Thailand, United Arab Emirates, Uzbekistan and Viet Nam have availed themselves of one or both of the faculties provided for in Arts. II and III of the Appendix until October 10, 2014. The United Kingdom, Germany and Norway have declared that they admit the application of the Appendix of the Paris Act to works of which they are the

---

[3] The Paris Act applies also to the Hong Kong and Macau Special Administrative Regions.

State of origin by States which have made a declaration under Article VI(1)(i) of the Appendix or a notification under Article 1 of the Appendix.

H. PRESENT MEMBERS OF THE COPYRIGHT UNION

Countries forming the Copyright Union. Delete and **substitute**: As of July 31 2007,[4] the following 163 countries form the Copyright Union: Albania, Algeria, Andorra, Antigua and Barbuda, Argentina, Armenia, Australia, Austria, Azerbaijan, Bahamas, Bahrain, Bangladesh, Barbados, Belarus, Belgium, Belize, Benin, Bhutan, Bolivia, Bosnia and Herzegovina, Botswana, Brazil, Brunei Darussalam, Bulgaria, Burkina Faso, Cameroon, Canada, Cape Verde, Central African Republic, Chad, Chile, China (China extended the application of the Paris Act of the Berne Convention to Hong Kong from July 1, 1997, and to Macao from December 20, 1999), Colombia, Comoros, Congo, Costa Rica, Côte d'Ivoire, Croatia, Cuba, Cyprus, Czech Republic, Democratic People's Republic of Korea, Democratic Republic of the Congo, Denmark, Djibouti, Dominica, Dominican Republic, Ecuador, Egypt, El Salvador, Equatorial Guinea, Estonia, Fiji, Finland, France (including overseas territories and the territorial entity of Mayotte), Gabon, Gambia, Georgia, Germany,[5] Ghana, Greece, Grenada, Guatemala, Guinea, Guinea-Bissau, Guyana, Haiti, Holy See, Honduras, Hungary, Iceland, India, Indonesia, Ireland, Israel, Italy, Jamaica, Japan, Jordan, Kazakhstan, Kenya, Kyrgyzstan (Kyrgyz Republic), Latvia, Lebanon (Lebanese Republic), Lesotho, Liberia, Libyan Arab Jamahiriya, Liechtenstein, Lithuania, Luxembourg, Madagascar, Malawi, Malaysia, Mali, Malta, Mauritania, Mauritius, Mexico, Micronesia (Federated States of), Monaco, Mongolia, Montenegro, Morocco, Namibia, Nepal, Netherlands, New Zealand, Nicaragua, Niger, Nigeria, Norway, Oman, Pakistan, Panama, Paraguay, Peru, Philippines, Poland, Portugal, Qatar, Republic of Korea, Republic of Moldova, Romania, Russian Federation, Rwanda, Saint Kitts and Nevis, Saint Lucia, Saint Vincent and the Grenadines, Samoa, Saudi Arabia, Senegal, Serbia, Singapore, Slovakia (Slovak Republic), Slovenia, South Africa, Spain, Sri Lanka, Sudan, Suriname, Swaziland, Sweden, Switzerland, Syrian Arab Republic, Tajikistan, Thailand, The former Yugoslav Republic of Macedonia, Togo, Tonga, Trinidad and Tobago, Tunisia, Turkey, Ukraine, United Arab Emirates, United Kingdom,[6] United Republic of Tanzania, United States of America (including the territories of American Samoa, Guam, the Northern Mariana Islands, Puerto Rico and the U.S. Virgin Islands), Uruguay, Uzbekistan, Venezuela (Bolivarian Republic of), Viet Nam, Zambia and Zimbabwe.

24–65

3. THE WIPO COPYRIGHT TREATY 1996

C. SIGNATORIES AND ENTRY INTO FORCE

Parties to the Treaty. Penultimate paragraph on page 1198. **Delete** and **substitute:** As of July 31, 2007, the following 64 countries had ratified or acceded to

24–75

---

[4] The situation is constantly changing and the current position can be obtained by consulting the World Intellectual Property Organization website: *http://www.wipo.int.treaties.*

[5] The Treaty of Union of August 31, 1990 (BGBL, 1990, Part II, 885 *et seq.*) between the former Federal Republic of Germany and the former German Democratic Republic, which effected the reunification of Germany, provided that, in the case of copyright, the law of the former Federal Republic of Germany (*i.e.* the Copyright Law of September 9, 1965, as amended), was to apply in the territory of the former German Democratic Republic with effect from October 3, 1990.

[6] The UK extended the application of the Paris Act of the Berne Convention to the Isle of Man with effect from March 18, 1996.

the Treaty: Albania, Argentina, Armenia, Australia, Azerbaijan, Bahrain, Belarus, Belgium, Benin, Botswana, Bulgaria, Burkina Faso, Chile, China, Colombia, Costa Rica, Croatia, Cyprus, Czech Republic, Dominican Republic, Ecuador, El Salvador, Gabon, Georgia, Ghana, Guatemala, Guinea, Honduras, Hungary, Indonesia, Jamaica, Japan, Jordan, Kazakhstan, Kyrgyzstan (Kyrgyz Republic), Latvia, Liechtenstein, Lithuania, Mali, Mexico, Mongolia, Montenegro, Nicaragua, Oman, Panama, Paraguay, Peru, Philippines, Poland, Qatar, Republic of Korea, Republic of Moldova, Romania, Saint Lucia, Senegal, Serbia (Republic of), Singapore, Slovakia (Slovak Republic), Slovenia, The former Yugoslav Republic of Macedonia, Togo, Ukraine, United Arab Emirates, United States of America.

D. PENDING ISSUES NOT ADDRESSED BY THE TREATY

24–78 **Databases.** Last sentence. **Delete** and **substitute:** Meanwhile, the issue has been discussed repeatedly under the auspices of WIPO, but to date no consensus on the need for or contents of a new international instrument on the subject has emerged and in 2005 it was decided to drop the matter for the time being.

NOTE 74. **Add:** In 2005, the WIPO Standing Committee for Copyright and Related Rights (SCCR) decided that the item would in future be put on the agenda only at the request of the Member States (SCCR/13/6 Prov., para.186).

4. THE UNIVERSAL COPYRIGHT CONVENTION AND ITS REVISION

A. HISTORY

24–80 **Object of Convention.** Last sentence. **Delete** and **substitute:** As of July 31, 2007, by contrast, the Berne Union comprises 163 Member States as compared with the100 Member States of the UCC (Geneva and Paris Acts). Since the publication of the Main Work, Montenegro has adhered to the Paris Act of the UCC.

D. ENTRY INTO FORCE OF THE 1952 AND 1971 CONVENTIONS

24–86 **Ratification or accession. Delete** and **substitute:** The following 65 countries have now ratified or acceded to the 1971 Convention as of July 31, 2007. Albania, Algeria, Australia, Austria, Bahamas, Bangladesh, Barbados, Bolivia, Bosnia and Herzogovina, Brazil, Bulgaria, Cameroon, China, Colombia, Costa Rica, Croatia, Cyprus, Czech Republic, Denmark, Dominican Republic, Ecuador, El Salvador, Finland, France, Germany, Guinea, the Holy See, Hungary, India, Italy, Japan, Kenya, Liechtenstein, Macedonia (the former Yugoslav Republic of), Mexico, Monaco, Montenegro, Morocco, the Netherlands, Niger, Norway, Panama, Peru, Poland, Portugal, Republic of Korea, Russian Federation, Rwanda, Saint Vincent and the Grenadines, Saudi Arabia, Senegal, Serbia (Republic of), Slovakia (Slovak Republic), Slovenia, Spain, Sri Lanka, Sweden, Switzerland, Togo, Trinidad and Tobago, Tunisia, United Kingdom, United States of America, Uruguay and Venezuela (Bolivarian Republic of).

The following countries have availed themselves of the exceptions in favour of developing countries: Algeria, Bangladesh, Bolivia, China, Mexico, Republic of Korea and Tunisia.

E. PARTIES TO THE UNIVERSAL COPYRIGHT CONVENTION

Convention countries. As of July 31, 2007, the following 100 countries are **24-87**
party to the Universal Copyright Convention 1952 (Geneva or Paris Acts).
Albania, Algeria, Andorra, Argentina, Australia, Austria, Azerbaijan, Bahamas,
Bangladesh, Barbados, Belarus, Belgium, Belize, Bolivia, Bosnia and Her-
zogovina, Brazil, Bulgaria, Cambodia, Cameroon, Canada, Chile, China,
Colombia, Costa Rica, Croatia, Cuba, Cyprus, Czech Republic, Denmark, Do-
minican Republic, Ecuador, El Salvador, Fiji, Finland, France, Germany,[7] Ghana,
Greece, Guatemala, Guinea, Haiti, the Holy See, Hungary, Iceland, India, Ireland,
Israel, Italy, Japan, Kazakhstan, Kenya, Lao People's Democratic Republic,
Lebanon, Liberia, Liechtenstein, Luxembourg, Macedonia (the former Yugoslav
Republic of), Mexico, Monaco, Montenegro, Morocco, the Netherlands, New
Zealand, Nicaragua, Niger, Nigeria, Norway, Pakistan, Panama, Paraguay, Peru,
Poland, Portugal, Republic of Korea, Republic of Moldova, Russian Federation,
Rwanda, Saint Vincent and the Grenadines, Saudi Arabia, Senegal, Serbia (Re-
public of), Slovakia (Slovak Republic), Slovenia, Spain, Sri Lanka, Sweden,
Switzerland, Tajikistan, Togo, Trinidad and Tobago, Tunisia, Ukraine, United
Kingdom[8] (extended to British Virgin Islands, Gibraltar, Isle of Man and Saint
Helena), United States of America (extended to American Samoa, Guam, the
Northern Mariana Islands, Puerto Rico, the US Virgin Islands), Uruguay and
Venezuela (Bolivarian Republic of).

5. THE ROME CONVENTION

A. HISTORY

Reasons for slow growth of membership. Last paragraph, last sentence. **Delete** **24-93**
and **substitute:** By its 20th anniversary in October 1981, its membership had
grown to 32 and, as of July 31, 2007, the Convention had 86 Member States.

Present relevance of the Convention. Last three sentences. **Delete** and **substi-** **24-94**
tute: A proposal for a WIPO Treaty on the Protection of Broadcasting Organizations has been the subject of two meetings in January and June 2007 of the WIPO
Standing Committee on Copyright and Related Rights (SCCR). The proposal
aimed at upgrading existing international standards relating to the rights of
broadcasting organisations and to ensure an appropriate balance between the different interests of all stakeholders and those of the general public. It was envisaged that following agreement on a revised proposal a diplomatic conference
would be held in November or December 2007 to conclude a treaty on the protection of traditional broadcasting organisations. However, at the June 2007 meeting, it was decided that more time was needed to bring negotiations to a successful conclusion. The matter will remain on the agenda of the SCCR, but a
diplomatic conference will be convened only after agreement on objectives,
specific scope and object of protection has been achieved.[9]

NOTE 8. **Delete** and **substitute:** The report of the SCCR meeting held in June
2007, and the working papers on this issue, are available on the WIPO website;
see documents SCCR/S1/3 and the "Non-Paper on the Draft WIPO Treaty on the
Protection of Broadcasting Organisations", April 20, 2007.

---

[7] See n.142, above.
[8] The effective date for the UK was September 27, 1957, and, as regards the 1971 Convention, it
was July 10, 1974.
[9] WIPO Press Release, PR/2007/498, June 25, 2007.

D. PARTIES TO THE ROME CONVENTION

24–108   **Present membership. Delete** and **substitute:** As of July 31, 2007, the following 86 States were party to the Convention: Albania, Algeria, Andorra, Argentina, Armenia, Australia, Austria, Azerbaijan, Bahrain, Barbados, Belarus, Belgium, Bolivia, Brazil, Bulgaria, Burkina Faso, Canada, Cape Verde, Chile, Colombia, Congo, Costa Rica, Croatia, Czech Republic, Denmark, Dominica, Dominican Republic, Ecuador, El Salvador, Estonia, Fiji, Finland, France, Georgia, Germany, Greece, Guatemala, Honduras, Hungary, Iceland, Ireland, Israel, Italy, Jamaica, Japan, Kyrgyzstan (Kyrgyz Republic), Latvia, Lebanon, Lesotho, Liechtenstein, Lithuania, Luxembourg, Mexico, Monaco, Montenegro, Netherlands (for the Kingdom in Europe), Nicaragua, Niger, Nigeria, Norway, Panama, Paraguay, Peru, Philippines, Poland, Portugal, Republic of Moldova, Romania, Russian Federation, Saint Lucia, Serbia (Republic of), Slovakia (Slovak Republic), Slovenia, Spain, Sweden, Switzerland, Syrian Arab Republic, The former Yugoslav Republic of Macedonia, Togo, Turkey, Ukraine, United Arab Emirates, United Kingdom, Uruguay, Venezuela (Bolivarian Republic of) and Viet Nam.

NOTE 33. **Delete** and **substitute:** Under the Rome Convention, Member States may make certain reservations. A complete list of these reservations appears in the General Table of Copyright and Related Rights Conventions in Ch.26.

6. THE PHONOGRAMS CONVENTION

D. PARTIES TO THE PHONOGRAMS CONVENTION

24–118   **Entry into force and membership.** Second sentence. **Delete** and **substitute:** Membership of the Convention grew relatively quickly and, as of July 31, 2007, the following 76 States were party to the Convention: Albania, Algeria, Argentina, Armenia, Australia, Austria, Azerbaijan, Barbados, Belarus, Brazil, Bulgaria, Burkina Faso, Chile, China,[10] Colombia, Costa Rica, Croatia, Cyprus, Czech Republic, Democratic Republic of the Congo, Denmark, Ecuador, Egypt, El Salvador, Estonia, Fiji, Finland,[11] France, Germany, Greece, Guatemala, Holy See, Honduras, Hungary, India, Israel, Italy,[12] Jamaica, Japan, Kazakhstan, Kenya, Kyrgyzstan (Kyrgyz Republic), Latvia, Liberia, Liechtenstein, Lithuania, Luxembourg, Mexico, Monaco, Montenegro, Netherlands (for the Kingdom in Europe), New Zealand, Nicaragua, Norway, Panama, Paraguay, Peru, Republic of Korea, Republic of Moldova, Romania, Russian Federation, Saint Lucia, Serbia (Republic of), Slovakia (Slovak Republic), Slovenia, Spain, Sweden, Switzerland, The former Yugoslav Republic of Macedonia, Togo, Trinidad and Tobago, Ukraine, United Kingdom, United States of America, Ukraine, Uruguay, Venezuela (Bolivarian Republic of) and Viet Nam.

---

[10] The Phonograms Convention applies also to the Hong Kong Special Administrative Region of China with effect from July 1, 1997 and to the Macao Special Administrative Region of China with effect from December 20, 1999.

[11] Finland has declared, in accordance with Art.7(4) of the Convention, that it will apply the criterion according to which it affords protection to producers of phonograms solely on the basis of the place of first fixation instead of the criterion of the nationality of the producer.

[12] Italy has declared, in accordance with Art.7(4) of the Convention, that it will apply the criterion according to which it affords protection to producers of phonograms solely on the basis of the place of first fixation instead of the criterion of the nationality of the producer.

7. WIPO PERFORMANCES AND PHONOGRAMS TREATY 1996

D. SIGNATORIES AND ENTRY INTO FORCE

Parties to the Treaty. Second paragraph. First sentence. **Delete** and **substitute:**   **24–133**
As of July 31, 2007, the following 62 States were parties to the Treaty:

Albania, Argentina, Armenia, Australia, Azerbaijan, Bahrain, Belarus, Belgium, Benin, Botswana, Bulgaria, Burkina Faso, Chile, China, Colombia, Costa Rica, Croatia, Cyprus, Czech Republic, Dominican Republic, Ecuador, El Salvador, Gabon, Georgia, Guatemala, Guinea, Honduras, Hungary, Indonesia, Jamaica, Japan, Jordan, Kazakhstan, Kyrgyzstan (Kyrgyz Republic), Latvia, Liechtenstein, Lithuania, Mali, Mexico, Mongolia, Montenegro, Nicaragua, Oman, Panama, Paraguay, Peru, Philippines, Poland, Qatar, Republic of Moldova, Romania, Saint Lucia, Senegal, Serbia (Republic of), Singapore, Slovakia (Slovak Republic), Slovenia, The former Yugoslav Republic of Macedonia, Togo, Ukraine, United Arab Emirates and the United States of America.

Add: NOTE 11A. Under the WPPT, Member States may make certain reservations. All such reservations are listed in the footnotes to the General Table of Copyright and Related Rights Conventions in Ch.26.

E. PENDING ISSUES NOT ADDRESSED BY THE TREATY

Problems left unresolved. Second paragraph, last sentence on page 1226. **Delete**   **24–134**
and **substitute:** Since then, informal consultations among Member States and key stakeholders in the private sector have continued under the auspices of WIPO, in order to identify ways and means for making progress on outstanding issues. The issue remains on the agenda of the General Assembly of WIPO for its session in September 2007.

8. THE TRIPS AGREEMENT

B. SUBSTANTIVE PROVISIONS

The Application of the 3–step test by a WTO Panel. NOTE 44. **Add:** See also   **24–142**
K.J. Koelman, "Fixing the Three-step Test" [2006] E.I.P.R. 28(8), 407–412.

Dispute prevention and settlement. NOTE 63. **Delete** and **substitute:** An   **24–147**
overview of the state of play of WTO disputes is available on the WTO website, *www.wto.org*. As of July 31, 2007, 24 TRIPs-related disputes had been settled or were still pending, of which nine concerned copyright or related rights issues.

D. PARTIES TO THE TRIPS AGREEMENT

Second sentence. **Delete** and **substitute:** As of July 31, 2007, there were 151   **24–152**
Members of the WTO and 30 Observer governments; the latter must start accession negotiations within five years of becoming observers.

9. OTHER CONVENTIONS OF RELEVANCE TO THE COPYRIGHT AND RELATED RIGHTS CONVENTIONS

B. THE SATELLITE CONVENTION

24–157 **Relationship to the Berne and Rome Conventions.** Penultimate sentence. **Delete** and **substitute**: In practice, problems in this connection do not appear to have arisen, the number of Member States of the Rome Convention having increased from 14 at the time of the adoption of the Satellites Convention in May 1974[13] to 86 States on July 31, 2007.

24–158 **Entry into force and parties to the Satellite Convention.** Second sentence. **Delete** and **substitute:** As of July 31, 2007, the following 30 States were party thereto: Armenia, Australia, Austria, Bahrain, Bosnia and Herzegovina, Costa Rica, Croatia, Germany, Greece, Italy, Jamaica, Kenya, Mexico, Montenegro, Morocco, Nicaragua, Panama, Peru, Portugal, Rwanda, Russian Federation, Serbia, Singapore, Slovenia, Switzerland, The former Yugoslav Republic of Macedonia, Togo, Trinidad and Tobago, United States of America and Viet Nam.

10. REGIONAL CONVENTIONS

B. COUNCIL OF EUROPE CONVENTIONS AND RECOMMENDATIONS

24–166 **Interest of the Council of Europe in Copyright and Related Rights.** End of first sentence. **Delete** and **substitute:** A table showing the parties to the Council of Europe Copyright and Related Rights Conventions as of July 31, 2007, follows paragraph 24–171 of this Supplement (see also the Council of Europe's website at *www.coe.int* for updated information).

Second paragraph. Second and third sentences. **Delete** and **substitute:** The value to the international community of the Council of Europe's involvement in these matters lies in its efforts to promote copyright and related rights throughout its 47 Member States in Western and Eastern Europe. The Agreements are also open to signature and ratification by non-signatory States which participate in their elaboration and to accession by other non-Member States.

NOTE 35. First sentence. **Add:** In May 2005 the Council of Europe Steering Committee on the Mass Media (CDMM) was renamed the Steering Committee on the Media and New Communications Services (CDMC) and its terms of reference were redefined. These no longer include matters of intellectual property. The new Committee will continue to monitor questions of copyright in the context of its work and , in particular, the impact of copyright on the exercise of the right to freedom of and access to information. The reports of the CDMC are available on the Council of Europe website.

NOTE 37. Following the accession of Montenegro on May 11, 2007, the Council of Europe has the following 47 Member States: Albania, Andorra, Armenia, Austria, Azerbaijan, Belgium, Bosnia and Herzegovina, Bulgaria, Croatia, Cyprus, Czech Republic, Denmark, Estonia, Finland, France, Georgia, Germany, Greece, Hungary, Iceland, Ireland, Italy, Latvia, Liechtenstein, Lithuania, Luxembourg, Malta, Moldova, Monaco, Montenegro, the Netherlands, Norway, Poland, Portugal, Romania, Russian Federation, San Marino, Serbia, Slovakia, Slovenia, Spain, Sweden, Switzerland, The former Yugoslav Republic of Macedonia, Turkey, Ukraine and the United Kingdom.

---

[13] [1975] *Copyright* 32.

European agreements on broadcasting. NOTE 38. Second sentence. **Delete** and **substitute:** As of July 31, 2007, the following 14 members of the Council of Europe were party to the European Agreement Concerning Programme Exchanges by means of Television Films: Belgium, Croatia, Cyprus, Denmark, France, Greece, Ireland, Luxembourg, the Netherlands, Norway, Spain, Sweden, Turkey and the United Kingdom. Non-Member States Israel and Tunisia have also ratified the Agreement. **24–167**

NOTE 39. Second sentence. **Delete**, and **substitute:** As of July 31, 2007, the following seven members of the Council of Europe were party thereto: Croatia, Denmark, France, Germany, Norway, Sweden and the United Kingdom.

NOTE 41. Second sentence. **Delete** and **substitute:** As of July 31, 2007, the following 19 members of the Council of Europe were party thereto: Belgium, Croatia, Cyprus, Denmark, France, Germany, Greece, Ireland, Italy, Liechtenstein, the Netherlands (including the Netherlands' Antilles and Aruba), Norway, Poland, Portugal, Spain, Sweden, Switzerland, Turkey and the United Kingdom.

Fourth paragraph. First sentence. **Delete** and **substitute:** The Convention was adopted on May 11, 1994, but as of July 31, 2007, it had not yet entered into force.

NOTE 42. First sentence. **Delete**, and **substitute:** As of July 31, 2007, the Convention had been signed by 10 Member States of the Council of Europe: Belgium, Bosnia and Herzegovina, Cyprus, Germany, Luxembourg, Norway, San Marino, Spain, Switzerland and the United Kingdom. It has been ratified by Cyprus and Norway.

Convention on Cybercrime. First paragraph. Last sentence. **Delete** and **substitute:** As of July 31, 2007, the Convention had been ratified by 20 Member States: Albania, Armenia, Bosnia and Herzegovina, Bulgaria, Croatia, Cyprus, Denmark, Estonia, Finland, France, Hungary, Iceland, Latvia, Lithuania, the Netherlands, Norway, Romania, Slovenia, The former Yugoslav Republic of Macedonia and Ukraine. One non-member State, the United States of America, has also ratified the convention. **24–168**

Second paragraph. Last sentence. **Delete** and **substitute:** The Protocol entered into force on March 1, 2006, and as of July 31, 2007, it had been ratified by 11 Member States: Albania, Armenia, Bosnia and Herzegovina, Cyprus, Denmark, France, Latvia, Lithuania, Slovenia, the former Yugoslav Republic of Macedonia and Ukraine.

NOTE 46. **Delete** and **substitute:** As of September 1, 2007, the Protocol had been signed by 30 Member States of the Council of Europe and Canada, and ratified by 11 Member States, Albania, Armenia, Bosnia and Herzogovina, Cyprus, Denmark, France, Latvia, Lithuania, Slovenia, the former Yugoslav Republic of Macedonia and the Ukraine.

European agreements on related topics, including the information society. Third paragraph. Last sentence. **Delete** and **substitute:** As of July 31, 2007, the Convention had not entered into force. **24–170**

First paragraph. Last sentence. **Delete** and **substitute:** As of July 31, 2007, the Convention had been ratified by five Member States and it will enter into force on January 1, 2008. The Protocol has not entered into force. **24–171**

Second paragraph. Last sentence. **Delete** and **substitute:** As of July 31, 2007, the Convention had the following eight Member States: Bulgaria, Croatia, Cyprus, France, Moldova, Netherlands, Romania and Switzerland.

Table of Council of Europe Copyright and Related Rights Conventions[1]

Member States of the Council of Europe	European Agreement Concerning Programme Exchanges by Means of Television Films 1958[2]	Agreement on the Protection of Television Broadcasts 1960[3]	European Agreement for the Prevention of Broadcasts Transmitted from Stations Outside National Territories 1965[4]	European Convention Relating to Questions of Copyright Law and Neighbouring Rights in the Framework of Transfrontier Broadcasting by Satellite 1994[5]	Convention on Cybercrime 2001[6] Additional Protocol 2003[7]
	Date of entry into force	(e) Date of entry into force (d) Date denunciation took effect	Date of entry into force	(a) Date of signature (b) Date of ratification	Date of entry into force of (a) Convention (b) Protocol
Albania					(a) July 1, 2004 (b) March 1, 2006
Andorra					
Armenia					(a) February 1, 2007 (b) February 1, 2007
Austria					
Azerbaijan					
Belgium	April 8, 1962	(e) March 8, 1968 (d) January 1, 1990	October 19, 1967	(a) August 6, 1998	
Bosnia and Herzegovina				(a) February 21, 2005	(a) & (b) September 1, 2006
Bulgaria					(a) August 1, 2005
Croatia	December 31, 2004	(e) December 31, 2004	December 31, 2004		(a) July 1, 2004
Cyprus	February 20, 1970	(e) February 22, 1970 (d) January 1, 1990	October 2, 1971	(a) February 10, 1995 (b) December 21, 1998	(a) May 1, 2005 (b) March 1, 2006

Member States of the Council of Europe	European Agreement Concerning Programme Exchanges by Means of Television Films 1958[2]	Agreement on the Protection of Television Broadcasts 1960[3]	European Agreement for the Prevention of Broadcasts Transmitted from Stations Outside National Territories 1965[4]	European Convention Relating to Questions of Copyright Law and Neighbouring Rights in the Framework of Transfrontier Broadcasting by Satellite 1994[5]	Convention on Cybercrime 2001[6] Additional Protocol 2003[7]
Czech Republic					
Denmark	November 25, 1961	(e) November 27, 1961	October 19, 1967		(a) October 1, 2005 (b) March 1, 2006.
Estonia					(a) July 1, 2004
Finland					(a) September 1, 2007
France	July 1, 1961	(e) July 1, 1961	April 6, 1968		(a) May 1, 2006 (b) May 1, 2006
Georgia					
Germany	February 9, 1962	(e) October 9, 1967	February 28, 1970	(a) April 18, 1997	
Greece			August 14, 1979		(a) July 1, 2004
Hungary					(a) May 1, 2007
Iceland	April 4, 1965		February 23, 1969		
Ireland			March 19, 1983		(a) June 1, 2007 (b) June 1, 2007
Italy					
Latvia			February 14, 1977		(a) July 1, 2004 (b) February 1, 2007
Liechtenstein					
Lithuania					

Member States of the Council of Europe	European Agreement Concerning Programme Exchanges by Means of Television Films 1958[2]	Agreement on the Protection of Television Broadcasts 1960[3]	European Agreement for the Prevention of Broadcasts Transmitted from Stations Outside National Territories 1965[4]	European Convention Relating to Questions of Copyright Law and Neighbouring Rights in the Framework of Transfrontier Broadcasting by Satellite 1994[5]	Convention on Cybercrime 2001[6] Additional Protocol 2003[7]
Luxembourg	October 31, 1963			(a) May 11, 1994	
Malta					
Moldova					
Montenegro					
Monaco					
Netherlands	March 5, 1967		September 27, 1974		(a) March 1, 2007
Norway	March 15, 1963	(e) August 10, 1968	October 17, 1971	(a) May 11, 1994 (b) June 19, 1998	(a) October 1, 2006
Poland			November 11, 1994		
Portugal			September 7, 1969		
Romania					(a) September 1, 2004
Russian Federation					
San Marino				(a) May 11, 1994	
Serbia					
Slovakia					
Slovenia					(a) January 1, 2005 (b) March 1, 2006
Spain	January 4, 1974	(e) October 23, 1971 (d) January 1, 1990	March 11, 1988	(a) May 11, 1994	
Sweden	July 1, 1961	(e) July 1, 1961	October 19, 1967	(a) May 11, 1994	
Switzerland			September 19, 1976	(a) May 11, 1994	

Member States of the Council of Europe	European Agreement Concerning Programme Exchanges by Means of Television Films 1958[2]	Agreement on the Protection of Television Broadcasts 1960[3]	European Agreement for the Prevention of Broadcasts Transmitted from Stations Outside National Territories 1965[4]	European Convention Relating to Questions of Copyright Law and Neighbouring Rights in the Framework of Transfrontier Broadcasting by Satellite 1994[5]	Convention on Cybercrime 2001[6] Additional Protocol 2003[7]
The former Yugoslav Republic of Macedonia					(a) January 1, 2005 (b) March 1, 2006
Turkey	March 28, 1964	(e) January 20, 1976 (d) January 1, 1990	February 17, 1975		
Ukraine					(a) July 1, 2006 (b) April 1, 2007
United Kingdom	July 1, 1961	(e) July 1, 1961	December 3, 1967	(a) October 2, 1996	
EC				(a) June 26, 1996	
Non-Member States[8]					
Belarus					
Canada					
Holy See					
Israel	February 15, 1978				
Japan					
Morocco					
South Africa					
Tunisia	February 22, 1969				
USA					(a) January 1, 2007

[1] See Chap. 24(10)(B). This Table is up to date as of July 31, 2007.
[2] CETS No. 027. The Agreement is open for accession by the following non-Member States: Israel, Morocco and Tunisia.

[3] CETS No. 034. As regards the Protocols to this Agreement (CETS No. 054, 1965) and the three additional Protocols thereto (CETS No. 081, 1974; CETS No. 113, 1983 and CETS No. 131, 1989), see paras 24–169 and 24–169.1, above.

[4] CETS No. 053. The Agreement is open for accession by Morocco.

[5] CETS No. 153. This Convention is open for signature and ratification by the Member States, the other States party to the European Cultural Convention (Belarus and the Holy See), and on behalf of the European Community. (Monaco, previously a non-member, joined the Council of Europe on October 5, 2004.)

[6] CETS No. 185. This Convention entered into force on July 1, 2004. It is open for signature and ratification by the Member States of the Council of Europe and by non-member States which participated in its elaboration, namely, Canada, Japan, South Africa and the United States of America. To date it has been signed by the following Member States: Albania, Armenia, Austria, Belgium, Bosnia and Herzegovina, Bulgaria, Croatia, Cyprus, Czech Republic, Denmark, Estonia, Finland, France, Germany, Greece, Hungary, Iceland, Ireland, Italy, Latvia, Lithuania, Luxembourg, Malta, Moldova, Montenegro, Netherlands, Norway, Poland, Portugal, Romania, Serbia, Slovakia, Slovenia, Spain, Sweden, Switzerland, the former Yugoslav Republic of Macedonia, Ukraine and the United Kingdom and the following Non-member States: Canada, Japan, South Africa and the United States of America.

[7] An Additional Protocol to the Convention on Cybercrime, concerning the criminalisation of acts of a racist and xenophobic nature committed through computer systems (CETS No. 189) was adopted on January 28, 2003, and entered into force on March 1, 2005. To date it has been signed by the following Member States: Albania, Armenia, Austria, Belgium, Bosnia and Herzegovina, Croatia, Cyprus, Denmark, Estonia, Finland, France, Germany, Greece, Iceland, Latvia, Lithuania, Luxembourg, Malta, Moldova, Montenegro, Netherlands, Poland, Portugal, Romania, Serbia, Slovenia, Sweden, Switzerland, the former Yugoslav Republic of Macedonia and the Ukraine and the following Non-member State: Canada.

[8] Note that some of the treaties listed are open for signature and ratification by one or more States not party to the Council of Europe (cf. nn. 2, 4, 5, 6 and 7 above).

CHAPTER TWENTY FIVE

COMMUNITY LAW

I. INTRODUCTION

Creation and enlargement of the EC and EEA. Second paragraph, first sentence: **Delete** and **substitute:** Subsequently, membership of the Community has expanded to 27.

25–01

Second paragraph. Fourth sentence. **Delete** and **substitute:** Finally on January 1, 2007, Bulgaria and Romania acceded to the EU.

Second paragraph. Last sentence: **Delete** and **substitute:** The Accession Treaties provided that the twelve new Member States had to have complied with EU law by the respective dates of their accession, including the *acquis communautaire* (existing body of Community law) with regard to copyright and related rights.

Sixth paragraph. **Add:** The Enlargement Agreement providing for the participation of Bulgaria and Romania in the European Economic Area was signed on July 25, 2007.[1]

Scope of the section. NOTE 14. **Add:** V. Korah, *Intellectual Property Rights and the EC Competition Rules*, Sweet and Maxwell, 2007.

25–02

---

[1] Press release 182 of the Council of the European Union,

3. CONFLICT BETWEEN COPYRIGHT AND RELATED RIGHTS AND THE FREE MOVEMENT OF GOODS AND SERVICES

25–08A   **Non-discrimination on the grounds of nationality.** The principle that copyright and related rights, which because of their effects on the free movement of goods and services fall within the scope of the EC Treaty, are also subject to the general principle of non-discrimination by reason of nationality laid down by Article 12 EC has long been established by the ECJ.[2] This principle prohibits not only overt discrimination by reason of nationality but also all covert forms of discrimination which, by the application of other distinguishing criteria, lead to the same result.[3] In a recent case, *Société Tod's SPA & Another v Heyraud SA*, the ECJ, applying this principle, has confirmed that the right of an author from one Member State to claim the copyright protection afforded by the law of another Member State may not be subject to a distinguishing criterion based on the country of origin of the work.[4] At issue was whether the proprietor of a design produced in Italy, where designs are not protected as artistic works but under a special law, could claim copyright protection in France. The Berne Convention for the Protection of Literary and Artistic Works[5] provides in such circumstances that "works protected in the country of origin solely as designs ... shall be entitled in another country of the Union only to such special protection as is granted in that country to designs ...", thereby subjecting the level of protection afforded to designs to the principle of reciprocity (Art.2(7)). The Court held that application of this provision of the Berne Convention in a Member State of the EU led to a distinction based on the criterion of the country of origin of the work and to an indirect discrimination on grounds of nationality. No obligations imposed on Member States by the EC Treaty or secondary legislation may be made subject to a condition of reciprocity.[6]

4. RESOLUTION OF THE CONFLICT BETWEEN INTELLECTUAL PROPERTY RIGHTS AND THE AIMS OF THE EC

A. CREATION OF COMMUNITY INTELLECTUAL PROPERTY RIGHTS

25–15   **Community Patent Convention.** Sixth sentence. **Delete** and **substitute:** The considerable progress which has been made since then in the harmonisation of national patent laws and the success of the 32-Member State European Patent Convention (EPC) removed any urgent need to establish a unitary Community patent.

Last sentence. **Delete.**

Add: In January 2006, the Commission launched a consultation process, asking industry and other stakeholders for their views on future patent policy in Europe. In April 2007, the Commission issued a Communication (COM(2007) 165 final) stating that the 2006 consultation had revealed broad consensus on the

---

[2] Joined Cases C–92/92 and C–326/92 *Phil Collins and Others* [1993] E.C.R. I–5145 and Case C–360/00 *Ricordi* [2002] E.C.R. I–5089.

[3] Case C–29/95 *Pastoors and Trans-Cap* [1997] E.C.R. I–285 and Case C–224/00 *Commission v Italy* [2002] E.C.R. I–2965.

[4] Case C–28/04 of June 30, 2005; reference for a preliminary ruling by the *Tribunal de Grande Instance de Paris*, December 5, 2003.

[5] See Ch.24, above.

[6] Case C–405/01 *Colegio de Oficiales de la Marina Mercante Espanola* [2003] E.C.R. I–1039.

need for a simple, cost-effective and high-quality one-stop-shop patent system in Europe, both for examination and grant as well as post-grant procedures, including litigation. There is still support for a Community patent, but only one which has clear advantages over the existing system in terms of cost and reliability. The language régime and jurisdictional arrangements proposed so far are unacceptable to stakeholders. Accordingly, the Communication focuses on suggestions for reinvigorating the Community patent project and on establishing an efficient EU-wide patent jurisdiction. It proposes compromise solutions aimed at securing the future of the European Patent Litigation Agreement (EPLA), promoted under the auspices of the European Patent Convention, and ensuring the ratification of the London Agreement (aimed at reducing translation costs). Other priorities include simplifying the structure and procedures for patent grant and litigation, decreasing the cost of obtaining a patent and improving the quality of patents. The Commission also announced its intention of presenting a comprehensive strategy communication on intellectual property rights (IPR) by early 2008. It will address the main outstanding non-legislative and horizontal issues in all fields of intellectual property.

5. HARMONISATION OF NATIONAL COPYRIGHT AND RELATED RIGHTS LAWS IN THE EUROPEAN UNION

B. The Challenge of Technology: The acquis communautaire 1991–1996

Follow-up to the Green Paper. Third paragraph. Second and third sentences. **Delete** and **substitute:** In the meantime, the Commission has legislated on all these issues, with the exception of moral rights.[7] Reprography was covered by the Directive on the harmonisation of certain aspects of copyright and related rights in the information society of May 22, 2001.[8] Artist's resale right was dealt with by the Directive on the resale right for the benefit of the author of an original work of art.[9] The collective management of copyright and related rights and collecting societies has been the subject not of a Directive, but of a Commission Recommendation dated May 18, 2005, on collective cross-border management of copyright and related rights for legitimate online music services.[10] The recommendation puts forward measures for improving the EU-wide licensing of copyright for online services.[11] To date, the Commission proposes to take no action with regard to moral rights.[12]

25–45

Legislative measures adopted to date. Second paragraph. **Delete** and **substitute:** The state of implementation of these Directives by the Member States as of July 31, 2007, is set out in the Table showing the implementation of the EC Directives on copyright and related rights in the Member States of the EU, EEA and Switzerland.

25–46

NOTE 12. **Add:** Repealed and replaced with effect from January 16, 2007, by Directive 2006/115/EC ([2006] O.J. L376).

NOTE 13. **Add:** Repealed and replaced with effect from January 16, 2007, by Directive 2006/116/EC ([2006] O.J. L372).

---

[7] See para.25–101.

[8] Directive 2001/29/EC ([2001] O.J. L 167/10). See Vol. 2 at H 11 and para.25–79 *et seq.,* below.

[9] Directive 2001/84/EC ([2001] O.J. L 272/32 of October 13, 2001); see also Ch.19A, above, and Vol. 2, H 12 (see para.25–72 *et seq.,* below).

[10] 2005/737/EC [2005] O.J. L 276/54.

[11] See para.25–100, below, and Ch. 28, para.28–20A.

[12] See para.25–101, below.

Add new paragraph:

25–50A ECJ Case Law. The decompilation exception permitted by Article 6 of the Directive has been the subject of dispute in the case *Microsoft Corporation v Commission*.[13] The exception permits reproduction of computer code when it is indispensable to obtain the information necessary to achieve the interoperability of an independently created computer program with other programs, subject to certain conditions. In the *Microsoft* case, the concept and definition of "interoperability" was at issue. Microsoft and the Commission disagreed as to whether the concept of interoperability employed in the contested decision of the Commission is or is not compatible with that envisaged by the Software Directive. The Court of First Instance in its decision found that the Commission's concept of interoperability, according to which interoperability between two software products means the capacity for them to exchange information and to use that information mutually in order to allow each of those software products to function in all the ways envisaged, is consistent with that envisaged by the Software Directive. The Court held also *inter alia* that what was at issue in the case was a decision adopted in application of Article 82 EC, a provision of higher rank than the Software Directive; thus, in the present case, the question was not so much whether the concept of interoperability in the contested decision was consistent with that directive as whether the Commission correctly determined the degree of interoperability that should be attainable in the light of the objectives of Article 82 EC.[14]

25–52 **Directive on Rental Right and Lending Right and on Certain Rights Related to Copyright in the Field of Intellectual Property (The Rental and Related Rights Directive).**

Add: This Directive, which had been amended by subsequent EC directives, was repealed and replaced by Directive 2006/115/EC, without prejudice to the obligations of the Member States relating to the time-limits for transposition into national law of the Directives, and their application. Directive 2006/115/EC is a consolidating measure only, being a codified text taking into account amendments already made to Directive 92/100 by other EC Directives. However, it should be noted that the numbering of the recitals and articles of the two directives differ somewhat. References in this supplement are to the new codified directive, unless otherwise indicated.

25–54 **Terms of the Directive.** NOTE 38. **Delete** and **substitute:** Directive 2006/115/EC, Art.3.

NOTE 40 **Delete** and **substitute:** Directive 2006/115/EC, Art.6.

Third paragraph. First sentence. **Delete** and **substitute:** Chapter II of Directive 92/100 concerned related rights and afforded the basic rights of the Rome Convention to its beneficiaries (performers, producers of phonograms and broadcasting organisations) in relation to rights of fixation[15], reproduction[16] and broadcasting and communication to the public[17]. The new Directive 2006/115/EC no longer includes provisions concerning the reproduction right because these

---

[13] Case T–201/04R, CFI (Grand Chamber) September 17, 2007.

[14] Judgment, paras. 225–227.

[15] Art.7.

[16] Directive 92/100, Art.7, repealed and replaced by Art.2(b)(c)(d)(e) of Directive 2001/29/EC (see para. 25–79, *et. seq*, below).

[17] Art.8.

have been replaced with similar, but somewhat broader provisions, in the Information Society Directive[18]

NOTE 46. First sentence. Directive 2006/115/EC, Art.9.

Last sentence. **Delete** and **substitute:** The Directive also provides a related right to authorise or prohibit distribution for film producers with respect to their films.

Authorship of cinematographic or audiovisual works. Second sentence. According to Article 2(2) of Directive 92/100: "For the purposes of the Directive" the principal director of a cinematographic or audiovisual work shall be considered as its author or one of its authors.   **25–55**

Second paragraph. Second sentence. The original text of Art. 2(2) was limited to "the purposes of this Directive", that is the harmonisation of the rental and lending right and related rights.

Public Lending Right. First paragraph. First sentence. The public lending right provisions of Directive 2006/115/EC are contained in Articles 1, 3 and 6 (previous Articles 1, 2 and 5). Article 1 provides for a right to authorise or prohibit the rental and lending of originals and copies of copyright works, and other subject-matter, namely, performers, producers of phonograms and film producers (Article 3). Member States may, however, derogate from the exclusive right in respect of public lending, provided that at least authors obtain remuneration for such lending (Article 6).   **25–56**

Last paragraph. **Delete** and **substitute:**

ECJ Case Law. Infringement proceedings under Article 226 of the Treaty have been taken against a number of Member States for failure to implement the PLR provisions of the Directive in due time. In particular, the Commission pursued infringement proceedings against a number of Member States on this issue, referring several to the European Court of Justice on the ground that they had failed to implement PLR fully or adequately into national legislation.[19] The Commission took action against Ireland (C–175/05), Italy (C–198/05), Portugal (C–53/05) and Spain (C–36/05) asking the ECJ to declare that by exempting all, or in the case of Spain almost all, categories of public lending establishments, including educational and academic institutions, from paying the public lending right remuneration these countries were in breach of their obligations under the Directive.[20] These cases resulted in court judgments declaring that these States had failed to fulfil their obligations under the Directive in these respects.[21]   **25–56A**

On a different issue concerning the rental right, the Commission laid a complaint before the ECJ because Portugal had created in its national law a rental right in favour of producers of videograms. The Court recently held that creating such a right was contrary to Portugal's obligations under the Directive. Moreover, creating the right in national legislation led to some doubt as to who is responsible for paying the remuneration owed to performers on assignment of the rental right.[22]

The ECJ recently handed down a decision in a case which raised questions arising out of both the Rental Right Directive and the Satellite and Cable Direc-

---

[18] Directive 2001/29/EC; see para.25–79 et seq., below.
[19] See Press releases IP/04/60 (January 16, 2004), IP/04 891 (July 13, 2004), IP/04/1519 (December 21, 2004), IP/05/347 (March 21, 2005), IP/05/921 (July 13, 2005).
[20] Cases C–175/05, C–198/05, C–53/05 and C–36/05.
[21] Judgments of the Court dated January 11, 2007 (Ireland), July 6, 2006 (Portugal) and October 26, 2006 (Italy and Spain).
[22] Case C–61/05, judgment of July 13, 2006.

tive (the *Lagardère* case)[23]. The French *Cour de Cassation* referred the following questions to the European Court:

(1) Where a broadcasting company transmitting from the territory of one Member state uses, in order to extend the transmission of its programmes to a part of its national audience, a transmitter situated nearby on the territory of another Member State, of which its majority-held subsidiary is the licence holder, does the legislation of the latter State govern the single equitable remuneration which is required by Article 8(2) of Directive 92/100 (the Rental Right Directive) ... and Article 4 of Directive 93/83 (the Satellite and Cable Directive) ... and is payable in respect of the phonograms published for commercial purposes included in the programmes retransmitted?

(2) If so, is the original broadcasting company entitled to deduct the sums paid by its subsidiary from the remuneration claimed from it in respect of all the transmissions received within national territory?

The Court held that:

(1) In the case of a broadcast of the kind at issue in this case, Council Directive 93/83 (the Satellite and Cable Directive) does not preclude the fee for phonogram use being governed not only by the law of the Member State in whose territory the broadcasting company is established but also by the legislation of the Member State in which, for technical reasons, the terrestrial transmitter broadcasting to the first State is located.

(2) Article 8(2) of Council Directive 92/100 (the Rental Right Directive) must be interpreted as meaning that, for determination of the equitable remuneration mentioned in that provision, the broadcasting company is not entitled unilaterally to deduct from the amount of the royalty paid or claimed in the Member State in whose territory the terrestrial transmitter broadcasting to the first State is located.

25–57   **Implementation in the United Kingdom. NOTE 53. Delete and substitute:** Case 458/2002, *Commission v UK*. On January 11, 2005, the Commission withdrew its action and on March 22, 2005, the Court of Justice ordered the case removed from the Register.

25–58   **Directive on the Co-ordination of Certain Rights Concerning Copyright and Rights Related to Copyright Applicable to Satellite Broadcasting and Cable Re-transmission (the Satellite and Cable Directive).**[24]

Add new paragraph:

25–60A   **ECJ Case Law.** On June 1, 2006, the ECJ held, on a reference from the Belgian *Cour de Cassation* for a preliminary ruling, that Article 9(2) of the Satellite and Cable Directive is to be interpreted as meaning that, where a collecting society is deemed to be mandated to manage the rights of a copyright owner or holder of related rights who has not transferred the management of his rights to a collecting society, that society has the power to exercise that right holder's right to grant or refuse authorisation to a cable operator for cable retransmission and, conse-

---

[23] *Lagardère Active Broadcast v Société pour la perception de la rémunération équitable (SPRE), Gesellschaft zur Verwertung von Leistungschutzrechten mbh (GVL); Compagnie européenne de radiodiffusion et de télévision Europe 1 SA (CERT) (Third Party)* [2006] E.C.D.R. 1.
[24] Council Directive 93/83/EEC [1993] O.J. L248.

quently, its mandate is not limited to management of the pecuniary aspects of those rights.[25] Another case decided by the ECJ relating to the Satellite and Cable Directive as well as the Rental Right Directive is described in paragraph 25–56A, above.

Directive Harmonising the Term of Protection of Copyright and Related Rights (the Term Directive). First paragraph. **Add:** This Directive, which had been amended by subsequent EC Directives, was repealed and replaced by a new codified text by means of Directive 2006/116/EC with effect from January 16, 2007.[26] Directive 2006/116/EC is a consolidating measure only, being a codified text taking into account amendments already made to Directive 93/98 by other EC Directives. However, it should be noted that the numbering of the recitals and articles of the two directives differ somewhat. References in this supplement are to the new codified directive unless otherwise indicated.   **25–62**

Terms of the Directive. NOTE 82. **Delete** and **substitute:** Directive 2006/116/ EC, Recital 6.   **25–64**

NOTE 83. **Delete** and **substitute:** Directive 2006/116/EC, Recital 10.

NOTE 86. **Delete** and **substitute:** Directive 2006/116/EC, Art.8.

NOTE 88. **Delete** and **substitute:** Directive 2006/116/EC, Art.6.

Directive on the Legal Protection of Databases (the Database Directive).[27]   **25–67**

Terms of the Directive. Add: In December 2005, the European Commission published an evaluation report on database protection in the EU.[28] The aim of the evaluation was to assess the extent to which the policy goals of the Database Directive had been achieved and, in particular, whether the introduction of the *sui generis* right led to an increase in the European database industry's rate of growth and in database production. The Commission pointed out also that the scope of the *sui generis* right had been severely curtailed in a series of judgments rendered by the European Court of Justice (ECJ) in November 2004.[29] The evaluation concluded that the economic impact of the *sui generis* right on database production is unproven. However, the European publishing industry argued that this protection is crucial to the continued success of their activities. In addition, most of those consulted believe that the *sui generis* right has brought about legal certainty, reduced the costs associated with the protection of databases, created more business opportunities and facilitated the marketing of databases. The evaluation is ongoing and stakeholders have been invited to submit their views and comments and to provide further evidence of the economic impact of the *sui generis* protection.   **25–69**

NOTE 17. **Add:** N. Thakur, "Database Protection in the European Union and the United States: The European Database Directive as an Optimum Global Model?" [2001] I.P.Q. 100.

ECJ Case Law. NOTE 26. **Add:** See also H. Meinberg, "From Magill to IMS Health: the new product requirement and the diversity of intellectual property rights" [2006] EIPR 398.   **25–70**

---

[25] Case C–169/05 [2006] O.J. C143.
[26] [2006] O.J. L372.
[27] Directive 96/9/EC of the European Parliament and of the Council [1996] O.J. L77/20.
[28] DG Internal Market and Services Working paper, First evaluation of Directive 96/9/EC on the legal protection of databases, December 12, 2005.
[29] See Supplement, para.25–70, below.

Last paragraph. **Delete** and **substitute:** The November 2004 judgments of the European Court of Justice relating to the interpretation of the *sui generis* protection afforded by the Database Directive in a series of cases referred by national courts and considered together are also of particular interest.[30]

The four judgments concern the scope of the *sui generis* protection of the Directive in the context of sporting databases (football fixture lists and a database containing a register of thoroughbred horses and information on horseracing). Fixtures Marketing Ltd. and the British Horseracing Board (BHB) alleged that other companies had infringed their rights in their databases. The Court held that the Directive reserves the protection of the *sui generis* right for databases which show that there has been, qualitatively or quantitatively, a substantial investment in the obtaining, verification or presentation of their contents. It then decided that the expression 'investment' in the obtaining of the contents of a database refers to the resources used to seek out existing materials and collect them in the database. It does not cover the resources used for the creation of materials which make up the contents of the database. The fact that the maker of a database is also the creator of the materials contained in it does not exclude that database from the protection of the *sui generis* right, provided that he establishes that the obtaining of those materials, their verification or their presentation required substantial investment in quantitative or qualitative terms, which was independent of the resources used to create those materials. Applying these principles, the Court then found that neither the obtaining, verification nor presentation of the contents of a football fixture list or a schedule of horse races constitutes substantial investment giving rise to protection against the use of the data by third parties. In the BHB case, the Court found also that the expression "substantial part", in quantitative terms, must be assessed in relation to the total volume of the contents of the database. In qualitative terms, it refers to the scale of the investment in the obtaining, verification or presentation of the contents extracted or re-utilised. It concluded that, since the materials extracted and re-utilised by William Hill did not require investment by BHB which was independent of the resources required for their creation, those materials did not constitute a substantial part of the contents of the BHB database.

As the Commission points out in its evaluation of the Database Directive,[31] the scope of the *sui generis* right was severely curtailed by these judgments. The protection for non-original databases has been decreased at least with respect to producers of databases that 'create' the data and information that comprises their databases, as opposed to obtaining the information from others.

Add new paragraph:

25–71A   The ECJ has recently been asked for a preliminary ruling on the question whether national provisions, which provide that an official database (in this case containing a collection of calls for tenders by a German regional authority) does not enjoy sui generis protection, is compatible with the database Directive.[32]

25–72   **Directive 2001/84/EC on the resale right for the benefit of the author of an original work of art (the Artists' Resale Right or *Droit de Suite* Directive).**

---

[30] Judgments of the Court in Cases C–46/02, C–203/02, C–338/02 and C–444/02, *Fixtures Marketing Ltd v Oy Veikkaus Ab, The British Horseracing Board Ltd and Others v William Hill Organisation Ltd, Fixtures Marketing Ltd v Svenska Spel AB, Fixtures Marketing Ltd v Organismos prognostikon agonon podosfairou (OPAP)*.

[31] See Supplement para. 25–69, above, and the conclusions to para.4.1 of the evaluation.

[32] C–215/07, *Verlag Schawe*.

Terms of the Directive. NOTE 43. **Delete** and **substitute:** Italy and Luxembourg   **25–74**
recognised the artists' resale right but did not yet apply it in practice. Austria,
Ireland, the Netherlands and the United Kingdom did not recognise the right. In
the meantime, the majority of Member States have brought their legislation into
line with the Directive. To date, the Commission is still examining whether the
laws of Belgium, Spain and Sweden are compatible with the Directive.

Implementation in the United Kingdom. Last sentence. **Delete** and **substitute:**   **25–75**
The Directive has been implemented in the United Kingdom by means of the
Artist's Resale Right Regulations 2006, which entered into force on February 14,
2006.[33]

C. THE INFORMATION SOCIETY

Directive on the harmonization of certain aspects of copyright and related   **25–79**
rights in the information society (the Information Society Directive). Sixth
sentence and rest of paragraph. **Delete** and **substitute:** In the meantime, the
Directive has been transposed into domestic law by all the Member States of the
enlarged European Union, including the latest new Members, Bulgaria and
Romania.

Distribution right. NOTE 8. **Add:** Confirmed by *Laserdisken v Kulturministeriet*   **25–84**
(Case C–479/04, ECJ judgment of September 12, 2006. See para.25–89A,
below).

Add new paragraph:

ECJ Case Law. Since the First Supplement was published in late 2006, the first   **25–89A**
decisions of the ECJ on issues arising from the Directive have been handed down.
    Concept of communication to the public. A reference for a preliminary rul-
ing was made to the ECJ by a Spanish court in the context of litigation between
the Spanish authors' society and a hotel chain. The question posed was whether
the communication of protected copyright works by means of television sets
installed in hotel rooms was a "communication to the public" within the meaning
of the Directive. The Court ruled that, while the mere provision of physical facilities does not as such amount to communication within the meaning of the Directive, the distribution of a signal by means of television sets by a hotel to customers staying in its rooms, whatever technique is used to transmit the signal,
constitutes communication to the public within the meaning of Article 3(1) of the
Directive.[34]
    Exhaustion of the distribution right. In *Laserdisken v Kulturministeriet* the
ECJ had to consider whether the Directive permitted Member States to legislate
for an international exhaustion of rights régime or to retain domestic law providing that the distribution right was exhausted when the first sale or other transfer
of ownership was made anywhere in the world. The ECJ held that Article 4(2) of
the Directive, in conjunction with recital 28 in the preamble to the Directive,
provides that it is not open to the Member States to provide for a rule of exhaustion other than the Community-wide exhaustion rule. The Directive is, therefore,
to be interpreted as precluding national rules providing for exhaustion of the dis-

---

[33] SI 2006/346; see Ch.19A.
[34] Case C–306/05, *Sociedad General de Autores y Editores de España (SGAE) v Rafael Hoteles SA*,
    judgment of December 7, 2006. See also, A. Bateman, "The Use of Televisions in Hotel Rooms"
    [2007] EIPR 22.

tribution right in respect of the original or copies of a work placed on the market outside the European Community by the right holder or with his consent.[35]

The distribution right. The following questions have been referred to the ECJ by the German *Bundesgerichtshof*: (a) Can it be assumed that there is a distribution to the public in any manner other than by sale within the terms of Article 4(1) of the Directive, in the case where it is made possible for third parties to make use of items of copyright-protected works without the grant of user involving a de facto power to dispose of those items. (b) Is there a distribution under the same provision also in the case in which items of copyright–protected works are shown publicly without the possibility of using those items being granted to third parties? If the answers are in the affirmative, can the protection accorded to the free movement of goods preclude, in the above mentioned cases, exercise of the distribution right if the items presented are not under copyright protection in the Member State in which they were manufactured and placed on the market?[36]

Add new paragraph:

25–90A   **Study on the implementation and effect of the Directive.** In 2006, the European Commission commissioned a major study carried out by the Institute for Information Law at the University of Amsterdam in cooperation with the Queen Mary Intellectual Property Research Centre of the University of London which examined the implementation and effect of the Information Society Directive in Member States' laws in the light of the development of the digital market[37] The study is in two parts: Part 1 provides an early and tentative assessment of the Directive on the development of on-line business models; Part II offers a comprehensive inventory of the actual implementation of the Directive in the 25 Member States covered. Part II also gives a summary of disparities and specific problems arising from the implementation of the Directive.

The purpose of the study was to assist the Commission in evaluating whether the Directive remains the appropriate response to the continuing challenges faced by the stakeholders concerned, such as rights holders, commercial users, consumers, educational and scientific users.

25–91   **Other EU Initiatives Relevant to the Information Society.** Second paragraph. **The EC Directive on the legal protection of conditional access services** (the Conditional Access Directive).[38]

Second paragraph, last sentence. **Add:** In April 2003, the Commission issued a report on the Implementation of the Directive[39] as part of the Commission's comprehensive Internal Market strategy to remove barriers to services. The report stressed that enforcement at national level had to be consolidated and that joint efforts were required to fight piracy effectively. Issues that deserved further reflection included the need to create a balanced and coherent enforcement framework

---

[35] Case C–479/04, judgment of September 12, 2006; see also Case Comment, "The ECJ has no Doubts Over Community Exhaustion" [2007] Ent. L.R. 70.

[36] Case C–456/06, reference of November 16, 2006, *Peek & Cloppenburg KG v Cassina S.p.A.*

[37] L. Guibault and G. Westkamp *et al.*, "Study on the Implementation and Effect in Member States' Laws of Directive 2001/29/EC on the Harmonisation of Certain Aspects of Copyright and Related Rights in the Information Society", Institute for Information Law, University of Amsterdam, and Queen Mary Intellectual Property Research Institute, Centre for Commercial Law Studies, University of London, February 2007.

[38] Directive 98/84/EC of the European Parliament and of the Council on the legal protection of services based on, or consisting of, conditional access (The Conditional Access Directive [1998] O.J. L 320/54 November 28, 1998). See Vol.2 at H9.

[39] COM (2003)198 final, of April 24, 2003; see also press release IP/03/583 of April 29, 2003.

applicable to all kinds of piracy and counterfeiting and the distribution of keys and illicit devices via the Internet.

EC Directive on Electronic Commerce(the E-Commerce Directive).[40]

Fourth paragraph. NOTES 62 TO 68. **Delete** and **substitute:** In November 2003, the Commission published a first report on the application of the Directive (COM (2003) 702 final of November 21, 2003; see also press release IP/03/1580 of the same date). The report concluded that the Internal Market objectives of the Directive had been met and that it had provided a sound legal framework for information society services in the Internal Market. It had also led to modernisation of existing national legislation, for example in contract law, to ensure the full validity of online transactions. The Commission concludes that revision of the Directive would be premature. Instead, it will focus on ensuring that the Directive is correctly applied and on collecting feedback from business and consumers alike. It proposes action to improve administrative co-operation between the Member States; to raise awareness amongst business and citizens of the EU; to collect information from businesses and citizens on their experience of the Directive in practice and to strengthen international cooperation.

Directive on the enforcement of intellectual property rights (the Enforcement Directive).[41]   25–92

Implementation of the Directive in the United Kingdom. Delete and **substitute:** The Directive has been implemented in the United Kingdom by means of The Intellectual Property (Enforcement, etc.) Regulations 2006,[42] which entered into force on April 29, 2006. In addition, changes to the court rules to implement the Directive were introduced by the 41st update to the Civil Procedure Rules, which came into force on April 6, 2006.   25–97

Other EU Initiatives Relevant to the Enforcement of Intellectual Property Rights.   25–97A

Council Regulation concerning customs action against goods suspected of infringing certain intellectual property rights and the measures to be taken against goods found to have infringed such rights.[43] The Regulation enables customs authorities, in cooperation with right holders to improve controls at external borders. It simplifies the procedure for the lodging of applications for action with the customs authorities, in particular for small and medium-sized enterprises (SMEs), and for the destruction of fraudulent goods. The Regulation lays down the conditions for customs action where goods are suspected of infringing intellectual property rights, and on the other hand the measures to be taken against goods that have been found to infringe intellectual property rights.

Commission Regulation laying down provisions for the implementation of Council Regulation (EC) No 1383/2003 concerning customs action against goods suspected of infringing certain intellectual property rights and the measures to be taken against goods found to have infringed such rights.[44] This regulation clarifies the provisions for the implementation of the above Council Regulation

---

[40] Directive 2000/31/EC of the European Parliament and of the Council of June 8, 2000, on certain legal aspects of information society services, in particular electronic commerce, in the Internal Market (the E-Commerce Directive [2001] O.J. L178/1, July 17, 2000).

[41] Directive 2004/48/EC of the European Parliament and of the Council of April 29, 2004, on the enforcement of intellectual property rights ([2004] O.J. L157 of April 30, 2004, as corrected in [2004] O.J.L195/16 of June 2, 2004).

[42] SI 2006/1028.

[43] (EC) No.1383/2003 of July 22, 2003 O.J. L196/7 August 2, 2003. The Regulation was applied with effect from July 1, 2004 and repealed Regulation (EC) No.3295/94 from that date.

[44] (EC) No.1891/2004, O.J. L 328 October 30, 2004.

concerning customs action. It defines the natural and legal persons who may represent the holder of a right or any other persons who may represent the holder of a right or any other person authorised to use the right. It is also necessary to specify the nature of the proof of ownership of intellectual property. The Regulation also lays down *inter alia* the procedures for the exchange of information between Member States and the Commission, so that it is possible for the Commission to monitor the effective application of the procedure and recognise patterns of fraud, and for the Member States to introduce appropriate risk analysis. The Regulation applied with effect from July 1, 2004.

In October 2005, a **Communication** from the Commission to the Council, the European Parliament and the European Economic and Social Committee on a customs response to latest trends in counterfeiting and piracy was published. The Commission proposes a series of customs measures aimed at protecting the EU more effectively against counterfeiting and piracy. These measures include improving legislation, strengthening partnership between customs and business and increasing international cooperation. The measures in question will be implemented by customs.[45]

Proposal for a directive on criminal sanctions. A further draft directive aiming at harmonising national criminal sanctions for the infringement of intellectual property rights other than patents has been put forward by the European Commission. It takes the view that a sufficiently dissuasive set of penalties applicable throughout the Community is needed to make the provisions laid down in the Enforcement Directive complete. The proposed new directive reflects the Commission's opinion that the Community legislature has the power to take the criminal law measures that are necessary where these are required for the effective implementation of Community law. The draft directive was considered and adopted by the European Parliament on April 25, 2007.[46]

D. FORECAST FOR FUTURE COMMUNITY INITIATIVES

25–99 **Private copying of sound and audiovisual recordings. Add:** Copyright levy reform was included in the Commission Work Program for 2006, with the aim of adopting a proposal for reform in the autumn of 2006. In October 2004, the Commission consulted Member States on the scope of the private copying exception and existing systems of remuneration. Replies from Member States were due in March 2006. The UK Government in reply stated *inter alia* that the private copying exceptions in UK law are so limited in their nature, scope and application that minimal prejudice to the right holder arises and no compensation is deemed necessary.

At the time, the Commission was concerned that copyright levies are being applied to digital equipment and media without due account being given to the impact on new technologies and equipment, especially the availability and use of so-called "digital rights management" technologies which can provide alternative ways of compensating right holders. Furthermore, it took the view that there is a lack of transparency about the application, collection and distribution of the copyright levies to right holders. The Commission's stated main policy objective was to ensure that the scope and level of systems for fair compensation established by Member States for acts of private copying take account of the application of digital rights management technologies.

---

[45] COM (2005) 479 final of October 11, 2005, not published in the O.J.

[46] Proposal for a directive of the European Parliament and of the Council on criminal measures aimed at ensuring the enforcement of intellectual property rights (COM(2006)0168); see also European Parliament legislative resolution and position adopted on April 25, 2007, concerning the amended proposal for the directive.

Following the consultation with Member States, in June 2006 the Commission launched a "Stakeholder Consultation on Copyright Levies in a Converging World", with the intention of consulting the public to ensure that any proposals for change were technically viable, practically workable and based on a bottom-up approach. This follow-up consultation was due to be completed by July 14, 2006. Meanwhile, in January 2007, the Commission decided to postpone all action on the subject indefinitely, without giving a reason.[47]

Collective Management of Copyright and Related Rights. Second paragraph.   **25–100**
Last two sentences: **Delete** and **substitute:** However, the Commission, following consultations with interested parties, has decided not to legislate for the time being on this controversial subject. Instead it has issued a Recommendation limited to the question of collective cross-border management of copyright and related rights for legitimate online music services.

Commission recommendation on collective cross-border management of   **25–100A**
copyright and related rights for legitimate online music services.[48] The recommendation puts forward measures for improving the EU-wide licensing of online rights in musical works. The aim of the Recommendation is to foster a climate where EU-wide licences are more readily available for online music service providers.[49] The recommendation sets out to promote multi-territorial licensing "in order to enhance greater legal certainty to commercial users in relation to their activity and to foster the development of legitimate online services, increasing, in turn, the revenue for right holders".[50] Up to now, collecting societies have operated on a territorial basis, entering into reciprocal agreements with collecting societies in other countries for mutual representation. Thus, users have been able to obtain licences for European or worldwide repertoire from any national collecting society. The Recommendation accepts this system and proposes that cooperation between collecting societies allowing each society in the EU to grant an EU-wide licence covering the other societies' repertoires should be improved. However, as an alternative, it provides that right holders should have the choice of appointing a collective rights manager anywhere in the EU for the online use of their musical works across the entire EU ("EU-wide direct licensing"). The Commission is seeking to promote collective management services which operate across national borders. Thus, right holders would be able to freely choose the collective rights manager or collecting society for the management of the rights necessary to operate legitimate online music services across the Community, irrespective of the Member State of residence or the nationality of either the collective rights manager or the rights holder.[51] For example, an Italian right holder seeking to licence his repertoire for online music services would be encouraged to entrust his rights to the UK Performing Rights Society (PRS), or another society within the EU, rather than to leave them with the Italian authors' society, SGAE. The aim clearly is to encourage competition between collecting societies.

According to the Commission, the recommendation reflects its view as to how

---

[47] Detailed information and documentation on this subject is available on the EU Internal Market Intellectual Property website.

[48] 2005/737/EC of May 18, 2005.

[49] For a more detailed discussion of the Commission's proposals and the Recommendation, see Chapter 28, para.28–20 *et seq.,* below.

[50] Recommendation, Recital 8.

[51] Directive, Recital 9.

the market should develop. In October 2005 it announced it would take tougher action if insufficient progress was made.[52]

In the meantime, on January 17, 2007, the Commission announced its intention to assess the development of Europe's online music sector in the light of the Recommendation. It therefore invited stakeholders to submit views and comments on their initial experience with the recommendation and, in general, on their views on how the online music sector has developed since its adoption. In this respect, the Commission identified several policy areas where views and opinions by the market players appeared essential to it and posed a series of questions to interested parties relating to the nature of the instrument, EU-wide licensing issues, the scope of the recommendation and governance and transparency.[53]

In the meantime, in March 2007, the Legal Affairs Committee of the European Parliament (EP) adopted an own-initiative report which is critical of the recommendation. The EP regards the Commission's choice of a soft law instrument as inappropriate and wants it to consult publicly and thereafter present a proposal for a flexible framework directive designed to regulate the collective management of copyright and related rights in cross-border online music services.

25–102   **Current Review of the EC Legal Framework in the Field of Copyright and Related Rights.** Second paragraph. Last three sentences. **Delete** and **substitute:** In this connection, the Commission announced in the paper that it was working on the objective of codifying the *acquis communautaire*. At the time it was working on the codification of the Software Directive, the Rental Right Directive and the Term Directive.[54] Meanwhile, the two latter directives have been repealed and replaced by codified texts.[55] On December 12, 2005, the Commission published an evaluation of the protection EU law gives to databases.[56]

Fourth paragraph. **Delete** and **substitute:** The Commission has consulted on these issues and two major studies have been commissioned and published: The first by the Institute for Information Law at the University of Amsterdam[57] examined the *acquis communautaire* with special focus on inconsistencies and lack of clarity, as well as a series of priority issues identified by the Commission as meriting special attention, including: the possible extension of the term of protection of phonograms; possible alignment of the term of protection of co-written musical works, the problems connected to multiple copyright ownership, including the issue of "orphan works", and copyright awareness among consumers. A second study carried out by the same institution in cooperation with the Queen Mary Intellectual Property Research Centre of the University of London examined the implementation and effect of the Information Society Directive in Member States' laws in the light of the development of the digital market[58] A focal point of the study is the development of on-line business models. Its purpose was to assist the Commission in evaluating whether the Directive

---

[52] Announcement of Internal Market and Services Commissioner, Charlie McCreavy, IP/05/1261, October 12, 2005.

[53] Call for comments, January 17, 2007.

[54] Detailed information and documentation on this subject is available on the EU Internal Market Intellectual Property website.

[55] Directive 2006/115/EC and Directive 2006/116/EC.

[56] DG Internal Market and Services Working paper, First Evaluation of Directive 96/9/EC on the legal protection of databases; see also Supplement para.25–69, above.

[57] B. Hugenholtz, *et al.* "The Recasting of Copyright and Related Rights for the Knowledge Economy", November 2006.

[58] L. Guibault *et al.* and G. Westkamp, "Study on the Implementation and Effect in Member States' Laws of Directive 2001/29/EC on the Harmonisation of Certain Aspects of Copyright and Related Rights in the Information Society", Institute for Information Law, University of Amsterdam, and Queen Mary Intellectual Property Research Institute, Centre for Commercial Law Studies, University of London, February 2007.

remains the appropriate response to the continuing challenges faced by the stakeholders concerned, such as rights holders, commercial users, consumers, educational and scientific users.

It is to be expected, therefore, that new proposals for legislation to amend the existing Directives and for further harmonisation will be put forward by the Commission in due course.

E. External Relations of the European Union

Community competence with respect to the TRIPs Agreement. Third paragraph. **Add:** In the case *Léon Van Parys NV v Belgisch Interventie- en Restitutiebureau*, the Court of Justice once again considered whether the WTO agreements, including the TRIPs Agreement, give Community nationals a right to rely on those agreements in legal proceedings challenging the validity of Community legislation.[59] It pointed out that the WTO agreements are not in principle among the rules which the Court must take into account when reviewing the legality of measures adopted by the Community institutions. It is only where the Community has intended to implement a particular obligation assumed in the context of the WTO, or where the Community measure refers expressly to particular provisions of the WTO agreements, that it is for the Court to review the legality of a Community measure in light of the WTO rules. Finding that these conditions were not met in this case, the Court went on to hold that a legal person cannot plead before a national court the incompatibility of Community legislation with certain rules of the WTO. That principle is not affected by the fact that the Dispute Settlement Body of the WTO has declared there to be such incompatibility, given the Commission's discretion to remedy the situation, for example, by means of a negotiated settlement.[60]

25–104

Add new paragraph:

The relationship between Community law and the TRIPs Agreement was considered most recently by the Court of First Instance in the case of *Microsoft Corporation v Commission*.[61] In this case, Microsoft had criticised the Commission for having interpreted Article 82 EC in a way that it considered inconsistent with Article 13 of the TRIPs Agreement, which confines limitations or exceptions to exclusive rights to certain special cases which do not conflict with a normal exploitation of the work and do not unreasonably prejudice the legitimate interests of the right holder.[62] The CFI recognised the principle laid down by the Court of Justice, according to which international agreements concluded by the Community take primacy over provisions of secondary Community legislation, which means that such provisions must, so far as is possible, be interpreted in a manner which is consistent with those agreements, but held that the principle applies only where the international agreement at issue prevails over the provision of Community law concerned.[63] It held that the TRIPs Agreement does not prevail over primary Community law and, therefore, does not apply to the interpretation

25–105

---

[59] Case C–377/02, Judgment of March 1, 2005.
[60] Case C–377/02, Judgment of March 1, 2005.
[61] Case T–201/04R, CFI (Grand Chamber) September 17, 2007
[62] Art.13 TRIPs embodies the principles of Art.9(2) of the Berne Convention and its so-called "three-step test" for permissible limitations; see paras 9–02 to 9–04 and paras 24–33 and 24–34 of the Main Work.
[63] Judgment, para.797.

of Article 82 EC,[64] Referring to the Court of Justice decision in *Portugal v Council*,[65] it relied on the case law referred to in paragraph 25–104, above, and held, therefore, that Microsoft could not rely on Article 13 TRIPs.

[64] Judgment, para.798.
[65] [1999] ECR I–8395.

Table Showing the Implementation of E.C. Directives on Copyright and Related Rights in the Member States of the E.U., EEA and Switzerland on July 31, 2007

Member States	Computer Programmes Directive 91/250/EEC (01.01.1993)	Rental and Lending Right Directive 92/100/EEC (repealed and replaced by Directive 2006/115/EC)[5]	Satellite Broadcasting & Cable Re-transmission Directive 93/83/EEC (01.01.1995)	Term of Copyright Protection Directive 93/98/EEC (repealed and replaced by Directive 2006/116/EC)[6]	Protection of Databases Directive 96/9/EC (31.12.1997)	Information Society Directive Directive 2001/29/EC (22.12.2002)	Artists' Resale Right Directive 2001/84/EC (01.01.2006)	Enforcement of Intellectual Property Rights Directive 2004/48/EC (29.04.2006)
EU Countries								
Austria	01.11.1993	11.02.1993	02.05.1996	29.03.1996	09.01.1998	06.06.2003	16.02.2006	21.06.2006
Belgium	27.07.1994	27.07.1994 14.05.2004	27.07.1994	27.07.1994	14.11.1998	27.05.2005	23.01.2007	10.05.2007
Bulgaria	09.12.2005	09.12.2005	09.12.2005	09.12.2005	09.12.2005	09.12.2005	09.12.2005	05.09.2006
Cyprus*	19.07.2002	19.07.2002 18.10.2002	19.07.2002	19.07.2002	19.07.2002	30.04.2004	28.07.2006	28.07.2006
Czech Republic*	12.05.2000	12.05.2000	12.05.2000	12.05.200	08.12.1961 05.03.1964 18.05.1990 18.12.1991 12.05.2000	08.12.1961 18.05.1990 01.12.1993 12.05.2000 23.02.2005 22.05.2006	12.05.2000 22.05.2006	26.05.2006

Member States	Computer Pro-grammes Directive 91/250/EEC (01.01.1993)	Rental and Lending Right Directive 92/100/EEC (repealed and replaced by Directive 2006/115/EC)[5]	Satellite Broadcast-ing & Cable Re-transmis-sion Directive 93/83/EEC (01.01.1995)	Term of Copyright Protection Directive 93/98/EEC (repealed and replaced by Directive 2006/116/EC)[6]	Protection of Databases Directive 96/9/EC (31.12.1997)	Informa-tion Society Directive Directive 2001/29/EC (22.12.2002)	Artists' Resale Right Directive 2001/84/EC (01.01.2006)	Enforce-ment of Intellectual Property Rights Directive 2004/48/EC (29.04.2006)
Denmark*	19.12.1992	13.06.1995 14.06.1995 17.12.2002	13.06.1995 12.03.2003	14.06.1995	26.06.1998	17.12.2002	21.12.2005	15.12.2005 05.04.2006
Estonia*	18.11.2002	18.11.2002 10.04.2004	18.11.2002	18.11.2002	18.11.2002	25.10.2004 13.02.2006 24.03.2006	27.06.2006 (Date of notification)	01.01.2006
Finland	07.05.1993 22.12.1993	24.03.1995 05.11.1997 27.12.2006	24.03.1995	22.12.1995	03.04.1998 22.10.2003	20.10.2005 20.12.2005	12.05.2006	04.08.2006
France	11.05.1994	01.07.1992 18.06.2003	28.03.1997	28.03.1997	01.07.1998	03.08.2006	03.08.2006 10.05.2007	—
Germany	23.06.1993	29.06.1995	20.05.1998	23.06.1995	28.07.1997	10.09.2003	15.11.2006	—
Greece	04.03.1993	04.03.1993	04.03.1993 24.12.1997	04.03.1993 24.12.1997	15.03.2000	10.10.2002	26.001.2007	26.01.2007
Hungary*	06.07.1999 27.11.2003	06.07.1999 27.11.2003	06.07.1999 27.11.2003	06.07.1999 27.11.2003	17.11.2001 27.11.2003	06.07.1999 27.11.2003	19.10.2005	08.05.2006
Ireland	02.02.1993	01.03.2001	01.03.2001	01.07.1995	01.03.2001	19.01.2004	23.06.2006	05.05.2006

Member States	Computer Pro-grammes Directive 91/250/EEC (01.01.1993)	Rental and Lending Right Directive 92/100/EEC (repealed and replaced by Directive 2006/115/EC)[5]	Satellite Broadcast-ing & Cable Re-transmis-sion Directive 93/83/EEC (01.01.1995)	Term of Copyright Protection Directive 93/98/EEC (repealed and replaced by Directive 2006/116/EC)[6]	Protection of Databases Directive 96/9/EC (31.12.1997)	Informa-tion Society Directive Directive 2001/29/EC (22.12.2002)	Artists' Resale Right Directive 2001/84/EC (01.01.2006)	Enforce-ment of Intellectual Property Rights Directive 2004/48/EC (29.04.2006)
Italy	31.12.1992	16.12.1994 28.11.2006	18.11.1996	27.02.1996 13.06.1997	30.04.1999 06.05.1999	14.04.2003	25.03.2006	07.04.2006
Latvia*	27.04.2000 01.05.2004	27.04.2000 01.05.2004	27.04.2000 01.05.2004	27.04.2000 01.05.2004	27.04.2000 01.05.2004	27.04.2000 01.05.2004	27.04.2000 01.05.2004	27.02.2007
Lithuania*	21.03.2003	21.03.2003	21.03.2003	21.03.2003	21.03.2003	21.03.2003	21.03.2003 31.10.2006	04.11.2006
Luxembourg	28.04.1995	16.09.1997 25.01.2007	16.09.1997 30.04.2001	16.09.1997	30.04.2001	29.04.2004	22.09.2006	—
Malta*	01.01.2001	01.01.2001	24.04.2000	01.01.2001	01.01.2001 10.01.2003	23.12.2003	14.08.2006	12.12.2006
Netherlands	07.07.1994	28.12.1995	18.07.1996	28.12.1995	21.07.1999	06.07.2004 18.08.2004 24.08.2004	16.02.2006 02.03.2006	22.03.2007
Poland*	23.05.1994 07.07.2000	23.05.1994 27.11.2002	23.05.1994 07.07.2000 27.11.2002	23.05.1994 07.07.2000 27.11.2002	23.05.1994 09.11.2001	26.09.2000 30.04.2004	21.04.2006	09.05.2007

Member States	Computer Programmes Directive 91/250/EEC (01.01.1993)	Rental and Lending Right Directive 92/100/EEC (repealed and replaced by Directive 2006/115/EC)[5]	Satellite Broadcasting & Cable Re-transmission Directive 93/83/EEC (01.01.1995)	Term of Copyright Protection Directive 93/98/EEC (repealed and replaced by Directive 2006/116/EC)[6]	Protection of Databases Directive 96/9/EC (31.12.1997)	Information Society Directive Directive 2001/29/EC (22.12.2002)	Artists' Resale Right Directive 2001/84/EC (01.01.2006)	Enforcement of Intellectual Property Rights Directive 2004/48/EC (29.04.2006)
Portugal	17.06.1994 20.10.1994	03.09.1997 27.11.1997 30.06.2006	03.09.1997 27.11.1997	03.09.1997 27.11.1997	04.07.2000	24.08.2004	29.06.2006	—
Romania	26.03.1996 30.06.2004 19.09.2005 31.07.2006	26.03.1996 30.06.2004 19.09.2005 31.07.2006	26.03.1996 30.06.2004 19.09.2005 31.07.2006	26.03.1996 30.06.2004 19.09.2005 31.07.2006	26.03.1996 30.06.2004 19.09.2005 31.07.2006	26.03.1996 30.06.2004 19.09.2005 31.07.2006	26.03.1996 30.06.2004 19.09.2005 31.07.2006	31.07.2006
Slovakia*	31.12.2003	31.12.2003	31.12.2003	31.12.2003	31.12.2003	31.12.2003 01.03.2007	31.12.2003	01.03.2007
Slovenia	14.04.1995	14.04.1995	14.04.1995	14.04.1995 09.02.2001	14.04.1995 09.02.2001	14.04.1995 09.02.2001	14.04.1995 17.02.2006	09.06.2006
Spain	24.12.1993	31.12.1994	13.10.1995 22.04.1996 07.03.1998	13.10.1995	07.03.1998	08.07.2006	16.12.1992 22.04.1996	06.06.2006
Sweden	01.01.1993	01.06.1995	07.12.1995	07.12.1995	01.01.1998	08.06.2005	—	—
United Kingdom	01.01.1993	01.12.1996	01.12.1996	19.12.1995	01.01.1998	31.10.2003 22.03.2005 (Gibraltar)	13.02.2006 01.06.2006 (Gibraltar)	29.04.2006

Member States	Computer Programmes Directive 91/250/EEC (01.01.1993)	Rental and Lending Right Directive 92/100/EEC (repealed and replaced by Directive 2006/115/EC)[5]	Satellite Broadcasting & Cable Re-transmission Directive 93/83/EEC (01.01.1995)	Term of Copyright Protection Directive 93/98/EEC (repealed and replaced by Directive 2006/116/EC)[6]	Protection of Databases Directive 96/9/EC (31.12.1997)	Information Society Directive Directive 2001/29/EC (22.12.2002)	Artists' Resale Right Directive 2001/84/EC (01.01.2006)	Enforcement of Intellectual Property Rights Directive 2004/48/EC (29.04.2006)
EFTA Countries								
Iceland	Fully implemented	Fully implemented	Fully implemented	Fully implemented	Fully implemented	?	?	?
Liechtenstein	Fully implemented	Fully implemented	Fully implemented	Fully implemented	Fully implemented	?	?	?
Norway	Fully implemented	Fully implemented	Fully implemented	Fully implemented	Fully implemented	Partially implemented	?	?
Switzerland	Compatible law	Partially implemented	Compatible law	Compatible law	No intention for implementation	Partially implemented	No intention for implementation	Intention for partial implementation

[1] The date refers to the date of publication in a State's official journal or, failing that, to the date of adoption or the date of entry into force (where the law so provides) — Concerning the new Member States (*), the implementing measures notified to the Commission have not yet been accepted as complete or in conformity with the respective Directive.

[2] See EFTA website: *www.efta.int.* As regards the EEA Agreement, see paras 25–01, 25–103 and n.47 of the Main Work.

[3] The revision of the Swiss national copyright law in 1994 contained provision to make the law compatible with E.C. copyright directives in force at that time. In June 2006, the Swiss Federal Government launched the legislative process for the revision of the current Copyright Law with a new draft to bring it into line with international standards and to enable Switzerland to ratify the WCT and WPPT. In August 2006, the Legal Committee of the Swiss *Ständesamt* decided to hold hearings on the draft which are currently under way (see *www.ige.ch*).

[4] The rental right applies to date only to computer programs.

[5] [2006] O.J. L376. The following Member States have already implemented the new Directive or declared their compliance: Bulgaria, Cyprus, Czech Republic, Germany, Spain, Hungary, Lithuania, Latvia, Poland, Slovakia.

[6] [2006] O.J. L372. The following Member States have already implemented the new Directive or declared their compliance: Bulgaria, Cyprus, Czech Republic, Germany, Spain, Hungary, Lithuania, Latvia, Poland, Slovakia.

CHAPTER TWENTY-SIX

THE PROTECTION OF COPYRIGHT WORKS ABROAD

General Table of Copyright and Related Rights Conventions and National   26–01
Laws. Delete and **substitute:** The following Table shows the extent to which
copyright works protected under the 1988 Act are protected in other countries in
accordance with the principal international treaties to which the United Kingdom
is party, and which have entered into force with respect to those countries on July
31, 2007. The substantive provisions of each of these treaties are discussed in
detail in Chapter 24, above. The aim of this Table is to present in a readily accessible form the basic information the reader requires to establish whether a work is
protected in the 191 countries listed. The information provided by the Table is
explained below.

The Berne Convention for the Protection of Literary and Artistic Works.   26–02
Last sentence. **Delete** and **substitute:** This column of the Table is up to date to
July 31, 2007.

Universal Copyright Convention, 1952. Last two sentences. **Delete** and **substi-**   26–03
tute: Countries which availed themselves of the exceptions to protection in favour of developing countries are also indicated. This column of the Table is up to
date to July 31, 2007.

Other treaties. Delete and **substitute:** The Table also gives the dates of the   26–04
adherences of each country (where appropriate) to the following additional treaties:

> The Agreement on Trade Related Aspects of Intellectual Property
> (TRIPs), 1994. This column of the Table is up to date to July 31, 2007.
> The Rome Convention for the Protection of Performers, Producers of
> Phonograms and Broadcasting Organisations (the Rome Convention),
> 1961. This column of the Table is up to date to July 31, 2007.
> The Convention for the Protection of Producers of Phonograms against
> the Unauthorised Duplication of their Phonograms (the Phonograms
> Convention), 1971. This column of the Table is up to date to July 31,
> 2007
> The Convention Relating to the Distribution of Programme-Carrying
> Signals Transmitted by Satellite (the Satellite Convention), 1974. This
> column of the Table is up to date to July 31, 2007.
> The WIPO Copyright Treaty, 1996. This column of the Table is up to date
> to July 31, 2007.
> The WIPO Performances and Phonograms Treaty, 1996. This column of
> the Table is up to date to July 31, 2007.

National Laws. Second and third paragraphs. **Delete** and **substitute:** Since the   26–05
Main Work was written in late 2004, it is of interest to note that, although only
six entirely new laws on copyright and related rights have been adopted, 21
national laws have been amended.

The period of protection for literary and artistic works (as defined in the Berne Convention, Art.2(1)) is shown also in the Table. Here it may be noted that the number of countries which now grant literary and artistic works a period of protection of 70 years pma or more has increased by 18 to a total of 68.

26–06   **Sources.** First sentence. **Delete** and **substitute:** The information given about the membership of the various conventions and treaties listed above is based on their current status as published on July 31, 2007, on the websites of WIPO (World Intellectual Property Organisation), Unesco (United Nations Organisation for Science, Education and Culture and the WTO (World Trade Organisation), as well as, in some cases, on additional more up to date information from the organisations themselves.

General Table of Copyright and Related Rights Conventions[1]

Signatories	Berne Convention[2] September 9, 1886 and Subsequent Acts	UCC[3] September 6, 1952 revised in Paris, July 24, 1971	TRIPS April 15, 1994	Rome Convention October 26, 1961	Geneva Phonograms Convention October 29, 1971	Satellite Convention May 21, 1974	WIPO Copyright Treaty[4]	WIPO Performances and Phonograms Treaty[5]	Date of Principal Law (most recent amendment)[6]	Period of Protection[6]
Afghanistan			Observer[7]							
Albania	Paris A	Paris	September 8, 2000	September 1, 2000	June 26, 2001		August 6, 2005	May 20, 2002	2005	70 years pma
Algeria	Paris A, C, H	Paris	Observer[4] &[7]	April 22, 2007[8]					2003	50 years from January 1, pma
Andorra	Paris A	Geneva	Observer[7]	May 25, 2004					1999	70 years pma
Angola			November 23, 1996						1990	50 years pma (from end of year)
Antigua and Barbuda	Paris A		January 1, 1995						2002	50 years pma
Argentina	Paris A	Geneva	January 1, 1995	March 2, 1992	June 30, 1973		March 6, 2002	May 20, 2002	1933 (2003)	70 years pma
Armenia	Paris A		February 5, 2003	January 31, 2003	January 31, 2003	December 13, 1993	March 6, 2005	March 6, 2005	2000	50 years from January 1, pma

Signatories	Berne Convention[2] September 9, 1886 and Subsequent Acts	UCC[3] September 6, 1952 revised in Paris, July 24, 1971	TRIPS April 15, 1994	Rome Convention October 26, 1961	Geneva Phonograms Convention October 29, 1971	Satellite Convention May 21, 1974	WIPO Copyright Treaty[4]	WIPO Performances and Phonograms Treaty[5]	Date of Principal Law (most recent amendment)[6]	Period of Protection[6]
Australia	Paris A	Paris	January 1, 1995	September 30, 1992[8]	June 22, 1974	October 26, 1990	July 26, 2007	July 26, 2007[16]	1968 (2007)	70 years pma (from end of year)
Austria	Paris A	Paris	January 1, 1995	June 9, 1973[8]	August 21, 1982	August 6, 1982			1936 (2005)	70 years pma
Azerbaijan	Paris A	Geneva	Observer[7]	October 8, 2005	September 1, 2001		April 11, 2006	April 11, 2006	1996	50 years pma
Bahamas	Brussels Paris, B, H	Paris	Observer[7]						1956	50 years pma (from end of year)
Bahrain	Paris A, C		January 1, 1995	January 18, 2006		May 1, 2007	December 15, 2005	December 15, 2005	1993	50 years pma
Bangladesh	Paris A, C, D	Paris	January 1, 1995						2000	60 years from January 1, pma
Barbados	Paris A	Paris	January 1, 1995	September 18, 1983	July 29, 1983				1998	50 years pma
Belarus	Paris A	Geneva	Observer[7]	May 27, 2003[8]	April 17, 2003		March 6, 2002	May 20, 2002	1996 (2003)	50 years pma
Belgium	Paris A	Geneva	January 1, 1995	October 2, 1999[8]			August 30, 2006	August 30, 2006	1994 (2006)	70 years from January, pma

Signatories	Berne Convention[2] September 9, 1886 and Subsequent Acts	UCC[3] September 6, 1952 revised in Paris, July 24, 1971	TRIPS April 15, 1994	Rome Convention October 26, 1961	Geneva Phonograms Convention October 29, 1971	Satellite Convention May 21, 1974	WIPO Copyright Treaty[4]	WIPO Performances and Phonograms Treaty[5]	Date of Principal Law (most recent amendment)[6]	Period of Protection[6]
Belize	Paris A	Geneva	January 1, 1995						2000	50 years pma (from end of year)
Benin	Paris A		February 22, 1996				April 16, 2006	April 16, 2006	1984	50 years pma (from end of year)
Bhutan	Paris A		Observer[7]						2001	50 years pma (from end of year)
Bolivia	Paris A	Paris	September 12, 1995	November 24, 1993					1992	50 years pma (from end of year)
Bosnia and Herzegovina	Paris A, E	Paris	Observer[7]			March 6, 1992			2002	70 years from January 1 pma
Botswana	Paris A		May 31, 1995				January 27, 2005	January 27, 2005	2000	50 years pma
Brazil	Paris A	Paris	January 1, 1995	September 29, 1965	November 28, 1975				1998 (2003)	70 years from January 1, pma

Signatories	Berne Convention² September 9, 1886 and Subsequent Acts	UCC³ September 6, 1952 revised in Paris, July 24, 1971	TRIPS April 15, 1994	Rome Convention October 26, 1961	Geneva Phonograms Convention October 29, 1971	Satellite Convention May 21, 1974	WIPO Copyright Treaty⁴	WIPO Performances and Phonograms Treaty⁵	Date of Principal Law (most recent amendment)⁶	Period of Protection⁶
Brunei Darussalam	Paris A [as of August 30, 2006]		January 1, 1995						1999	50 years pma (from end of year)
Bulgaria	Paris A	Paris	December 1, 1996	August 31, 1995⁸	September 6, 1995		March 6, 2002	May 20, 2002	1993 (2002)	70 years pma
Burkina Faso	Paris A		June 3, 1995	January 14, 1988	January 30, 1988		March 6, 2002	May 20, 2002	1997 (1999)	50 years pma (from end of year)
Burundi			July 23, 1995						1978	50 years pma (from end of year)
Cambodia		Geneva	October 13, 2004						2003	50 years pma
Cameroon	Paris A	Paris	December 13, 1995						2000	50 years pma (from end of year)
Canada	Paris A	Geneva	January 1, 1995	June 4, 1998⁸					1985 (2007)	50 years pma (from end of year)

Signatories	Berne Convention[2] September 9, 1886 and Subsequent Acts	UCC[3] September 6, 1952 revised in Paris, July 24, 1971	TRIPS April 15, 1994	Rome Convention October 26, 1961	Geneva Phonograms Convention October 29, 1971	Satellite Convention May 21, 1974	WIPO Copyright Treaty[4]	WIPO Performances and Phonograms Treaty[5]	Date of Principal Law (most recent amendment)[6]	Period of Protection[6]
Cape Verde	Paris A		Observer[5] &[7]	July 3, 1997					1990	50 years from January 1, pma
Central African Republic	Paris A		May 31, 1995						1985	50 years pma (from end of year)
Chad	Stockholm B Brussels		October 19, 1996						Unknown	50 years pma minimum of BC
Chile	Paris A[9]	Geneva	January 1, 1995	September 5, 1974	March 24, 1977		March 6, 2002	May 20, 2002[9]	1970 (1992)	50 years pma
China	Paris A[9]	Paris*	December 11, 2001		April 30, 1993[9]		June 9, 2007[18]	June 9, 2007[18]	1990 (2002)	50 years pma
Colombia	Paris A	Paris	April 30, 1995	September 17, 1976	May 16, 1994		March 6, 2002	May 20, 2002	1982 (1993)	80 years pma
Comoros	Paris A								1957	50 years pma minimum of BC
Congo	Paris A		March 27, 1997	May 18, 1964[8]	June 17, 1982				1982 (1999)	70 years pma
Costa Rica	Paris A	Paris	January 1, 1995	September 9, 1971	June 17, 1982	June 25, 1999	March 6, 2002	May 20, 2002	2000	70 years pma

Signatories	Berne Convention[2] September 9, 1886 and Subsequent Acts	UCC[3] September 6, 1952 revised in Paris, July 24, 1971	TRIPS April 15, 1994	Rome Convention October 26, 1961	Geneva Phonograms Convention October 29, 1971	Satellite Convention May 21, 1974	WIPO Copyright Treaty[4]	WIPO Performances and Phonograms Treaty[5]	Date of Principal Law (most recent amendment)[6]	Period of Protection[6]
Côte d'Ivoire	Paris A		January 1, 1995						1996	99 years pma (from end of year)
Croatia	Paris A	Paris	November 30, 2000	April 20, 2000[8]	April 20, 2000	October 8, 1991	March 6, 2002	May 20, 2002	2003	50 years from January 1, pma
Cuba	Paris A, C, D, H	Geneva	April 20, 1995						1977 (1994)	50 years from January 1, pma
Cyprus	Paris A, E	Paris	July 30, 1995		September 30, 1993		November 4, 2003	December 2, 2005	1976 (2004)	50 years pma (from end of year)
Czech Republic	Paris A	Paris	January 1, 1995	January 1, 1993[8]	January 1, 1993		March 6, 2002	May 20, 2002	2000 (2005)	70 years pma (from January 1 pma)
Democratic People's Republic of Korea	Paris A, C, H								2001	50 years pma minimum of BC

Signatories	Berne Convention[2] September 9, 1886 and Subsequent Acts	UCC[3] September 6, 1952 revised in Paris, July 24, 1971	TRIPS April 15, 1994	Rome Convention October 26, 1961	Geneva Phonograms Convention October 29, 1971	Satellite Convention May 21, 1974	WIPO Copyright Treaty[4]	WIPO Performances and Phonograms Treaty[5]	Date of Principal Law (most recent amendment)[6]	Period of Protection[6]
Democratic Republic of the Congo	Paris A		January 1, 1997		November 29, 1977				1986	50 years pma (from end of year)
Denmark	Paris A	Paris	January 1, 1995	September 23, 1965[8]	March 24, 1977				1995 (2006)	70 years pma
Djibouti	Paris A		May 31, 1995						1996	25 years pma
Dominica	Paris A		January 1, 1995	November 9, 1999					2003	70 years pma
Dominican Republic	Paris A	Paris	March 9, 1995	January 27, 1987			January 10, 2006	January 10, 2006	2000	50 years from January 1 pma
Ecuador	Paris A	Paris	January 21, 1996	May 18, 1964	September 14, 1974		March 6, 2002	May 20, 2002	1998	70 years pma
Egypt	Paris A, H		June 30, 1995		April 23, 1978				1954 (2002)	50 years pma
El Salvador	Paris A	Paris	May 7, 1995	June 29, 1979	February 9, 1979		March 6, 2002	May 20, 2002	1993	50 years pma
Equatorial Guinea	Paris A		Observer[5]						Unknown	50 years pma minimum of BC
Estonia	Paris A		November 13, 1999	April 28, 2000[8]	May 28, 2000				1992 (2004)	70 years pma

Signatories	Berne Convention[2] September 9, 1886 and Subsequent Acts	UCC[3] September 6, 1952 revised in Paris, July 24, 1971	TRIPS April 15, 1994	Rome Convention October 26, 1961	Geneva Phonograms Convention October 29, 1971	Satellite Convention May 21, 1974	WIPO Copyright Treaty[4]	WIPO Performances and Phonograms Treaty[5]	Date of Principal Law (most recent amendment)[6]	Period of Protection[6]
Ethiopia			Observer[7]						1960	50 years pma (from end of year)
European Communities			January 1, 1995						Directives cf. Ch. 25, above	70 years pma Dir. 93/98/ EEC
Fiji	Stockholm B Brussels	Geneva	January 14, 1996	April 11, 1972[8]	April 18, 1973				1999	50 years pma
Finland	Paris A	Paris	January 1, 1995	October 21, 1983[8]	April 18, 1973				1961 (1998)	70 years pma (from end of year)
France	Paris A	Paris	January 1, 1995	July 3, 1987[8]	April 18, 1973				1992 (2006)	70 years pma (from end of year)
Gabon	Paris A		January 1, 1995				March 6, 2002	May 20, 2002	1987	
Gambia	Paris A		October 23, 1996						Unknown	50 years pma minimum of BC

Signatories	Berne Convention[2] September 9, 1886 and Subsequent Acts	UCC[3] September 6, 1952 revised in Paris, July 24, 1971	TRIPS April 15, 1994	Rome Convention October 26, 1961	Geneva Phonograms Convention October 29, 1971	Satellite Convention May 21, 1974	WIPO Copyright Treaty[4]	WIPO Performances and Phonograms Treaty[5]	Date of Principal Law (most recent amendment)[6]	Period of Protection[6]
Georgia	Paris A		June 14, 2000	August 14, 2004			March 6, 2002	May 20, 2002	1999	70 years from January 1, pma
Germany	Paris A, I	Paris	January 1, 1995	October 21, 1966[8]	May 18, 1974	August 25, 1979			1965 (2006)	70 years pma (from end of year)
Ghana	Paris A	Geneva	January 1, 1995				November 18, 2006		2005	70 years pma
Greece	Paris A	Geneva	January 1, 1995	January 6, 1993	February 9, 1994	October 22, 1991			1993 (2002)	70 years pma (from end of year)
Grenada	Paris A		February 22, 1996						1989	50 years pma
Guatemala	Paris A, H	Geneva	July 21, 1995	January 14, 1977	February 1, 1977		February 4, 2003	January 8, 2003	1998 (2000)	75 years pma
Guinea	Paris A	Paris	October 25, 1995				May 25, 2002	May 25, 2002	1980	80 years pma (from end of year), thereafter paying public domain

Signatories	Berne Convention[2] September 9, 1886 and Subsequent Acts	UCC[3] September 6, 1952 revised in Paris, July 24, 1971	TRIPS April 15, 1994	Rome Convention October 26, 1961	Geneva Phonograms Convention October 29, 1971	Satellite Convention May 21, 1974	WIPO Copyright Treaty[4]	WIPO Performances and Phonograms Treaty[5]	Date of Principal Law (most recent amendment)[6]	Period of Protection[6]
Guinea-Bissau	Paris A		May 31, 1995						Unknown	50 years pma minimum of BC
Guyana	Paris A		January 1, 1995						1999	50 years pma
Haiti	Paris A	Geneva	January 30, 1996						1968 (1988)	25 years pma (50 years under BC)
Holy See	Paris A	Paris	Observer[7]		July 18, 1977				1960 (1996)	70 years pma (from end of year)
Honduras	Paris A		January 1, 1995	February 16, 1990	March 6, 1990		May 20, 2002	May 20, 2002	1999	75 years pma
Hong Kong (SAR of China)[10]	Paris A	Paris	January 1, 1995		July 1, 1997				1997 (2001)	50 years pma
Hungary	Paris A	Paris	January 1, 1995	February 10, 1995	May 28, 1975		March 6, 2002	May 20, 2002	1999 (2001)	70 years from January 1, pma

Signatories	Berne Convention[2] September 9, 1886 and Subsequent Acts	UCC[3] September 6, 1952 revised in Paris, July 24, 1971	TRIPS April 15, 1994	Rome Convention October 26, 1961	Geneva Phonograms Convention October 29, 1971	Satellite Convention May 21, 1974	WIPO Copyright Treaty[4]	WIPO Performances and Phonograms Treaty[5]	Date of Principal Law (most recent amendment)[6]	Period of Protection[6]
Iceland	Paris A	Geneva	January 1, 1995	June 15, 1994[8]					1972 (2000)	70 years pma (from end of year)
India	Paris A, F, H	Paris	January 1, 1995		February 12, 1975				1957 (1999)	60 years from January 1, pma
Indonesia	Paris A, H		January 1, 1995				March 6, 2002	February 15, 2005	2002	50 years from January 1, pma
Iran (Islamic Republic of)			Observer[7]						1970	30 years pma
Iraq			Observer[7]						1971 (2004)	50 years pma
Ireland	Paris A	Geneva	January 1, 1995	September 19, 1979[8]					2000 (2004)	70 years pma
Israel	Paris A, H	Geneva	April 21, 1995	December 20, 2002[8]	May 1, 1978				1911 (2005)	70 years from January 1, pma
Italy	Paris A, H	Paris	January 1, 1995	April 8, 1975[8]	March 24, 1977	July 7, 1981			1941 (2003)	70 years from January 1, pma

Signatories	Berne Convention[2] September 9, 1886 and Subsequent Acts	UCC[3] September 6, 1952 revised in Paris, July 24, 1971	TRIPS April 15, 1994	Rome Convention October 26, 1961	Geneva Phonograms Convention October 29, 1971	Satellite Convention May 21, 1974	WIPO Copyright Treaty[4]	WIPO Performances and Phonograms Treaty[5]	Date of Principal Law (most recent amendment)[6]	Period of Protection[6]
Jamaica	Paris A		March 9, 1995	January 27, 1994	January 11, 1994	January 12, 2000	June 12, 2002	June 12, 2002	1993 (1999)	50 years pma
Japan	Paris A	Paris	January 1, 1995	October 26, 1989[8]	October 14, 1978		March 6, 2002	October 9, 2002[11]	1970 (2004)	50 years from January 1, pma
Jordan	Paris A, C, D, H		April 11, 2000				April 27, 2004	May 24, 2004	1992 (2005)	50 years from January 1, pma
Kazakhstan	Paris A	Geneva	Observer[7]		August 3, 2001		November 12, 2004	November 12, 2004	1996	50 years pma
Kenya	Paris A	Paris	January 1, 1995		April 21, 1976	August 25, 1979			2001	50 years pma (from end of year)
Kuwait			January 1, 1995						1999	50 years pma
Kyrgyzstan (Kyrgyz Republic)	Paris A		December 20, 1998	August 13, 2003	October 12, 2002		March 6, 2002	August 15, 2002	1998 (2001)	50 years from January 1 pma
Lao People's Democratic Republic		Geneva	Observer[7]						No legislation	25 years pma minimum of UCC

Signatories	Berne Convention[2] September 9, 1886 and Subsequent Acts	UCC[3] September 6, 1952 revised in Paris, July 24, 1971	TRIPS April 15, 1994	Rome Convention October 26, 1961	Geneva Phonograms Convention October 29, 1971	Satellite Convention May 21, 1974	WIPO Copyright Treaty[4]	WIPO Performances and Phonograms Treaty[5]	Date of Principal Law (most recent amendment)[6]	Period of Protection[6]
Latvia	Paris A		February 10, 1999	August 20, 1999[8]	August 23, 1997		March 6, 2002	May 20, 2002	2000 (2004)	70 years from January 1, pma
Lebanon (Lebanese Republic)	Rome	Geneva	Observer[7]	August 12, 1997					1999	50 years pma (from end of year)
Lesotho	Paris A, H		May 31, 1995	January 26, 1990[8]					1989	50 years pma (from end of year)
Liberia	Paris A, H	Geneva			December 16, 2005				1972	25 years pma (50 years under BC)
Libyan Arab Jamahiriya	Paris A, H		Observer[7]						1968 (1984)	50 years pma (from end of year)
Liechtenstein	Paris A	Paris	September 1, 1995	October 12, 1999[8]	October 12, 1999		April 30, 2007	April 30, 2007	1999	70 years pma
Lithuania	Paris A, H		May 31, 2001	July 22, 1999[8]	January 27, 2000		March 6, 2002	May 20, 2002	1999 (2003)	70 years pma

Signatories	Berne Convention[2] September 9, 1886 and Subsequent Acts	UCC[3] September 6, 1952 revised in Paris, July 24, 1971	TRIPS April 15, 1994	Rome Convention October 26, 1961	Geneva Phonograms Convention October 29, 1971	Satellite Convention May 21, 1974	WIPO Copyright Treaty[4]	WIPO Performances and Phonograms Treaty[5]	Date of Principal Law (most recent amendment)[6]	Period of Protection[6]
Luxembourg	Paris A	Geneva	January 1, 1995	February 25, 1976[8]	March 8, 1976				2001 (2004)	70 years from January 1, pma
Macau (SAR of China)[10]	Paris A	Paris	January 1, 1995		December 20, 1999				1999 (2000))	50 years pma
Madagascar	Brussels		November 17, 1995						1995	70 years pma (from end of year)
Malawi	Paris A	Geneva	May 31, 1995						1989	50 years pma (from end of year)
Malaysia	Paris A		January 1, 1995						1987 (2000)	50 years pma
Maldives			May 31, 1995						No legislation	50 years pma minimum of TRIPs
Mali	Paris A		May 31, 1995				April 24, 2002	May 20, 2002	1977 (1994)	50 years pma
Malta	Rome Paris B, H	Geneva	January 1, 1995						2000 (2003)	70 years pma (from end of year)

Signatories	Berne Convention[2] September 9, 1886 and Subsequent Acts	UCC[3] September 6, 1952 revised in Paris, July 24, 1971	TRIPS April 15, 1994	Rome Convention October 26, 1961	Geneva Phonograms Convention October 29, 1971	Satellite Convention May 21, 1974	WIPO Copyright Treaty[4]	WIPO Performances and Phonograms Treaty[5]	Date of Principal Law (most recent amendment)[6]	Period of Protection[6]
Mauritania	Paris A		May 31, 1995						Unknown	50 years pma minimum of BC
Mauritius	Paris A, H	Geneva	January 1, 1995						1997	50 years pma
Mexico	Paris A	Paris*	January 1, 1995	May 18, 1964	December 21, 1973	August 25, 1979	March 6, 2002	May 20, 2002	1997 (2005)	75 years pma
Micronesia (Federated States of)	Paris A								1982 (2001)	50 years pma
Monaco	Paris A	Paris		December 6, 1985[8]	December 2, 1974				1948	50 years pma
Mongolia	Paris A, C, D, H		January 29, 1997				October 25, 2002	October 25, 2002	1993 (1999)	50 years pma
Montenegro	Paris A, E	Paris	Observer	June 3, 2006	June 3, 2006	June 3, 2006	June 3, 2006	June 3, 2006	2005	70 years pma
Morocco	Paris A	Paris	January 1, 1995			June 30, 1983			2000	50 years pma (from end of year)
Mozambique			August 26, 1995						2001	70 years pma
Myanmar			January 1, 1995						1914 (2001)	50 years pma

Signatories	Berne Convention[2] September 9, 1886 and Subsequent Acts	UCC[3] September 6, 1952 revised in Paris, July 24, 1971	TRIPS April 15, 1994	Rome Convention October 26, 1961	Geneva Phonograms Convention October 29, 1971	Satellite Convention May 21, 1974	WIPO Copyright Treaty[4]	WIPO Performances and Phonograms Treaty[5]	Date of Principal Law (most recent amendment)[6]	Period of Protection[6]
Namibia	Paris A		January 1, 1995						1978 (1997)	50 years pma (from end of year)
Nauru									1956 (1971)	50 years pma
Nepal	Paris A, H		April 23, 2004						2002	50 years pma
Netherlands	Paris A[12]	Paris	January 1, 1995[12]	October 7, 1993[12] &[8]	October 12, 1993[12] &[8]				1912 (2006)	70 years pma (from end of year)
New Zealand	Rome	Geneva	January 1, 1995		August 13, 1976				1994 (2005)	50 years pma (from end of year)
Nicaragua	Paris A	Geneva	September 3, 1995	August 10, 2000	August 10, 2000	August 25, 1979	March 6, 2003	March 6, 2003	1999	70 years from January 1 pma
Niger	Paris A	Paris	December 13, 1996	May 18, 1964[8]					1993	50 years pma (from end of year)

Signatories	Berne Convention[2] September 9, 1886 and Subsequent Acts	UCC[3] September 6, 1952 revised in Paris, July 24, 1971	TRIPS April 15, 1994	Rome Convention October 26, 1961	Geneva Phonograms Convention October 29, 1971	Satellite Convention May 21, 1974	WIPO Copyright Treaty[4]	WIPO Performances and Phonograms Treaty[5]	Date of Principal Law (most recent amendment)[6]	Period of Protection[6]
Nigeria	Paris A	Geneva	January 1, 1995	October 29, 1993[8]					1988 (1999)	70 years pma (from the end of the year)
Norway	Paris A, I	Paris	January 1, 1995	July 10, 1978[8]	August 1, 1978				1961 (2005)	70 years pma (from end of year); 50 years for certain works
Oman	Paris A, D, H		November 9, 2000				September 20, 2005	September 20, 2005	2000	50 years from January 1, pma
Pakistan	Rome Stockholm B	Geneva	January 1, 1995						1962 (2000)	50 years from January 1, pma
Panama	Paris A	Paris	September 6, 1997	September 2, 1983	June 29, 1974	September 25, 1985	March 6, 2002	May 20, 2002	1994 (2000)	50 years pma
Papua New Guinea			June 9, 1996						2000	50 years pma

Signatories	Berne Convention[2] September 9, 1886 and Subsequent Acts	UCC[3] September 6, 1952 revised in Paris, July 24, 1971	TRIPS April 15, 1994	Rome Convention October 26, 1961	Geneva Phonograms Convention October 29, 1971	Satellite Convention May 21, 1974	WIPO Copyright Treaty[4]	WIPO Performances and Phonograms Treaty[5]	Date of Principal Law (most recent amendment)[6]	Period of Protection[6]
Paraguay	Paris A	Geneva	January 1, 1995	February 26, 1970	February 13, 1979		March 6, 2002	May 20, 2002	1998 (1999)	70 years pma
Peru	Paris A	Paris	January 1, 1995	August 7, 1985	August 24, 1985	August 7, 1985	March 6, 2002	July 18, 2002	1996	70 years pma
Philippines	Paris A, D		January 1, 1995	September 25, 1984			October 4, 2002	October 4, 2002	1998	50 years pma
Poland	Paris A	Paris	July 1, 1995	June 13, 1997[8]			March 23, 2004	October 21, 2003	1994 (2005)	70 years pma
Portugal	Paris A, G	Paris	January 1, 1995	July 17, 2002		March 11, 1996			1985 (2004)	70 years pma
Qatar	Paris A		January 13, 1996				October 28, 2005	October 28, 2005	2002	50 years pma
Republic of Korea	Paris A	Paris*	January 1, 1995		October 10, 1987		June 24, 2004		1986 (1998)	50 years from January 1, pma
Republic of Moldova	Paris A	Geneva	July 26, 2001	December 5, 1995[8]	July 17, 2000		March 6, 2002	May 20, 2002	1994 (2004)	50 years from January 1, pma
Romania	Paris A		January 1, 1995	October 22, 1998[8]	October 1, 1998		March 6, 2002	May 20, 2002	1996	70 years pma
Russian Federation	Paris A	Paris	Observer[7]	May 26, 2003[8]	March 13, 1995	January 20, 1989			1993 (2004)	70 years from January 1, pma

Signatories	Berne Convention[2] September 9, 1886 and Subsequent Acts	UCC[3] September 6, 1952 revised in Paris, July 24, 1971	TRIPS April 15, 1994	Rome Convention October 26, 1961	Geneva Phonograms Convention October 29, 1971	Satellite Convention May 21, 1974	WIPO Copyright Treaty[4]	WIPO Performances and Phonograms Treaty[5]	Date of Principal Law (most recent amendment)[6]	Period of Protection[6]
Rwanda	Paris A	Paris	May 22, 1996			July 25, 2001			1983	50 years pma
Saint Kitts and Nevis	Paris A		February 21, 1996						1919	50 years pma minimum of BC
Saint Lucia	Paris A, H		January 1, 1995	August 17, 1996[8]	April 2, 2001		March 6, 2002	May 20, 2002	1995 (2000)	50 years pma
Saint Vincent and the Grenadines	Paris A	Paris	January 1, 1995						2003	70 year pma (from end of year)
Samoa	Paris A, D		Observer[7]						1998	75 years pma
San Marino									1991	50 years pma (from end of year)
Sao Tome and Principe			Observer[7]						Unknown	
Saudi Arabia	Paris A	Paris	December 11, 2005						2004	50 years pma
Senegal	Paris A	Paris	January 1, 1995				May 18, 2002	May 20, 2002	1973 (1986)	50 years pma (from end of year)

Signatories	Berne Convention[2] September 9, 1886 and Subsequent Acts	UCC[3] September 6, 1952 revised in Paris, July 24, 1971	TRIPS April 15, 1994	Rome Convention October 26, 1961	Geneva Phonograms Convention October 29, 1971	Satellite Convention May 21, 1974	WIPO Copyright Treaty[4]	WIPO Performances and Phonograms Treaty[5]	Date of Principal Law (most recent amendment)[6]	Period of Protection[6]
Serbia (Republic of)	Paris A, E	Paris	Observer[7]	June 10, 2003	June 10, 2003	April 27, 1992	June 13, 2003	June 13, 2003	2005	70 years pma
Seychelles			Observer[7]						1984 (1991)	25 years pma (from end of year)
Sierra Leone			July 23, 1995						1965	50 years pma (from end of the year)
Singapore	Paris A, C		January 1, 1995			April 27, 2005	April 17, 2005	April 17, 2005[13]	1987 (2005)	50 years pma (from end of the year)
Slovakia (Slovak Republic)	Paris A	Paris	January 1, 1995	January 1, 1993[8]	January 1, 1993		March 6, 2002	May 20, 2002	2003	70 years from January 1, pma
Slovenia	Paris A, E	Paris	July 30, 1995	October 9, 1996[8]	October 15, 1996	June 25, 1991	March 6, 2002	May 20, 2002	1995 (2004)	70 years pma

Signatories	Berne Convention[2] September 9, 1886 and Subsequent Acts	UCC[3] September 6, 1952 revised in Paris, July 24, 1971	TRIPS April 15, 1994	Rome Convention October 26, 1961	Geneva Phonograms Convention October 29, 1971	Satellite Convention May 21, 1974	WIPO Copyright Treaty[4]	WIPO Performances and Phonograms Treaty[5]	Date of Principal Law (most recent amendment)[6]	Period of Protection[6]
Solomon Islands			July 26, 1996						1987 (1996)	50 years pma (from end of year)
South Africa	Brussels Paris B, H		January 1, 1995						1978 (2002)	50 years pma (from end of year)
Spain	Paris A	Paris	January 1, 1995	November 14, 1991[8]	August 24, 1974				1996 (2000)	70 years pma
Sri Lanka	Paris A, D	Paris	January 1, 1995						2003	70 years pma
Sudan	Paris A, D		Observer[7]						1996	50 years pma; 25 years pma for certain works
Suriname	Paris A		January 1, 1995						1913 (1984)	50 years pma
Swaziland	Paris A		January 1, 1995						No legislation	50 years pma minimum of BC
Sweden	Paris A	Paris	January 1, 1995	May 18, 1964[8]	April 18, 1973				1960 (2005)	70 years pma

Signatories	Berne Convention[2] September 9, 1886 and Subsequent Acts	UCC[3] September 6, 1952 revised in Paris, July 24, 1971	TRIPS April 15, 1994	Rome Convention October 26, 1961	Geneva Phonograms Convention October 29, 1971	Satellite Convention May 21, 1974	WIPO Copyright Treaty[4]	WIPO Performances and Phonograms Treaty[5]	Date of Principal Law (most recent amendment)[6]	Period of Protection[6]
Switzerland	Paris A	Paris	July 1, 1995	September 24, 1993[8]	September 30, 1993	September 24, 1993			1992 (2002)	70 years pma, 50 years for certain works (both from end of year)
Syrian Arab Republic	Paris A, D			May 13, 2006					2001	50 years pma
Taipei (China)			January 1, 2002						Unknown	50 years pma minimum of TRIPs
Taiwan									1992 (2004)	50 years pma
Tajikistan	Paris A	Geneva	Observer[7]						1998 (2003)	50 years pma
Thailand	Paris A, D, H,		January 1, 1995						1994	50 years pma
The former Yugoslav Republic of Macedonia	Paris A	Paris	April 4, 2003	March 2, 1998[8]	March 2, 1998	November 17, 1991	February 4, 2004	March 20, 2005[14]	1996 (1998)	70 years pma

Signatories	Berne Convention[2] September 9, 1886 and Subsequent Acts	UCC[3] September 6, 1952 revised in Paris, July 24, 1971	TRIPS April 15, 1994	Rome Convention October 26, 1961	Geneva Phonograms Convention October 29, 1971	Satellite Convention May 21, 1974	WIPO Copyright Treaty[4]	WIPO Performances and Phonograms Treaty[5]	Date of Principal Law (most recent amendment)[6]	Period of Protection[6]
Togo	Paris A	Paris	May 31, 1995	June 10, 2003	June 10, 2003	June 10, 2003	May 21, 2003	May 21, 2003	1991	50 years pma (from end of year)
Tonga	Paris A		Observer[7]						1985 (1988)	50 years pma (from end of year)
Trinidad and Tobago	Paris A	Paris	March 1, 1995		October 1, 1988	November 1, 1996			1997 (2000)	50 years pma; 75 years from publication for certain works
Tunisia	Paris A, H	Paris	March 29, 1995						1994	50 years from January 1, pma
Turkey	Paris A, H		March 26, 1995	April 8, 2004					1951 (2006)	70 years pma

Signatories	Berne Convention[2] September 9, 1886 and Subsequent Acts	UCC[3] September 6, 1952 revised in Paris, July 24, 1971	TRIPS April 15, 1994	Rome Convention October 26, 1961	Geneva Phonograms Convention October 29, 1971	Satellite Convention May 21, 1974	WIPO Copyright Treaty[4]	WIPO Performances and Phonograms Treaty[5]	Date of Principal Law (most recent amendment)[6]	Period of Protection[6]
Uganda			January 1, 1995						1964	50 years pma or from publication, whichever ever latest
Ukraine	Paris A	Geneva	Observer[7]	June 12, 2002	February 18, 2000		March 6, 2002	May 20, 2002	2001 (2003)	70 years pma
United Arab Emirates	Paris A, D		April 10, 1996	January 14, 2005			July 14, 2004	June 9, 2005	2002	50 years from January 1, pma
United Kingdom	Paris A, I (extended to the Isle of Man from March 18, 1996)	Paris	January 1, 1995	May 18, 1964 (extended to Isle of Man from July 28, 1999)[8]	April 18, 1973				1988 (2007)	70 years pma
United Republic of Tanzania	Paris A, H		January 1, 1995						1999 (2003)	50 years pma (from end of year)

Signatories	Berne Convention[2] September 9, 1886 and Subsequent Acts	UCC[3] September 6, 1952 revised in Paris, July 24, 1971	TRIPS April 15, 1994	Rome Convention October 26, 1961	Geneva Phonograms Convention October 29, 1971	Satellite Convention May 21, 1974	WIPO Copyright Treaty[4]	WIPO Performances and Phonograms Treaty[5]	Date of Principal Law (most recent amendment)[6]	Period of Protection[6]
United States of America	Paris A	Paris	January 1, 1995		March 10, 1974	March 7, 1985	March 6, 2002	May 20, 2002[15]	1976 (2006)	70 years pma; for works made for hire 95 years from first publication or 120 years from creation, whichever expires first
Uruguay	Paris A	Paris	January 1, 1995	July 4, 1977	January 18, 1983				1937 (2003)	50 years pma
Uzbekistan	Paris A, D		Observer[7]						1996	50 years from January 1, pma
Vanuatu			Observer[7]							

Signatories	Berne Convention[2] September 9, 1886 and Subsequent Acts	UCC[3] September 6, 1952 revised in Paris, July 24, 1971	TRIPS April 15, 1994	Rome Convention October 26, 1961	Geneva Phonograms Convention October 29, 1971	Satellite Convention May 21, 1974	WIPO Copyright Treaty[4]	WIPO Performances and Phonograms Treaty[5]	Date of Principal Law (most recent amendment)[6]	Period of Protection[6]
Venezuela (Bolivarian Republic of)	Paris A, H	Paris	January 1, 1995	January 30, 1996	November 18, 1982				1993 (1999)	60 years from January 1, pma
Viet Nam	Paris A, D, H		January 11, 2007	March 1, 2007[8]	July 6, 2005	January 12, 2006			1995 (2006)	50 years pma (from end of year)
Yemen			Observer[7]						1994	30 years from January 1, pma or 25 years from January 1, of year of production for certain works

Signatories	Berne Convention[2] September 9, 1886 and Subsequent Acts	UCC[3] September 6, 1952 revised in Paris, July 24, 1971	TRIPS April 15, 1994	Rome Convention October 26, 1961	Geneva Phonograms Convention October 29, 1971	Satellite Convention May 21, 1974	WIPO Copyright Treaty[4]	WIPO Performances and Phonograms Treaty[5]	Date of Principal Law (most recent amendment)[6]	Period of Protection[6]
Zambia	Paris A	Geneva	January 1, 1995						1994	50 years pma (from end of year)
Zimbabwe	Rome Paris B		March 5, 1995						1967 (1982)	50 years pma (from end of year)
Total number of Member States	163	Paris 65 Geneva 35 Total 100	Member States 151 Observers 30	86	76	30	64	62	178 laws 8 unknown 3 no legislation	

[1] This table reflects the status of ratifications and accessions to the Conventions as of July 31, 2007. The authors are indebted to WIPO, Unesco and the WTO for the information used in compiling this table. For more up to date information, see the following web pages: *www.wipo.org*; *www.portal.unesco.org/culture*; and *http://www.wto.org*.

[2] Berne Convention: "Paris" means the Berne Convention as revised at Paris on July 24, 1971 (Paris Act); "Stockholm" means the said Convention as revised at Stockholm on July 14, 1967 (Stockholm Act); "Brussels" means the said Convention as revised at Brussels on June 26, 1948 (Brussels Act); "Rome" means the said Convention as revised at Rome on June 2, 1928 (Rome Act). Paris Revision Countries which have ratified or acceded to the entire Paris Act of the Berne Convention, including the Appendix, are indicated as "Paris A". Countries which have declared that their ratification or accession does not apply to Arts. 1–21 and the Appendix are indicated as "Paris B". Countries which availed themselves of one or both of the faculties provided for in Arts II and III of the Appendix until October 10, 2004, are indicated as "Paris C". Countries which have availed themselves of one or both of the faculties provided for in Arts II and III of the Appendix until October 10, 2014, are indicated as "Paris D". Countries which made a declaration concerning the right of translation under Art. V of the Appendix are indicated as "Paris E". Countries which made a declaration under Art. 14*bis*(2) (b) are indicated as "Paris F" (presumption of legitimation for some authors who have brought contributions to the making of the cinematographic work). Countries which have made a declaration under Art. 14*bis*(2)(c) are indicated as "Paris G" (undertaking by authors to bring contributions to the making of a cinematographic work must be in writing). Countries which made a declaration under Art. 33(2) relating to the International Court of Justice are indicated as "Paris H". Countries which made a declaration that they admit the application of the Appendix of the Paris Act to works of which it is the State of origin are indicated as Paris I.

Stockholm Revision: The substantive provisions of the Stockholm revision did not, and now cannot, come into force. However, previous Acts remain in force in relations with those countries of the Union which have not ratified or acceded to the Paris Act. For countries which have ratified or acceded to the whole of the Paris Act and the Appendix, no reference is made to either Stockholm or earlier revisions. Countries which declared that their ratification or accession does not apply to Arts. 1–21 of the Stockholm Act and the Protocol Regarding Developing Countries are indicated as "Stockholm B". This also indicates countries which ratified or acceded to the entire Stockholm Act, the substantive provisions of which have not come into force.

[3] UCC: Countries which have ratified or acceded to the 1971 Paris revised Convention are indicated as "Paris" (most of these are party also to the Geneva Convention); others are shown as "Geneva". Countries which have availed themselves of the exceptions in favour of developing countries are indicated as "Paris*".

[4] The WIPO Copyright Treaty entered into force on March 6, 2002. See para. 24–82 above.

[5] The WIPO Performances and Phonograms Treaty entered into force on May 20, 2002. See para. 24–138 above.

[6] The date of the principal law is given, with the date of the most recent amendment in brackets. The period of protection is for literary and artistic works (as defined in Art. 2(1) of the Berne Convention), and is indicated as either *post mortem auctoris* (pma), pma from the end of the calendar year, or pma from January 1 of the following year. Many countries have different periods of protection for different works, *e.g.* for photographs, computer programs, collective works,

works where the author is a legal entity and for the subject-matter of related rights. For some works the period of protection runs from the date of publication. In some countries the period of protection is less than that required by international convention. In such cases the indicated period does not apply to foreign works. This Table is up-to-date as of July 31, 2007. It is intended as a general guide only, and more detailed information can be obtained at *http://wipo.org/ clea/en/index.html* and *http://portal.unesco.org/culture* (Collection of National Copyright Laws).

[7] An "observer" State must start accession negotiations within five years of becoming an observer (except Holy See).

[8] The instruments of ratification or accession, or subsequent notifications, deposited with the Secretary-General of the United Nations by the following States contain declarations made under the articles mentioned hereafter (with reference to publication in *Le Droit d'auteur* (Copyright) for the years 1962 to 1964, in *Copyright* for the years 1965 to 1994, in *Industrial Property and Copyright* until May 1998 and, in *Intellectual Property Laws and Treaties* from June 1998 until December 2001). Thereafter, notifications may be consulted on the WIPO website: *www.wipo.int/treaties*.

Algeria, Articles 5(3) (concerning Article 5(1)(c), Article 6(2) and Article 16(1)(a)(iii) and (iv)).

Australia, Articles 5(3) (concerning Article 5(1)(c)), 6(2), 16(1)(a)(i) and 16(1)(b) [1992, p. 301];

Austria, Article 16(1)(a)(iii) and (iv) and 1(b) [1973, p. 67];

Belarus, Articles 5(3) (concerning Article 5(1)(b)), 6(2), 16(1)(a)(iii) and (iv);

Belgium, Articles 5(3) (concerning Article 5(1)(c)), 6(2), 16(1)(a)(iii) and (iv) [1999, p. 119];

Bulgaria, Article 16(1)(a)(iii) and (iv) [1995, p. 262];

Canada, Article 5(3) (concerning Articles 5(1)(b) and (c)), 6(2) (concerning Article 6(1)) and 16(1)(a)(iv) [1998, p. 42]

Congo, Articles 5(3) (concerning Article 5(1)(c)) and 16(1)(a)(i) [1964, p. 127];

Croatia, Articles 5(3) (concerning Article 5(1)(b)) and 16(1)(a)(iii) and (iv) [2000, p. 14];

Czech Republic, Article 16(1)(a)(iii) and (iv) [1964, p. 110];

Denmark, Articles 5(3) (concerning Article 5(1)(c)), 6(2), 16(1)(a)(ii) and (iv) [1965, p. 214];

Estonia, Articles 5(3) (concerning Articles 5(1) (c)), and 6(2), and as from October 9, 2003, Article 16(1)(a)(iv);

Fiji, Articles 5(3) (concerning Article 5(1)(b)), 6(2) and 16(1) (a)(i) [1972, pp. 88 and 178];

Finland, Articles 16(1)(a)(i), (ii) and (iv) and 17 [1983, p. 287 and 1994, p. 152];

France, Articles 5(3) (concerning Article 5(1)(c)) and 16(1)(a)(iii) and (iv) [1987, p. 184];

Germany, Articles 5(3) (concerning Article 5(1)(b)) and 16(1)(a)(iv) [1966, p. 237];

Iceland, Articles 5(3) (concerning Article 5(1)(b)), 6(2) and 16(1)(a)(i), (ii), (iii) and (iv) [1994, p. 152];

Ireland, Articles 5(3) (concerning Article 5(1)(b)), 6(2) and 16(1)(a)(ii) [1979, p. 218];

Israel, Articles 5(3) (concerning Article 5(1)(b)), 6(2) (concerning Article 6(1)) and 16(1)(a)(iii), (iv) and 16(1)(b);

Italy, Articles 6(2), 16(1)(a)(ii), (iii) and (iv), 16(1)(b) and 17 [1975, p. 44];

Japan, Articles 5(3) (concerning Article 5(1)(c)) and 16(1)(a)(ii) and (iv) [1989, p. 288];

Latvia, Article 16(1)(a)(iii) [1999, p. 76];

Lesotho, Article 16(1)(a)(ii) and (1)(b) [1990, p. 95];

Liechtenstein, Article 5(3) (concerning Article 5(1)(b)) and Article 16(1)(a)(iii) and (iv) [1999, p. 119];

Lithuania, Article 16(1)(a)(iii) [1999, p. 76];

Luxembourg, Articles 5(3) (concerning Article 5(1)(c)), 16(1)(a)(i) and 16(1)(b) [1976, p. 24];

Monaco, Articles 5(3) (concerning Article 5(1)(c)), 16(1)(a)(i) and 16(1)(b) [1985, p. 422];

Netherlands, Article 16(1)(a)(iii) and (iv) [1993, p. 253];

Niger, Articles 5(3) (concerning Article 5(1)(c)) and 16(1)(a)(i) [1963, p. 155];

Nigeria, Articles 5(3) (concerning Article 5(1)(c)), 6(2) and 16(1)(a)(ii), (iii) and (iv) [1993, p. 253];

Norway, Articles 6(2) and 16(1)(a)(iii) and (iv) [1978, p. 133; in respect of 16(1)(a)(ii) modified: 1989, p. 288];

Poland, Articles 5(3) (concerning Article 5(1) (c)), 6(2), and 16(1)(a)(ii), (iii) and (iv) and 16(1)(b) [1997 p. 170];

Republic of Moldova, Articles 5(3) (concerning Article 5(1)(b)), 6(2), 16(1)(a)(iii), (iii) and (iv) [1996, p. 40];

Romania, Articles 5(3), 6(2), 16(1)(a)(iii) and (iv) [1998, p. 54];

Russian Federation, Articles 5(3) (concerning Article 5(1)(b)), 6(2) and 16(1)(a)(iii) and (iv);

Saint Lucia, Articles 5(3) (concerning Article 5(1)(c)) and 16(1)(a)(iii);

Slovakia, Article 16(1)(a)(iii) and (iv) [1964, p. 110];

Slovenia, Articles 5(3) (concerning Article 5(1)(c)) and 16(1)(a)(i) [1996, p. 318];

Spain, Articles 5(3) (concerning Article 5(1)(c)), 6(2) and 16(1)(a)(iii) and (iv) [1991, p. 221];

Sweden, Article 16(1)(a)(iv) [1962, p. 211; 1986, p. 382];

Switzerland, Articles 5(3) (concerning Article 5(1)(b)) and 16(1)(a)(iii) and (iv) [1993, p. 254];

The former Yugoslav Republic of Macedonia, Articles 5(3) (concerning Article 5(1)(c)) and 16(1)(a)(i) [1998, p. 42];

United Kingdom, Articles 5(3) (concerning Article 5(1)(b)), 6(2) and 16(1)(a)(ii), (iii) and (iv) [1963, p. 244]; the same declarations were made for Gibraltar and Bermuda [1967, p. 36; 1970, p. 108].

Viet Nam, Articles 16(1)(a)(i) and 16(1)(b) concerning Articles 12 and 13(d).

[9] Pursuant to Art.15, para.3 of the Treaty, the Republic of Chile will apply the provisions of Art.15, para.1 of the Treaty only in respect of direct uses of phonograms published for commercial purposes for broadcasting or for any communication to the public. Pursuant to Art.15, para.3 of the Treaty, as regards Phonograms the producer or performer of which is a national of another Contracting Party which has made a declaration under Art.15, para.3 of the Treaty, the Republic of Chile will apply, notwithstanding the provisions of the preceding declaration, the provisions of Art.15, para.1 of the Treaty to the extent that Party grants the protection provided for by the provisions of Art.15, para.1 of the Treaty.

[10] The Paris Act of the Berne Convention and the Geneva Phonograms Convention have applied to Hong Kong from July 1, 1997 and to Macao from December 20, 1999.

[11] Pursuant to Art.3(3), Japan will not apply the criterion of publication concerning the protection of producers of phonograms. Pursuant to Art.15(3), Japan will apply the provisions of Art.15(1) to the extent that Party grants the protection provided for by Art.15(1); and Japan will apply the provisions of Art.15(1) in respect of direct uses for broadcasting or for wire diffusion, but Japan will not apply the provisions of Art.15(1) to the phonograms made available to the public, by wire or wireless means, in such a way that members of the public may access them from a place and at a time individually chosen by them.

[12] Accession for the Kingdom in Europe. Arts 22–38 of the Paris Act of the Berne Convention apply also to the Netherlands Antilles and Aruba.

[13] Pursuant to Art.15(3), Singapore will limit the provisions of Art.15(1) in the following ways: (i) Producers of phonograms have the exclusive right to make available to the public a sound recording by means of, or as part of, a digital audio transmission; and (ii) Performers can bring an action of unauthorised communication of a live performance to the public (on a network or otherwise) in such a way that the recording may be accessed by any person from a place and at a time chosen by him. In this context, "communication" includes broadcasting, inclusion in a cable programme service and the making available of the live performance in such a way that the performance may be accessed by any person from a place and at a time chosen by him.

[14] Pursuant to Art.3(3) of the treaty, the FYRM shall not apply the provision on the criterion of publication in respect of the national treatment on protection of phonogram producers in relation to the expressed reservation of the FRYM on Art.5(3) of the International Convention Protection of Performers, Phonograms Producers and Broadcasting Organization (Rome Convention). Pursuant to Art.15(3) of the WPPT, the FRYM shall also not apply the provision on single equitable remuneration for the performers and for the phonogram producers for direct or indirect use of phonograms published for commercial purposes for broadcasting or for any other communication to the public, in relation to the expressed reservation of the FYRM on Art.16(1)(a)(i) of the Rome Convention.

[15] Pursuant to Art.15(3) of the WIPO Performances and Phonograms Treaty, the United States will apply the provisions of Art.15(1) of the WIPO Performances and Phonograms Treaty only in respect of certain acts of broadcasting and communication to the public by digital means for which a direct or indirect fee is charged for reception, and for other retransmissions and digital phonrecord deliveries, as provided under the United States law.

[16] Pursuant to Article 3(3) of the treaty, Australia will not apply the criterion of publication concerning the protection of producers of phonograms. Further, it will not apply the provisions of Article 15(1) in respect of: (a) the use of phonograms for (i) radio broadcasting, and (ii) communication to the public within the meaning of the first sentence of Article 2(g), and (b) the communication to the public of phonograms by way of making the sounds of the phonograms available to the public by means of the operation of equipment to receive a broadcast or other transmission of the phonograms.

[17] Pursuant to Article 3(3) of the treaty, Belgium will not apply the criterion of publication with effect from August 30, 2006.

[18] The WCT and WPPT shall not apply to the Hong Kong Special Administrative Region and the Macao Special Administrative Region of the People's Republic of China. Further, China does not consider itself bound by Article 15(1) WPPT.

Chapter Twenty Seven

EXPLOITATION OF RIGHTS IN PARTICULAR INDUSTRIES

Contents

Contents   *Para.*

1. THE PUBLISHING INDUSTRY

A. THE GENERAL NATURE OF THE PUBLISHING INDUSTRY

Book publishing. Developments in print-on-demand technology and the Internet **27–02** have led to a growth in self-publishing opportunities. Websites such as Lulu.com and Author-House offer authors the opportunity to publish their works at minimal cost to themselves, but with the opportunity of wide availability, including through Internet booksellers, such as Amazon and Barnes & Noble, and through conventional bookshops. These websites allow authors to retain full control over their work, including design, ownership of rights and pricing. Books are printed only when orders are received, so there is no inventory.

Perhaps the most significant development in this area is the launch by Amazon, through its US website Amazon.com, of its self-publishing service branded "CreateSpace". Authors upload their work in PDF form, the files are checked to ensure that they comply with the CreateSpace technical submission requirements, and once that hurdle has been successfully cleared, a proof is ordered so that the author can check and be satisfied with the book. Once the book is finished, it can be available for sale on Amazon.com within 15 business days. Authors can choose the sales channels through which the book is available, which could be just the author's own CreateSpace E-Store or can also include Amazon.com. However, the books cannot at present be listed for sale on any of Amazon's other international websites. This can have implications for the amount which the author receives from each sale, because CreateSpace charges a percentage of the list price (20 per cent on sales through the author's CreateSpace E-Store but 30 per cent on sales through Amazon.com) plus a fixed charge (currently US$3.15 per copy) plus a charge per page.

27–03   Book Distribution.

(f) *Internet sales*

Add: *Amazon.co.uk* is the dominant online UK-based bookseller. Other online booksellers, such as Borders, Books Etc and Waterstone's, use *Amazon.co.uk* to manage their online retail sales operation. Many independent booksellers, publishers and individuals also use *Amazon.co.uk* to reach new markets by listing stock and selling books on the *Amazon.co.uk* Marketplace platform, which can also provide an opportunity to buy rare and out of print books. *Amazon.co.uk*'s Associates scheme enables third-party websites to link to *Amazon.co.uk* and be paid a proportion of any sales that are made as a result of the link. This option has been popular with individual booksellers, publishers and other organisations, such as schools, fan sites and charities, as well as private individuals. For Amazon's digitisation programme, see Supplement paragraph 27–78B, below.

A UK website The Book Depository (*www.bookdepositoiy.co.uk*) has the aim of "making 'All books available to All' through pioneering supply chain initiatives, republishing and digitising of content", and is both a book distributor and also a publisher in that it reprints a substantial (and increasing) number of titles that are out of print and can supply them within a few days. The Book Depository claims to be the fastest growing book distributor in Europe.

A new development, reported in *The Bookseller* in September 2007, sees major publishers competing with, and even undercutting, retailers in selling books direct from their own revamped websites. Random House UK, Penguin and Pan Macmillan are all now selling books directly to consumers, offering online discounts. Hachette Livre is overhauling all of its websites with a view to commencing direct sales to consumers. HarperCollins is expected to relaunch its website with direct sales to consumers in time for Christmas 2007. How all of this will affect booksellers remains to be seen, but the Booksellers Association is clearly concerned. Publishers are trying to reassure the industry that they are not intending to take sales away from booksellers, but rather add some extra value, for example in terms of additional content. But unless publishers are actually generating new business by their direct-to-consumer sales, it is hard to see how this can do anything but harm to booksellers' sales. Concern has also been expressed by the Booksellers Association that consumers might be confused by the multiplicity of places to buy books online, and that their response may be simply to default to purchasing from Amazon, rather than, for example, independent booksellers' websites.

Magazine distribution. For the latest available statistics of the UK magazine   **27–05**
publishing industry, see the website of The Periodical Publishers' Association at
www.ppa.co.uk.

Journal publishing. For the latest available statistics of the UK journal publish-   **27–06**
ing industry, see the website of The Association of Learned and Professional Society Publishers at *www.alpsp.org.* However, the statistics available here are not
terribly up-to-date.

E. COLLECTING SOCIETIES AND LICENSING AGENCIES RESPONSIBLE FOR
ADMINISTERING RIGHTS

Educational users. The Educational Recording Agency Ltd scheme has been   **27–32**
superseded a number of times. The present scheme is set out in SI 2007/266. See
Supplement at **B2.i.**

F. PUBLISHING AGREEMENTS

(ii) Formal agreements: common forms of publishing arrangements

Agreements conferring licences. The industry continues to debate whether or   **27–36**
not recommended retail prices should continue to be shown on book covers. At
the annual Booksellers' Association Conference in May 2006 it was decided to
continue with the practice of printing prices on books, but the debate looks likely
to go on. Whether the practice of stipulating recommended retail prices could
infringe competition law, given that in the vast majority of cases books will be
sold in retail shops at the recommended retail prices specified by publishers, especially if printed on the book covers, is yet to be decided.

G. MATTERS TO BE CONSIDERED IN DRAFTING PUBLISHING AGREEMENTS

(ii) Minimum Terms Agreements

The Society of Authors continues to have MTAs with most of the major trade   **27–44**
publishers (*e.g.* Penguin, Random House, HarperCollins, Bloomsbury) but they
could benefit from some updating to reflect the latest industry practice. The Society of Authors assists its members who negotiate their own contracts with
publishers by issuing its "Quick Guide to Publishing Contracts" and by providing
detailed advice.

I. CONSEQUENCES OF BREACH OF A PUBLISHING AGREEMENT

(iii) Breach of contract to ghost-write an autobiography

In *Sadler v Reynolds* [2005] EWHC QB 309, it was held that Reynolds had   **27–73A**
breached a contract with Sadler under which Sadler was to write Reynolds'
autobiography and to share the proceeds equally. The breach consisted of entering into a contract with another ghost-writer for the same purpose. The publisher
with whom Sadler had negotiated a contract for publication of Reynolds'
autobiography gave evidence that the advance agreed (£70,000 to be shared
equally between Sadler and Reynolds) was intended to represent their likely
royalties from the book, and the judge accordingly awarded Sadler £35,000 for
loss of royalties and a further sum of £1,000 for loss of the opportunity to enhance
his reputation by publication of the book.

J. PARTICULAR PROBLEMS OR POINTS WHICH CONFRONT THE PUBLISHING INDUSTRY

27–74   **Territorial rights.** UK trade publishers are facing a number of difficulties, including:

- increasing parallel importation of US "open market" editions entering the UK via Europe;
- the value of UK English language rights being diminished by parallel importation of US editions via other European countries;
- the growth of internet bookselling facilitating parallel importation;
- parallel importation of "open market" editions facilitating the trade in illegal (infringing) editions which have not entered the EU lawfully.

In response, UK publishers are increasingly seeking from authors and agents Exclusive English Language Rights to Europe as a practical way of protecting their home market, where previously they had held exclusive UK territorial rights. It is anticipated that with more countries joining the EU, the incentive for UK publishers, authors and authors' agents to acquire and sell Exclusive European Rights, which can be operated effectively within the Community regime of Exhaustion of Rights, is likely to increase.

Following discussions between representatives of The Publishers Association and Amazon.co.uk, a new notice-and-take-down procedure has been introduced to deal with territorial (or other) rights infringements both for main catalogue items and items being resold on Marketplace on Amazon.co.uk. This should help UK publishers protect their UK exclusivity from being infringed by the importation of American editions via the Internet.

27–76   **Site licensing of journals. Add:** A series of model licences has been developed for the acquisition of electronic journals and other electronic resources by libraries of various types: single academic institutions; academic consortia; public libraries; and corporate and other special libraries. They are available free of charge from *www.licensingmodels.com*.

A group made up of publishers and members of the Pharma Documentation Ring (which comprises companies in the pharmaceutical industry) has produced a new Model Licence for the licensing of digital journal content to the pharmaceutical industry. The Model Licence, along with a background document outlining the history of the Model Licence and explanations of the rationale behind some of the clauses, can be downloaded from the ALPSP website.

27–78   **Electronic publishing generally.** A Trial Scanning Licence for Further Education was introduced by the Copyright Licensing Agency ("CLA") in 2003 and a Trial Photocopying and Scanning Licence for Higher Education was introduced by CLA in 2005. In September 2006 CLA announced that it has extended its standard licence for independent Higher Education Institutions ("HEIs") to permit them and their registered students to make digital copies of documents, as well as physical photocopies. This brings the licence into line with the standard licence for the HEIs which are members of Universities UK or the Standing Conference of Principals. The new licences will run for an initial two-year trial period until August 31, 2008. Details and copies of these licences and associated documents (such as a User Guide) can be obtained from the CLA website *www.cla.co.uk*.

In March 2007 CLA announced that following lengthy negotiations, it has agreed a central photocopying and scanning licence for the NHS in England.

In April 2007 CLA clarified the distinction between the photocopying and scanning licences granted to HEIs and to the NHS in England, Wales, Scotland and Northern Ireland. CLA stated that it recognised that there is a significant degree of co-operation, collaboration and partnership between HEIs and NHS Trusts—especially in respect of Teaching Hospitals, joint library facilities and staff engaged in delivering teaching and/or participating in courses of study in one or both sectors, and made clear that the principles underpinning the making of licensed copies are that:

- copies made by, for or on behalf of staff and students of a university or College of Higher Education are subject to the terms of the HE Licence;
- copies made by, for, or on behalf of, staff employed by the NHS are subject to the terms and conditions of the NHS Licence;
- all copying activity should retain an intimate link between the collection of printed books, journals and magazines owned by the respective HEI or NHS Trust and its delivery to an authorised user contracted to/enrolled with that HEI or contracted to that NHS Trust.

CLA announced on October 15, 2007 that it has introduced a new licence to the Adult Education sector. The enhanced Trial Scanning Licence is now available to all Adult and Community Education and Learning providers. The enhanced licence permits the creation of digital copies made from print originals owned by the licensee and for those digital copies to be used with technologies such as digital whiteboards, within Virtual Learning Environments, including email and fax.

This is the first licence of its type to include digital uses such as scanning and retyping of print resources.

This licence will run on a trial basis and will come into effect from November 1, 2007.

e-books. For a number of years now, electronic books (or "e-books") have been a   **27–78A** commercial reality, available in a variety of formats for reading either on a dedicated e-book reader or on a hand-held palmtop computer, a laptop or a desktop computer. Unfortunately, at present there is no common standard used by producers and manufacturers. As a result, customers cannot read a Palm e-book on a Microsoft Reader, for example. To correct this situation, many of the major software companies and device manufacturers in the e-book market are backing new common standards that are being drafted by the International Digital Publishing Forum ("IDPF"), which will address how e-books are produced and read. Working groups have been created to establish the new specifications, which are now being made available for public consultation. The IDPF is the trade and standards association for the digital publishing industry. Its members consist of academic, trade and professional publishers, hardware and software companies, digital content retailers, libraries, educational institutions, accessibility advocates and related organisations whose common goals are to advance the competitiveness and exposure of digital publishing.

The IDPF announced on October 30, 2006 the release of a new technical standard to facilitate digital content creation, distribution and use by consumers. In addition to the Open eBook Publication Structure (OEBPS), an XML standard for authoring digital books, the IDPF has now released a new standard for packaging a digital publication, including the contents of the publication, metadata, signatures, encryption, rights and other information into one standard file. The new IDPF standard is called the Open eBook Publication Structure Container Format (OCF) and will allow publishers to release a single standard file into their sales and distribution channels and will also enable consumers to exchange unencrypted eBooks and other digital publications between reading systems that support the new standard. But Digital Rights Management ("DRM") will remain an issue on which there is unlikely to be a common solution.

In a bid to stimulate demand for e-books, the German scientific and professional publisher Springer is now offering all of its new titles as e-books and is selling digital versions of its yearly copyrighted collections dating from 2004. Further, it is moving to a more open business model that allows libraries and institutions to make e-books available to all users simultaneously at all times and permits remote access, as well as providing sophisticated management tools for librarians. Springer is not the first scientific and professional publisher to offer e-books. It is reported that John Wiley & Sons started offering electronic titles in 2001 with a range of 300 titles, and that it now has about 1,800 titles available electronically, and plans to add 500 electronic titles per year.

Sony launched an electronic bookstore on the Internet at the end of September 2006: *http://ebooks.connect.com*. It announced that it will carry about 10,000 titles from the top six publishers, including HarperCollins and Simon & Schuster. In addition, Sony has launched its new portable Reader device to go with the electronic bookstore.

27–78B   **Google and Amazon digitisation programmes.** Google and Amazon (and others, such as Microsoft and Yahoo) have been busy trying to persuade publishers and libraries to allow them to scan large quantities of books and make the digitised texts available to be searched on the Google search engine and browsed on the Amazon website.

Google: There are two aspects to the Google Print project (now known as the Google Book Search project): the Print Publisher Program and the Print Library Project.

The **Print Publisher Program** enables publishers who control the relevant rights in the book to authorise Google to scan the full text of the book into Google's search database. Then when a user does a Google search, books that contain their search terms will show up in the search results. Users will be able to preview a limited number of pages to determine whether they have found what they were looking for, and they will be provided with links to online bookstores to buy the book. This program is being put to publishers as free promotion for their books and a means to generate more sales.

The **Print Library Project** involves Google scanning into its search database millions of published books from the libraries of Harvard University, Stanford University, the University of Michigan, the University of Wisconsin-Madison, the University of Virginia, Universidad Complutense of Madrid and the University of California. The Bodleian Library, Oxford and the New York Public Library are also participating in the Print Library Project, but are only making available works that are out of copyright. In response to search queries, users will be able to browse the full text of materials that are out of copyright, but for materials that are still in copyright, users will only be able to see a few sentences of the text surrounding the search term.

Copies of Google's contracts with the University of California and the University of Michigan have become available on the Internet. Both contracts acknowledge that some of the works affected by the contract will be in copyright and others will be out of copyright, and that this may vary from jurisdiction to jurisdiction. Both contracts contain a statement that the parties intend to perform the contracts in compliance with copyright law. The sheer scale of what is involved is vast. For example, the contract with the University of California covers more than 100 libraries on the 10 campuses of the University, and the

University is required to provide no fewer than two and a half million volumes for digitisation.

The Print Library Project has given rise to litigation in the United States alleging copyright infringement. Separate lawsuits have been brought by The Authors Guild and by the Association of American Publishers on behalf of five major publisher members of its organisation: The McGraw-Hill Companies, Pearson Education, Penguin Group (USA), Simon & Schuster and John Wiley & Sons. Google claims to be entitled to scan and digitise copyright works under the "fair use" provisions of US copyright law, which are considered to be considerably wider than the "fair dealing" provisions of UK copyright law. It carries out the scanning in the US, claiming that it is entitled to do so under US law, notwithstanding that the publishers of some of the works in question may be based in other countries. It then argues that the display of only very small portions from in-copyright works does not infringe the copyrights subsisting in other countries on the test of substantiality. In the UK, organisations representing rights owners have not so far considered it necessary to take legal action. The Society of Authors wants to see digitisation conducted under licence, as does The Publishers Association. The Publishers Association has had discussions with Google, but at the time of writing, no consensus has yet emerged. In France and Germany, legal actions have been commenced against Google in respect of the Print Library Project, but the German action has reportedly been withdrawn after Google removed the titles of the German publisher in question. It has also been reported that Google China has signed up four Chinese publishers as part of the Google Book Search program.

Amazon: Amazon operates its Search Inside program in a way similar to the Google Print Publisher Program. Publishers are asked to allow Amazon to reproduce all of the authorised books in digital form so that they will be searchable by visitors to the various Amazon websites, enabling visitors to display portions of each such book on the Amazon websites.

In the UK, Penguin Books have joined the Search Inside program, after Penguin in the US had deemed it a success. Apparently, in the US Penguin found that sales of books included in the Search Inside program were between 7 and 10 per cent up. Random House and HarperCollins are reported to be "in discussions" but apparently have yet to make a firm decision on this.

Yahoo, in conjunction with Adobe Systems, Hewlett-Packard and the libraries of the University of California and the University of Toronto, has also announced a book-scanning project that would make digitised texts searchable through the Yahoo search engine. The works to be included in the project would only be those for which rights holders' permission has been obtained or works that are in the public domain.

Microsoft has also announced a similar project, limited to works that are out of copyright or, in the case of books that are in copyright, only by agreement with rights-holders. The **Windows Live Books Publisher Program** was launched in May 2006, and should be available to the general public later in 2006. As with the other digitisation programmes, books that comply with their criteria for inclusion in the programme will be scanned by Microsoft and indexed, and rights-holders can define the amount of a book that can be viewed by users. Rights-holders will receive reports to enable them to track the results of Windows Live searches on their titles. Microsoft has agreements to scan books from Cornell University's library, the British Library, the University of California and the University of Toronto.

Scientific publications: free for all. The debate about Open Access (the provision of free online access for all to scholarly research articles) continues. There   **27–79A**

are primarily two ways of achieving the objective of Open Access: the first is Open Access publishing itself; and the second is self-archiving.

Open Access publishing requires that the funding comes otherwise than from the subscribers to the Journal. Usually, there will be a subsidy (for example, from the publication's parent organisation or from a third-party grant) or from the author or his or her research funder. In a recent survey, the Association of Learned and Professional Society Publishers ("ALPSP") found that over 20 per cent of publishers were experimenting with Open Access journals. One variation on Open Access publishing is "Delayed Open Access", whereby the content of a journal is made freely available to all after a certain period—sometimes as short as six months. The idea of the delay is to protect subscription income. However, this might work for some journals but not for others. If material were made Open Access after, say, only six months, the publisher might be giving away a very significant part of the value of the material. For example, if librarians know that the articles in the journal would be free in six months' time, they might decide not to subscribe to the journal, and just wait for the material to be available free of charge. That could damage the publisher's financial viability and could also be damaging to the research process, since researchers would not have access to the most up-to-date material until it became Open Access.

Self-archiving involves authors being allowed to self-archive pre-publication versions of their own work or sometimes a PDF version of the published article. However, this can give rise to a number of problems. Some publishers have found that where all or most of a journal's content can be found in an archive, users appear content to use that version rather than the one on the publisher's website, even though only the version on the publisher's website has undergone peer review and editing, and despite the fact that the version on the publisher's website also has additional functionality, such as reference linking. The other serious problem it is that self-archiving will result in different versions of the material appearing in different places, and researchers may not know whether any particular version is or is not the official version or even whether it has actually been peer reviewed and published. This problem never arose with printed paper journals, since publication in the printed journal necessarily constituted the definitive version of the work. ALPSP wants publishers to retain the ability to control the manner and timing of self-archiving, in order to preserve the journals and the valuable functions they perform for the scientific community.

K. DEPOSIT OF PRINTED AND NON-PRINTED PUBLICATIONS

27–89   **Further developments in preserving electronic works.** As part of the European Commission's digital libraries initiative, the High Level Expert Group (HLEG) on European Digital Libraries published in April 2007 a report on digital preservation, orphan works and out-of-print works, together with a model licence agreement on digitisation of out-of-print works. The report (which can be downloaded at *ec.europa.eu/information_society/newsroom/cf/ document.cfm?action=display&doc_id=295*) contains a number of practical recommendations for rights-holders and libraries to consider, and follows on from an Interim Report presented by the Copyright Subgroup of the HLEG in October 2006. The model licence can be downloaded at *ec.europa.eu/ information_society/newsroom/cf/ document.cfm?action=display&doc_id=296.*

2. THE NEWSPAPER INDUSTRY

A. GENERAL NATURE OF THE INDUSTRY

National and regional press sectors. Average net circulation of national newspapers for the period May 28, 2007 to July 1, 2007 was 16,608,911 for the dailies and 8,039,924 for the Sunday newspapers (figures from the Audit Bureau of Circulations, *www.abc.org.uk*).

27–94

B. SOURCES OF COPYRIGHT

General. NOTE 80. *Newspaper Licensing Agency Ltd v Marks & Spencer Plc* is reported at [2003] 1 A.C. 551; [2002] R.P.C. 4; [2001] E.M.L.R. 43.

27–98

Other material obtained from other sources. Newspapers publish a huge range of other material obtained from a wide variety of sources. In doing so, reliance is often placed on the 'fair dealing' defences. While the defence of 'fair dealing' for the purposes of reporting current events is to be construed liberally, there are limits to its scope. Where extracts quoted from a private journal form a substantial part of the whole, the copy of the journal has been obtained via a breach of confidence, and the articles are not confined to current events, their purpose being to report on the revelation of the contents of the journal as itself as an event of interest, the defence is unlikely to apply: *HRH Prince of Wales v Associated Newspapers Ltd* [2006] EWHC 522; [2006] E.C.D.R. 20. Newspaper content is itself as much prone to 'fair dealing' uses by third parties as it is likely to benefit from such uses: *Fraser-Woodward Ltd v BBC* [2005] EWHC 472; [2005] E.M.L.R. 22. It is not however fair dealing for the purposes of criticism and review to reproduce the entire front page of a title published by a competitor in a comparative advertisement where a simple identification of the original title would have sufficed: *IPC Media Ltd v News Group Newspapers Ltd* [2005] EWHC 317; [2005] E.M.L.R. 23.

27–104A

C. RIGHTS REQUIRED FOR EXPLOITATION

Photographs. NOTE 15. **Delete** and **substitute**: *Von Hannover v Germany* (59320/00) [2004] E.M.L.R. 21.

27–110

D. REPRESENTATIVE COLLECTING SOCIETIES AND LICENSING AGENCIES RESPONSIBLE FOR ADMINISTERING THE RIGHTS

The Newspaper Licensing Agency. Second sub-paragraph. **Delete** second sentence and **substitute:** It is estimated that the NLA distributes over £12m each year to national and regional newspapers in respect of copyright works. See "Information for Publishers", *www.nla.co.uk*.

27–117

Add at end: In March 2006 the NLA launched eclips, a digital database of newspaper clippings allowing Press Clippings Agencies (PCAs) and their clients direct access to original quality national and regional press articles. See "NLA launches eClips", published by the NLA on March 31, 2006; *www.nla.co.uk*. End users receive a link from their PCAs which takes them directly to a PDF of the press clipping, thereby removing the need for scanning and making it easier to adhere to copyright laws. The service (to which two of the largest PCAs signed up in January 2007) also allows end users to retain online access to digital cuttings for a full year. See "Market signs up to eclips', published by the NLA on January 30, 2007; *www.nla.co.uk*.

E. Other industry controls

27–118   **Self-regulatory controls. Note 35. Delete** and **substitute:** The current Code of Practice was framed by the newspaper and periodical industry and was ratified by the PCC on June 13, 2005. It can be seen at *www.pcc.org.uk/cop/practice.html*.

    Note 37. **Delete** and **substitute:** Advertising Standards Authority, Mid City Place, 71 High Holborn, London WC1V 6QT. Tel. 020 7492 2222.

F. Current industry issues

27–121   **Electronic databases copyright litigation. Add** after third sentence: Due to an appeal against the terms of the settlement by a small group of class members, the settlement is not yet final and so, pending the hearing of the appeal, UK newspaper publishers have not received any claims for payment.

27–121A   **Possible withdrawal of the *sui generis* right.** Following *The British Horse Racing Board Limited v William Hill Organisation Limited* (in the ECJ Case C–203/02 and then in the Court of Appeal [2005] EWCA Civ 863; [2005] R.P.C. 35; see also the *Fixtures Marketing* cases *Fixtures Marketing Ltd v Svenska Spel AB* (C–338/02) [2005] E.C.D.R. 4; *Fixtures Marketing Ltd v Organismos Prognostikon Agonon Podosfairou* [2005] E.C.D.R. 3; and *Fixtures Marketing Ltd v Oy Veikkaus AB* (C–46/02) [2005] E.C.D.R. 2) the European Commission published a draft Evaluation on the future of the *sui generis* right: see *http://europa.eu.int/comm/internal_market/copyright/docs/docs/evaluation-databases-draft_en.pdf*. Noting that the UK had maintained its primacy as the foremost producer of databases in the EU, it nevertheless appeared to conclude that database protection under the Database Directive had failed in its objective of increasing the global competitiveness of the EU database publishing industry, particularly by comparison with the USA. Newspaper and periodical publishers have lobbied to support the retention of database protection. Newspaper publishers publish aggregated data (whether in their newspaper titles or as separate products) that are susceptible to protection by database right. Newspapers are themselves databases within the definition, as are newspaper websites. At the same time, published databases are a source of information for journalists in a wide range of areas, including, for example, sports listings and fixtures. In that context, while the right lacks a defence permitting extraction or re-utilisation of a database for the reporting of current events, the *British Horse Racing Board* and *Fixtures Marketing* decisions can be seen to have reduced the risk of infringement of database right by newspapers publishing sports listings information.

3. THE MUSIC INDUSTRY

A. Overview

27–124   First paragraph. **Delete** first sentence and **substitute: Size and economic impact of the industry.** The music industry is a major cultural and economic force in the UK, accounting for more than £3.6 billion in economic activity (measured by Gross Value Added), 29,000 businesses and 236,300 direct and related jobs.[51]

    Note 51. **Delete** and **substitute:** Department for Culture, Media and Sport, Creative Industries Economic Estimates: Statistical Bulletin, September 2006.

    Third paragraph. **Add:** The five major group companies (Universal, EMI, Sony, Warner and BMG) continue to account for more than a 65 per cent market share of music publishing and 73.5 per cent of recorded music sales world-wide (source: Music & Copyright, Warner Music SEC 10–K Report).

The European Commission has approved for a second time the joint venture that combined the Sony and BMG recorded music operations (but not their publishing arms) in 2004. On July 13, 2006, the European Court of First Instance upheld the complaint of Impala, the European independent record company association, against the merger. See Case T–464/04, *Independent Music Publishers and Labels Association (Impala) v. Commission.* Following a detailed reassessment, the Commission re-approved the deal on October 3, 2007 (source: Commission press release).

Universal agreed to purchase the publishing arm of BMG in September 2006, which the European Commission's competition directorate approved in May 2007 subject to divestiture of certain Anglo-American music catalogue (source: European Commission).

After months of discussions and speculation about a possible merger between Warner Music and EMI, including a controversial decision by the independent labels' associations Impala and AIM to support such a merger subject to certain guarantees, Warner issued an announcement in July 2007 that "it has decided not to make an offer for EMI" (source: Warner Music, AIM).

NOTE 52. **Delete** second sentence.

NOTE 53. **Delete**.

Add at end:

Market trends. The UK still represents about 10 per cent of the world-wide market for recorded music sales. Sales of music in physical formats have continued to decline in the UK, but online, mobile and broadcasting revenues as well as public performance royalties all rose in 2006. Retail revenues from sales of recorded music (physical and digital sales combined) fell 6.7 per cent to £1,109 million at trade value in the UK in 2006. This reflected a 73 per cent growth in digital sales to £66.4 million, but a 9 per cent drop in physical CD and music DVD sales to £1,042.7 million. This compares with an average 11 per cent drop in revenues from physical sales of recorded music world-wide in 2006. Digital music now accounts for 6 per cent of recorded music sales in the UK, with internet downloads and subscriptions outpacing mobile music sales by approximately two to one. The various UK collection societies reported growth in overall broadcasting, public performance and digital revenues in 2006, albeit with some declines in mechanical and commercial radio broadcasting revenues (source: IFPI, BPI, MCPS, PRS, PPL).

Continued integration of digital business models. The major legal and business developments among the three major groupings of music industry rights owners—composers ("authors"), record labels ("producers") and artists ("performers")—principally relate to the ongoing integration of new digital uses into the music business. There has been significant progress such that many "digital issues" are now largely settled and routine, for example, the delineation and application of copyright rights to online and mobile uses of music; the inclusion of digital uses in the industry's various agreements; and the licensing of a variety of digital uses by rights owners and their collection societies. Major unresolved issues are highlighted in this Supplement.

Possible changes to legislation. The Gowers Review of Intellectual Property, commissioned by the Treasury and released in December 2006, examined several possible changes in legislation relevant to the music industry that are being lobbied at the time of writing. These include (1) extension of the term of copyright protection for performers and producers from 50 years to 70 years or longer; (2) responsibility of internet service providers with respect to internet users that infringe copyright; (3) damages rules and other copyright enforcement-related issues; and (4) private copying (along the lines of a "format shifting" exception to protection). Most sectors of the music industry support the first three proposals in some form, and have secured support from the House of Commons' Culture, Media and Sport Committee in its May 2007 report *New Media and the Cultural Industries*. (The Government announced on July 27, 2007 that it would not support extending copyright term, however (source: Department of Culture, Media and Sport).) The industry is divided on whether, or how, to implement a broader copyright exception for private copying, which under the 2001 EU Copyright Directive would require "fair compensation" for the rights holders subjected to such an exception. See Directive 2001/29/EC, Article 5(2)(b).

B. THE MUSIC PUBLISHING BUSINESS

Collecting Societies

27–127   **Add:** The UK Copyright Tribunal issued its interim decision with respect to the MCPS/PRS combined licence for various online and mobile download and streaming services (the "Joint Online Licence") in July 2007. MCPS/PRS had initially sought a headline royalty rate of 12 per cent of gross retail revenues for such services, temporarily discounted to 8 per cent. The Tribunal approved tariffs of 8 per cent of gross revenues for on-demand music services, 6.5 per cent for interactive webcasting services, and 5.75 per cent for non-interactive webcasting, subject to certain minimums. The BPI, mobile telecommunication companies and iTunes had settled most of their issues with the MCPS/PRS, including applicable rates (8 per cent for on-demand services, and 6.5 per cent for non-interactive services) in September 2006. The Tribunal decision resolved remaining issues with respect to the definition of gross revenues and the internet music service providers' objections to the rates. See *BPI & Ors v MCPS/PRS*, No. CT84–90/05 (Copyright Tribunal, July 19, 2007).

Ringtone services are currently licensed by the MCPS and PRS separately, although a combined licence may be introduced. The MCPS and PRS are in the process of reviewing the range of licence schemes offered in view of the continued proliferation of means of exploitation introducing for example so-called "podcasting" and "mobile TV" trial licence schemes.

NOTE 73. **Delete** and **substitute:** Universal Group's recording arm entered into a three-year agreement with the Belgian publishers' society SABAM in July 2004 to license physical, digital and mobile uses Europe-wide. The digital and mobile aspects of the licence proved controversial among the other collecting societies. See para. 27–180.

Publishing Agreements

Types of Agreement

27–134A   **Add:**
(v) **Library Music.** This type of agreement generally assigns rights in specified works and compositions together with recordings thereof to a library music publisher primarily for the purpose of exploitation in conjunction with audio visual productions. Library music (both the sound recordings and the underlying works) is typically available for exploitation in synchronisation with television and other audio visual programmes without restrictions or rights of approval and is collectively licensed on standard terms making it easy to clear and therefore commercially attractive where its use is appropriate.

Rights

Add after fourth sentence: Until the 1980s, rights periods under exclusive song- **27–135**
writing agreements for the life of copyright were relatively common. However,
such lengthy periods are now very rare, even in the case of independent
publishers. Competition between major publishers for high profile or desirable
writers and catalogues has led to rights periods falling (in some cases significantly
below 10 years after the expiry of the term of the agreement). Life of copyright
remains the standard duration of rights under a commissioning or library music
agreement.

NOTE 90. **Add:** As to dealer price see para.27–147 of the Main Work.   **27–136**

Remuneration

NOTE 1. **Add:** The royalty rate in respect of library music is typically 50 per cent   **27–137**
of receipts in respect of all income except income collected by PRS where the
publisher typically receives the 50 per cent "publisher's share" and the writer
collects directly the 50 per cent "writer's share" from PRS (as to the writer's
share and publisher's share see n.92 to para.27–136 of the Main Work).

Representative Bodies

First paragraph: **Delete** BASCA and **substitute:** BACS.   **27–138**
    NOTE 2. **Delete** and **substitute:** British Academy of Composers & Songwrit-
ers, 26 Berners Street, London W1T 3LR. Telephone: 020 7636 2929. Fax: 020
7636 2212.
    NOTE 3. **Delete** and **substitute:** MPA, 6th Floor, British Music House, 26
Berners Street, London, W1T 3LR. Tel: 020 7580 0126. Fax: 020 7637 3929.

C. THE RECORDING BUSINESS

Delete last sentence and **substitute:** In 2006 the global recorded music market   **27–139**
was worth US$31.8 billion at retail value, $19.6 billion at trade value.[9]
    NOTE 9. **Delete** and **substitute:** IFPI, Recording Industry in Numbers (June
2007).

Collecting Societies

Add: PPL has substantially expanded its reciprocal arrangements with other pro-   **27–141**
ducer collecting societies outside the UK to enable the collection of public performance, broadcast and certain online royalties in multiple territories on behalf
of member record companies and performers. At the time of writing, PPL had bilateral agreements with 33 other producer collecting societies (source: PPL).
    Some of these agreements involve arrangements authorising PPL and the other
society to collect traditional broadcasting and public performance royalties on
each other's behalf. So far, this has had principal relevance for independent record companies that are members of PPL but not members of producer collection
societies in other countries.
    More broadly, these agreements set up "one-stop shops" for internet simulcast-
ing and webcasting licences valid throughout these territories. The agreements
establish reciprocal representation for each participating society to license
"simulcasting" (internet streaming of traditional broadcast stations' programming) as well as non-interactive "webcasting" (internet-originated streaming) in
the participating territories. As approved by the European Commission, the
simulcasting and webcasting tariffs are based upon the relevant tariff of the
country into which each recording is streamed (the "country of destination"

principle). Under these agreements there are no territorial restrictions within the EU as to which collection society a licensee can go to get a licence. See paragraph 29–243 of the Main Work.

PPL is expanding the online uses that it will license on behalf of its members, and launched a new online licensing scheme in 2006 that would offer webcasters licences for archive programming, certain interactive functions and other customised services. At the time of writing PPL is asking its record company members to enter into new membership agreements, among other things, to mandate a wider set of licensing activities—in particular with respect to such on-line uses.

Three PPL tariffs remain under review by the Copyright Tribunal at the time of writing. The Secretary of State referred PPL's tariffs for factories and offices; public houses, bars, restaurants and cafes; and shops and stores to the Tribunal under section 128A of the CDPA 1988. See Copyright Tribunal referral nos. CT 91/05, 92/05, 93/05.

Video Performance Limited ("VPL") administers licences for audio visual recordings for public performances and broadcast on behalf of record companies. VPL's address is 1 Upper James Street, London, W1F 9DE. Tel: 020 7534 1400. Fax: 020 7534 1414.

Independent record companies announced in January 2007 that they would be creating the global licensing agency Merlin, "outside the space occupied by collecting societies", through which independent record companies could jointly license "new media deals". Details remain sketchy at the time of writing (source: AIM).

Record Companies

27–142   **Add:** Despite widely touted predictions that new technologies and digital distribution would make physical distribution and the traditional role of record companies redundant, however, at the time of writing this had not happened. Digital sales remain a growing but small but part of overall sales—6 per cent in the UK) (source: IFPI). Artists and record companies are finding that online promotion can boost physical and digital sales. For example, the artist Gnarls Barkley achieved a number one status with the single "Crazy" before the release of the recording in physical format. The artist The Arctic Monkeys achieved the highest ever number of first week album sales in the UK with their first album, in part as the result of building a reputation through online communities such as *myspace.com*.

Acquiring rights in recordings—exclusive recording agreements

Exclusivity, term and minimum commitment

27–144   **Add:** Whilst major label recording agreements have for some time governed all audio or audio-visual recordings of an artist's musical performances and included requirements for the delivery of audio-visual performances in the context of promotional videos of singles, the scope of such agreements typically now also includes obligations to create and grant rights over a broader range of audio and audio-visual recordings and other products of the artist's services embodying the artist's name and image. This is intended to provide the record label with material that can be used and offered in a wider variety of new media, including for example internet video streaming and mobile videotones. Some artists have sought to retain rights over such audio-visual material, with limited success.

Rights

Add: In a few cases, record companies have agreed with an artist to participate in the artist's other revenue streams including, for example, income from live performances and merchandise. EMI Records entered into such an agreement with the artist Robbie Williams in October 2002 pursuant to which EMI and the artist invested in a joint entity entitled to a broad range of the artist's services and income. EMI has entered into other such deals with the band Korn and a few artists in Asia, and Interscope struck a deal in 2003 with the Pussycat Dolls by which the two sides split the profits from all the act's ventures (source: CFOEurope.com, The Economist). Such agreements are still uncommon, do not readily fit every artist's situation, and are resisted by many artists and their managers.

27–145

Remuneration

(i) Royalties based on the price of records. Add: Some record companies have sought to apply the royalty rate applicable to the sale of physical records to digital distribution (audio and audio-visual downloading and/or streaming), whilst featured performers have tried to increase their remuneration for such digital distribution. The MMF has taken out advertisements in the industry and national press, and made a submission to the Gowers Review, to the effect that performers' remuneration should be raised for digital uses given the lower attendant manufacturing and distribution costs. Record companies argue that digital distribution benefits from all of their other activities in artist and repertoire development, marketing and physical distribution, and thus does not merit a different royalty treatment. At the time of writing, this debate has not been resolved, given the difficulty at this stage of the development of new media to reach a solution that is both equitable in the current market and also "future-proof".

27–147

(ii) Royalties based on net receipts. Add: An independent record company's basis of accounting does not on the face of it require change in the context of the development of new forms of exploitation.

27–148

D. Performers

Moral Rights

Delete second sentence and **substitute:** The WIPO Performances and Phonograms Treaty has now been ratified by 62 States. The UK has signed but not ratified the treaty, but plans to do so together with the other EU countries and the European Community. Performers' moral rights have now been introduced in the United Kingdom by the Performances (Moral Rights, etc.) Regulations 2006 (SI 2006/18), which enacted new sections 205 C to N into the 1988 Act.

27–157

The clearance of performer's rights

The right to receive equitable remuneration

Delete second paragraph and **substitute:** PPL now collects and distributes all equitable remuneration payments for all broadcasting and public performance, and certain internet uses, on behalf of performers in the UK. PAMRA and AURA have merged into PPL following approval by the Office of Fair Trading in May 2006. PPL has established a new Performer Board, which includes former PAMRA and AURA directors as well as Equity and Musicians' Union representatives. The merged entity, properly mandated on behalf of and responsible to both the record companies and performers, is expected to be more effective in terms of cost savings that should result from rationalising the func-

27–160

tions of the three societies, and also in terms of the merged society's ability to secure better and more comprehensive collection of revenues from sister societies throughout the world.

Note 58. **Delete**.

Note 59. **Delete**.

H. New threats or new opportunities

Piracy—the digital age and Peer-to-Peer networks

27–168   **Add** to the second paragraph: Recent statistics indicate that approximately 11 per cent of internet users in the UK engage in infringing "file sharing" (source: Jupiter Research, IFPI).

The P2P networks:

27–170   **Delete** last two sentences of second paragraph and **substitute:** Despite some initial successes by these "decentralised" P2P services, copyright litigation against them has taken a very different path from earlier hardware-related cases, including the *Amstrad* case in the UK and the *Sony* Betamax case in the US.

Grokster. The United States Supreme Court's unanimous ruling against the P2P services Grokster and Streamcast (*MGM Studios Inc. v. Grokster, Ltd.*, 545 U.S. 913 (2005)), overturned the decision of the US Court of Appeals for the 9th Circuit and found that the P2P services could not escape liability if they *promoted* the infringement of copyright. In the view of the US Supreme Court, such promotion need not be subjective or overt to result in liability—it could be proven by the presence of more than one objective activity evidencing such promotion, including communications (*e.g.* soliciting infringing users), failure to prevent or curtail infringement (*i.e.* to filter), or profiting from the infringement. In such circumstances, actual or potentially lawful uses, even if substantial, would be no defence.

Universal v Sharman. Within the Commonwealth, companies and individuals involved in the Kazaa P2P service have paid a reported US$100 million in settlement damages to record company claimants and agreed to filter their P2P service after being found liable for "authorising infringement" by the Federal Court in Australia following a protracted and costly lawsuit. Rejecting familiar "blindness" defences, the court found in September 2005 that six of the Kazaa-related respondents had "long known" that the system was "widely used" for sharing copyright files; had encouraged infringement; had offered a system the "primary", "major" or "predominant" use of which was to share infringing material; had a financial interest in maximising infringement; and had failed to take steps to prevent or curtail infringement. The court had issued an injunction ordering the Kazaa service to filter out users' infringing copies of music files. The settlement was reached prior to the court's determination of damages. See *Universal Music Australia Pty Ltd v. Sharman License Holdings Ltd* [2005] F.C.A. 1242 (September 5, 2005); *Kazaa to pay record groups $100m*, Financial Times (July 27, 2006).

Both the *Grokster* and the *Sharman* decisions indicate that the greater the knowledge, proximity, intention and involvement of a service provider in a third party's infringement, the less likely the service will be able to avoid liability and obligations to prevent such infringement through such measures as filtering.

The individual users:

Delete and **substitute:** The record industry has pursued and continues to pursue   **27–171**
claims against individual users of P2P networks in addition to the networks
themselves. At the time of writing, the industry has brought more than 36,000
cases against such individuals in 20 countries including the UK. Most of these
cases have been settled, for an average of approximately US$3,400 each. Nine
such cases have gone to court in the UK, all of which have resulted in judgements
for the record companies. *Polydor Limited v Brown* [2005] EWHC 3191,
explicitly confirmed that unauthorised uploading of music files for use on P2P
networks constitutes an infringement of the copyright owner's rights by the individual user. Despite some public criticism, the record industry claims that the litigation is producing its desired effect: "While broadband household penetration
is rapidly rising, the percent of internet users engaged in frequent unauthorised
P2P usage is actually falling". (See IFPI, *Digital Music Report* 2007.)

NOTE 86. **Delete**.

Developing and licensing legitimate services:

Add: Although there has been tremendous growth among licensed legitimate   **27–172**
services, there have been some complaints in the UK and elsewhere about the
lack of interoperability between the different services' DRM technologies. The
Gowers Review recommended that better information on DRM be made available to consumers through such vehicles as an easier complaint procedure or a
labelling system. No new legislation has been recommended in the UK to date.

EMI was the first major record company to offer DRM-free tracks for download
on iTunes, announcing in April 2007 that it would offer unprotected tracks in the
MP3 format with a higher quality but at a 20p premium. EMI is continuing to offer DRM-protected tracks at the normal iTunes price of 79p in the UK. (See *EMI
and Apple agree iTunes music deal, Financial Times*, April 1, 2007).

Legitimate new forms of exploitation—new opportunities

The Online Boom

Delete and **substitute:** Apple's iTunes online music download service has sold   **27–173**
over two billion music tracks since its launch in April 2003, one billion in 2006
alone.[88] Apple has sold more than 100 million iPods and retains an estimated 80
per cent market share of the legitimate online music market.[89] A fair amount of
diversity remains available, however, with an estimated 500 legitimate online
services in over 40 countries, and new ones announced on a regular basis
(*www.pro-music.org*).

NOTE 88. **Delete** and **substitute:** IFPI, June 2007.

NOTE 89. **Delete** and **substitute:** *Financial Times*, May 17, 2007, July 2, 2007.

(i) Download services. Add: In addition to the now relatively established   **27–174**
download services for audio recordings there has been a growth in the delivery of
audio-visual recordings (assisted by Apple's launch of video enabled versions of
its iPod player) as well as the development of new download products such as
podcasts. Podcasts consist of a downloadable audio or audio visual programme
which may be a radio or television programme made available for download or
may be specially created for download purposes.

Mobile music

Add before last sentence: The mobile music market is growing, but perhaps less   **27–176**
quickly than originally expected in the UK. eMarketer (*emarketer.com*) predicted
in April 2005 that the global mobile music market will make up 65 per cent of the

digital music market which itself will make up 35 per cent of overall music industry income by 2010. This would represent a growth from US$434 million in 2005 to US$7.7 billion.

The mobile music market in the UK remains in relative infancy, representing 34 per cent of digital sales in 2006 (down from 38 per cent in 2005). All digital sales—mobile and online—still represent only 6 per cent of total sales in the UK at trade value. In Japan, mobile music represented about 90 per cent of digital sales in 2006 (source: IFPI).

27–177   **(i) Ringtones. Delete** first sentence and **substitute:** Continued growth in the ringtone market in 2006 coincided with the increased availability and consumer take up of mastertones as well as videotones (an audio visual recording as opposed to audio only). Mastertones accounted for 16 per cent of all digital sales in the UK in 2006.[92]

NOTE 92. **Delete** and **substitute:** IFPI, June 2007.

27–178   **(ii) Ring-back. Add:** At the time of writing, and despite success in some territories including Japan, ringback tones have yet to achieve a significant market in the UK.

Changes in the industry

(i) *The publishing business*

27–180   **Delete** last two sentences and **substitute:** The publishers' collection societies let this multi-territorial reciprocal licensing system for internet-based activities lapse, however, following the European Commission's Statement of Objections in 2001 to the effect that these societies' "Santiago" and "Barcelona" agreements contained anti-competitive territorial and membership restrictions. See paragraph 29–244 of the Main Work. This has effectively eliminated any "one-stop shops" where online music services might otherwise have secured publishing licences to cover their activities in Europe, instead requiring that music services clear publisher rights for multi-territorial services country by country.

The issue has arisen again in the context of RTL's and Music Choice Europe's EU competition complaint against these societies' traditional reciprocal agreements covering "communication to the public". The complainants originally sought pan-European licences for traditional broadcasting, and objected to restrictions in these reciprocal agreements that they claimed precluded such licences. Given that internet-based activities have been defined as "communication to the public" by the 2001 EU Copyright Directive (Directive 2001/29/EC, Art.3(1)), the allegations expanded to include claims that the societies also were restricting membership and licensing territories in ways that prohibit pan-European licensing of online services. The Commission announced a Statement of Objections against these traditional reciprocal agreements in February 2006, and in June 2007 began publicly "market testing" the societies' proposed commitments to address the Commission's objections. (See European Commission, *Press Release: Antitrust—Commission market tests commitments from CISAC and 18 EEA collecting societies concerning reciprocal representation contracts* (June 14, 2007).)

Against this backdrop the major publishers and the collection societies are considering alternative licensing regimes in connection with online and mobile services. MCPS/PRS and GEMA have announced an agreement with EMI Music Publishing whereby these two national societies would have mandates for and license EMI's Anglo-American catalogue for online and mobile usage Europe-wide through a joint venture called CELAS (source: MCPS/PRS). If implemented as planned, this would appear to involve a partial withdrawal of EMI licensing mandates from other European publishers' societies, and the set up of a "one-stop" shop at least with respect to this particular catalogue of this particular publisher. Other catalogue and other publishers' repertoire would continue to be licensed territory by territory—with the result that another "stop" would be *added* to the publishers' "multi-stop shopping". MCPS/PRS are encouraging other music publishers to enter into similar arrangements through their Alliance Digital programme (source: MCPS/PRS).

The Universal record company agreed with SABAM (Belgium) to clear publisher licensing for online and mobile activities Europe-wide in 2003. In a complaint filed with the European Commission in 2004, however, Universal alleged that the other societies punished SABAM for "breaking rank", with some major publishers and societies reportedly threatening to withdraw rights from SABAM, and the French society SACEM suing Universal in 2004 for failing to secure those rights in France. (See *Universal Files Antitrust Complaint Against Euro Collecting Agencies*, Billboard (October 22, 2005).) The Commission has not taken any action or made any allegation of illegal activity on the part of the collection societies in response to the complaint.

Online music service eMusic hit a similar glitch when it tried to clear Europe-wide publishing rights through Dutch society Buma/Stemra in 2006. The MCPS/PRS Alliance reportedly objected, saying that eMusic had to obtain licences from the Alliance to offer downloads in the UK: "[The Alliance] has made it clear to eMusic and to Dutch collecting society Buma/Stemra that it (Buma/Stemra) is not able to grant such a pan-European licence since it does not have the MCPS or PRS rights to do so." *MCPS-PRS Rebukes eMusic's Pan-Europe System*, Billboard.biz (September 15, 2006).

The publisher societies' tariffs for digital services have been the subject of debate, negotiation and, in some cases, litigation in several key markets including the UK, USA and Germany. The record companies' and music service providers' challenge to the MCPS/PRS combined licence for various online and mobile download and streaming services has been resolved by a September 2006 settlement with the record companies and a July 2007 interim decision of the Copyright Tribunal with respect to other parties and issues. (See para.27–127, above.)

(ii) *The record companies*

Add: Digital sales continue to boom, growing by 73 per cent in the UK to £66.4m, and nearly doubling world-wide to US$2.1 billion, between 2005 and 2006. Sales of digital singles now account for 72 per cent of all singles sold in the UK, and 85 per cent of all singles sold world-wide (source: IFPI). **27–181**

NOTE 97. **Delete** and **substitute:** Down by 11 per cent in 2006 (source: IFPI, June 2007).

(iii) *The performers*

Add to the end of first paragraph: Featured performers' efforts to increase their remuneration under recording agreements have been given new impetus with the success of new digital uses, however. (See para.27–147, above.) **27–182**

(iv) *The distributors and retailers*

Add: The environment for these traditional businesses is becoming even more challenging. Iconic US music retailer, Tower Records, filed for Chapter 11 bankruptcy protection in 2004 citing illegal music downloading as one of the main causes (source: BBC, February 9, 2004). In the UK, in the year to the end of **27–183**

April 2007, the HMV chain of records stores' profits fell by more than 70 per cent (source: *Financial Times*, June 28, 2007). HMV chief executive Simon Fox pointed to downloading and other new ways of consuming music as putting pressure on traditional retail traffic (source: BBC, June 28, 2007).

4. THE FILM INDUSTRY

A. The General nature of the industry

27–184 Statistics from the Department for Culture, Media and Sport (DCMS) show that in 2006, 145 films received British Film Certificates from the DCMS, of which 76 were wholly United Kingdom-produced and 69 were co-productions. The US continues to be a big investor in larger budget British films. The total costs of the 145 films certified as British in 2006 was £864 million. Although only 19 of the 145 certified films had US investment, the total costs of these 19 films was £419 million, amounting to 48.5 per cent of the overall costs.

(ii) Production

27–187 Second paragraph. **Add:** If a number of financiers are involved in the financing of a film, each will require a security interest over the production company and/or the film. The priority and enforcement procedures for their respective security interests will be dealt with in an intercreditor agreement.

27–187A **Producer Tax Credits.** In his budget in March 2005 the Chancellor announced that the Government would replace the previous film tax reliefs with a new regime aimed directly at filmmakers. Chapter 3 of the Finance Act 2006 reformed the taxation of the film industry and introduced a new tax relief for the production of "British" films. The new provisions were brought into force from January 1, 2007 by the Finance Act 2006, section 53(1) (Films and Sound Recordings) (Appointed Day) Order 2006 (SI 2006/3399)). Certain transitional provisions were included in the Corporation Tax (Taxation of Films) (Transitional Provisions) Regulations 2007 (SI 2007/1050). The new film tax credit is available for films that (i) commenced principal photography on or after January 1, 2007; or (ii) commenced principal photography before January 1, 2007 but were still uncompleted on that date (subject to meeting the conditions listed in (a), (b) and (c) below). This replaces the relief previously given under section 42 of the Finance (No.2) Act 1992 and section 48 of the Finance (No.2) Act 1997. The new tax relief is given to film production companies (not individuals or partnerships nor to investors, financial institutions or those whose involvement in filmmaking is confined to providing or arranging finance).

Such companies only receive the relief in respect of their films if:

(a) the film is intended for theatrical release (*i.e.* exhibition to the paying public at the commercial cinema). The film is only regarded as intended for theatrical release if it is intended that a significant proportion of the earnings of the film should be obtained from such exhibition (the timing and measurement of this "intention" is set out in detail in the HMRC Guidance Notes on Film Tax Relief); and

(b) it is British Qualifying, *i.e.* if it is certified by the DCMS (or the Film Council from April 2007, see para.27–219) as a British film under the revised Schedule 1 to the Films Act 1985 (see para.27–219 below) or as an official co-production (see para.27–222 of the Main Work); and

(c) at least 25 per cent of the film's core expenditure is incurred in the United Kingdom. Core expenditure is production expenditure on activities involved in pre-production, principal photography and post production of a film. It excludes expenditure on development and distribution.

To qualify as a film production company, a company must, in general, be responsible for:
  (a) the pre-production, principal photography and post production of the film; and
  (b) the delivery of the film on completion.

The film tax relief consists of two elements being an enhanced deduction and a payable tax credit. The amount of the film tax relief is based on the UK core expenditure, up to a maximum of 80 per cent of the total core expenditure incurred by the film production company. This means that a film production company can claim film tax relief on whichever is the lower of: (i) 80 per cent of the total core expenditure or (ii) the actual UK core expenditure incurred.

UK core expenditure is the amount of the core expenditure incurred by the film production company, which is also UK expenditure. UK expenditure is defined as that which is incurred on goods and services which are used or consumed in the UK. The nationality of those providing such goods and services has no bearing on whether the expenditure qualifies as UK expenditure.

The Finance Act makes provision for the film production company to claim the tax relief in instalments during production of the film rather than only upon completion.

In March 2007 HM Revenue and Customs announced that it was severely restricting "sideways loss relief" which allows partners to use losses in one business to set off against income derived elsewhere for tax purposes. This relief formed a backbone of much of the investment made by film finance partnerships into British films. The question to be answered in the forthcoming years is whether the film tax relief will compensate for the restriction of the sideways loss relief.

(iii) Distribution

Second paragraph. **Add:** Under the Finance Act 2006 (see para.27–187A, above)   **27–188** there is no requirement for the film production company to own the master negative of the film. This contrasts with the previous tax regime where the film production company had to own the master negative at the time when the sale and leaseback took place.

B. THE SOURCES AND RIGHTS

(i) Underlying works

(iv) and NOTE 16. **Delete** and **substitute:** communicate the work to the public: **27–190** CDPA 1988, s.20 as amended by the Copyright and Related Rights Regulations 2003 (SI 2003/2498). See generally paras 7–105 *et seq.* of the Main Work;

C. THE WORKS WHICH ARE CREATED AND THE MAIN RIGHTS WHICH ARE REQUIRED FOR EXPLOITATION

The film

27–199   Second sentence. **Add:** In addition, video or near video on demand services have increased over recent years. It is likely that digital downloading via the internet will increase as a method of exploitation of films in the forthcoming years. Hollywood studios have previously been wary of putting films on the internet for fear of piracy and undermining DVD sales. In April 2006 six studios began selling online and in May 2006 the remake of "King Kong" became the first significant DVD release to offer a downloading option in the United Kingdom. Several companies now rent digital films online. In June 2007 Warner Bros announced its plans to release selected video on demand services at the same time as certain films come out on DVD. This deviates from the traditional windows of exploitation adopted by the US studios. In March 2007 the first authorised "download to burn" service for films was offered in Britain.

Performers' property rights

27–203   The recent Court of Appeal case of *Experience Hendrix LLC v (1) Purple Haze Records Ltd* [2007] EWCA Civ 501 confirmed that performers' rights exist in performances that predate the CDPA 1988.

E. THE TRADE UNIONS OR TRADE ASSOCIATIONS WHICH REPRESENT VARIOUS INTERESTS

27–207   (a). On July 1, 2004, AFMA adopted a new name, The Independent Film and Television Alliance (IFTA), in recognition of its new global membership. IFTA's membership includes 160 companies from 22 countries.

Guild agreements

27–213   **PACT—Equity agreement for cinema.** This has been revised so that artists are no longer engaged on a buy out basis but have the right to share in the profits of a film.

NOTE 47: **Delete** and **substitute:** The PACT—Equity agreement for cinema is dated March 2002 and was revised in September 2003.

NOTE 48: **Delete** and **substitute:** The PACT—WGGB Agreement is dated February 2002.

NOTE 49: **Delete** and **substitute:** The PACT—BECTU Agreement is dated November 1, 2003 and was revised in 2005.

G. RELEVANT INDUSTRY CONTROLS

Licensing of films

27–217   Fourth sentence. **Add:** The BBFC classifies films on behalf of the local authorities who license cinemas under the Licensing Act 2003.

Tenth sentence. **Add:** Uc is an additional classification category that indicates that a film is particularly suitable for pre-school children.

Quotas

The Commission is proposing revisions to culminate in a new Directive (the Au-   **27–218**
diovisual Content Directive). In June 2006 DCMS launched a three month
consultation on the proposed Directive. On May 24, 2007 political agreement
was reached on the new Audiovisual Media Services Directive. The Directive
should enter into force by the end of 2007. Member States will be given 24
months to transpose the new provisions into national law.

Films Act 1985

Schedule 1 to the Films Act 1985 sets out the requirements to be satisfied for a   **27–219**
film to be a British film for the purpose of that Schedule. Schedule 1 to the Films
Act 1985 was modified by the Films (Definition of "British Film") Order 2006
(SI 2006/643), which was further modified by the Films (Definition of a "British
Film") (No.2) Order (SI 20063430). These orders introduce a requirement to pass
the cultural test before a film can be certified as "British". The reason a new test
was required was that the tax relief is a form of state aid which needs to be cleared
by the European Commission. The promotion of culture is an exceptional reason
for the granting of state aid and therefore the new test ensures that the tax relief is
more clearly aimed at promoting culture.

On June 13, 2007 the European Commission adopted a Communication
extending until December 31, 2009 at the latest the current rules on state aid to
cinematographic and other audiovisual works. This Communication extends the
rules laid down in the previous Cinema Communications of 2001 and 2004. This
Communication requires the "general legality principle" to be respected and sets
out four additional specific compatibility criteria according to which aid for the
production of films for cinema and TV can be approved as cultural aid. These
criteria are that:

  (i) aid must benefit a cultural product;
  (ii) the producer must be free to spend at least 20 per cent of the production
       budget in other Member States without suffering any reduction in the aid
       provided under the scheme;
  (iii) the aid intensity in principle must be limited to 50 per cent of the produc-
       tion budget (except for difficult and low budget films); and
  (iv) aid supplements for specific filmmaking activities are not allowed.

In September 2005 the United Kingdom submitted a state aid notification to
obtain approval from the Commission for the new tax relief. The existing cultural
test (set out in SI 2006/43) was submitted to the Commission. However, in
September 2006 the Commission indicated that they had concerns about the
existing cultural test in that it placed too much emphasis on the economic elements of film making. The Government then agreed a revised test with the Commission, which is set out in SI 2006/3430. This new test changed the allocation of
points within the existing categories and introduced a new category to reflect the
contribution a film makes to British culture.

A film will pass the cultural test if it is awarded 16 out of a possible 31 points.
There are four categories of points, namely:
  (i) cultural content (16 points) assessing the British subject matter of the
       film;
  (ii) cultural contribution (4 points) assessing the contribution of the film to the
       promotion, development and enhancement of British culture;
  (iii) cultural hubs (3 points) assessing the use of the United Kingdom's film
       making facilities;

(iv) cultural practitioners (8 points) assessing the use of all personnel with creative input.

The Order sets out how the points will be allocated.

As from April 1, 2007 the DCMS transferred its film certification function to the UK Film Council.

H. Problems which confront the industry in practice

(iii) Co-productions

27–222   Fourth sentence. **Add:** The UK is currently party to bi-lateral agreements with Australia, Canada, France, New Zealand and South Africa. The UK's Co-production treaty with Germany ended on December 31, 2006. The UK's Co-production treaty with Italy ended on May 2, 2006. The UK's co-production treaty with Norway was terminated on May 24, 2007. The UK/South Africa Co-production treaty was signed in May 2006. The main body of a co-production treaty with India was signed in New Delhi on December 5, 2005 but the Annex, which contains much of the detail for co-producing, is still being negotiated. Both the Treaty and the Annex will need to be agreed, signed and ratified by the respective governments before it can enter into force.

The European Convention on Cinematographic Co-productions remains in place.

(vi) ISAN system

27–225   The ISAN system has now been introduced.

5. THE BROADCASTING INDUSTRY

A. Overview

27–235   In 2006, the UK radio and television broadcasters paid the Performing Right Society some £104.3 million for the right to broadcast musical works, representing 46.1 per cent of the PRS's revenues in that year from its UK licensing activity.

The turnover of BBC Worldwide Limited from programme distribution and channel licensing in 2006/2007 was £385.4 million.

B. The structure of the Broadcasting industry in the United Kingdom

Regulation

27–236   The BBC's main object as set out in its new Charter of September 19, 2006 is the promotion of its Public Purposes. These are defined as:

  (a) sustaining citizenship and civil society;
  (b) promoting education and learning;
  (c) stimulating creativity and cultural excellence;
  (d) representing the UK, its nations, regions and communities;
  (e) bringing the UK to the World and the World to the UK;
  (f) in pursuing its other purposes, helping to deliver to the public the benefit of emerging communications technologies and services and, in addition, taking a leading role in the switchover to digital television.

The EC Television Without Frontiers Directive 89/552/EC is to be superseded by the Audiovisual Media Services Directive. The new Directive will reiterate the social, cultural and political purposes of the Directive it replaces.

Range of services

First bullet point. **Delete:** "around 2010–2012". **Substitute:** ", region–by–region, between 2008 and 2012."   **27–239**

Third bullet point. Granada is now known as ITV plc.

Tenth bullet point. At the time of writing, BSkyB's own channels are not retransmitted on cable networks as a result of failure to agree on licence fees.

Programme production

Add: Independent radio productions now make up some 10 per cent of programming broadcast on the BBC's national services.   **27–240**

Cable

First sentence. **Delete:** March 2004. **Substitute:** March 2007. **Delete:** over 3.3 million. **Substitute:** 3.4 million.   **27–241**

Add: Over 3.1 million of these homes received digital cable broadcasts. See Ofcom Digital Television Update—2007 Q1.

C. THE USE OF COPYRIGHT WORKS AND PROTECTED PERFORMANCES IN
BROADCASTING

Acquisition of rights

Add: A considerable amount of information about collecting societies' licensing terms is now available on their respective websites.   **27–245**

Table on page 1485.

Second column against "Source Material". **Delete:** "and for the radio channel BBC7".

Second column against "Screenplays and radio drama scripts". **Delete:** "and for radio channel BBC7".

Table on page 1486.

Second column against "Directors". **Add** at end: "and makes distributions to directors in respect of sales of programmes out of an annual payment made by the broadcasters and PACT under the agreements referred to here."

First column against "Commissioned Composers". **Delete** entry and **substitute:** Yes, other than for broadcasting, cable, public performance and on-demand rights pre-assigned by the composer to the Performing Right Society ("PRS")

Table on page 1487.

Third column against "Existing Music". **Delete** (b) and (c) and **substitute:** The PRS (see para.28–59 of the Main Work) and MCPS (see para.28–56 of the Main Work) now negotiate jointly with broadcasters to offer a licence of broadcasting rights

Table on page 1488.

Third column against "Commercial sound recordings". **Add:** The Association of Independent Music also offers certain rights agreements on behalf of the record companies it represents.

D. REGULATORY CONTROLS RELEVANT TO RIGHTS-CLEARANCES

Copyright Tribunal

27–246   **Add:** As many broadcasters now simulcast their services and make programmes available on-demand online, the recent decision by the Copyright Tribunal in the reference made by record companies, online music service providers and mobile networkoperators in respect of the Joint Online Licence offered by the PRS/MCPS Alliance has been of particular interest.

E. RIGHTS-CLEARANCE ISSUES IN THE BROADCASTING FIELD

EC copyright harmonisation Directives

Exemption from collective licensing

27–257   Under commitments which CISAC and certain EEA performing rights societies have proposed to give to the European Commission in response to the Commission's statement of objections in case COMP/38698, it would become possible in certain circumstances for satellite broadcasters to obtain a licence from a single performing rights society covering both the satellite broadcasting of copyright music and the cable retransmission of it in the countries in which those other EEA societies are located.

H. INTERNATIONAL PROTECTION OF BROADCASTERS' RIGHTS

27–267   **Add:** For reasons unrelated to the need for copyright law reform, progress towards the adoption of a new treaty covering broadcasters' rights slowed in 2004 and 2005. The WIPO Standing Committee on Copyright and Related Rights at its meeting in May 2006 made progress that enabled the General Assembly in September to recommend the convening of the necessary Diplomatic Conference in November 2007 to negotiate the final terms of the Treaty. The key to progress lay in the United States of America dropping its insistence that the Treaty should give webcasters equivalent rights.

The broadcasters' hopes for a new treaty were dashed, however, when in June 2007 the WIPO General Assembly decided that there was insufficient agreement to justify the convening of a Diplomatic Conference to adopt a treaty. Brazil and India led the opposition to the treaty proposals, the harshest critics arguing that the creation of new rights for broadcasters would overlay other copyrights in broadcast content, restrict access to programmes in the public domain, prevent legitimate copying for private use and stifle technological innovation.

6. THE THEATRE, THE OPERA AND THE BALLET

A. THE AUTHORS OF COPYRIGHT MATERIALS

(i) Writer and composers

27–269   NOTE 55. As to copyright in a "composite work", see paras 27–282 and 27–299 of this Supplement.

Delete: "4–47 *et seq.*" and **substitute:** "4–37 *et seq.*" *Brighton v Jones* is now reported at [2004] E.M.L.R. 26 and [2005] F.S.R. 16.

Add: As to implied licences to re-use existing material, see *Brighton v Jones* at paragraphs 72 to 77.

(ii) The creative team

NOTE 67. *Intercase UK Ltd v Time Computers Ltd* is now reported at [2004]   **27–270**
E.C.D.R. 8. *Ultraframe (UK) Ltd v Fielding* is now reported at [2004] R.P.C. 24.

(a) *Directors*

NOTE 71. *Brighton v Jones* is now reported at [2004] E.M.L.R. 26 and [2005]   **27–271**
F.S.R. 16.
   Add: See also D. Michael Rose, "Copyright in stage production elements:
requirements of originality and record under English law" [1998] Ent. L.R. 30.
Also on the issue of substantiality see *Baigent and Anor v Random House Group
Limited* [2007] All ER (D) 456; [2007] EWCA Civ 247, (the Da Vinci Code
case) where Mummery L.J. (with whose judgment Rix L.J. agreed) said that the
resolution of this issue in that case required a careful assessment or evaluation of
all the relevant evidence by the fact-finding tribunal in the context of the pleaded
case [143]. This observation seems particularly apposite in its application to a
claim for infringement of that part of the copyright in a dramatic work which
consists of stage directions.

(b) *Choreographers and musical stagers*

British Actors Equity Association is now called, simply, Equity.   **27–272**

(c) *Designers*

Lighting design. NOTE 84. **Add:** See also D. Michael Rose, "Copyright in stage   **27–275**
production elements: requirements of originality and record under English law"
[1998] Ent. L.R. 30.

Sound design. Add: See also D. Michael Rose, "Copyright in stage production   **27–276**
elements: requirements of originality and record under English law" [1998] Ent.
L.R. 30.

(d) *Orchestrators*

NOTES 86 and 88. *Sawkins v Hyperion Records Ltd* is now reported at [2004]   **27–277**
E.M.L.R. 27 and [2005] R.P.C. 4; and on appeal ([2005] EWCA Civ 565) at
[2005] 1 W.L.R. 3281; [2005] E.M.L.R. 29 and [2005] R.P.C. 32.

(iii) Logo and artwork designers

NOTE 89. *R Griggs Group Ltd v Evans* is now reported at [2004] F.S.R. 31; on   **27–278**
appeal [2005] EWCA Civ 11.

(iv) Performers

First sentence. For performers' rights, see paragraph 27–304, below and Chapter   **27–279**
12.
   Second paragraph. First sentence. **Delete:** "Theatre Managers Association"
and **substitute:** "Theatrical Management Association".
   Performers now have statutory, non-assignable moral rights to be identified as
the performer, and to object to derogatory treatment, subject to certain exceptions
and supplementary provisions. See CDPA 1988, sections 205C(1) and 205F(1),
inserted with effect from February 1, 2006 by the Performances (Moral Rights
etc) Regulations 2006 (SI 2006/18). See also paragraph 27–294 and Chapter 12
of this supplement.

(v) Translators

27–280   NOTE 94. *R Griggs Group Ltd v Evans* is now reported at [2004] F.S.R. 31; see also the judgment on appeal ([2005] EWCA Civ 11).

(vi) The producer

27–282   **Add** at end of second paragraph: However, a producer who commissions for value various production elements of a composite dramatic work, for example, in the case of a ballet, the stage direction, music or choreography, is likely, in the absence of agreement to the contrary, to be the owner of the copyright in the composite work and can thereby claim copyright in "his production". See paragraphs 4–24 and 27–299 of the Main Work and *Massine v de Basil* [1936–45] Mac C.C. 223. The latter decision predated the 1956 Act. Accordingly, to the extent that it suggests that the copyright in a dramatic work extends to the scenic designs and costumes for that work, it should be treated with caution. See paragraphs 3–33 and 3–35 of the Main Work and *Copinger* (8th Ed.) pages 61 to 63. If scenic designs and costumes are not protected by the copyright in the dramatic work they may of course qualify for separate protection as artistic works.

B. LICENCE OR ASSIGNMENT?

27–285   **The creative team.** NOTE 2. At end of text **add:** and the TMA/Equity Agreement for Subsidised Repertory and Commercial Theatres (2004). Interestingly, and in contrast to most other creative team collective agreements, the last two mentioned agreements contain, in addition to the option for an outright assignment of copyright, alternative terms for a licence covering not just the United Kingdom but also the rest of the world, which in the case of the TMA/Equity Agreement is described as being for "the copyright period". Why provision for a similarly broad licence is not included in corresponding collective agreements for other members of the creative team between SOLT/TMA and Equity is not explained.

27–286   **Commissioned work.** NOTE 3. *R Griggs Group Ltd v Evans* is now reported at [2004] F.S.R. 31; see also the judgment on appeal ([2005] EWCA Civ 11).

   Add: A factor which may induce an agreement to assign, rather than license, is if the writer is being commissioned to adapt a pre-existing work (*e.g.* a film or novel into a stage play), so that the commissioned work will have no stand-alone life of its own without the consent of the owner of the adaptation rights (usually the intended producer who is doing the commissioning).

   If the contract between a producer and an independent contractor for creation by the latter for value of material capable of forming part of a composite copyright work is silent as to ownership of the commissioned material, the facts of the case are likely to give rise to a "necessary implication" that the producer, as the paying party, is the equitable owner of that part of the copyright and accordingly has the right to require it to be assigned to him. This is analogous to the American doctrine of "work for hire" which carries a similar implication, but such an implication will not necessarily be made in every case of a commissioned work. See paragraphs 5–32 and 5–173 to 5–175 of the Main Work, and also *Massine v de Busil* [1936-45] Mac C.C. 223, in which such a term was held to be implied.

D. MORAL RIGHTS

27–294   NOTE 13. Note that CDPA 1988, ss. 205C(1) and 205F(1), inserted with effect from February 1, 2006 by the Performances (Moral Rights etc) Regulations 2006 (SI 2006/18), created two new statutory, non-assignable moral rights for performers, similar to those already existing for copyright owners, namely a right to be identified as the performer, and a right to object to derogatory treatment. These new rights are subject to certain exceptions and supplementary provisions. See Ch.12 of this Supplement.

THOMSON
™
SWEET & MAXWELL

Thank you for purchasing **Copinger & Skone James on Copyright**, 2nd supplement to the 15th edition.

☑ Don't miss important updates

So that you have all the latest information, **Copinger & Skone James on Copyright** is supplemented regularly. Sign up today for a Standing Order to ensure you receive the updating supplements as soon as they publish.

Setting up your Standing Order with Sweet & Maxwell is hassle-free, simply complete and return this FREEPOST card and we'll do the rest. You can cancel your request at any time by writing to us at Sweet & Maxwell, PO Box 1000, Andover SP10 9AF stating the standing order you wish to cancel.

Alternatively if you have purchased your copy of **Copinger & Skone James on Copyright** from a bookshop or other supplier, please ask your supplier to ensure that you are registered to receive your supplements.

Yes, please send me new editions and/or supplements to **Copinger & Skone James on Copyright** to be invoiced on publication, until I cancel the standing order in writing. Please tick:

☐ All supplements to current edition
☐ All new editions
☐ All new editions and supplements

Name:

Organisation:

Address:

Postcode:

Telephone:

Email:

S&M account number: (if known)

All orders are accepted subject to the terms of this order form, our Terms of Trading (see our website www.sweetandmaxwell.thomson.com) and relevant Service Terms (available with the product or on request).

By submitting this order form, I confirm that I accept these terms and am authorised to sign on behalf of the customer.

Signed: Date:

Print name: Job title:

STANDING ORDERS

SWEET & MAXWELL

FREEPOST

PO BOX 2000

ANDOVER

SP10 9AH

E. THEATRE PREMISES AND DEPOSIT OF SCRIPTS

Add: For a more detailed treatment of this topic see paragraph 27–90 *et seq.* of the Main Work.   **27–295**

F. UNIONS, TRADE ASSOCIATIONS AND OTHER ORGANISATIONS

First sentence. **Delete:** "Cinematograph" and **substitute:** "Cinematography".   **27–296**
    Second sentence. The Theatres National Committee (TNC) no longer exists.
    Second paragraph. First sentence. The British Academy of Songwriters, Composers and Authors (BASCA) has now been renamed British Academy of Composers and Songwriters (BACS).

H. COLLECTIVE BARGAINING AGREEMENTS

1987. The 1987 SOLT/TMA/Equity Agreement for Producers and Directors of   **27–298**
Opera in the United Kingdom has been replaced by a new 2006 Agreement for Opera Directors and Staff Directors.
    1989. The 1989 SOLT/Equity Agreement for West End of London Theatre Designers is currently in renegotiation and is likely very shortly to be replaced, as also is the 1995 SOLT/TMA/ITC/Equity Agreement for Fight Directors.
    1993. In relation to the TNC/Writers' Guild of GB/Theatre Writers Union Agreement, the TNC no longer exists and the Theatre Writers Union has since merged with the Writers' Guild of GB. The Agreement is thus between the Writers' Guild of GB and the "English Stage Companies", namely Royal National Theatre, Royal Shakespeare Company and Royal Court Theatre and is applicable to productions staged at those theatres.
    1993. In relation to the TMA/Writers' Guild of GB/Theatre Writers Union/ Scottish Society of Playwrights Agreement, the Theatre Writers Union has since merged with the Writers' Guild of GB, and the expression "provinces" is no longer used in this context, instead of which the Agreement is regarded as relating to works to be produced by members using the TMA/Equity Subsidised Repertory Agreement.
    1995. The TNC/Equity Agreement for Fight Directors is now the SOLT/TMA/ ITC/Equity Agreement for Fight Directors. The TNC no longer exists.
    2000. The TMA/Equity Agreement for Choreographers in subsidised repertory and provincial commercial contracts has now been replaced by a 2004 TMA/ Equity Agreement for Choreographers for Subsidised Repertory and Commercial Theatres, in which the word "provincial" is no longer used.
    2001. The 2001 SOLT/Equity Agreement for Engagement of Freelance Directors and Assistant Directors at a West End of London Theatre (and any pre-West End Tour) has been replaced by a new 2006 SOLT/Equity Agreement for West End Directors.
    2002. The TMA/Equity Agreement for Directors and Assistant Directors of subsidised repertory and provincial theatres is now the 2002 TMA/Equity Agreement for Theatre Directors in Subsidised Repertory and Commercial Theatres. Assistant directors are no longer covered by the Agreement and the word "provincial" is no longer used.
    2002. **Delete:** "2002 SOLT/Equity Agreement for West End Theatre chChoreographers" (sic). **Substitute:** "2003 SOLT/Equity Agreement for West End Theatre Choreographers".
    2003. In relation to the ITC/Writers' Guild of GB/Theatre Writers' Union Agreement, note that the Theatre Writers' Union has merged with the Writers' Guild of GB. **Delete:** "professioanlly" (sic) and **substitute:** "professionally".

Add: The ITC (Independent Theatre Council) also has a number of other collective agreements with various bodies, on similar lines to those of SOLT/TMA, which are regarded as compulsory for ITC members registered as "approved managers". The ITC has over 600 members (only a proportion of whom have "approved manager" status), who are concerned principally with small to medium sized stage performances outside the West End of London, including non-traditional performance spaces. Its collective agreements for owners of copyright material comprise :

1993 ITC/Equity Agreement for Resident and Freelance Theatre Directors.

1993 ITC/Equity Agreement for Freelance Designers.

2002 ITC/Equity Agreement for Theatre Writers.

2004 ITC/Equity agreement for Freelance Choreographers.

Unlike SOLT/TMA, doubtless because the latter focus on larger productions of completed dramatico-musical works, ITC in its 1993 Agreement with Equity for Theatre Directors grapples, where applicable and in considerable detail, with contractual issues relating to so-called "devised plays" which have no working script at commencement of the workshop/rehearsal period but are allowed to develop and devolve during such period from contributions by various participants in the creative process including, prominently, the Director. Reference should be made to this agreement for its somewhat complex treatment of the copyright issues concerned.

I. OPERA AND BALLET

27–299   **Add** at end: Before the passing of the 1956 Act, a ballet in its entirety was treated by the Court as a composite work protected by copyright, comprising collectively the elements of music, story, choreography, scenery and costumes, in which case there seems to be no reason in principle why the same should not apply to an opera or, indeed, to any other dramatic work, even though depending on the facts a separate copyright might subsist in some of the individual elements. Thus, the combination of an element such as music with a particular dramatic work might (if sufficiently original) give rise to a separate work which is protected separately from its component parts. See paragraph 3–26 of the Main Work and *Massine v de Basil* [1936-45] Mac C.C. 223. However, to the extent that it suggests that the copyright in a dramatic work extends to the scenic designs and costumes for that work, the decision in *Massine v Basil* should be treated with caution. See paragraphs 3–33 and 3–35 of the Main Work and *Copinger* (8th Ed.) pages 61 to 63. Of course, if scenic designs and costumes are not protected by the copyright in the dramatic work they may qualify for separate protection as artistic works.

Furthermore, it is important to bear in mind that copyright may not subsist in contributions to the mere interpretation and theatrical presentation of a dramatic work: *Brighton v Jones* [2004] EWHC 1157; [2004] EMLR 26 at [34] and [56].

27–300   **The creative team.** NOTE 25. *Intercase UK Ltd v Time Computers Ltd* is now reported at [2004] E.C.D.R. 8. *Ultraframe (UK) Ltd v Fielding* is now reported at [2004] R.P.C. 24.

Add at end of first sub-paragraph: However, if the contract with an independent contractor is silent as to ownership of copyright, it is likely that the circumstances will give rise to a "necessary implication" that copyright in the material concerned should in equity be the property of the paying party who should in that event be entitled to have the rights assigned to him. See *Massine v de Basil* [1936-45] Mac C.C. 223.

NOTE 26. **After "1987" add:** (updated in 2006).

Third sub-paragraph. **After "1987" add:** (updated in 2006).

7. THE ADVERTISING INDUSTRY

A. COMPONENTS OF ADVERTISING

(i) Television, radio and cinema commercials

Production companies. NOTE 36. **Delete** and **substitute:** The Advertising Producers Association (*www.a-p-a.net*), the Institute of Practitioners in Advertising (*www.ipa.co.uk*) and the Incorporated Society of British Advertisers (*www.isba.org.uk*).   27–302
NOTES 37 and 38. In each case **delete** "2003" and **substitute:** "2004".
Fifth paragraph. **Delete** the third sentence starting "The standard contract ...".
NOTES 39 and 40. In each case **delete** "2003" and **substitute:** "2004".

Music. Second paragraph. Second sentences and NOTES 43 to 45. **Delete** and **substitute:** Under the terms of the standard agreements approved by the trade associations of the music production companies (Producers and Composers of Applied Music, *www.pcam.co.uk*) and advertising agencies, the copyrights in both the sound recording and any original composition are retained by the music production company (as between the production company and the composer, the production company will usually have taken the copyright either as the composer's employer or under the terms of his engagement). In the case of a rerecording of an existing musical work, the music production company retains the copyright in the sound recording but the copyright in any arrangement of the existing musical work becomes the property of the owner of the copyright in the work that has been arranged. The standard agreements are the Agreement for the Production and Licensing of Original Musical Composition and the Agreement for the Licensing and Re-Recording of an Existing Copyright Work (February 2003).   27–303
Second paragraph. Last sentence. **Delete:** "With one limited qualification" and **substitute:** "With limited qualifications".
NOTE 46. **Add** at end: An arranger is entitled to a credit in such circumstances "wherever possible".
Third paragraph. Second sentence. **Delete** and **substitute:** "See the Synchronisation Licence for Music in Commercials, approved by the Music Publishers Association and the Institute of Practitioners in Advertising (December 2005)."

Actors. NOTE 52. **Delete** and **substitute:** Agreement for the Employment of Featured Artists in Television Commercials (November 1, 1991). This agreement is not officially approved but is used in practice, as supplemented by a Form of Engagement approved by the Advertising Producers Association, the Institute of Practitioners in Advertising and the Incorporated Society of British Advertisers (July 2004).   27–304
First paragraph. **Add** at end: The Form of Engagement covers overseas use and gives "the right to use such commercial(s) for agency/production company promotion, awards entries and websites, and for use in all showreels".

Performers' moral rights. Performers of qualifying performances now have the right to be identified as such (CDPA 1988, s.205C(1)) and the right to object to derogatory treatment of their performance (s.205F(1)). The right to be identified does not apply where it is not reasonably practicable to identify the performer (s.205E(2)), nor does it apply in relation to performances given for the purposes of advertising any goods or services (s.205E(4)).   27–304A

(ii) Printed Advertisements

Photographs and illustrations. NOTE 57. **Delete** and **substitute:** *www.the-aop.org*.   27–307

B. ISSUES BETWEEN RIGHTS OWNERS

(iii) Rights of advertisers vis-á-vis agencies

27–310   First sentence. **Delete** "2002" and **substitute:** "2005".
NOTE 61. **Delete** and **substitute:** *www.isba.org.uk.*
NOTE 62. **Delete** and **substitute:** *www.cips.org.*
Second sentence to end of paragraph. **Delete** and **substitute:** However, the suggested contract no longer includes provisions concerning ownership of copyright in advertising. A menu of options and guidance for clauses dealing with copyright is now contained in a separate document to the standard agreement: Handbook of Intellectual Property Clauses.
NOTE 63. The decision in *R Griggs Group Ltd v Evans* (reported at [2004] F.S.R. 31) was upheld on appeal: [2005] EWCA Civ 11.

C. COPYING OF OTHER ADVERTISEMENTS

(i) Copyright and passing off

27–311   **Copyright. Add** at end: There is no equivalent in copyright law to the provisions in trade mark law allowing the use of marks in comparative advertising (Trade Marks Act 1994, s. 10(6)). Reproduction in an advertisement of a competitor's copyright work is unlikely to be fair dealing for the purposes of criticism or review: *IPC Media v News Group Newspapers Ltd* [2005] EWHC 317 (Ch); (2005) EMLR 532; (2005) FSR 35; and see *IPC Magazines v MGN Ltd* [1998] FSR 431.

(ii) Advertising codes

27–314   NOTE 72. **Delete** and **substitute:** *www.asa.org.uk.*

NOTE 73. **Delete** and **substitute:** *www.ofcom.org.uk.*

D. REFERENCES TO INDIVIDUALS

(i) Defamation and passing off

27–317   **Passing off.** NOTE 80. *Irvine v Talksport Ltd* is now reported at [2002] 1 W.L.R. 2355; [2002] E.M.L.R. 32; [2002] F.S.R. 60 (liability at first instance); [2003] E.M.L.R. 6 (damages); and [2003] F.S.R. 25 and [2003] E.M.L.R. 26 (on appeal).

8. THE COMPUTER SOFTWARE INDUSTRY

A. THE INDUSTRY

27–320   Second sub-paragraph starting "Some software is bespoke". **Delete** fifth sentence starting "Traditionally". **Substitute:** Traditionally, this mainly occurred by means of the supply of copies in electronic form on physical media such as tape, floppy discs or CD-ROMs, often through intermediary wholesalers and retailers.
Third sub-paragraph starting "More recently". First sentence. After "direct electronic distribution," **add:** "for example by internet download from the software vendor's own website",. Last but one line. **Delete:** "may". **Substitute:** "are likely to".
Add at end: Open source concepts can now be seen in evolving practices in

other areas of collaborative endeavour, such as the Creative Commons movement, and the web encyclopaedia, Wikipedia.

B. Writing software

(i) Authorship/ownership

Add at end of first sub-paragraph: For more recent cases dealing with disputes over ownership as between software developers and their customers see *Cyprotex Discovery Ltd v University of Sheffield* [2004] EWCA Civ 380 (CA); [2004] R.P.C. 44; *Clearsprings Management Ltd v Businesslinx Ltd* [2005] EWHC 1487 (Ch); [2006] F.S.R. 3 and *Wrenn Integrated Multi-Media Solutions Ltd v Landamore* [2007] EWHC 1833 (Ch).

27–321

Second sub-paragraph starting "The mobility of programmers". Second line. After "employer" **add** "or customer". **Delete** second sentence and **substitute:** This may be a clear infringement resulting from programmers innocently or deliberately re-using copied software.

Add at end: In *Navitaire Inc v easyJet Airline Co Ltd* [2004] EWHC 1725 (Ch); [2006] R.P.C. 3. Pumfrey J. held that character-based screens in dispute in that action were properly viewed as tables and therefore literary in character, while other screen layouts were artistic works. The claimants succeeded in respect of the screens held to be artistic works, but not in respect of the screens held to be literary works. In *Nova Productions Ltd v Mazooma Games Ltd* [2006] EWHC 24 (Ch); [2006] R.P.C. 14; [2006] E.M.L.R. 14, Kitchin J held that, insofar as composite frames displayed on screen during game play were computer-generated by reason of having been created by a computer program from a series of bitmap files stored in computer memory, the human author of the program and bitmap frames was the deemed author.

C. Relevant works

NOTE 93. **Add:** In *Navitaire Inc v easyJet Airline Co Ltd* [2004] EWHC 1725 (Ch); [2006] R.P.C. 3 Pumfrey J. considered the dividing line between program copying and database copyright. This arose in respect of data migration and the design of a substitute database.

27–324

NOTE 94. *Sony v Ball* is now reported as *Kabushiki Kaisha Sony Computer Entertainment Inc v Ball* at [2005] F.S.R. 9; [2004] E.C.D.R. 33.

Second sub-paragraph, starting "At the user interface level". **Delete** second sentence. **Substitute:** Program protection may be argued, for example, to extend to input commands, screen layout, text or images on screen generated by the program, or other forms of data output to devices to which the computer is connected. In *Navitaire Inc v easyJet Airline Co Ltd* [2004] EWHC 1725 (Ch); [2006] R.P.C. 3 Pumfrey J. held that individual commands in issue in that case were not copyright works and that the compilation of commands should also not be protected. In his view, to protect these amounted to protecting ideas, which is excluded under Recital 14 of Directive 91/250. On his analysis, computer languages, as opposed to computer programs written in specific languages, are not themselves protected by copyright. However, he acknowledged that the exclusion of programming languages from protection was not entirely clear, and would require to be referred to the Court of Justice.

Add at end of fourth sentence: In *Navitaire Inc v easyJet Airline Co Ltd* [2004] EWHC 1725 (Ch); [2006] R.P.C. 3 Pumfrey J. held that character-based screens in dispute in that action were properly viewed as tables and therefore literary in character, while other screen layouts were artistic works. The claimants succeeded in respect of the screens held to be artistic works, but not in respect of the screens held to be literary works. In *Nova Productions Ltd v Mazooma Games Ltd* [2006] EWHC 24 (Ch); [2006] R.P.C. 14; [2006] E.M.L.R. 14, a case relating to computer games based on the game pool, Kitchin J. held that each of bitmap files stored in computer memory and composite frames generated from those files during game play were artistic works within CDPA 1988, section 4. On appeal, [2007] R.P.C. 25, it was common ground between the parties that the individual frames stored in memory were "graphic works". Jacob L.J. found the case based on graphic works "falls at the first hurdle" given the concession that there was no frame-for-frame reproduction, and that the similarity was in the sequence of events depicted through the series of frames. The appellant did not pursue its claims based on rights in film or dramatic works on appeal.

Third line from the end. **Delete:** could. **Substitute:** may.

D. RELEVANT TRADE ASSOCIATIONS, COLLECTING SOCIETIES/LICENSING AGENCIES

27–325   NOTE 1. The postal address of FAST is now York House, 18 York Road, Maidenhead, Berkshire SL6 1SF.

NOTE 2. The postal address of ELSPA Ltd is now 167 Wardour Street, London W1F 8WL.

Add at end: The address of BCS is 1st Floor, Block D, North Star House, North Star Avenue, Swindon SN2 1FA; *www.bcs.org*.

F. PROBLEMS AND ISSUES

(i) Problems of subsistence and infringement inherent in the nature of software

27–327   Add at end: In *Navitaire Inc v easyJet Airline Co Ltd* [2004] EWHC 1725 (Ch); [2006] R.P.C. 3 Pumfrey J. rejected the claimant's argument based on infringement by copying of the "business logic" underlying its programs, in circumstances where the disputed systems had been specifically designed to replace the claimant's software. The defendant's software acted upon identical or very similar inputs and produced very similar results but without copying code.

(iii) Compatibility; protection of interfaces; reverse engineering

27–329   Third sub-paragraph beginning "The defendants' main argument". **Add** after fourth sentence: In *Navitaire Inc v easyJet Airline Co Ltd* [2004] EWHC 1725 (Ch); [2006] R.P.C. 3. See also [2005] EWHC 0282 (Ch); [2006] R.P.C. 4. Pumfrey J. had to consider whether the defendants had infringed program copyright, and/or database copyright in designing and developing a replacement system to perform similar functions on the same data types, and/or in migrating data to the new system. He held most of the acts done by the defendants in this process were permitted uses under section 50B (acts necessary for the purpose of access to and use of the contents of the database by a lawful user).

(v) Enforceability of shrink-wrap licences

27–331   Last line. **Delete:** may increase. **Substitute:** is now widespread.

CHAPTER TWENTY EIGHT

COLLECTING SOCIETIES

1. INTRODUCTION

A. RATIONALE FOR COLLECTING SOCIETIES

28–02 **Need for collective administration of certain rights.** Last sentence. **Add:** NOTE 3A. D. Gervais (ed.) *Collective Management of Copyright and Related Rights*, Sweet and Maxwell, London, 2007.

28–06 **The public interest.** NOTE 13. First two lines. **Delete** and **substitute:** Directive on rental right and lending right and on certain rights related to copyright in the field of intellectual property (Directive 92/100 [1992] O.J. L346/61), repealed and replaced by Directive 2006/115/EC (codified version) [2006] O.J. L376 of December 27, 2006.

Fourth paragraph. Last sentence. **Delete** and **substitute:** Other examples of rights in respect of which legislation makes their exercise conditional on collective administration are the reprographic reproduction right, the right to remuneration in respect of private copying of works (a right which has been introduced in a majority of Member States of the EU and elsewhere but which is not yet part of the law of the United Kingdom), and the artist's resale right (*droit de suite*), which has only recently been introduced in the law of the United Kingdom (see Ch.19A of this Supplement).

Fifth paragraph. **Delete**.

B. ORIGINS OF COLLECTING SOCIETIES

28–10 **Collecting societies operating in the United Kingdom in 2007.** First paragraph. **Delete** and **substitute:** Today, the following additional collective licensing bodies are operating in the United Kingdom; their activities, as well as those of the MCPS, PRS and PPL, are described in more detail in Section 4 of this Chapter, below:

(a) Artists' Collecting Society (ACS) collects artists' resale right royalties (*droit de suite*) on behalf of UK artists;

(b) Authors' Licensing and Collecting Society Ltd (ALCS) administers a wide variety of rights in literary and dramatic works on behalf of authors, including *inter alia* the reprographic right, the cable distribution right and the private recording right;

(c) British Equity Collecting Society Ltd (BECS) administers performers' remuneration;

(d) Compact Collections Ltd (CCL) collects secondary television royalties for film and television content owners;

(e) Copyright Licensing Agency Ltd (CLA) licenses the reprographic rights of authors and publishers in published literary and artistic works;

(f) Design and Artists Copyright Society Ltd (DACS) administers rights in artistic works, including the artists' resale right;

(g) Directors and Producers Rights Society (1992) Ltd (DPRS) administers certain rights on behalf of film and television directors and producers;

(h) Educational Recording Agency Ltd (ERA) licenses the recording by educational establishments of broadcasts and cable programmes;

(i) Newspaper Licensing Agency Ltd (NLA) licenses the reprographic rights of newspaper publishers in news articles;

(j) Video Performance Ltd (VPL) administers the rights of producers of music videos.

Add: The Association of United Recording Artists (AURA) and the Performing Artists Media Rights Association Ltd (PAMRA) both of which previously collected equitable remuneration arising from the exploitation of sound recordings on behalf of performers went into voluntary liquidation in late 2006, following a merger with PPL.

C. CHARACTERISTICS OF EFFECTIVE COLLECTING SOCIETIES

Structure and functions of collecting societies. NOTE 23. **Add:** M. Ficsor, *Collective Management of Copyright and Related Right* (WIPO Publication no.855). 28–11

Benefits of a single organisation representing a single category of rights owner. NOTE 25. **Delete** and **substitute:** As noted in para.9-1 of the MMC PRS report (see n.22, above), there are only two major jurisdictions, Brazil and the USA, where there are competing societies. In Brazil, there are 13: ABRAC (Associação Brasileira de Autores, Compositores, Intérpretes e Músicos), ABRAMUS (*Associação Brasileira de Músicos*); ACIMBRA (*Associação de Compositóres e Intérpretes Musicais do Brasil*), AMAR (*Associação de Músicos, Arranjadores e Regentes*); ANACIM (*Associação Nacional de Autores, Compositores e Intérpretes de Música*); ASSIM (*Associação de Intérpretes e Músicos*); ATIDA (*Associação de Titulares de Direitos Autorais*), SADEMBRA (*Sociedade Administradora de Direitos de Execução Musical do Brasil*); SBACEM (*Sociedade Brasileira de Autores, Compositores e Escritores de Música*); SBAT (*Sociedade Brasileira de Autores Teatrais*) which administers "grand rights"; SICAM (*Sociedade Independente de Compositores e Autores Musicais*); SOCINPRO (*Sociedade Brasileira de Administração e Protecão de Direitos Intelectuais*) and UBC (*União Brasileira de Compositores*). In the USA, there are three: ASCAP (American Society of Composers, Authors and Publishers), BMI (Broadcast Music Inc.) and SESAC (Society of European Stage Authors and Composers). In Brazil, so far as performing rights in musical works and phonograms are concerned, the situation is different from that in the USA. Collection on behalf of all the societies, with the exception of SBAT, is effected by one organisation, ECAD. ECAD is a private monopoly organisation imposed by law, which collects remuneration on behalf of the societies it represents and distributes it to rights owners through the specific society to which the rights owner is affiliated (Law no.9.610/98). The following societies are affiliated to ECAD: AMAR, ABRAMUS, SPACEM, SICAM, SOCINPRO and UBC. As to the position in the USA, see para.28–17. 28–12

E. COLLECTIVE ADMINISTRATION AND EC LAW

Community action on collecting societies. First paragraph. Second and third sentences. **Delete** and **substitute:** To date, no firm proposals for legislation relating to collective administration generally have been published by the Commission. A legislative proposal was foreshadowed in a communication published in April 2004 entitled "The Management of Copyright and Related Rights in the Internal Market".[1] However, in May 2005, the Commission issued a Recommendation on collective cross-border management of copyright and related rights for legitimate online music services, see paragraph 28–20A, below.[2] The Recommendation is limited in its scope to the management of online music 28–20

---

[1] Communication from the Commission to the Council, The European Parliament and the European Economic and Social Committee, document COM (2004) 261 final, of April 16, 2004.
[2] 2005/737/EC [2005] O.J. L276/54.

rights. However, further and tougher action, presumably in the form of legislation, will be taken by the Commission if sufficient progress is not made.[3]

The 2004 communication remains relevant, therefore. It was the result of a wide-ranging process of consultation with interested parties begun in 1995/6 and continued through 2002 on the basis of its Green Paper entitled: *Copyright and Related Rights in the Information Society*, published in July 1995.[4]

Second paragraph. First sentence. **Delete** and **substitute:** In its April 2004 communication, the Commission announced that it had concluded that Community legislation on the collective management of rights, and particularly on the governance of collecting societies, would be highly desirable, stating that the marketing of intellectual property rights needed to be facilitated in order to create a true single market in this area.[5]

28–20A **Commission recommendation on management of online rights in musical works.**[6] Presenting the recommendation to the public, the Commission stated that it "puts forward measures for improving the EU-wide licensing of copyright and related rights for on-line services. Improvements are necessary because new Internet-based services such as webcasting or on-demand music downloads need a licence that covers their activities throughout the EU. The absence of EU-wide copyright licences has been one factor that has made it difficult for new Internet-based music services to develop their full potential…".[7] In order to improve EU-wide online licensing of music, which it considered unsatisfactory due to the cost and complexity of clearing online rights in musical works on a territory-by-territory basis, the Commission considered three options: (1) do nothing; (2) improve cooperation among collecting societies allowing each society in the EU to grant a EU-wide licence covering the other societies' repertoires; or (3) give right holders the choice to appoint a collective rights manager for the online use of their musical works across the entire EU ("EU-wide direct licensing"). Having reached a consensus with right holders, collecting societies and commercial users, that doing nothing was not an option, views were divided as regards the other two options. The Commission concluded that right holders and commercial users of copyright-protected material should be given a choice as to their preferred model of licensing and that different online services might require different forms of EU-wide licensing policies. Multi-territorial licensing should be provided for in order to enhance greater legal certainty to commercial users in relation to their activity and to foster the development of legitimate online services, increasing, in

---

[3] Statement of Internal Market and Services Commissioner Charlie McCreevy, October 12, 2005, IP/05/1261.

[4] Green Paper, *Copyright and Related Rights in the Information Society*, Brussels, July 19, 1995, COM (95) 382, final.

[5] COM (2004) 261, final of April 16, 2004. Note also that the European Parliament adopted a resolution on January 15, 2004, on a Community framework for collective management societies in the field of copyright and neighbouring rights. The resolution noted *inter alia* "that collecting societies require a degree of regulation, bringing greater harmonisation, democratisation and transparency in relation to the management of copyright and neighbouring rights, and … a Community approach in the area of the exercise and management of copyright and neighbouring rights must be pursued while respecting and complying with the principles of copyright and competition law and in accordance with the principles of subsidiarity and proportionality", Bull. EU 1/2-2004, para.1.3.61. See also Report on a Community Framework for collecting societies for authors' rights adopted by the Committee on Legal Affairs and the Internal Market, December 11, 2003 (doc.A5-0578/2003, final).

[6] Recommendation on collective cross-border management of copyright and related rights for legitimate online music services, see the Supplement to Vol.2, Part IA (2005/737/EC [2005] O.J. L276/54).

[7] IP/05/1261.

turn, the revenue stream for right holders.[8] The recommendation invites Member States to facilitate the growth of legitimate online services[9] and states that right holders should have the right to entrust the management of any of the online rights necessary to operate legitimate online music services, on a territorial scope of their choice, irrespective of the Member State of residence or the nationality of either the collective rights manager or the right holder.[10] The recommendation also includes provisions on the governance of collecting societies, the distribution of royalties, equal treatment of right holders, transparency, dispute settlement and accountability of collective rights managers, aimed at introducing "a culture of transparency and good governance enabling all relevant stakeholders to make an informed decision as to the licensing model best suited to their needs".[11] The recommendation is addressed to EU Member States as well as to all economic operators involved in the clearance of copyright across the European Union.[12] The Commission will continue to assess the development of the online music sector and the need for further action at Community level.[13]

Future EC legislative action. Delete and **substitute:** The adoption of the Commission recommendation referred to in paragraphs 28–20 and 28–20A, above, does not mean that binding legislation on the governance of collecting societies in Europe may not be introduced in the future. The legislative proposal foreshadowed in the Commission's communication on the management of copyright and related rights in the internal market already referred to therefore remains relevant. The proposal came to four main conclusions[14]:   **28–22**

— An internal market for collective rights management will be more firmly established if a legislative framework on the governance of collecting societies is implemented at Community level. Such a framework would address the issues surrounding the establishment and use of collecting societies, the relationship they have with right holders and commercial users, and lastly, their external supervision. This would make it possible to ensure that collecting societies are transparent, and that established Community law in the field of intellectual property is properly applied. It would foster the emergence of Community-wide licensing for the exploitation of rights via one-stop shops.

— The development of Digital Rights Management (DRM) systems should, in principle, be based on their acceptance by all stakeholders, including consumers, as well as on copyright policy of the legislature. A prerequisite to ensure Community-wide accessibility to DRM systems and services by right holders as well as users and, in particular, consumers, is that DRM systems and services are interoperable.

— For the time being, there is no need for action at Community level with regard to individual rights management as differences in national law have not given rise to concern with respect to the functioning of the Internal Market; national developments will, however, be kept under review.[15] An internal market in the collective management of rights can be best achieved if the monitoring of collecting societies under competi-

---

[8] Recommendation, Recital 8.
[9] Art.2.
[10] Art.3.
[11] IP/05/1261.
[12] Art.19.
[13] Arts 17 and 18.
[14] Commission Press release IP/04/492.
[15] COM (96) 568 final, para.2.

tion rules is complemented by the establishment of a legislative framework on good governance. Common ground on the following features of collective rights management would be required: the establishment and status of collecting societies (persons who may establish a society, the status thereof, the necessary evidence of efficiency, operability, accounting obligations, and a sufficient number of represented right holders); the relation of collecting societies to users (users must be in a position to contest tariffs, through the courts, specially created mediation tribunals or with the assistance of public authorities); however, use without payment should not be permitted. These principles would promote and safeguard access to protected works on appropriate terms.[16]

F. RELATIONS WITH FOREIGN COLLECTING SOCIETIES

28–23   **Application of principle of national treatment.** NOTE 75. **Delete** and **substitute:** The Copyright and Performers' (Application to Other Countries) Order (SI 2007/273), which entered into force on April 6, 2007, see Vol. 2 at **C1.iv** as amended in this Supplement.

28–24   **Need for international co-operation to implement national treatment.** Fifth sentence. **Delete** and **substitute:** Co-operation developed rapidly between these organisations and in 1926 an international confederation of such societies was established, the International Confederation of Societies of Authors and Composers (CISAC), which groups 219 societies in 115 countries,[17] representing rights owners of musical, dramatic, literary and audio-visual works and works of graphic and visual art.[18] It has five Regional Committees (Africa and Caribbean, Ibero-America, Asia-Pacific, Canada/USA and Europe) to facilitate co-operation between societies in the same region.

Second paragraph. **First to fourth sentences.** A second powerful international organisation, which groups 50 national societies in 54 countries concerned with the collective administration of authors' rights to authorise the reproduction of works in the form of recordings (sound recordings or audiovisual fixations), sometimes referred to as mechanical rights, is the International Bureau of Societies Administering the Rights of Mechanical Recording and Reproduction (BIEM—*Bureau international des Sociétés gérant les droits d'enregistrement et de reproduction mécanique)*, founded in 1929.[19] BIEM's principal function is to act as a centralised negotiating body fixing the conditions for the use of the repertoire of its member societies. Its main negotiating partner is the International Federation of the Phonographic Industry (IFPI), established in 1933.[20] As at July 31, 2007, IFPI has more than 1,400 members in 75 countries and affiliated industry associations in 49 countries.[21]

Third paragraph. **First sentence.** Other international organisations represent-

---

[16] COM (96) 568 final, para.3.5.
[17] As at July 31, 2007.
[18] The address of CISAC is 20–26 Boulevard du Parc, 92200 Neuilly-sur-Seine, France; *www.cisac.org.*
[19] Membership as at July 31, 2006. The address of BIEM is 20–26 Boulevard du Parc, 92200 Neuilly-sur-Seine, France; *www.BIEM.org.*
[20] The IFPI Secretariat is located at 10 Piccadilly, London, W1J 0DD, UK. It has regional offices also in Brussels, Hong Kong, Miami (for Latin America) and Moscow.
[21] The RIAA (Recording Industry of America) is affiliated to IFPI. See *www.ifpi.org* and *www.riaa.org.*

ing collecting societies operating in non-musical fields include AGICOA[22] and IFFRO.[23]

NOTE 85. **Delete** and **substitute:** Agicoa By-Laws, Art.3.

NOTE 87. **Delete** and **substitute:** Countries affording protection for sound recordings and performers, including performing rights, are listed in the Schedule of the Copyright and Performances (Application to Other Countries) Order 2007 (SI 2007/273).

NOTE 88. **Delete** and **substitute:** As at March 8, 2006, FIM , founded in 1948, has more than 200,000 members who are members of 72 musicians' organisations in 66 countries. It has two regional groups: one for Africa and the other for Latin America. Its objects are to protect and further the economic, social and artistic interests of musicians organised in its member unions. Its address is 21*bis*, rue Victor Massé, 75009 Paris, France; *www.Fim-musicians.com*.

NOTE 89. **Delete** and **substitute:** FIA, established in 1952, has 100 member organisations in 70 countries. Its objects are the protection and promotion of the artistic, economic, social and legal interests of the actors, singers, dancers, variety and circus artists, choreographers, directors, professional broadcasters, etc. organised in its affiliated or associated unions. It has offices in London at Guild House, Upper St. Martin's Lane, London, WC2H 9EG, U.K. and in Brussels at 31 rue de l'Hôpital, B-1000, Brussels, Belgium;*www.fia-actors.com*.

2. THE CONTROL OF COLLECTING SOCIETIES IN THE UNITED KINGDOM

C. THE COPYRIGHT TRIBUNAL

The Copyright Tribunal. Third and fourth sentences. **Delete** and **substitute:** 28–34
Since the 1988 Act came into force, the functions of the Copyright Tribunal have more than doubled as a result of new legislation, including *inter alia* the Broadcasting Act 1996 and the Copyright and Related Rights Regulations 1996 and 2003. Broadly, the Tribunal's jurisdiction is such that anyone who has unreasonably been refused a licence by a collecting society or considers the terms of an offered licence to be unreasonable may refer the matter the matter to the Tribunal. At present, the Patent Office is considering whether improvements could be made in the way in which the Copyright Tribunal works.

Add new paragraph:

At present, the UK Intellectual Property Office (new operating name of the Patent 28–34A
Office) is considering whether improvements could be made in the way in which the Copyright Tribunal works and recently published a "Review of the Copyright Tribunal" (CT), which recommends extensive changes to the existing system as regards the jurisdiction of the Tribunal, its practice, the location, resources and composition of the Tribunal and the subject-matter to be referred to it. The most important of the 30 recommendations include the following: a proposal to repeal the Copyright Tribunal Rules 1989 and for the proceedings of the Tribunal to be governed by the Civil Procedure Rules (CPR) and practice directions; the fees of

---

[22] As at May 22, 2007, Agicoa had 45 member associations in 29 countries. Its address is 1, rue Pestalozzi, CH-1202, Geneva, Switzerland; *www.agicoa.org*.

[23] As at February 2, 2007, IFFRO grouped 50 member organisations and 60 associate members in more than 50 countries. Its address is rue du Prince Royal 87, B-1050 Brussels, Belgium; *www.iffro.org*.

the CT to be abolished; the emphasis should be on written rather than oral evidence; expert evidence to be allowed only if strictly necessary; Alternative Dispute Resolution (ADR) should be used when appropriate; the CT should have a permanent staff of two located at permanent premises to be made available at the offices of the UK Intellectual Property Office in London; the chairman should be called the President and the position should be salaried and filled by an open recruitment exercise; there should be no restriction on the number of deputy chairmen but lay members should be abolished.[24]

3. THE FUTURE OF COLLECTING SOCIETIES

A. THE IMPACT OF TECHNICAL DEVELOPMENT AND THE INFORMATION SOCIETY ON COLLECTING SOCIETIES AND THE MARKET

28–38 **Expansion of fields of collective administration. Add:** Most recently, the artist's resale right has been introduced into the law of the UK; this right may only be exercised through a collecting society.[25]

28–39 **The impact of digital technology on the market. NOTE 37. Add:** See also P. Gilliéron, "Collecting Societies and the Digital Environment" [2006] I.I.C. 939 and para.28–44, below.

28–40 **The challenge to collecting societies. Add:** A further challenge to right owners and collecting societies is the problem of reconciling the use of technological protection measures and rights management information with the need to respect the limitations and exceptions provided for by copyright legislation. Technical protection measures and rights management systems are crucial to a secure and balanced distribution of content in the electronic environment and, following the adoption of the 1996 WIPO Internet Treaties,[26] have found wide acceptance in national legislation. However, the Internet Treaties and, indeed, the Information Society Directive,[27] also establish principles for the development of limitations and exceptions in national legislation, laying the ground work for adaptation of limitations and exceptions to the digital environment. Future avenues of work towards facilitating the coexistence of limitations and technological measures have been identified in a recent WIPO Study.[28]

28–41 **Supranational central licensing schemes. Add:** The EC Recommendation of May 18, 2005, on cross-border management of copyright and related rights for legitimate online music services aims to promote collective licensing across borders.[29]

28–43 **The concept of a one-stop-shop. Last sentence. Delete and substitute:** In the past, the European Commission took the view that the creation and development of one stop shops for "Multimedia Rights Clearance Systems" should be left to

---

[24] The Review is available on the website of the UK Intellectual Property Office, *www.ipo.gov.uk*.
[25] The Artist's Resale Right Regulations 2006, s.14.
[26] See Ch.24, above.
[27] See Ch.25, above.
[28] N. Garnett, *Automated Rights Management Systems and Copyright Limitations and Exceptions* (WIPO document SCCR/14/5, April 27, 2006).
[29] 2005/737/EC.

the market and limited itself to supporting studies and pilot projects financially.[30] The collecting societies responded to the need for one-stop-shops by means of reciprocal representation agreements so that each authors' society offered in its territory a one-stop-shop for users to obtain licences for a world-wide repertoire from a single source. The European Commission, however, takes the view that in the on-line environment it is appropriate to provide for multi-territorial licensing and that there should be freedom to provide collective management services across national borders. This entails that right holders are able to freely choose the collective rights manager for the management of the rights necessary to operate legitimate online music services across the Community. As the Commission Recommendation on collective cross-border management of copyright and related rights for legitimate online music services makes clear "That right implies the possibility to entrust or transfer all or a part of the online rights to another collective rights manager irrespective of the member state of residence or the nationality of either the collective rights manager or the rights holder."[31]

B. EU APPROACH TO THE ROLE OF COLLECTING SOCIETIES IN THE INFORMATION SOCIETY

The approach of the EU. Add: The European Commission Competition Department sent a Statement of Objections to CISAC, the International Federation of Societies of Authors and Composers, and to 24 of its members in the EEA, on January 31, 2006. The objections followed complaints filed by RTL in 2000 and Music Choice Europe in 2003. The objections deal with the transmission of music by cable, satellite and the Internet and targeted aspects of the reciprocal representation agreements signed between authors' societies alleging that these were in breach of EC competition laws. This action of the Competition authorities together with the adoption of the Recommendation on collective cross-border management of copyright and related rights for legitimate online music services[32] indicate that the European Commission is determined to encourage multi-territorial licensing by pan-European collecting societies.

28–44

Meanwhile, CISAC, along with 18 EEA authors' societies, has announced that it has reached an agreement in principle with the European Commission in response to the issues raised in the statement of objections. *Exclusivity*: CISAC agreed formally to reconfirm the absence of exclusivity from its Model Contract, whilst the societies agreed to ensure such an absence from their representation contracts with other EEA-based societies. *Membership*: CISAC agreed that the Model Contract would re-emphasise the right of an EEA creator and publisher to move freely between EEA authors' societies, whilst the societies agreed to ensure that such a right was present in their representation contract with other EEA-based societies. *Territoriality*: The societies agreed to mandate each other to grant multi-territorial EEA Internet, satellite and cable retransmission service licenses (subject to certain qualifications aimed at protecting the creative community and ensuring that authors and their works do not suffer the effects of a potentially harmful downward spiral in royalty rates). In June 2007, the European Commission has invited comments from interested parties on the commitments proposed by CISAC. If the results of the market test are positive, the Commis-

---

[30] See M. Shippan, "Purchase and Licensing of Digital Rights: The VERDI Project and the Clearing of Multimedia Rights in Europe" [2000] E.I.P.R. 24; *Multimedia Rights Clearance Systems* (European Commission, DG XIII/E).

[31] Recommendation 2005/737/EC, Recitals 9 and 10.

[32] See paras 28–20, 28–20A and 28–43, above.

sion has indicated that it would adopt a decision under Article 9 of Regulation 1/2003, rendering the commitments legally binding.[33]

In April 2007, IFPI announced that in response to the 2005 Recommendation arrangements had been put in place between IFPI and more than 40 collecting societies representing the record industry to facilitate online music and broadcasting services. Two new licensing agreements will create the framework for collective licensing of producers' rights for certain streaming and podcast services across several markets. In practice, the participating collecting societies will be able to license rights in each others' territories and repertoire. Online music services and broadcasters established in the EEA will be able to approach any European society for a licence, which will enable them to approach and choose the society they consider provides the best service for their needs. Users will continue also to have the option to approach record companies directly for a licence.[34]

In January 2007, the Commission announced its intention to assess the development of Europe's online music sector in the light of the Commission Recommendation referred to in paragraph 28–41, above[35] and issued an invitation to Member States and collective rights managers to report to the Commission by July 1, 2007, on measures they have taken in relation to the recommendation and on the management, at Community level, of copyright and related rights for the provision of legitimate online music services.

4. INDIVIDUAL COLLECTING SOCIETIES OPERATING IN THE UNITED KINGDOM

AA. ARTISTS' COLLECTING SOCIETY

Add new paragraph:

28–47A   The Artists' Collecting Society (ACS) was formally established as a collecting society in June 2006 in response to the EC's Directive 2001/84/EC and the new UK legislation on artists' resale right. ACS is an independent collecting society, established to collect resale royalties for British artists in the UK. Its aim is to provide artists with an alternative agency which maximises revenue due to its members, while minimising interference in the art trade. It is run on a not-for-profit basis and will charge 18 per cent for administration costs but has undertaken to reimburse artists with any excess money on a pro-rata basis. Its members are artists represented by the Society of London Art Dealers and the British Art Market Federation. As at July 31, 2007, ACS had some 200 members. ACS's website is at *www.artistscollectingsociety.org.uk.*

A. ASSOCIATION OF UNITED RECORDING ARTISTS ("AURA")

28–48   In the second half of 2006 AURA went into members' voluntary liquidation following a merger with PPL and PAMRA. See paragraph 28–60, below for details of the merger.

The editors are grateful to Sam Moorhouse, Legal and Business Affairs Executive, for his assistance in updating this paragraph.

---

[33] Details of the proposed commitments have been published at [2007] O.J. C128.
[34] IFPI Press Release, April 27, 2007.
[35] Recommendation 2005/737/EC [2005] O.J. L276.

B. AUTHORS' LICENSING & COLLECTING SOCIETY LTD ("ALCS")

Eighth sentence. **Add:** ALCS now administers fees from the Austrian Public   **28–49**
Lending Right scheme as well as those in Germany and the Netherlands.

NOTE 84. **Add:** ALCS now collects monies from blank tape levies in Italy,
Denmark and the Netherlands.

NOTE 85. **Add:** ALCS no longer collects remuneration from the schemes for
the collection of fees from Norwegian "blind readers" and the BBC PRIME/
WORLD licence.

Eleventh sentence. **Add:** As at July 2007 ALCS had over 50,000 members of
whom 35,000 were Ordinary Members. ALCS has removed the distinction between Ordinary and Associate Members and is currently undergoing a transition
process whereby those that were Associate Members become Ordinary Members.

Eleventh sentence. **Delete:** 38 and **substitute:** 39.

NOTE 87. **Add:** Norway.

Fourteenth sentence. **Delete** and **substitute:** ALCS now charges a one-off £25
joining fee for new members and has abolished the £10 annual fee previously
charged.

Fifteenth sentence: **Add:** As at July 2007 the ALCS levied a commission of
9.5 per cent.

NOTE 89. **Delete**.

Sixteenth sentence. **Add:** In the year 2006/7, the ALCS distributed royalties of
about £19 million gross.

The editors are grateful to Richard Combes, Head of Rights and Licensing, for
his assistance in updating this paragraph.

C. BRITISH EQUITY COLLECTING SOCIETY LTD ("BECS")

Third Sentence. **Add:** For example BECS is now responsible for administering   **28–50**
the revenue generated from contractual licences with BBC 7 (Digital Archive
Radio) and BBC TV Plus trials.

The Board of Management has granted its approval for BECS to act as agent
for Equity to receive sums negotiated between Equity and UK broadcasters for
clearing the use of performances by Equity members in programmes made available in "new media trials". These have included the BBC's High Definition trials
and Catch up Television Video on Demand trials.

Fourth Sentence. **Add:** In 2005 BECS collected in excess of £3 million for its
members.

Fifth sentence. **Delete:** , the amount of which depends on the source of revenue, but may be as much as 15.6 per cent. **Substitute:** . BECS commission levels
vary according to approved distribution policies and take into account the level
of data input and checking carried out by BECS (as opposed to third party collecting societies). Commission is not levied on all sources of revenue. Where
performances are identified individually by a foreign society, BECS does not
generally charge commission. However, where commission is charged, it is solely
for the purpose of covering BECS's overheads. For BECS members rates of
commission vary up to 10 per cent. Payments made to non members are subject
to higher commission rates.

Sixth Sentence. **Add:** As at July 2007 BECS had over 20,000 members.

Seventh Sentence. **Add:** As at July 2007 BECS had reciprocal arrangements
with 14 foreign collecting societies, in Denmark (two collecting societies), the
Netherlands, Belgium, France, Spain, Italy, Greece, Switzerland, Germany, Sweden Portugal, Romania and Norway. Further reciprocal arrangements with col-

lecting societies in Austria and the Czech Republic are close to agreement. At European level, BECS is affiliated to aepo-artis (see *www.aepo-artis.org*). At UK level, it is affiliated to the British Copyright Council.

The editors are grateful to Andrew Yeates for his assistance in updating this paragraph.

D. COMPACT COLLECTIONS LIMITED

28–51   Third sentence. **Add:** As at April 2007 Compact represented over 250 media companies worldwide including production companies, distributors, sales agents and broadcasters.

Fourth sentence. **Delete:** the cable retransmission right. **Substitute:** the cable and satellite retransmission right.

Sixth sentence. **Delete** and **substitute:** It is anticipated that during 2007 Compact will begin collecting royalties in respect of the exercise of rights in audio visual works in the United Kingdom.

Seventh sentence. **Delete** and **substitute:** Compact provides a full administration service from registering the audio-visual works of its clients with each of the rights societies through to distributing the collected returns. In order to facilitate this process, the relevant right is assigned by the right holder. This enables Compact to furnish warranties to the rights societies and to collect receipts. The member retains all other rights.

The editors are grateful to Cate Hemmings, Head of Commercial Affairs, for her assistance in updating this paragraph.

E. COPYRIGHT LICENSING AGENCY LTD ("CLA")

28–52   Fourth sentence. **Add:** As at April 2006 CLA represented some 1,900 mandating publishers. As at July 2007 CLA had bilateral agreements with similar societies in 24 countries.

Fifth sentence. **Add:** As at April 2006 CLA represented just over 50,000 ACLS author members.

NOTE 8. The *Universities UK* decision is reported at [2002] R.P.C. 36; [2002] E.M.L.R. 35.

Eleventh sentence. **Add:** During 2005/06 licences were agreed with American Express Europe, Cadbury Schweppes, ABN AMRO, Telewest Communications, and Bupa among others.

NOTE 10. **Add:** As at October 2006 the current rates for business licences ranged from £10.44 to £31.31 per year per professional, managerial or technical employee depending upon the type of business which is determined according to the SIC (Standard Industry Classification) code .

NOTE 15. **Delete:** February 1998. **Substitute:**June 2007.

Third sentence from end. **Add:** In 2005/6 CLA received royalties totalling £47 million and distributed £48 million. During the year CLA's administration costs were £5.6 million.

F. DESIGN AND ARTISTS COPYRIGHT SOCIETY LTD ("DACS")

28–53   Second sentence. **Add:** DACS is currently governed by a board of non-executive directors comprising representatives from a range of artistic disciplines alongside others from business and the legal profession.

Third sentence. **Add** at end: (DACS now refers to Individual Rights Management (IRM) and Collective Rights Management (CRM)).

Fourth sentence. **Add** at end: Representation is authorised by way of direct agreements with UK artists and through reciprocal agreements with the Associated Societies.

Seventh sentence. **Delete** and **substitute:** Since February 2006 DACS has administered the Artist's Resale Right.

Eighth sentence. **Add:** As at February 2006 DACS had a membership of over 40,000 artists and their successors in title for its Individual Rights Management service.

Ninth sentence. **Delete** and **substitute:** Licence fees received in respect of collective rights management are distributed annually through the DACS Payback service, from which in 2006, 11,179 visual creators successfully claimed a share of £2.2m of collective licensing revenue collected in 2004. All visual creators, whether or not they are members of DACS, are entitled to seek a share of annual collective licensing revenue, and are entitled to a royalty subject to certain criteria.

Tenth sentence. **Add** at end: Also included are associate members (individuals or organisations which own, manage, administer or otherwise control relevant rights), and governing members (any person appointed as a director of DACS): see Articles 3.2 and 3.3 of the Articles of Association respectively.

Eleventh sentence. **Add:** However, since March 2006 new members have been able to join DACS without payment of a membership fee.

Fourth sentence from the end. **Add:** As at July 2007 DACS retained a commission of 25 per cent of all copyright revenue collected through IRM and CRM and 15 per cent of all Artists' Resale Right royalties in the UK.

Second sentence from the end. **Add:** DACS's total turnover for 2006 was over £5.7 million.

Add at end: The Artist's Resale Right Service (ARR) is a new service of collection and distribution of resale royalties launched by DACS in February 2006 as a result of the United Kingdom implementation of the Artist's Resale Right Directive. The ARR service is offered to all artists and visual creators, and with its online facility is designed to offer administrative ease in the collection and distribution of the royalties for both art market professionals and artists. In particular DACS is aiming to ensure that all artists are eligible to receive royalties through DACS whether or not DACS manages their copyright through the Individual Rights Management Service. Artists can mandate DACS to act on their behalf in respect of resale royalties by completing a simple registration form. Distribution is not yet "real time": an artist who has registered does not receive an immediate payment if a resale generates a royalty. Art market professionals have a certain period of time within which to provide information on completed sales to DACS via its online portal. On receipt of that information DACS will calculate any royalty liability and invoice them accordingly.

DACS belongs to an international network of visual artists' organisations and currently holds reciprocal agreements with 32 other copyright societies ("Associated Societies") in 27 countries. All agreements cover individual and collective rights management (including the administration of artist's resale right). DACS also belongs to the following international federations: EVA (European Visual Artists: *www.europeanvisualartists.org*), IFRRO (International Federation of Reproduction Rights Organisations: *www.ifrro.org*) and CISAC (International Confederation of Authors and Composers Societies). In the first year of administering the Artists' Resale Right, DACS distributed over £1 million to artists and visual creators.

The editors are grateful to John Robinson, Director of Legal & International, for his assistance in updating this paragraph.

G. DIRECTORS AND PRODUCERS RIGHTS SOCIETY (1992) LTD ("DPRS")

28–54   First sentence. **Add:** The producers represented by the DPRS are individual documentary makers who produce, direct, and write their works and frequently take an on screen credit as "producer".

Third sentence. **Delete:** in the United Kingdom. **Substitute:** throughout the world.

Sixth sentence. **Add** at end: The agreement also covers sales and DVD releases.

Last but one sentence. **Add:** As at April 2006 DPRS had in excess of 3000 members.

H. EDUCATIONAL RECORDING AGENCY LTD ("ERA")

28–55   First sentence. **Delete:** cable or broadcast programmes. **Substitute:** broadcasts.

Second sentence. **Add** at end: Similar provision is made in respect of rights in performances by paragraph 6 of Schedule 2 to the 1988 Act. See the Main Work at paragraph 12–83.

Delete fifth sentence and NOTES 42 and 43 and **substitute:** This scheme was replaced by a new one, which was brought into effect on April 1, 2005 by the Copyright (Certification of Licensing Scheme for Educational Recording of Broadcasts) (Educational Recording Agency Ltd) Order 2005,[36] which should be read in conjunction with The Copyright (Educational Establishments) Order 2005[37] which has updated the description of "Educational Establishments" for the purposes of Part 1 of the 1988 Act. SI 2005/222 was made by the Secretary of State in the exercise of the powers conferred on her by section 43 of and paragraph 16 of Schedule 2A to the 1988 Act as a result of an application by ERA. Accordingly, with effect from April 6, 2006, the Copyright (Certification of Licensing Scheme for Educational Recording of Broadcasts and Cable Programmes) (Educational Recording Agency Ltd) Order 1990, and the various subsequent amending Orders relating to the ERA licensing scheme in operation prior to April 1, 2005 have been revoked by the Copyright (Certification of Licensing Scheme for Educational Recording of Broadcasts and Cable Programmes) (Educational Recording Agency Ltd) (Revocation) Order 2006.[38]

This scheme itself was replaced (with effect from April 1, 2007) by the scheme set out in the Copyright (Certification of Licensing Scheme for the Educational Recording of Broadcasts) (Educational Recording Agency Limited) Order 2007 (SI 2007/266).

The schemes which have applied since April 1, 2005 both have substantially the same text. The main changes effected in 2007 are to the royalty rates. These two schemes differ from their predecessors in three main ways, all of which result from the implementation of the Information Society Directive by the Copyright and Related Rights Regulations 2003.[39]

First, there are changes consequential on the deletion of references to cable programmes in section 35 of and paragraph 6 of Schedule 2 to the 1988 Act.

Second, there are changes consequential on the fact that the rights licensed by the ERA now include the communication of recordings and copies of recordings to students and teachers within the premises of licensed educational establishments.

---

[36] SI 2005/222.
[37] SI 2005/223.
[38] SI 2006/35.
[39] SI 2003/2498.

Third, there are changes consequential on other amendments to Schedule 2 to the 1988 Act. Before the Regulations were introduced, paragraph 6(1) of Schedule 2 simply provided that the making of off-air recordings by educational establishments was a permitted act. There was no exception to this if or to the extent that there was a licensing scheme in force. The current position is as follows: the making of such recordings remains a permitted act: see paragraph 6(1) of Schedule 2 to the 1988 Act. The communication of such recordings to the public within the premises of the educational establishment is also now a permitted act: see paragraph 6(1A) of Schedule 2. However, such acts cease to be permitted if or to the extent that there is a licensing scheme in force: see paragraph 6(1B) of Schedule 2. Thus, rights in performances are placed on the same footing as copyright. The new licensing scheme extends to rights in performances and accordingly, Equity, the Musician's Union and The Incorporated Society of Musicians are now licensor members of the ERA and are specified in the Scheme as licensing rights on behalf of their members.

The Scheme is limited to specified categories of material, the copyright in which is owned or controlled by specified Licensor Members of the ERA and to performances by persons represented by other specified Licensor Members. The Licensor Members are: ALCS, BBC Worldwide Ltd, Channel Four Television Corporation, Channel Five Broadcasting Limited, DACS, Equity, Incorporated Society of Musicians, BPI, ITV Network Limited, MCPS, Musicians Union, PRS, PPL and Sianel Pedwar, Cymru: see paragraph 8 of the Scheme, which is the Schedule to SI 2007/266.

In addition, ERA has admitted DPRS (see para.28–54 of the Main Work) and AGICOA (the Association of International Collective Management of Audiovisual Works—Association de Gestion Internationale Collective des Oeuvres Audiovisuelles) as Licensor Members with effect from July 1, 2007, although these changes have not been formally given effect to in a Statutory Instrument.

NOTE 44. **Delete** and **substitute:** ERA Scheme, para.8.

Seventh sentence. **Delete** and **substitute:** The ERA Scheme permits licensees to cause or authorise the making of recordings of a broadcast and copies of such a recording and (only as a direct result of their inclusion in a broadcast) of copyright works and/or performances contained in the recorded broadcast by or on behalf of an Educational Establishment for the educational purposes of that Educational Establishment ("ERA Recordings") (para.7(a)); and to authorise ERA Recordings to be communicated to the public by a person situated within the premises of an Educational Establishment but only to the extent that the communication cannot be received by any person situated outside the premises of that Educational Establishment (para.7(b)).

Eighth sentence. **Delete**.

NOTE 46. **Delete** and **substitute:** Rates for ERA licences were last adjusted from April 1, 2005 to reflect the extended grant of rights and broader repertoire. They have since been further increased: see SI 2007/266. Further, the increased use of computers in the classroom and the use of broadband Internet access by many schools have reduced the difference between the opportunities for use of recordings of broadcast material in primary schools on the one hand and in secondary schools on the other. Accordingly, the initial differential between the tariff for primary school students and secondary school students has become increasingly less relevant.

The annual tariff for licences issued between April 1, 2007 and March 31, 2008 is as follows: 30p per head for primary schools; 52p per head for secondary schools; 98p per head for further education establishments; and £1.55 per head for higher education establishments. The equivalent figures for licences taking effect on or after April 1, 2008 will be 31p, 54p, £1.01 and £1.60 (see SI 2007/

266). ERA has negotiated discounted licence fees with umbrella organisations representing large numbers of educational establishments. As a result some educational establishments may be covered by one centrally held blanket licence.

NOTE 48. **Delete** and **substitute:** see para.11 of the ERA Scheme.

Eleventh sentence. **Add** at end: When ERA recordings are made and stored in digital form for access through a computer, labelling must take the form of a written opening credit or webpage which must be viewed or listened to before access to the recording is permitted.

NOTE 49. **Delete** and **substitute:** see para.13 of the ERA Scheme.

NOTE 50 **Delete** and **substitute:** see para.14 of the ERA Scheme.

Twelfth sentence. **Add** at end: If fees are not paid when due or a licensee is in substantial breach of the licence terms, for example by permitting an unauthorised use of an ERA recording, the ERA may give the licensee 28 days' notice of termination. The notice will take effect at the end of the 28-day period unless the licensee has paid the outstanding fees or remedied the breach: see paragraph 20 of the Scheme. Interest may be charged at the rate prescribed by the Late Payment of Commercial Debts (Interest) Act 1998: see paragraph 22.

Third sentence from end. **Add:** For the year ending March 31, 2005 the turnover of the ERA was £5.62 million.

Last sentence but one. **Delete** and **substitute:** Overheads are recouped against a budget approved by members which equates to a commission of around 6.5 per cent.

In December 2006 the Gowers Review published its recommendations. These included that steps should be taken to enable educational provisions to cover distance learning and interactive white boards by 2008 by amending section 35 of the Copyright Designs and Patents Act 1988. As a result, from August 1, 2007 ERA will offer a new "ERA Plus Licence". This will permit Licensor Members to authorise ERA Recordings to be accessed by students and teachers online whether they are on the premises of their school, college or university, at home, or working elsewhere in the UK.

Educational establishments and bodies acting on behalf of educational establishments which hold ERA licences will be eligible for ERA Plus licences. The right to record broadcasts for non-commercial educational purposes by making ERA Recordings will continue to be governed by the terms of the ERA licence.

The annual tariff for the ERA Plus Licence will be calculated according to the number of full-time or full-time equivalent students who have the benefit of the licence. For licences taking effect before March 30, 2008 the tariffs are as follows: Primary/Preparatory schools: 15p per head; secondary schools: 26p per head; further education establishments: 49p per head; and higher education establishments: 78p per head. For licences taking effect on or after April 1, 2008 the equivalent figures will be 16p, 27p, 51p and 80p. The ERA Plus Licence will offer the same discounts as an ordinary licence where blanket licences have been taken out.

The editors are grateful to Andrew Yeates, General Counsel of the ERA, for his assistance in updating this paragraph.

I. MECHANICAL-COPYRIGHT PROTECTION SOCIETY LTD ("MCPS")

28–56   Third sentence. **Add:** As at July 2007 MCPS had about 15,200 composer members and 5,300 publisher members.

Fourth sentence. **Add:** As at July 2007 MCPS had 40 reciprocal agreements with societies in foreign countries.

NOTE 63. As at July 2006 about 180 record companies and associated labels were parties to an AP.1 Agreement.

Twenty-first sentence. **Add:** As at July 2007 commission rates were fixed at between 3.4 per cent and 25 per cent depending on the product and the nature of the licensing agreement with the average rate being 9.73 per cent.

Twenty-third sentence. **Add:** In 2006, royalties of £210m were collected, over £209m was distributed and commission of over £16.2m was levied.

The editors are grateful to members of the MCPS legal team for their assistance in updating this paragraph.

J. NEWSPAPER LICENSING AGENCY LTD ("NLA")

Second sentence. **Add:** As at March 2006 its repertoire had increased to some   **28–57** 1,300 titles including "The Economist" which was added in 2005.

Sixth sentence. **After** each instance of the word "copying", **add:** for internal management purposes.

Twelfth sentence. **Add:** By March 2006, the NLA had issued over 6,143 licences representing over 150,000 businesses.

Thirteenth sentence. **Add:** In the last financial year (2005) the NLA collected royalties of over £15 million.

The editors are grateful to Susan Dowley, Marketing Manager of the NLA, and Martin Stevenson, Managing Director of the NLA, for their assistance in updating this paragraph.

K. PERFORMING ARTISTS' MEDIA RIGHTS ASSOCIATION LIMITED ("PAMRA")

In the second half of 2006 PAMRA went into members' voluntary liquidation   **28–58** following a merger with PPL and AURA. See paragraph 28–60, below.

The editors are grateful to Sam Moorhouse, Legal and Business Affairs Executive for his assistance in updating this paragraph.

L. PERFORMING RIGHT SOCIETY LTD ("PRS")

Third sentence. **Add:** As at July 2007 the PRS had a combined membership   **28–59** including living composer members and music publishers of 47,500.

Fourth sentence. **Add:** In 2006, the PRS had 91 affiliations with societies in foreign countries with £62.6 million allocated to copyright owners abroad.

Seventeenth sentence. **Add:** In 2006 the PRS collected royalties of £336 million and distributed royalties of £291 million.

The editors are grateful to members of MCPS legal team for their assistance in updating this paragraph.

M. PHONOGRAPHIC PERFORMANCE LIMITED ("PPL")

Third sentence. **Add:** As at July 2007, PPL had over 3,500 record company   **28–60** members.

Fourth sentence. **Add:** Members may also appoint PPL as their agent to administer and license their "new media" rights, which are the right to communicate any sound recording, via the Internet or otherwise, to the public and the right to make copies for the purpose of such communication. Members may also appoint PPL as their agent to exploit their repertoire overseas and collect payment from overseas collecting societies.

Fifth sentence. **After** "By its Articles of Association" **add:** and by virtue of these assignments. **Add** at end: PPL licenses over 200,000 premises for public performance. It also grants licences to radio and television broadcasters who wish to incorporate sound recordings in their broadcasts; licences for the simultaneous transmission over the Internet of a radio station's broadcasts as well as archived programmes available on demand via the Internet; and licences to commercial suppliers of background music, who wish to dub sound recordings for subsequent public performance in their customers' premises.

Sixth sentence. **Delete** from "Like the PRS" to "licensing schemes". **Substitute:** PPL has about 60 different tariffs.

Delete seventh to fourteenth sentences and **substitute:** The revenue is distributed to members and performers according to the way in which the sound recordings were used, which is determined by a variety of means including detailed track-based usage reports received from licensees and specialist chart data. Once PPL has received all of this information, it compares it with its sound recording database called CatCo, to identify exactly which tracks have been played. (As at July 2007 the CatCo database contained information relating to over 9 million sound recordings. For each track on CatCo a substantial amount of information is held, such as the record company that owns the track and the full performer line-up, which often includes many orchestral and other performers as well as the featured artist(s).) PPL allocates money to each track depending upon the amount of use each has received. PPL then distributes this to members and performers along with information showing how much each track has earned.

PPL offers international services to collect overseas public performance, broadcast and associated income from a growing number of territories on behalf of record company members and registered performers. This service involves the member or performer giving PPL a legal mandate to collect overseas income, either in all territories or on a country-by-country basis. As at July 2007 PPL had 24 arrangements with foreign producer societies and 12 arrangements with foreign performer societies. As at July 2007 PPL had collected £16.54 million in total from foreign performer societies.

Sixteenth sentence **Add:** As at May 2006, PPL collected and distributed royalties to over 40,000 performers who had registered with it.

Nineteenth sentence. **Add:** By May 2006, the proposed merger of PAMRA, AURA and PPL had received clearance from the Office of Fair Trading. Following this clearance and the receipt of approvals from the respective companies' members, in the second half of 2006 the businesses of PAMRA and AURA were transferred to PPL. PPL will now pay performers formerly represented by PAMRA and AURA directly in respect of equitable remuneration arising in the UK. This has removed a duplication of work by the three societies and has thereby reduced administration costs. It is also expected to enable PPL to offer improved services to performers generally, including a more streamlined and effective international revenue collection service. Shortly after the merger, both PAMRA and AURA went into members' voluntary liquidation.

At the same time as the merger, in June 2006 PPL's members voted to change the Company's Memorandum and Articles of Association in order to increase performer representation within the organisation. Pursuant to this change, a "Performer Board" controlled by performer representatives has been established to oversee the distribution of income and secure the repatriation of overseas earnings. In addition, a Director of Performer Affairs has been appointed and Annual Performer Meetings will be held.

Twentieth sentence. **Add:** In the year ending December 31, 2006, PPL's gross revenue amounted to £98.33 million while its administration costs were £16.38 million.

The editors are grateful to Sam Moorhouse, Legal and Business Affairs Executive, for his assistance in updating this paragraph.

N. VIDEO PERFORMANCE LTD ("VPL")

Third sentence. **Add:** As at July 2007, VPL had over 1,000 members (including   **28–61** major record companies in the United Kingdom) and controlled the copyright in over 60,000 music videos.

Fifth sentence. **Add:** VPL's gross revenue for the year ending December 31, 2006 was £13.8 million and its administrative costs were £2.03 million.

The editors are grateful to Sam Moorhouse, Legal and Business Affairs Executive, for his assistance in updating this paragraph.

CHAPTER TWENTY NINE

CONTROL OF THE EXERCISE OF COPYRIGHTS AND RELATED RIGHTS

1. COMPULSORY LICENCES

C. EXISTING COMPULSORY LICENCES

(i) Information about programmes

The Database Regulations. NOTE 39. The *Fixtures Marketing* cases are now   **29–24**
reported as follows: *Fixtures Marketing Ltd v Oy Veikkaus AB* at [2005] E.C.D.R.
2; *Fixtures Marketing Ltd v Svenska Spel AB* at [2005] E.C.D.R. 4; and *Fixtures
Marketing Ltd v OPAP* at [2005] C.M.L.R. 16; [2005] E.C.D.R. 3. *British Horseracing Board Ltd v William Hill Ltd* is reported at [2005] 1 C.M.L.R. 15; [2005]
R.P.C. 13 and [2005] E.C.D.R. 1.

(ix) Control of monopoly: European law

IMS Health. NOTE 25. **Add**: Ong, "Anti-competitive Refusals to Grant Copy-   **29–60**
right Licences: Reflections on the *IMS* Saga" [2004] 11 E.I.P.R. 505; Ridyard,
"Compulsory Access Under EC Competition Law—A New Doctrine of "Conve-
nient Facilities" and the Case for Price Regulation" [2004] E.C.L.R. 669; Ong,
"Building Brick Barricades and other Barriers to Entry: Abusing a Dominant Po-
sition by Refusing to Licence Intellectual Property Rights" [2005] E.C.L.R. 215;
Meinberg, "From *Magill* to *IMS Health*: The New Product Requirement and the
Diversity of Intellectual Property Rights" [2006] 7 E.I.P.R. 398.

Indispensability: the decision. On this issue, see also Case T–201/04 *Microsoft*,   **29–62**
para.29–251A below.

29–63   **Abuse: the three conditions.** In Case T–201/04 *Microsoft*, para.29–251A, below, the Court of First Instance restated the conditions (or, as it held, circumstances) listed in *IMS Health* in a more logical order as follows. First, the refusal relates to a product or service which is indispensable to the exercise of a particular activity on a neighbouring market. Second, the refusal is of such a kind as to exclude any effective competition on that neighbouring market. Third, the refusal prevents the appearance of a new product for which there is potential consumer demand. Finally, there is no objective justification for the refusal.

NOTES 33 and 34. *Intel Corp v Via Technologies Inc* is reported at [2003] F.S.R. 33

Add at end: In *Wireless Group Plc v Radio Joint Audience Research Ltd* [2004] EWHC 2925; [2005] E.M.L.R. 27 at paragraph 45, Lloyd J. stated that a proposition that it is sufficient to satisfy three conditions cannot be read as equivalent to saying that it is necessary to satisfy them. To the same effect, see Case T–201/04 *Microsoft*, para.29–251A, below.

29–64   **The first condition: new product or service. Add** at end: In Case T–201/04 *Microsoft*, para.29–251A below, the Court of First Instance apparently took the view that a technical development of an existing product amounts to a new product for these purposes.

29–65   **The second condition: unjustified. Add** at end: In Case T–201/04 *Microsoft*, para.29–251A below, the Court of First Instance held that the fact that the interoperability information was covered by intellectual property rights or was secret, valuable and innovative did not provide objective justification for the refusal.

29–66   **The third condition: exclusion of competition on a secondary market.** NOTE 39. *Intel Corp v Via Technologies Inc* is reported at [2003] F.S.R. 33.

NOTE 40. *Intel Corp v Via Technologies Inc* is reported at [2003] F.S.R. 33.

Add: In Case T–201/04 *Microsoft*, para.29–251A below, the Court of First Instance held that it was sufficient that all effective competition is liable to or likely to be excluded in the future.

29–67   **Application in the United Kingdom.** NOTES 41 to 44. *Intel Corp v Via Technologies Inc* is reported at [2003] F.S.R. 33.

29–68   **Enforcement by the Commission.** NOTE 46. For subsequent developments in the *Microsoft* case, see paras 29–251—29–251B below.

2. MISCELLANEOUS CONTROLS ON THE EXERCISE OF RIGHTS

A. COMPULSORY COLLECTIVE ADMINISTRATION OF RIGHTS: THE CABLE RETRANSMISSION RIGHT

29–75   **Section 144A of the 1988 Act.** NOTE 89. The European Court of Justice has held that the effect of Art.9(2) of the Directive (which is implemented by s.144A(3)) is that the licensing body is deemed to have the right not only to collect royalties but also to grant or refuse licences: Case C–169/05, *Uradex SCRL v Union Professionelle de la Radio et de la Télédistribution (RTD)* [2006] E.C.D.R. 23.

C. CERTIFICATION OR NOTIFICATION OF LICENSING SCHEMES FOR PURPOSES OF EXCLUDING PERMITTED ACTS

Certification of licensing schemes. NOTE 19. The 1990 scheme for the   **29–78**
educational recording of broadcasts and cable programmes has now been replaced
by a new scheme scheduled to the Copyright (Certification of Licensing Scheme
for Educational Recording of Broadcasts) (Educational Recording Agency
Limited) Order 2005 (SI 2005/222). SI 1990/879 and its amending SIs have been
revoked by the Copyright (Certification of Licensing Scheme for Educational Recording of Broadcasts and Cable Programmes) (Educational Recording Agency
Limited) (Revocation) Order 2006 (SI 2006/35).

D. COMPULSORY NOTIFICATION OF SOUND RECORDING LICENSING SCHEMES TO THE SECRETARY OF STATE

Decision to the Copyright Tribunal. Second sentence. **Delete** and **substitute:**   **29–86**
The Tribunal has now published a Practice Direction setting out how it proposes
to deal with notifications under section 128A: *www.patent.gov.uk/copy/tribunal/*
tribpractice.htm. Within 21 days of receipt of notice that the Secretary of State
has notified a proposed licence or licensing scheme to the Tribunal, the licensing
body is obliged to serve on all other parties which to its knowledge have made
representations to it or to the Secretary of State copies of all documents it has put
before the Secretary of State. At the same time, it is obliged to serve on the Secretary to the Tribunal (with copies to all such other parties) such other representations as it may wish to make to the Tribunal, together with a list of the names and
addresses of the other parties (para.1). The other parties then have 21 days to
make any further representations (para.2) and the licensing body has a further 14
days to reply (para.3). The Tribunal will then address such questions (if any) as it
considers appropriate to the licensing body and/or any of the other parties and
will inform any third party that it considers should be notified of the existence of
the reference. At the same time the Tribunal will set such time limits for the
answering of such questions or for the making of representations by the third parties or further representations by the licensing body and/or the other parties as it
sees fit (para.4). Following this process, the Tribunal will issue its formal decision (para.5). The Practice Direction states that the Tribunal will only hold an
oral hearing in exceptional circumstances.

3. CONTROL OF THE EXERCISE OF COPYRIGHT AND RELATED RIGHTS BY THE COPYRIGHT TRIBUNAL

A. INTRODUCTION

Proposals for reform. Add at end: A Review of the Copyright Tribunal has   **29–92**
recently been carried out for the UK Intellectual Property Office. The review
recommends a large number of procedural changes, including the application of
the Civil Procedure Rules to the Tribunal. See *www.ipo.gov.uk/*
ctribunalreview.pdf.

B. THE COPYRIGHT TRIBUNAL

Factors the Copyright Tribunal has taken into consideration. In *The British*   **29–99**
Phonographic Industry Ltd v Mechanical-Copyright Protection Society Ltd, CT
84–90/05, the Tribunal dealt with a number of references relating to the terms of
licences issued by two collecting societies, PRS and MCPS (collectively called
"the Alliance"), which enable music legitimately to be made available online to
members of the public.

The webcaster parties complained that by making allegedly excessive demands the Alliance were exploiting a serendipitous right to participate in developments in information technology in which they had played no part and in respect of which they had taken no risks [45]. The Tribunal stated that the proper "general approach" was that copyright (and thus the régime under which collecting societies operate), exists for the benefit of right holders [44]. Collecting societies have been accorded statutory (and international) recognition in order to advance the proprietary interests of the right holders who comprise their membership. But the effects of that responsibility may sometimes have to be tempered. An important purpose of the Tribunal is therefore to curb any tendency to unwarranted gain as a result of the de facto monopoly position in which the collecting societies find themselves. Overall, however, the Tribunal's job is not to favour one side or the other [45] but to maintain a balance between copyright owners and users. There is no presumption in favour of the referred scheme nor is there a presumption that a referred scheme should be varied [46].

The Tribunal went on to identify the following general guidance in the authorities:

(1) Fairness. The Tribunal must determine whether the legitimate financial expectations of the licensor, acting on behalf of its right holders, are reasonable in all the relevant circumstances. The Tribunal performs a discretionary, balancing exercise wherein the result must be fair in the sense identified in the *AEI* case (see NOTE 50 in the Main Work) [48].

(2) The willing buyer/seller test. This is "a classic test in this jurisdiction" (the Tribunal referred to the Working Men's Club case referred to in NOTE 51 in the Main Work). However, a recent, freely negotiated tariff in respect of comparable subject matter may be the best record of the market value of the rights [49].

(3) Comparators. In practice comparators appear to have been more of a legitimate quarry (or template) for particular terms and figures rather than full precedents for a particular licence [50–51].

(4) A simple and workable tariff. The tariff should be simple and workable having regard to the service being licensed, with a straightforward rate structure based on straightforward definitions [57].

(5) The revenue-based approach to royalty. Where the parties have agreed on a revenue-based approach there must also be a nexus (or "direct causal connection") between use of the licensor's repertoire and revenues earned by the licensee, however "imperfect" a measure that may appear [61].

(6) Risk sharing. The fact that the licensor has borne no risk in issuing to the public the material in issue is a material factor [71].

C. CONTROL BY THE COPYRIGHT TRIBUNAL OF LICENSING SCHEMES AND LICENSING BODIES DEALING WITH COPYRIGHT LICENCES

(i) Definitions

29–106   **Licensing scheme.** NOTES 85 to 87. The *Universities UK* decision is reported at [2002] R.P.C. 36 and [2002] E.M.L.R. 35.

(ii) Refences and applications with respect to licensing schemes

29–116   **Application for individual licence where scheme exists.** NOTE 26. The *Universities UK* decision is reported at [2002] R.P.C. 36; [2002] E.M.L.R. 35.

E. CONTROL BY THE COPYRIGHT TRIBUNAL OF PERFORMERS' RIGHTS AND OVER EQUITABLE REMUNERATION PAYABLE TO PERFORMERS

(ii) Control by the Copyright Tribunal of performers' rights to equitable remuneration and other performers' rights

Section 182D of the 1988 Act: playing in public and communication to the public. NOTE 83. **Add:** See also Case C–28/04, *Lagardère Active Broadcast v Société pour la perception de la rémunération équitable (SPRE)*.   29–152

G. PROCEDURE BEFORE THE COPYRIGHT TRIBUNAL

Provisions governing procedure. Add: Although the Civil Procedure Rules are not expressly applied to the Tribunal, they are applied in practice. For a recent example, see the reference to the "overriding objective" in *The British Phonographic Industry Ltd v Mechanical-Copyright Protection Society Ltd*, CT 84–90/05 at [282].   29–159

Directions. NOTE 86. The *Universities UK* decision is reported at [2002] R.P.C. 36; [2002] E.M.L.R. 35.   29–167

In *The British Phonographic Industry Ltd v Mechanical-Copyright Protection Society Ltd*, CT 84–90/05, there were four expert witnesses, three of whose bills totalled over £2.2m, an amount described by the Tribunal as "seriously disproportionate" [111] and "overkill" [284]. The Tribunal also criticised the amount of inter partes correspondence [284].

Add at end: In *The British Phonographic Industry Ltd v Mechanical-Copyright Protection Society Ltd*, CT 84–90/05 at [107–108], the Tribunal applied the Civil Procedure Rules and authorities in ordinary civil proceedings to the duties of experts. It also addressed (at [121]) the scope of the evidence which a forensic accountant could give to the Tribunal, stating that such an expert would be free to give evidence on matters such as costs, investments, revenue streams and their relevance; to provide comment and criticism of industry reports on topics such as statistics, revenue sources and similar technical matters; and to express an opinion about which licence agreements might or might not be relevant comparables. However, the Tribunal thought it "not helpful" for such a witness to opine on what rates of royalty (or minima) were reasonable for a particular service, what deductions should apply and so on.

Costs. NOTE 17. The substantive *Universities UK* decision is reported at [2002] R.P.C. 36; [2002] E.M.L.R. 35. The decision on costs is reported at [2002] I.P.D. 25043.   29–170

4. COMPETITION LAW AND THE EXERCISE OF COPYRIGHT AND OTHER RIGHTS COVERED IN THIS WORK

A. EUROPEAN COMMUNITY COMPETITION LAW

(i) Article 81: general

Apparently unilateral behaviour. For the practical implications of the *Bayer* case, see Stothers, "Who Needs Intellectual Property? Competition Law and Restrictions on Parallel Trade within the European Economic Area" [2005] 12   29–176

E.I.P.R. 458. For a summary by the English Court of Appeal of the European cases in this area, see *Argos Ltd v OFT* [2006] EWCA Civ 1318; [2006] U.K.C.L.R. at [21].

29–177   **Undertakings.** NOTE 44. Add at end of first sentence: See also Case C–205/03 P, *Federación Española de Empresas de Tecnología Sanitaria (FENIN) v Commission*, para.25, emphasising that it is the activity consisting in offering goods and services on a given market which is the characteristic feature of an economic activity.

NOTE 49. **Add:** Amongst Eurocontrol's activities are the defining and adopting of common standards and specifications in the air navigation sector. In Case T–155/04, *SELEX Sistemi Integrati SpA v Commission* [2007] 4 C.M.L.R. 10, the CFI upheld the Commission's findings that this did not amount to an economic activity. The standards were produced within Eurocontrol and adopted by its Council of Member States. This did not involve the offering of goods or services on a market [61]. Eurocontrol also acquires prototypes of air traffic management equipment and systems, funds their development by third parties and licenses the fruits of the development to interested parties at no cost. This too was not an economic activity: it was ancillary to the promotion of technical development, forming part of the aims of Eurocontrol's public service tasks and not being pursued in Eurocontrol's own interest, separable from those aims (applying, by analogy, Joined Cases C-264/01, C 306/01, C-354/01 and C-355/01 *AOK Bundesverband and Others* [2004] ECR I–2493; [2004] 4 C.M.L.R. 22) [77]. By contrast, Eurocontrol's provision for remuneration of services for its Member States in connection with public tenders, did amount to an economic activity [92] but there was no abuse of a dominant position [108].

29–178   **Single economic entity.** NOTE 49. **Add**: See also Joined Cases T–71/03, T–74/03, T–87/03 and T–91/03 *Tokai Carbon Co. Ltd and others v Commission* (CFI): the Commission can generally assume that a wholly-owned subsidary essentially follows the instructions given to it by its parent company without needing to check whether the parent company has in fact exercised that power. An agent too may be considered to be part of the same economic unit as its principal for these purposes, see *e.g.* Case T–325/01, *DaimlerChrysler AG v Commission* (CFI) paras 86–88. See Treacy and Lawrance, "An Agent of Change? The Court of First Instance Considers the Competition Law Treatment of Agents" [2006] C.T.L.R. 52.

29–183   **Proof of anti-competitive effect.** NOTE 64. See, however, *The Racehorse Association v OFT* [2005] CAT 29 in which it is suggested that it is difficult to resolve the *Métropole* approach with earlier and later cases of the ECJ, including *Wouters v Algemene Raad van de Nederlandse Orde van Advocaten* [2002] ECR I–1577.

29–184   **Market analysis.** NOTE 71. *Crehan v Inntrepreneur Pub Company CPC* is reported at [2004] E.C.C. 28. See also the judgment of the House of Lords, [2006] UKHL 38, also following *Delimitis* but reinstating the Judge's original decision.

29–188   **Effect on trade between Member states.** NOTE 90. **Add:** see also Joined Cases C–295/04 to C–298/04, *Manfredi v Lloyd Adriatico Assicurazioni SpA* (ECJ).

NOTE 94. **Add:** see also Joined Cases C–295/04 to C–298/04, *Manfredi v Lloyd Adriatico Assicurazioni SpA* (ECJ), emphasising that the fact that an agreement, decision or practice relates only to the marketing of products in a single Member State does not exclude the possibility that trade between Member States may be affected (para.44); and that an agreement or practice extending over the whole of the territory of a Member State has by its very nature the effect of reinforcing the partitioning of markets on a national basis, thereby holding up the economic interpenetration which the Treaty is designed to bring about (para.45).

(ii) Article 82: general

Article 82. See, generally DG Competition's Discussion Paper on the Applica-   **29–193**
tion of Article 82 to Exclusionary Abuses (defined as "behaviours by dominant firms which are likely to have a foreclosure effect on the Market") (December 2005),   *http://europa.eu.int/comm/competition/antitrust/others/ article_82_review.html*; and Dethmers and Dodoo, "The abuse of Hoffmann-La Roche: the meaning of dominance under EC Competition Law" [2006] E.C.L.R. 537.

Essential facilities. NOTE 59. **Add:** See, more recently, *Attheraces Ltd v The*   **29–203**
British Horseracing Board [2005] EWHC 3015 (Ch); [2006] F.S.R. 20; [2006] E.C.D.R. 13 (pre-race information not protected by database right; this decision is discussed in Penny, "Dominance: Excessive Pricing, Access to Data and Essential Facilities Attheraces Ltd v British Horseracing Board" [2006] 4 Ent. L.R. 128). The decision in this case that there was abuse was overturned on appeal: [2007] EWCA Civ 38; [2007] E.C.C. 7. See Edwards, "Not Such a Good Day at the races" [2007] 5 Ent. L.R. 180.

Miscellaneous abuses. NOTE 61. **Add:** See also Case T–201/04 *Microsoft.*   **29–204**

(iii) Enforcement and direct effect of Articles 81(1) and 82

Enforcement. For the operation of the Modernisation Regulation in 2005, see   **29–205**
the Commission's Report on Competition Policy 2005 (SEC (2006) 761, final), page 7. See *http://europa.eu.int/comm/competition/antitrust/others/ article_82_review.html.*

NOTE 69. First sentence. **Add** at end: In this case, binding commitments were accepted. See the Commission's decision on January 19, 2005, *http:// europa.eu.int/comm/competition/antitrust/cases/decisions/37214/en.pdf* and paras 96 to 104 of the Commission's Report on Competition Policy 2005 (SEC (2006) 761 final), *http://europa.eu.int/comm/competition/antitrust/others/ article_82_review.html.*

Relationship between the work of the Commission and the national competi-   **29–206**
tion authorities: general. NOTE 77. **Add:** : See also *Inntrepreneur Pub Company (CPC) v Crehan* [2006] UKHL 38.

For an account by the Commission of cooperation between the Commission and national competition authorities in 2005, see the Commission's Report on Competition Policy 2005 (SEC (2006) 761, final), page 8 and paragraphs 201 to 218:   *http://europa.eu.int/comm/competition/antitrust/others/ article_82_review.html.*

Relationship between the work of the Commission and litigation in the   **29–208**
national courts. For the operation of Article 15 of the Modernisation Regulation in 2005, see paragraphs 219 to 236 of the Commission's Report on Competition Policy 2005 (SEC (2006) 761, final), *http://europa.eu.int/comm/competition/ antitrust/others/article_82_review.html.*

Direct effect. As to the application of the Judgments Regulation to claims under   **29–209**
Article 82, see *Sandisk Corporation v Koninklijke Philips Electronics NV* [2007] EWHC 332; [2007] F.S.R. 22 (Pumfrey J.).

NOTE 4. *Crehan v Inntrepreneur Pub Company CPC* is reported at [2004] E.C.C. 28. **Add:** See also Joined Cases C–295/04 to C–298/04, *Manfredi v Lloyd Adriatico Assicurazioni SpA* (ECJ), paras 56 to 63 ("*Manfredi*") and the Commission's Green Paper *Damages actions for breach of the EC antitrust rules* (COM (2005) 672, final), *http://ec.europa.eu/comm/competition/antitrust/others/ actions_for_damages/gp_en.pdf*. The Commission starts from the premise that this area of law in the Member States presents a picture of "total underdevelopment" and goes on to invite submissions on proposals in a number of areas: procedure and evidence; the quantification of damages; the "passing on" defence and the position of indirect purchasers; collective actions for the benefit of consumers; costs; the coordination of public and private enforcement; jurisdiction and applicable law; court-appointed experts; limitation periods; and causation.

NOTE 5. *Crehan v Inntrepreneur Pub Company CPC* is reported at [2004] E.C.C. 28. **Add:** In *Manfredi* (above) the Court of Justice held that "the detailed procedural rules" included the applicable limitation period (para.82) and the rules for the assessment of damages (para.98).

NOTES 6 to 9. *Crehan v Inntrepreneur Pub Company CPC* is reported at [2004] E.C.C. 28.

NOTE 10. **Add:** The question of the quantification of damages did not arise on the appeal to the House of Lords: *Inntrepreneur Pub Company (CPC) v Crehan* [2006] UKHL 38 para.73.

NOTE 11. **Add:** In *Manfredi* (above) the Court of Justice held (at para.61) that individuals could claim compensation for the harm suffered "where there is a causal relationship between that harm and an agreement or practice prohibited under Article 81 EC" but that in the absence of Community rules governing the matter it was for domestic legal systems to prescribe the detailed rules on the application of the concept of "causal relationship" provided that the principles of equivalence and effectiveness are observed (para.64).

Delete last sentence and **substitute:** The Court may grant an injunction to prevent a breach of threatened breach of Articles 81 or 82. Where a mandatory injunction is sought normal principles apply: *AAH Pharmaceuticals Ltd v Pfizer Ltd* [2007] EWHC 565 (Ch).

(iv) Application of Community competition law to copyright and related rights

29–210   **Introduction. Add:** The existence of anti-competitive conduct may be raised as a defence to infringement proceedings. However, before such a defence can succeed, it is necessary for the defendant establish a nexus between the abuse and the claimant's cause of action. Thus, for example, the mere fact that an intellectual property right is being used by a dominant undertaking to secure a market environment in which price fixing may occur will not prevent the enforcement of that right, *e.g.* to prevent unlawful importation of infringing goods: *Hewlett Packard Development Company LP v Expansys UK Ltd* [2005] EWHC 1495; [2005] E.T.M.R. 1111. Contrast *Sportswear SpA v Stonestyle Ltd* [2006] EWCA Civ 380, in which it was held well arguable that to be able to prove that a relevant agreement was in breach of Article 81 would give a defendant a stronger basis for saying that a claimant did not have legitimate reasons to oppose further dealings in the goods for the purposes of section 12(2) of the Trade Marks Act 1994.

(b) *Application of Article 81 to assignments or licences of copyright and related rights: relevant block exemptions*

The technology transfer block exemption ("TTBER"): background. Add: 29–213
See Hansen and Shah, "The Hew EU Technology Transfer Regime—Out of the
Straightjacket into the Safe Harbour?" [2004] E.C.L.R. 465; Treacy and Heide,
"The New EC Technology Transfer Block Exemption Regulation" [2004] 9
E.I.P.R. 414; Vollebregt, "The New Technology Transfer Block Exemption:
From Straitjacket to Moving Targets" [2004] C.T.L.R. 123; Batchelor, "Applica-
tion of the Technology Transfer Block Exemption to Software Licensing Agree-
ments" [2004] C.T.L.R. 166; Treacy, "Intellectual Property Transactions and
Block Exemptions—The Future?" [2005] C.T.L.R. 191; and Bird and Toutoungi,
"The New EC Technology Transfer Regulation: Two Years On" [2006] 5 E.I.P.R.
292.

(c) *Application of Article 81 to assignments or licences of copyright and related
rights: relevant case law and Commission decisions*

Other objectionable provisions in the case-law and Commission decisions. 29–241
Add at end of first sub-paragraph: The Commission has issued a statement of
objections in relation to the major record companies' agreements with Apple in
respect of downloads through its iTunes on-line stores. It appears that there is a
separate iTunes store in each country in the EEA. In order to buy a download
from a store in a particular country it is necessary to use a credit card issued by a
bank with an address in that country. According to the Commission, this means
that in violation of Article 81: "consumers can only buy music from the iTunes
on-line store in their country of residence. Consumers are thus restricted in their
choice of where to buy music, and consequently what music is available, and at
what price." Case COMP/39.154—*iTunes*. See MEMO/07/126.

Add: Typically, the studios sell to broadcasters their entire film production for
a given period of years. The MFN clauses give the studios the right to enjoy the
most favourable terms agreed between a pay television company and any one of
them. According to the Commission's preliminary assessment (COMP/38.427),
the cumulative effect of the clauses was an alignment of the prices paid to the
studios. Without admitting a violation of competition law, all but two of the studios waived the MFN clauses in their existing agreements. The investigation
remains open in respect of NPB Universal and Paramount Pictures Corp Inc. See
Commission Press Release IP/04/1314 and the Commission's Report on Competition Policy 2004, paras 88–91.

For a discussion of the competition implications of so-called "Copyleft"
licences, see Välimäki, "Copyleft Licensing and EC Competition Law" [2006]
E.C.L.R. 130.

Sports broadcasting and Article 81. Second paragraph. **Add:** However, this de- 29–242
cision was annulled by the Court of First Instance on the ground that the system
of sublicensing did not guarantee access to non EBU members and therefore
failed to avoid the elimination of competition in the market: Joined Cases T–185/
00, T–216/00, T–299/00 and T–300/00. An appeal to the Court of Justice was
dismissed: Case C470/02.

Last sentence. **Delete:** has.

NOTE 95. First sentence. **Add:** Following clarification of these commitments,
they have now been made binding by the Commission: see Commission Press
Release IP/06/356.

Add at end: In the *Bundesliga* case, binding commitments were accepted. See
the Commission's decision of January 19, 2005, *http://europa.eu.int/comm/
competition/antitrust/cases/decisions/37214/en.pdf* and paragraphs 96 to 104 of
the Commission's Report on Competition Policy.

In September 2005 the Commission concluded a sector inquiry into the market for new systems of mobile communication that are able to transmit audiovisual content (3G). The inquiry involved a comprehensive review of the behaviour of all parties involved in the acquisition, resale and exploitation of mobile rights to sports events

Four main areas of concern were identified. First, bundling: situations where powerful media operators have bought all audiovisual rights to premium sports in a bundle in order to secure exclusivity over all platforms with no view to exploiting or sublicensing 3G rights. Second, embargoes: situations where overly restrictive conditions (serious time embargoes or unnecessary limitations of clip length) are imposed upon mobile rights that limit the practical availability of 3G content. Third, joint selling: situations where 3G rights remain unexploited because collective selling organisations do not manage to sell the 3G rights of individual sports clubs. Fourth, exclusivity: the exclusive attribution of 3G rights in situations leading to the monopolisation of premium content by powerful operators.

The report invited market players to review their business practices and to redress possible anticompetitive effects resulting from them. See the report at *http://europa.eu.int/comm/competition/antitrust/others/sector_inquiries/ new_media/3g/*. Its contents are summarised at paragraphs 78 to 83 of the Commission's Report on Competition Policy 2005 (SEC (2006) 761 final): *http:// europa.eu.int/comm/competition/antitrust/others/article_82_review.html*.

See also Penny, "Sports Rights—How Mobile are they?" [2005] 8 Ent. L.R. 201 and Hatton, Wagner and Armengod, "Fair Play: How Competition Authorities have regulated the Sale of Football Media Rights in Europe" [2007] E.C.L.R. 346.

In *The Racehorse Association v OFT* [2005] CAT 29 it was held that the joint selling of media rights to horse races did not infringe the Chapter I prohibition being necessary to secure a proper commercial objective, namely the creation of a new broadcasting channel and linked interactive betting website.

29–244 **The Santiago Agreement. Add:** In April and May 2005, two of the parties to the Santiago agreement (BUMRA and SABEM) undertook to the Commission pursuant to Article 9(1) of the Modernisation Regulation not to be party to any agreement in relation to the licensing of public performance of music on the Internet which contained an "economic residency" clause of the type to which the Commission objected. The Commission has invited comments: Cases COMP/C2/ 39152—*BUMRA* and COMP/C2/39151—*SABEM* [2005] O.J. C 200/11. See also Commission Recommendation on collective cross-border management of copyright and related rights for legitimate online music services: [2005] O.J. L 276/ 54. This recommendation covers most forms of online distribution of musical works (see Article 1(f)). Article 3 provides that "Right-holders should have the right to entrust the management of any of the online rights necessary to operate legitimate online music services, on a territorial scope of their choice, to a collective rights manager of their choice, irrespective of the Member State of residence or the nationality of either the collective rights manager or the right-holder." For a detailed assessment by the Commission of some of the competition issues relevant to the European music industry, see decision C(2007)2160 in the merger case COMP/M.4402—*Universal/BMG Publishing*.

29–244A **The Cannes Extension Agreement.** This is an agreement between 13 European mechanical copyright collecting societies and the five major music publishers which was notified to the Commission under Regulation 17. On January 24, 2006, the Commission notified the parties of its preliminary assessment within the meaning of Article 9(1) of the Modernisation Regulation. The Commission raised two serious concerns. The first concerned Clause 9(a), which made provision for the grant of rebates to record companies who negotiated Central Licensing Agreements (defined by the Commission as "multi-repertoire one stop shop licences for the whole EEA territory"). Clause 9(a) provided that a collecting society would have to obtain the consent of all its members before granting such a rebate. Given that each collecting society might have thousands of members, the Commission took the view that Clause 9(a) would effectively prevent the grant of rebates. The second concerned Clause 7(a)(i), which provided that collecting societies should never engage in activities which might be the activities of a publisher or record company. The Commission took the view that this clause had the object and might have the effect of crystallising current market structures and preventing future competition. The parties to the agreement have now offered commitments. Clause 9(a) will be modified to permit a collecting society to grant a rebate if so decided by the competent body of the society and to provide that all rebates will be included in the Rate (as defined in the agreement) and will not reduce the income of the members. Clause 7(a)(i) will be deleted. The Commission invited comments in accordance with Article 27(4) of the Modernisation Regulation: see its Notice [2006] O.J. C122/02 in Case COMP/C.2/38.681 *Universal International Music BV/MCPS and others (the Cannes Extension Agreement).* Those commitments have now been accepted: see the Commission's Press Release IP/06/1311.

CISAC. CISAC (International Confederation of Societies of Authors and   **29–244B** Composers) is the international association of authors' collecting societies. It has 24 members in the EEA including PRS in the United Kingdom (as to which see para.28–59 of the Main Work) and GEMA in Germany. The relations between its members are governed by a standard model contract for reciprocal representation in relation to the management of public performance rights.

On November 30, 2000, the RTL Group filed a complaint to the Commission against GEMA concerning GEMA's refusal to grant a Community-wide licence for all RTL Group's music broadcasting activities. On April 4, 2003, Music Choice Europe plc filed a complaint to the Commission concerning CISAC's model contract. The two cases were later merged as the *CISAC* Case (COMP 38.698).

At the time of the complaints, each member of CISAC enjoyed an exclusive position on its domestic market and had its own portfolio of works (or "repertoire"). Each EEA member of CISAC had a reciprocal representation contract with each of the other EEA members, giving it a "global portfolio" of musical works ("a multirepertoire") which enabled each member to deliver a multirepertoire licence to be exploited in its domestic market only.

For the purposes of this case, there were two important categories of clause in the CISAC model contract. The "membership clause" provided that while a reciprocal representation contract was in force neither of the contracting collecting societies might without the consent of the other accept as a member any member of the other society or any natural or legal person having the nationality of one of the countries in which the other collecting society operated. The "territoriality clauses" provided first that the reciprocal representation was done on an exclusive basis for the respective territories of the societies ("the exclusivity clause"); and secondly that the licence was limited to the domestic territory of the society which granted it ("the territorial delineation"). This limitation applied even for the internet, cable retransmission and (with certain exceptions) satellite transmission.

On February 7, 2006 the Commission announced that it had sent a statement of objections to CISAC concerning three forms of copyright exploitation: internet, satellite transmission and cable retransmission of music. The Commission was not concerned about the reciprocal representation agreements as such, but considered that the membership clause and the territoriality clauses might infringe Article 81. The Commission also expressed concerns about the "network effect" of the agreements. It stated that it believed that the effect of the network of these agreements was that the membership and territorial restrictions multiplied and guaranteed to collecting societies an absolutely exclusive position on their domestic market, thus strengthening their historical de facto monopoly and preventing new entrants from entering the market for the management of copyright.

Following written replies and an oral hearing, CISAC and 18 of its members (including PRS) offered commitments. The commitments involve the removal of the "membership clause" and the "exclusivity clause". As to the "territorial delineation", each society has offered either to license its own repertoire directly across the EEA or to mandate under certain conditions each signatory society which fulfils certain criteria to grant multirepertoire multi territorial licences. The Commission has indicated its intention, subject to market testing, to adopt a decision under Article 9 of the Modernisation Regulation. See the Commission's Announcement [2007] O.J. C128/12.

29–244C   **Future regulation of collecting societies.** For the Commission's proposals in this area, see paragraphs 25–100 and 28–20—28–22 of the Main Work.

(d) *Application of Article 82 to the exercise of copyright and related rights*

29–248   **Infringement actions.** NOTE 19. **Add:** See also Case T–111/96 *ITT Promedia NV v. Commission* [1998] ECR II–2937; [1998] 5 C.M.L.R. 491, discussed in *Sandisk Corporation v Koninklijke Philips Electronics NV* [2007] EWHC 332; [2007] F.S.R. 22.

29–251   **The *Magill* line of cases.** NOTE 28. **Add:** On June 7, 2004, Microsoft applied for annulment of this decision (Case T–201/04 R). On June 25, 2004, Microsoft also applied for suspension of operation of parts of the decision. The President of the Court of First Instance ruled on the latter application on December 22, 2004 ([2005] E.C.D.R. 19). Although Microsoft's application for interim measures was refused, the President ruled that Microsoft had a prima facie case in relation to its application for annulment. On September 17, 2007, the Court of First Instance granted Microsoft's application for annulment so far as it related to the Commission's appointment of an independent trustee to monitor compliance with its decision, but otherwise refused the application.

29–251A   **Supply of interoperability information.** The abuse identified by the Commission was the refusal to supply the specifications for the protocols used by Windows workgroup servers in order to provide file, print and group and user administration services to Windows work group networks and allow third parties to implement such specifications for the purpose of developing and distributing interoperable work group server operating system products (recital 546). The Commission summarised its reasoning as follows. Microsoft had had a dominant (quasi-monopoly) position on the client PC operating system market for many years. This had enabled Microsoft to determine to a large extent the set of coherent communications rules that would govern the de facto standard of interoperability in work group networks. As such, interoperability with the Windows domain architecture was necessary for a work group server operating system vendor in order viably to stay in the market (recital 779). Microsoft had refused to disclose to third parties the information necessary to achieve such interoperability (recital 780). As a result of the interoperability advantage enjoyed by Microsoft, it had reached a dominant position in the market. There was no actual or potential substitute for disclosures by Microsoft (recital 781). Microsoft's refusal to supply such information had the result of stifling innovation in the market and of diminishing consumers' choices by locking them into a homogeneous Microsoft solution. This was inconsistent with Article 82 (b) (recital 782). On balance, the possible negative impact on Microsoft's incentives to innovate which would result from a disclosure order was outweighed by the positive effects of such an order on the level of innovation in the whole industry (including Microsoft). For this and other reasons there was no objective justification for Microsoft's conduct (recital 783). There was an appreciable effect on trade between Member States and between the Contracting Parties to the EEA (recital 993). Accordingly, applying the pre-*IMS Health* case law, Microsoft was ordered to disclose the information (recital 998 *et seq.*).

On July 12, 2006, the European Commission imposed a penalty payment of €280.5m on Microsoft for its continued failure to comply with the obligation to provide complete and accurate technical documentation (see IP/06/979 and MEMO/06/277). Microsoft then submitted new documentation which it has continued to improve. The Commission also decided on July 12, 2006 that should Microsoft continue to fail to comply with its obligations, the amount of the daily penalty payment to which it could be subject would be increased from up to €2m to up to €3m per day with effect from July 31, 2006. As at November 23, 2006, revised documentation had been supplied: MEMO/06/445.

The Commission's decision that there had been abuse was upheld by the Court of First Instance. In reaching its decision, the Court, like the Commission, assumed that the interoperability information was subject to intellectual property rights [289]. It seems that Microsoft sought to contend that a refusal by a person in a dominant position to license an intellectual property right would only be abusive if the conditions identified in the previous case law (and in particular in *Magill*, *IMS Health* and *Bronner*) were met [315]. By contrast, the Commission contended that the enquiry needed to be more general, taking account of all the particular circumstances and not merely those identified in the existing case law [316]. This was potentially a significant issue because the Commission was relying on factors other than those in the existing case law albeit it was contending in the alternative that the conditions identified in that case law were met [317]–[318].

The Court appears to have found in favour of the Commission on this point. After emphasising that a refusal by a person in a dominant position to license an intellectual property right would only be abusive in exceptional circumstances [331], it went on to say that the following circumstances, in particular, must be considered to be exceptional: first, the refusal relates to a product or service indispensable to the exercise of a particular activity on a neighbouring market; second, the refusal is of such a kind as to exclude any effective competition on that neighbouring market; third, the refusal prevents the appearance of a new product for which there is potential consumer demand ("the *Magill/IMS* circumstances") [332]. Once it is established that the *Magill/IMS* circumstances are present, the refusal by the holder of a dominant position to grant a licence may infringe Article 82 EC unless the refusal is objectively justified [333]. The Court went on to say that in this particular case the correct approach was to decide whether the *Magill/IMS* conditions were present but that if one or more of the conditions were absent it would proceed to assess the particular circumstances invoked by the Commission [336]. In the event, the Court held that Microsoft had not satisfied it that any of the *Magill/IMS* circumstances were absent or that there was any objective justification for the refusal to license [436], [620], [665], [711], [712]. Accordingly, it did not examine the other particular circumstances invoked by the Commission. See also [691], in which the Court appeared to state that the *Magill/IMS* circumstances were examples of the type of circumstances in which a refusal might be abusive.

As to the *Magill/IMS* circumstances, the Court made the following legal findings.

Indispensability. The Court upheld the Commission's approach, which was first to consider what degree of interoperability with the Windows domain architecture non-Microsoft work group server operating systems must achieve in order for competitors to be able to remain viably on the market and secondly to appraise whether the information that Microsoft refused to disclose was indispensable to the attainment of that degree of interoperability [370 *et seq.*].

Exclusion of effective competition. Microsoft criticised the Commission on the ground that it had considered that this condition would be met if there was a "risk", rather than a "likelihood" or "high probability", that competition on the work group operating systems market would be eliminated [560]. The Court rejected this argument. It stated that the expressions "risk of elimination of competition" and "likely to eliminate competition" are used without distinction by the Community judicature to reflect the same idea, namely that Article 82 does not apply only from the time when there is no more, or practically no more, competition on the market. If the Commission were required to wait until competitors were eliminated from the market, or until their elimination was sufficiently imminent, before being able to take action under Article 82, that would run counter to the objective of that provision, which is to maintain undistorted competition in the common market and, in particular, to safeguard the competition that still exists on the relevant market [561]. In this case it had been particularly important for the Commission to act when it did because the market in question was characterised by significant network effects [562]. The Court made the further point that it is not necessary to demonstrate that *all* competition on the market will be eliminated. What matters is that the refusal at issue is liable to, or is likely to, eliminate all *effective* competition on the market. The fact that the competitors of the dominant undertaking retain a marginal presence in certain niches on the market cannot suffice to substantiate the existence of such competition [563].

New product. There were already a number of server operating systems in the market. The Commission's case was that the supply of the interoperability information would enable the products of Microsoft's competitors to behave in the same way as Windows server operating systems [623] and to develop the advanced features of their existing products [624]. Microsoft contended that the Commission had therefore failed to identify a new product which would be developed as a result of the supply of the information [624]. The Commission contended that in order to be described as new, it was sufficient for a product to contain substantial elements contributed by the licensee's own efforts [626], [631]. The Court held that the "new product" requirement must seen in the context of Article 82(b), which gives, as an example of abusive conduct, "limiting production, markets or technical development to the prejudice of consumers" [643]. Accordingly, "the circumstance relating to the appearance of a new product, as envisaged in *Magill* and *IMS Health* … cannot be the only parameter which determines whether a refusal to license an intellectual property right is capable of causing prejudice to consumers within the meaning of Article 82(b)" [647]. Thus, the Commission had been entitled to find that the "new product" condition was satisfied because the refusal limited technical development to the prejudice of consumers [648], [665]. It appears, therefore, that the Court took the view that a technical development of an existing product amounts to a new product for these purposes. There is clearly scope for argument as to whether this is a correct interpretation of the earlier case-law or whether by reason of this finding the Court effectively held that there were exceptional circumstances other than the *Magill/ IMS* circumstances.

Objective justification. The Court made the preliminary point that it was necessary for the dominant undertaking to raise any plea of objective justification supported by argument and evidence and for the Commission to rebut such a plea [688]. Microsoft's only argument had been that the interoperability information was covered by intellectual property rights and the Court held that this was inconsistent with the raison d'être of the *Magill* exception [690]. It made no difference that the material was secret, valuable and innovative [693-695]. Further, Microsoft had failed to establish that the order for disclosure would have a sufficient negative effect on its incentives to innovate [701].

Having upheld the Commission's findings of abuse, the Court went on to reject Microsoft's arguments that the Commission's decision was inconsistent with Article 13 of TRIPS on the following grounds. First, international agreements such as TRIPS do not prevail over primary Community law, such as Article 82 [798]. Second, and in any event, the Commission was not obliged to make a choice between different constructions of a Community text [799]. Third, it is only where the Community has intended to implement a particular obligation assumed under the WTO or where the Community measure refers expressly to specific provisions of the WTO agreements that the Community judicature is obliged to review the legality of the Community measure in question in the light of the WTO rules. That was not the case here [802].

Tying. The Commission held that through tying Windows Media Player with   **29–251B**
Windows, Microsoft used Windows as "a distribution channel to anti-competitively ensure for itself a significant competition advantage in the media player market", placing competitors at a disadvantage irrespective of the quality of their products (recital 979). This interfered with the normal competitive process which would benefit users in terms of quicker cycles of innovation due to unfettered competition on the merits (recitals 980 and 981). Moreover, tying enabled Microsoft "to anti-competitively expand its position in adjacent media-related software markets and weaken effective competition to the eventual detriment of consumers" (recital 982). The tying also deterred innovation in any technologies which Microsoft could conceivably take an interest in and tie with Windows in future (recital 983). There was therefore a reasonable likelihood that the tying would lead to a lessening of competition so that the maintenance of an effective competition structure would not be ensured for the foreseeable future. Accordingly, there was a violation of Article 82(d) (recital 984). There was an appreciable effect on trade between Member States and between the Contracting Parties to the EEA (recital 993). Accordingly, Microsoft was ordered to offer a version of Windows for client PCs which did not include Windows Media Player (recital 1011) and to refrain from using any technological, commercial, contractual or other means which would have the equivalent effect of tying Windows Media Player to Windows (recital 1012).

For an account of the enforcement of the *Microsoft* decision in 2005, see paragraphs 106 to 112 of the Commission's Report on Competition Policy 2005 (SEC (2006) 761, final). See *http://europa.eu.int/comm/competition/antitrust/ others/article_82_review.html*.

This decision was upheld by the Court of First Instance. The Commission had adopted a four-stage analysis (Recital 794). First, the tying product (Windows client PC operating systems) and the tied product (Windows Media Player) were two separate products. Second, Microsoft was dominant in the market for the tying product. Third, Microsoft did not give customers a choice to obtain the tying product without the tied product. Fourth, the practice in question foreclosed competition.

Microsoft criticised the Commission's third step on the grounds that it amounted to a departure from Article 82(d), which provides as an example of abusive conduct "making the conclusion of contracts subject to acceptance by the other parties of supplementary obligations which, by their nature or according to commercial usage, have no connection with the subject of such contracts". The Court observed that Article 82(d) is not intended to be exhaustive [861] but held in any event that the Commission's third step merely expressed in different words the concept that "bundling assumes that consumers are compelled, directly or indirectly, to accept 'supplementary obligations', such as those referred to in Article 82(d)" [864].

Microsoft also criticised the Commission's fourth step as introducing a new requirement, not justified in the case law. The Court dismissed this argument: "the fact remains that, in principle, conduct will be regarded as abusive only if it is capable of restricting competition" (applying *Michelin III* [2003] E.C.R. II–4071).

Again, the Court rejected arguments based on TRIPS. In this instance, Microsoft's arguments included a contention that the Commission's decision infringed its rights—protected by TRIPS—to authorise adaptations, arrangements and other alterations of its works, to authorise the reproduction of its works, in any manner or form, and to distribute copies of Windows to the public. It contended that the decision forced it to create an adaptation of Windows which was not of its own design and which represented a substantial alteration of its copyright work, and also to license the use of copies of that "compelled adaptation of its copyrighted work". It asserted that the compulsory licensing of a copyright work is authorised by the TRIPS Agreement only on the conditions laid down in Article 13 of that agreement, which were not fulfilled in this case [1175]. The Court held that Microsoft could not rely on TRIPS for the reasons stated in relation to the interoperability information [1190] but went on to state that there was nothing in TRIPS to prevent the competition authorities of the members of the WTO from imposing remedies which limit or regulate the exploitation of intellectual property rights held by an undertaking in a dominant position where that undertaking exercises those rights in an anti-competitive manner (referring to Art.40(2) of TRIPS) [1192].

On the Commission's decision, see Ridyard, "Compulsory Access Under EC Competition Law—A New Doctrine of 'Convenient Facilities' and the Case for Price Regulation" [2004] E.C.L.R. 669; Art and McCurdy, "The European Commission's Media Player Remedy in its Microsoft decision: Compulsory Code Removal despite the Absence of Tying or Foreclosure" [2004] E.C.L.R. 694; Le, "What Does 'Capable of Eliminating all Competition' Mean?" [2005] E.C.L.R. 6; Hart, "Interoperability Information and the Microsoft decision" [2006] 7 E.I.P.R. 361; and Apon, "Cases Against Microsoft: Similar Cases, Different Remedies" [2007] E.C.L.R. 327.

29–252   **The Berne Convention.** For the application of TRIPS, see paras 29–251A and 29–251B, above.

29–253   **Collecting Societies.** NOTE 40. **Add:** The French Competition Council case *SACD* (reported at [2005] E.C.L.R. N–132) is to the same effect.

B. UNITED KINGDOM COMPETITION LAW

(i) Introduction

Current United Kingdom legislation. Add: In Joined Cases C–295/04 to   29–254
C–298/04, *Manfredi v Lloyd Adriatico Assicurazioni SpA*, the Court of Justice
emphasised that Community competition law and national competition law apply
in parallel, since they consider restrictive practices from different points of view.
Whereas Articles 81 and 82 regard them in the light of the obstacles which may
result for trade between Member States, national law proceeds on the basis of
considerations peculiar to it and considers restrictive practices only in that
context.

(ii) The Competition Act 1998

(a) *Transitional arrangements and general principles*

The Competition Act: transitional provisions: general. NOTE 57. Second and   29–256
third sentences. **Delete** and **substitute:** It was intended that this Guideline should
be updated by a new Guideline on the major provisions (a draft of which was
published as OFT 400a in April 2004). In fact, however, OFT 400a was never finalised and both it and Guideline OFT 406 have been removed from the OFT's
website. The OFT's understanding of the transitional provisions is now set out in
Modernisation, OFT Guideline 442 (December 2004), paras 11.8 *et seq*. See
www.oft.gov.uk.

Transitional periods. NOTE 60. **Delete:** OFT 400a, para.12.15. **Substitute:** OFT   29–257
442, para.11.15.
    Sixth sentence. **Delete:** draft.
    NOTE 64. **Delete** and **substitute:** OFT 442, para.11.13.
    Eighth sentence. **Delete:** draft.
    NOTE 66. **Delete** and **substitute:** OFT 442, para.11.25.
    Tenth sentence. **Delete:** draft.
    NOTE 68. **Delete** and **substitute:** OFT 442, para.11.28.

General principles of interpretation. NOTE 77. **Delete** and **substitute:** In the   29–259
OFT's view, this is limited to decisions or statements which have the authority of
the European Commission as a whole, such as, for example, decisions on individual cases under Arts 81 and/or 82; European Commission Notices; and clear
statements about its policy approach which the European Commission has
published in its Annual Reports on Competition Policy: *Modernisation*: OFT
Guideline 442 (December 2004).
    Add: In *Microsoft Corp v Ling* [2006] EWHC 1619 (Ch), H.H. Judge Havery
Q.C. rejected a submission that where a defendant alleged that a licensing system
infringed one of the prohibitions in the Act the burden lay on the licensor to
prove that it did not infringe.

(b) *The Chapter I prohibition*

The Chapter I prohibition. NOTE 80. **Delete** and **substitute:** In December 2004   29–261
the OFT published a Guideline as to its interpretation of the Ch.1 prohibition
(OFT 401).
    NOTE 82. Second sentence onwards. **Delete** and **substitute:** According to the
OFT: "Agreement has a wide meaning and covers agreements whether legally

enforceable or not, written or oral; it includes so-called gentlemen's agreements. There does not have to be a physical meeting of the parties for an agreement to be reached: an exchange of letters or telephone calls may suffice." See OFT 401 para.2.7. The OFT has published a Guideline on the application of the Ch.I and Ch.II prohibitions to the activities of trade association, professional bodies and self-regulating bodies: OFT 408 (December 2004).

NOTE 83. **Delete** and **substitute:** According to the OFT, the term "undertaking" "covers any natural or legal person engaged in economic activity, regardless of its legal status and the way in which it is financed. It includes companies, firms, businesses, partnerships, individuals operating as sole traders, agricultural co-operatives, associations of undertakings (*e.g.* trade associations), non profit-making organisations and (in some circumstances) public entities that offer goods or services on a given market." See OFT 401, para.2.5. As under Community law, the prohibition is not applied to agreements between entities which form a single economic unit: *ibid.*, para.2.6.

NOTE 84. **Delete:** para.2.16 of Guideline OFT 401. **Substitute:** para.2.25 of Guideline OFT 401. **Delete:** (para.2.21 of OFT 401a is to the same effect).

Add: In *P&S Amusements Ltd v Valley House Leisure Ltd* [2006] EWHC 1510 (Ch) it was submitted that as a result of the Competition Appeal Tribunal's decision in *Aberdeen Journals Ltd v OFT* [2003] CAT 11 (see para.29–272, below), there was no requirement that the effect on trade in the United Kingdom should be appreciable. Morritt C (*obiter*) expressed considerable misgivings about the *Aberdeen Journals* decision on this point and stated that he would need "much persuasion" that it should be transposed into the different context of section 2.

29–263   **Appreciability.** Second sentence onwards and NOTES 86 to 93. **Delete** and **substitute:** In determining whether an agreement has an appreciable effect on competition for the purposes of the Chapter I prohibition (or indeed Article 81), the OFT will have regard to the Commission's approach as set out in its Notice on Agreements of Minor Importance (as to which see paras 29–185 and 29–186 of the Main Work): see Guideline OFT 401, paragraph 2.18. As a matter of practice the OFT is likely to consider that an agreement will not fall within the Chapter I prohibition when it is covered by the Commission's Notice: *ibid.*, paragraph 2.19. Furthermore, where the OFT considers that undertakings have relied in good faith on the terms of the Notice it will not impose financial penalties: *ibid.* The mere fact that the parties' market shares exceed the thresholds provided for in the Notice does not mean that the effect on competition is appreciable. Other factors, such as the content of the agreement and the structure of the market, will be considered: OFT 401 paragraph 2.20. In *Burgess v The OFT* [2005] CAT 25, the CAT was prepared to accept that a material effect on competition must be shown, but rejected the OFT's submission that it was necessary to show "substantial harm".

29–267   **Vertical agreements: scope of the exclusion.** NOTE 15. **Delete** and **substitute:** See *Vertical agreements*, OFT Guideline 419.

29–269   **Guidance from the OFT.** NOTE 25. **Delete** and **substitute:** See *Modernisation*, OFT Guideline 442, para.11.3.

NOTE 29. **Delete** and **substitute:** See *Modernisation*, OFT Guideline 442, para.3.5.

NOTE 30. **Delete** and **substitute:** See *Modernisation*, OFT Guideline 442, para.7.4.

NOTE 31. **Delete** and **substitute:** See *Modernisation*, OFT Guideline 442, para.7.18.

NOTE 32. **Delete** and **substitute:** See *Modernisation*, OFT Guideline 442, para.7.19.

The OFT's draft guideline on intellectual property rights: general. First sentence. **Add** at end: This draft guideline was never finalised and has now been withdrawn from the OFT's website. It seems doubtful whether it is of any value other than as an indication of the OFT's thinking on the subject in November 2001. Nevertheless, an account follows.   **29–270**

The OFT's draft guideline on intellectual property rights: specific provisions in licences. Add at start: This paragraph should be read subject to the caveat that since the draft guideline was never finalised and has now been withdrawn from the OFT's website, it seems doubtful whether it is of any value other than as an indication of the OFT's thinking on the subject in November 2001.   **29–271**

(c) *The Chapter II prohibition*

The Chapter II prohibition. NOTE 46. **Delete** and **substitute:** The OFT has published a guideline as to its interpretation of the Ch. II prohibition: *Abuse of a Dominant Position*, OFT 402 (December 2004).   **29–272**

NOTE 47. **Add:** In *Aberdeen Journals Ltd v OFT* [2003] CAT 11, the Competition Appeal Tribunal held that there was no requirement that the effect on trade should be appreciable. In *P&S Amusements Ltd v Valley House Leisure Ltd* [2006] EWHC 1510 (Ch) Morritt C. (*obiter*) expressed considerable misgivings about this.

Enforcement. NOTE 54. Second sentence. **Delete** and **substitute:** see OFT's Guidance as to the appropriate amount of a penalty, OFT 423 (December 2004).   **29–275**

Last sentence. **Delete** "the Competition Commission established by section 45 and Schedule 7" and NOTE 57 and **substitute:** the Competition Appeal Tribunal established by section 12 of and Schedule 2 to the Enterprise Act 2002.

Add at end: In *Argos Ltd v OFT* [2006] EWCA Civ 1318; [2006] U.K.C.L.R. 1135 at [163] the Court of Appeal approved the approach of the Competition Appeal Tribunal to the OFT's guidance on penalties. That approach is to make its own assessment of the penalty, on the basis of a "broad brush" approach, taking the case as a whole and then to carry out a "cross check" to see whether the amount so arrived at would be within the parameters set out in the Guidance. The Court of Appeal went on to say (at [165]) that it recognised that the Tribunal is an expert and specialised body, and that, subject to any difference in the basis on which the infringements are to be considered as a result of any appeal on liability, the Court of Appeal should hesitate before interfering with the Tribunal's assessment of the appropriate penalty.

Civil liability. Add: Interim relief will be granted in appropriate cases and where a mandatory injunction is sought normal principles apply: see *AAH Pharmaceuticals Ltd v Pfizer Ltd* [2007] EWHC 565 (Ch) and *Software Cellular Network Ltd v T-Mobile (UK) Ltd,* Robin Knowles Q.C. July 17, 2007 (mandatory injunction).   **29–276**

The OFT's draft guideline on intellectual property rights: general points about the Chapter II prohibition. First sentence. **Add** at end: This draft guideline was never finalised and has now been withdrawn from the OFT's website. It seems doubtful whether it is of any value other than as an indication of the OFT's thinking on the subject in November 2001. Nevertheless, an account follows.   **27–277**

NOTE 63. **Delete** fourth sentence and **substitute:** Both OFT 403 and OFT 402 were reissued in December 2004.

29–278   **The OFT's draft guideline: specific types of conduct. Add** at start: This paragraph should be read subject to the caveat that since the draft guideline was never finalised and has now been withdrawn from the OFT's website, it seems doubtful whether it is of any value other than as an indication of the OFT's thinking on the subject in November 2001.

(iii) Mergers: Part 3 of the Enterprise Act 2002.

29–280   **When the OFT may make a reference.** NOTE 76. *OFT v IBA Health Ltd* is now reported at [2004] 4 All E.R. 1003 and [2005] E.C.C. 1.

29–282   **Undertakings in lieu of reference.** In *Tetra Laval* the OFT accepted in lieu of a reference undertakings to grant to a suitable purchaser an exclusive irrevocable EEA-wide licence of intellectual property rights relating to cheese equipment. See Press Release 162/06.

29–283   **Determination by the Competition Commission.** NOTE 93. *OFT v IBA Health Ltd* is now reported at [2004] 4 All E.R. 1003 and [2005] E.C.C. 1.

(iv) Market investigations: Part 4 of the Enterprise Act 2002

29–291   **Power of OFT and Minister to make references.** NOTE 42. **Delete:** March 2003. **Substitute:** March 2006.

5. RESTRAINT OF TRADE

29–304   **General principles. Add** at end of first sub-paragraph: In *Peer International Corporation v Termidor Music Publishers Ltd* [2006] EWHC 2883 (Ch); [2007] E.C.D.R. 1, the question arose as to whether the doctrine of restraint of trade could be relied on by a stranger to a contract in circumstances where the "innocent" party was not represented in the proceedings. Lindsay J. noted that standing in contractual matters is normally confined to the parties to the contract but that the public interest in every person being able to carry on his trade freely arguably justified a broader approach. However, he concluded that the public interest did not provide a "wholly compelling reason" for such an approach. Even if there was scope for such an approach, on the particular facts of the case there was no basis for holding that the third party should have standing to challenge the agreements in question [31].

Add at end: The doctrine of restraint of trade may have an impact on the construction of agreements. Thus, in *Taylor v Rive Droite Music Ltd* [2005] EWCA Civ 1300; [2006] E.M.L.R. 4 at para.142. Neuberger L.J. stated that there was no principle requiring a court to lean in favour of a construction of a recording agreement which would give the production company a monopoly over all the output of an artist during its term. He concluded on the facts of that case that if there was any presumption it was to the opposite effect, for two reasons. First, the agreement was in a standard form prepared by the production company and accordingly the *contra proferentem* rule applied against the company. Second, any bias in the court's approach should be one which is "against monopoly, restraint of trade and impairing an artist's freedom to exploit his work commercially".

CHAPTER THIRTY

TAXATION

Contents

1. INCOME TAX

A. INTRODUCTION

Add new paragraphs:

30–01A   **The Tax Law Rewrite.** In the 1995 Budget, the Chancellor announced a long-term project to rewrite the whole of the primary legislation imposing income and other direct taxes. Called the Tax Law Rewrite, the purpose of the project was not to change the meaning of the law, but to reorder and rewrite it using simpler language and structure and taking into account current case law, concessions and practices. The consequence will eventually be the repeal of the entirety of the Income and Corporation Taxes Act 1988 ("ICTA 1988") to which much of the Taxation chapter in the Main Work refers, replacing it with a series of separate Acts which collectively will form the income tax code.

Since April 6, 2003, the relevant changes to date can briefly be summarised as follows:

(1) The Income Tax (Earnings and Pensions) Act 2003 ("ITEPA 2003") repealed the former Schedule E charge and imposed a separate charge on employment income from April 6, 2003 (with effect for income tax purposes, for the tax year 2003–04 and subsequent tax years and, with effect for corporation tax, for accounting periods ending after April 5, 2003);

(2) The Income Tax (Trading and Other Income) Act 2005 ("ITTOIA 2005") repealed Schedule D in respect of individuals and imposed separate charges on trading and miscellaneous income from April 6, 2005 (with effect for income tax purposes, for the tax year 2005–06 and subsequent tax years and for corporation tax purposes, for accounting periods ending after April 5,2005); and

(3) The Income Tax Act 2007 ("ITA 2007") repeals miscellaneous sections of ICTA 1988 that have not so far been rewritten, including the basic provisions, specific reliefs and rules and general definitions from April 6, 2007 (with effect for income tax purposes, for the tax year 2007–08 and subsequent tax years and, for corporation tax purposes, for accounting periods ending after April 5,2007).

As the project is so far only partially complete, the rewrite of the income tax principles according to which corporation tax is computed is in the form of a sixth bill, yet to be enacted.

Accordingly, this supplement includes references to the new legislation for income tax purposes. The scheduler system and certain other provisions of ICTA 1988 continue in force for corporation tax purposes and this will be stated where relevant.

Merger of the Inland Revenue and HM Customs & Excise. On April 18, 2005,   **30–01B**
the Inland Revenue merged with HM Customs & Excise to form a combined
department—HM Revenue & Customs. All references to the separate departments in the Main Work should now be read accordingly.

Recognition of Civil Partnerships. Following the Civil Partnership Act 2004   **30–01C**
and the Tax and Civil Partnership Regulations (SI 2005/3229), which came into
force on December 5, 2005, there is now the same or similar tax treatment for
civil partners as there is for spouses. Accordingly, references to "spouse" in the
Main Work should now be read as "spouse or civil partner".

B. TRADES, PROFESSIONS AND VOCATIONS

First sub-paragraph. First sentence. **Add** at end: for corporation tax purposes. For   **30–02**
income tax purposes, the profits of a trade, profession or vocation are charged
collectively under ITTOIA 2005, s.5.

NOTE 1. **Add:** for corporation tax purposes. ITITOIA, s.5 for income tax
purposes.

First sub-paragraph. Second sentence. **Delete** and **substitute:** However, as
there was no material difference between the rules applicable to Cases I and II of
Schedule D and the present ITTOIA 2005 provisions largely apply to professions
and vocations as they apply to trades, it is convenient to classify as "traders" not
only persons who carry on a trade which involves the creation or exploitation of
intellectual property, for example, persons involved in publishing, film and record production or distribution, etc. but also individuals who carry on a profession
or vocation which involves the creation or exploitation of intellectual property
for example, authors, composers and designers.

First sub-paragraph. Penultimate sentence. **Delete** and **substitute:** The employee is taxable under the employment income provisions of ITEPA 2003 (Parts
2 to 7) on his general earnings and specific employment income.

H. DEDUCTIBLE EXPENSES

First sub-paragraph. Second sentence. **Add** at end: and ITTOIA 2005.   **30–09**

First sub-paragraph. Third sentence. **Add** at end: for corporation tax purposes.
This rule has not been explicitly rewritten into ITTOIA 2005 for income tax
purposes; instead disallowances are contained primarily in Chapter 4 of ITTOIA
2005 and elsewhere throughout the Act.

NOTE 22. **Add:** for corporation tax purposes. ITTOIA 2005, s.34(l)(a) for
income tax purposes.

NOTE 23. **Add:** for corporation tax purposes. ITTOIA 2005, s.33 for income
tax purposes.

NOTE 24. **Add:** S.74(l)(m) has not been rewritten for income tax purposes, but
note that ITTOIA 2005, s.29 expressly provides that interest on loans is an item
of revenue nature, and so is deductible.

Second sub-paragraph. **Delete:** 30–00. **Substitute:** 30–33.

I. EXPENDITURE ON FILMS, TAPES AND DISCS

Following the 2005 Budget, which announced the intended replacement of exist-   **30–10**
ing tax relief for films with a new relief which targeted film production
companies, there was a period of formal consultation. The results of this consultation were announced in the December 2005 Pre-Budget Report and are enacted
in sections 31 to 48 of and Schedules 4 and 5 to the Finance Act 2006. The new
rules for film tax relief replace the existing rules for tax relief set out in sections

40A to 43 of the Finance (No.2) Act 1992 and section 48 of the Finance (No.2) Act 1997 for corporation tax purposes. They also replace the existing rules for tax relief for income tax purposes (re-enacted in sections 130 to 144 of the Income Tax (Trading and Other Income) Act 2005).

The relief ("film tax relief") applies only to a "film production company" in respect of expenditure on a film that commences principal photography on or after January 1, 2007, or to acquisition expenditure that is incurred on or after October 1, 2007 on a film (whenever made) and which is expenditure that qualifies for relief. It is clear, therefore, that this relief does not apply to individuals or to partners in partnerships.

Expenditure qualifies for relief if it satisfies three conditions (set out in ss.39 to 41 inclusive), namely, that the film is "intended for theatrical release", that it is a "British film" and that the expenditure is "UK expenditure". These are defined terms. A film is "intended for theatrical release" where, broadly, it is intended to be exhibited to the paying public at a commercial cinema and it is intended that a significant proportion of the earnings from the film are to arise from such exhibition. A film is a "British film" if it is so certified under Schedule 1 to the Films Act 1985. "UK expenditure" is expenditure on services performed in the UK or on goods supplied in the UK. In order for the third condition (as to UK expenditure) to be satisfied, it is necessary that not less than 25 per cent of the core expenditure on the film is UK expenditure.

Where these conditions are satisfied, the film production company is entitled to an additional deduction in respect of "qualifying expenditure" in calculating the profit and loss of its trade. "Qualifying expenditure" is, broadly, the core expenditure of the film, being UK expenditure, as is taken into account by Schedule 4 to the Finance Act 2006. Paragraph 4 of Schedule 5 to the Finance Act 2006 provides a formula for calculating the amount of the additional deduction: $E \times R$, where E is the lesser of the amount of qualifying expenditure that is UK expenditure and 80 per cent of the total amount of qualifying expenditure and R is the rate of enhancement. The R figure (the rate of enhancement) is set at 100 per cent for films with budgets of less than £20m and at 80 per cent for films with budgets of over £20m.

A film production company qualifying for the additional deduction is also entitled to a payable tax credit (Sch.5, para.6 to Finance Act 2006). A film production company is entitled to claim the payable tax credit where it has a "surrenderable loss" in an accounting period. The "surrenderable loss" is either the trading loss of the company or the available qualifying expenditure, whichever is less. The amount of the available qualifying expenditure is the figure for "E" in para.4 of Schedule 5 to the Finance Act 2006—in other words, the lesser of the qualifying expenditure that is UK expenditure and 80 per cent of the total amount of the qualifying expenditure. Paragraph 7 provides that a film production company may surrender all or part of its surrenderable loss for a period. The amount of the payable tax credit is determined by using the formula at para.7 of Schedule 5 to the Finance Act 2006: $L \times R$, where L is the amount of loss surrendered and R is the payable credit rate. The payable credit rate for films with budgets of less than £20m is 25 per cent and for films with budgets of over £20m it is 20 per cent.

The payable tax credit is not automatic but must be claimed. The credit may be set against the corporation tax liability of the film production company.

There are, not surprisingly, anti-avoidance provisions built into the new film tax relief. These provisions deny film tax relief (the additional deduction and the payable tax credit) if, and to the extent that, the relief arises from arrangements entered into wholly or partly for a disqualifying purpose, *i.e.* arrangements where the main object, or one of the main objects, is to enable the film production company to obtain an additional deduction or a payable tax credit to which it would not otherwise have been entitled or one greater than the one to which it would otherwise have been entitled.

The Corporation Tax (Taxation of Films) (Transitional Provisions) Regulations 2007 came into effect on March 29, 2007 and apply the tax relief for films contained in Finance Act 2006 to films that commenced principal photography before January 1, 2007 but were not completed before that date.

Draft legislation is contained in clause 57 of Finance Bill 2007 to allow companies to opt out of the provisions for relief in Finance Act 2006 and into general tax treatment. To do this, the clause allows a company to make an election in its tax return to be regarded as not meeting the conditions to be a Film Production Company in respect of any present or future film. Once an election has been made, it may be withdrawn only within the time limit for amending the return in which it is contained.

J. TOP-SLICING RELIEF

The rules set out in paragraphs 30–16 to 30–18 of the Main Work relating to top-slicing relief (namely, ss.534, 535 and 537 ICTA 1988) were superseded by the Finance Act 2001, which added a new section 95A and Schedule 4A to ICTA 1988 for payments comprising royalties or lump sums actually receivable after April 5, 2001 (see para.30–20 of the Main Work).   **30–15**

These provisions have themselves been rewritten by ITTOIA 2005, sections 221 to 225 for the tax year 2005–06 and onwards for income tax and accounting periods ending after April 5, 2005 for corporation tax. The current rules contained in ITTOIA 2005 are far more straightforward than the rules relating to top-slicing relief and are set out below.

Sections 221 to 225 provide relief for the fluctuating profits of creative artists by averaging profits over consecutive years. Taxpayers can qualify for relief if their profits are derived wholly or mainly from creative works (s.221(2)(c)) and their profits fluctuate from one tax year to the next (s.221(l)(b)). "Creative works" mean literary, dramatic, musical or artistic works or designs created by the taxpayer either personally or in partnership (s.221(3)).

Relief takes the form of an "averaging claim" which can be made if the taxpayer has been carrying on a qualifying trade for two consecutive years and either (a) the relevant profits for one of the tax years are less than 75 per cent of the taxpayer's relevant profits for the other, or (b) the taxpayer's relevant profits for one (but not both) of the years are nil (s.222(1)). For these purposes, "profits" are taken to mean profits before making any deduction for losses in any tax year (s.221(4)) and are regarded as nil if the taxpayer makes a loss in one of the tax years in question (s.221(5)).

An averaging claim may be made in relation to a tax year which was the later tax year on a previous claim (s.222(2)) (*i.e.* a claim for years 2 and 3 can be made even if a claim has been made for years 1 and 2). However an averaging claim may not be made for a tax year if an averaging claim has already been made in relation to the same trade for a later tax year (s.222(3)). Furthermore, an averaging claim may not be made in relation to a tax year in which the trader starts or permanently ceases to carry on the trade or in which the trade begins or ceases to be a qualifying trade (s.222(4)).

Relief must be claimed no later than 12 months after January 31 following the end of the second of those years whose profits are to be averaged (s.222(5)). If, after an averaging claim has been made, the profits of either of the years concerned are adjusted for any other reason, the averaging claim is nullified and a new claim must be made if necessary, no later than 12 months after the January 31 following the end of the tax year in which the adjustment was made (s.225).

Where an averaging claim is made, the method for calculating the adjustment depends on the proportion of profits between the two years in question. Where the relevant profit for one of the two years is not more than 70 per cent of the relevant profit of the other year, or the relevant profit for one (but not both) of the years is nil, the adjusted profit for each year is the average of the two amounts (s.223(3)). Where the relevant profits for one of the two years is between 70 and 75 per cent of the profits of the other year, the adjusted profits are calculated by applying the formula:

$$(D \times 3) - (P \times 0.75)$$
where,

D is the difference between the relevant profits for the two years; and
P is the profit for the higher year (s.223(4)).

The result is added to the relevant profit of the lower year and deducted from the relevant profit of the higher year.

The adjusted profits are treated as the relevant profits of the two tax years to which the claim relates for all income tax purposes (s.224(1)). However, if the relevant profits in one of the tax years is nil, these rules do not prevent the taxpayer from claiming loss relief in that or any other tax year (s.224(3)).

K. Post-cessation receipts

30–21   **Add** at start: Under generally accepted accounting practice, since the tax year 1999/2000, traders must normally make up their accounts under the accruals basis for the purposes of establishing taxable profits. This means that income is taxed as soon as it is earned (accrued) even if not yet received. In that case, receipts after discontinuance do not normally give rise to any tax liability as they would have already been accounted for in a prior period of account.

Note 3. **Add** at end: for corporation tax purposes. ITTOIA 2005, ss.98 and 251 for income tax purposes.

Note 5. **Add** at end: for corporation tax purposes. ITTOIA 2005, ss.241 to 253 for income tax purposes, which treat such receipts as chargeable to income tax.

Note 6. **Add** at end: for corporation tax purposes. ITTOIA 2005, ss. 243(1) and 246(1) for income tax purposes, which apply to any sums "… received after a person permanently ceases to canyon a trade … which arise from the carrying on of the trade before cessation" only insofar as such sums are not otherwise chargeable to income or corporation tax.

L. Non-residents: Trading in the United Kingdom

30–22   Note 9. **Add:** Nor does it matter that the party contracting with the taxpayer may itself be non-resident and the taxpayer receives no income in the United Kingdom pursuant to that contract: see *Agassi v Robinson (H.M. Inspector of Taxes)* 77 TC 686. See also *IR Manuals International Manual*, para. INTM263000 for the current HMRC guidance on non-residents trading in the United Kingdom, the determining factors and a discussion of the case law.

Note 11. **Add** at end: for corporation tax purposes. ITTOIA 2005, s.243(3) for income tax purposes.

M. Residence

30–23   Note 15. **Add:** References to ignoring days of arrival and departure when counting the number of days spent in the United Kingdom should now be treated with caution following *Gaines-Cooper v Revenue and Customs Commissioners* [2007] STC (SCD) 23, where the Special Commissioners chose not to follow IR 20, but instead counted the number of nights the taxpayer spent in the United Kingdom.

NOTE 16. **Add:** In *Gaines-Cooper v Revenue and Customs Commissioners* [2007] STC (SCD) 23, the taxpayer's presence in the United Kingdom for the years under appeal was held not to have been for a temporary purpose, notwithstanding that he had no subjective intention of establishing a residence in the United Kingdom.

NOTE 18. **Add:** See the recent cases of *Wood and another v Holden (Inspector of in Taxes)* [2006] EWCA Civ 26; [2006] STC 443 and *News Datacom Ltd and another v Atkinson (Inspector of Taxes)* [2006] STC (SCD) 732 as to what constitutes central management and control.

N. FOREIGN TRADES, PROFESSIONS, ETC.

NOTE 19. **Add:** Though see *Clark (Inspector of Taxes) v Oceanic Contractors Inc.* [1983] 2 A.C. 130 as referred to in *Agassi v Robinson (HM. Inspector of Taxes)* 77 TC 686 for subsequent limitations to this principle.   **30–24**

Second sub-paragraph. **Delete** second sentence to end and **substitute:** If he is domiciled here, he is subject to income tax on all his income arising worldwide under ITTOIA 2005, section 6; but under ITTOIA 2005, section 243(3), the post-cessation receipts rules (as to which, see para.30–21) do not apply where the trade was carried on wholly outside the United Kingdom. Accordingly, sums arising after the discontinuance of the trade, profession or vocation escape the charge to tax.

NOTE 21. **Add:** See ITTOIA 2005, s.831.

NOTE 22. **Delete** and **substitute:** ITTOIA 2005, s.832: the "remittance" basis of taxation.

NOTE 23. **Delete** and **substitute:** ITTOIA 2005, ss.833 to 834.

O. ROYALTIES RECEIVED OTHERWISE THAN IN THE COURSE OF A TRADE, PROFESSION OR VOCATION

NOTE 24. **Add:** References to Cases III and VI of Schedule D remain in force for corporation tax purposes. For income tax purposes, so far as is relevant to this work, the charge to tax now arises under Pt V of ITTOIA 2005 (Miscellaneous Income), specifically: Ch.2 (receipts from intellectual property), Ch.3 (films and sound recordings: non-trade businesses) and Ch.8 (income not otherwise charged) or, exceptionally, Ch.7 (annual payments not otherwise charged) if the subject matter of the charge is not pure income. The principles derived from the case law remain unchanged.   **30–25**

First sub-paragraph. Last sentence. **Delete:** 30–00 to 30–00, below. **Substitute:** 30–27 to 30–31, below.

Second sub-paragraph. **Add** at end: For income purposes, the FA 2004 exemption is now at ITTOIA 2005, sections 757 to 767.

P. LUMP SUMS RECEIVED OTHERWISE THAN IN THE COURSE OF A TRADE, PROFESSION OR VOCATION

Last line. **Delete:** 30–00. **Substitute:** 30–35.   **30–26**

Q. ANTI-AVOIDANCE PROVISIONS

(i) Section 775: Sale of income derived from personal activities

Section 775 has been repealed by Schedule 3 of ITA 2007 and is rewritten at ITA 2007, Part 13, Chapter 4.   **30–28**

NOTE 34. **Delete** and **substitute:** Under ITA 2007, s.776.

NOTE 35. **Delete** and **substitute:** ITA 2007, s.773(2). The taxpayer has a statutory right to recover tax payable under s.776 from the person who actually receives the capital sum: ITA 2007, s.786.

(ii) Part XV of the Taxes Act: The settlement provisions

30–29   The settlement provisions have been repealed by Schedule 3 of ITTOIA 2005 and are rewritten at ITTOIA 2005, Part 5, Chapter 5.

NOTE 36. **Delete** and **substitute:** ITTOIA 2005, s.624(1). A person has an interest in settled property if it may become payable to or applicable for the benefit of him or his spouse or civil partner: s.625(1) and note the exceptions in s.625(2)–(4). Capital sums paid to the settlor out of undistributed income which is not otherwise taxable in his hands are also charged to income tax: ss.633–64.

NOTE 37. **Delete** and **substitute:** ITTOIA 2005, s.629. Payments out of accumulated income are also caught: s.631.

Third sentence. **Delete:** section 660G of ICTA 1988. **Substitute:** ITTOIA 2005, section 620(1).

NOTE 39. **Delete:** ICTA 1988, s.660G(l), (2). **Substitute:** ITTOIA 2005, s.620(1), (2).

(iii) Sections 739 and 740: Transfers of assets abroad

30–30   Sections 739 and 740 have been repealed by Schedule 3 to ITA 2007 and are rewritten at ITA 2007, Part 13, Chapter 2, in particular ITA 2007, sections 721, 728 and 732. The rewritten section 721 imposes a charge to income tax on "individuals with a power to enjoy income as a result of relevant transactions", section 728 on "individuals receiving capital sums as a result of relevant transactions" (the old s.739) and section 732 on "non-transferors receiving a benefit as a result of relevant transactions" (the old s.740). References to sections 739 and 740 in the remainder of paragraph 30–30 should be read accordingly.

NOTE 41. **Delete:** ICTA 1988, ss.739(1A)(b) and 741 and **substitute:** ITA 2007, ss.721(5), 728(3), 737 and 739.

NOTE 42. **Delete** and **substitute:** ITA 2007, ss.721(5) and 728(3).

First sub-paragraph. **Delete** last sentence and NOTE 43. **Add** new sub-paragraph: Individuals will not be liable for income tax under these provisions if they fall into one of the categories for exemption or partial exemption at ITA 2007, sections 736–742. Broadly, the exemptions apply where there is no tax avoidance purpose or the transactions are genuine commercial transactions (as defined in ITA 2007, s.738). There are separate exemptions for wholly pre-December 5, 2005 transactions (ITA 2007, s.739), wholly post-December 4, 2005 transactions (ITA 2007, ss.737 and 738) and transactions comprising a mixture of the two (ITA 2007, s.740). The conditions for exemption post-December 4, 2005 are more stringent (in particular, in relation to associated operations: s.737(8)) and they effectively clarify that the existence or otherwise of a tax avoidance purpose must be determined objectively in light of all the circumstances and not subjectively. Where an individual satisfies only the pre-December 5, 2005 conditions, a reduced liability to tax may be available under the partial exemption rules: ITA 2007, sections 741 and 742.

(iv) Post-cessation receipts

30–31   First sentence. **Delete:** 30–00. **Substitute:** 30–21.

NOTE 46. **Add** at end: for corporation tax purposes. ITTOIA 2005, ss.98 and 251 for income tax purposes.

NOTE 48. **Delete** and **substitute:** ITTOIA 2005, s.253(1). This exclusion also has effect in relation to assignments of public lending rights (s.253(1)(b)) and there is a corresponding provision relating to design rights: s.253(2).

R. ANTI-AVOIDANCE: LIMITED PARTNERSHIPS

ICTA 1988, sections 117 and 118 have been repealed by ITA 2007 for 2007–08   **30–32** onwards and rewritten at ITA 2007, Part 4, Chapter 3. The new provisions also make a number of clarifications as to what is included in a partner's contribution to the firm (broadly speaking, contributed capital and capitalised undrawn profits): ITA 2007, section 105.

S. POSITION OF THE PAYER

First sub-paragraph. First sentence. **Add** at end: for corporation tax purposes or   **30–33** by Chapter 4 of ITTOIA 2005, or elsewhere in that Act.

NOTE 61. **Add** at end: for corporation tax purposes, ITA 2007, ss.843 and 904 for income tax purposes.

NOTE 62. First sentence. **Delete** and **substitute:** ITA 2007, s.906, which also applies to a public lending right (s.907(l)(c)) and a "right in a design", which means the design right in a design or the right in a registered design: s.907(1)(b) and s.907(2). Last sentence. **Delete:** s.536(2) as substituted by CDPA 1988, Sch.7, para.36(5) and **substitute:** ITA 2007, s.907(2).

NOTE 63. First sentence. **Delete** and **substitute:** ITA 2007, s.906(5), which does not apply to payments in respect of copies of works, or articles, which have been exported from the United Kingdom for distribution outside the United Kingdom: ITA 2007, s.906(4).

Delete third sub-paragraph and NOTE 67.

NOTE 64. **Delete** and **substitute:** ITA 2007, s.909(2).

NOTE 65. First sentence. **Delete** and **substitute:** ITA 2007, s.908(1).

NOTE 66. **Delete** and **substitute:** ITA 2007, s.908(2).

T. DOUBLE TAXATION RELIEF

Add at end: The United Kingdom's provisions for unilateral relief are at ICTA   **30–34** 1988, section 790.

2. CAPITAL GAINS TAX

C. GIFTS

NOTE 97. **Add** at end: Though note *Jerome v Kelly (Inspector of Taxes)* [2004]   **30–38** UKHL 25; [2004] 2 All E.R. 835 at 849, paragraph 42, where the necessity for an asset to *exist* at the time of a disposal was distinguished from the case where the disposal of an asset for capital gains tax purposes may properly *precede* its acquisition, such as where an investor sells short.

E. ALLOWABLE EXPENDITURE

Add at end: Where the asset in question is intangible (as will be the case with   **30–41** intellectual property), "state or nature" has been held to mean something more than merely the value of the asset (see *Trustees of the F D Fenston Will Trusts v Revenue and Customs Commissioners* [2007] STC (SCD) 316 where the words were held to require a change in the rights or restrictions attaching to the asset—here, shares. However, the author believes that this may be too narrow a construction).

3. INHERITANCE TAX

A. DEATH

30–44   NOTE 16. **Add:** For new interest in possession settlements, *i.e.* those created after March 22, 2006, the value of the settled property in which the interest in possession subsists will no longer be deemed to fall within the person's estate on death (para.4 of Sch.20 to the Finance Act 2006). This ties in with the aim of ensuring that all new interest in possession settlements are taxed in the same way as discretionary settlements.

B. LIFETIME GIFTS AND SETTLEMENTS BY THE HOLDER

30–45   NOTE 22. **Add:** For new interest in possession settlements, *i.e.* those created after March 22, 2006, the value of the settled property in which the interest in possession subsists will no longer be deemed to fall within the person's estate on death (para. 4 of Sch.20 to the Finance Act 2006).

NOTE 23. **Add:** The Finance Act 2006 has made significant erosions into the realm of potentially exempt transfers. No transfers made after March 22, 2006 are potentially exempt transfers unless, broadly, they are to an individual or to a disabled trust (defined by s.89 of IHTA 1984). The concept of accumulation and maintenance trusts has been abolished for assets settled after March 22, 2006.

C. EXEMPTIONS

30–47   As a result of the Finance Act 2006, no new *inter vivos* settlements in favour of the spouse will attract the spouse exemption. For *inter vivos* gifts, it will now only be possible to attract the spouse exemption on outright gifts to the spouse.

5. VALUE ADDED TAX

A. THE SOURCES OF VAT LAW

30–51   First sub-paragraph. Second sentence. **Delete:** the Commissioners of Customs and Excise. **Substitute:** HM Revenue & Customs.

Second sub-paragraph. **Delete** and **substitute:** The principal current source of United Kingdom VAT legislation is the consolidating Value Added Tax Act ("VATA 1994"), together with Regulations made under Statutory Instrument. Domestic legislation is designed to give effect to the common system of VAT which predominantly originated as the Sixth Directive of May 17, 1977 and was required to be implemented in all Member States' VAT legislation. On December 11, 2006, the revised versions of the First and Sixth Directives were published: [2006] O.J. L347/1. The newly approved Council Directive 2006/112/EC entered into force on January 1, 2007 (Art.413 of the Directive). In general, the new Directive does not bring any major changes to the current VAT rules and principles and domestic legislation will continue to be construed accordingly. In case of conflict between domestic and directly applicable Community legislation, taxpayers (but not HM Revenue & Customs) may rely on the latter.

B. THE CHARGE TO VAT

NOTE 47. **Delete** and **substitute:** £64,000 from April 1,2007.   **30–54**
    Last sentence. **Delete:** £60,000. **Substitute:** £70,000.

Penultimate sentence. **Delete:** the Commissioners of Customs and Excise. **Substi-**   **30–55**
tute: HM Revenue & Customs.

MATERIALS

The following list indicates only those sections where changes or additions have been made.

Where a statutory instrument which was reproduced in the Main Work has been completely superseded, its title is shown in square brackets followed by the title of the instrument which superseded it.

PART A

COPYRIGHT, DESIGNS AND PATENTS ACT 1988 AND RELATED MATERIALS

A1. COPYRIGHT, DESIGNS AND PATENTS ACT 1988

Films

p.22 Section 5B(3) has been amended to read as follows:

"(3) Without prejudice to the generality of subsection (2), where that subsection applies.

    (a) references in this Part to showing a film include playing the film sound track to accompany the film,

    [(b) references in this Part to playing a sound recording, or to communicating a sound recording to the public, do not include playing or communicating the film sound track to accompany the film,

    (c) references in this Part to copying a work, so far as they apply to a sound recording, do not include copying the film sound track to accompany the film, and

    (d) references in this Part to the issuing, rental or lending of copies of a work, so far as they apply to a sound recording, do not include the issuing, rental or lending of copies of the sound track to accompany the film.]"

Note: Subsection (3)(b) was substituted and (3)(c) and (d) were inserted by the Performances (Moral Rights, etc.) Regulations 2006 (SI 2006/18), Sch. para.2, with effect from February 1, 2006.

Duration of copyright in literary, dramatic, musical or artistic works

p.28 Section 12(9) has been amended to read as follows:

"(9) This section does not apply to Crown copyright or Parliamentary copyright (see sections 163 to [166D]) or to copyright which subsists by virtue of section 168 (copyright of certain international organisations)."

Note: The words in square brackets in s.12(9) were substituted by the Government of Wales Act 2006 (c.32), Sch.10 para.23, with effect from May 4, 2007.

Material communicated to the Crown in the course of public business

p.57 Section 48(6) is amended to read as follows:

"(6) In this section "the Crown" includes a health service body, as defined in section 60(7) of the National Health Service and Community Care Act 1990, [a Primary Care Trust established under [section 18 of the National Health Service Act 2006],] [the Commission for Social Care Inspection,] [the Commission for Healthcare Audit and Inspection] and a National Health Service trust established under [section 25 of the National

Health Service Act 2006, section 18 of the National Health Service (Wales) Act 2006] or the National Health Service (Scotland) Act 1978 [and an NHS foundation trust] [and also includes a health and social services body, as defined in Article 7(6) of the Health and Personal Social Services (N.I.) Order 1991, and a Health and Social Services trust established under that Order]; and the reference in subsection (1) above to public business shall be construed accordingly."

Note: The references to the 2006 Acts in s.48(6) were substituted for former references to the 1977 Act by the National Health Service (Consequential Provisions) Act 2006 (c.43), Sch.1 para.112, with effect from March 1, 2007.

Public records

Section 49 has been amended to read as follows: **p.58**

"**49.** Material which is comprised in public records within the meaning of the Public Records Act 1958, the Public Records (Scotland) Act 1937 or the Public Records Act (Northern Ireland) 1923 [, or in Welsh public records (as defined in the [Government of Wales Act 2006]),] which are open to public inspection in pursuance of that Act, may be copied, and a copy may be supplied to any person, by or with the authority of any officer appointed under that Act, without infringement of copyright."

Note: The words in the internal square brackets in s.49 were substituted by the Government of Wales Act 2006 (c.32), Sch.10 para.24, with effect from May 4, 2007.

Enforcement by local weights and measures authority

Section 107A has been inserted by section 165 of the Criminal Justice and Public   **p.95**
Order Act 1994, with effect from April 6, 2007 (see SI 2007/621).

Search warrants

Section 109(3)(b) has been amended to read as follows: **p.97**

"(b) remains in force for [three months] from the date of its issue."

Note: The words in square brackets in subs.(3)(b) were substituted for the former words "28 days" by the Serious Organised Crime and Police Act 2005 (c.15), Sch.16 para.6, with effect from January 1, 2006.

Section 109(4) should read:

"(4) In executing a warrant issued under this section a constable may seize an article if he reasonably believes that it is evidence that any offence under section [107(1), (2) or (2A)] has been or is about to be committed."

Power of Commissioners of Customs and Excise to make regulations

Section 112(5) has been repealed.   **p.99**

Note: Subs.(5) was repealed by the Commissioners for Revenue and Customs Act 2005 (c.11), Sch.5, with effect from April 18, 2005.

Order as to disposal of infringing copy or other article

p.100 Section 114(6) has been amended to read as follows:

"(6) References in this section to a person having an interest in a copy or other article include any person in whose favour an order could be made in respect of it

[(a) under this section or under section 204 or 231 of this Act;

(b) under section 24D of the Registered Designs Act 1949;

(c) under section 19 of Trade Marks Act 1994 (including that section as applied by regulation 4 of the Community Trade Mark Regulations 2006 (SI 2006/1027)); or

(d) under regulation 1C of the Community Design Regulations 2005 (SI 2005/2339).]"

Note: S.114(6) was amended by the Intellectual Property (Enforcement, etc.) Regulations 2006 (SI 2006/1028), Sch.2 para.7, with effect from April 29, 2006.

Collective exercise of certain rights in relation to cable re-transmission

p.123 In section 144A(1), the word "member" has been repealed.

Note: In subs.(1) the word "member" was repealed by the Intellectual Property (Enforcement, etc.) Regulations 2006 (SI 2006/1028), Sch.4, with effect from April 29, 2006.

Membership of the Tribunal

p.125 Section 146(7) to (11) has been inserted and section 146(8) has been amended to read as follows:

"(7) The Lord Chancellor may exercise his powers to remove a person under subsection (3) or to appoint a person under subsection (4) only with the concurrence of the appropriate senior judge.

(8) The appropriate senior judge is the Lord Chief Justice of England and Wales, unless—

(a) the person to be removed exercises functions [, or the person to be appointed is to exercise functions,] wholly or mainly in Scotland, in which case it is the Lord President of the Court of Session, or

(b) the person to be removed exercises functions [, or the person to be appointed is to exercise functions,] wholly or mainly in Northern Ireland, in which case it is the Lord Chief Justice of Northern Ireland.

(9) The Lord Chief Justice of England and Wales may nominate a judicial office holder (as defined in section 109(4) of the Constitutional Reform Act 2005) to exercise his functions under subsection (7) in relation to the appointment of a person under subsection (4).

(10) The Lord President of the Court of Session may nominate a judge of the Court of Session who is a member of the First or Second Division of the Inner House of that Court to exercise his functions under subsection (7) in relation to the appointment of a person under subsection (4).

(11) The Lord Chief Justice of Northern Ireland may nominate any of the following to exercise his functions under subsection (7) in relation to the appointment of a person under subsection (4)—

(a) the holder of one of the offices listed in Schedule 1 to the Justice (Northern Ireland) Act 2002;

(b) a Lord Justice of Appeal (as defined in section 88 of that Act)."

Note: Subs.(7) to (11) were inserted by the Constitutional Reform Act 2005 (c.4), Sch.4 para.199, with effect from April 3, 2006.

The words in square brackets in s.146(8) were inserted by the Lord Chancellor (Transfer of Functions and Supplementary Provisions) (No.2) Order 2006 (SI 2006/1016), Sch.3, with effect from April 3, 2006.

Qualification for copyright protection

Section 153(2) has been amended to read as follows: p.129

"(2) Subsection (1) does not apply in relation to Crown copyright or Parliamentary copyright (see sections 163 to [166D]) or to copyright subsisting by virtue of section 168 (copyright of certain international organisations)."

Note: The words in square brackets in s.153(2) were substituted by the Government of Wales Act 2006 (c.32), Sch.10 para.25, with effect from May 4, 2007.

Crown copyright

Section 163(1A) has been omitted and section 163(6) has been amended to read   p.134
as follows:

"(6) This section does not apply to a work if, or to the extent that, Parliamentary copyright subsists in the work (see sections 165 and [166D])."

Note: S.163(1A) was omitted and the words in square brackets in s.163(6) were substituted by the Government of Wales Act 2006 (c.32), Sch.10 para.26, with effect from May 4, 2007.

Section 164 has been amended to read as follows: p.134

Copyright in Acts and Measures

"**164.**—(1) Her Majesty is entitled to copyright in every Act of Parliament [, Act of the Scottish Parliament][, [Measure of the National Assembly for Wales, Act of the National Assembly for Wales,] Act of the Northern Ireland Assembly] or Measure of the General Synod of the Church of England.

(2) The copyright subsists
  [(a) in the case of an Act or a Measure of the General Synod of the Church of England, until the end of the period of 50 years from the end of the calendar year in which Royal Assent was given, and
  (b) in the case of a Measure of the National Assembly for Wales, until the end of the period of 50 years from the end of the calendar year in which the Measure was approved by Her Majesty in Council.]"

Note: The words "Measure of the National Assembly for Wales, Act of the National Assembly for Wales," in s.164(1) were inserted and the words in square brackets in s.164(2) were substituted by the Government of Wales Act 2006 (c.32), Sch.10 para.27, with effect from May 4, 2007.

After s.166B, the following have been inserted: p.137

"Copyright in proposed Measures of the National Assembly for Wales

166C.—(1) Copyright in every proposed Assembly Measure introduced into the National Assembly for Wales belongs to the National Assembly for Wales Commission.

(2) Copyright under this section subsists from the time when the text of the proposed Assembly Measure is handed in to the Assembly for introduction—

(a) until the proposed Assembly Measure is approved by Her Majesty in Council, or

(b) if the proposed Assembly Measure is not approved by Her Majesty in Council, until it is withdrawn or rejected or no further proceedings of the Assembly may be taken in respect of it.

(3) References in this Part to Parliamentary copyright (except in section 165) include copyright under this section; and, except as mentioned above, the provisions of this Part apply in relation to copyright under this section as to other Parliamentary copyright.

(4) No other copyright, or right in the nature of copyright, subsists in a proposed Assembly Measure after copyright has once subsisted under this section; but without prejudice to the subsequent operation of this section in relation to a proposed Assembly Measure which, not having been approved by Her Majesty in Council, is later reintroduced into the Assembly.

Copyright in Bills of the National Assembly for Wales

166D.—(1) Copyright in every Bill introduced into the National Assembly for Wales belongs to the National Assembly for Wales Commission.

(2) Copyright under this section subsists from the time when the text of the Bill is handed in to the Assembly for introduction—

(a) until the Bill receives Royal Assent, or

(b) if the Bill does not receive Royal Assent, until it is withdrawn or rejected or no further proceedings of the Assembly may be taken in respect of it.

(3) References in this Part to Parliamentary copyright (except in section 165) include copyright under this section; and, except as mentioned above, the provisions of this Part apply in relation to copyright under this section as to other Parliamentary copyright.

(4) No other copyright, or right in the nature of copyright, subsists in a Bill after copyright has once subsisted under this section; but without prejudice to the subsequent operation of this section in relation to a Bill which, not having received Royal Assent, is later reintroduced into the Assembly."

Note: SS.166C and 166D were inserted by the Government of Wales Act 2006 (c.32), Sch.10 para.28, with effect from May 4, 2007.

Meaning of EEA and related expressions

p.139 Section 172A has been amended to read as follows:

"(1) In this Part—

"the EEA" means the European Economic Area; and

"EEA state" means a member State, Iceland, Liechtenstein or Norway.

(2) References in this Part to a person being [a national of an EEA State] shall be construed in relation to a body corporate as references to its being incorporated under the law of an EEA state.

(3) [...]"

Note: Subs.(1) was substituted, in subs.(2) the words in square brackets were substituted for the former words "an EEA national" and subs.(3) was repealed by the Intellectual Property (Enforcement, etc.) Regulations 2006 (SI 2006/1028), Sch.2 para.8 and Sch.4, with effect from April 29, 2006.

Minor definitions

The definitions of "the Crown" and "parliamentary proceedings" in section 178   **p.142**
have been amended to read as follows:

> "the Crown" includes the Crown in right [of the Scottish Administration [, of the Welsh Assembly Government] or of] Her Majesty's Government in Northern Ireland or in any country outside the United Kingdom to which this Part extends;
>
> "parliamentary proceedings" includes proceedings of the Northern Ireland Assembly [...] [of the Scottish Parliament] or of the European Parliament [and Assembly proceedings within the meaning of section 1(5) of the Government of Wales Act 2006];

Note: The words in the internal square brackets in the definition of "the Crown" and the words in square brackets at the end of the definition of "parliamentary proceedings" were inserted by the Government of Wales Act 2006 (c.32), Sch.10 para.29, with effect from May 4, 2007.

Index of defined expressions

In section 179 the entry for "EEA, EEA national and EEA state" has been   **p.145**
substituted and the definition of "Parliamentary copyright" has been amended to
read as follows:

"the EEA, EEA state and national of an EEA state	section 172A"
Parliamentary copyright	sections 165(2) and (7), [166(6) [, 166A(3) [166B(3) 166C(3) and 166D(3)]]]

Note: S.179 was amended by the Intellectual Property (Enforcement, etc.) Regulations 2006 (SI 2006/1028), Sch.2 para.9, with effect from April 29, 2006.

The definition of "Parliamentary copyright" was further amended by the Government of Wales Act 2006 (c.32), Sch.10 para.30, with effect from May 4, 2007.

Rights in Performances

For Part II of the Act, substitute the following: **p.147**

PART II

RIGHTS IN PERFORMANCES

[CHAPTER 1

INTRODUCTORY]

Rights conferred on performers and persons having recording rights

180.—(1) [Chapter 2 of this Part (economic rights)] confers rights—
  (a) on a performer, by requiring his consent to the exploitation of his performances (see sections 181 to 184), and
  (b) on a person having recording rights in relation to a performance, in relation to recordings made without his consent or that of the performer (see sections 185 to 188),

and creates offences in relation to dealing with or using illicit recordings and certain other related acts (see sections 198 and 201).

[(1A) Rights are also conferred on a performer by the following provisions of Chapter 3 of this Part (moral rights)—

    (a) section 205C (right to be identified);

    (b) section 205F (right to object to derogatory treatment of performance).]

(2) In this Part—

    "performance" means—

        (a) a dramatic performance (which includes dance and mime),

        (b) a musical performance,

        (c) a reading or recitation of a literary work, or

        (d) a performance of a variety act or any similar presentation,

which is, or so far as it is, a live performance given by one or more individuals; and

"recording", in relation to a performance, means a film or sound recording—

        (a) made directly from the live performance.

        (b) made from a broadcast of [...] the performance, or

        (c) made, directly or indirectly, from another recording of the performance.

(3) The rights conferred by this Part apply in relation to performances taking place before the commencement of this Part; but no other act done before commencement, or in pursuance of arrangements made before commencement, shall be regarded as infringing those rights.

(4) The rights conferred by this Part are independent of—

    (a) any copyright in, or moral rights relating to, any work performed or any film or sound recording of, or broadcast including [...] the performance, and

    (b) any other right or obligation arising otherwise than under this Part.

Note:

    (1) The words in square brackets at the beginning of subs.(1) were substituted for the former words "This Part" and subs.(1A) was inserted by the Performances (Moral Rights, etc.) Regulations 2006 (SI 2006/18), reg.5, with effect from February 1, 2006.

    (2) The words ", or cable programme including," in the definition of "recording" in subs.(2) and the words "or cable programme" in subs.(4)(a) were repealed by the Copyright and Related Rights Regulations 2003 (SI 2003/2498), Sch.2 with effect from October 31, 2003. For savings and transitional provisions, see Part 3 of those Regulations.

Qualifying performances

181. A performance is a qualifying performance for the purposes of the provisions of this Part relating to performers' rights if it is given by a qualifying individual (as defined in section 206) or takes place in a qualifying country (as so defined).

Note: Ss.180 and 181 became Chapter 1 of Part 2, the existing cross-headings before ss.180 and 181 were omitted and the cross-heading before s.180 was inserted by the Performances (Moral Rights, etc.) Regulations 2006 (SI 2006/18), reg.4(2), (3), with effect from February 1, 2006.

[CHAPTER 2

ECONOMIC RIGHTS

Performers' rights]

[Consent required for recording, &c. of live performance

182.—(1) A performer's rights are infringed by a person who, without his consent—

(a) makes a recording of the whole or any substantial part of a qualifying performance directly from the live performance,

(b) broadcasts live [...] the whole or any substantial part of a qualifying performance,

(c) makes a recording of the whole or any substantial part of a qualifying performance directly from a broadcast of [...] the live performance.

[...]

(3) In an action for infringement of a performer's rights brought by virtue of this section damages shall not be awarded against a defendant who shows that at the time of the infringement he believed on reasonable grounds that consent had been given.]

Note:

(1) This section was inserted by the Copyright and Related Rights Regulations 1996 (SI 1996/2967), which replaced the old section 182 with effect from December 1, 1996. For savings and transitional provisions, see Part III of those Regulations.

(2) The words", or includes live in a cable programme service," in subs.(1)(b), the words ", or cable programme including," in subs.(1)(c) and subs.(2) were repealed by the Copyright and Related Rights Regulations 2003 (SI 2003/2498), Sch.2 with effect from October 31, 2003. For savings and transitional provisions, see Part 3 of those Regulations. The former subs.(2) provided:

(2) *A performer's rights are not infringed by the making of any such recording by a person for his private and domestic use.*

[Consent required for copying of recording

182A.—(1) A performer's rights are infringed by a person who, without his consent, makes [...] a copy of a recording of the whole or any substantial part of a qualifying performance.

(1A) In subsection (1) making a copy of a recording includes making a copy which is transient or is incidental to some other use of the original recording.

(2) It is immaterial whether the copy is made directly or indirectly.

(3) The right of a performer under this section to authorise or prohibit the making of such copies is referred to in [this Chapter] as "reproduction right".]

Note:

(1) This section was inserted by the Copyright and Related Rights Regulations 1996 (SI 1996/2967), with effect from December 1, 1996. For savings and transitional provisions, see Part III of those Regulations.

(2) The words ", otherwise than for his private and domestic use," in subs.(1) were repealed by the Copyright and Related Rights Regulations 2003 (SI 2003/2498), Sch.2 with effect from October 31, 2003. For savings and transitional provisions, see Part 3 of those Regulations.

(3) Section (1A) was inserted by the Copyright and Related Rights Regulations 2003 (SI2003/2498), Reg.8 with effect from October 31, 2003. For savings and transitional provisions, see Part 3 of those Regulations.

(4) In subs. (3) the words "this Chapter" were substituted for the former words "this Part" by the Performances (Moral Rights, etc.) Regulations 2006 (SI 2006/18), Sch. para.8, with effect from February 1, 2006.

[Consent required for issue of copies to public

182B.—(1) A performer's rights are infringed by a person who, without his consent, issues to the public copies of a recording of the whole or any substantial part of a qualifying performance.

(2) References in this Part to the issue to the public of copies of a recording are to—

    (a) the act of putting into circulation in the EEA copies not previously put into circulation in the EEA by or with the consent of the performer, or

    (b) the act of putting into circulation outside the EEA copies not previously put into circulation in the EEA or elsewhere.

(3) References in this Part to the issue to the public of copies of a recording do not include—

    (a) any subsequent distribution, sale, hiring or loan of copies previously put into circulation (but see section 182C: consent required for rental or lending), or

    (b) any subsequent importation of such copies into the United Kingdom or another EEA state,

except so far as paragraph (a) of subsection (2) applies to putting into circulation in the EEA copies previously put into circulation outside the EEA.

(4) References in this Part to the issue of copies of a recording of a performance include the issue of the original recording of the live performance.

(5) The right of a performer under this section to authorise or prohibit the issue of copies to the public is referred to in [this Chapter] as "distribution right".]

Note:

    (1) This section was inserted by the Copyright and Related Rights Regulations 1996 (SI 1996/2967), with effect from December 1, 1996. For savings and transitional provisions, see Part III of those Regulations.

    (2) In subs.(5) the words "this Chapter" were substituted for the former words "this Part" by the Performances (Moral Rights, etc.) Regulations 2006 (SI 2006/18), Sch. para.8, with effect from February 1, 2006.

[Consent required for rental or lending of copies to public

182C.—(1) A performer's rights are infringed by a person who, without his consent, rents or lends to the public copies of a recording of the whole or any substantial part of a qualifying performance.

(2) In [this Chapter], subject to the following provisions of this section—

    (a) "rental" means making a copy of a recording available for use, on terms that it will or may be returned, for direct or indirect economic or commercial advantage, and

    (b) "lending" means making a copy of a recording available for use, on terms that it will or may be returned, otherwise than for direct or indirect economic or commercial advantage, through an establishment which is accessible to the public.

(3) The expressions "rental" and "lending" do not include—

    (a) making available for the purpose of public performance, playing or showing in public [or communication to the public];

    (b) making available for the purpose of exhibition in public; or

    (c) making available for on-the-spot reference use.

(4) The expression "lending" does not include making available between establishments which are accessible to the public.

(5) Where lending by an establishment accessible to the public gives rise to a payment the amount of which does not go beyond what is necessary to cover the operating costs of the establishment, there is no direct or indirect economic or commercial advantage for the purposes of this section.

(6) References in [this Chapter] to the rental or lending of copies of a recording of a performance include the rental or lending of the original recording of the live performance.

(7) In [this Chapter]—

"rental right" means the right of a performer under this section to authorise or prohibit the rental of copies to the public, and

"lending right" means the right of a performer under this section to authorise or prohibit the lending of copies to the public.]

Note:

(1) This section was inserted by the Copyright and Related Rights Regulations 1996 (SI 1996/2967), with effect from December 1, 1996. For savings and transitional provisions, see Part III of those Regulations.

(2) The words in square brackets in subs.(3)(a) were substituted for the former words ", broadcasting or inclusion in a cable programme service" by the Copyright and Related Rights Regulations 2003 (SI 2003/2498), Sch.1, para.6 with effect from October 31, 2003. For savings and transitional provisions, see Part 3 of those Regulations.

(3) In subs.(2), (6) and (7) the words "this Chapter" were substituted for the former words "this Part" by the Performances (Moral Rights, etc.) Regulations 2006 (SI 2006/18), Sch. para.8, with effect from February 1, 2006.

[Consent required for making available to the public

182CA.—(1) A performer's rights are infringed by a person who, without his consent, makes available to the public a recording of the whole or any substantial part of a qualifying performance by electronic transmission in such a way that members of the public may access the recording from a place and at a time individually chosen by them.

(2) The right of a performer under this section to authorise or prohibit the making available to the public of a recording is referred to in [this Chapter] as "making available right".]

Note:

(1) This section was inserted by the Copyright and Related Rights Regulations 2003 (SI 2003/2498), reg.7 with effect from October 31, 2003. For savings and transitional provisions, see Part 3 of those Regulations.

(2) In subs.(2) the words "this Chapter" were substituted for the former words "this Part" by the Performances (Moral Rights, etc.) Regulations 2006 (SI 2006/18), Sch. para.8, with effect from February 1, 2006.

[Right to equitable remuneration for exploitation of sound recording

182D.—(1) Where a commercially published sound recording of the whole or any substantial part of a qualifying performance—

(a) is played in public, or

[(b) is communicated to the public otherwise than by its being made available to the public in the way mentioned in section 182CA(1),]

the performer is entitled to equitable remuneration from the owner of the copyright in the sound recording.

[(1A) In subsection (1), the reference to publication of a sound recording includes making it available to the public by electronic transmission in such a way that members of the public may access it from a place and at a time individually chosen by them.]

(2) The right to equitable remuneration under this section may not be assigned by the performer except to a collecting society for the purpose of enabling it to enforce the right on his behalf.

The right is, however, transmissible by testamentary disposition or by operation of law as personal or moveable property; and it may be assigned or further transmitted by any person into whose hands it passes.

(3) The amount payable by way of equitable remuneration is as agreed by or on behalf of the persons by and to whom it is payable, subject to the following provisions.

(4) In default of agreement as to the amount payable by way of equitable remuneration, the person by or to whom it is payable may apply to the Copyright Tribunal to determine the amount payable.

(5) A person to or by whom equitable remuneration is payable may also apply to the Copyright Tribunal—

(a) to vary any agreement as to the amount payable, or

(b) to vary any previous determination of the Tribunal as to that matter;

but except with the special leave of the Tribunal no such application may be made within twelve months from the date of a previous determination.

An order made on an application under this subsection has effect from the date on which it is made or such later date as may be specified by the Tribunal.

(6) On an application under this section the Tribunal shall consider the matter and make such order as to the method of calculating and paying equitable remuneration as it may determine to be reasonable in the circumstances, taking into account the importance of the contribution of the performer to the sound recording.

(7) An agreement is of no effect in so far as it purports—

(a) to exclude or restrict the right to equitable remuneration under this section, or

(b) to prevent a person questioning the amount of equitable remuneration or to restrict the powers of the Copyright Tribunal under this section.

[(8) In this section "collecting society" means a society or other organisation which has as its main object, or one of its main objects, the exercise of the right to equitable remuneration on behalf of more than one performer.]

Note:

(1) This section was inserted by the Copyright and Related Rights Regulations 1996 (SI 1996/2967), with effect from December 1, 1996. For savings and transitional provisions, see Part III of those Regulations.

(2) Subsection (1)(b) was substituted by the Copyright and Related Rights Regulations 2003 (SI 2003/2498), reg.7 with effect from October 31, 2003. For savings and transitional provisions, see Part 3 of those Regulations. The former subs.(1)(b) provided:

(b) *is included in a broadcast or cable programme service,*

(3) Subs.(1A) and (8) were inserted by the Performances (Moral Rights, etc.) Regulations 2006 (SI 2006/18), Sch. para.3, with effect from February 1, 2006.

Infringement of performer's rights by use of recording made without consent

183. A performer's rights are infringed by a person who, without his consent—

(a) shows or plays in public the whole or any substantial part of a qualifying performance, or

(b) [communicates to the public] the whole or any substantial part of a qualifying performance,

by means of a recording which was, and which that person knows or has reason to believe was, made without the performer's consent.

Note: The words in square brackets in subs.(b) were substituted for the former words "broadcasts or includes in a cable programme service" by the Copyright and Related Rights Regulations 2003 (SI 2003/2498), Sch.1, para.13 with effect from October 31, 2003. For savings and transitional provisions, see Part 3 of those Regulations.

Infringement of performer's rights by importing, possessing or dealing with illicit recording

184.—(1) A performer's rights are infringed by a person who, without his consent—

(a) imports into the United Kingdom otherwise than for his private and domestic use, or

(b) in the course of a business possesses, sells or lets for hire, offers or exposes for sale or hire, or distributes,

a recording of a qualifying performance which is, and which that person knows or has reason to believe is, an illicit recording.

(2) Where in an action for infringement of a performer's rights brought by virtue of this section a defendant shows that the illicit recording was innocently acquired by him or a predecessor in title of his, the only remedy available against him in respect of the infringement is damages not exceeding a reasonable payment in respect of the act complained of.

(3) In subsection (2) "innocently acquired" means that the person acquiring the recording did not know and had no reason to believe that it was an illicit recording.

Rights of person having recording rights

Exclusive recording contracts and persons having recording rights

185.—(1) In [this Chapter] an "exclusive recording contract" means a contract between a performer and another person under which that person is entitled to the exclusion of all other persons (including the performer) to make recordings of one or more of his performances with a view to their commercial exploitation.

(2) References in this Part to a "person having recording rights", in relation to a performance, are (subject to subsection (3)) to a person—

(a) who is party to and has the benefit of an exclusive recording contract to which the performance is subject, or

(b) to whom the benefit of such a contract has been assigned,

and who is a qualifying person.

(3) If a performance is subject to an exclusive recording contract but the person mentioned in subsection (2) is not a qualifying person, references in [this Chapter] to a "person having recording rights" in relation to the performance are to any person—

(a) who is licensed by such a person to make recordings of the performance with a view to their commercial exploitation, or

(b) to whom the benefit of such a licence has been assigned,

and who is a qualifying person.

(4) In this section "with a view to commercial exploitation" means with a view to the recordings being sold or let for hire, or shown or played in public.

Note: In subs. (1) to (3) the words "this Chapter" were substituted for the former words "this Part" by the Performances (Moral Rights, etc.) Regulations 2006 (SI 2006/18), Sch. para.8, with effect from February 1, 2006.

Consent required for recording of performance subject to exclusive contract

186.—(1) A person infringes the rights of a person having recording rights in relation to a performance who, without his consent or that of the performer, makes a recording of the whole or any substantial part of the performance [...].

(2) In an action for infringement of those rights brought by virtue of this section damages shall not be awarded against a defendant who shows that at the time of the infringement he believed on reasonable grounds that consent had been given.

Note: The words ", otherwise that for his private and domestic use" were repealed from subs.(1) by the Copyright and Related Rights Regulations 2003 (SI 2003/2498), Sch.2 with effect from October 31, 2003. For savings and transitional provisions, see Part 3 of those Regulations.

Infringement of recording rights by use of recording made without consent

187.—(1) A person infringes the rights of a person having recording rights in relation to a performance who, without his consent or, in the case of a qualifying performance, that of the performer—

(a) shows or plays in public the whole or any substantial part of the performance, or

(b) [communicates to the public] the whole or any substantial part of the performance,

by means of a recording which was, and which that person knows or has reason to believe was, made without the appropriate consent.

(2) The reference in subsection (1) to "the appropriate consent" is to the consent of—

(a) the performer, or

(b) the person who at the time the consent was given had recording rights in relation to the performance (or, if there was more than one such person, of all of them).

Note: The words in square brackets in subs.(1)(b) were substituted for the former words "broadcasts or includes in a cable programme service" by the Copyright and Related Rights Regulations 2003 (SI 2003/2498), Sch.1, para.13 with effect from October 31, 2003. For savings and transitional provisions, see Part 3 of those Regulations.

Infringement of recording rights by importing, possessing or dealing with illicit recording

188.—(1) A person infringes the rights of a person having recording rights in relation to a performance who, without his consent or, in the case of a qualifying performance, that of the performer—

(a) imports into the United Kingdom otherwise than for his private and domestic use, or

(b) in the course of a business possesses, sells or lets for hire, offers or exposes for sale or hire, or distributes,

a recording of the performance which is, and which that person knows or has reason to believe is, an illicit recording.

(2) Where in an action for infringement of those rights brought by virtue of this section a defendant shows that the illicit recording was innocently acquired by him or a predecessor in title of his, the only remedy available against him in respect of the infringement is damages not exceeding a reasonable payment in respect of the act complained of.

(3) In subsection (2) "innocently acquired" means that the person acquiring the recording did not know and had no reason to believe that it was an illicit recording.

Exceptions to rights conferred

Acts permitted notwithstanding rights conferred by [this Chapter]

189. The provisions of Schedule 2 specify acts which may be done notwithstanding the rights conferred by [this Chapter], being acts which correspond broadly to certain of those specified in Chapter III of Part I (acts permitted notwithstanding copyright).

Note: In s.189 and the heading preceding it the words "this Chapter" were substituted in each place for the former words "this Part" by the Performances (Moral Rights, etc.) Regulations 2006 (SI 2006/18), Sch. para.8, with effect from February 1, 2006.

Power of tribunal to give consent on behalf of performer in certain cases

190.—[(1) The Copyright Tribunal may, on the application of a person wishing to make a copy of a recording of a performance, give consent in a case where the identity or whereabouts of the person entitled to the reproduction right cannot be ascertained by reasonable inquiry.]

(2) Consent given by the Tribunal has effect as consent of [the person entitled to the reproduction right] for the purposes of—
    (a) the provisions of [this Chapter] relating to performers' rights, and
    (b) section 198(3)(a) (criminal liability: sufficient consent in relation to qualifying performances),
and may be given subject to any conditions specified in the Tribunal's order.

(3) The Tribunal shall not give consent under subsection (1)(a) except after the service or publication of such notices as may be required by rules made under section 150 (general procedural rules) or as the Tribunal may in any particular case direct.

(4) [...]

(5) In any case the Tribunal shall take into account the following factors—
    (a) whether the original recording was made with the performer's consent and is lawfully in the possession or control of the person proposing to make the further recording;
    (b) whether the making of the further recording is consistent with the obligations of the parties to the arrangements under which, or is otherwise consistent with the purposes for which, the original recording was made.

(6) Where the Tribunal gives consent under this section it shall, in default of agreement between the applicant and [the person entitled to the reproduction right], make such order as it thinks fit as to the payment to be made to [that person] in consideration of consent being given.

Note:

(1) Subsection (1) was inserted, subss.(2) and (6) were amended and subs.(4) deleted by the Copyright and Related Rights Regulations 1996 (SI 1996/2967), with effect from December 1, 1996. The old subss.(1) and (4) provided:

> (1) *The Copyright Tribunal may, on the application of a person wishing to make a recording from a previous recording of a performance, give consent in a case where—*
>> (a) *the identity or whereabouts of a performer cannot be ascertained by reasonable enquiry, or*
>> (b) *a performer unreasonably withholds his consent.*
> (4) *The Tribunal shall not give consent under subsection (1)(b) unless satisfied that the performer's reasons for withholding consent do not include the protection of any legitimate interest of his; but it shall be for the performer to show what his reasons are for withholding consent, and in default of evidence as to his reasons the Tribunal may draw such inferences as it thinks fit.*

For savings and transitional provisions, see Part III of those Regulations.

(2) In subs.(2)(a) the words "this Chapter" were substituted for the former words "this Part" by the Performances (Moral Rights, etc.) Regulations 2006 (SI 2006/18), Sch. para.8, with effect from February 1, 2006.

[Duration of rights]

Duration of rights

[**191.**—(1) The following provisions have effect with respect to the duration of the rights conferred by [this Chapter].

(2) The rights conferred by [this Chapter] in relation to a performance expire—

(a) at the end of the period of 50 years from the end of the calender year in which the performance takes place, or

(b) if during that period a recording of the performances is released, 50 years from the end of the calendar year in which it is released,

subject as follows.

(3) For the purposes of subsection (2) a recording is "released" when it is first published, played or shown in public [or communicated to the public]; but in determining whether a recording has been released no account shall be taken of any unauthorised act.

(4) Where a performer is not a national of an EEA state, the duration of the rights conferred by [this Chapter] in relation to his performance is that to which the performance is entitled in the country of which he is a national, provided that does not exceed the period which would apply under subsections (2) and (3).

(5) If or to the extent that the application of subsection (4) would be at variance with an international obligation to which the United Kingdom became subject prior to 29th October 1993, the duration of the rights conferred by [this Chapter] shall be as specified in subsections (2) and (3).]

Note:

(1) The heading preceding this section was amended by the Copyright and Related Rights Regulations 1996 (SI 1996/2967), with effect from December 1, 1996. For savings and transitional provisions, see Part III of theose Regulations.

(2) This section was inserted by the Duration of Copyright and Rights in Performances Regulations 1995 (SI 1995/3297), which replaced the old s.191 with effect from January 1, 1996. The old s.191 and heading preceding it provided:

> *Duration and transmission of rights; consent*

> **Duration of rights**
> **191.** *The rights conferred by this Part continue to subsist in relation to a performance until the end of the period of 50 years from the end of the calendar year in which the performance takes place.*

For savings and transitional provisions, see Part III of those Regulations.

(3) The words in square brackets in subs.(3) were substituted for the former words ", broadcast or included in a cable programme service" by the Copyright and Related Rights Regulations 2003 (SI 2003/2498), Sch.1, para.8 with effect from October 31, 2003. For savings and transitional provisions, see Part 3 of those Regulations.

(4) In subs. (1), (2), (4) and (5) the words "this Chapter" were substituted for the former words "this Part" by the Performances (Moral Rights, etc.) Regulations 2006 (SI 2006/18), Sch. para.8, with effect from February 1, 2006.

[Performers' property rights

Performers' property rights

191A.—(1) The following rights conferred by [this Chapter] on a performer—
reproduction right (section 182A),
distribution right (section 182B),
rental right and lending right (section 182C),
[making available right (section 182CA),]
are property rights ("a [...] performer's property rights").

(2) References in [this Chapter] to the consent of the performer shall be construed in relation to a performer's property rights as references to the consent of the rights owner.

(3) Where different persons are (whether in consequence of a partial assignment or otherwise) entitled to different aspects of a performer's property rights in relation to a performance, the rights owner for any purpose of [this Chapter] is the person who is entitled to the aspect of those rights relevant for that purpose.

(4) Where a performer's property rights (or any aspect of them) is owned by more than one person jointly, references in [this Chapter] to the rights owner are to all the owners, so that, in particular, any requirement of the licence of the rights owner requires the licence of all of them.]

Note:

(1) This section and the heading preceding it were inserted by the Copyright and Related Rights Regulations 1996 (SI 1996/2967), with effect from December 1, 1996. For savings and transitional provisions, see Part III of those Regulations.

(2) The words in square brackets in subs.(1) were inserted by the Copyright and Related Rights Regulations 2003 (SI 2003/2498), reg.7 with effect from October 31, 2003. For savings and transitional provisions, see Part 3 of those Regulations.

(3) In subs.(1) to (4) the words "this Chapter" were substituted for the former words "this Part" by the Performances (Moral Rights, etc.) Regulations 2006 (SI 2006/18), Sch. para.8, with effect from February 1, 2006.

(4) In subs.(1) the word "a" formerly appearing before the words "performers' property rights" was omitted by the Performances (Moral Rights, etc.) Regulations 2006 (SI 2006/18), Sch. para.4, with effect from February 1, 2006.

[Assignment and licences

191B.—(1) A performer's property rights are transmissible by assignment, by testamentary disposition or by operation of law, as personal or moveable property.

(2) An assignment or other transmission of a performer's property rights may be partial, that is, limited so as to apply—

(a) to one or more, but not all, of the things requiring the consent of the rights owner;

(b) to part, but not the whole, of the period for which the rights are to subsist.

(3) An assignment of a performer's property rights is not effective unless it is in writing signed by or on behalf of the assignor.

(4) A licence granted by the owner of a performer's property rights is binding on every successor in title to his interest in the rights, except a purchaser in good faith for valuable consideration and without notice (actual or constructive) of the licence or a person deriving title from such a purchaser; and references in [this Chapter] to doing anything with, or without, the licence of the rights owner shall be construed accordingly.]

> *Note:*
>
> (1) This section was inserted by the Copyright and Related Rights Regulations 1996 (SI 1996/2967), with effect from December 1, 1996. For savings and transitional provisions, see Part III of those Regulations.
>
> (2) In subs.(4) the words "this Chapter" were substituted for the former words "this Part" by the Performances (Moral Rights, etc.) Regulations 2006 (SI 2006/18), Sch. para.8, with effect from February 1, 2006.

[Prospective ownership of a performer's property rights

191C.—(1) This section applies where by an agreement made in relation to a future recording of a performance, and signed by or on behalf of the performer, the performer purports to assign his performer's property rights (wholly or partially) to another person.

(2) If on the rights coming into existence the assignee or another person claiming under him would be entitled as against all other persons to require the rights to be vested in him, they shall vest in the assignee or his successor in title by virtue of this subsection.

(3) A licence granted by a prospective owner of a performer's property rights is binding on every successor in title to his interest (or prospective interest) in the rights, except a purchaser in good faith for valuable consideration and without notice (actual or constructive) of the licence or a person deriving title from such a purchaser.

References in [this Chapter] to doing anything with, or without, the licence of the rights owner shall be construed accordingly.

(4) In subsection (3) "prospective owner" in relation to a performer's property rights means a person who is prospectively entitled to those rights by virtue of such an agreement as is mentioned in subsection (1).]

> *Note:*
>
> (1) This section was inserted by the Copyright and Related Rights Regulations 1996 (SI 1996/2967), with effect from December 1, 1996. For savings and transitional provisions, see Part III of those Regulations.
>
> (2) In subs.(3) the words "this Chapter" were substituted for the former words "this Part" by the Performances (Moral Rights, etc.) Regulations 2006 (SI 2006/18), Sch. para.8, with effect from February 1, 2006.

[Exclusive licences

191D.—(1) In [this Chapter] an "exclusive licence" means a licence in writing signed by or on behalf of the owner of a performer's property rights authorising the licensee to the exclusion of all other persons, including the person granting the licence, to do anything requiring the consent of the rights owner.

(2) The licensee under an exclusive licence has the same rights against a successor in title who is bound by the licence as he has against the person granting the licence.]

Note:
(1) This section was inserted by the Copyright and Related Rights Regulations 1996 (SI 1996/2967), with effect from December 1, 1996. For savings and transitional provisions, see Part III of those Regulations.
(2) In subs.(1) the words "this Chapter" were substituted for the former words "this Part" by the Performances (Moral Rights, etc.) Regulations 2006 (SI 2006/18), Sch. para.8, with effect from February 1, 2006.

[Performer's property right to pass under will with unpublished original recording

191E. Where under a bequest (whether general or specific) a person is entitled beneficially or otherwise to any material thing containing an original recording of a performance which was not published before the death of the testator, the bequest shall, unless a contrary intention is indicated in the testator's will or a codicil to it, be construed as including any performer's rights in relation to the recording to which the testator was entitled immediately before his death.]

Note: This section was inserted by the Copyright and Related Rights Regulations 1996 (SI 1996/2967), with effect from December 1, 1996. For savings and transitional provisions, see Part III of those Regulations.

[Presumption of transfer of rental right in case of film production agreement

191F.—(1) Where an agreement concerning film production is concluded between a performer and a film producer, the performer shall be presumed, unless the agreement provides to the contrary, to have transferred to the film producer any rental right in relation to the film arising from the inclusion of a recording of his performance in the film.

(2) Where this section applies, the absence of signature by or on behalf of the performer does not exclude the operation of section 191C (effect of purported assignment of future rights).

(3) The reference in subsection (1) to an agreement concluded between a performer and a film producer includes any agreement having effect between those persons, whether made by them directly or though intermediaries.

(4) Section 191G (right to equitable remuneration on transfer of rental right) applies where there is a presumed transfer by virtue of this section as in the case of an actual transfer.]

Note: This section was inserted by the Copyright and Related Rights Regulations 1996 (SI 1996/2967), with effect from December 1, 1996. For savings and transitional provisions, see Part III of those Regulations.

[Right to equitable remuneration where rental right transferred

191G.—(1) Where a performer has transferred his rental right concerning a sound recording or a film to the producer of the sound recording or film, he retains the right to equitable remuneration for the rental.

The reference above to the transfer of rental right by one person to another includes any arrangement having that effect, whether made by them directly or through intermediaries.

(2) The right to equitable remuneration under this section may not be assigned by the performer except to a collecting society for the purpose of enabling it to enforce the right on his behalf.

The right is, however, transmissible by testamentary disposition or by operation of law as personal or moveable property; and it may be assigned or further transmitted by any person into whose hands it passes.

(3) Equitable remuneration under this section is payable by the person for the time being entitled to the rental right, that is, the person to whom the right was transferred or any successor in title of his.

(4) The amount payable by way of equitable remuneration is as agreed by or on behalf of the persons by and to whom it is payable, subject to section 191H (reference of amount to Copyright Tribunal).

(5) An agreement is of no effect in so far as it purports to exclude or restrict the right to equitable remuneration under this section.

(6) In this section a "collecting society" means a society or other organisation which has as its main object, or one of its main objects, the exercise of the right to equitable remuneration on behalf of more than one performer.]

Note: This section was inserted by the Copyright and Related Rights Regulations 1996 (SI 1996/2967), with effect from December 1 1996. For savings and transitional provisions, see Part III of those Regulations.

[Equitable remuneration: reference of amount to Copyright Tribunal

191H.—(1) In default of agreement as to the amount payable by way of equitable remuneration under section 191G, the person by or to whom it is payable may also apply to the Copyright Tribunal to determine the amount payable.

(2) A person to or by whom equitable remuneration is payable may also apply to the Copyright Tribunal—

(a) to vary any agreement as to the amount payable, or

(b) to vary any previous determination of the Tribunal as to that matter;

but except with the special leave of the Tribunal no such application may be made within twelve months from the date of a previous determination.

An order made on an application under this subsection has effect from the date on which it is made or such later date as may be specified by the Tribunal.

(3) On an application under this section the Tribunal shall consider the matter and make such order as to the method of calculating and paying equitable remuneration as it may determine to be reasonable in the circumstances, taking into account the importance of the contribution of the performer to the film or sound recording.

(4) Remuneration shall not be considered inequitable merely because it was paid by way of a single payment or at the time of the transfer of the rental right.

(5) An agreement is of no effect in so far as it purports to prevent a person questioning the amount of equitable remuneration or to restrict the powers of the Copyright Tribunal under this section.]

Note: This section was inserted by the Copyright and Related Rights Regulations 1996 (SI 1996/2967), with effect from December 1, 1996. For savings and transitional provisions, see Part III of those Regulations.

[Infringement actionable by rights owner

191I.—(1) An infringement of a performer's property rights is actionable by the rights owner.

(2) In an action for infringement of a performer's property rights all such relief by way of damages, injunctions, accounts or otherwise is available to the plaintiff as is available in respect of the infringement of any other property right.

(3) This section has effect subject to the following provisions of [this Chapter].]

Note:

(1) This section was inserted by the Copyright and Related Rights Regulations 1996 (SI 1996/2967), with effect from December 1, 1996. For savings and transitional provisions, see Part III of those Regulations.

(2) In subs.(3) the words "this Chapter" were substituted for the former words "this Part" by the Performances (Moral Rights, etc.) Regulations 2006 (SI 2006/18), Sch. para.8, with effect from February 1, 2006.

[Provisions as to damages in infringement action

191J.—(1) Where in an action for infringement of a performer's property rights it is shown that at the time of the infringement the defendant did not know, and had no reason to believe, that the rights subsisted in the recording to which the action relates, the plaintiff is not entitled to damages against him, but without prejudice to any other remedy.

(2) The court may in an action for infringement of a performer's property rights having regard to all the circumstances, and in particular to—

(a) the flagrancy of the infringement, and

(b) any benefit accruing to the defendant by reason of the infringement,

award such additional damages as the justice of the case may require.]

Note: This section was inserted by the Copyright and Related Rights Regulations 1996 (SI 1996/2967), with effect from December 1, 1996. For savings and transitional provisions, see Part III of those Regulations.

[Injunctions against service providers

191JA.—(1) The High Court (in Scotland, the Court of Session) shall have power to grant an injunction against a service provider, where that service provider has actual knowledge of another person using their service to infringe a performer's property right.

(2) In determining whether a service provider has actual knowledge for the purpose of this section, a court shall take into account all matters which appear to it in the particular circumstances to be relevant and, amongst other things, shall have regard to—

(a) whether a service provider has received a notice through a means of contact made available in accordance with regulation 6(1)(c) of the Electronic Commerce (EC Directive) Regulations 2002 (SI 2002/2013); and

(b) the extent to which any notice includes—

(i) the full name and address of the sender of the notice;

(ii) details of the infringement in question.

(3) In this section "service provider" has the meaning given to it by regulation 2 of the Electronic Commerce (EC Directive) Regulations 2002.

(4) Section 177 applies in respect of this section as it applies in respect of Part 1.]

Note: This section was inserted by Copyright and Related Rights Regulations 2003 (SI 2003/2498), reg.27 with effect from October 31, 2003. For savings and transitional provisions, see Part 3 of those Regulations.

[Undertaking to take licence of right in infringement proceedings

191K.—(1) If in proceedings for infringement of a performer's property rights in respect of which a licence is available as of right under paragraph 17 of Schedule 2A (powers exercisable in consequence of competition report) the defendant undertakes to take a licence on such terms as may be agreed or, in default of agreement, settled by the Copyright Tribunal under that paragraph—

    (a) no injunction shall be granted against him,

    (b) no order for delivery up shall be made under section 195, and

    (c) the amount recoverable against him by way of damages or on an account of profits shall not exceed double the amount which would have been payable by him as licensee if such a licence on those terms had been granted before the earliest infringement.

(2) An undertaking may be given at any time before final order in the proceedings, without any admission of liability.

(3) Nothing in this section affects the remedies available in respect of an infringement committed before licences of right were available.]

Note: This section was inserted by the Copyright and Related Rights Regulations 1996 (SI 1996/2967), with effect from December 1, 1996. For savings and transitional provisions, see Part III of those Regulations.

[Rights and remedies for exclusive licensee

191L.—(1) An exclusive licensee has, except against the owner of a performer's property rights, the same rights and remedies in respect of matters occurring after the grant of the licence as if the licence had been an assignment.

(2) His rights and remedies are concurrent with those of the rights owner; and references in the relevant provisions of [this Chapter] to the rights owner shall be construed accordingly.

(3) In an action brought by an exclusive licensee by virtue of this section a defendant may avail himself of any defence which would have been available to him if the action had been brought by the rights owner.]

Note:

    (1) This section was inserted by the Copyright and Related Rights Regulations 1996 (SI 1996/2967), with effect from December 1, 1996. For savings and transitional provisions, see Part III of those Regulations.

    (2) In subs.(2) the words "this Chapter" were substituted for the former words "this Part" by the Performances (Moral Rights, etc.) Regulations 2006 (SI 2006/18), Sch. para.8, with effect from February 1, 2006.

[Exercise of concurrent rights

191M.—(1) Where an action for infringement of a performer's property rights brought by the rights owner or an exclusive licensee relates (wholly or partly) to an infringement in respect of which they have concurrent rights of action, the rights owner or, as the case may be, the exclusive licensee may not, without the leave of the court, proceed with the action unless the other is either joined as plaintiff or added as a defendant.

(2) A rights owner or exclusive licensee who is added as a defendant in pursuance of subsection (1) is not liable for any costs in the action unless he takes part in the proceedings.

(3) The above provisions do not affect the granting of interlocutory relief on an application by the rights owner or exclusive licensee alone.

(4) Where an action for infringement of a performer's property rights is brought which relates (wholly or partly) to an infringement in respect of which the rights owner and an exclusive licensee have or had concurrent rights of action—

    (a) the court shall in assessing damages take into account—

  (i) the terms of the licence, and
  (ii) any pecuniary remedy already awarded or available to either of
       them in respect of the infringement;
  (b) no account of profits shall be directed if an award of damages has been
      made, or an account of profits has been directed, in favour of the other of
      them in respect of the infringement; and
  (c) the court shall if an account of profits is directed apportion the profits be-
      tween them as the court considers just, subject to any agreement be-
      tween them;
and these provisions apply whether or not the rights owner and the exclusive licensee are both parties to the action.

(5) The owner of a performer's property rights shall notify any exclusive licensee having concurrent rights before applying for an order under section 195
(order for delivery up) or exercising the right conferred by section 196 (right of
seizure); and the court may on the application of the licensee make such order
under section 195 or, as the case may be, prohibiting or permitting the exercise
by the rights owner of the right conferred by section 196, as it thinks fit having
regard to the terms of the licence.]

Note: This section was inserted by the Copyright and Related Rights Regulations 1996
(SI 1996/2967), with effect from December 1, 1996. For savings and transitional provisions, see Part III of those Regulations.

[Non property rights

Performers' non-property rights

  192A.—(1) The rights conferred on a performer by—
    section 182 (consent required for recording, &c. of live performance),
    section 183 (infringement of performer's rights by use of recording made
       without consent), and
    section 184 (infringement of performer's rights importing, possessing or
       dealing with illicit recording),
are not assignable or transmissible, except to the following extent.
  They are referred to in [this Chapter] as "[…] performer's non-property rights".
  (2) On the death of a person entitled to any such right—
    (a) the right passes to such person as he may by testamentary disposition
        specifically direct, and
    (b) if or to the extent that there is no such direction, the right is exercisable
        by his personal representatives.
  (3) References in [this Chapter] to the performer, in the context of the person
having any such right, shall be construed as references to the person for the time
being entitled to exercise those rights.
  (4) Where by virtue of subsection (2)(a) a right becomes exercisable by more
than one person, it is exercisable by each of them independently of the other or
others.
  (5) Any damages recovered by personal representatives by virtue of this section in respect of an infringement after a person's death shall devolve as part of
his estate as if the right of action had subsisted and been vested in him immediately before his death.]

Note:

  (1) See the Note to section 192B.
  (2) In subs.(1) the word "a" formerly appearing before the words "performers' non-

property rights" was omitted by the Performances (Moral Rights, etc.) Regulations 2006 (SI 2006/18), Sch. para.5, with effect from February 1, 2006.

(3) In s.192A(1) and (3) the words "this Chapter" were substituted for the former words "this Part" by the Performances (Moral Rights, etc.) Regulations 2006 (SI 2006/18), Sch. para.8, with effect from February 1, 2006

[Transmissibility of rights of person having recording rights

192B.—(1) The rights conferred by [this Chapter] on a person having recording rights are not assignable or transmissible.

(2) This does not affect section 185(2)(b) or (3)(b), so far as those provisions confer rights under [this Chapter] on a person to whom the benefit of a contract or licence is assigned.]

Note:

(1) Sections 192A and 192B and the heading preceding them were inserted by the Copyright and Related Rights Regulations 1996 (SI 1996/2967), replaced the old s.192 with effect from December 1, 1996. The old s.192 provided:

> **Transmission of rights**
>
> **192.**—(1) *The rights conferred by this Part are not assignable or transmissible, except to the extent that performers' rights are transmissible in accordance with the following provisions.*
>
> (2) *On the death of a person entitled to performer's rights—*
> (a)
> *the rights pass to such person as he may by testamentary disposition specifically direct, and*
> (b)
> *if or to the extent that there is no such direction, the rights are exercisable by his personal representatives;*
> *and references in this Part to the performer, in the context of the person having performers' rights, shall be construed as references to the person for the time being entitled to exercise those rights.*
>
> (3) *Where by virtue of subsection (2)(a) a right becomes exercisable by more than one person, it is exercisable by each of them independently of the other or others.*
>
> (4) *The above provisions do not affect section 185(2)(b) or (3)(b), so far as those provisions confer rights under this Part on a person to whom the benefit of a contract or licence is assigned.*
>
> (5) *Any damages recovered by personal representatives by virtue of this section in respect of an infringement after a person's death shall devolve as part of his estate as if the right of action had subsisted and been vested in him immediately before his death.*

For savings and transitional provisions, see Part III of those Regulations.

(2) In subs.(1) and (2) the words "this Chapter" were substituted for the former words "this Part" by the Performances (Moral Rights, etc.) Regulations 2006 (SI 2006/18), Sch. para.8, with effect from February 1, 2006.

Consent

193.—(1) Consent for the purposes of [this Chapter] [by a person having a performer's non-property rights, or by a person having recording rights,] may be given in relation to a specific performance, a specified description of performances or performances generally, and may relate to past or future performances.

(2) A person having recording rights in a performance is bound by any consent given by a person through whom he derives his rights under the exclusive record-

ing contract or licence in question, in the same way as if the consent had been given by him.

(3) Where [a performer's non-property right] passes to another person, any consent binding on the person previously entitled binds the person to whom the right passes in the same way as if the consent had been given by him.

Note:

(1) Subsections (1) and (3) are printed as amended by the Copyright and Related Rights Regulations 1996 (SI 1996/2967), with effect from December 1, 1996. For savings and transitional provisions, see Part III of thesoe Regulations.

(2) In subs.(1) the words "this Chapter" were substituted for the former words "this Part" by the Performances (Moral Rights, etc.) Regulations 2006 (SI 2006/18), Sch. para.8, with effect from February 1, 2006.

Remedies for infringement

Infringement actionable as breach of statutory duty

194. An infringement of [—
   (a) a performer's non-property rights, or
   (b) any right conferred by [this Chapter] on a person having recording rights,]
is actionable by the person entitled to the right as a breach of statutory duty.

Note:

(1) Section 194 is printed as amended by the Copyright and Related Rights Regulations 1996 (SI 1996/2967), with effect from December 1, 1996, which also deleted the heading before the section: *"Remedies for infringement"*. For savings and transitional provisions, see Part III of those Regulations.

(2) In subs.(b) the words "this Chapter" were substituted for the former words "this Part" by the Performances (Moral Rights, etc.) Regulations 2006 (SI 2006/18), Sch. para.8, with effect from February 1, 2006.

[Delivery up or seizure of illicit recordings]

Order for delivery up

195.—(1) Where a person has in his possession, custody or control in the course of a business an illicit recording of a performance, a person having performer's rights or recording rights in relation to the performance under [this Chapter] may apply to the court for an order that the recording be delivered up to him or to such other person as the court may direct.

(2) An application shall not be made after the end of the period specified in section 203; and no order shall be made unless the court also makes, or it appears to the court that there are grounds for making, an order under section 204 (order as to disposal of illicit recording).

(3) A person to whom a recording is delivered up in pursuance of an order under this section shall, if an order under section 204 is not made, retain it pending the making of an order, or the decision not to make an order, under that section.

(4) Nothing in this section affects any other power of the court.

Note:

(1) The heading preceding this section was inserted by the Copyright and Related Rights Regulations 1996 (SI 1996/2967), with effect from December 1, 1996.

(2) In subs.(1) the words "this Chapter" were substituted for the former words "this

Part" by the Performances (Moral Rights, etc.) Regulations 2006 (SI 2006/18), Sch. para.8, with effect from February 1, 2006.

Right to seize illicit recordings

196.—(1) An illicit recording of a performance which is found exposed or otherwise immediately available for sale or hire, and in respect of which a person would be entitled to apply for an order under section 195, may be seized and detained by him or a person authorised by him.

The right to seize and detain is exercisable subject to the following conditions and is subject to any decision of the court under section 204 (order as to disposal of illicit recording).

(2) Before anything is seized under this section notice of the time and place of the proposed seizure must be given to a local police station.

(3) A person may for the purpose of exercising the right conferred by this section enter premises to which the public have access but may not seize anything in the possession, custody or control of a person at a permanent or regular place of business of his and may not use any force.

(4) At the time when anything is seized under this section there shall be left at the place where it was seized a notice in the prescribed form containing the prescribed particulars as to the person by whom or on whose authority the seizure is made and the grounds on which it is made.

(5) In this section—

"premises" includes land, buildings, fixed or moveable structures, vehicles, vessels, aircraft and hovercraft; and

"prescribed" means prescribed by order of the Secretary of State.

(6) An order of the Secretary of State under this section shall be made by statutory instrument which shall be subject to annulment in pursuance of a resolution of either House of Parliament.

Meaning of "illicit recording"

197.—(1) In [this Chapter] "illicit recording", in relation to a performance, shall be construed in accordance with this section.

(2) For the purposes of a performer's rights, a recording of the whole or any substantial part of a performance of his is an illicit recording if it is made, otherwise than for private purposes, without his consent.

(3) For the purposes of the rights of a person having recording rights, a recording of the whole or any substantial part of a performance subject to the exclusive recording contract is an illicit recording if it is made, otherwise than for private purposes, without his consent or that of the performer.

(4) For the purposes of sections 198 and 199 (offences and orders for delivery up in criminal proceedings), a recording is an illicit recording if it is an illicit recording for the purposes mentioned in subsection (2) or subsection (3).

(5) In [this Chapter] "illicit recording" includes a recording falling to be treated as an illicit recording by virtue of any of the following provisions of Schedule 2—

paragraph 4(3) (recordings made for the purposes of instruction or examination),

paragraph 6(2) (recordings made by educational establishments for educational purposes),

paragraph 12(2) (recordings of performance in electronic form retained on transfer of principal recording),

paragraph 16(3) (recordings made for purposes of broadcast [...]),

[paragraph 17A(2) (recording for the purposes of time-shifting),or
paragraph 17B(2) (photographs of broadcasts),]
but otherwise does not include a recording made in accordance with any of the
provisions of that Schedule.

(6) It is immaterial for the purposes of this section where the recording was
made.

Note:
  (1) In subs.(5), the words "or cable programme" were repealed and the entries for
      paragraphs 17A(2) and 17B(2) inserted by the Copyright and Related Rights
      Regulations 2003 (SI 2003/2498), reg.20 and Sch.2, with effect from October 31,
      2003. For savings and transitional provisions, see Part 3 of those Regulations.
  (2) In subs.(1) and (5) the words "this Chapter" were substituted for the former words
      "this Part" by the Performances (Moral Rights, etc.) Regulations 2006 (SI 2006/
      18), Sch. para.8, with effect from February 1, 2006.

Presumptions relevant to recordings of performances

[**197A.**—(1) In proceedings brought by virtue of this Part with respect to the
rights in a performance, where copies of a recording of the performance as issued
to the public bear a statement that a named person was the performer, the statement shall be admissible as evidence of the fact stated and shall be presumed to
be correct until the contrary is proved.

(2) Subsection (1) does not apply to proceedings for an offence under section
198 (criminal liability for making etc. illicit recordings); but without prejudice to
its application in proceedings for an order under section 199 (order for delivery
up in criminal proceedings).]

Note: S.197A was inserted by the Intellectual Property (Enforcement, etc.) Regulations
2006 (SI 2006/1028), Sch.2 para.10, with effect from April 29, 2006.

Offences

Criminal liability for making, dealing with or using illicit recordings

198.—(1) A person commits an offence who without sufficient consent—
  (a) makes for sale or hire, or
  (b) imports into the United Kingdom otherwise than for his private and do-
      mestic use, or
  (c) possesses in the course of a business with a view to committing any act
      infringing the rights conferred by [this Chapter], or
  (d) in the course of a business—
        (i) sells or lets for hire, or
        (ii) offers or exposes for sale or hire, or
        (iii) distributes,
a recording which is, and which he knows or has reason to believe is, an illicit
recording.

[(1A) A person who infringes a performer's making available right—
  (a) in the course of a business, or
  (b) otherwise than in the course of a business to such an extent as to affect
      prejudicially the owner of the making available right,
commits an offence if he knows or has reason to believe that, by doing so, he is
infringing the making available right in the recording.]

(2) A person commits an offence who causes a recording of a performance
made without sufficient consent to be—

    (a) shown or played in public, or

    [(b) communicated to the public,]

thereby infringing any of the rights conferred by [this Chapter], if he knows or has reason to believe that those rights are thereby infringed.

    (3) In subsections (1) and (2) "sufficient consent" means—

      (a) in the case of a qualifying performance, the consent of the performer, and

      (b) in the case of a non-qualifying performance subject to an exclusive recording contract—

        (i) for the purposes of subsection (1)(a) (making of recording), the consent of the performer or the person having recording rights, and

        (ii) for the purposes of subsection (1)(b), (c) and (d) and subsection (2) (dealing with or using recording), the consent of the person having recording rights.

The references in this subsection to the person having recording rights are to the person having those rights at the time the consent is given or, if there is more than one such person, to all of them.

    (4) No offence is committed under subsection (1) or (2) by the commission of an act which by virtue of any provision of Schedule 2 may be done without infringing the rights conferred by [this Chapter].

    (5) A person guilty of an offence under subsection (1)(a), (b) or (d)(iii) is liable—

      (a) on summary conviction to imprisonment for a term not exceeding six months or a fine not exceeding the statutory maximum, or both;

      (b) on conviction on indictment to a fine or imprisonment for a term not exceeding two years, or both.

    [(5A) A person guilty of an offence under subsection (1A) is liable—

      (a) on summary conviction to imprisonment for a term not exceeding three months or a fine not exceeding the statutory maximum, or both;

      (b) on conviction on indictment to a fine or imprisonment for a term not exceeding [ten] years, or both.]

    (6) A person guilty of any other offence under this section is liable on summary conviction to a fine not exceeding level 5 on the standard scale or imprisonment for a term not exceeding six months, or both.

Note:

    (1) The word in square brackets in Subs.(5)(b) was substituted for the former word "two" by the Copyright, etc. and Trade Marks (Offences and Enforcement) Act 2002 (c.25), s.1, with effect from November 20, 2002 (Copyright, etc. and Trade Marks (Offences and Enforcement) Act 2002 (Commencement) Order 2002 (SI 2002/2749)).

    (2) Subsection (2A) and (5A) were inserted and Subs.(2)(b) was substituted by Reg.26 of para.4(5) of Sch.1 to the Copyright and Related Rights Regulations 2003 (SI 2003/2498).

    (3) In subs.(1)(c), (2) and (4) the words "this Chapter" were substituted for the former words "this Part" by the Performances (Moral Rights, etc.) Regulations 2006 (SI 2006/18), Sch. para.8, with effect from February 1, 2006.

Enforcement by local weights and measures authority

    [198A.—(1) It is the duty of every local weights and measures authority to enforce within their area the provisions of section 198.

    (2) The following provisions of the Trade Descriptions Act 1968 apply in relation to the enforcement of that section by such an authority as in relation to the enforcement of that Act—

section 27 (power to make test purchases),

section 28 (power to enter premises and inspect and seize goods and documents),

section 29 (obstruction of authorised officers), and

section 33 (compensation for loss, &c. of goods seized).

(3) Subsection (1) above does not apply in relation to the enforcement of section 198 in Northern Ireland, but it is the duty of the Department of Economic Development to enforce that section in Northern Ireland.

For that purpose the provisions of the Trade Descriptions Act 1968 specified in subsection (2) apply as if for the references to a local weights and measures authority and any officer of such an authority there were substituted references to that Department and any of its officers.

(4) Any enactment which authorises the disclosure of information for the purpose of facilitating the enforcement of the Trade Descriptions Act 1968 shall apply as if section 198 were contained in that Act and as if the functions of any person in relation to the enforcement of that section were functions under that Act.

(5) Nothing in this section shall be construed as authorising a local weights and measures authority to bring proceedings in Scotland for an offence.]

Note: This section was inserted by s.165 of the Criminal Justice and Public Order Act 1994 with effect from April 6, 2007.

Order for delivery up in criminal proceedings

199.—(1) The court before which proceedings are brought against a person for an offence under section 198 may, if satisfied that at the time of his arrest or charge he had in his possession, custody or control in the course of a business an illicit recording of a performance, order that it be delivered up to a person having performers' rights or recording rights in relation to the performance or to such other person as the court may direct.

(2) For this purpose a person shall be treated as charged with an offence—

(a) in England, Wales and Northern Ireland, when he is orally charged or is served with a summons or indictment;

(b) in Scotland, when he is cautioned, charged or served with a complaint or indictment.

(3) An order may be made by the court of its own motion or on the application of the prosecutor (or, in Scotland, the Lord Advocate or procurator-fiscal), and may be made whether or not the person is convicted of the offence, but shall not be made—

(a) after the end of the period specified in section 203 (period after which remedy of delivery up not available), or

(b) if it appears to the court unlikely that any order will be made under section 204 (order as to disposal of illicit recording).

(4) An appeal lies from an order made under this section by a magistrates' court—

(a) in England and Wales, to the Crown Court, and

(b) in Northern Ireland, to the county court;

and in Scotland, where an order has been made under this section, the person from whose possession, custody or control the illicit recording has been removed may, without prejudice to any other form of appeal under any rule of law, appeal against that order in the same manner as against sentence.

(5) A person to whom an illicit recording is delivered up in pursuance of an order under this section shall retain it pending the making of an order, or the decision not to make an order, under section 204.

(6) Nothing in this section affects the powers of the court under [section 143 of the Powers of Criminal Courts (Sentencing) Act 2000], [Part II of the Proceeds of Crime (Scotland) Act 1995] or [Article 11 of the Criminal Justice (Northern Ireland) Order 1994] (general provisions as to forfeiture in criminal proceedings).

Note:

(1) The official version of this Act has the word "in" twice at the start of subs.(6), presumably in error.

(2) In subs.(6), the words in the first set of square brackets were substituted for the former words "section 43 of the Powers of Criminal Courts Act 1973" by the Powers of Criminal Courts (Sentencing) Act 2000 (c.6), s.165 and Sch.9, para 116, with effect from August 25, 2000. Subsection (6) had previously been amended by the Criminal Procedure (Consequential Provisions) (Scotland) Act 1995, with effect from April 1, 1996 by virtue of that Act, which inserted the words in the first set of square brackets in place of "Chapter II of Part II of the Criminal Justice (Scotland) Act 1995", such words having been inserted into Subsection (6) by the Criminal Justice (Scotland) Act 1995 with effect from September 26, 1995 by virtue of the Criminal Justice (Scotland) Act 1995 (Commencement No.1 Transitional Provisions and Savings) Order 1995 (SI 1995/2995).

(3) Subsection (6) is printed as further amended by the Criminal Justice (Northern Ireland) Order 1994 (SI 1994/2795 (N.I.15)) with effect from January 9, 1995 by virtue of the Criminal Justice (1994 Order) (Commencement) Order (Northern Ireland) 1994 (SI 1994/446).

Search warrants

200.—(1) Where a justice of the peace (in Scotland, a sheriff or justice of the peace) is satisfied by information on oath given by a constable (in Scotland, by evidence on oath) that there are reasonable grounds for believing—

(a) that an offence under [section 198(1) or (1A)] (offences of making, importing [, possessing, selling etc.] or distributing illicit recordings) has been or is about to be committed in any premises, and

(b) that evidence that such an offence has been or is about to be committed is in those premises,

he may issue a warrant authorising a constable to enter and search the premises, using such reasonable force as is necessary.

(2) The power conferred by subsection (1) does not, in England and Wales, extend to authorising a search for material of the kinds mentioned in section 9(2) of the Police and Criminal Evidence Act 1984 (certain classes of personal or confidential material).

(3) A warrant under subsection (1)—

(a) may authorise persons to accompany any constable executing the warrant, and

(b) remains in force for [three months] from the date of its issue.

[(3A) In executing a warrant issued under subsection (1) a constable may seize an article if he reasonably believes that it is evidence that any offence under section 198(1) has been or is about to be committed.]

(4) In this section "premises" includes land, buildings, fixed or moveable structures, vehicles, vessels, aircraft and hovercraft.

Note:

(1) In subs.(1)(a), the words in square brackets were substituted for the former words "section 198(1)" by the Copyright and Related Rights Regulations 2003 (SI 2003/2498), reg.26 with effect from October 31, 2003. For savings and transitional provisions, see Part 3 of those Regulations. The words "198(1)" were previously substituted for the original words "198(1)(a), (b) or (d)(iii)" by the Copyright, etc.

and Trade Marks (Offences and Enforcement) Act 2002 (c.25), s.2, with effect from November 20, 2002 (Copyright, etc. and Trade Marks (Offences and Enforcement) Act 2002 (Commencement) Order 2002 (SI 2002/2749)).

(2) Subsection (3A) was inserted by the Copyright, etc. and Trade Marks (Offences and Enforcement) Act 2002 (c.25), s.2, with effect from November 20, 2002 (Copyright, etc. and Trade Marks (Offences and Enforcement) Act 2002 (Commencement) Order 2002 (SI 2002/2749)).

(3) The words in square brackets in subs.(3)(b) were substituted for the former words "28 days" by the Serious Organised Crime and Police Act 2005 (c.15), Sch.16 para.6, with effect from January 1, 2006.

False representation of authority to give consent

201.—(1) It is an offence for a person to represent falsely that he is authorised by any person to give consent for the purposes of [this Chapter] in relation to a performance, unless he believes on reasonable grounds that he is so authorised.

(2) A person guilty of an offence under this section is liable on summary conviction to imprisonment for a term not exceeding six months or a fine not exceeding level 5 on the standard scale or both.

Note: In subs.(1) the words "this Chapter" were substituted for the former words "this Part" by the Performances (Moral Rights, etc.) Regulations 2006 (SI 2006/18), Sch. para.8, with effect from February 1, 2006.

Offence by body corporate: liability of officers

202.—(1) Where an offence under [this Chapter] committed by a body corporate is proved to have been committed with the consent or connivance of a director, manager, secretary or other similar officer of the body, or a person purporting to act in any such capacity, he as well as the body corporate is guilty of the offence and liable to be proceeded against and punished accordingly.

(2) In relation to a body corporate whose affairs are managed by its members "director" means a member of the body corporate.

Note: In s.202(1) the words "this Chapter" were substituted for the former words "this Part" by the Performances (Moral Rights, etc.) Regulations 2006 (SI 2006/18), Sch. para.8, with effect from February 1, 2006.

Supplementary provisions with respect to delivery up and seizure

Period after which remedy of delivery up not available

203.—(1) An application for an order under section 195 (order for delivery up in civil proceedings) may not be made after the end of the period of six years from the date on which the illicit recording in question was made, subject to the following provisions.

(2) If during the whole or any part of that period a person entitled to apply for an order—

(a) is under a disability, or

(b) is prevented by fraud or concealment from discovering the facts entitling him to apply,

an application may be made by him at any time before the end of the period of six years from the date on which he ceased to be under a disability or, as the case may be, could with reasonable diligence have discovered those facts.

(3) In subsection (2) "disability"—

(a) in England and Wales, has the same meaning as in the Limitation Act 1980;

(b) in Scotland, means legal disability within the meaning of the Prescription and Limitations (Scotland) Act 1973;

(c) in Northern Ireland, has the same meaning as in the Statute of Limitation (Northern Ireland) 1958.

(4) An order under section 199 (order for delivery up in criminal proceedings) shall not, in any case, be made after the end of the period of six years from the date on which the illicit recording in question was made.

Order as to disposal of illicit recording

204.—(1) An application may be made to the court for an order that an illicit recording of a performance delivered up in pursuance of an order under section 195 or 199, or seized and detained in pursuance of the right conferred by section 196, shall be—

(a) forfeited to such person having performer's rights or recording rights in relation to the performance as the court may direct, or

(b) destroyed or otherwise dealt with as the court may think fit,

or for a decision that no such order should be made.

(2) In considering what order (if any) should be made, the court shall consider whether other remedies available in an action for infringement of the rights conferred by [this Chapter] would be adequate to compensate the person or persons entitled to the rights and to protect their interests.

(3) Provision shall be made by rules of court as to the service of notice on persons having an interest in the recording, and any such person is entitled—

(a) to appear in proceedings for an order under this section, whether or not he was served with notice, and

(b) to appeal against any order made, whether or not he appeared;

and an order shall not take effect until the end of the period within which notice of an appeal may be given or, if before the end of that period notice of appeal is duly given, until the final determination or abandonment of the proceedings on the appeal.

(4) Where there is more than one person interested in a recording, the court shall make such order as it thinks just and may (in particular) direct that the recording be sold, or otherwise dealt with, and the proceeds divided.

(5) If the court decides that no order should be made under this section, the person in whose possession, custody or control the recording was before being delivered up or seized is entitled to its return.

(6) References in this section to a person having an interest in a recording include any person in whose favour an order could be made in respect of the recording

[(a) under this section or under section 114 or 231 of this Act;

(b) under section 24D of the Registered Designs Act 1949;

(c) under section 19 of Trade Marks Act 1994 (including that section as applied by regulation 4 of the Community Trade Mark Regulations 2006 (SI 2006/1027)); or

(d) under regulation 1C of the Community Design Regulations 2005 (SI 2005/2339).]

Note:

(1) Subsection (6) is printed as amended by the Trade Marks Act 1994 with effect from October 31, 1994 by virtue of the Trade Marks Act 1994 (Commencement) Order 1994 (SI 1994/2550).

(2) In subs.(2) the words "this Chapter" were substituted for the former words "this Part" by the Performances (Moral Rights, etc.) Regulations 2006 (SI 2006/18), Sch. para.8, with effect from February 1, 2006.

(3) The words in square brackets in subs.(6) were substituted by the Intellectual Property (Enforcement, etc.) Regulations 2006 (SI 2006/1028), Sch.2 para.11, with effect from April 29, 2006.

[Forfeiture of illicit recordings: England and Wales or Northern Ireland

204A.—(1) In England and Wales or Northern Ireland where illicit recordings of a performance have come into the possession of any person in connection with the investigation or prosecution of a relevant offence, that person may apply under this section for an order for the forfeiture of the illicit recordings.

(2) For the purposes of this section "relevant offence" means—

  (a) an offence under [section 198(1) or (1A)] (criminal liability for making or dealing with illicit recordings),

  (b) an offence under the Trade Descriptions Act 1968 (c. 29), or

  (c) an offence involving dishonesty or deception.

(3) An application under this section may be made—

  (a) where proceedings have been brought in any court for a relevant offence relating to some or all of the illicit recordings, to that court, or

  (b) where no application for the forfeiture of the illicit recordings has been made under paragraph (a), by way of complaint to a magistrates' court.

(4) On an application under this section, the court shall make an order for the forfeiture of any illicit recordings only if it is satisfied that a relevant offence has been committed in relation to the illicit recordings.

(5) A court may infer for the purposes of this section that such an offence has been committed in relation to any illicit recordings if it is satisfied that such an offence has been committed in relation to illicit recordings which are representative of the illicit recordings in question (whether by reason of being part of the same consignment or batch or otherwise).

(6) Any person aggrieved by an order made under this section by a magistrates' court, or by a decision of such a court not to make such an order, may appeal against that order or decision—

  (a) in England and Wales, to the Crown Court, or

  (b) in Northern Ireland, to the county court.

(7) An order under this section may contain such provision as appears to the court to be appropriate for delaying the coming into force of the order pending the making and determination of any appeal (including any application under section 111 of the Magistrates' Courts Act 1980 (c. 43) or Article 146 of the Magistrates' Courts (Northern Ireland) Order 1981 (SI 1987/1675 (N.I. 26)) (statement of case)).

(8) Subject to subsection (9), where any illicit recordings are forfeited under this section they shall be destroyed in accordance with such directions as the court may give.

(9) On making an order under this section the court may direct that the illicit recordings to which the order relates shall (instead of being destroyed) be forfeited to the person having the performers' rights or recording rights in question or dealt with in such other way as the court considers appropriate.]

Note:

  (1) Section 204A was inserted by the Copyright, etc. and Trade Marks (Offences and Enforcement) Act 2002 (c.25), s.4, with effect from November 20, 2002 (Copyright, etc. and Trade Marks (Offences and Enforcement) Act 2002 (Commencement) Order 2002 (SI 2002/2749)).

  (2) The words in square brackets in subs.(2)(a) were substituted for the former words "section 198(1)" by the Copyright and Related Rights Regulations 2003 (SI 2003/

2498), reg.26, with effect from October 31, 2003. For savings and transitional provisions, see Part 3 of those Regulations.

[Forfeiture: Scotland

204B.—(1) In Scotland the court may make an order under this section for the forfeiture of any illicit recordings.

(2) An order under this section may be made—

> (a) on an application by the procurator-fiscal made in the manner specified in section 134 of the Criminal Procedure (Scotland) Act 1995 (c. 46), or
>
> (b) where a person is convicted of a relevant offence, in addition to any other penalty which the court may impose.

(3) On an application under subsection (2)(a), the court shall make an order for the forfeiture of any illicit recordings only if it is satisfied that a relevant offence has been committed in relation to the illicit recordings.

(4) The court may infer for the purposes of this section that such an offence has been committed in relation to any illicit recordings if it is satisfied that such an offence has been committed in relation to illicit recordings which are representative of the illicit recordings in question (whether by reason of being part of the same consignment or batch or otherwise).

(5) The procurator-fiscal making the application under subsection (2)(a) shall serve on any person appearing to him to be the owner of, or otherwise to have an interest in, the illicit recordings to which the application relates a copy of the application, together with a notice giving him the opportunity to appear at the hearing of the application to show cause why the illicit recordings should not be forfeited.

(6) Service under subsection (5) shall be carried out, and such service may be proved, in the manner specified for citation of an accused in summary proceedings under the Criminal Procedure (Scotland) Act 1995.

(7) Any person upon whom notice is served under subsection (5) and any other person claiming to be the owner of, or otherwise to have an interest in, illicit recordings to which an application under this section relates shall be entitled to appear at the hearing of the application to show cause why the illicit recordings should not be forfeited.

(8) The court shall not make an order following an application under subsection (2)(a)—

> (a) if any person on whom notice is served under subsection (5) does not appear, unless service of the notice on that person is proved, or
>
> (b) if no notice under subsection (5) has been served, unless the court is satisfied that in the circumstances it was reasonable not to serve such notice.

(9) Where an order for the forfeiture of any illicit recordings is made following an application under subsection (2)(a), any person who appeared, or was entitled to appear, to show cause why the illicit recordings should not be forfeited may, within 21 days of the making of the order, appeal to the High Court by Bill of Suspension.

(10) Section 182(5)(a) to (e) of the Criminal Procedure (Scotland) Act 1995 shall apply to an appeal under subsection (9) as it applies to a stated case under Part 2 of that Act.

(11) An order following an application under subsection (2)(a) shall not take effect—

> (a) until the end of the period of 21 days beginning with the day after the day on which the order is made, or
>
> (b) if an appeal is made under subsection (9) above within that period, until the appeal is determined or abandoned.

(12) An order under subsection (2)(b) shall not take effect—

    (a) until the end of the period within which an appeal against the order could be brought under the Criminal Procedure (Scotland) Act 1995 (c. 46), or

    (b) if an appeal is made within that period, until the appeal is determined or abandoned.

(13) Subject to subsection (14), illicit recordings forfeited under this section shall be destroyed in accordance with such directions as the court may give.

(14) On making an order under this section the court may direct that the illicit recordings to which the order relates shall (instead of being destroyed) be forfeited to the person having the performers' rights or recording rights in question or dealt with in such other way as the court considers appropriate.

(15) For the purposes of this section—

    "relevant offence" means an offence under [section 198(1) or (1A)] (criminal liability for making or dealing with illicit recordings), or under the Trade Descriptions Act 1968 (c. 29) or any offence involving dishonesty or deception;

    "the court" means—

        (a) in relation to an order made on an application under subsection (2)(a), the sheriff, and

        (b) in relation to an order made under subsection (2)(b), the court which imposed the penalty.]

Note:

  (1) Section 204B was inserted by the Copyright, etc. and Trade Marks (Offences and Enforcement) Act 2002 (c.25), s.4, with effect from November 20, 2002 (Copyright, etc. and Trade Marks (Offences and Enforcement) Act 2002 (Commencement) Order 2002 (SI 2002/2749)).

  (2) The words in square brackets in subs.(15) were substituted for the former words "section 198(1)" by the Copyright and Related Rights Regulations 2003 (SI 2003/2498), reg.26, with effect from October 31, 2003. For savings and transitional provisions, see Part 3 of those Regulations.

Jurisdiction of county court and sheriff court

205.—(1) In England, Wales and Northern Ireland a county court may entertain proceedings under—

    section 195 (order for delivery up of illicit recording), or

    section 204 (order as to disposal of illicit recording),

[save that, in Northern Ireland, a county court may entertain such proceedings only] where the value of the illicit recordings in question does not exceed the county court limit for actions in tort.

(2) In Scotland proceedings for an order under either of those provisions may be brought in the sheriff court.

(3) Nothing in this section shall be construed as affecting the jurisdiction of the High Court or, in Scotland, the Court of Session.

Note: Subsection (1) is printed as amended by the High Court and County Courts Jurisdiction Order 1991 (SI 1991/724).

[Licensing of performers' property rights

Licensing of performers' property rights

205A. The provisions of Schedule 2A have effect with respect to the licensing of performers' property rights.]

Note: This section and the heading preceding it were inserted by the Copyright and Related Rights Regulations 1996 (SI 1996/2967), with effect from December 1, 1996. For savings and transitional provisions, see Part III of those Regulations.

[Jurisdiction of Copyright Tribunal

Jurisdiction of Copyright Tribunal

205B—(1) The Copyright Tribunal has jurisdiction under [this Chapter] to hear and determine proceedings under—

    (a) section 182D (amount of equitable remuneration for exploitation of commercial sound recording);

    (b) section 190 (application to give consent on behalf of owner of reproduction right);

    (c) section 191H (amount of equitable remuneration on transfer of rental right);

[(cc) paragraph 19 of Schedule 2 (determination of royalty or other remuneration to be paid with respect to re-transmission of broadcast including performance or recording);]

    (d) paragraph 3, 4 or 5 of Schedule 2A (reference of licensing scheme);

    (e) paragraph 6 or 7 of that Schedule (application with respect to licence under licensing scheme);

    (f) paragraph 10, 11 or 12 of that Schedule (reference or application with respect to licensing by licensing body);

    (g) paragraph 15 of that Schedule (application to settle royalty for certain lending);

    (h) paragraph 17 of that Schedule (application to settle terms of licence available as of right).

(2) The provisions of Chapter VIII of Part I (general provisions relating to the Copyright Tribunal) apply in relation to the Tribunal when exercising any jurisdiction under [this Chapter].

(3) Provision shall be made by rules under section 150 prohibiting the Tribunal from entertaining a reference under paragraph 3, 4 or 5 of Schedule 2A (reference of licensing scheme) by a representative organisation unless the Tribunal is satisfied that the organisation is reasonably representative of the class of persons which it claims to represent.]

Note:

    (1) This section and the heading preceding it were inserted by the Copyright and Related Rights Regulations 1996 (SI 1996/2967), with effect from December 1, 1996. For savings and transitional provisions, see Part III of those Regulations.

    (2) Subsection (1)(cc) was inserted by s.138 and Sch.9 to the Broadcasting Act 1996 with effect from October 1, 1996 by virtue of the Broadcasting Act 1996 (Commencement No.1 and Transitional Provisions) Order 1996 (SI 1996/2120).

    (3) In subs.(1) and (2) the words "this Chapter" were substituted for the former words "this Part" by the Performances (Moral Rights, etc.) Regulations 2006 (SI 2006/18), Sch. para.8, with effect from February 1, 2006.

Note: Ss.182 to 205B became Chapter 2 of Part 2 and the cross-heading before s.182 was inserted by the Performances (Moral Rights, etc.) Regulations 2006 (SI 2006/18), reg.4(4), (5), with effect from February 1, 2006.

[CHAPTER 3

MORAL RIGHTS

Right to be identified as performer

Right to be identified as performer

205C.—(1) Whenever a person—

(a) produces or puts on a qualifying performance that is given in public,

(b) broadcasts live a qualifying performance,

(c) communicates to the public a sound recording of a qualifying performance, or

(d) issues to the public copies of such a recording,

the performer has the right to be identified as such.

(2) The right of the performer under this section is—

(a) in the case of a performance that is given in public, to be identified in any programme accompanying the performance or in some other manner likely to bring his identity to the notice of a person seeing or hearing the performance,

(b) in the case of a performance that is broadcast, to be identified in a manner likely to bring his identity to the notice of a person seeing or hearing the broadcast,

(c) in the case of a sound recording that is communicated to the public, to be identified in a manner likely to bring his identity to the notice of a person hearing the communication,

(d) in the case of a sound recording that is issued to the public, to be identified in or on each copy or, if that is not appropriate, in some other manner likely to bring his identity to the notice of a person acquiring a copy,

or (in any of the above cases) to be identified in such other manner as may be agreed between the performer and the person mentioned in subsection (1).

(3) The right conferred by this section in relation to a performance given by a group (or so much of a performance as is given by a group) is not infringed—

(a) in a case falling within paragraph (a), (b) or (c) of subsection (2), or

(b) in a case falling within paragraph (d) of that subsection in which it is not reasonably practicable for each member of the group to be identified,

if the group itself is identified as specified in subsection (2).

(4) In this section "group" means two or more performers who have a particular name by which they may be identified collectively.

(5) If the assertion under section 205D specifies a pseudonym, initials or some other particular form of identification, that form shall be used; otherwise any reasonable form of identification may be used.

(6) This section has effect subject to section 205E (exceptions to right).

Requirement that right be asserted

205D.—(1) A person does not infringe the right conferred by section 205C (right to be identified as performer) by doing any of the acts mentioned in that section unless the right has been asserted in accordance with the following provisions so as to bind him in relation to that act.

(2) The right may be asserted generally, or in relation to any specified act or description of acts—

(a) by instrument in writing signed by or on behalf of the performer, or

(b) on an assignment of a performer's property rights, by including in the instrument effecting the assignment a statement that the performer asserts in relation to the performance his right to be identified.

(3) The persons bound by an assertion of the right under subsection (2) are—

(a) in the case of an assertion under subsection (2)(a), anyone to whose notice the assertion is brought;

(b) in the case of an assertion under subsection (2)(b), the assignee and anyone claiming through him, whether or not he has notice of the assertion.

(4) In an action for infringement of the right the court shall, in considering remedies, take into account any delay in asserting the right.

Exceptions to right

205E.—(1) The right conferred by section 205C (right to be identified as performer) is subject to the following exceptions.

(2) The right does not apply where it is not reasonably practicable to identify the performer (or, where identification of a group is permitted by virtue of section 205C(3), the group).

(3) The right does not apply in relation to any performance given for the purposes of reporting current events.

(4) The right does not apply in relation to any performance given for the purposes of advertising any goods or services.

(5) The right is not infringed by an act which by virtue of any of the following provisions of Schedule 2 would not infringe any of the rights conferred by Chapter 2—

(a) paragraph 2(1A) (news reporting);

(b) paragraph 3 (incidental inclusion of a performance or recording);

(c) paragraph 4(2) (things done for the purposes of examination);

(d) paragraph 8 (parliamentary and judicial proceedings);

(e) paragraph 9 (Royal Commissions and statutory inquiries).

Right to object to derogatory treatment

Right to object to derogatory treatment of performance

205F.—(1) The performer of a qualifying performance has a right which is infringed if—

(a) the performance is broadcast live, or

(b) by means of a sound recording the performance is played in public or communicated to the public, with any distortion, mutilation or other modification that is prejudicial to the reputation of the performer.

(2) This section has effect subject to section 205G (exceptions to right).

Exceptions to right

205G.—(1) The right conferred by section 205F (right to object to derogatory treatment of performance) is subject to the following exceptions.

(2) The right does not apply in relation to any performance given for the purposes of reporting current events.

(3) The right is not infringed by modifications made to a performance which are consistent with normal editorial or production practice.

(4) Subject to subsection (5), the right is not infringed by anything done for the purpose of—

(a) avoiding the commission of an offence,

(b) complying with a duty imposed by or under an enactment, or

(c) in the case of the British Broadcasting Corporation, avoiding the inclusion in a programme broadcast by them of anything which offends against good taste or decency or which is likely to encourage or incite crime or lead to disorder or to be offensive to public feeling.

(5) Where—

(a) the performer is identified in a manner likely to bring his identity to the notice of a person seeing or hearing the performance as modified by the act in question; or

(b) he has previously been identified in or on copies of a sound recording issued to the public, subsection (4) applies only if there is sufficient disclaimer.

(6) In subsection (5) "sufficient disclaimer", in relation to an act capable of infringing the right, means a clear and reasonably prominent indication—

(a) given in a manner likely to bring it to the notice of a person seeing or hearing the performance as modified by the act in question, and

(b) if the performer is identified at the time of the act, appearing along with the identification, that the modifications were made without the performer's consent.

Infringement of right by possessing or dealing with infringing article

205H.—(1) The right conferred by section 205F (right to object to derogatory treatment of performance) is also infringed by a person who—

(a) possesses in the course of business, or

(b) sells or lets for hire, or offers or exposes for sale or hire, or

(c) distributes, an article which is, and which he knows or has reason to believe is, an infringing article.

(2) An "infringing article" means a sound recording of a qualifying performance with any distortion, mutilation or other modification that is prejudicial to the reputation of the performer.

Supplementary

Duration of rights

205I.—(1) A performer's rights under this Chapter in relation to a performance subsist so long as that performer's rights under Chapter 2 subsist in relation to the performance.

(2) In subsection (1) "performer's rights" includes rights of a performer that are vested in a successor of his.

Consent and waiver of rights

205J.—(1) It is not an infringement of the rights conferred by this Chapter to do any act to which consent has been given by or on behalf of the person entitled to the right.

(2) Any of those rights may be waived by instrument in writing signed by or on behalf of the person giving up the right.

(3) A waiver—

(a) may relate to a specific performance, to performances of a specified description or to performances generally, and may relate to existing or future performances, and

(b) may be conditional or unconditional and may be expressed to be subject to revocation, and if made in favour of the owner or prospective owner of a performer's property rights in the performance or performances to which it relates, it shall be presumed to extend to his licensees and successors in title unless a contrary intention is expressed.

(4) Nothing in this Chapter shall be construed as excluding the operation of the general law of contract or estoppel in relation to an informal waiver or other transaction in relation to either of the rights conferred by this Chapter.

Application of provisions to parts of performances

205K.—(1) The right conferred by section 205C (right to be identified as performer) applies in relation to the whole or any substantial part of a performance.

(2) The right conferred by section 205F (right to object to derogatory treatment of performance) applies in relation to the whole or any part of a performance.

Moral rights not assignable

205L. The rights conferred by this Chapter are not assignable.

Transmission of moral rights on death

205M.—(1) On the death of a person entitled to a right conferred by this Chapter—
- (a) the right passes to such person as he may by testamentary disposition specifically direct,
- (b) if there is no such direction but the performer's property rights in respect of the performance in question form part of his estate, the right passes to the person to whom the property rights pass,
- (c) if or to the extent that the right does not pass under paragraph (a) or (b) it is exercisable by his personal representatives.

(2) Where a performer's property rights pass in part to one person and in part to another, as for example where a bequest is limited so as to apply—
- (a) to one or more, but not all, of the things to which the owner has the right to consent, or
- (b) to part, but not the whole, of the period for which the rights subsist, any right which by virtue of subsection (1) passes with the performer's property rights is correspondingly divided.

(3) Where by virtue of subsection (1)(a) or (1)(b) a right becomes exercisable by more than one person—
- (a) it is, in the case of the right conferred by section 205F (right to object to derogatory treatment of performance), a right exercisable by each of them and is satisfied in relation to any of them if he consents to the treatment or act in question, and
- (b) any waiver of the right in accordance with section 205J by one of them does not affect the rights of the others.

(4) A consent or waiver previously given or made binds any person to whom a right passes by virtue of subsection (1).

(5) Any damages recovered by personal representatives by virtue of this section in respect of an infringement after a person's death shall devolve as part of his estate as if the right of action had subsisted and been vested in him immediately before his death.

Remedies for infringement of moral rights

205N.—(1) An infringement of a right conferred by this Chapter is actionable as a breach of statutory duty owed to the person entitled to the right.

(2) Where—

(a) there is an infringement of a right conferred by this Chapter,

(b) a person falsely claiming to act on behalf of a performer consented to the relevant conduct or purported to waive the right, and

(c) there would have been no infringement if he had been so acting, that person shall be liable, jointly and severally with any person liable in respect of the infringement by virtue of subsection (1), as if he himself had infringed the right.

(3) Where proceedings for infringement of the right conferred on a performer by this Chapter, it shall be a defence to prove—

(a) that a person claiming to act on behalf of the performer consented to the defendant's conduct or purported to waive the right, and

(b) that the defendant reasonably believed that the person was acting on behalf of the performer.

(4) In proceedings for infringement of the right conferred by section 205F the court may, if it thinks it an adequate remedy in the circumstances, grant an injunction on terms prohibiting the doing of any act unless a disclaimer is made, in such terms and in such manner as may be approved by the court, dissociating the performer from the broadcast or sound recording of the performance.]

Note: Ss.205C to 205N were inserted by the Performances (Moral Rights, etc.) Regulations 2006 (SI 2006/18), reg.6; those sections became Chapter 3 of Part 2 and the cross heading for that Chapter was inserted by reg.4(6) of those Regulations, both with effect from February 1, 2006.

[CHAPTER 4

QUALIFICATION FOR PROTECTION, EXTENT AND INTERPRETATION]

Qualification for protection and extent

Qualifying countries, individuals and persons

206.—(1) In this Part—

"qualifying country" means—

(a) the United Kingdom,

(b) another member State of the European Economic Community, or

(c) to the extent that an Order under section 208 so provides, a country designated under that section as enjoying reciprocal protection;

"qualifying individual" means a citizen or subject of, or an individual resident in, a qualifying country; and

"qualifying person" means a qualifying individual or a body corporate or other body having legal personality which—

(a) is formed under the law of a part of the United Kingdom or another qualifying country, and

(b) has in any qualifying country a place of business at which substantial business activity is carried on.

(2) The reference in the definition of "qualifying individual" to a person's being a citizen or subject of a qualifying country shall be construed—

(a) in relation to the United Kingdom, as a reference to his being a British citizen, and

(b) in relation to a colony of the United Kingdom, as a reference to his being a British Dependent Territories' citizen by connection with that colony.

(3) In determining for the purpose of the definition of "qualifying person" whether substantial business activity is carried on at a place of business in any country, no account shall be taken of dealings in goods which are at all material times outside that country.

Countries to which this Part extends

207. This Part extends to England and Wales, Scotland and Northern Ireland.

Countries enjoying reciprocal protection

208.—(1) Her Majesty may by Order in Council designate as enjoying reciprocal protection under this Part—

(a) a Convention country, or

(b) a country as to which Her Majesty is satisfied that provision has been or will be made under its law giving adequate protection for British performances.

(2) A "Convention country" means a country which is a party to a Convention relating to performers' rights to which the United Kingdom is also a party.

(3) A "British performance" means a performance—

(a) given by an individual who is a British citizen or resident in the United Kingdom, or

(b) taking place in the United Kingdom.

(4) If the law of that country provides adequate protection only for certain descriptions of performance, an Order under subsection (1)(b) designating that country shall contain provision limiting to a corresponding extent the protection afforded by this Part in relation to performances connected with that country.

(5) The power conferred by subsection (1)(b) is exercisable in relation to any of the Channel Islands, the Isle of Man or any colony of the United Kingdom, as in relation to a foreign country.

(6) A statutory instrument containing an Order in Council under this section shall be subject to annulment in pursuance of a resolution of either House of Parliament.

Territorial waters and the continental shelf

209.—(1) For the purposes of this Part the territorial waters of the United Kingdom shall be treated as part of the United Kingdom.

(2) This Part applies to things done in the United Kingdom sector of the continental shelf on a structure or vessel which is present there for purposes directly connected with the exploration of the sea bed or subsoil or the exploitation of their natural resources as it applies to things done in the United Kingdom.

(3) The United Kingdom sector of the continental shelf means the areas designated by order under section 1(7) of the Continental Shelf Act 1964.

British ships, aircraft and hovercraft

210.—(1) This Part applies to things done on a British ship, aircraft or hovercraft as it applies to things done in the United Kingdom.

(2) In this section—

"British ship" means a ship which is a British ship for the purposes of the Merchant Shipping Act [1995] otherwise than by virtue of registration in a country outside the United Kingdom; and

"British aircraft" and "British hovercraft" mean an aircraft or hovercraft registered in the United Kingdom.

Note: Subsection (2) is printed as amended by the Merchant Shipping Act 1995.

[210A.—(1) (1) The requirement in the following provisions that an instrument be signed by or on behalf of a person is also satisfied in the case of a body corporate by the affixing of its seal—

      section 191B(3) (assignment of performer's property rights);

      section 191C(1) (assignment of future performer's property rights);

      section 191D(1) (grant of exclusive licence).

(2) The requirement in the following provisions that an instrument be signed by a person is also satisfied in the case of a body corporate by signature on behalf of the body or by the affixing of its seal—

      section 205D(2)(a) (assertion of performer's moral rights);

      section 205J(2) (waiver of performer's moral rights).]

Note: S.210A was inserted by the Performances (Moral Rights, etc.) Regulations 2006 (SI 2006/18), reg.7, with effect from February 1, 2006.

Interpretation

Expressions having same meaning as in copyright provisions

211.—(1) The following expressions have the same meaning in this Part as in Part I (copyright)—

    [assignment (in Scotland),]
    broadcast,
    business,
    [communication to the public,]
    country,
    defendant (in Scotland),
    delivery up (in Scotland),
    [the EEA,]
    [EEA State,]
    film,
    [injunction (in Scotland)]
    literary work,
    published,
    [signed,]
    [sound recording, and]
    [wireless broadcast.]

(2) [The provisions of—

  (a) section 5B(2) and (3) (supplementary provisions relating to films), and

  (b) section 6(3) to (5A) and section 19(4) (supplementary provisions relating to broadcasting),

apply] for the purposes of this Part, and in relation to an infringement of the rights conferred by this Part, as they apply for the purposes of Part I and in relation to an infringement of copyright.

Note:

(1) Subsection (1) is printed as amended by the Duration of Copyright and Rights in Performances Regulations 1995 (SI 1995/3297), which added "EEA national" with effect from January 1, 1996.

(2) In subs.(1), the entries for "communication to the public", "injunction (Scotland)" and "wireless broadcast" were inserted, the entry for "sound recording" amended and the entries for "cable programme" and "cable programme service" repealed by the Copyright and Related Rights Regulations 2003 (SI 2003/2498), Sch.1, para.15, Sch.2, with effect from October 31, 2003. For savings and transitional provisions, see Part 3 of those Regulations.

(3) In subs.(2) the words in square brackets were substituted for the former words "6(3) to (5), section 7(5) and 19(4)" and the words "and cable programme services" repealed by the Copyright and Related Rights Regulations 2003 (SI 2003/2498), Sch.1, para.15, Sch.2, with effect from October 31, 2003. For savings and transitional provisions, see Part 3 of those Regulations.

(4) The expressions "assignment (in Scotland)," and "signed," were inserted into subs.(1) and the words in square brackets in subs.(2) were substituted by the Performances (Moral Rights, etc.) Regulations 2006 (SI 2006/18), Sch. para.6, with effect from February 1, 2006. Also in subs.(1) the expressions "the EEA" and "EEA State" were substituted for the former expression "EEA national" by the Intellectual Property (Enforcement, etc.) Regulations 2006 (SI 2006/1028), Sch.2 para.12, with effect from April 29, 2006.

Index of defined expressions

212. The following Table shows provisions defining or otherwise explaining expressions used in this Part (other than provisions defining or explaining an expression used only in the same section)—

[assignment (in Scotland)	section 211(1) (and section 177);]
broadcast (and related expressions)	section 211(1) (and section 6)
business	section 211(1) (and section 178)
[communication to the public	section 211(1) (and section 20)]
[consent of performer (in relation to performer's property rights)	section 191A(2)]
country	section 211(1) (and section 178)
defendant (in Scotland)	section 211(1) (and section 177)
delivery up (in Scotland)	section 211(1) (and section 177)
[distribution right	section 182B(5)]
[the EEA and EEA State	section 211(1) (and section 172A)]
exclusive recording contract	section 185(1)
film	section 211(1) (and [section 5B])
[group	section 205C(4);]
illicit recording	section 197
[injunction (in Scotland)	section 211(1) (and section 177)]
[issue to the public	section 182B;]
[lending right	section 182C(7)]
literary work	section 211(1) (and section 3(1))

[making available right	section 182CA]
performance	section 180(2)
[performer's non-property rights	section 192A(1)]
[performer's property rights	section 191A(1)]
published	section 211(1) (and section 175)
qualifying country	section 206(1)
qualifying individual	section 206(1) and (2)
qualifying performance	section 181
qualifying person	section 206(1) and (3)
recording (of a performance)	section 180(2)
recording rights (person having)	section 185(2) and (3)
[rental right	section 182C(7)]
[reproduction right	section 182A(3)]
[rights owner (in relation to performer's property rights)	section 191A(3) and (4)]
[signed	section 211(1) (and section 176);]
sound recording	section 211(1) (and [section 5A]).
[wireless broadcast	section 211(1) (and section 178).]

Note:

(1) The references to "film" and "sound recording" were amended by, and the reference to "EEA national" was inserted by the Duration of Copyright and Rights in Performances Regulations 1995 (SI 1995/3297), with effect from January 1, 1996.

(2) The references to "consent of performer (in relation to performer's property rights)", "distribution right","lending right","performer's non-property rights", "performer's property rights","rental right","reproduction right", and "rights owner (in relation to performers' property rights)" were inserted by the Copyright and Related Rights Regulations 1996 (SI 1996/2967), with effect from December 1, 1996.

(3) The entries for "communication to the public", "injunction (Scotland)" and "making available right" were inserted and the entry for "cable programme" repealed by the Copyright and Related Rights Regulations 2003 (SI 2003/2498), Sch.1, para.15, Sch.2, with effect from October 31, 2003. For savings and transitional provisions, see Part 3 of those Regulations. The former entry for "cable programme" provided:

> *cable programme, cable programme*   section 211(1) (and section 7)
> *service (and related expressions)*

(4) The expressions "assignment (in Scotland)" "group", "issue to the public", "signed" and "wireless broadcast" were inserted into s.212 by the Performances (Moral Rights, etc.) Regulations 2006 (SI 2006/18), Sch. para.7, with effect from February 1, 2006. Also in s.212 the expression "the EEA and EEA State" was substituted for the former expression "EEA national" by the Intellectual Property (Enforcement, etc.) Regulations 2006 (SI 2006/1028), Sch.2 para.13, with effect from April 29, 2006.

Note: Ss.206 to 212 became Chapter 4 and the cross heading before s.206 was inserted by the Performances (Moral Rights, etc.) Regulations 2006 (SI 2006/18), reg.4(7), with effect from February 1, 2006.

Order as to disposal of infringing articles, &c.

p.184 Section 231(5) has been repealed and subsection (6) has been amended to read as follows:

"(6) References in this section to a person having an interest in an article or other thing include any person in whose favour an order could be made in respect of it [—

(a) under this section or under section 114 or 204 of this Act;

(b) under section 24D of the Registered Designs Act 1949;

(c) under section 19 of Trade Marks Act 1994 (including that section as applied by regulation 4 of the Community Trade Mark Regulations 2006 (SI 2006/1027)); or

(d) under regulation 1C of the Community Design Regulations 2005 (SI 2005/2339).]"

Note: Subs.(5) was repealed and in subs.(6) the words in square brackets were substituted by the Intellectual Property (Enforcement, etc.) Regulations 2006 (SI 2006/1028), Sch.2 para.14 and Sch.4, with effect from April 29, 2006.

Crown use of designs

p.188 Section 240(4) has been amended to read as follows (*sic*):

"(4) The reference to the supply of articles for "health service purposes" are to their supply for the purposes of providing—

[(za) primary medical services or primary dental services under [the National Health Service Act 2006 or the National Health Service (Wales) Act 2006,] [or primary medical services under Part 1 of the National Health Service (Scotland) Act 1978];]]

[(a) pharmaceutical services, general medical services or general dental services under—

(i) [Chapter 1 of Part 7 of the National Health Service Act 2006, or Chapter 1 of Part 7 of the National Health Service (Wales) Act 2006 (in the case of pharmaceutical services),]

(ii) Part II of the National Health Service (Scotland) Act 1978 [(in the case of pharmaceutical services or general dental services)], or

(iii) the corresponding provisions of the law in force in Northern Ireland; or

(b) personal medical services [. . .] in accordance with arrangements made under—

(i) [...]

(ii) section 17C of the 1978 Act [(in the case of personal dental services)], or

(iii) the corresponding provisions of the law in force in Northern Ireland.]

[(c) local pharmaceutical services provided under [the National Health Service Act 2006 or the National Health Service (Wales) Act 2006.]]"

Note: The words in the second set of square brackets in subs.4(za), and in the square brackets in subs.(a)(ii) and (b)(ii) were inserted by the Primary Medical Services (Scotland) Act 2004 (Consequential Modifications) Order 2004 (SI 2004/957), Sch.1 para.5, with effect from April 1, 2004.

The words in the first set of square brackets in subs.(4)(za), in the square brackets in subs.(4)(a)(i) and in the internal square brackets in subs.(4)(c) were substituted by the National Health Service (Consequential Provisions) Act 2006 (c.43), Sch.1 para.113, with effect from March 1, 2007.

Minor definitions

In section 263(1), the definitions of "the Crown" and "government department" **p.199**
have been amended to read as follows:

> "the Crown" includes the Crown in right of Her Majesty's Govern-
> ment in Northern Ireland [and the Crown in right of the Scot-
> tish Administration] [and the Crown in right of the Welsh As-
> sembly Government];
>
> "government department" includes a Northern Ireland department
> [and any part of the Scottish Administration] [and any part of
> the Welsh Assembly Government].

Note: The words in the second set of square brackets in the definitions of "the Crown"
and "government department" were inserted by the Government of Wales Act 2006 (c.32),
Sch.10 para.31, with effect from May 4, 2007.

Patents county courts: special jurisdiction

Section 287(1) will prospectively be amended to begin as follows: **p.208**

> "(1) The Lord Chancellor [, with the concurrence of the Lord Chief Justice,]
> may by order made by statutory instrument..."

Section 287(6) has been inserted to read as follows:

> "(6) The Lord Chief Justice of England and Wales may nominate a judicial
> office holder (as defined in section 109(4) of the Constitutional Reform Act
> 2005) to exercise his functions under this section."

Note: The words in square brackets in subs.(1) are prospectively inserted and in subs.(6)
were inserted by the Constitutional Reform Act 2005 (c.4), Sch.4 para.200, with effect
from April 3, 2006.

Proceedings in patents county court

Section 291(1) has been amended to read as follows: **p.209**

> "(1) Where a county court is designated a patents county court, the[Lord
> Chief Justice shall, after consulting the Lord Chancellor,] nominate a person
> entitled to sit as a judge of that court as the patents judge."

Section 291(6) has been inserted to read as follows:

> "(6) The Lord Chief Justice may nominate a judicial office holder (as
> defined in section 109(4) of the Constitutional Reform Act 2005) to exercise
> his functions under subsection (1)."

Note: The words in square brackets in subs.(1) were substituted for the former words
"Lord Chancellor shall" and subs.(6) is prospectively inserted by the Constitutional
Reform Act 2005 (c.4), Sch.4 para.201, with effect from April 3, 2006.

**Rights and duties of registered patent agents in relation to proceedings in
patents county court**

In section 292(1), the words "Senior Courts" will prospectively be substituted for **p.210**
the existing words "Supreme Court".

In section 292, subsections (2A) and (7) have been inserted to read as follows:

> "(2A) The Lord Chancellor may make regulations under subsection (2)
> only with the concurrence of the Lord Chief Justice."

"(7) The Lord Chief Justice may nominate a judicial office holder (as defined in section 109(4) of the Constitutional Reform Act 2005) to exercise his functions under this section."

Note: In subs.(1) the words "Senior Courts" are prospectively substituted for the existing words "Supreme Court" and subs.(2A) and (7) were inserted by the Constitutional Reform Act 2005 (c.4), Sch.4 para.202 and Sch.11 para.4, with effect from April 3, 2006.

Circumvention of technical devices applied to computer programs

p.213 In section 296(7)(b), the words "Senior Courts Act 1981" will prospectively be substituted for the existing words "Supreme Court Act 1981".

Note: In subs.(7)(b) the words "Senior Courts Act 1981" are prospectively substituted for the existing words "Supreme Court Act 1981" by the Constitutional Reform Act 2005 (c.4), Sch.11 para.1, from a date to be appointed.

Rights and remedies in respect of devices and services designed to circumvent technological measures

p.216 In section 296ZD(6)(b), the words "Senior Courts Act 1981" will prospectively be substituted for the existing words "Supreme Court Act 1981".

Note: In subs.(6)(b) the words "Senior Courts Act 1981" are prospectively substituted for the existing words "Supreme Court Act 1981" by the Constitutional Reform Act 2005 (c.4), Sch.11 para.1, from a date to be appointed.

Electronic rights management information

p.218 After section 296ZF, the following section has been inserted:

296ZG.—(1) This section applies where a person (D), knowingly and without authority, removes or alters electronic rights management information which—

(a) is associated with a copy of a copyright work, or

(b) appears in connection with the communication to the public of a copyright work, and where D knows, or has reason to believe, that by so doing he is inducing, enabling, facilitating or concealing an infringement of copyright.

(2) This section also applies where a person (E), knowingly and without authority, distributes, imports for distribution or communicates to the public copies of a copyright work from which electronic rights management information—

(a) associated with the copies, or

(b) appearing in connection with the communication to the public of the work, has been removed or altered without authority and where E knows, or has reason to believe, that by so doing he is inducing, enabling, facilitating or concealing an infringement of copyright.

(3) A person issuing to the public copies of, or communicating, the work to the public, has the same rights against D and E as a copyright owner has in respect of an infringement of copyright.

(4) The copyright owner or his exclusive licensee, if he is not the person issuing to the public copies of, or communicating, the work to the public, also has the same rights against D and E as he has in respect of an infringement of copyright.

(5) The rights conferred by subsections (3) and (4) are concurrent, and sections 101(3) and 102(1) to (4) apply, in proceedings under this section, in relation to persons with concurrent rights as they apply, in proceedings mentioned in those provisions, in relation to a copyright owner and exclusive licensee with concurrent rights.

(6) The following provisions apply in relation to proceedings under this section as in relation to proceedings under Part 1 (copyright)—

(a) sections 104 to 106 of this Act (presumptions as to certain matters relating to copyright); and

(b) section 72 of the Supreme Court Act 1981, section 15 of the Law Reform (Miscellaneous Provisions) (Scotland) Act 1985 and section 94A of the Judicature (Northern Ireland) Act 1978 (withdrawal of privilege against self-incrimination in certain proceedings relating to intellectual property).

(7) In this section—

(a) expressions which are defined for the purposes of Part 1 of this Act (copyright) have the same meaning as in that Part; and

(b) "rights management information" means any information provided by the copyright owner or the holder of any right under copyright which identifies the work, the author, the copyright owner or the holder of any intellectual property rights, or information about the terms and conditions of use of the work, and any numbers or codes that represent such information.

(8) Subsections (1) to (5) and (6)(b), and any other provision of this Act as it has effect for the purposes of those subsections, apply, with any necessary adaptations, to rights in performances, publication right and database right.

(9) The provisions of regulation 22 (presumptions relevant to database right) of the Copyright and Rights in Databases Regulations 1997 (SI 1997/3032) apply in proceedings brought by virtue of this section in relation to database right.

Note: S.296ZG was inserted by the Copyright and Related Rights Regulations 2003 (SI 2003/2498), Pt 2 reg.25, subject to the savings specified reg.32.

Search warrants

Section 297B(3)(b) has been amended to read as follows: **p.222**

"(b) remains in force for [three months] from the date of its issue."

Note: The words in square brackets in subs.(3)(b) were substituted for the former words "28 days" by the Serious Organised Crime and Police Act 2005 (c.15), Sch.16 para.6, with effect from January 1, 2006.

SCHEDULE 2

Rights in Performances: Permitted Acts

Throughout Schedule 2, for the words "Part 2" (or "Part II") (except the reference in **p.239–250** paragraph 17(2)(b) to Part II of the Broadcasting Act 1990) substitute "this Chapter".

Note: In Sch.2 the words "this Chapter" were substituted for the former words "Part 2" (or "Part II") by the Performances (Moral Rights, etc.) Regulations 2006 (SI 2006/18), Sch. para.9, with effect from February 1, 2006.

Public records

Schedule 2 paragraph 10(1) has been amended to read as follows: **p.242**

"(1) Material which is comprised in public records within the meaning of the Public Records Act 1958, the Public Records (Scotland) Act 1937 or the Public Records Act (Northern Ireland) 1923 [, or in Welsh public records (as defined in [the Government of Wales Act 2006]),] which are open to public inspection in pursuance of that Act, may be copied, and a copy may be supplied to any person, by or with the authority of any officer appointed under that Act, without infringing any right conferred by Part II."

Note: The words in the internal square brackets were substituted by the Government of Wales Act 2006 (c.32), Sch.10 para.32, with effect from May 4, 2007.

Transfer of copies of works in electronic form

p.242 In Schedule 2 paragraph 12(2), for the words "this Part" substitute "this Chapter".

Note: In para.12(2) the words "this Chapter" were substituted for the former words "this Part" by the Performances (Moral Rights, etc.) Regulations 2006 (SI 2006/18), Sch. para.8, with effect from February 1, 2006.

Incidental recording for purposes of broadcast

p.244 In Schedule 2 paragraph 16(1), for the words "that Part" substitute "this Chapter".

Note: In para.16(1) the words "this Chapter" were substituted for the former words "that Part" by the Performances (Moral Rights, etc.) Regulations 2006 (SI 2006/18), Sch. para.10, with effect from February 1, 2006.

SCHEDULE 2A

Licensing of Performers' Property Rights

Licensing schemes and licensing bodies

p.250 In Schedule 2A paragraph 1(1) and (2), for the words "Part 2" (or "Part II") substitute "this Chapter".
In Schedule 2A paragraph 1(4), for the words "this Part" substitute "this Chapter".

Note:

(1) In para.1(1) and (2) the words "this Chapter" were substituted for the former words "Part 2" (or "Part II") by the Performances (Moral Rights, etc.) Regulations 2006 (SI 2006/18), Sch. para.9, with effect from February 1, 2006.

(2) In para.1(4) the words "this Chapter" were substituted for the former words "this Part" by the Performances (Moral Rights, etc.) Regulations 2006 (SI 2006/18), Sch. para.8, with effect from February 1, 2006.

SCHEDULE 6

Provisions for the Benefit of the Hospital for Sick Children

Interpretation

p.258 In Schedule 6 paragraph 1(1), the definition of "the trustees" has been amended to read as follows:

"the trustees" means the special trustees appointed for the Hospital under the National Health Service Act 1977 [or the National Health Service Act 2006];

Note: The words in square brackets in the definition of "the trustees" in Sch.6 para.1(1) were inserted by the National Health Service (Consequential Provisions) Act 2006 (c.43), Sch.1 para.114, with effect from March 1, 2007.

p.258 Schedule 6 paragraph 7(2) has been amended to read as follows:

Right only for the benefit of the Hospital

"(2) The right may not be the subject of an order under [section 213 of the National Health Service Act 2006 or section 161 of the National Health Service (Wales) Act 2006] (transfers of trust property by order of the Secretary of State) and shall cease if the Hospital ceases to have a separate identity or ceases to have purposes which include the care of sick children."

Note: The words in square brackets in Sch.6 para.7(2) were substituted by the National

Health Service (Consequential Provisions) Act 2006 (c.43), Sch.1 para.114, with effect from March 1, 2007.

SCHEDULE 7

CONSEQUENTIAL AMENDMENTS: GENERAL

Marine, etc., Broadcasting (Offences) Act 1967 (c. 41)

Schedule 7 paragraph 9 has been repealed.   **p.265**

Note: Sch.7 para.9 was repealed by the Wireless Telegraphy Act 2006 (c.36), Sch.9 Pt 1, with effect from February 8, 2007.

Income and Corporation Taxes Act 1988 (c.1)

Schedule 7 paragraph 36(3) has been repealed.   **p.265**

Note: Sch.7 para.36(3) was repealed by the Income Tax (Trading & Other Income Act 2005 (c.5), Sch.3, with effect from April 6, 2005.

A3. REGULATIONS AMENDING CDPA 1988 AND TRANSITIONAL PROVISIONS

A3.ii The Duration of Copyright and Rights in Performances Regulations 1995

(SI 1995/3297)

Interpretation

In regulation 2 the definition of "EEA State" has been substituted to read as fol-   **p.281**
lows:

" "EEA state" means a member State, Iceland, Liechtenstein or Norway."

Note: In reg.2 the definition of "EEA state" was substituted by the Intellectual Property (Enforcement, etc.) Regulations 2006 (SI 2006/1028), Sch.3 para.1, with effect from April 29, 2006.

A3.iii The Duration of Copyright and Rights in Performances Regulations 1996

(SI 1996/2967)

Interpretation

In regulation 2 the definition of "EEA State" has been substituted to read as fol-   **p.291**
lows:

" "EEA state" means a member State, Iceland, Liechtenstein or Norway."

Note: In reg.2 the definition of "EEA state" was substituted by the Intellectual Property (Enforcement, etc.) Regulations 2006 (SI 2006/1028), Sch.3 para.1, with effect from April 29, 2006.

Publication right

p.292   Regulation 16(7) has been amended to read as follows:

> "(7) In this regulation [and regulation 17A] a "work" means a literary, dramatic, musical or artistic work or a film."

Note: In reg.16(7) the words in square brackets were inserted by the Intellectual Property (Enforcement, etc.) Regulations 2006 (SI 2006/1028), Sch.3 para.4, with effect from April 29, 2006.

Presumptions relevant to works subject to publication right

p.293   After regulation 17 there has been inserted:

"Presumptions relevant to works subject to publication right

17A. In proceedings brought by virtue of Chapter 6 of Part 1 of the Copyright, Designs and Patents Act 1988, as applied to publication right by regulation 17, with respect to a work, where copies of the work as issued to the public bear a statement that a named person was the owner of publication right in the work at the date of issue of the copies, the statement shall be admissible as evidence of the fact stated and shall be presumed to be correct until the contrary is proved.

Application of presumptions in relation to an order for delivery up in criminal proceedings

17B. Regulation 17A does not apply to proceedings for an offence under section 107 of the Copyright, Designs and Patents Act 1988 as applied and modified by regulation 17 in relation to publication right; but without prejudice to its application in proceedings for an order under section 108 of the Copyright, Designs and Patents Act 1988 as that section applies to publication right by virtue of regulation 17."

Note: Regs 17A and 17B were inserted by the Intellectual Property (Enforcement, etc.) Regulations 2006 (SI 2006/1028), Sch.3 para.5, with effect from April 29, 2006.

A3.iv The Copyright and Rights in Databases Regulations 1997

(SI 1997/3032)

Application of copyright provisions to database right

p.302   Regulation 23 has been substituted to read as follows:

"Application of copyright provisions to database right

23. The following provisions of the 1988 Act apply in relation to database right and databases in which that right subsists as they apply in relation to copyright and copyright works—
>   sections 90 to 93 (dealing with rights in copyright works)
>   sections 96 to 102 (rights and remedies of copyright owner and exclusive licensee)
>   sections 113 and 114 (supplementary provisions relating to delivery up)
>   section 115 (jurisdiction of county court and sheriff court)."

Note: Reg 23 was substituted by the Intellectual Property (Enforcement, etc.) Regulations 2006 (SI 2006/1028), Sch.3 para.6, with effect from April 29, 2006.

A4. REGULATIONS MADE UNDER CDPA 1988 RELATING TO COPYRIGHT, PERFORMANCES AND FRAUDULENT RECEPTION

A4.v The Copyright (Educational Establishments) (No.2) Order 1989

(SI 1989/1068)

This Order has been revoked and replaced by the Copyright (Educational **p.317** Establishments) Order 2005 (SI 2005/223), art.3, with effect from April 1, 2005 which is reproduced below:

The Copyright (Educational Establishments) Order 2005

(SI 2005/223)

Made	*2nd February 2005*
Laid before Parliament	*8th February 2005*
Coming into Force	*1st April 2005*

The Secretary of State, in exercise of the powers conferred upon her by section 174(1)(b) of the Copyright, Designs and Patents Act 1988, hereby makes the following Order:

1. This Order may be cited as the Copyright (Educational Establishments) Order 2005 and shall come into force on 1st April 2005.

2. The descriptions of educational establishments mentioned in the Schedule to this Order are specified for the purposes of Part I of the Copyright, Designs and Patents Act 1988.

3. The Copyright (Educational Establishments) (No.2) Order 1989 is hereby revoked.

SCHEDULE
Article 2

HIGHER EDUCATION

1. Any university empowered by Royal Charter or Act of Parliament to award degrees and any college, or institution in the nature of a college, in such a university.

2. Any institution in England and Wales which provides a course of any description mentioned in Schedule 6 to the Education Reform Act 1988.

3. Any institution in Scotland which provides higher education within the meaning of section 38 of the Further and Higher Education (Scotland) Act 1992.

4. Any institution in Northern Ireland—

(a) which provides a course of any description mentioned in Schedule 1 to the Further Education (Northern Ireland) Order 1997; or

(b) which is a college of education within the meaning of article 2(2) of the Education and Libraries (Northern Ireland) Order 1986.

FURTHER EDUCATION

5. Any institution in England and Wales the sole or main purpose of which is to provide further education within the meaning of section 2 of the Education Act 1996.

6. Any institution in Scotland the sole or main purpose of which is to provide further education within the meaning of either section 1(5)(b) of the Education (Scotland) Act 1980 or section 1(3) of the Further and Higher Education (Scotland) Act 1992.

7. Any institution in Northern Ireland the sole or main purpose of which is to provide further education within the meaning of article 3 of the Further Education (Northern Ireland) Order 1997.

THEOLOGICAL COLLEGES

8. Any theological college.

A4.ix The Copyright, Designs and Patents Act 1988 (Isle of Man) (No. 2) Order 1989

(SI 1989/1292)

p.325   Article 2(1)(a) and (c) have been revoked by the Registered Designs (Isle of Man) Order 2001 (SI 2001/3678), art.4 and Sch.4, with effect from December 9, 2001.

A4.xv The Copyright (Application to the Isle of Man) Order 1992

(SI 1992/1313)

p.332   This Order has been revoked and replaced by the Copyright and Performances (Application to Other Countries) Order 2005 (SI 2005/852), art.8, with effect from May 1, 2005, which was in turn revoked and replaced by the Copyright and Performances (Application to Other Countries) Order 2006 (SI 2006/316), art.1(3), with effect from April 6, 2006. The 2006 Order was in turn revoked and replaced by SI 2007/273, which is reproduced at **C1.iv**.

PART B

RELATED LEGISLATION AND MATERIALS

B1. THE COPYRIGHT TRIBUNAL

After **B1.iii** insert:

p.382

B1.iv Copyright Tribunal Practice Direction 2006

References to the Copyright Tribunal ("the Tribunal") under s.128(A) and (B) of the Copyright, Designs and Patents Act 1988 ("the Act").

This Practice Direction sets out the procedure that the Tribunal intends to adopt in considering references that are made to it by the Secretary of State for Trade and Industry under s. 128(A) of the Act and in the exercise of the powers conferred on the Tribunal pursuant to s.128(B) of the Act.

1. The licensing body shall within 21 days of receipt of notice that the Secretary of State has referred a proposed licence or licensing scheme to the Tribunal:—

a. serve on all other parties which to its knowledge have made representations to it or to the Secretary of State copies of all documents it has put before the Secretary of State; and

b. serve on the Secretary to the Tribunal (with copies to all such other parties) such other representations as it may wish to make to the Tribunal, together with a list of the names and addresses of the other parties.

2. Within 21 days of service of the documents specified in paragraph 1 above the other parties shall serve on the Secretary to the Tribunal (with copies to the licensing body) any further representations that they may wish to make to the Tribunal.

3. Within 14 days of service on it of any further representations pursuant to paragraph 2 above, the licensing body may make representations strictly in reply to any new matters raised in such further representations.

4. The Tribunal will then address such questions (if any) as it considers appropriate to the licensing body and/or any of the other parties and will inform any third party that it considers should be notified of the existence of the reference and shall set such time limits for the answering of such questions or for the making of representations by the third parties or further representations by the licensing body and/or the other parties as it sees fit.

5. The Tribunal, after considering all relevant materials, will issue its formal decision.

It should be noted that:—

    a. save in exceptional circumstances, the Tribunal will not hold any hearings; and

    b. where the Tribunal has pursuant to s. 128B(3) confirmed or varied a licence or licensing scheme, it is open to any relevant person to:—

        (i) lodge an appeal to the High Court pursuant to s. 152 of the Act; and/or

(ii) refer such licence or licensing scheme to the Tribunal pursuant to s.120 of the Act.

Dated: 3 January 2006

Christopher Tootal

Christopher Floyd, QC

Simon Thorley, QC

B2. LICENSING SCHEMES

B2.i The Copyright (Certification of Licensing Scheme for Educational Recording of Broadcasts and Cable Programmes) (Educational Recording Agency Limited) Order 1990

(SI 1990/879)

p.383   *Note:* This Order was revoked by the Copyright (Certification of Licensing Scheme for Educational Recording of Broadcasts and Cable Programmes) (Educational Recording Agency Limited) (Revocation) Order 2006 (SI 2006/35), art.2 with effect from January 9, 2006. The scheme was superseded by the scheme set out in SI 2005/222 which has in turn been superseded by the scheme set out in SI 2007/266, which is set out below:

The Copyright (Certification of Licensing Scheme for Educational Recording of Broadcasts) (Educational Recording Agency Limited) Order 2007

(SI 2007/266)

Made   *1st February 2007*

The Educational Recording Agency Limited (company number 2423219), whose registered office is at New Premier House, 150 Southampton Row, London WC1B 5AL has applied to the Secretary of State to certify, for the purposes of section 35 of, and paragraph 6 of Schedule 2 to, the Copyright, Designs and Patents Act 1988 ("the Act"), a licensing scheme to be operated by it:

The Secretary of State is satisfied that the scheme enables the works to which it relates to be identified with sufficient certainty by persons likely to require licences and that it sets out clearly the charges (if any) payable and the other terms on which licences will be granted:

Accordingly, the Secretary of State, in exercise of the powers conferred upon him by section 143 of, and paragraph 16 of Schedule 2A to, the Act, hereby makes the following Order:

1. This Order may be cited as the Copyright (Certification of Licensing Scheme for Educational Recording of Broadcasts) (Educational Recording Agency Limited) Order 2007.

2. The licensing scheme set out in the Schedule to this Order is certified for the purposes of section 35 of, and paragraph 6 of Schedule 2 to, the Copyright, Designs and Patents Act 1988.

3. The certification under article 2 shall come into operation on 1st April 2007.

Article 2

SCHEDULE

THE EDUCATIONAL RECORDING AGENCY LIMITED LICENSING SCHEME

NATURE OF THE LICENCE

1. The Educational Recording Agency Limited (known as "ERA") is authorised to operate a Licensing Scheme for the purposes of both section 35 of, and paragraph 6 of Schedule 2 to the Copyright, Designs and Patents Act 1988.

2. "The Act" refers to the Copyright, Designs and Patents Act 1988 or any relevant law amending, modifying or re-enacting it from time to time.

3. Set out below are the terms of the Licensing Scheme which ERA has been authorised to operate to the extent that the same has been certified for the purposes of both section 35 of the Act and paragraph 6 of Schedule 2 to the Act ("the Licensing Scheme").

4. These terms shall form part of licences issued under the Licensing Scheme ("the Licence").

5. The Licensing Scheme and Licences issued under it shall apply only to Relevant Rights when used for non-commercial educational purposes within or on behalf of an Educational Establishment. All licensees under the Licensing Scheme shall either be or represent an Educational Establishment ("Licensee").

6. "Educational Establishment" shall mean any school and any other description of educational establishment as may be specified by order of the Secretary of State for the purposes of section 174 of the Act.

ERA REPERTOIRE AND LICENSOR MEMBERS

7.—(1) The copyright works and rights in performances relevant to a Licence granted under the Licensing Scheme ("ERA Repertoire") are the works and performances in respect of which and to the extent which the Licensor Members of ERA (or persons represented by the Licensor Members) own or control Relevant Rights.

(2) "Relevant Rights" shall comprise the right:

    (a) to cause or authorise the making of recordings of a broadcast and copies of such a recording and (only as a direct result of their inclusion in a broadcast) of copyright works and/or performances contained in the recorded broadcast by or on behalf of an Educational Establishment for the educational purposes of that Educational Establishment ("ERA Recordings"); and

    (b) to authorise ERA Recordings to be communicated to the public by a person situated within the premises of an Educational Establishment but only to the extent that the communication cannot be received by any person situated outside the premises of that Educational Establishment.

8. The Licensor Members of ERA and the works and performances forming part of ERA Repertoire in respect of which the Relevant Rights are owned or controlled by such Licensor Members will for the purposes of Licences issued under the Licensing Scheme comprise:

AUTHORS' LICENSING AND COLLECTING SOCIETY LIMITED ("ALCS")

Those literary and dramatic works which are owned by or controlled by persons represented by ALCS and which are included in any broadcast.

BBC WORLDWIDE LIMITED

The broadcasts of the British Broadcasting Corporation and all those copyright works owned or controlled by the British Broadcasting Corporation which are included in any broadcast.

CHANNEL FOUR TELEVISION CORPORATION ("Channel 4")

The broadcasts made on Channel 4, E4 and/or Film Four and/or any other broadcast service operated by Channel 4 or any of its subsidiary companies and all those copyright works owned or controlled by Channel 4 or any of its subsidiary companies included in any broadcast.

CHANNEL 5 BROADCASTING LIMITED ("Channel 5")

The broadcasts made on Five and/or any other broadcast service operated by Channel 5 or any of its subsidiary companies and all those copyright works owned or controlled by Channel 5 or any of its subsidiary companies included in any broadcast

DESIGN AND ARTISTS COPYRIGHT SOCIETY LIMITED ("DACS")

Those artistic works (as defined in the Act) in which the copyright is owned or controlled by the members of DACS or the members of copyright societies represented by DACS and which are included in any broadcast.

EQUITY

The performances by persons represented by Equity which are included in any broadcast.

THE INCORPORATED SOCIETY OF MUSICIANS ("ISM")

The literary and musical works which are owned by or controlled by persons represented by ISM and the performances by persons who are represented by ISM which are included in any broadcast.

THE BRITISH PHONOGRAPHIC INDUSTRY LIMITED ("BPI")

Those sound recordings which are owned or controlled by persons represented by BPI and which are included in any broadcast from which an ERA Recording is made.

ITV NETWORK LIMITED ("ITV Network")

The broadcasts made on the channel branded as ITV1 in England and Wales, as the STV regions (formerly known as Grampian TV and Scottish TV) in Scotland, as Ulster in Northern Ireland, and as Channel TV in the Channel Islands, on ITV 2, on ITV 3, on the ITV News Channel and/or any other broadcast service operated by ITV Network Limited or any of its associated or subsidiary companies and all those copyright works owned or controlled by ITV Network Limited or any of its subsidiary or associated companies included in any broadcast.

MECHANICAL COPYRIGHT PROTECTION SOCIETY LIMITED ("MCPS")

Those musical works and sound recordings which are owned or controlled by members of MCPS and entrusted by its members to MCPS and which are included in any broadcast from which an ERA Recording is made.

MUSICIANS' UNION ("the MU")

The performances by persons represented by the MU which are included in any broadcast.

THE PERFORMING RIGHT SOCIETY LIMITED ("PRS")

The musical works which are owned or controlled by the PRS or by persons represented by the PRS and which are included in any broadcast from which an ERA Recording has been made.

PHONOGRAPHIC PERFORMANCE LIMITED ("PPL")

Those sound recordings which are owned or represented by PPL and which are included in any broadcast from which an ERA Recording is made.

SIANEL PEDWAR CYMRU ("S4C")

The broadcasts made on S4C, S4C Digital and/or S4C2 and/or any other broadcast service operated by S4C or any of its subsidiary companies and all those copyright works owned or controlled by S4C or any of its subsidiary companies included in any broadcast.

For the above purposes "broadcast" shall have the meaning provided by section 6 of the Act.

However, Licences under the Licensing Scheme shall not authorise the recording of Open University programmes. If the Licensee is in any doubt as to whether a Licence covers a particular right or a particular copyright work the Licensee shall be entitled to contact ERA who shall be obliged within a reasonable time (by one of the Licensor Members) to confirm whether or not a particular right is owned or controlled by one of the Licensors.

9. No recording or copying of a broadcast under any Licence shall be made except by or on behalf of an Educational Establishment and any such recording or copying shall be made either:

(a) on the premises of the Educational Establishment by or under the direct supervision of a teacher or employee of the Licensee; or

(b) at the residence of a teacher employed by the Licensee by that teacher; or

(c) at the premises of a third party authorised by the Licensee to make recordings or copies on behalf of the Licensee under written contractual terms and conditions which prevent the retention or use of any recordings or copies by that third party or any other third party unless ERA shall have expressly agreed that a specific third party may retain any recordings or copies for subsequent use only by authorised Licensees of ERA in accordance with the provisions of the Licensing Scheme.

MAINTAINING RECORDS

10. Licensees shall be required to ensure that all ERA Recordings or copies comprising ERA Recordings made under a Licence provide for sufficient acknowledgement of the broadcast relevant to the ERA Recording to be given with each ERA Recording being marked with the name of the broadcaster, the date upon which the broadcast took place and the title of the recording.

To provide sufficient acknowledgement all copies shall be marked with a statement in clear and bold lettering reading:

"This recording is to be used only for non-commercial educational purposes under the terms of the ERA Licence"

or such other wording or statement as ERA shall reasonably require from time to time.

Physical copies shall include the statement on the exterior of the copy, and /or its packaging.

When under the Licence copies are made and stored in digital form for access through a computer server, the statement shall also be included as a written opening credit or webpage which must be viewed or listened to before access to the ERA Recording is permitted.

11. Licensees may be required to record and maintain at the request of ERA details of broadcasts and television or radio programmes or any part or parts of such programmes which are made as ERA Recordings and the number of copies of such recordings made under a Licence and to make available to ERA such records for inspection.

12. Licensees shall undertake that if and when any ERA Recordings are communicated to the public by a person situated within the premises of an Educational Establishment under the Licence suitable password, and other digital rights management or technological protection systems are operated and applied by the Licensee to ensure that such communication is not received or receivable by persons situated outside the premises of the licensed Educational Establishment.

13. Licensees may be required to maintain further records and answer questionnaires or surveys as ERA may reasonably require for the proper operation of the Licensing Scheme.

14. ERA shall be entitled to inspect and Licensees shall provide for ERA to have access to all records that Licensees and licensed Educational Establishments are required to maintain under the above provisions, and further to have access to all ERA Recordings however stored under the terms of a Licence, in order to inspect the same to check compliance with the Licence.

PERIOD OF LICENCE AND FEES

15. Licences shall be granted in consideration of payment of the agreed Licence fees and may be granted for such period or periods as may from time to time be specified by or agreed with ERA.

16. The Licence fee shall be calculated by reference to the period for which the Licence is granted and to the tariff applicable in respect of that period.

17. The annual tariff shall be calculated on a full-time or full-time equivalent per head basis by category of student in an Educational Establishment.

For Licences taking effect on or after 1st April 2007 the annual tariff shall be:	
Students in Primary schools (including Educational Establishments known as Preparatory Schools)	30p per head
Students in Secondary schools	52p per head
Students in Educational Establishments of Further Education (including former Sixth Form Colleges)	98p per head
Students in Educational Establishments of Higher Education (including Higher Education Colleges, Theological Colleges and Universities)	£1.55 per head

Students in Educational Establishments not listed above specified from time to time by the Secretary of State under section 174 of the Act	£1.55 per head

For Licences taking effect on or after 1st April 2008 the annual tariff shall be:	
Students in Primary schools (including Educational Establishments known as Preparatory Schools)	31p per head
Students in Secondary schools	54p per head
Students in Educational Establishments of Further Education (including former Sixth Form Colleges)	£1.01 per head
Students in Educational Establishments of Higher Education (including Higher Education Colleges, Theological Colleges and Universities)	£1.60 per head
Students in Educational Establishments not listed above specified from time to time by the Secretary of State under section 174 of the Act	£1.60 per head

Discounted rates may be negotiated at ERA's discretion to cover groups of Educational Establishments.

18. Licence fees for Licences running for a period of less than one year shall be calculated on a pro-rata basis against the applicable annual tariff.

19. Licensees shall pay agreed Licence fees together with any VAT and any other Government tax which may be applicable from time to time in addition to such Licence Fee on such a date or dates as may from time to time be required by ERA in the Licence and within 28 days of invoice.

TERMINATION

20. ERA shall be entitled to terminate Licences granted:

    (a) if Licence Fees are not paid when due; or

    (b) for any other substantial breach of the conditions of the Licence,

provided that ERA shall have given to the Licensee written notice identifying the nature of late payment or the nature of the breach.

The termination will become effective twenty eight days after receipt of the written notice unless during the relevant period of twenty eight days the Licensee makes payment of outstanding fees or remedies the breach.

21. Licences will automatically terminate:

    (a) if and when an administrator, receiver, administrative receiver or other encumbrancer takes possession of, or is appointed over, the whole or any substantial part of the assets of a Licensee;

    (b) if the Licensee enters into an arrangement or composition with or for the benefit of its creditors (including any voluntary arrangement under the Insolvency Act 1986);

    (c) if a petition is presented for the purpose of considering a resolution for the making of an administration order, the winding-up or dissolution of the Licensee.

22. If punctual payment of agreed Licence Fees is not made, ERA shall be entitled to charge interest on amounts unpaid at the rate of statutory interest prescribed under section 6 of the Late Payment of Commercial Debts (Interest) Act 1998.

23. Upon expiry of a Licence without renewal or when a Licence is terminated by ERA it shall be entitled to require a Licensee to delete all ERA Recordings or copies made by the Educational Establishment to which the Licence related.

24. If a Licensee is in breach of the terms of a Licence and ERA incurs costs and expenses either in monitoring and discovering any breach of the terms of a Licence or in enforcing the conditions of any Licence, the Licensee shall be required to indemnify ERA in respect of any such costs and expenses so incurred.

25. Licensees shall be required to take all reasonable steps to ensure that rights granted by a Licence are not exceeded or abused by teachers, employees, pupils or other persons.

26. Licences issued shall be governed and interpreted in accordance with the laws of England and Wales.

B3. PUBLIC LENDING RIGHT

B3.ii Public Lending Right Scheme 1982 (Commencement of Variations) Order 1990

(SI 1990/2360)

Designation of sampling points

Article 38(2)(f) and (g) have been amended to read as follows: **p.416**

> "(f) during each sampling year at least [7] operative sampling points shall be replaced by new such points; and
> (g) no operative sampling point shall remain as such for a continuous period of more than 4 years[, unless it is in Group H in Schedule 2]."

Note: The words in square brackets in Art.38(2)(f) were substituted and in (g) were inserted by the Public Lending Right Scheme 1982 (Commencement of Variations) Order 2005 (SI 2005/1519), Appendix para.1, with effect from July 1, 2005.

Determination of the sum due in respect of Public Lending Right

The figure in article 46(1)(a) has been amended as follows: **p.419**

From 4.85p to 5.26p by the Public Lending Right Scheme 1982 (Commencement of Variation) (No.2) Order 2004 (SI 2004/3128), with effect from December 23, 2004.
From 5.26p to 5.57p by the Public Lending Right Scheme 1982 (Commencement of Variation) (No.2) Order 2005 (SI 2005/3351), with effect from December 29, 2005.
From 5.57p to 5.98p by the Public Lending Right Scheme 1982 (Commencement of Variations) Order 2006 (SI 2006/3294), with effect from January 2, 2007.

The figure in article 46(2)(b) has been amended from £5 to £1 by the Public Lending Right Scheme 1982 (Commencement of Variations) Order 2005 (SI 2005/1519) with effect from September 1, 2006.

B8. DESIGNS

B8.i Registered Designs Act 1949

(12, 13 & 14 Geo. 6, c.88)

Substantive grounds for refusal of registration

Section 1A has been omitted.   **p.501**

Note: S.1A was omitted by the Regulatory Reform (Registered Designs) Order 2006 (SI 2006/1974), art.3, with effect from October 1, 2006.

Applications for registration

Section 3(1) to (3) has been amended to read as follows: **p.503**

"**3.**—(1) An application for the registration of a design [or designs] shall be made in the prescribed form and shall be filed at the Patent Office in the prescribed manner.

(2) An application for the registration of a design [or designs] shall be made by the person claiming to be the proprietor of the design [or designs].

(3) An application for the registration of a design [or designs] in which national unregistered design right subsists shall be made by the person claiming to be the design right owner."

Section 3(4) has been omitted.

Note: The words in square brackets in s.3(1) to (3) were inserted and s.3(4) was omitted by the Regulatory Reform (Registered Designs) Order 2006 (SI 2006/1974), art.4 and art.11, with effect from October 1, 2006.

Determination of applications for registration

p.503 Section 3A has been amended to read as follows:

"**3A.**—(1) Subject as follows, the registrar shall not refuse [to register a design included in an application under this Act].

(2) If it appears to the registrar that an application for the registration of a design [or designs] has not been made in accordance with any rules made under this Act, he may refuse [to register any design included in it].

(3) If it appears to the registrar that [the applicant is not under section 3(2) or (3) or 14 entitled to apply for the registration of a design included in the application, he shall refuse to register that design.]

[(4) If it appears to the registrar that the application for registration includes—

(a) something which does not fulfil the requirements of section 1(2) of this Act;

(b) a design that does not fulfil the requirements of section 1C or 1D of this Act; or

(c) a design to which a ground of refusal mentioned in Schedule A1 to this Act applies, he shall refuse to register that thing or that design.]"

Note: The words in square brackets in s.3A(1) to (3) were inserted and s.3A(4) was substituted by the Regulatory Reform (Registered Designs) Order 2006 (SI 2006/1974), art.5 and art.12, with effect from October 1, 2006. Read literally, the effect of Art. 12(3)(a) of SI 2006/1974 is to substitute the words "or designs" in s. 3A(2) for the words "a design". It seems clear that this is an error and Art. 12(3)(a) should have provided for the *addition* of the words "or designs" after "a design". In this supplement the text of s. 3A(2) has been amended so as to give effect to this clear intention.

Modification of applications for registration

p.504 Section 3B(1) to (4) has been amended to read as follows:

"**3B.**—(1) The registrar may, at any time before an application for the registration of a design [or designs] is determined, permit the applicant to make such modifications of the application as the registrar thinks fit.

(2) Where an application for the registration of a design [or designs] has been modified before it has been determined in such a way that [any design included in the application] has been altered significantly, the registrar may, for the purpose of deciding whether and to what extent the design is new or has individual character, direct that the application [so far as relating to that design] shall be treated as having been made on the date on which it was so modified.

(3) Where—

(a) an application for the registration of [more than one design] has been modified before it has been determined to exclude one or more designs from the application; and

(b) a subsequent application for the registration of a design so excluded has, within such period (if any) as has been prescribed for such applications, been made by the person who made the earlier application or his successor in title,

the registrar may, for the purpose of deciding whether and to what extent the design is new or has individual character, direct that the subsequent application shall be treated as having been made on the date on which the earlier application was, or is treated as having been, made.

(4) Where [. . .] the registration of a design has been refused on any ground mentioned in [section 3A(4)(b) or (c)] of this Act, the application [for the design-]may be modified by the applicant if it appears to the registrar that—

(a) the identity of the design is retained; and

(b) the modifications have been made in accordance with any rules made under this Act."

Note: The words in square brackets in s.3B(1) to (4) were substituted or inserted by the Regulatory Reform (Registered Designs) Order 2006 (SI 2006/1974), art.6 and art.13, with effect from October 1, 2006.

Restoration of lapsed right in design

Section 8A(4) has been amended to read as follows: **p.511**

"(4) If the registrar is satisfied that the [failure of the proprietor] to see that the period for which the right subsisted was extended in accordance with section 8(2) or (4) [was unintentional], he shall, on payment of any unpaid renewal fee and any prescribed additional fee, order the restoration of the right in the design."

Note: The words in square brackets in s.8A(4) were inserted by the Regulatory Reform (Registered Designs) Order 2006 (SI 2006/1974), art.17, with effect from October 1, 2006.

Exemption of innocent infringer from liability for damages

Section 9 has been repealed.   **p.511**

Note: S.9 was repealed by the Intellectual Property (Enforcement, etc.) Regulations 2006 (SI 2006/1028), Sch.4, with effect from April 29, 2006.

Grounds for invalidity of registration

Section 11ZA(1) has been amended and section 11ZA(1A) and (1B) have been   **p.513**
inserted to read as follows:

"(1) The registration of a design may be declared invalid

[(a) on the ground that it does not fulfil the requirements of section 1(2) of this Act;

(b) on the ground that it does not fulfil the requirements of sections 1B to 1D of this Act; or

(c) where any ground of refusal mentioned in Schedule A1 to this Act applies.]

[(1A) The registration of a design ("the later design") may be declared invalid if it is not new or does not have individual character when compared to a design which—

(a) has been made available to the public on or after the relevant date; but

(b) is protected as from a date prior to the relevant date by virtue of registration under this Act or the Community Design Regulation or an application for such registration.

(1B) In subsection (1A) "the relevant date" means the date on which the application for the registration of the later design was made or is treated by virtue of section 3B(2), (3) or (5) or 14(2) of this Act as having been made.]"

Note: The words in square brackets in s.11ZA(1) and s.11ZA(1A) and (1B) were inserted by the Regulatory Reform (Registered Designs) Order 2006 (SI 2006/1974), art.7, with effect from October 1, 2006.

Applications for declaration of invalidity

p.513   Section 11ZB(1), (2), (3) and (5) have been amended to read as follows:

"**11ZB.**—(1) Any person interested may make an application to the registrar for a declaration of invalidity [under section 11ZA(1)(a) or (b)] of this Act.

(2) Any person concerned by the use in question may make an application to the registrar for a declaration of invalidity [under section 11ZA(1)(c)] of this Act.

(3) The relevant person may make an application to the registrar for a declaration of invalidity [under section 11ZA(1A)] of this Act.

(4) In subsection (3) above "the relevant person" means, in relation to an earlier design protected by virtue of registration under this Act or an application for such registration, the registered proprietor of the design or (as the case may be) the applicant.

(5) The person able to make an objection under subsection (2), (3) or (4) of section 11ZA of this Act may make an application to the registrar for a declaration of invalidity [under] that subsection.

(6) An application may be made under this section in relation to a design at any time after the design has been registered."

Note: The words in square brackets in s.11ZB(1), (2), (3) and (5) were substituted by the Regulatory Reform (Registered Designs) Order 2006 (SI 2006/1974), art.8, with effect from October 1, 2006.

Modification of registration

p.514   Section 11ZD(1) has been amended to read as follows:

"(1) Subsections (2) and (3) below apply where the registrar intends to declare the registration of a design invalid [under section 11ZA(1)(b) or (c), (1A), (3) or (4)] of this Act."

Note: The words in square brackets in s.11ZD(1) were substituted by the Regulatory Reform (Registered Designs) Order 2006 (SI 2006/1974), art.9, with effect from October 1, 2006.

Registration of design where application for protection in convention country has been made

p.517   Section 14(1) and (2) have been amended to read as follows:

"(1) An application for registration of a design [or designs] in respect of which protection has been applied for in a convention country may be made in accordance with the provisions of this Act by the person by whom the application for protection was made or his personal representative or assignee:

Provided that no application shall be made by virtue of this section after the expiration of six months from the date of the application for protection in a convention country or, where more than one such application for protection has been made, from the date of the first application.

(2) Where an application for registration of a design [or designs] is made by virtue of this section, the application shall be treated, for the purpose of determining whether [(and to what extent)] that or any other design is new [or has individual character], as made on the date of the application for protection in the convention country or, if more than one such application was made, on the date of the first such application."

Note: The words "or designs" in square brackets in s.14(1) and (2) were inserted by the Regulatory Reform (Registered Designs) Order 2006 (SI 2006/1974), art.14, with effect from October 1, 2006.

Property in and dealing with registered designs and applications

After section 15 there has been inserted: **p.519**

"Property in and dealing with registered designs and applications

The nature of registered designs

15A. A registered design or an application for a registered design is personal property (in Scotland, incorporeal moveable property).

Assignment, &c of registered designs and applications for registered designs

15B.—(1) A registered design or an application for a registered design is transmissible by assignment, testamentary disposition or operation of law in the same way as other personal or moveable property, subject to the following provisions of this section.

(2) Any transmission of a registered design or an application for a registered design is subject to any rights vested in any other person of which notice is entered in the register of designs, or in the case of applications, notice is given to the registrar.

(3) An assignment of, or an assent relating to, a registered design or application for a registered design is not effective unless it is in writing signed by or on behalf of the assignor or, as the case may be, a personal representative.

(4) Except in Scotland, the requirement in subsection (3) may be satisfied in a case where the assignor or personal representative is a body corporate by the affixing of its seal.

(5) Subsections (3) and (4) apply to assignment by way of security as in relation to any other assignment.

(6) A registered design or application for a registered design may be the subject of a charge (in Scotland, security) in the same way as other personal or moveable property.

(7) The proprietor of a registered design may grant a licence to use that registered design.

(8) Any equities (in Scotland, rights) in respect of a registered design or an application for a registered design may be enforced in like manner as in respect of any other personal or moveable property.

Exclusive licences

15C.—(1) In this Act an "exclusive licence" means a licence in writing signed by or on behalf of the proprietor of the registered design authorising the licensee to the exclusion of all other persons, including the person granting the licence, to exercise a right which would otherwise be exercisable exclusively by the proprietor of the registered design.

(2) The licensee under an exclusive licence has the same rights against any successor in title who is bound by the licence as he has against the person granting the licence."

Note: Ss.15A–15C were inserted by the Intellectual Property (Enforcement, etc.) Regulations 2006 (SI 2006/1028), Sch.1 para.2, with effect from April 29, 2006.

Registration of assignments, etc.

p.521   Section 19(4) has been repealed.

Note:

S.19(4) was repealed by the Intellectual Property (Enforcement, etc.) Regulations 2006 (SI 2006/1028), Sch.4, with effect from April 29, 2006.

Rectification of register

p.522   Section 20(1A) has been amended to read as follows:

"(1A) In subsection (1) above "the relevant person" means—
- (a) in the case of an application invoking any ground referred to in [section 11ZA(1)(c)] of this Act, any person concerned by the use in question;
- (b) in the case of an application invoking the ground mentioned in [section 11ZA(1A)] of this Act, the appropriate person;
- (c) in the case of an application invoking any ground mentioned in section 11ZA(2), (3) or (4) of this Act, the person able to make the objection;
- (d) in any other case, any person aggrieved."

Note: The words in square brackets in s.20(1A) were substituted by the Regulatory Reform (Registered Designs) Order 2006 (SI 2006/1974), art.10, with effect from October 1, 2006.

Inspection of registered designs

p.523   Section 22 has been amended to read as follows:

"**22.**—(1) Where a design has been registered under this Act, there shall be open to inspection at the Patent Office on and after the day on which the certificate of registration is [granted]—
- (a) the representation or specimen of the design,

[...]

This subsection has effect subject to [subsection (4)] and to any rules made under section 5(2) of this Act.

(2) [...]

(3) [...]

[(4) Where registration of a design has been refused pursuant to an application under this Act, or an application under this Act has been abandoned in relation to any design—
- (a) the application, so far as relating to that design, and
- (b) any representation, specimen or other document which has been

filed and relates to that design, shall not at any time be open to inspection at the Patent Office or be published by the registrar.]"

Note: S.22(2) and (3) were omitted, s.22(4) and the words in square brackets in s.22(1) were substituted by the Regulatory Reform (Registered Designs) Order 2006 (SI 2006/1974), arts.15 and 16, with effect from October 1, 2006.

Legal proceedings and appeals

Before section 25 there has been inserted: **p.524**

"Action for infringement

24A.—(1) An infringement of the right in a registered design is actionable by the registered proprietor.

(2) In an action for infringement all such relief by way of damages, injunctions, accounts or otherwise is available to him as is available in respect of the infringement of any other property right.

(3) This section has effect subject to section 24B of this Act (exemption of innocent infringer from liability).

Exemption of innocent infringer from liability

24B.—(1) In proceedings for the infringement of the right in a registered design damages shall not be awarded, and no order shall be made for an account of profits, against a defendant who proves that at the date of the infringement he was not aware, and had no reasonable ground for supposing, that the design was registered.

(2) For the purposes of subsection (1), a person shall not be deemed to have been aware or to have had reasonable grounds for supposing that the design was registered by reason only of the marking of a product with—

   (a) the word "registered" or any abbreviation thereof, or

   (b) any word or words expressing or implying that the design applied to, or incorporated in, the product has been registered,

unless the number of the design accompanied the word or words or the abbreviation in question.

(3) Nothing in this section shall affect the power of the court to grant an injunction in any proceedings for infringement of the right in a registered design.

Order for delivery up

24C.—(1) Where a person—

   (a) has in his possession, custody or control for commercial purposes an infringing article, or

   (b) has in his possession, custody or control anything specifically designed or adapted for making articles to a particular design which is a registered design, knowing or having reason to believe that it has been or is to be used to make an infringing article,

the registered proprietor in question may apply to the court for an order that the infringing article or other thing be delivered up to him or to such other person as the court may direct.

(2) An application shall not be made after the end of the period specified in the following provisions of this section; and no order shall be made unless the court also makes, or it appears to the court that there are grounds for making, an order under section 24D of this Act (order as to disposal of infringing article, &c.).

(3) An application for an order under this section may not be made after the end of the period of six years from the date on which the article or thing in question was made, subject to subsection (4).

(4) If during the whole or any part of that period the registered proprietor—

(a) is under a disability, or

(b) is prevented by fraud or concealment from discovering the facts entitling him to apply for an order,

an application may be made at any time before the end of the period of six years from the date on which he ceased to be under a disability or, as the case may be, could with reasonable diligence have discovered those facts.

(5) In subsection (4) "disability"—

(a) in England and Wales, has the same meaning as in the Limitation Act 1980;

(b) in Scotland, means legal disability within the meaning of the Prescription and Limitation (Scotland) Act 1973;

(c) in Northern Ireland, has the same meaning as in the Statute of Limitations (Northern Ireland) 1958.

(6) A person to whom an infringing article or other thing is delivered up in pursuance of an order under this section shall, if an order under section 24D of this Act is not made, retain it pending the making of an order, or the decision not to make an order, under that section.

(7) The reference in subsection (1) to an act being done in relation to an article for "commercial purposes" are to its being done with a view to the article in question being sold or hired in the course of a business.

(8) Nothing in this section affects any other power of the court.

Order as to disposal of infringing articles, &c

24D.—(1) An application may be made to the court for an order that an infringing article or other thing delivered up in pursuance of an order under section 24C of this Act shall be—

(a) forfeited to the registered proprietor, or

(b) destroyed or otherwise dealt with as the court may think fit,

or for a decision that no such order should be made.

(2) In considering what order (if any) should be made, the court shall consider whether other remedies available in an action for infringement of the right in a registered design would be adequate to compensate the registered proprietor and to protect his interests.

(3) Where there is more than one person interested in an article or other thing, the court shall make such order as it thinks just and may (in particular) direct that the thing be sold, or otherwise dealt with, and the proceeds divided.

(4) If the court decides that no order should be made under this section, the person in whose possession, custody or control the article or other thing was before being delivered up is entitled to its return.

(5) References in this section to a person having an interest in an article or other thing include any person in whose favour an order could be made in respect of it—

(a) under this section;

(b) under section 19 of Trade Marks Act 1994 (including that section as applied by regulation 4 of the Community Trade Mark Regulations 2006 (SI 2006/1027));

(c) under section 114, 204 or 231 of the Copyright, Designs and Patents Act 1988; or

    (d) under regulation 1C of the Community Design Regulations 2005 (SI 2005/2339).

Jurisdiction of county court and sheriff court

24E.—(1) In Northern Ireland a county court may entertain proceedings under the following provisions of this Act—

    section 24C (order for delivery up of infringing article, &c.),

    section 24D (order as to disposal of infringing article, &c.), or

    section 24F(8) (application by exclusive licensee having concurrent rights),

where the value of the infringing articles and other things in question does not exceed the county court limit for actions in tort.

(2) In Scotland proceedings for an order under any of those provisions may be brought in the sheriff court.

(3) Nothing in this section shall be construed as affecting the jurisdiction of the Court of Session or the High Court in Northern Ireland.

Rights and remedies of exclusive licensee

24F.—(1) In relation to a registered design, an exclusive licensee has, except against the registered proprietor, the same rights and remedies in respect of matters occurring after the grant of the licence as if the licence had been an assignment.

(2) His rights and remedies are concurrent with those of the registered proprietor; and references to the registered proprietor in the provisions of this Act relating to infringement shall be construed accordingly.

(3) In an action brought by an exclusive licensee by virtue of this section a defendant may avail himself of any defence which would have been available to him if the action had been brought by the registered proprietor.

(4) Where an action for infringement of the right in a registered design brought by the registered proprietor or an exclusive licensee relates (wholly or partly) to an infringement in respect of which they have concurrent rights of action, the proprietor or, as the case may be, the exclusive licensee may not, without the leave of the court, proceed with the action unless the other is either joined as a claimant or added as a defendant.

(5) A registered proprietor or exclusive licensee who is added as a defendant in pursuance of subsection (4) is not liable for any costs in the action unless he takes part in the proceedings.

(6) Subsections (4) and (5) do not affect the granting of interlocutory relief on the application of the registered proprietor or an exclusive licensee.

(7) Where an action for infringement of the right in a registered design is brought which relates (wholly or partly) to an infringement in respect of which the registered proprietor and an exclusive licensee have concurrent rights of action—

    (a) the court shall, in assessing damages, take into account—

        (i) the terms of the licence, and

        (ii) any pecuniary remedy already awarded or available to either of them in respect of the infringement;

    (b) no account of profits shall be directed if an award of damages has been made, or an account of profits has been directed, in favour of the other of them in respect of the infringement; and

    (c) the court shall if an account of profits is directed apportion the profits between them as the court considers just, subject to any agreement between them;

and these provisions apply whether or not the proprietor and the exclusive licensee are both parties to the action.

(8) The registered proprietor shall notify any exclusive licensee having concurrent rights before applying for an order under section 24C of this Act (order for delivery up of infringing article, &c); and the court may on the application of the licensee make such order under that section as it thinks fit having regard to the terms of the licence.

Meaning of "infringing article"

24G.—(1) In this Act "infringing article", in relation to a design, shall be construed in accordance with this section.

(2) An article is an infringing article if its making to that design was an infringement of the right in a registered design.

(3) An article is also an infringing article if—
  (a) it has been or is proposed to be imported into the United Kingdom, and
  (b) its making to that design in the United Kingdom would have been an infringement of the right in a registered design or a breach of an exclusive licensing agreement relating to that registered design.

(4) Where it is shown that an article is made to a design which is or has been a registered design, it shall be presumed until the contrary is proved that the article was made at a time when the right in the registered design subsisted.

(5) Nothing in subsection (3) shall be construed as applying to an article which may be lawfully imported into the United Kingdom by virtue of an enforceable Community right within the meaning of section 2(1) of the European Communities Act 1972."

Note: Ss.24A–24G inserted by the Intellectual Property (Enforcement, etc.) Regulations 2006 (SI 2006/1028), Sch.1 para.3, with effect from April 29, 2006.

Remedy for groundless threats of infringement proceedings

p.525 Section 26(2) has been amended to read as follows:

"(2) Unless in any action brought by virtue of this section the defendant proves that the acts in respect of which proceedings were threatened constitute or, if done, would constitute, an infringement of the right in a registered design the registration of which is not shown by the [claimant] to be invalid, the [claimant] shall be entitled to the following relief, that is to say:
  (a) a declaration to the effect that the threats are unjustifiable;
  (b) an injunction against the continuance of the threats; and
  (c) such damages, if any, as he has sustained thereby."

Note: S.26(2) was amended by the Intellectual Property (Enforcement, etc.) Regulations 2006 (SI 2006/1028), Sch.1 para.4, with effect from April 29, 2006.

The Court

p.525 Section 27(2) has been amended to read as follows:

"(2) Provision may be made by rules of court with respect to proceedings in the High Court in England and Wales for references and applications under this Act to be dealt with by such judge of that court as the [Lord Chief Justice of England and Wales may, after consulting the Lord Chancellor, select] for the purpose."

Section 27(3) has been inserted to read as follows:

"(3) The Lord Chief Justice may nominate a judicial office holder (as defined in section 109(4) of the Constitutional Reform Act 2005) to exercise his functions under subsection (2)."

Note: Subs.(2) was amended and subs.(3) was inserted by the Constitutional Reform Act 2005 (c.4), Sch.4 para.36, with effect from April 3, 2006.

The Appeal Tribunal

Section 28(2) has been amended to read as follows: **p.525**

"(2) The Appeal Tribunal shall consist of
(a) one or more judges of the High Court nominated [by the Lord Chief Justice of England and Wales after consulting the Lord Chancellor], and
(b) one judge of the Court of Session nominated by the Lord President of that Court."

Section 28(5) has been amended to read as follows:

"(5) Upon any appeal under this Act the Appeal Tribunal may by order award to any party such costs [.   .   .] as the Tribunal may consider reasonable and direct how and by what parties the costs [.   .   .] are to be paid; and any such order may be enforced
(a) in England and Wales or Northern Ireland, in the same way as an order of the High Court;
(b) in Scotland, in the same way as a decree for expenses granted by the Court of Session."

Section 28(11) has been inserted to read as follows:

"(11) The Lord Chief Justice may nominate a judicial office holder (as defined in section 109(4) of the Constitutional Reform Act 2005) to exercise his functions under subsection (2)(a)."

Note:
(1) Subs.(2) was amended and subs.(11) was inserted by the Constitutional Reform Act 2005 (c.4), Sch.4 para.37, with effect from April 3, 2006.
(2) In s.28(5) the words "or expenses" were repealed in both places by the Intellectual Property (Enforcement, etc.) Regulations 2006 (SI 2006/1028), Sch.4, with effect from April 29, 2006.

Fine for falsely representing a design as registered

Section 35(3) has been inserted to read as follows: **p.528**

"(3) For the purposes of this section, the use in the United Kingdom in relation to a design—
(a) of the word "registered", or
(b) of any other word or symbol importing a reference (express or implied) to registration, shall be deemed to be a representation as to registration under this Act unless it is shown that the reference is to registration elsewhere than in the United Kingdom and that the design is in fact so registered."

Note: Subs.(3) was inserted by the Community Design Regulations 2005 (SI 2005/2339), reg.6, with effect from October 1, 2005.

Use of electronic communications

p.529 After section 37, insert:

Use of electronic communications

37A.—(1) The registrar may give directions as to the form and manner in which documents to be delivered to the registrar—

    (a) in electronic form; or

    (b) using electronic communications, are to be delivered to him.

(2) A direction under subsection (1) may provide that in order for a document to be delivered in compliance with the direction it shall be accompanied by one or more additional documents specified in the direction.

(3) Subject to subsections (11) and (12), if a document to which a direction under subsection (1) or (2) applies is delivered to the registrar in a form or manner which does not comply with the direction the registrar may treat the document as not having been delivered.

(4) Subsection (5) applies in relation to a case where—

    (a) a document is delivered using electronic communications, and

    (b) there is a requirement for a fee to accompany the document.

(5) The registrar may give directions specifying—

    (a) how the fee shall be paid; and

    (b) when the fee shall be deemed to have been paid.

(6) The registrar may give directions specifying that a person who delivers a document to the registrar in electronic form or using electronic communications cannot treat the document as having been delivered unless its delivery has been acknowledged.

(7) The registrar may give directions specifying how a time of delivery is to be accorded to a document delivered to him in electronic form or using electronic communications.

(8) A direction under this section may be given—

    (a) generally;

    (b) in relation to a description of cases specified in the direction;

    (c) in relation to a particular person or persons.

(9) A direction under this section may be varied or revoked by a subsequent direction under this section.

(10) The delivery using electronic communications to any person by the registrar of any document is deemed to be effected, unless the registrar has otherwise specified, by transmitting an electronic communication containing the document to an address provided or made available to the registrar by that person as an address of his for the receipt of electronic communications; and unless the contrary is proved such delivery is deemed to be effected immediately upon the transmission of the communication.

(11) A requirement of this Act that something must be done in the prescribed manner is satisfied in the case of something that is done—

    (a) using a document in electronic form, or

    (b) using electronic communications, only if the directions under this section that apply to the manner in which it is done are complied with

(12) In the case of an application made as mentioned in subsection (11)(a) or (b) above, a reference in this Act to the application not having been made in accordance with rules under this Act includes a reference to its not having been made in accordance with any applicable directions under this section.

(13) This section applies—

    (a) to delivery at the Patent Office as it applies to delivery to the registrar; and

    (b) to delivery by the Patent Office as it applies to delivery by the registrar.

Note: S.37A was inserted by the Registered Designs Act 1949 and Patents Act 1977 (Electronic Communications) Order 2006 (SI 2006/1229), art.2, with effect from October 1, 2006.

Interpretation

At the appropriate place in section 44(1) the following definition has been inserted: **p.531**

" "electronic communication" has the same meaning as in the Electronic Communications Act 2000;"

Note: In s.44(1), the definition of "electronic communication" was inserted by the Registered Designs Act 1949 and Patents Act 1977 (Electronic Communications) Order 2006 (SI 2006/1229), art.3, with effect from October 1, 2006.

Application to Scotland

Section 45 has been substituted to read as follows: **p.532**

"Application to Scotland

45.—(1) In the application of this Act to Scotland—
"account of profits" means accounting and payment of profits;
"accounts" means count, reckoning and payment;
"arbitrator" means arbiter;
"assignment" means assignation;
"claimant" means pursuer;
"costs" means expenses;
"defendant" means defender;
"delivery up" means delivery;
"injunction" means interdict;
"interlocutory relief" means interim remedy.
(2) References to the Crown shall be construed as including references to the Crown in right of the Scottish Administration."

Note: S.45 was substituted by the Intellectual Property (Enforcement, etc.) Regulations 2006 (SI 2006/1028), Sch.1 para.5, with effect from April 29, 2006.

Application to Northern Ireland

After section 46(4) there has been inserted: **p.532**

"(4A) Any reference to a claimant includes a reference to a plaintiff."

Note: S.46(4A) was inserted by the Intellectual Property (Enforcement, etc.) Regulations 2006 (SI 2006/1028), Sch.1 para.6, with effect from April 29, 2006.

B8.iii The Design Right (Proceedings before Comptroller) Rules 1989

(SI 1989/1130)

General

Rule 23 is amended to read as follows: **p.546**

"**23.**—(1) Every person concerned in any proceedings to which these Rules relate shall furnish to the Comptroller an address for service […], and that address may be treated for all purposes connected with such proceedings as the address of the person concerned.

[(1A) The address for service shall be an address in the United Kingdom, unless in a particular case the comptroller otherwise directs.]

(2) Where any document or part of a document which is in a language other than English is served on the Comptroller or any party to proceedings or filed with the Comptroller in pursuance of these Rules, it shall be accompanied by a translation into English of the document or part, verified to the satisfaction of the Comptroller as corresponding to the original text.

Note: R.23(1) was repealed in part and r.23(1A) was inserted by the Patents, Trade Marks and Designs (Address For Service and Time Limits, etc) Rules 2006 (SI 2006/760), r.3, with effect from April 6, 2006.

B8.iv The Patents County Court (Designation and Jurisdiction) Order 1994

(SI 1994/1609)

Designation as Patents County Court

p.551   Article 3 has been amended to read as follows:

3. As a patents country court, the Central London County Court shall have jurisdiction, subject to [article 4 below—

(a)] to hear and determine any action or matter relating to patents or designs over which the High Court would have jurisdiction, together with any claims or matters ancillary to, or arising from, such proceedings[; and

(b) under the following provisions of the Trade Marks Act 1994—

     (i) sections 15, 16, 19, 23(5), 25(4)(b), 30, 31, 46, 47, 64, 73 and 74;

     (ii) paragraph 12 of Schedule 1; and

     (iii) paragraph 14 of Schedule 2,

to include jurisdiction to hear and determine any claims or matters ancillary to, or arising from proceedings brought under such provisions]."

Note: Article 3 was amended by the High Court and County Courts Jurisdiction (Amendment) Order 2005 (SI 2005/587), art.5, with effect from April 1, 2005.

B8.v The Registered Design Rules 1995

(SI 1995/2912)

p.551   These Rules have been repealed.

Note: These Rules were repealed by the Registered Designs Rules 2006 (SI 2006/1975), Sch.3, with effect from April 6, 2006.

p.604   After **B8.ix**, insert the following:

B8.x The Community Designs (Designation of Community Design Courts) Regulations 2005

(SI 2005/696)

Made	*10th March 2005*
Laid before Parliament	*16th March 2005*
Coming into force	*6th April 2005*

The Secretary of State, being a Minister designated for the purposes of section 2(2) of the European Communities Act 1972 in relation to measures relating to the legal protection of designs, in exercise of powers conferred on her by that section makes the following Regulations:

1. These Regulations may be cited as the Community Designs (Designation of Community Design Courts) Regulations 2005 and shall come into force on 6th April 2005.

2.—(1) For the purposes of Article 80 of the Council Regulation (EC) No. 6/2002 of 12th December 2001 on Community designs, the following courts are designated as Community design courts–

    (a) in England and Wales–

        (i) the High Court; and

        (ii) any county court designated as a patents county court under section 287(1) of the Copyright, Designs and Patents Act 1988;

    (b) in Scotland, the Court of Session; and

    (c) in Northern Ireland, the High Court.

    (2) For the purpose of hearing appeals from judgments of the courts designated by paragraph (1), the following courts are designated as Community design courts–

    (a) in England and Wales, the Court of Appeal;

    (b) in Scotland, the Court of Session;

    (c) in Northern Ireland, the Court of Appeal.

B8.xi The Community Design Regulations 2005

(SI 2005/2339)

Made	*15th August 2005*
Laid before Parliament	*23rd August 2005*
Coming into force	*1st October 2005*

The Secretary of State, being a Minister designated for the purposes of section 2(2) of the European Communities Act 1972 in relation to measures relating to the legal protection of designs, in exercise of the powers conferred on him by that section makes the following Regulations:

Introductory and interpretation

1.—(1) These Regulations may be cited as the Community Design Regulations 2005 and shall come into force on 1st October 2005.

    (2) In these Regulations—

    "the Community Design Regulation" means Council Regulation (EC) 6/2002 of 12th December 2001 on Community Designs; and

    ["Community design court" means a court designated as such by the Community Designs (Designation of Community Design Courts) Regulations 2005;] and

    "Community design", "registered Community design" and "unregistered Community design" have the same meanings as in the Community Design Regulation.

Note: In reg.1(2) the definition of "Community design court" was inserted by the Intellectual Property (Enforcement, etc.) Regulations 2006 (SI 2006/1028), Sch.3 para.8, with effect from April 29, 2006.

[Infringement proceedings

1A.—(1) This regulation and regulations 1B to 1D are without prejudice to the duties of the Community design court under the provisions of Article 89(1)(a) to (c) of the Community Design Regulation.

(2) In an action for infringement of a Community design all such relief by way of damages, injunctions, accounts or otherwise is available to the holder of the Community design as is available in respect of the infringement of any other property right.

Order for delivery up

1B.—(1) Where a person—

  (a) has in his possession, custody or control for commercial purposes an infringing article, or

  (b) has in his possession, custody or control anything specifically designed or adapted for making articles to a particular design which is a Community design, knowing or having reason to believe that it has been or is to be used to make an infringing article,

the holder of the Community design in question may apply to the Community design court for an order that the infringing article or other thing be delivered up to him or to such other person as the court may direct.

(2) An application shall not be made after the end of the period specified in the following provisions of this regulation; and no order shall be made unless the court also makes, or it appears to the court that there are grounds for making, an order under regulation 1C (order as to disposal of infringing articles, &c.).

(3) An application for an order under this regulation may not be made after the end of the period of six years from the date on which the article or thing in question was made, subject to paragraph (4).

(4) If during the whole or any part of that period the holder of the Community design—

  (a) is under a disability, or

  (b) is prevented by fraud or concealment from discovering the facts entitling him to apply for an order,

an application may be made at any time before the end of the period of six years from the date on which he ceased to be under a disability or, as the case may be, could with reasonable diligence have discovered those facts.

(5) In paragraph (4) "disability"—

  (a) in England and Wales, has the same meaning as in the Limitation Act 1980;

  (b) in Scotland, means legal disability within the meaning of the Prescription and Limitation (Scotland) Act 1973;

  (c) in Northern Ireland, has the same meaning as in the Statute of Limitations (Northern Ireland) 1958.

(6) A person to whom an infringing article or other thing is delivered up in pursuance of an order under this regulation shall, if an order under regulation 1C is not made, retain it pending the making of an order, or the decision not to make an order, under that regulation.

(7) The reference in paragraph (1) to an act being done in relation to an article for "commercial purposes" are to its being done with a view to the article in question being sold or hired in the course of a business.

(8) Nothing in this regulation affects any other power of the court.

Order as to disposal of infringing articles, &c

1C.—(1) An application may be made to the Community design court for an order that an infringing article or other thing delivered up in pursuance of an order under regulation 1B shall be—

(a) forfeited to the holder of the Community design, or

(b) destroyed or otherwise dealt with as the court may think fit,

or for a decision that no such order should be made.

(2) In considering what order (if any) should be made, the court shall consider whether other remedies available in an action for infringement of the right in a Community design would be adequate to compensate the holder and to protect his interests.

(3) Where there is more than one person interested in an article or other thing, the court shall make such order as it thinks just and may (in particular) direct that the thing be sold, or otherwise dealt with, and the proceeds divided.

(4) If the court decides that no order should be made under this regulation, the person in whose possession, custody or control the article or other thing was before being delivered up is entitled to its return.

(5) References in this regulation to a person having an interest in an article or other thing include any person in whose favour an order could be made in respect of it—

(a) under this regulation;

(b) under section 24D of the Registered Designs Act 1949;

(c) under section 114, 204 or 231 of the Copyright, Designs and Patents Act 1988; or

(d) under section 19 of the Trade Marks Act 1994 (including that section as applied by regulation 4 of the Community Trade Mark Regulations 2006 (SI 2006/1027)).

Meaning of "infringing article"

1D.—(1) In these Regulations "infringing article", in relation to a design, shall be construed in accordance with this regulation.

(2) An article is an infringing article if its making to that design was an infringement of a Community design.

(3) An article is also an infringing article if—

(a) it has been or is proposed to be imported into the United Kingdom, and

(b) its making to that design in the United Kingdom would have been an infringement of a Community design or a breach of an exclusive licensing agreement relating to that Community design.

(4) Where it is shown that an article is made to a design which is or has been a Community design, it shall be presumed until the contrary is proved that the article was made at a time when the right in the Community design subsisted.

(5) Nothing in paragraph (3) shall be construed as applying to an article which may be lawfully imported into the United Kingdom by virtue of an enforceable Community right within the meaning of section 2(1) of the European Communities Act 1972.]

Note: Regs 1A—1D were inserted by the Intellectual Property (Enforcement, etc.) Regulations 2006 (SI 2006/1028), Sch.3 para.9, with effect from April 29, 2006.

Remedy for groundless threats of infringement proceedings

2.—(1) Where any person (whether entitled to or interested in a Community design or not) by circulars, advertisements or otherwise threatens any other person with proceedings for infringement of a Community design, any person aggrieved thereby may bring an action against him for any such relief as is mentioned in paragraph (2).

(2) Subject to paragraphs (3) and (4), the claimant shall be entitled to the following relief—

(a) a declaration to the effect that the threats are unjustifiable;

(b) an injunction against the continuance of the threats; and

(c) such damages, if any, as he has sustained by reason of the threats.

(3) If the defendant proves that the acts in respect of which proceedings were threatened constitute or, if done, would constitute an infringement of a registered Community design the claimant shall be entitled to the relief claimed only if he shows that the registration is invalid.

(4) If the defendant proves that the acts in respect of which proceedings were threatened constitute or, if done, would constitute an infringement of an unregistered Community design the claimant shall not be entitled to the relief claimed.

(5) Proceedings may not be brought under this regulation in respect of a threat to bring proceedings for an infringement alleged to consist of the making or importing of anything.

(6) Mere notification that a design is—

(a) a registered Community design; or

(b) protected as an unregistered Community design,

does not constitute a threat of proceedings for the purpose of this regulation.

(7) [...]

Note: Reg.2(7) was revoked by the Intellectual Property (Enforcement, etc.) Regulations 2006 (SI 2006/1028), Sch.4, with effect from April 29, 2006.

Falsely representing a design as a registered Community design

3.—(1) It is an offence for a person falsely to represent that a design applied to, or incorporated in, any product sold by him is a registered Community design.

(2) It is an offence for a person, after a registered Community design has expired, to represent (expressly or by implication) that a design applied to, or incorporated in, any product sold is still registered in the manner provided for in the Community Design Regulation.

(3) A person guilty of an offence under paragraph (1) is liable on summary conviction to a fine not exceeding level 3 on the standard scale.

(4) A person guilty of an offence under paragraph (2) is liable on summary conviction to a fine not exceeding level 1 on the standard scale.

Privilege for communications with those on the special list of professional design representatives

4.—(1) This regulation applies to communications as to any matter relating to the protection of any design.

(2) Any such communication—

(a) between a person and his professional designs representative, or

(b) for the purposes of obtaining, or in response to a request for, information which a person is seeking for the purpose of instructing his professional designs representative,

is privileged from, or in Scotland protected against, disclosure in legal proceedings in the same way as a communication between a person and his solicitor or, as the case may be, a communication for the purpose of obtaining, or in response to a request for, information which a person is seeking for the purpose of instructing his solicitor.

(3) In paragraph (2) "professional designs representative" means a person who is on the special list of professional representatives for design matters referred to in Article 78 of the Community Design Regulation.

Use of Community design for services of the Crown

5. The provisions of the Schedule to these Regulations shall have effect with respect to the use of registered Community designs and unregistered Community designs for the services of the Crown and the rights of third parties in respect of such use.

[Application to Scotland and Northern Ireland

5A.—(1) In the application of these Regulations to Scotland—
"accounts" means count, reckoning and payment;
"claimant" means pursuer;
"defendant" means defender;
"delivery up" means delivery;
"injunction" means interdict.

(2) In the application of these Regulations to Northern Ireland, "claimant" includes plaintiff.]

Note: Reg.5A was inserted by the Intellectual Property (Enforcement, etc.) Regulations 2006 (SI 2006/1028), Sch.3 para.10, with effect from April 29, 2006.

Amendment of section 35 of the Registered Designs Act 1949

6. [Section 35 of the Registered Designs Act 1949 amended].

Regulation 5

SCHEDULE

USE OF COMMUNITY DESIGNS FOR SERVICES OF THE CROWN

Use of Community design for services of the Crown

1.—(1) A government department, or a person authorised in writing by a government department, may without the consent of the holder of a Community design—
  (a) do anything for the purpose of supplying products for the services of the Crown, or
  (b) dispose of products no longer required for the services of the Crown;
and nothing done by virtue of this paragraph infringes the Community design.

(2) References in this Schedule to "the services of the Crown" are limited to those which are necessary for essential defence or security needs.

(3) In this Schedule—
  "Crown use", in relation to a Community design, means the doing of anything by virtue of this paragraph which would otherwise be an infringement of the Community design; and
  "the government department concerned", in relation to such use, means the government department by whom or on whose authority the act was done.

(4) The authority of a government department in respect of Crown use of a Community design may be given to a person either before or after the use and whether or not he is authorised, directly or indirectly, by the holder of the Community design to do anything in relation to the design.

(5) A person acquiring anything sold in the exercise of powers conferred by this paragraph, and any person claiming under him, may deal with it in the same manner as if the Crown was the holder of the Community design.

Settlement of terms for Crown use

2.—(1) Where Crown use is made of a Community design, the government department concerned shall—

(a) notify the holder of the Community design as soon as practicable, and

(b) give him such information as to the extent of the use as he may from time to time require,

unless it appears to the department that it would be contrary to the public interest to do so or the identity of the holder of the Community design cannot be ascertained on reasonable inquiry.

(2) Crown use of a Community design shall be on such terms as, either before or after the use, are agreed between the government department concerned and the holder of the Community design with the approval of the Treasury or, in default of agreement, are determined by the court.

(3) In the application of sub-paragraph (2) to Northern Ireland the reference to the Treasury shall, where the government department referred to in that sub-paragraph is a Northern Ireland department, be construed as a reference to the Department of Finance and Personnel.

(4) In the application of sub-paragraph (2) to Scotland, where the government department referred to in that sub-paragraph is any part of the Scottish Administration, the words "with the approval of the Treasury" are omitted.

(5) Where the identity of the holder of the Community design cannot be ascertained on reasonable inquiry, the government department concerned may apply to the court who may order that no royalty or other sum shall be payable in respect of Crown use of the Community design until the holder agrees terms with the department or refers the matter to the court for determination.

Rights of third parties in case of Crown use

3.—(1) The provisions of any licence, assignment or agreement made between the holder of the Community design (or anyone deriving title from him or from whom he derives title) and any person other than a government department are of no effect in relation to Crown use of a Community design, or any act incidental to Crown use, so far as they—

(a) restrict or regulate anything done in relation to the Community design, or the use of any model, document or other information relating to it, or

(b) provide for the making of payments in respect of, or calculated by reference to such use;

and the copying or issuing to the public of copies of any such model or document in connection with the thing done, or any such use, shall be deemed not to be an infringement of any copyright in the model or document.

(2) Sub-paragraph (1) shall not be construed as authorising the disclosure of any such model, document or information in contravention of the licence, assignment or agreement.

(3) Where an exclusive licence is in force in respect of the Community design—

(a) if the licence was granted for royalties—

(i) any agreement between the holder of the Community design and a government department under paragraph 2 (settlement of terms for Crown use) requires the consent of the licensee, and

(ii) the licensee is entitled to recover from the holder of the Community design such part of the payment for Crown use as may be agreed between them or, in default of agreement, determined by the court;

(b) if the licence was granted otherwise than for royalties—

(i) paragraph 2 applies in relation to anything done which but for paragraph 1 (Crown use) and sub-paragraph (1) would be an infringement of the rights of the licensee with the substitution for references to the holder of the Community design of references to the licensee, and

(ii) paragraph 2 does not apply in relation to anything done by the licensee by virtue of an authority given under paragraph 1.

(4) Where the Community design has been assigned to the holder of the Community design in consideration of royalties—

(a) paragraph 2 applies in relation to Crown use of the Community design as if the references to the holder of the Community design included the assignor, and any payment for Crown use shall be divided between them in such proportion as may be agreed or, in default of agreement, determined by the court; and

(b) paragraph 2 applies in relation to any act incidental to Crown use as it applies in relation to Crown use of the Community design.

(5) Where any model, document or other information relating to a Community design is used in connection with Crown use of the design, or any act incidental to Crown use, paragraph 2 applies to the use of the model, document or other information with the substitution for the references to the holder of the Community design of references to the person entitled to the benefit of any provision of an agreement rendered inoperative by sub-paragraph (1).

(6) In this paragraph—

"act incidental to Crown use" means anything done for the services of the Crown to the order of a government department by the holder of the Community design in respect of a design;

"payment for Crown use" means such amount as is payable by the government department concerned by virtue of paragraph 2; and

"royalties" includes any benefit determined by reference to the use of the Community design.

Crown use: compensation for loss of profit

4.—(1) Where Crown use is made of a Community design, the government department concerned shall pay—

(a) to the holder of the Community design, or

(b) if there is an exclusive licence in force in respect of the Community design, to the exclusive licensee,

compensation for any loss resulting from his not being awarded a contract to supply the products to which the Community design is applied or in which it is incorporated.

(2) Compensation is payable only to the extent that such a contract could have been fulfilled from his existing manufacturing capacity; but is payable notwithstanding the existence of circumstances rendering him ineligible for the award of such a contract.

(3) In determining the loss, regard shall be had to the profit which would have been made on such a contract and to the extent to which any manufacturing capacity was under-used.

(4) No compensation is payable in respect of any failure to secure contracts for the supply of products to which the Community design is applied or in which it is incorporated otherwise than for the services of the Crown.

(5) The amount payable shall, if not agreed between the holder of the Community design or licensee and the government department concerned with the approval of the Treasury, be determined by the court on a reference under paragraph 5; and it is in addition to any amount payable under paragraph 2 or 3.

(6) In the application of this paragraph to Northern Ireland, the reference in sub-paragraph (5) to the Treasury shall, where the government department concerned is a Northern Ireland department, be construed as a reference to the Department of Finance and Personnel.

(7) In the application of this paragraph to Scotland, where the government department referred to in sub-paragraph (5) is any part of the Scottish Administration, the words "with the approval of the Treasury" in that sub-paragraph are omitted.

Reference of disputes relating to Crown use

5.—(1) A dispute as to any matter which falls to be determined by the court in default of agreement under—

(a) paragraph 2 (settlement of terms for Crown use),

(b) paragraph 3 (rights of third parties in case of Crown use), or

(c) paragraph 4(Crown use: compensation for loss of profit),

may be referred to the court by any party to the dispute.

(2) In determining a dispute between a government department and any person as to the terms for Crown use of a Community design the court shall have regard to—

(a) any sums which that person or a person from whom he derives title has received or is entitled to receive, directly or indirectly, from any government department in respect of the Community design; and

(b) whether that person or a person from whom he derives title has in the court's opinion without reasonable cause failed to comply with a request of the department for the use of the Community design on reasonable terms.

(3) One of two or more joint holders of the Community design may, without the concurrence of the others, refer a dispute to the court under this paragraph, but shall not do so unless the others are made parties; and none of those others is liable for any costs unless he takes part in the proceedings.

(4) Where the consent of an exclusive licensee is required by paragraph 3(3)(a)(i) to the settlement by agreement of the terms for Crown use of a Community design, a determination by the court of the amount of any payment to be made for such use is of no effect unless the licensee has been notified of the reference and given an opportunity to be heard.

(5) On the reference of a dispute as to the amount recoverable as mentioned in paragraph 3(3)(a)(ii) (right of exclusive licensee to recover part of amount payable to holder of Community design) the court shall determine what is just having regard to any expenditure incurred by the licensee—

    (a) in developing the design, or

    (b) in making payments to the holder of the Community design in consideration of the licence (other than royalties or other payments determined by reference to the use of the design).

(6) In this Schedule "the court" means—

    (a) in England and Wales, the High Court or any patents county court having jurisdiction by virtue of an order under section 287 of the Copyright, Designs and Patents Act 1988,

    (b) in Scotland, the Court of Session, and

    (c) in Northern Ireland, the High Court.

B9. SEMICONDUCTOR TOPOGRAPHIES

B9.i The Design Right (Semiconductor Topographies) Regulations 1989

(SI 1989/1100)

Qualification

p.605   Regulation 4(2) has been substituted to read as follows:

"(2) Part III of the Act has effect as if for section 217(3) there was substituted the following—

"(3) In this section "qualifying country" means—

    (a) the United Kingdom,

    (b) another member State,

    (c) the Isle of Man, Gibraltar, the Channel Islands or any colony,

    (d) a country listed in the Schedule to the Design Right (Semiconductor Topographies) Regulations 1989."".

Note: Reg.4(2) was substituted by the Design Right (Semiconductor Topographies) (Amendment) Regulations 2006 (SI 2006/1833), reg.3 with effect from August 1, 2006.

Schedule has been substituted to read as follows:

"SCHEDULE

QUALIFYING COUNTRIES

Albania
Angola

Antigua and Barbuda
Argentina
Armenia
Australia
Bahrain, Kingdom of
Bangladesh
Barbados
Belize
Benin
Bolivia
Botswana
Brazil
Brunei Darussalam
Bulgaria
Burkina Faso
Burundi
Cambodia
Cameroon
Canada
Central African Republic
Chad
Chile
China
Colombia
Congo
Costa Rica
Côte d'Ivoire
Croatia
Cuba
Democratic Republic of the Congo
Djibouti
Dominica
Dominican Republic
Ecuador
Egypt
El Salvador
Fiji
Former Yugoslav Republic of Macedonia
French overseas territories
Gabon
The Gambia
Georgia
Ghana
Grenada
Guatemala
Guinea
Guinea Bissau
Guyana
Haiti
Honduras
Hong Kong
Iceland
India
Indonesia
Israel
Jamaica
Japan
Jordan
Kenya
Korea, Republic of

Kuwait
Kyrgyz Republic
Lesotho
Liechtenstein
Macao, China
Madagascar
Malawi
Malaysia
Maldives
Mali
Mauritania
Mauritius
Mexico
Moldova
Mongolia
Morocco
Mozambique
Myanmar
Namibia
Nepal
Netherlands Antilles
New Zealand
Nicaragua
Niger
Nigeria
Norway
Oman
Pakistan
Panama
Papua New Guinea
Paraguay
Peru
Philippines
Qatar
Romania
Rwanda
Saint Kitts and Nevis
Saint Lucia
Saint Vincent & the Grenadines
Saudi Arabia
Senegal
Sierra Leone
Singapore
Solomon Islands
South Africa
Sri Lanka
Suriname
Swaziland
Switzerland
Chinese Taipei
Tanzania
Thailand
Togo
Trinidad and Tobago
Tunisia
Turkey
Uganda
United Arab Emirates
United States of America
Uruguay

Venezuela
Zambia
Zimbabwe"

Note: Schedule was substituted by the Design Right (Semiconductor Topographies) (Amendment) Regulations 2006 (SI 2006/1833), reg.4 with effect from August 1, 2006.

After **B10 E-Commerce** insert: **p.614**

B11. ENFORCEMENT

B11.i The Intellectual Property (Enforcement, etc.) Regulations 2006

(SI 2006/1028)

Made	*5th April 2006*
Laid before Parliament	*6th April 2006*
Coming into force	*29th April 2006*

The Secretary of State has been designated for the purposes of section 2(2) of the European Communities Act 1972 in relation to intellectual property (including both registered and unregistered rights).

He makes the following Regulations under the powers conferred by that section:

Citation and commencement

1. These Regulations may be cited as the Intellectual Property (Enforcement, etc.) Regulations 2006 and shall come into force on 29th April 2006.

Amendments of legislation

2.—(1) Schedule 1 (amendments to the Registered Designs Act 1949) shall have effect.

(2) Schedule 2 (amendments to other primary legislation) shall have effect.

(3) Schedule 3 (amendments to secondary legislation) shall have effect.

(4) The enactments set out in Schedule 4 (repeals) shall be repealed or revoked to the extent specified.

Assessment of damages

3.—(1) Where in an action for infringement of an intellectual property right the defendant knew, or had reasonable grounds to know, that he engaged in infringing activity, the damages awarded to the claimant shall be appropriate to the actual prejudice he suffered as a result of the infringement.

(2) When awarding such damages—
- (a) all appropriate aspects shall be taken into account, including in particular—
    - (i) the negative economic consequences, including any lost profits, which the claimant has suffered, and any unfair profits made by the defendant; and
    - (ii) elements other than economic factors, including the moral prejudice caused to the claimant by the infringement; or
- (b) where appropriate, they may be awarded on the basis of the royalties or fees which would have been due had the defendant obtained a licence.

(3) This regulation does not affect the operation of any enactment or rule of law relating to remedies for the infringement of intellectual property rights except to the extent that it is inconsistent with the provisions of this regulation.

(4) In the application of this regulation to—

    (a) Scotland, "claimant" includes pursuer; "defendant" includes defender; and "enactment" includes an enactment comprised in, or an instrument made under, an Act of the Scottish Parliament; and

    (b) Northern Ireland, "claimant" includes plaintiff.

Order in Scotland for disclosure of information

4.—(1) This regulation applies to proceedings in Scotland concerning an infringement of an intellectual property right.

(2) The pursuer may apply to the court for an order that information regarding the origin and distribution networks of goods or services which infringe an intellectual property right shall be disclosed to him by the relevant person.

(3) The court may only order the information to be disclosed where it considers it just and proportionate having regard to the rights and privileges of the relevant person and others; such an order may be subject to such conditions as the court thinks fit.

(4) The relevant person is—

    (a) the alleged infringer,

    (b) any person who—

        (i) was found in possession of the infringing goods on a commercial scale,

        (ii) was found to be using the infringing services on a commercial scale, or

        (iii) was found to be providing services on a commercial scale, which are used in activities which infringe an intellectual property right, or

    (c) any person who has been identified by a person specified in sub-paragraph (b) as being involved in—

        (i) the production, manufacture or distribution of the infringing goods, or

        (ii) the provision of the infringing services.

(5) For the purposes of paragraph (3), the court may order the disclosure of any of the following types of information—

    (a) the names and addresses of—

        (i) each producer, manufacturer, distributor or supplier of the infringing goods or services;

        (ii) any person who previously possessed the infringing goods; and

        (iii) the intended wholesaler and retailer of the infringing goods or services; and

    (b) information relating to—

        (i) the quantities of infringing goods or the amount of infringing services provided, produced, manufactured, delivered, received or ordered; and

        (ii) the price paid for the infringing goods or infringing services in question.

(6) Nothing in this regulation affects—

    (a) any right of the pursuer to receive information under any other enactment (including an enactment comprised in, or an instrument made under, an Act of the Scottish Parliament) or rule of law; and

    (b) any other power of the court.

(7) For the purposes of this regulation and regulation 5, "court" means the Court of Session or the sheriff.

Order in Scotland for publication of judgments

5. In Scotland, where the court finds that an intellectual property right has been infringed, the court may, at the request of the pursuer, order appropriate measures for the dissemination and publication of the judgment to be taken at the defender's expense.

Schedules 1–4

[Not reproduced]

PART C

ORDERS IN COUNCIL

C1. PART I

C1.iv The Copyright (Application to Other Countries) Order 1999

p.621 This order has been revoked.

Note: This order was revoked by the Copyright and Performances (Application to Other Countries) Order 2005 (SI 2005/852), art.8, with effect from May 1, 2005, which was in turn revoked by the Copyright and Performances (Application to Other Countries) Order 2006 (SI 2006/316), art.1(3), with effect from April 6, 2006. The Copyright and Performances (Application to Other Countries) Order 2006 was in turn revoked by the Copyright and Performances (Application to Other Countries) Order 2007 (SI 2007/273), art.1(3), with effect from April 6, 2007.

SI 2007/273 is reproduced below:

The Copyright and Performances (Application to Other Countries) Order 2007

(SI 2007/273)

Made	*7th February 2007*
Laid before Parliament	*14th February 2007*
Coming into force	*6th April 2007*

At the Court at Buckingham Palace, the 7th day of February 2007

Present,

The Queen's Most Excellent Majesty in Council

Her Majesty is satisfied that provision has been or will be made giving adequate protection for British performances and to the owners of British copyright works under the laws of the Isle of Man and for British performances under the laws of Gibraltar.

Her Majesty is further satisfied that provision has been or will be made giving adequate protection to the owners of the copyright in British sound recordings and wireless broadcasts under the laws of Indonesia and Malaysia and to the owners of the copyright in British sound recordings under the laws of Bangladesh, Botswana, Gabon, Georgia, Ghana, Guinea, India, Jordan, Kazakhstan, Mali, Mongolia, New Zealand, Pakistan, Senegal, Taiwan, Thailand and the United States of America.

Accordingly, Her Majesty, by and with the advice of Her Privy Council, in exercise of the powers conferred upon Her by sections 159 and 208 of the Copyright, Designs and Patents Act 1988 and by section 2(2) of the European Communities Act 1972, makes the following Order:

Introductory

1.—(1) This Order may be cited as the Copyright and Performances (Application to Other Countries) Order 2007 and shall come into force on 6th April 2007.

(2) In this Order "the Act" means the Copyright, Designs and Patents Act 1988.

(3) The Copyright and Performances (Application to Other Countries) Order 2006 is revoked.

Literary, dramatic, musical and artistic works, films and the typographical arrangement of published editions

2.—(1) All the provisions of Part 1 of the Act, insofar as they relate to literary, dramatic, musical and artistic works, films and the typographical arrangement of published editions, apply in relation to the countries indicated in the second column of the table set out in the Schedule so that those provisions apply—

(a) in relation to persons who are citizens or subjects of, or are domiciled or resident in, those countries as they apply to persons who are British citizens or are domiciled or resident in the United Kingdom,

(b) in relation to bodies incorporated under the laws of those countries as they apply in relation to bodies incorporated under the law of a part of the United Kingdom, and

(c) in relation to works first published in those countries as they apply in relation to works first published in the United Kingdom,

subject to paragraph (2).

(2) Where a literary, dramatic, musical or artistic work was first published before 1st June 1957 it shall not qualify for copyright protection by reason of section 154 (qualification by reference to author).

Sound recordings

3.—(1) Except for the provisions listed in paragraph (2)(a), all the provisions of Part 1 of the Act, insofar as they relate to sound recordings, apply in relation to the countries indicated in the third column of the table set out in the Schedule so that those provisions apply—

(a) in relation to persons who are citizens or subjects of, or are domiciled or resident in, those countries as they apply to persons who are British citizens or are domiciled or resident in the United Kingdom,

(b) in relation to bodies incorporated under the laws of those countries as they apply in relation to bodies incorporated under the law of a part of the United Kingdom, and

(c) in relation to works first published in those countries as they apply in relation to works first published in the United Kingdom.

(2) Where in the third column of the table set out in the Schedule the entry for a country—

(a) includes an asterisk (*), the following provisions of Part 1 of the Act, insofar as they relate to sound recordings, also apply to that country—

(i) section 18A (infringement by rental or lending of work to the public) insofar as it applies to lending;

(ii) section 19 (infringement by playing of work in public);

(iii) section 20 (infringement by communication to the public);

(iv) section 26 (secondary infringement: provision of apparatus for infringing performance, &c); and

(v) section 107(2A) and (3) (criminal liability for communicating to the public or playing a sound recording);

(b) includes a hash (#), the following provisions of Part 1 of the Act, insofar as they relate to sound recordings, also apply to that country—

(i) section 20 (infringement by communication to the public), except that references to communication to the public do not include the broadcasting of a sound recording; and

(ii) section 107(2A) (criminal liability for communicating to the public), except that it does not apply in relation to the broadcasting of a sound recording.

Wireless broadcasts

4.—(1) Except for the provisions listed in paragraph (2), all the provisions of Part 1 of the Act, insofar as they relate to wireless broadcasts, apply in relation to the countries indicated in the fourth column of the table set out in the Schedule so that those provisions apply—

(a) in relation to persons who are citizens or subjects of, or are domiciled or resident in, those countries as they apply to persons who are British citizens or are domiciled or resident in the United Kingdom,

(b) in relation to bodies incorporated under the laws of those countries as they apply in relation to bodies incorporated under the law of a part of the United Kingdom, and

(c) in relation to broadcasts made from those countries as they apply in relation to broadcasts made from the United Kingdom,

subject to paragraphs (3) to (5).

(2) The following provisions of Part 1 of the Act, insofar as they relate to wireless broadcasts, also apply in relation to a country where its entry in the fourth column of the table set out in the Schedule does not include an asterisk (*)—

(a) section 18A (infringement by rental or lending of work to the public);

(b) section 19 (infringement by showing or playing of work in public), but only insofar as it relates to broadcasts other than television broadcasts;

(c) section 20 (infringement by communication to the public), except in relation to broadcasting by wireless telegraphy;

(d) section 26 (secondary infringement: provision of apparatus for infringing performance, &c), but only insofar as it relates to broadcasts other than television broadcasts;

(e) section 107(2A) (criminal liability for communicating to the public), except in relation to broadcasting by wireless telegraphy.

(3) The provisions of Part 1 of the Act do not apply in relation to a wireless broadcast made from a place in a country, referred to in paragraph (4), before the relevant date.

(4) The relevant date in relation to a country—

(a) where its entry in the fourth column of the table set out in the Schedule includes an "(X)", is 1st June 1957;

(b) where its entry in the fourth column of the table set out in the Schedule includes a "(Y)", is 1st January 1996; or

(c) where there is a date next to its entry in the fourth column of the table set out in the Schedule, is that date.

(5) For the purposes of section 14(5) of the Act (duration of copyright in repeats) any wireless broadcast which does not qualify for copyright protection shall be disregarded.

Other broadcasts

5. All the provisions of Part 1 of the Act, insofar as they relate to broadcasts (other than wireless broadcasts), apply in relation to the countries indicated in the fifth column of the table set out in the Schedule so that those provisions apply—

    (a) in relation to persons who are citizens or subjects of, or are domiciled or resident in, those countries as they apply to persons who are British citizens or are domiciled or resident in the United Kingdom,

    (b) in relation to bodies incorporated under the laws of those countries as they apply in relation to bodies incorporated under the law of a part of the United Kingdom, and

    (c) in relation to broadcasts made from those countries as they apply in relation to broadcasts made from the United Kingdom.

Performances

6.—(1) The countries in respect of which the word "designated" is included in the sixth column of the table set out in the Schedule are designated as enjoying reciprocal protection under Part 2 of the Act.

(2) The countries in respect of which the word "deemed" is included in the sixth column of the table set out in the Schedule shall be treated as if they were designated as enjoying reciprocal protection under Part 2 of the Act, except that—

    (a) in that Part the term "recording" shall be construed as applying only to sound recordings (and not to films);

    (b) the following provisions of Part 2 of the Act shall not apply—

        (i) section 182C (consent required for rental or lending of copies to public), insofar as it relates to lending;

        (ii) section 182D (right to equitable remuneration for exploitation of sound recording);

        (iii) section 183 (infringement of performer's rights by use of recording made without consent);

        (iv) sections 185 to 188 (rights of person having recording rights);

        (v) section 198(2) (criminal liability for playing or communicating to the public); and

    (c) where in the sixth column of the table set out in the Schedule the entry for a country includes an asterisk (*), the following provisions of Part 2 of the Act shall also not apply—

        (i) section 182CA (consent required for making available to the public);

        (ii) section 198(1A) (criminal liability for making available to the public).

Savings

7.—(1) For the purposes of this article an act is an "excluded act" where—

    (a) a person (A) has incurred any expenditure or liability in connection with the act; and

    (b) he—

        (i) began in good faith to do the act, or

        (ii) made in good faith effective and serious preparations to do the act,

at a time when the act neither infringed nor was restricted by the relevant rights in the work or performance.

(2) Where another person (B) acquires those relevant rights pursuant to this Order, A has the right—

    (a) to continue to do the excluded act, or

    (b) to do the excluded act,

notwithstanding that the excluded act infringes or is restricted by those relevant rights.

(3) Where B, or his exclusive licensee, pays reasonable compensation to A paragraph (2) no longer applies.

(4) Where—

    (a) B offers to pay compensation to A under paragraph (3); but

    (b) A and B cannot agree on what compensation is reasonable,

either person may refer the matter to arbitration.

(5) In this article "relevant rights" means copyright, the rights conferred by Chapter 4 of Part 1 of the Act and the rights conferred by Part 2 of the Act.

Articles 2 to 6

SCHEDULE

Country	Article 2 (literary, dramatic, musical and artistic works, films and typographical arrangements)	Article 3 (sound recordings)	Article 4 (wireless broadcasts)	Article 5 (other broadcasts)	Article 6 (performances)
Albania	Applies	Applies (*)	Applies (1st September 2000)		Designated
Algeria	Applies	Applies			
Andorra	Applies	Applies (*)	Applies (25th May 2004)		Designated
Angola	Applies	Applies	Applies (*) (23rd November 1996)		Deemed (*)
Antigua and Barbuda	Applies	Applies	Applies (*)(Y)		Deemed (*)
Argentina	Applies	Applies (*)	Applies (2nd March 1992)		Designated
Armenia	Applies	Applies (*)	Applies (31st January 2003)		Designated
Australia (including Norfolk Island)	Applies	Applies (*)	Applies (30th September 1992)		Designated
Austria	Applies	Applies (*)	Applies (X)	Applies	
Azerbaijan	Applies	Applies (*)	Applies (5th October 2005)		Designated
Bahamas	Applies	Applies			

Country	Article 2 (literary, dramatic, musical and artistic works, films and typographical arrangements)	Article 3 (sound recordings)	Article 4 (wireless broadcasts)	Article 5 (other broadcasts)	Article 6 (perfor-mances)
Bahrain	Applies	Applies (*)	Applies (Y)		Designated
Bangladesh	Applies	Applies (*)	Applies (*)(Y)		Deemed (*)
Barbados	Applies	Applies (*)	Applies (18th September 1983)		Designated
Belarus	Applies	Applies (*)	Applies (27th May 2003)		Designated
Belgium	Applies	Applies (*)	Applies (X)	Applies	
Belize	Applies	Applies	Applies (*)(Y)		Deemed (*)
Benin	Applies	Applies (#)	Applies (*) (22nd February 1996)		Deemed
Bhutan	Applies	Applies			
Bolivia	Applies	Applies (*)	Applies (24th November 1993)		Designated
Bosnia and Herzegovina	Applies	Applies			
Botswana	Applies	Applies (#)	Applies (*)(Y)		Deemed
Brazil	Applies	Applies (*)	Applies (29th September 1965)		Designated
Brunei Darussalam	Applies	Applies	Applies (*)(Y)		Deemed (*)
Bulgaria	Applies	Applies (*)	Applies (X)	Applies	
Burkina Faso	Applies	Applies (*)	Applies (14th January 1988)		Designated
Burundi	Applies	Applies	Applies (*)(Y)		Deemed (*)

Country	Article 2 (literary, dramatic, musical and artistic works, films and typographical arrangements)	Article 3 (sound recordings)	Article 4 (wireless broadcasts)	Article 5 (other broadcasts)	Article 6 (performances)
Cambodia	Applies	Applies	Applies (*) (13th October 2004)		Deemed (*)
Cameroon	Applies	Applies	Applies (*)(Y)		Deemed (*)
Canada	Applies	Applies (*)	Applies (Y)		Designated
Cape Verde	Applies	Applies (*)	Applies (3rd July 1997)		Designated
Central African Republic	Applies	Applies	Applies (*)(Y)		Deemed (*)
Chad	Applies	Applies	Applies (*) (19th October 1996)		Deemed (*)
Chile	Applies	Applies (*)	Applies (5th September 1974)		Designated
China	Applies	Applies	Applies (*) (11th December 2001)		Deemed (*)
Columbia	Applies	Applies (*)	Applies (17th September 1976)		Designated
Comoros	Applies	Applies			
Congo	Applies	Applies (*)	Applies (18th May 1964)		Designated
Costa Rica	Applies	Applies (*)	Applies (9th September 1971)		Designated
Cote d'Ivoire	Applies	Applies	Applies (*)(Y)		Deemed (*)
Croatia	Applies	Applies (*)	Applies (20th April 2000)		Designated
Cuba	Applies	Applies	Applies (*)(Y)		Deemed (*)

Country	Article 2 (literary, dramatic, musical and artistic works, films and typographical arrangements)	Article 3 (sound recordings)	Article 4 (wireless broadcasts)	Article 5 (other broadcasts)	Article 6 (performances)
Cyprus	Applies	Applies (*)	Applies (X)	Applies	
Czech Republic	Applies	Applies (*)	Applies (X)	Applies	
Democratic Republic of the Congo	Applies	Applies	Applies (*) (1st January 1997)		Deemed (*)
Denmark	Applies	Applies (*)	Applies (X)	Applies	
Djibouti	Applies	Applies	Applies (*)(Y)		Deemed (*)
Dominica	Applies	Applies (*)	Applies (Y)		Designated
Dominican Republic	Applies	Applies (*)	Applies (27th January 1987)		Designated
Ecuador	Applies	Applies (*)	Applies (18th May 1964)		Designated
Egypt	Applies	Applies	Applies (*)(Y)		Deemed (*)
El Salvador	Applies	Applies (*)	Applies (29th June 1979)		Designated
Equatorial Guinea	Applies	Applies			
Estonia	Applies	Applies (*)	Applies (X)	Applies	
Faeroe Islands	Applies	Applies	Applies (1st February 1962)		Designated
Fiji	Applies	Applies (*)	Applies (11th April 1972)		Designated
Finland	Applies	Applies (*)	Applies (X)	Applies	

Country	Article 2 (literary, dramatic, musical and artistic works, films and typographical arrangements)	Article 3 (sound recordings)	Article 4 (wireless broadcasts)	Article 5 (other broadcasts)	Article 6 (performances)
France (including Overseas Departments and Territories)	Applies	Applies (*)	Applies (X)	Applies	
Gabon	Applies	Applies (#)	Applies (*)(Y)		Deemed
Gambia	Applies	Applies	Applies (*) (23rd October 1996)		Deemed (*)
Georgia	Applies	Applies (#)	Applies (*) (14th June 2000)		Deemed
Germany	Applies	Applies (*)	Applies (X)	Applies	
Ghana	Applies	Applies (*)	Applies (*)(Y)		Deemed (*)
Gibraltar	Applies	Applies (*)	Applies (X)	Applies	Designated
Greece	Applies	Applies (*)	Applies (X)	Applies	
Greenland	Applies	Applies	Applies (1st February 1962)		Designated
Grenada	Applies	Applies	Applies (*) (22nd February 1996)		Deemed (*)
Guatemala	Applies	Applies (*)	Applies (14th January 1977)		Designated
Guinea	Applies	Applies (#)	Applies (*)(Y)		Deemed
Guinea-Bissau	Applies	Applies	Applies (*)(Y)		Deemed (*)
Guyana	Applies	Applies	Applies (*)(Y)		Deemed (*)
Haiti	Applies	Applies	Applies (*) (30th January 1996)		Deemed (*)

Country	Article 2 (literary, dramatic, musical and artistic works, films and typographical arrangements)	Article 3 (sound recordings)	Article 4 (wireless broadcasts)	Article 5 (other broadcasts)	Article 6 (perfor-mances)
Holy See	Applies	Applies			
Honduras	Applies	Applies (*)	Applies (16th February 1990)		Designated
Hong Kong	Applies	Applies (*)	Applies (X)		Deemed (*)
Hungary	Applies	Applies (*)	Applies (X)	Applies	
Iceland	Applies	Applies (*)	Applies (X)	Applies	Designated
India	Applies	Applies (*)	Applies (*)(Y)		Deemed (*)
Indonesia	Applies	Applies (*)	Applies (X)	Applies	Deemed
Ireland	Applies	Applies (*)	Applies (X)	Applies	
Isle of Man	Applies	Applies (*)	Applies (X)	Applies	Designated
Israel	Applies	Applies (*)	Applies (Y)		Designated
Italy	Applies	Applies (*)	Applies (X)	Applies	
Jamaica	Applies	Applies (*)	Applies (27th January 1994)		Designated
Japan	Applies	Applies (*)	Applies (26th October 1989)		Designated
Jordan	Applies	Applies (#)	Applies (*) (11th April 2000)		Deemed
Kazakhstan	Applies	Applies (#)			Deemed
Kenya	Applies	Applies	Applies (*)(Y)		Deemed (*)
Korea, Democratic People's Republic of	Applies	Applies			
Korea, Republic of	Applies	Applies	Applies (*)(Y)		Deemed (*)

Country	Article 2 (literary, dramatic, musical and artistic works, films and typographical arrangements)	Article 3 (sound record-ings)	Article 4 (wireless broadcasts)	Article 5 (other broadcasts)	Article 6 (perfor-mances)
Kuwait	Applies	Applies	Applies (*)(Y)		Deemed (*)
Kyrgyzstan	Applies	Applies (*)	Applies (20th December 1998)		Designated
Lao People's Democratic Republic	Applies	Applies			
Latvia	Applies	Applies (*)	Applies (X)	Applies	
Lebanon	Applies	Applies (*)	Applies (12th August 1997)		Designated
Lesotho	Applies	Applies (*)	Applies (26th January 1990)		Designated
Liberia	Applies	Applies			
Libyan Arab Jamahiriya	Applies	Applies			
Liechtenstein	Applies	Applies (*)	Applies (X)	Applies	Designated
Lithuania	Applies	Applies (*)	Applies (X)	Applies	
Luxembourg	Applies	Applies (*)	Applies (X)	Applies	
Macao	Applies	Applies	Applies (*)(Y)		Deemed (*)
Macedonia, The Former Yugoslav Republic of	Applies	Applies (*)	Applies (2nd March 1998)		Designated
Madagascar	Applies	Applies	Applies (*)(Y)		Deemed (*)
Malawi	Applies	Applies (*)	Applies (22nd June 1989)		Deemed (*)
Malaysia	Applies	Applies (*)	Applies (X)		Deemed (*)
Maldives	Applies	Applies	Applies (*)(Y)		Deemed (*)
Mali	Applies	Applies (#)	Applies (*)(Y)		Deemed

Country	Article 2 (literary, dramatic, musical and artistic works, films and typographical arrangements)	Article 3 (sound recordings)	Article 4 (wireless broadcasts)	Article 5 (other broadcasts)	Article 6 (performances)
Malta	Applies	Applies (*)	Applies (X)	Applies	
Mauritania	Applies	Applies	Applies (*)(Y)		Deemed (*)
Mauritius	Applies	Applies	Applies (*)(Y)		Deemed (*)
Mexico	Applies	Applies (*)	Applies (18th May 1964)		Designated
Micronesia, Federated States of	Applies	Applies			
Moldova, Republic of	Applies	Applies (*)	Applies (5th December 1995)		Designated
Monaco	Applies	Applies (*)	Applies (6th December 1985)		Designated
Mongolia	Applies	Applies (#)	Applies (*) (29th January 1997)		Deemed
Montenegro	Applies	Applies (*)	Applies (10th June 2003)		Designated
Morocco	Applies	Applies	Applies (*)(Y)		Deemed (*)
Mozambique	Applies	Applies	Applies (*)(Y)		Deemed (*)
Myanmar	Applies	Applies	Applies (*)(Y)		Deemed (*)
Namibia	Applies	Applies	Applies (*)(Y)		Deemed (*)
Nepal	Applies	Applies	Applies (*) (23rd April 2004)		Deemed (*)
Netherlands	Applies	Applies (*)	Applies (X)	Applies	
Netherlands Antilles and Aruba	Applies	Applies	Applies (*)(Y)		Deemed

Country	Article 2 (literary, dramatic, musical and artistic works, films and typographical arrangements)	Article 3 (sound recordings)	Article 4 (wireless broadcasts)	Article 5 (other broadcasts)	Article 6 (performances)
New Zealand	Applies	Applies (*)	Applies (*)(Y)		Deemed (*)
Nicaragua	Applies	Applies (*)	Applies (Y)		Designated
Niger	Applies	Applies (*)	Applies (18th May 1964)		Designated
Nigeria	Applies	Applies (*)	Applies (29th October 1993)		Designated
Norway	Applies	Applies (*)	Applies (X)	Applies	Designated
Oman	Applies	Applies	Applies (*) (9th November 2000)		Deemed
Pakistan	Applies	Applies (*)	Applies (*)(Y)		Deemed (*)
Panama	Applies	Applies (*)	Applies (2nd September 1983)		Designated
Papua New Guinea	Applies	Applies	Applies (*) (9th June 1996)		Deemed (*)
Paraguay	Applies	Applies (*)	Applies (26th February 1970)		Designated
Peru	Applies	Applies (*)	Applies (7th August 1985)		Designated
Philippines	Applies	Applies (*)	Applies (25th September 1984)		Designated
Poland	Applies	Applies (*)	Applies (X)	Applies	
Portugal	Applies	Applies (*)	Applies (X)	Applies	

Country	Article 2 (literary, dramatic, musical and artistic works, films and typographical arrangements)	Article 3 (sound recordings)	Article 4 (wireless broadcasts)	Article 5 (other broadcasts)	Article 6 (performances)
Qatar	Applies	Applies	Applies (*) (13th January 1996)		Deemed
Romania	Applies	Applies (*)	Applies (X)	Applies	
Russian Federation	Applies	Applies (*)	Applies (26th May 2003)		Designated
Rwanda	Applies	Applies	Applies (*) (22nd May 1996)		Deemed (*)
Saint Kitts and Nevis	Applies	Applies	Applies (*) (21st February 1996)		Deemed (*)
Saint Lucia	Applies	Applies (*)	Applies (Y)		Designated
Saint Vincent and the Grenadines	Applies	Applies	Applies (*)(Y)		Deemed (*)
Samoa	Applies	Applies			
Saudi Arabia	Applies	Applies			
Senegal	Applies	Applies (#)	Applies (*)(Y)		Deemed
Serbia	Applies	Applies (*)	Applies (10th June 2003)		Designated
Sierra Leone	Applies	Applies	Applies (*)(Y)		Deemed (*)
Singapore	Applies	Applies (#)	Applies (X)	Applies	Deemed
Slovak Republic	Applies	Applies (*)	Applies (X)	Applies	
Slovenia	Applies	Applies (*)	Applies (X)	Applies	
Solomon Islands	Applies	Applies	Applies (*) (26th July 1996)		Deemed (*)
South Africa	Applies	Applies	Applies (*)(Y)		Deemed (*)

Country	Article 2 (literary, dramatic, musical and artistic works, films and typographical arrangements)	Article 3 (sound recordings)	Article 4 (wireless broadcasts)	Article 5 (other broadcasts)	Article 6 (performances)
Spain	Applies	Applies (*)	Applies (X)	Applies	
Sri Lanka	Applies	Applies	Applies (*)(Y)		Deemed (*)
Sudan	Applies	Applies			
Suriname	Applies	Applies	Applies (*)(Y)		Deemed (*)
Swaziland	Applies	Applies	Applies (*)(Y)		Deemed (*)
Sweden	Applies	Applies (*)	Applies (X)	Applies	
Switzerland	Applies	Applies (*)	Applies (X)	Applies	Designated
Syrian Arab Republic	Applies	Applies (*)	Applies (13th May 2006)		Designated
Taiwan	Applies	Applies (*)	Applies (*) (1st January 2002)		Deemed (*)
Tajikistan	Applies	Applies			
Tanzania, United Republic of	Applies	Applies	Applies (*)(Y)		Deemed (*)
Thailand	Applies	Applies (*)	Applies (*)(Y)		Deemed (*)
Togo	Applies	Applies (*)	Applies (Y)		Designated
Tonga	Applies	Applies			
Trinidad and Tobago	Applies	Applies	Applies (*)(Y)		Deemed (*)
Tunisia	Applies	Applies	Applies (*)(Y)		Deemed (*)
Turkey	Applies	Applies (*)	Applies (Y)		Designated
Uganda	Applies	Applies	Applies (*)(Y)		Deemed (*)
Ukraine	Applies	Applies (*)	Applies (12th June 2002)		Designated
United Arab Emirates	Applies	Applies (*)	Applies (10th April 1996)		Designated

Country	Article 2 *(literary, dramatic, musical and artistic works, films and typographical arrangements)*	Article 3 *(sound recordings)*	Article 4 *(wireless broadcasts)*	Article 5 *(other broadcasts)*	Article 6 *(performances)*
United States of America (including Puerto Rico and all territories and possessions)	Applies	Applies (#)	Applies (*)(Y)		Deemed
Uruguay	Applies	Applies (*)	Applies (4th July 1977)		Designated
Uzbekistan	Applies	Applies			
Venezuela	Applies	Applies (*)	Applies (Y)		Designated
Viet Nam	Applies	Applies			
Zambia	Applies	Applies	Applies (*)(Y)		Deemed (*)
Zimbabwe	Applies	Applies	Applies (*)(Y)		Deemed (*)

C1.v The Performances (Reciprocal Protection) (Convention Countries and Isle of Man) Order 2003

p.632

This order has been revoked.

Note: This order was revoked by the Copyright and Performances (Application to Other Countries) Order 2005 (SI 2005/852), art.8, with effect from May 1, 2005.

PART D

PARLIAMENTARY DEBATES ON COPYRIGHT, DESIGNS AND PATENTS ACT 1988 AND SUBSEQUENT AMENDMENTS

D1. TABLE OF PARLIAMENTARY DEBATES ON THE COPYRIGHT, DESIGNS AND PATENTS ACT 1988 AND SUBSEQUENT AMENDMENTS

COPYRIGHT, DESIGNS AND PATENTS ACT 1988

PART E

REPEALED STATUTES

E4. COMPARATIVE TABLES III AND IV

COMPARATIVE TABLE—IV

Copyright Act, 1956 compared with Copyright Act, 1911

In the column headings to Table IV, for 1956 substitute 1911, and for 1911 **p.779** substitute 1956.

PART F

COPYRIGHT CONVENTIONS AND AGREEMENTS

F3. EUROPEAN AGREEMENT ON THE PROTECTION OF TELEVISION BROADCASTS

p.863   After **F3.iii** insert:

F3.iv Additional Protocol to the Protocol to the European Agreement on the Protection of Television Broadcasts

Strasbourg, April 20, 1989

The member States of the Council of Europe, signatories hereto,

Having regard to the European Agreement on the Protection of Television Broadcasts of 22 June 1960, hereinafter called "the Agreement", as modified by the Protocol of 22 January 1965 and the Additional Protocols of 14 January 1974 and of 21 March 1983;

Having regard to the fact that the date given in Article 13, paragraph 2, of the Agreement was extended by the said Additional Protocols of 14 January 1974 and of 21 March 1983;

Considering the desirability of further extending this date for the benefit of States which are not yet Parties to the International Convention for the Protection of Performers, Producers of Phonograms and Broadcasting Organisations, signed in Rome on 26 October 1961,

Have agreed as follows:

Article 1

Paragraph 2 of Article 3 of the Protocol to the Agreement and, consequently, paragraph 2 of Article 13 of the Agreement are replaced by the following text:

"2. Nevertheless, as from 1 January 1995, no State may remain or become a Party to this Agreement unless it is also a Party to the International Convention for the Protection of Performers, Producers of Phonograms and Broadcasting Organisations, signed in Rome on 26 October 1961."

Article 2

1. This Additional Protocol shall be open for signature by the member States of the Council of Europe which have signed or acceded to the Agreement, which may become Parties to this Additional Protocol by:

   (a) signature without reservation as to ratification, acceptance or approval, or

   (b) signature subject to ratification, acceptance or approval, followed by ratification, acceptance or approval.

2. No member State of the Council of Europe shall sign without reservation as to ratification, acceptance or approval, or deposit an instrument of ratification, acceptance or approval, unless it is already or becomes simultaneously a Party to the Agreement.

3. Any State, not a member of the Council of Europe, which has acceded to the Agreement may also accede to this Additional Protocol.

4. Instruments of ratification, acceptance, approval or accession shall be deposited with the Secretary General of the Council of Europe.

Article 3

This Additional Protocol shall enter into force on the first day of the month following the date on which all the Parties to the Agreement have expressed their consent to be bound by this Additional Protocol in accordance with the provisions of Article 2.

Article 4

From the date of entry into force of this Additional Protocol, no State may become a Party to the Agreement without at the same time becoming a Party to this Additional Protocol.

Article 5

The Secretary General of the Council of Europe shall notify the member States of the Council of Europe, any State having acceded to the Agreement and the Director General of the World Intellectual Property Organisation of:

(a) any signature of this Additional Protocol;

(b) the deposit of any instrument of ratification, acceptance, approval or accession;

(c) the date of entry into force of this Additional Protocol in accordance with Article 3.

In witness whereof the undersigned, being duly authorised thereto, have signed this Additional Protocol.

Done at Strasbourg, the 20th April 1989 in English and in French, both texts being equally authentic, in a single copy which shall be deposited in the archives of the Council of Europe. The Secretary General of the Council of Europe shall transmit certified copies to each member State of the Council of Europe, to any State invited to accede to the Agreement and to the Director General of the World Intellectual Property Organisation.

Signed by the United Kingdom on December 18, 1989 without reservation as to ratification.

F11 AGREEMENT ON TRADE-RELATED ASPECTS OF INTELLECTUAL PROPERTY RIGHTS[1]

For **F11** substitute the following:

p.917

TABLE OF CONTENTS

PART I

GENERAL PROVISIONS AND BASIC PRINCIPLES

---

[1] Annex 1C to the Agreement Establishing the World Trade Organisation, done at Marrakesh, April 15, 1994.

Members,

Desiring to reduce distortions and impediments to international trade, and taking into account the need to promote effective and adequate protection of intellectual property rights, and to ensure that measures and procedures to enforce intellectual property rights do not themselves become barriers to legitimate trade;

Recognizing, to this end, the need for new rules and disciplines concerning:

(a) the applicability of the basic principle of the GATT 1994 and of relevant international intellectual property agreements or conventions;

(b) the provision of adequate standards and principles concerning the availability, scope and use of trade-related intellectual property rights;

(c) the provisions of effective and appropriate means for the enforcement of trade-related intellectual property rights, taking into account differences in national legal systems;

(d) the provision of effective and expeditious procedures for the multilateral prevention and settlement of disputes between governments; and

(e) transitional arrangements aiming at the fullest participation in the results of the negotiations;

Recognizing the need for a multilateral framework of principles, rules and disciplines dealing with international trade in counterfeit goods;

Recognizing that intellectual property rights are private rights;

Recognizing the underlying public policy objectives of national systems for the protection of intellectual property, including developmental and technological objectives;

Recognizing also the special needs of the least-developed country Members in respect of maximum flexibility in the domestic implementation of laws and regulations in order to enable them to create a sound and viable technological base;

Emphasizing the importance of reducing tensions by reaching strengthened commitments to resolve disputes on trade-related intellectual property issues through multilateral procedures;

Desiring to establish a mutually supportive relationship between the WTO and the World Intellectual Property Organization (referred to in this Agreement as "WIPO") as well as other relevant international organisations;

Hereby agree as follows:

PART I

GENERAL PROVISIONS AND BASIC PRINCIPLES

Article 1
Nature and Scope of Obligations

1. Members shall give effect to the provisions of this Agreement. Members may, but shall not be obliged to, implement in their law more extensive protection than is required by this Agreement, provided that such protection does not contravene the provisions of this Agreement. Members shall be free to determine the appropriate method of implementing the provisions of this Agreement within their own legal system and practice.

2. For the purposes of this Agreement, the term "intellectual property" refers to all categories of intellectual property that are the subject of Sections 1 through 7 of Part II.

3. Members shall accord the treatment provided for in this Agreement to the nationals of other Members.[2] In respect of the relevant intellectual property right, the nationals of other Members shall be understood as those natural or legal persons that would meet the criteria for eligibility for protection provided for in the Paris Convention (1967), the Berne Convention (1971), the Rome Convention and the Treaty on Intellectual Property in Respect of Integrated Circuits, were all Members of the WTO members of those conventions.[3] Any Member availing itself of the possibilities provided in paragraph 3 of Article 5 or paragraph 2 of Article 6 of the Rome Convention shall make a notification as foreseen in those provisions to the Council for Trade-Related Aspects of Intellectual Property Rights (the "Council for Trips").

Article 2
Intellectual Property Conventions

1. In respect of Parts II, III and IV of this Agreement, Members shall comply with Articles 1 through 12, and Article 19, of the Paris Convention (1967).

---

[2] When "nationals" are referred to in this Agreement, they shall be deemed, in the case of a separate customs territory Member of the WTO, to mean persons, natural or legal, who are domiciled or who have a real and effective industrial or commercial establishment in that customs territory.

[3] In this Agreement, "Paris Convention" refers to the Paris Convention for the Protection of Industrial Property: "Paris Convention (1967)" refers to the Stockholm Act of this Convention of 14 July 1967. "Berne Convention" refers to the Berne Convention for the Protection of Literary and Artistic Works: "Berne Convention (1971)" refers to the Paris Act of this Convention of 24 July 1971. "Rome Convention" refers to the International Convention for the Protection of Performers, Producers of Phonograms and Broadcasting Organisations, adopted at Rome on 26 October 1961. "Treaty on Intellectual Property in Respect of Integrated Circuits" (IPIC Treaty) refers to the Treaty on Intellectual Property in Respect of Integrated Circuits, adopted at Washington on 26 May 1989. "WTO Agreement" refers to the Agreement Establishing the WTO.

2. Nothing in Parts I to IV of this Agreement shall derogate from existing obligations that Members may have to each other under the Paris Convention, the Berne Convention, the Rome Convention and the Treaty on Intellectual Property in Respect of Integrated Circuits.

Article 3

National Treatment

1. Each Member shall accord to the nationals of other Members treatment no less favourable than that it accords to its own nationals with regard to the protection[4] of intellectual property, subject to the exceptions already provided in, respectively, the Paris Convention (1967), the Berne Convention (1971), the Rome Convention or the Treaty on Intellectual Property in Respect of Integrated Circuits. In respect of performers, producers of phonograms and broadcasting organizations, this obligation only applies in respect of the rights provided under this Agreement. Any Member availing itself of the possibilities provided in Article 6 of the Berne Convention (1971) or paragraph 1(b) of Article 16 of the Rome Convention shall make a notification as foreseen in those provisions to the Council for TRIPS.

2. Members may avail themselves of the exceptions permitted under paragraph 1 in relation to judicial and administrative procedures, including the designation of an address for service or the appointment of an agent within the jurisdiction of a Member, only where such exceptions are necessary to secure compliance with laws and regulations which are not inconsistent with the provisions of this Agreement and where such practices are not applied in a manner which would constitute a disguised restriction on trade.

Article 4

Most-Favoured-Nation Treatment

With regard to the protection of intellectual property, any advantage, favour, privilege or immunity granted by a Member to the nationals of any other country shall be accorded immediately and unconditionally to the nationals of all other Members. Exempted from this obligation are any advantage, favour, privilege or immunity accorded by a Member:

(a) deriving from international agreements on judicial assistance or law enforcement of a general nature and not particularly confined to the protection of intellectual property;

(b) granted in accordance with the provisions of the Berne Convention (1971) or the Rome Convention authorizing that the treatment accorded be a function not of national treatment but of the treatment accorded in another country;

(c) in respect of the rights of performers, producers of phonograms and broadcasting organizations not provided under this Agreement;

(d) deriving from international agreements related to the protection of intellectual property which entered into force prior to the entry into force of the WTO Agreement, provided that such agreements are notified to the Council for TRIPS and do not constitute an arbitrary or unjustifiable discrimination against nationals of other Members.

---

[4] For the purposes of Articles 3 and 4, "protection" shall include matters affecting the availability, acquisition, scope, maintenance and enforcement of intellectual property rights as well as those matters affecting the use of intellectual property rights specifically addressed in this Agreement.

Article 5

Multilateral Agreements on Acquisition or Maintenance of Protection

The obligations under Articles 3 and 4 above do not apply to procedures provided in multilateral agreements concluded under the auspices of WIPO relating to the acquisition or maintenance of intellectual property rights.

Article 6

Exhaustion

For the purposes of dispute settlement under this Agreement, subject to the provisions of Articles 3 and 4 nothing in this Agreement shall be used to address the issue of the exhaustion of intellectual property rights.

Article 7

Objectives

The protection and enforcement of intellectual property rights should contribute to the promotion of technological innovation and to the transfer and dissemination of technology, to the mutual advantage of producers and users of technological knowledge and in a manner conducive to social and economic welfare, and to a balance of rights and obligations.

Article 8

Principles

1. Members may, in formulating or amending their laws and regulations, adopt measures necessary to protect public health and nutrition, and to promote the public interest in sectors of vital importance to their socio-economic and technological development, provided that such measures are consistent with the provisions of this Agreement.

2. Appropriate measures, provided that they are consistent with the provisions of this Agreement, may be needed to prevent the abuse of intellectual property rights by right holders or the resort to practices which unreasonably restrain trade or adversely affect the international transfer of technology.

PART II

STANDARDS CONCERNING THE AVAILABILITY, SCOPE AND USE OF INTELLECTUAL PROPERTY RIGHTS

SECTION 1

COPYRIGHT AND RELATED RIGHTS

Article 9

Relation to the Berne Convention

1. Members shall comply with Articles 1 through 21 and the Berne Convention (1971) and the Appendix thereto. However, Members shall not have rights or obligations under this Agreement in respect of the rights conferred under Article 6bis of that Convention or of the rights derived therefrom.

2. Copyright protection shall extend to expressions and not to ideas, procedures, methods of operation or mathematical concepts as such.

Article 10

Computer Programs and Compilations of Data

1. Computer programs, whether in source or object code, shall be protected as literary works under the Berne Convention (1971).

2. Compilations of data or other material, whether in machine readable or other form, which by reason of the selection or arrangement of their contents constitute intellectual creations shall be protected as such. Such protection, which shall not extend to the data or material itself, shall be without prejudice to any copyright subsisting in the data or material itself.

Article 11

Rental Rights

In respect of at least computer programs and cinematographic works, a Member shall provide authors and their successors in title the right to authorize or to prohibit the commercial rental to the public of originals or copies of their copyright works. A Member shall be excepted from this obligation in respect of cinematographic works unless such rental has led to widespread copying of such works which is materially impairing the exclusive right of reproduction conferred in that Member on authors and their successors in title. In respect of computer programs, this obligation does not apply to rentals where the program itself is not the essential object of the rental.

Article 12

Term of Protection

Whenever the term of protection of a work, other than a photographic work or a work of applied art, is calculated on a basis other than the life of a natural person, such term shall be no less than 50 years from the end of the calendar year of authorized publication or, failing such authorised publication within 50 years from the making of the work, 50 years from the end of the calendar year of making.

Article 13

Limitations and Exceptions

Members shall confine limitations or exceptions to exclusive rights to certain special cases which do not conflict with a normal exploitation of the work and do not unreasonably prejudice the legitimate interests of the right holder.

Article 14

Protection of Performers, Producers of Phonograms (Sound Recordings) and Broadcasting Organizations

1. In respect of a fixation of their performance on a phonogram, performers shall have the possibility of preventing the following acts when undertaken without their authorization: the fixation of their unfixed performance and the reproduction of such fixation. Performers shall also have the possibility of preventing the following acts when undertaken without their authorization: the broadcasting by wireless means and the communication to the public of their live performance.

2. Producers of phonograms shall enjoy the right to authorize or prohibit the direct or indirect reproduction of their phonograms.

3. Broadcasting organizations shall have the right to prohibit the following acts when undertaken without their authorization: the fixation, the reproduction of fixations, and the rebroadcasting by wireless means of broadcasts, as well as the communication to the public of television broadcasts of the same. Where Members do not grant such rights to broadcasting organizations, they shall provide owners of copyright in the subject matter of broadcasts with the possibil-

ity of preventing the above acts, subject to the provisions of the Berne Convention (1971).

4. The provisions of Article 11 in respect of computer programs shall apply *mutatis mutandis* to producers of phonograms and any other right holders in phonograms as determined in a Member's law. If on 15 April 1994 a Member has in force a system of equitable remuneration of right holders in respect of the rental of phonograms, it may maintain such system provided that the commercial rental of phonograms is not giving rise to the material impairment of the exclusive rights of reproduction of right holders.

5. The term of the protection available under this Agreement to performers and producers of phonograms shall last at least until the end of a period of 50 years computed from the end of the calendar year in which the fixation was made or the performance took place. The term of protection granted pursuant to paragraph 3 shall last for a least 20 years from the end of the calendar year in which the broadcast took place.

6. Any Member may, in relation to the rights conferred under paragraphs 1, 2 and 3, provide for conditions, limitations, exceptions and reservations to the extent permitted by the Rome Convention. However, the provisions of Article 18 of the Berne Convention (1971) shall also apply, *mutatis mutandis*, to the rights of performers and producers of phonograms in phonograms.

SECTION 2

TRADEMARKS

Article 15
Protectable Subject-Matter

1. Any sign, or any combination of signs, capable of distinguishing the goods or services of one undertaking from those of other undertakings, shall be capable of constituting a trademark. Such signs, in particular words including personal names, letters, numerals, figurative elements and combinations of colours as well as any combination of such signs, shall be eligible for registration as trademarks. Where signs are not inherently capable of distinguishing the relevant goods or services, Members may make registrability depend on distinctiveness acquired through use. Members may require, as a condition of registration, that signs be visually perceptible.

2. Paragraph 1 shall not be understood to prevent a Member from denying registration of a trademark on other grounds, provided that they do not derogate from the provisions of the Paris Convention (1967).

3. Members may make registrability depend on use. However, actual use of a trademark shall not be a condition for filing an application for registration. An application shall not be refused solely on the ground that intended use has not taken place before the expiry of a period of three years from the date of application.

4. The nature of the goods or services to which a trademark is to be applied shall in no case form an obstacle to registration of the trademark.

5. Members shall publish each trademark either before it is registered or promptly after it is registered and shall afford a reasonable opportunity for petitions to cancel the registration. In addition, Members may afford an opportunity for the registration of a trademark to be opposed.

Article 16

Rights Conferred

1. The owner of a registered trademark shall have the exclusive right to prevent all third parties not having the owners' consent from using in the course of trade identical or similar signs for goods or services which are identical or similar to those in respect of which the trademark is registered where such use would result in a likelihood of confusion. In case of the use of an identical sign for identical goods or services, a likelihood of confusion shall be presumed. The rights described above shall not prejudice any existing prior rights, nor shall they affect the possibility of Members making rights available on the basis of use.

2. Article 6*bis* of the Paris Convention (1967) shall apply, *mutatis mutandis*, to services. In determining whether a trademark is well-known, Members shall take account of the knowledge of the trademark in the relevant sector of the public, including knowledge in the Member concerned which has been obtained as a result of the promotion of the trademark.

3. Article 6*bis* of the Paris Convention (1967) shall apply, *mutatis mutandis*, to goods or services which are not similar to those in respect of which a trademark is registered, provided that use of that trademark in relation to those goods or services would indicate a connection between those goods or services and the owner of the registered trademark and provided that the interests of the owner of the registered trademark are likely to be damaged by such use.

Article 17

Exceptions

Members may provide limited exceptions to the rights conferred by a trademark, such as fair use of descriptive terms, provided that such exceptions take account of the legitimate interests of the owner of the trademark and of third parties.

Article 18

Term of Protection

Initial registration, and each renewal of registration, of a trademark shall be for a term of no less than seven years. The registration of a trademark shall be renewable indefinitely.

Article 19

Requirement of Use

1. If use is required to maintain a registration, the registration may be cancelled only after an uninterrupted period of at least three years of non-use, unless valid reasons based on the existence of obstacles to such use are shown by the trademark owner. Circumstances arising independently of the will of the owner of the trademark which constitute an obstacle to the use of the trademark, such as import restrictions on or other government requirements for goods or services protected by the trademark, shall be recognized as valid reasons for non-use.

2. When subject to the control of its owner, use of a trademark by another person shall be recognized as use of the trademark for the purpose of maintaining the registration.

Article 20

Other Requirements

The use of a trademark in the course of trade shall not be unjustifiably encumbered by special requirements, such as use with another trademark, use in a special form or use in a manner detrimental to its capability to distinguish the goods or services of one undertaking form those of other undertakings, This will not preclude a requirement prescribing the use of the trademark identifying the undertaking producing the goods or services along with, but without linking it to, the trademark distinguishing the specific goods or services in question of that undertaking.

Article 21

Licensing and Assignment

Members may determine conditions on the licensing and assignment of trademarks, it being understood that the compulsory licensing of trademarks shall not be permitted and that the owner of a registered trademark shall have the right to assign his trademark with or without the transfer of the business to which the trademark belongs.

SECTION 3

GEOGRAPHICAL INDICATIONS

Article 22

Protection of Geographical Indications

1. Geographical indications are, for the purposes of this Agreement, indications which identify a good as originating in the territory of a Member, or a region or locality in that territory, where a given quality, reputation or other characteristic of the good is essentially attributable to its geographical origin.

2. In respect of geographical indications, Members shall provide the legal means for interested parties to prevent:

(a) the use of any means in the designation or presentation of a good that indicates or suggests that the good in question originates in a geographical area other than the true place of origin in a manner which misleads the public as to the geographical origin of the good;

(b) any use which constitutes an act of unfair competition within the meaning of Article 10*bis* of the Paris Convention (1967).

3. A Member shall, *ex officio* if its legislation so permits or at the request of an interested party, refuse or invalidate the registration of a trademark which contains or consists of a geographical indication with respect to goods not originating in the territory indicated, if use of the indication in the trademark for such goods in that Member is of such a nature as to mislead the public as to the true place of origin.

4. The protection under paragraphs 1, 2 and 3 shall be applicable against a geographical indication which, although literally true as to the territory, region or locality in which the goods originate, falsely represents to the public that the goods originate in another territory.

Article 23

Additional Protection for Geographical Indications for Wines and Spirits

1. Each Member shall provide the legal means for interested parties to prevent use of a geographical indication identifying wines for wines not originating in the place indicated by the geographical indication in question or identifying spirits for spirits not originating in the place indicated by the geographical indication in question, even where the true origin of the goods is indicated or the geographical

indication is used in translation or accompanied by expressions such as "kind", "type", "style", "imitation" or the like.[5]

2. The registration of a trademark for wines which contains or consists of a geographical indication identifying wines or for spirits which contains or consists of a geographical indication identifying spirits shall be refused or invalidated, *ex officio* if a Member's legislation so permits or at the request of an interested party, with respect to such wines or spirits not having this origin.

3. In the case of homonymous geographical indications for wines, protection shall be accorded to each indication, subject to the provisions of paragraph 4 of Article 22. Each Member shall determine the practical conditions under which the homonymous indications in question will be differentiated from each other, taking into account the need to ensure equitable treatment of the producers concerned and that consumers are not misled.

4. In order to facilitate the protection of geographical indications for wines, negotiations shall be undertaken in the Council for TRIPS concerning the establishment of a multilateral system of notification and registration of geographical indications for wines eligible for protection in those Members participating in the system.

Article 24
International Negotiations; Exceptions

1. Members agree to enter into negotiations aimed at increasing the protection of individual geographical indications under Article 23. The provisions of paragraphs 4 through 8 below shall not be used by a Member to refuse to conduct negotiations or to conclude bilateral or multilateral agreements. In the context of such negotiations, Members shall be willing to consider the continued applicability of these provisions to individual geographical indications whose use was the subject of such negotiations.

2. The Council for TRIPS shall keep under review the application of the provisions of this Section; the first such review shall take place within two years of the entry into force of the WTO Agreement. Any matter affecting the compliance with the obligations under these provisions may be drawn to the attention of the Council, which, at the request of a Member, shall consult with any Member or Members in respect of such matter in respect of which it has not been possible to find a satisfactory solution through bilateral or plurilateral consultations between the Members concerned. The Council shall take such action as may be agreed to facilitate the operation and further the objectives of this Section.

3. In implementing this Section, a Member shall not diminish the protection of geographical indications that existed in that Member immediately prior to the date of entry into force of the WTO Agreement.

4. Nothing in this Section shall require a Member to prevent continued and similar use of a particular geographical indication of another Member identifying wines or spirits in connection with goods or services by any of its nationals or domiciliaries who have used that geographical indication in a continuous manner with regard to the same or related goods or services in the territory of that Member either (*a*) for at least 10 years preceding 15 April 1994 or (*b*) in good faith preceding that date.

5. Where a trademark has been applied for or registered in good faith, or where rights to a trademark have been acquired through use in good faith either:

   (a) before the date of application of these provisions in that Member as defined in Part VI; or

---

[5] Notwithstanding the first sentence of Article 42, Members may, with respect to these obligations, instead provide for enforcement by administrative action.

(b) before the geographical indication is protected in its country of origin;

measures adopted to implement this Section shall not prejudice eligibility for or the validity of the registration of a trademark, or the right to use a trademark, on the basis that such a trademark is identical with, or similar to, a geographical indication.

6. Nothing in this Section shall require a Member to apply its provisions in respect of a geographical indication of any other Member with respect to goods or services for which the relevant indication is identical with the term customary in common language as the common name for such goods or services in the territory of that Member. Nothing in this Section shall require a Member to apply its provisions in respect of a geographical indication of any other Member with respect to products of the vine for which the relevant indication is identical with the customary name of a grape variety existing in the territory of that Member as of the date of entry into force of the WTO Agreement.

7. A Member may provide that any request made under this Section in connection with the use or registration of a trademark must be presented within five years after the adverse use of the protected indication has become generally known in that Member or after the date of registration of the trademark in that Member provided that the trademark has been published by that date, if such date is earlier than the date on which the adverse use became generally known in that Member, provided that the geographical indication is not used or registered in bad faith.

8. The provisions of this Section shall in no way prejudice the right of any person to use, in the course of trade, that person's name or the name of that person's predecessor in business, except where such name is used in such a manner as to mislead the public.

9. There shall be no obligation under this Agreement to protect geographical indications which are not or cease to be protected in their country of origin, or which have fallen into disuse in that country.

SECTION 4

INDUSTRIAL DESIGNS

Article 25

Requirements for Protection

1. Members shall provide for the protection of independently created industrial designs that are new or original. Members may provide that designs are not new or original if they do not significantly differ from known designs or combinations of known design features. Members may provide that such protection shall not extend to designs dictated essentially by technical or functional considerations.

2. Each Member shall ensure that requirements for securing protection for textile designs, in particular in regard to any cost, examination or publication, do not unreasonably impair the opportunity to seek and obtain such protection. Members shall be free to meet this obligation through industrial design law or through copyright law.

Article 26

Protection

1. The owner of a protected industrial design shall have the right to prevent third parties not having the owner's consent from making, selling or importing articles bearing or embodying a design which is a copy, or substantially a copy, of the protected design, when such acts are undertaken for commercial purposes.

2. Members may provide limited exceptions to the protection of industrial designs, provided that such exceptions do not unreasonably conflict with the normal exploitation of protected industrial designs and do not unreasonably prejudice the legitimate interests of the owner of the protected design, taking account of the legitimate interests of third parties.

3. The duration of protection available shall amount to at least 10 years.

SECTION 5

PATENTS

Article 27

Patentable Subject-Matter

1. Subject to the provisions of paragraphs 2 and 3, patents shall be available for any inventions, whether products or processes, in all fields of technology, provided that they are new, involve an inventive step and are capable of industrial application.[6] Subject to paragraph 4 of Article 65, paragraph 8 of Article 70 and paragraph 3 of this Article, patents shall be available and patent rights enjoyable without discrimination as to the place of invention, the field of technology and whether products are imported or locally produced.

2. Members may exclude from patentability inventions, the prevention within their territory of the commercial exploitation of which is necessary to protect *ordre public* or morality, including to protect human, animal or plant life or health or to avoid serious prejudice to the environment, provided that such exclusion is not made merely because the exploitation is prohibited by their law.

3. Members may also exclude from patentability:

(a) diagnostic, therapeutic and surgical methods for the treatment of humans or animals;

(b) plants and animals other than micro-organisms, and essentially biological processes for the production of plants or animals other than non-biological and microbiological processes. However, Members shall provide for the protection of plant varieties either by patents or by an effective *sui generis* system or by any combination thereof. The provisions of this subparagraph shall be reviewed four years after the date of entry into force of the WTO Agreement.

Article 28

Rights Conferred

1. A patent shall confer on its owner the following exclusive rights:

(a) where the subject matter of a patent is a product, to prevent third parties not having the owner's consent from the acts of: making, using, offering for sale, selling, or importing[7] for these purposes that product;

(b) where the subject matter of a patent is a process, to prevent third parties not having the owner's consent from the act of using the process, and from the acts of: using, offering for sale, selling, or importing for these purposes at least the product obtained directly by that process.

---

[6] For the purposes of this Article, the terms "inventive step" and "capable of industrial application" may be deemed by a Member to be synonymous with the terms "non-obvious" and "useful" respectively.

[7] This right, like all other rights conferred under this Agreement in respect of the use, sale, importation or other distribution of goods, is subject to the provisions of Article 6.

2. Patent owners shall also have the right to assign, or transfer by succession, the patent and to conclude licensing contracts.

Article 29
Conditions on Patent Applicants

1. Members shall require that an applicant for a patent shall disclose the invention in a manner sufficiently clear and complete for the invention to be carried out by a person skilled in the art and may require the applicant to indicate the best mode for carrying out the invention known to the inventor at the filing date or, where priority is claimed, at the priority date of the application.

2. Members may require an applicant for a patent to provide information concerning the applicant's corresponding foreign applications and grants.

Article 30
Exceptions to Rights Conferred

Members may provide limited exceptions to the exclusive rights conferred by a patent, provided that such exceptions do not unreasonably conflict with a normal exploitation of the patent and do not unreasonably prejudice the legitimate interests of the patent owner, taking account of the legitimate interests of third parties.

Article 31
Other Use Without Authorization of the Right Holder

Where the law of a Member allows for other use[8] of the subject matter of a patent without the authorization of the right holder, including use by the government or third parties authorized by the government, the following provisions shall be respected:

(a) authorization of such use shall be considered on its individual merits;

(b) such use may only be permitted if, prior to such use, the proposed user has made efforts to obtain authorization from the right holder on reasonable commercial terms and conditions and that such efforts have not been successful within a reasonable period of time. This requirement may be waived by a Member in the case of a national emergency or other circumstances of extreme urgency or in cases of public non-commercial use. In situations of national emergency or other circumstances of extreme urgency, the right holder shall, nevertheless, be notified as soon as reasonably practicable. In the case of public non-commercial use, where the government or contractor, without making a patent search, knows or has demonstrable grounds to know that a valid patent is or will be used by or for the government, the right holder shall be informed promptly;

(c) the scope and duration of such use shall be limited to the purpose for which it was authorized, and in the case of semi-conductor technology shall only be for public non-commercial use or to remedy a practice determined after judicial or administrative process to be anti-competitive.

(d) such use shall be non-exclusive;

(e) such use shall be non-assignable, except with that part of the enterprise or goodwill which enjoys such use;

---

[8] "Other use" refers to use other than that allowed under Article 30.

(f) any such use shall be authorized predominantly for the supply of the domestic market of the Member authorizing such use;

(g) authorization for such use shall be liable, subject to adequate protection of the legitimate interests of the persons so authorized, to be terminated if and when the circumstances which led to it cease to exist and are unlikely to recur. The competent authority shall have the authority to review, upon motivated request, the continued existence of these circumstances;

(h) the right holder shall be paid adequate remuneration in the circumstances of each case, taking into account the economic value of the authorization;

(i) the legal validity of any decision relating to the authorization of such use shall be subject to judicial review or other independent review by a distinct higher authority in that Member;

(j) any decision relating to the remuneration provided in respect of such use shall be subject to judicial review or other independent review by a distinct higher authority in that Member;

(k) Members are not obliged to apply the conditions set forth in subparagraphs (b) and (f) where such use is permitted to remedy a practice determined after judicial or administrative process to be anti-competitive. The need to correct anti-competitive practices may be taken into account in determining the amount of remuneration in such cases. Competent authorities shall have the authority to refuse termination of authorization if and when the conditions which led to such authorization are likely to recur;

(l) where such use is authorized to permit the exploitation of a patent ("the second patent") which cannot be exploited without infringing another patent ("the first patent"), the following additional conditions shall apply:

    (i) the invention claimed in the second patent shall involve an important technical advance of considerable economic significance in relation to the invention claimed in the first patent;

    (ii) the owner of the first patent shall be entitled to a cross-licence on reasonable terms to use the invention claimed in the second patent; and

    (iii) the use authorized in respect of the first patent shall be non-assignable except with the assignment of the second patent.

Article 32

Revocation/Forfeiture

An opportunity for judicial review of any decision to revoke or forfeit a patent shall be available.

Article 33

Term of Protection

The term of protection available shall not end before the expiration of a period of twenty years counted from the filing date.[9]

---

[9] It is understood that those Members which do not have a system of original grant may provide that the term of protection shall be computed from the filing date in the system of original grant.

Article 34

Process Patents: Burden of Proof

1. For the purposes of civil proceedings in respect of the infringement of the rights of the owner referred to in paragraph 1(b) of Article 28, if the subject matter of a patent is a process for obtaining a product, the judicial authorities shall have the authority to order the defendant to prove that the process to obtain an identical product is different from the patented process. Therefore, Members shall provide, in at least one of the following circumstances, that any identical product when produced without the consent of the patent owner shall, in the absence of proof to the contrary, be deemed to have been obtained by the patented process:

    (a) if the product obtained by the patented process is new;

    (b) if there is a substantial likelihood that the identical product was made by the process and the owner of the patent has been unable through reasonable efforts to determine the process actually used.

2. Any Member shall be free to provide that the burden of proof indicated in paragraph 1 shall be on the alleged infringer only if the condition referred to in subparagraph (a) is fulfilled or only if the condition referred to in subparagraph (b) is fulfilled.

3. In the adduction of proof to the contrary, the legitimate interests of defendants in protecting their manufacturing and business secrets shall be taken into account.

Section 6

Layout-Designs (Topographies) of Integrated Circuits

Article 35

Relation to the IPIC Treaty

Members agree to provide protection to the layout-designs (topographies) of integrated circuits (referred to in this Agreement as "layout-designs") in accordance with Articles 2 through 7 (other than paragraph 3 of Article 6), Article 12 and paragraph 3 of Article 16 of the Treaty on Intellectual Property in Respect of Integrated Circuits and, in addition, to comply with the following provisions.

Article 36

Scope of the Protection

Subject to the provisions of paragraph 1 of Article 37 below, Members shall consider unlawful the following acts if performed without the authorization of the right holder[10]: importing, selling, or otherwise distributing for commercial purposes a protected layout-design, an integrated circuit in which a protected layout-design is incorporated, or an article incorporating such an integrated circuit only in so far as it continues to contain an unlawfully reproduced layout-design.

---

[10] The term "right holder" in this Section shall be understood as having the same meaning as the term "holder of the right" in the IPIC Treaty.

Article 37

Acts Not Requiring the Authorization of the Right Holder

1. Notwithstanding Article 36, no Member shall consider unlawful the performance of any of the acts referred to in that Article in respect of an integrated circuit incorporating an unlawfully reproduced layout-design or any article incorporating such an integrated circuit where the person performing or ordering such acts did not know and had no reasonable ground to know, when acquiring the integrated circuit or article incorporating such an integrated circuit, that it incorporated an unlawfully reproduced layout-design. Members shall provide that, after the time that such person has received sufficient notice that the layout-design was unlawfully reproduced, that person may perform any of the acts with respect to the stock on hand or ordered before such time, but shall be liable to pay to the right holder a sum equivalent to a reasonable royalty such as would be payable under a freely negotiated licence in respect of such a layout-design.

2. The conditions set out in subparagraphs (a) through (k) of Article 31 shall apply *mutatis mutandis* in the event of any non-voluntary licensing of a layout-design or of its use by or for the government without the authorization of the right holder.

Article 38

Term of Protection

1. In Members requiring registration as a condition of protection, the term of protection of layout-design shall not end before the expiration of a period of 10 years counted from the date of filing an application for registration or from the first commercial exploitation wherever in the world it occurs.

2. In Members not requiring registration as a condition for protection, layout-designs shall be protected for a term of no less than 10 years from the date of the first commercial exploitation wherever in the world it occurs.

3. Notwithstanding paragraphs 1 and 2, a Member may provide that protection shall lapse 15 years after the creation of the layout-design.

SECTION 7

PROTECTION OF UNDISCLOSED INFORMATION

Article 39

1. In the course of ensuring effective protection against unfair competition as provided in Article 10*bis* of the Paris Convention (1967), Members shall protect undisclosed information in accordance with paragraph 2 and data submitted to governments or governmental agencies in accordance with paragraph 3.

2. Natural and legal persons shall have the possibility of preventing information lawfully within their control from being disclosed to, acquired by, or used by others without their consent in a manner contrary to honest commercial practices[11] so long as such information:

(a) is secret in the sense that it is not, as a body or in the precise configuration and assembly of its components, generally known among or readily accessible to persons within the circles that normally deal with the kind of information in question:

---

[11] For the purpose of this provision, "a manner contrary to honest commercial practices" shall mean at least practices such as breach of contract, breach of confidence and inducement to breach, and includes the acquisition of undisclosed information by third parties who knew, or were grossly negligent in failing to know, that such practices were involved in the acquisition.

(b) has commercial value because it is secret; and

(c) has been subject to reasonable steps under the circumstances, by the person lawfully in control of the information, to keep it secret.

3. Members, when requiring, as a condition of approving the marketing of pharmaceutical or of agricultural chemical products which utilize new chemical entities, the submission of undisclosed test or other data, the origination of which involves a considerable effort, shall protect such data against unfair commercial use. In addition, Members shall protect such data against disclosure, except where necessary to protect the public, or unless steps are taken to ensure that the data are protected against unfair commercial use.

SECTION 8

CONTROL OF ANTI-COMPETITIVE PRACTICES IN CONTRACTUAL LICENCES

Article 40

1. Members agree that some licensing practices or conditions pertaining to intellectual property rights which restrain competition may have adverse effects on trade and may impede the transfer and dissemination of technology.

2. Nothing in this Agreement shall prevent Members from specifying in their legislation licensing practices or conditions that may in particular cases constitute an abuse of intellectual property rights having an adverse effect on competition in the relevant market. As provided above, a Member may adopt, consistently with the other provisions of this Agreement, appropriate measures to prevent or control such practices, which may include for example exclusive grantback conditions, conditions preventing challenges to validity and coercive package licensing, in the light of the relevant laws and regulations of that Member.

3. Each Member shall enter, upon request, into consultations with any other Member which has cause to believe that an intellectual property right owner that is a national or domiciliary of the Member to which the request for consultations has been addressed is undertaking practices in violation of the requesting Member's laws and regulations on the subject-matter of this Section, and which wishes to secure compliance with such legislation, without prejudice to any action under the law and to the full freedom of an ultimate decision of either Member. The Member addressed shall accord full and sympathetic consideration to, and shall afford adequate opportunity for, consultations with the requesting Member, and shall cooperate through supply of publicly available non-confidential information of relevance to the matter in question and of other information available to the Member, subject to domestic law and to the conclusion of mutually satisfactory agreements concerning the safeguarding of its confidentiality by the requesting Member.

4. A Member whose nationals or domiciliaries are subject to proceedings in another Member concerning alleged violation of that other Member's laws and regulations on the subject matter of this Section shall, upon request, be granted an opportunity for consultations by the other Member under the same conditions as those foreseen in paragraph 3.

PART III

ENFORCEMENT OF INTELLECTUAL PROPERTY RIGHTS

SECTION 1

GENERAL OBLIGATIONS

Article 41

1. Members shall ensure that enforcement procedures as specified in this Part are available under their law so as to permit effective action against any act of infringement of intellectual property rights covered by this Agreement, including expeditious remedies to prevent infringements and remedies which constitute a deterrent to further infringements. These procedures shall be applied in such a manner as to avoid the creation of barriers to legitimate trade and to provide for safeguards against their abuse.

2. Procedures concerning the enforcement of intellectual property rights shall be fair and equitable. They shall not be unnecessarily complicated or costly, or entail unreasonable time-limits or unwarranted delays.

3. Decisions on the merits of a case shall preferably be in writing and reasoned. They shall be made available at least to the parties to the proceeding without undue delay. Decisions on the merits of a case shall be based only on evidence in respect of which parties were offered the opportunity to be heard.

4. Parties to a proceeding shall have an opportunity for review by a judicial authority of final administrative decisions and, subject to jurisdictional provisions in a Member's law concerning the importance of a case, of at least the legal aspects of initial judicial decisions on the merits of a case. However, there shall be no obligation to provide an opportunity for review of acquittals in criminal cases.

5. It is understood that this Part does not create any obligation to put in place a judicial system for the enforcement of intellectual property rights distinct from that for the enforcement of law in general, nor does it affect the capacity of Members to enforce their law in general. Nothing in this Part creates any obligation with respect to the distribution of resources as between enforcement of intellectual property rights and the enforcement of law in general.

SECTION 2

CIVIL AND ADMINISTRATIVE PROCEDURES AND REMEDIES

Article 42

Fair and Equitable Procedures

Members shall make available to right holders[12] civil judicial procedures concerning the enforcement of any intellectual property right covered by this Agreement. Defendants shall have the right to written notice which is timely and contains sufficient detail, including the basis of the claims. Parties shall be allowed to be represented by independent legal counsel, and procedures shall not impose overly burdensome requirements concerning mandatory personal appearances. All parties to such procedures shall be duly entitled to substantiate their claims and to present all relevant evidence. The procedure shall provide a

---

[12] For the purpose of this Part, the term "right holder" includes federations and associations having legal standing to assert such rights.

means to identify and protect confidential information, unless this would be contrary to existing constitutional requirements.

Article 43
Evidence

1. The judicial authorities shall have the authority, where a party has presented reasonably available evidence sufficient to support its claims and has specified evidence relevant to substantiation of its claims which lies in the control of the opposing party, to order that this evidence be produced by the opposing party, subject in appropriate cases to conditions which ensure the protection of confidential information.

2. In cases in which a party to a proceeding voluntarily and without good reason refuses access to, or otherwise does not provide necessary information within a reasonable period, or significantly impedes a procedure relating to an enforcement action, a Member may accord judicial authorities the authority to make preliminary and final determinations, affirmative or negative, on the basis of the information presented to them, including the complaint or the allegation presented by the party adversely affected by the denial of access to information, subject to providing the parties an opportunity to be heard on the allegations or evidence.

Article 44
Injunctions

1. The judicial authorities shall have the authority to order a party to desist from an infringement, *inter alia* to prevent the entry into the channels of commerce in their jurisdiction of imported goods that involve the infringement of an intellectual property right, immediately after customs clearance of such goods. Members are not obliged to accord such authority in respect of protected subject matter acquired or ordered by a person prior to knowing or having reasonable grounds to know that dealing in such subject matter would entail the infringement of an intellectual property right.

2. Notwithstanding the other provisions of this Part and provided that the provisions of Part II specifically addressing use by governments, or by third parties authorized by a government, without the authorization of the right holder are complied with, Members may limit the remedies available against such use to payment of remuneration in accordance with subparagraph (h) of Article 31. In other cases, the remedies under this Part shall apply or, where these remedies are inconsistent with a Member's law, declaratory judgments and adequate compensation shall be available.

Article 45
Damages

1. The judicial authorities shall have the authority to order the infringer to pay the right holder damages adequate to compensate for the injury the right holder has suffered because of an infringement of that person's intellectual property right by an infringer who knowingly, or with reasonable grounds to know, engaged in infringing activity.

2. The judicial authorities shall also have the authority to order the infringer to pay the right holder expenses, which may include appropriate attorney's fees. In appropriate cases, Members may authorize the judicial authorities to order recovery of profits and/or payment of pre-established damages even where the infringer did not knowingly, or with reasonable grounds to know, engage in infringing activity.

Article 46

Other Remedies

In order to create an effective deterrent to infringement, the judicial authorities shall have the authority to order that goods that they have found to be infringing be, without compensation of any sort, disposed of outside the channels of commerce in such a manner as to avoid any harm caused to the right holder, or, unless this would be contrary to existing constitutional requirements, destroyed. The judicial authorities shall also have the authority to order that materials and implements the predominant use of which has been in the creation of the infringing goods be, without compensation of any sort, disposed of outside the channels of commerce in such a manner as to minimize the risks of further infringements. In considering such requests, the need for proportionality between the seriousness of the infringement and the remedies ordered as well as the interests of third parties shall be taken into account. In regard to counterfeit trademark goods, the simple removal of the trademark unlawfully affixed shall not be sufficient, other than in exceptional cases, to permit release of the goods into the channels of commerce.

Article 47

Right of Information

Members may provide that the judicial authorities shall have the authority, unless this would be out of proportion to the seriousness of the infringement, to order the infringer to inform the right holder of the identity of third persons involved in the production and distribution of the infringing goods or services and of their channels of distribution.

Article 48

Indemnification of the Defendant

1. The judicial authorities shall have the authority to order a party at whose request measures were taken and who has abused enforcement procedures to provide to a party wrongfully enjoined or restrained adequate compensation for the injury suffered because of such abuse. The judicial authorities shall also have the authority to order the applicant to pay the defendant expenses, which may include appropriate attorney's fees.

2. In respect of the administration of any law pertaining to the protection or enforcement of intellectual property rights, Members shall only exempt both public authorities and officials from liability to appropriate remedial measures where actions are taken or intended in good faith in the course of the administration of that law.

Article 49

Administrative Procedures

To the extent that any civil remedy can be ordered as a result of administrative procedures on the merits of a case, such procedures shall conform to principles equivalent in substance to those set forth in this Section.

Section 3

Provisional Measures

Article 50

1. The judicial authorities shall have the authority to order prompt and effective provisional measures:

   (a) to prevent an infringement of any intellectual property right from occurring, and in particular to prevent the entry into the channels of commerce in their jurisdiction of goods, including imported goods immediately after customs clearance;

   (b) to preserve relevant evidence in regard to the alleged infringement.

2. The judicial authorities shall have the authority to adopt provisional measures *inaudita altera parte* where appropriate, in particular where any delay is likely to cause irreparable harm to the right holder, or where there is a demonstrable risk of evidence being destroyed.

3. The judicial authorities shall have the authority to require the applicant to provide any reasonably available evidence in order to satisfy themselves with a sufficient degree of certainty that the applicant is the right holder and that the applicant's right is being infringed or that such infringement is imminent, and to order the applicant to provide a security or equivalent assurance sufficient to protect the defendant and to prevent abuse.

4. Where provisional measures have been adopted *inaudita altera parte*, the parties affected shall be given notice, without delay after the execution of the measures at the latest. A review, including a right to be heard, shall take place upon request of the defendant with a view to deciding, within a reasonable period after the notification of the measures, whether these measures shall be modified, revoked or confirmed.

5. The applicant may be required to supply other information necessary for the identification of the goods concerned by the authority that will execute the provisional measures.

6. Without prejudice to paragraph 4, provisional measures taken on the basis of paragraphs 1 and 2 shall, upon request by the defendant, be revoked or otherwise cease to have effect, if proceedings leading to a decision on the merits of the case are not initiated within a reasonable period, to be determined by the judicial authority ordering the measures where a Member's law so permits or, in the absence of such a determination, not to exceed 20 working days or 31 calendar days, whichever is the longer.

7. Where the provisional measures are revoked or where they lapse due to any act or omission by the applicant, or where it is subsequently found that there has been no infringement or threat of infringement of an intellectual property right, the judicial authorities shall have the authority to order the applicant, upon request of the defendant, to provide the defendant appropriate compensation for any injury caused by these measures.

8. To the extent that any provisional measure can be ordered as a result of administrative procedures, such procedures shall conform to principles equivalent in substance to those set forth in this Section.

Section 4

Special Requirements Related to Border Measures[13]

Article 51

Suspension of Release by Customs Authorities

Members shall, in conformity with the provisions set out below, adopt procedures[14] to enable a right holder, who has valid grounds for suspecting that the importation of counterfeit trademark or pirated copyright goods[15] may take place, to lodge an application in writing with competent authorities, administrative or judicial, for the suspension by the customs authorities of the release into free circulation of such goods. Members may enable such an application to be made in respect of goods which involve other infringements of intellectual property rights, provided that the requirements of this Section are met. Members may also provide for corresponding procedures concerning the suspension by the customs authorities of the release of infringing goods destined for exportation from their territories.

Article 52

Application

Any right holder initiating the procedures under Article 51 above shall be required to provide adequate evidence to satisfy the competent authorities that, under the laws of the country of importation, there is *prima facie* an infringement of the right holder's intellectual property right and to supply a sufficiently detailed description of the goods to make them readily recognizable by the customs authorities. The competent authorities shall inform the applicant within a reasonable period whether they have accepted the application and, where determined by the competent authorities, the period for which the customs authorities will take action.

Article 53

Security or Equivalent Assurance

1. The competent authorities shall have the authority to require an applicant to provide a security or equivalent assurance sufficient to protect the defendant and the competent authorities and to prevent abuse. Such security or equivalent assurance shall not unreasonably deter recourse to these procedures.

2. Where pursuant to an application under this Section the release of goods involving industrial designs, patents, layout-designs or undisclosed information into free circulation has been suspended by customs authorities on the basis of a decision other than by a judicial or other independent authority, and the period

---

[13] Where a Member has dismantled substantially all controls over movement of goods across its border with another Member with which it forms part of a customs union, it shall not be required to apply the provisions of this Section at that border.

[14] It is understood that there shall be no obligation to apply such procedures to imports of goods put on the market in another country by or with the consent of the right holder, or to goods in transit.

[15] For the purposes of this Agreement: (a) "counterfeit trademark goods" shall mean any goods, including packaging, bearing without authorization a trademark which is identical to the trademark validly registered in respect of such goods, or which cannot be distinguished in its essential aspects from such a trademark, and which thereby infringes the rights of the owner of the trademark in question under the law of the country of importation; (b) "pirated copyright goods" shall mean any goods which are copies made without the consent of the right holder or person duly authorized by the right holder in the country of production and which are made directly or indirectly from an article where the making of that copy would have constituted an infringement of a copyright or a related right under the law of the country of importation.

provided for in Article 55 has expired without the granting of provisional relief by the duly empowered authority, and provided that all other conditions for importation have been complied with, the owner, importer, or consignee of such goods shall be entitled to their release on the posting of a security in an amount sufficient to protect the right holder for any infringement. Payment of such security shall not prejudice any other remedy available to the right holder, it being understood that the security shall be released if the right holder fails to pursue the right of action within a reasonable period of time.

Article 54

Notice of Suspension

The importer and the applicant shall be promptly notified of the suspension of the release of goods according to Article 51.

Article 55

Duration of Suspension

If, within a period not exceeding 10 working days after the applicant has been served notice of the suspension, the customs authorities have not been informed that proceedings leading to a decision on the merits of the case have been initiated by a party other than the defendant, or that the duly empowered authority has taken provisional measures prolonging the suspension of the release of the goods, the goods shall be released, provided that all other conditions for importation or exportation have been complied with; in appropriate cases, this time-limit may be extended by another 10 working days. If proceedings leading to a decision on the merits of the case have been initiated, a review, including a right to be heard, shall take place upon request of the defendant with a view to deciding, within a reasonable period, whether these measures shall be modified, revoked or confirmed. Notwithstanding the above, where the suspension of the release of goods is carried out or continued in accordance with a provisional judicial measure, the provisions of paragraph 6 of Article 50 shall apply.

Article 56

Indemnification of the Importer and of the Owner of the Goods

Relevant authorities shall have the authority to order the applicant to pay the importer, the consignee and the owner of the goods appropriate compensation for any injury caused to them through the wrongful detention of goods or through the detention of goods released pursuant to Article 55.

Article 57

Right of Inspection and Information

Without prejudice to the protection of confidential information, Members shall provide the competent authorities the authority to give the right holder sufficient opportunity to have any goods detained by the customs authorities inspected in order to substantiate the right holder's claims. The competent authorities shall also have authority to give the importer an equivalent opportunity to have any such product inspected. Where a positive determination has been made on the merits of a case, Members may provide the competent authorities the authority to inform the right holder of the names and addresses of the consignor, the importer and the consignee and of the quantity of the goods in question.

Article 58

Ex Officio Action

Where Members require competent authorities to act upon their own initiative and to suspend the release of goods in respect of which they have acquired *prima facie* evidence that an intellectual property right is being infringed:

   (a) the competent authorities may at any time seek from the right holder any information that may assist them to exercise these powers:

   (b) the importer and the right holder shall be promptly notified of the suspension. Where the importer has lodged an appeal against the suspension with the competent authorities, the suspension shall be subject to the conditions, *mutatis mutandis*, set out at Article 55;

   (c) Members shall only exempt both public authorities and officials from liability to appropriate remedial measures where actions are taken or intended in good faith.

Article 59

Remedies

Without prejudice to other rights of action open to the right holder and subject to the right of the defendant to seek review by a judicial authority, competent authorities shall have the authority to order the destruction or disposal of infringing goods in accordance with the principles set out in Article 46. In regard to counterfeit trademark goods, the authorities shall not allow the re-exportation of the infringing goods in an unaltered state or subject them to a different customs procedure, other than in exceptional circumstances.

Article 60

De Minimis Imports

Members may exclude from the application of the above provisions small quantities of goods of a non-commercial nature contained in travellers' personal luggage or sent in small consignments.

SECTION 5

CRIMINAL PROCEDURES

Article 61

Members shall provide for criminal procedures and penalties to be applied at least in cases of wilful trademark counterfeiting or copyright piracy on a commercial scale. Remedies available shall include imprisonment and/or monetary fines sufficient to provide a deterrent, consistently with the level of penalties applied for crimes of a corresponding gravity. In appropriate cases, remedies available shall also include the seizure, forfeiture and destruction of the infringing goods and of any materials and implements the predominant use of which has been in the commission of the offence. Members may provide for criminal procedures and penalties to be applied in other cases of infringement of intellectual property rights, in particular where they are committed wilfully and on a commercial scale.

PART IV

ACQUISITION AND MAINTENANCE OF INTELLECTUAL PROPERTY RIGHTS AND RELATED INTER-PARTES PROCEDURES

Article 62

1. Members may require, as a condition of the acquisition or maintenance of the intellectual property rights provided for under Sections 2 through 6 of Part II, compliance with reasonable procedures and formalities. Such procedures and formalities shall be consistent with the provisions of this Agreement.

2. Where the acquisition of an intellectual property right is subject to the right being granted or registered, Members shall ensure that the procedures for grant or registration, subject to compliance with the substantive conditions for acquisition of the right, permit the granting or registration of the right within a reasonable period of time so as to avoid unwarranted curtailment of the period of protection.

3. Article 4 of the Paris Convention (1967) shall apply *mutatis mutandis* to service marks.

4. Procedures concerning the acquisition or maintenance of intellectual property rights and, where a Member's law provides for such procedures, administrative revocation and *inter partes* procedures such as opposition, revocation and cancellation, shall be governed by the general principles set out in paragraphs 2 and 3 of Article 41.

5. Final administrative decisions in any of the procedures referred to under paragraph 4 shall be subject to review by a judicial or quasi-judicial authority. However, there shall be no obligation to provide an opportunity for such review of decisions in cases of unsuccessful opposition or administrative revocation, provided that the grounds for such procedures can be the subject of invalidation procedures.

PART V

DISPUTE PREVENTION AND SETTLEMENT

Article 63

Transparency

1. Laws and regulations, and final judicial decisions and administrative rulings of general application, made effective by a Member pertaining to the subject matter of this Agreement (the availability, scope, acquisition, enforcement and prevention of the abuse of intellectual property rights) shall be published, or where such publication is not practicable made publicly available, in a national language, in such a manner as to enable governments and right holders to become acquainted with them. Agreements concerning the subject matter of this Agreement which are in force between the government or a governmental agency of a Member and the government or a governmental agency of another Member shall also be published.

2. Members shall notify the laws and regulations referred to in paragraph 1 to the Council for TRIPS in order to assist that Council in its review of the operation of this Agreement. The Council shall attempt to minimize the burden on Members in carrying out this obligation and may decide to waive the obligation to notify such laws and regulations directly to the Council if consultations with WIPO on the establishment of a common register containing these laws and regulations are successful. The Council shall also consider in this connection any action required regarding notifications pursuant to the obligations under this

Agreement stemming from the provisions of Article 6*ter* of the Paris Convention (1967).

3. Each Member shall be prepared to supply, in response to a written request from another Member, information of the sort referred to in paragraph 1. A Member, having reason to believe that a specific judicial decision or administrative ruling or bilateral agreement in the area of intellectual property rights affects its rights under this Agreement, may also request in writing to be given access to or be informed in sufficient detail of such specific judicial decisions or administrative rulings or bilateral agreements.

4. Nothing in paragraphs 1, 2 and 3 shall require Members to disclose confidential information which would impede law enforcement or otherwise be contrary to the public interest or would prejudice the legitimate commercial interests of particular enterprises, public or private.

Article 64

Dispute Settlement

1. The provisions of Articles XXII and XXIII of GATT 1994 as elaborated and applied by the Dispute Settlement Understanding shall apply to consultations and the settlement of disputes under this Agreement except as otherwise specifically provided herein.

2. Sub-paragraphs 1(b) and 1(c) of Article XXIII of GATT 1994 shall not apply to the settlement of disputes under this Agreement for a period of five years from the entry into force of the WTO Agreement.

3. During the time period referred to in paragraph 2, the Council for TRIPS shall examine the scope and modalities for complaints of the type provided for under subparagraphs 1(b) and 1(c) of Article XXIII of GATT 1994 made pursuant to this Agreement, and submit its recommendations to the Ministerial Conference for approval. Any decision of the Ministerial Conference to approve such recommendations or to extend the period in paragraph 2 shall be made only by consensus, and approved recommendations shall be effective for all Members without further formal acceptance process.

Part VI

Transitional Arrangements

Article 65

Transitional Arrangements

1. Subject to the provisions of paragraphs 2, 3 and 4, no Member shall be obliged to apply the provisions of this Agreement before the expiry of a general period of one year following the date of entry into force of the WTO Agreement.

2. Any developing country Member is entitled to delay for a further period of four years the date of application, as defined in paragraph 1, of the provisions of this Agreement other than Article 3, 4, and 5.

3. Any other Member which is in the process of transformation from a centrally-planned into a market, free-enterprise economy and which is undertaking structural reform of its intellectual property system and facing special problems in the preparation and implementation of intellectual property laws and regulations, may also benefit from a period of delay as foreseen in paragraph 2.

4. To the extent that a developing country Member is obliged by this Agreement to extend product patent protection to areas of technology not so protectable in its territory on the general date of application of this Agreement for that

Member, as defined in paragraph 2, it may delay the application of the provisions on product patents of Section 5 of Part II to such areas of technology for an additional period of five years.

5. A Member availing itself of a transitional period under paragraphs 1, 2, 3 or 4 shall ensure that any changes in its laws, regulations and practice made during that period do not result in a lesser degree of consistency with the provisions of this Agreement.

Article 66

Least-Developed Country Members

1. In view of their special needs and requirements of least-developed country Members, their economic, financial and administrative constraints, and their need for flexibility to create a viable technological base, such Members shall not be required to apply the provisions of this Agreement, other than Articles 3, 4 and 5, for a period of 10 years from the date of application as defined under paragraph 1 of Article 65. The Council for TRIPS shall, upon duly motivated request by a least-developed country Member, accord extensions of this period.

2. Developed country Members shall provide incentives to enterprises and institutions in their territories for the purpose of promoting and encouraging technology transfer to least-developed country Members in order to enable them to create a sound and viable technological base.

Article 67

Technical Cooperation

In order to facilitate the implementation of this Agreement, developed country Members shall provide, on request and on mutually agreed terms and conditions, technical and financial cooperation in favour of developing and least-developed country Members. Such cooperation shall include assistance in the preparation of laws and regulations on the protection and enforcement of intellectual property rights as well as on the prevention of their abuse, and shall include support regarding the establishment or reinforcement of domestic offices and agencies relevant to these matters, including the training of personnel.

PART VII

INSTITUTIONAL ARRANGEMENTS; FINAL PROVISIONS

Article 68

Council for Trade-Related Aspects of Intellectual Property Rights

The Council for TRIPS shall monitor the operation of this Agreement and, in particular, Members' compliance with their obligations hereunder, and shall afford Members the opportunity of consulting on matters relating to the trade-related aspects of intellectual property rights. It shall carry out such other responsibilities as assigned to it by the Members, and it shall, in particular, provide any assistance requested by them in the context of dispute settlement procedures. In carrying out its functions, the Council for TRIPS may consult with and seek information from any source it deems appropriate. In consultation with WIPO, the Council shall seek to establish, within one year of its first meeting, appropriate arrangements for cooperation with bodies of that Organization.

Article 69
International Cooperation

Members agree to cooperate with each other with a view to eliminating international trade in goods infringing intellectual property rights. For this purpose, they shall establish and notify contact points in their administrations and be ready to exchange information on trade in infringing goods. They shall, in particular, promote the exchange of information and cooperation between customs authorities with regard to trade in counterfeit trademark goods and pirated copyright goods.

Article 70
Protection of Existing Subject-Matter

1. This Agreement does not give rise to obligations in respect of acts which occurred before the date of application of the Agreement for the Member in question.

2. Except as otherwise provided for in this Agreement, this Agreement gives rise to obligations in respect of all subject matter existing at the date of application of this Agreement for the Member in question, and which is protected in that Member on the said date, or which meets or comes subsequently to meet the criteria for protection under the terms of this Agreement. In respect of this paragraph and paragraphs 3 and 4, copyright obligations with respect to existing works shall be solely determined under Article 18 of the Berne Convention (1971), and obligations with respect to the rights of producers of phonograms and performers in existing phonograms shall be determined solely under Article 18 of the Berne Convention (1971) as made applicable under paragraph 6 of Article 14 of this Agreement.

3. There shall be no obligation to restore protection to subject matter which on the date of application of this Agreement for the Member in question has fallen into the public domain.

4. In respect of any acts in respect of specific objects embodying protected subject matter which become infringing under the terms of legislation in conformity with this Agreement, and which were commenced, or in respect of which a significant investment was made, before the date of acceptance of the WTO Agreement by that Member, any Member may provide for a limitation of the remedies available to the right holder as to the continued performance of such acts after the date of application of this Agreement for that Member. In such cases the Member shall, however, at least provide for the payment of equitable remuneration.

5. A Member is not obliged to apply the provisions of Article 11 and of paragraph 4 of Article 14 with respect to originals or copies purchased prior to the date of application of this Agreement for that Member.

6. Members shall not be required to apply Article 31, or the requirement in paragraph 1 of Article 27 that patent rights shall be enjoyable without discrimination as to the field of technology, to use without the authorization of the right holder where authorization for such use was granted by the government before the date this Agreement became known.

7. In the case of intellectual property rights for which protection is conditional upon registration, applications for protection which are pending on the date of application of this Agreement for the Member in question shall be permitted to be amended to claim any enhanced protection provided under the provisions of this Agreement. Such amendments shall not include new matter.

8. Where a Member does not make available as of the date of entry into force

of the WTO Agreement patent protection for pharmaceutical and agricultural chemical products commensurate with its obligations under Article 27, that Member shall:

(a) notwithstanding the provisions of Part VI, provide as from the date of entry into force of the WTO Agreement a means by which applications for patents for such inventions can be filed;

(b) apply to these applications, as of the date of application of this Agreement, the criteria for patentability as laid down in this Agreement as if those criteria were being applied on the date of filing in that Member or, where priority is available and claimed, the priority date of the application; and

(c) provide patent protection in accordance with this Agreement as from the grant of the patent and for the remainder of the patent term, counted from the filing date in accordance with Article 33 of this Agreement, for those of these applications that meet the criteria for protection referred to in subparagraph (b) above.

9. Where a product is the subject of a patent application in a Member in accordance with paragraph 8(a), exclusive marketing rights shall be granted, notwithstanding the provisions of Part VI, for a period of five years after obtaining market approval in that Member or until a product patent is granted or rejected in that Member, whichever period is shorter, provided that, subsequent to the entry into force of the WTO Agreement, a patent application has been filed and a patent granted for that product in another Member and marketing approval obtained in such other Member.

Article 71

Review and Amendment

1. The Council for TRIPS shall review the implementation of this Agreement after the expiration of the transitional period referred to in paragraph 2 of Article 65. The Council shall, having regard to the experience gained in its implementation, review it two years after that date, and at identical intervals thereafter. The Council may also undertake reviews in the light of any relevant new developments which might warrant modification or amendment of this Agreement.

2. Amendments merely serving the purpose of adjusting to higher levels of protection of intellectual property rights achieve, and in force, in other multilateral agreements and accepted under those agreements by all Members of the WTO may be referred to the Ministerial Conference for action in accordance with paragraph 6 of Article X of the WTO Agreement on the basis of a consensus proposal from the Council for TRIPS.

Article 72

Reservations

Reservations may not be entered in respect of any of the provisions of this Agreement without the consent of the other Members.

Article 73

Security Exceptions

Nothing in this Agreement shall be construed:

(a) to require any Member to furnish any information the disclosure of which it considers contrary to its essential security interests; or

(b) to prevent a Member from taking any action which it considers necessary for the protection of its essential security interests:

      (i) relating to fissionable materials or the materials from which they are derived;

     (ii) relating to the traffic in arms, ammunition and implements of war and to such traffic in other goods and materials as is carried on directly or indirectly for the purpose of supplying a military establishment;

    (iii) taken in time of war or other emergency in international relations; or

  (c) to prevent a Member from taking any action in pursuance of its obligations under the United Nations Charter for the maintenance of international peace and security.

PART H

EC DIRECTIVES

H3. COUNCIL DIRECTIVE 92/100/EEC

Council Directive 92/100/EEC of November 19, 1992 on rental right and lending right and on certain rights related to copyright in the field of intellectual property

This Directive has been repealed.

Note:

This Directive was repealed by Directive 2006/115/EC of the European Parliament and of the Council of 12 December 2006 on rental right and lending right and on certain rights related to copyright in the field of intellectual property [2006] O.J. L376/28, Art.14, with effect from January 8, 2007. The text of Directive 2006/115/EC is at **H15** below.

H5. COUNCIL DIRECTIVE 93/98/EEC

Council Directive 93/98/EEC of October 29, 1993 harmonizing the term of protection of copyright and certain related rights

This Directive has been repealed.

Note:

This Directive was repealed by Directive 2006/116/EC of the European Parliament and of the Council of 12 December 2006 on the term of protection of copyright and certain related rights [2006] O.J. L372/12, Art.12, with effect from January 8, 2007. The text of Directive 2006/116/EC is at **H16** below.

H11. DIRECTIVE 2001/29

Directive 2001/29/EC of the European Parliament and of the Council of 22 May 2001 on the harmonisation of certain aspects of copyright and related rights in the information society

Technical adaptations

Article 11(1) was repealed by Directive 2006/115/EC of the European Parliament and of the Council of 12 December 2006 on rental right and lending right and on certain rights related to copyright in the field of intellectual property [2006] O.J. L376/28, Annex I, with effect from January 8, 2007.

Article 11(2) was repealed by Directive 2006/116/EC of the European Parliament and of the Council of 12 December 2006 on the term of protection of copyright and certain related rights [2006] O.J. L372/12, Annex I, with effect from January 8, 2007.

p.1140

After **H14**, insert

H15. DIRECTIVE 2006/115

Directive 2006/115/EC of the European Parliament and of the Council of 12 December 2006 on rental right and lending right and on certain rights related to copyright in the field of intellectual property

([2006] O.J. L376/28)

THE EUROPEAN PARLIAMENT AND THE COUNCIL OF THE EUROPEAN UNION,

Having regard to the Treaty establishing the European Community, and in particular Articles 47(2), 55 and 95 thereof,

Having regard to the proposal from the Commission,

Having regard to the opinion of the European Economic and Social Committee,

Acting in accordance with the procedure laid down in Article 251 of the Treaty[1],

(1) Council Directive 92/100/EEC of 19 November 1992 on rental right and lending right and on certain rights related to copyright in the field of intellectual property[2] has been substantially amended several times.[3] In the interests of clarity and rationality the said Directive should be codified.

(2) Rental and lending of copyright works and the subject matter of related rights protection is playing an increasingly important role in particular for authors, performers and producers of phonograms and films. Piracy is becoming an increasing threat.

(3) The adequate protection of copyright works and subject matter of related rights protection by rental and lending rights as well as the protection of the subject matter of related rights protection by the fixation right, distribution right, right to broadcast and communication to the public can accordingly be considered as being of fundamental importance for the economic and cultural development of the Community.

(4) Copyright and related rights protection must adapt to new economic developments such as new forms of exploitation.

(5) The creative and artistic work of authors and performers necessitates an adequate income as a basis for further creative and artistic work, and the investments required particularly for the production of phonograms and films are especially high and risky. The possibility of securing that income and recouping that investment can be effectively guaranteed only through adequate legal protection of the rightholders concerned.

(6) These creative, artistic and entrepreneurial activities are, to a large extent, activities of self-employed persons. The pursuit of such activities should be made

---

[1] Opinion of the European Parliament delivered on 12 October 2006 (not yet published in the Official Journal).

[2] OJ L 346, 27.11.1992, p. 61. Directive as last amended by Directive 2001/29/EC of the European Parliament and of the Council (OJ L 167, 22.6.2001, p. 10).

[3] See Annex I, Part A.

easier by providing a harmonised legal protection within the Community. To the extent that these activities principally constitute services, their provision should equally be facilitated by a harmonised legal framework in the Community.

(7) The legislation of the Member States should be approximated in such a way as not to conflict with the international conventions on which the copyright and related rights laws of many Member States are based.

(8) The legal framework of the Community on the rental right and lending right and on certain rights related to copyright can be limited to establishing that Member States provide rights with respect to rental and lending for certain groups of rightholders and further to establishing the rights of fixation, distribution, broadcasting and communication to the public for certain groups of rightholders in the field of related rights protection.

(9) It is necessary to define the concepts of rental and lending for the purposes of this Directive.

(10) It is desirable, with a view to clarity, to exclude from rental and lending within the meaning of this Directive certain forms of making available, as for instance making available phonograms or films for the purpose of public performance or broadcasting, making available for the purpose of exhibition, or making available for on-the-spot reference use. Lending within the meaning of this Directive should not include making available between establishments which are accessible to the public.

(11) Where lending by an establishment accessible to the public gives rise to a payment the amount of which does not go beyond what is necessary to cover the operating costs of the establishment, there is no direct or indirect economic or commercial advantage within the meaning of this Directive.

(12) It is necessary to introduce arrangements ensuring that an unwaivable equitable remuneration is obtained by authors and performers who must remain able to entrust the administration of this right to collecting societies representing them.

(13) The equitable remuneration may be paid on the basis of one or several payments at any time on or after the conclusion of the contract. It should take account of the importance of the contribution of the authors and performers concerned to the phonogram or film.

(14) It is also necessary to protect the rights at least of authors as regards public lending by providing for specific arrangements. However, any measures taken by way of derogation from the exclusive public lending right should comply in particular with Article 12 of the Treaty.

(15) The provisions laid down in this Directive as to rights related to copyright should not prevent Member States from extending to those exclusive rights the presumption provided for in this Directive with regard to contracts concerning film production concluded individually or collectively by performers with a film producer. Furthermore, those provisions should not prevent Member States from providing for a rebuttable presumption of the authorisation of exploitation in respect of the exclusive rights of performers provided for in the relevant provisions of this Directive, in so far as such presumption is compatible with the International Convention for the Protection of Performers, Producers of Phonograms and Broadcasting Organisations (hereinafter referred to as the Rome Convention).

(16) Member States should be able to provide for more farreaching protection for owners of rights related to copyright than that required by the provisions laid down in this Directive in respect of broadcasting and communication to the public.

(17) The harmonised rental and lending rights and the harmonised protection in the field of rights related to copyright should not be exercised in a way which constitutes a disguised restriction on trade between Member States or in a way

which is contrary to the rule of media exploitation chronology, as recognised in the judgment handed down in Société Cinéthèque v. FNCF.[4]

(18) This Directive should be without prejudice to the obligations of the Member States relating to the time-limits for transposition into national law of the Directives as set out in Part B of Annex I,

HAVE ADOPTED THIS DIRECTIVE:

CHAPTER I

RENTAL AND LENDING RIGHT

Article 1

Object of harmonisation

1. In accordance with the provisions of this Chapter, Member States shall provide, subject to Article 6, a right to authorise or prohibit the rental and lending of originals and copies of copyright works, and other subject matter as set out in Article 3(1).

2. The rights referred to in paragraph 1 shall not be exhausted by any sale or other act of distribution of originals and copies of copyright works and other subject matter as set out in Article 3(1).

Article 2

Definitions

1. For the purposes of this Directive the following definitions shall apply:

  (a) 'rental' means making available for use, for a limited period of time and for direct or indirect economic or commercial advantage;
  (b) 'lending' means making available for use, for a limited period of time and not for direct or indirect economic or commercial advantage, when it is made through establishments which are accessible to the public;
  (c) 'film' means a cinematographic or audiovisual work or moving images, whether or not accompanied by sound.

2. The principal director of a cinematographic or audiovisual work shall be considered as its author or one of its authors. Member States may provide for others to be considered as its co-authors.

Article 3

Rightholders and subject matter of rental and lending right

1. The exclusive right to authorise or prohibit rental and lending shall belong to the following:

  (a) the author in respect of the original and copies of his work;
  (b) the performer in respect of fixations of his performance;
  (c) the phonogram producer in respect of his phonograms;
  (d) the producer of the first fixation of a film in respect of the original and copies of his film.

2. This Directive shall not cover rental and lending rights in relation to buildings and to works of applied art.

3. The rights referred to in paragraph 1 may be transferred, assigned or subject to the granting of contractual licences.

---

[4] Joined Cases 60/84 and 61/84 [1985] ECR 2 605.

4. Without prejudice to paragraph 6, when a contract concerning film production is concluded, individually or collectively, by performers with a film producer, the performer covered by this contract shall be presumed, subject to contractual clauses to the contrary, to have transferred his rental right, subject to Article 5.

5. Member States may provide for a similar presumption as set out in paragraph 4 with respect to authors.

6. Member States may provide that the signing of a contract concluded between a performer and a film producer concerning the production of a film has the effect of authorising rental, provided that such contract provides for an equitable remuneration within the meaning of Article 5. Member States may also provide that this paragraph shall apply mutatis mutandis to the rights included in Chapter II.

Article 4

Rental of computer programs

This Directive shall be without prejudice to Article 4(c) of Council Directive 91/250/EEC of 14 May 1991 on the legal protection of computer programs.[5]

Article 5

Unwaivable right to equitable remuneration

1. Where an author or performer has transferred or assigned his rental right concerning a phonogram or an original or copy of a film to a phonogram or film producer, that author or performer shall retain the right to obtain an equitable remuneration for the rental.

2. The right to obtain an equitable remuneration for rental cannot be waived by authors or performers.

3. The administration of this right to obtain an equitable remuneration may be entrusted to collecting societies representing authors or performers.

4. Member States may regulate whether and to what extent administration by collecting societies of the right to obtain an equitable remuneration may be imposed, as well as the question from whom this remuneration may be claimed or collected.

Article 6

Derogation from the exclusive public lending right

1. Member States may derogate from the exclusive right provided for in Article 1 in respect of public lending, provided that at least authors obtain a remuneration for such lending. Member States shall be free to determine this remuneration taking account of their cultural promotion objectives.

2. Where Member States do not apply the exclusive lending right provided for in Article 1 as regards phonograms, films and computer programs, they shall introduce, at least for authors, a remuneration.

3. Member States may exempt certain categories of establishments from the payment of the remuneration referred to in paragraphs 1 and 2.

---

[5] OJ L 122, 17.5.1991, p. 42. Directive as amended by Directive 93/98/EEC (OJ L 290, 24.11.1993, p. 9).

CHAPTER II

RIGHTS RELATED TO COPYRIGHT

Article 7

Fixation right

1. Member States shall provide for performers the exclusive right to authorise or prohibit the fixation of their performances.

2. Member States shall provide for broadcasting organisations the exclusive right to authorise or prohibit the fixation of their broadcasts, whether these broadcasts are transmitted by wire or over the air, including by cable or satellite.

3. A cable distributor shall not have the right provided for in paragraph 2 where it merely retransmits by cable the broadcasts of broadcasting organisations.

Article 8

Broadcasting and communication to the public

1. Member States shall provide for performers the exclusive right to authorise or prohibit the broadcasting by wireless means and the communication to the public of their performances, except where the performance is itself already a broadcast performance or is made from a fixation.

2. Member States shall provide a right in order to ensure that a single equitable remuneration is paid by the user, if a phonogram published for commercial purposes, or a reproduction of such phonogram, is used for broadcasting by wireless means or for any communication to the public, and to ensure that this remuneration is shared between the relevant performers and phonogram producers. Member States may, in the absence of agreement between the performers and phonogram producers, lay down the conditions as to the sharing of this remuneration between them.

3. Member States shall provide for broadcasting organisations the exclusive right to authorise or prohibit the rebroadcasting of their broadcasts by wireless means, as well as the communication to the public of their broadcasts if such communication is made in places accessible to the public against payment of an entrance fee.

Article 9

Distribution right

1. Member States shall provide the exclusive right to make available to the public, by sale or otherwise, the objects indicated in points (a) to (d), including copies thereof, hereinafter 'the distribution right':

   (a) for performers, in respect of fixations of their performances;
   (b) for phonogram producers, in respect of their phonograms;
   (c) for producers of the first fixations of films, in respect of the original and copies of their films;
   (d) for broadcasting organisations, in respect of fixations of their broadcasts as set out in Article 7(2).

2. The distribution right shall not be exhausted within the Community in respect of an object as referred to in paragraph 1, except where the first sale in the Community of that object is made by the rightholder or with his consent.

3. The distribution right shall be without prejudice to the specific provisions of Chapter I, in particular Article 1(2).

4. The distribution right may be transferred, assigned or subject to the granting of contractual licences.

Article 10
Limitations to rights

1. Member States may provide for limitations to the rights referred to in this Chapter in respect of:

(a) private use;

(b) use of short excerpts in connection with the reporting of current events;

(c) ephemeral fixation by a broadcasting organisation by means of its own facilities and for its own broadcasts;

(d) use solely for the purposes of teaching or scientific research.

2. Irrespective of paragraph 1, any Member State may provide for the same kinds of limitations with regard to the protection of performers, producers of phonograms, broadcasting organisations and of producers of the first fixations of films, as it provides for in connection with the protection of copyright in literary and artistic works.

However, compulsory licences may be provided for only to the extent to which they are compatible with the Rome Convention.

3. The limitations referred to in paragraphs 1 and 2 shall be applied only in certain special cases which do not conflict with a normal exploitation of the subject matter and do not unreasonably prejudice the legitimate interests of the rightholder.

CHAPTER III

COMMON PROVISIONS

Article 11
Application in time

1. This Directive shall apply in respect of all copyright works, performances, phonograms, broadcasts and first fixations of films referred to in this Directive which were, on 1 July 1994, still protected by the legislation of the Member States in the field of copyright and related rights or which met the criteria for protection under this Directive on that date.

2. This Directive shall apply without prejudice to any acts of exploitation performed before 1 July 1994.

3. Member States may provide that the rightholders are deemed to have given their authorisation to the rental or lending of an object referred to in points (a) to (d) of Article 3(1) which is proven to have been made available to third parties for this purpose or to have been acquired before 1 July 1994.

However, in particular where such an object is a digital recording, Member States may provide that rightholders shall have a right to obtain an adequate remuneration for the rental or lending of that object.

4. Member States need not apply the provisions of Article 2(2) to cinematographic or audiovisual works created before 1 July 1994.

5. This Directive shall, without prejudice to paragraph 3 and subject to paragraph 7, not affect any contracts concluded before 19 November 1992.

6. Member States may provide, subject to the provisions of paragraph 7, that when rightholders who acquire new rights under the national provisions adopted in implementation of this Directive have, before 1 July 1994, given their consent for exploitation, they shall be presumed to have transferred the new exclusive rights.

7. For contracts concluded before 1 July 1994, the unwaivable right to an equi-

table remuneration provided for in Article 5 shall apply only where authors or performers or those representing them have submitted a request to that effect before 1 January 1997. In the absence of agreement between rightholders concerning the level of remuneration, Member States may fix the level of equitable remuneration.

Article 12

Relation between copyright and related rights

Protection of copyright-related rights under this Directive shall leave intact and shall in no way affect the protection of copyright.

Article 13

Communication

Member States shall communicate to the Commission the main provisions of national law adopted in the field covered by this Directive.

Article 14

Repeal

Directive 92/100/EEC is hereby repealed, without prejudice to the obligations of the Member States relating to the time-limits for transposition into national law of the Directives as set out in Part B of Annex I.

References made to the repealed Directive shall be construed as being made to this Directive and should be read in accordance with the correlation table in Annex II.

Article 15

Entry into force

This Directive shall enter into force on the twentieth day following that of its publication in the Official Journal of the European Union.

Article 16

Addressees

This Directive is addressed to the Member States.

Done at Strasbourg, 12 December 2006.

For the European Parliament	*For the Council*
The President	*The President*
J. BORRELL FONTELLES	M. PEKKARINEN

ANNEX I

PART A

REPEALED DIRECTIVE WITH ITS SUCCESSIVE AMENDMENTS

Council Directive 92/100/EEC
(OJ L 346, 27.11.1992, p. 61)

Council Directive 93/98/EEC   Article 11(2) only
(OJ L 290, 24.11.1993, p.9)

Directive 2001/29/EC of the European Parliament   Article 11(1) only
and of the Council
(O) L 167, 22.6.2001, p.10)

PART B

LIST OF TIME-LIMITS FOR TRANSPOSITION INTO NATIONAL LAW

(referred to in Article 14)

Directive	Time-limit for transposition
92/100/EEC	1 July 1994
93/98/EEC	30 June 1995
2001/29/EC	21 December 2002

ANNEX II

CORRELATION TABLE

Directive 92/100/EEC	This Directive
Article 1(1)	Article 1(1)
Article 1(2)	Article 2(1), introductory words and point (a)
Article 1(3)	Article 2(1), point (b)
Article 1(4)	Article 1(2)
Article 2(1), introductory words	Article 3(1), introductory words
Article 2(1), first indent	Article 3(1)(a)
Article 2(1), second indent	Article 3(1)(b)
Article 2(1), third indent	Article 3(1)(c)
Article 2(1), fourth indent, first sentence	Article 3(1)(d)
Article 2(1), fourth indent, second sentence	Article 2(1), point (c)
Article 2(2)	Article 2(2)
Article 2(3)	Article 3(2)
Article 2(4)	Article 3(3)
Article 2(5)	Article 3(4)
Article 2(6)	Article 3(5)
Article 2(7)	Article 3(6)
Article 3	Article 4
Article 4	Article 5
Article 5(1) to (3)	Article 6(1) to (3)
Article 5(4)	—
Article 6	Article 7
Article 8	Article 8
Article 9(1), introductory words and final words	Article 9(1), introductory words
Article 9(1), first indent	Article 9(1)(a)
Article 9(1), first indent	Article 9(1)(a)
Article 9(1), second indent	Article 9(1)(b)
Article 9(1), third indent	Article 9(1)(c)
Article 9(1), fourth indent	Article 9(1)(d)

Directive 92/100/EEC	This Directive
Article 9(2), (3) and (4)	Article 9(2), (3) and (4)
Article 10(1)	Article 10(1)
Article 10(2), first sentence	Article 10(2), first subparagraph
Article 10(2), second sentence	Article 10(2), second subparagraph
Article 10(3)	Article 10(3)
Article 13(1), and (2)	Article 11(1), and (2)
Article 13(3), first sentence	Article 11(3), first subparagraph
Article 13(3), second sentence	Article 11(3), second subparagraph
Article 13(4)	Article 11(4)
Article 13(5)	—
Article 13(6)	Article 11(5)
Article 13(7)	Article 11(6)
Article 13(8)	—
Article 13(9)	Article 11(7)
Article 14	Article 12
Article 15(1)	—
Article 15(2)	Article 13
—	Article 14
—	Article 15
Article 16	Article 16
—	Annex I
—	Annex II

H16. DIRECTIVE 2006/116

Directive 2006/116/EC of the European Parliament and of the Council of 12 December 2006 on the term of protection of copyright and certain related rights

([2006] O.J. L372/12)

THE EUROPEAN PARLIAMENT AND THE COUNCIL OF THE EURO-PEAN UNION,

Having regard to the Treaty establishing the European Community, and in particular Articles 47(2), 55 and 95 thereof,

Having regard to the proposal from the Commission,

Having regard to the opinion of the European Economic and Social Committee[6],

Acting in accordance with the procedure laid down in Article 251 of the Treaty[7],

Whereas:

(1) Council Directive 93/98/EEC of 29 October 1993 harmonising the term of

---

[6] Opinion of 26 October 2006 (not yet published in the Official Journal).

[7] Opinion of the European Parliament of 12 October 2006 (not yet published in the Official Journal) and Council Decision of 30 November 2006.

protection of copyright and certain related rights[8] has been substantially amended.[9] In the interests of clarity and rationality the said Directive should be codified.

(2) The Berne Convention for the protection of literary and artistic works and the International Convention for the protection of performers, producers of phonograms and broadcasting organisations (Rome Convention) lay down only minimum terms of protection of the rights they refer to, leaving the Contracting States free to grant longer terms. Certain Member States have exercised this entitlement. In addition, some Member States have not yet become party to the Rome Convention.

(3) There are consequently differences between the national laws governing the terms of protection of copyright and related rights, which are liable to impede the free movement of goods and freedom to provide services and to distort competition in the common market. Therefore, with a view to the smooth operation of the internal market, the laws of the Member States should be harmonised so as to make terms of protection identical throughout the Community.

(4) It is important to lay down not only the terms of protection as such, but also certain implementing arrangements, such as the date from which each term of protection is calculated.

(5) The provisions of this Directive should not affect the application by the Member States of the provisions of Article 14 bis (2)(b), (c) and (d) and (3) of the Berne Convention.

(6) The minimum term of protection laid down by the Berne Convention, namely the life of the author and 50 years after his death, was intended to provide protection for the author and the first two generations of his descendants. The average lifespan in the Community has grown longer, to the point where this term is no longer sufficient to cover two generations.

(7) Certain Member States have granted a term longer than 50 years after the death of the author in order to offset the effects of the world wars on the exploitation of authors' works.

(8) For the protection of related rights certain Member States have introduced a term of 50 years after lawful publication or lawful communication to the public.

(9) The Diplomatic Conference held in December 1996, under the auspices of the World Intellectual Property Organization (WIPO), led to the adoption of the WIPO Performances and Phonograms Treaty, which deals with the protection of performers and producers of phonograms. This Treaty took the form of a substantial up-date of the international protection of related rights.

(10) Due regard for established rights is one of the general principles of law protected by the Community legal order. Therefore, the terms of protection of copyright and related rights established by Community law cannot have the effect of reducing the protection enjoyed by rightholders in the Community before the entry into force of Directive 93/98/ EEC. In order to keep the effects of transitional measures to a minimum and to allow the internal market to function smoothly, those terms of protection should be applied for long periods.

(11) The level of protection of copyright and related rights should be high, since those rights are fundamental to intellectual creation. Their protection ensures the maintenance and development of creativity in the interest of authors, cultural industries, consumers and society as a whole.

(12) In order to establish a high level of protection which at the same time

---

[8] OJ L 290, 24.11.1993, p. 9. Directive as amended by Directive 2001/ 29/EC of the European Parliament and of the Council (OJ L 167, 22.6.2001, p. 10).
[9] See Annex I, Part A.

meets the requirements of the internal market and the need to establish a legal environment conducive to the harmonious development of literary and artistic creation in the Community, the term of protection for copyright should be harmonised at 70 years after the death of the author or 70 years after the work is lawfully made available to the public, and for related rights at 50 years after the event which sets the term running.

(13) Collections are protected according to Article 2(5) of the Berne Convention when, by reason of the selection and arrangement of their content, they constitute intellectual creations. Those works are protected as such, without prejudice to the copyright in each of the works forming part of such collections. Consequently, specific terms of protection may apply to works included in collections.

(14) In all cases where one or more physical persons are identified as authors, the term of protection should be calculated after their death. The question of authorship of the whole or a part of a work is a question of fact which the national courts may have to decide.

(15) Terms of protection should be calculated from the first day of January of the year following the relevant event, as they are in the Berne and Rome Conventions.

(16) The protection of photographs in the Member States is the subject of varying regimes. A photographic work within the meaning of the Berne Convention is to be considered original if it is the author's own intellectual creation reflecting his personality, no other criteria such as merit or purpose being taken into account. The protection of other photographs should be left to national law.

(17) In order to avoid differences in the term of protection as regards related rights it is necessary to provide the same starting point for the calculation of the term throughout the Community. The performance, fixation, transmission, lawful publication, and lawful communication to the public, that is to say the means of making a subject of a related right perceptible in all appropriate ways to persons in general, should be taken into account for the calculation of the term of protection regardless of the country where this performance, fixation, transmission, lawful publication, or lawful communication to the public takes place.

(18) The rights of broadcasting organisations in their broadcasts, whether these broadcasts are transmitted by wire or over the air, including by cable or satellite, should not be perpetual. It is therefore necessary to have the term of protection running from the first transmission of a particular broadcast only. This provision is understood to avoid a new term running in cases where a broadcast is identical to a previous one.

(19) The Member States should remain free to maintain or introduce other rights related to copyright in particular in relation to the protection of critical and scientific publications. In order to ensure transparency at Community level, it is however necessary for Member States which introduce new related rights to notify the Commission.

(20) It should be made clear that this Directive does not apply to moral rights.

(21) For works whose country of origin within the meaning of the Berne Convention is a third country and whose author is not a Community national, comparison of terms of protection should be applied, provided that the term accorded in the Community does not exceed the term laid down in this Directive.

(22) Where a rightholder who is not a Community national qualifies for protection under an international agreement, the term of protection of related rights should be the same as that laid down in this Directive. However, this term should not exceed that fixed in the third country of which the rightholder is a national.

(23) Comparison of terms should not result in Member States being brought into conflict with their international obligations.

(24) Member States should remain free to adopt provisions on the interpretation, adaptation and further execution of contracts on the exploitation of protected works and other subject matter which were concluded before the extension of the term of protection resulting from this Directive.

(25) Respect of acquired rights and legitimate expectations is part of the Community legal order. Member States may provide in particular that in certain circumstances the copyright and related rights which are revived pursuant to this Directive may not give rise to payments by persons who undertook in good faith the exploitation of the works at the time when such works lay within the public domain.

(26) This Directive should be without prejudice to the obligations of the Member States relating to the time-limits for transposition into national law and application of the Directives, as set out in Part B of Annex I,

HAVE ADOPTED THIS DIRECTIVE:

Article 1
Duration of authors' rights

1. The rights of an author of a literary or artistic work within the meaning of Article 2 of the Berne Convention shall run for the life of the author and for 70 years after his death, irrespective of the date when the work is lawfully made available to the public.

2. In the case of a work of joint authorship, the term referred to in paragraph 1 shall be calculated from the death of the last surviving author.

3. In the case of anonymous or pseudonymous works, the term of protection shall run for 70 years after the work is lawfully made available to the public. However, when the pseudonym adopted by the author leaves no doubt as to his identity, or if the author discloses his identity during the period referred to in the first sentence, the term of protection applicable shall be that laid down in paragraph 1.

4. Where a Member State provides for particular provisions on copyright in respect of collective works or for a legal person to be designated as the rightholder, the term of protection shall be calculated according to the provisions of paragraph 3, except if the natural persons who have created the work are identified as such in the versions of the work which are made available to the public. This paragraph is without prejudice to the rights of identified authors whose identifiable contributions are included in such works, to which contributions paragraph 1 or 2 shall apply.

5. Where a work is published in volumes, parts, instalments, issues or episodes and the term of protection runs from the time when the work was lawfully made available to the public, the term of protection shall run for each such item separately.

6. In the case of works for which the term of protection is not calculated from the death of the author or authors and which have not been lawfully made available to the public within 70 years from their creation, the protection shall terminate.

Article 2
Cinematographic or audiovisual works

1. The principal director of a cinematographic or audiovisual work shall be considered as its author or one of its authors. Member States shall be free to designate other co-authors.

2. The term of protection of cinematographic or audiovisual works shall expire

70 years after the death of the last of the following persons to survive, whether or not these persons are designated as co-authors: the principal director, the author of the screenplay, the author of the dialogue and the composer of music specifically created for use in the cinematographic or audiovisual work.

Article 3
Duration of related rights

1. The rights of performers shall expire 50 years after the date of the performance. However, if a fixation of the performance is lawfully published or lawfully communicated to the public within this period, the rights shall expire 50 years from the date of the first such publication or the first such communication to the public, whichever is the earlier.

2. The rights of producers of phonograms shall expire 50 years after the fixation is made. However, if the phonogram has been lawfully published within this period, the said rights shall expire 50 years from the date of the first lawful publication. If no lawful publication has taken place within the period mentioned in the first sentence, and if the phonogram has been lawfully communicated to the public within this period, the said rights shall expire 50 years from the date of the first lawful communication to the public.

However, this paragraph shall not have the effect of protecting anew the rights of producers of phonograms where, through the expiry of the term of protection granted them pursuant to Article 3(2) of Directive 93/98/EEC in its version before amendment by Directive 2001/29/EEC, they were no longer protected on 22 December 2002.

3. The rights of producers of the first fixation of a film shall expire 50 years after the fixation is made. However, if the film is lawfully published or lawfully communicated to the public during this period, the rights shall expire 50 years from the date of the first such publication or the first such communication to the public, whichever is the earlier. The term 'film' shall designate a cinematographic or audiovisual work or moving images, whether or not accompanied by sound.

4. The rights of broadcasting organisations shall expire 50 years after the first transmission of a broadcast, whether this broadcast is transmitted by wire or over the air, including by cable or satellite.

Article 4
Protection of previously unpublished works

Any person who, after the expiry of copyright protection, for the first time lawfully publishes or lawfully communicates to the public a previously unpublished work, shall benefit from a protection equivalent to the economic rights of the author. The term of protection of such rights shall be 25 years from the time when the work was first lawfully published or lawfully communicated to the public.

Article 5
Critical and scientific publications

Member States may protect critical and scientific publications of works which have come into the public domain. The maximum term of protection of such rights shall be 30 years from the time when the publication was first lawfully published.

Article 6
Protection of photographs

Photographs which are original in the sense that they are the author's own intellectual creation shall be protected in accordance with Article 1. No other criteria shall be applied to determine their eligibility for protection. Member States may provide for the protection of other photographs.

Article 7
Protection vis-à-vis third countries

1. Where the country of origin of a work, within the meaning of the Berne Convention, is a third country, and the author of the work is not a Community national, the term of protection granted by the Member States shall expire on the date of expiry of the protection granted in the country of origin of the work, but may not exceed the term laid down in Article 1.

2. The terms of protection laid down in Article 3 shall also apply in the case of rightholders who are not Community nationals, provided Member States grant them protection. However, without prejudice to the international obligations of the Member States, the term of protection granted by Member States shall expire no later than the date of expiry of the protection granted in the country of which the rightholder is a national and may not exceed the term laid down in Article 3.

3. Member States which, on 29 October 1993, in particular pursuant to their international obligations, granted a longer term of protection than that which would result from the provisions of paragraphs 1 and 2 may maintain this protection until the conclusion of international agreements on the term of protection of copyright or related rights.

Article 8
Calculation of terms

The terms laid down in this Directive shall be calculated from the first day of January of the year following the event which gives rise to them.

Article 9
Distribution right

Moral rights This Directive shall be without prejudice to the provisions of the Member States regulating moral rights.

Article 10
Application in time

1. Where a term of protection which is longer than the corresponding term provided for by this Directive was already running in a Member State on 1 July 1995, this Directive shall not have the effect of shortening that term of protection in that Member State.

2. The terms of protection provided for in this Directive shall apply to all works and subject matter which were protected in at least one Member State on the date referred to in paragraph 1, pursuant to national provisions on copyright or related rights, or which meet the criteria for protection under [Council Directive 92/100/EEC of 19 November 1992 on rental right and lending right and on certain rights related to copyright in the field of intellectual property].[10]

3. This Directive shall be without prejudice to any acts of exploitation performed before the date referred to in paragraph 1. Member States shall adopt the necessary provisions to protect in particular acquired rights of third parties.

---

[10] OJ L 346, 27.11.1992, p. 61. Directive as last amended by Directive 2001/29/EC.

4. Member States need not apply the provisions of Article 2(1) to cinematographic or audiovisual works created before 1 July 1994.

Article 11

Notification and communication

1. Member States shall immediately notify the Commission of any governmental plan to grant new related rights, including the basic reasons for their introduction and the term of protection envisaged.

2. Member States shall communicate to the Commission the texts of the provisions of internal law which they adopt in the field governed by this Directive.

Article 12

Repeal

Directive 93/98/EEC is hereby repealed, without prejudice to the obligations of the Member States relating to the time-limits for transposition into national law, as set out in Part B of Annex I, of the Directives, and their application.

References made to the repealed Directive shall be construed as being made to this Directive and should be read in accordance with the correlation table in Annex II.

Article 13

Entry into force

This Directive shall enter into force on the twentieth day following that of its publication in the *Official Journal of the European Union*.

Article 14

Addressees

This Directive is addressed to the Member States.
Done at Strasbourg, 12 December 2006.

For the European Parliament	*For the Council*
The President	*The President*
J. BORRELL FONTELLES	M. PEKKARINEN

ANNEX I

PART A

REPEALED DIRECTIVE WITH ITS AMENDMENT

Council Directive 93/98/EEC
(OJ L 290, 24.11.1993, p. 9)

Article 11(2) only

Directive 2001/29/EC of the European Parliament
and of the Council (OJ L 167, 22.6.2001, p. 10)

PART B

LIST OF TIME-LIMITS FOR TRANSPOSITION INTO NATIONAL LAW AND APPLICATION

(referred to in Article 12)

Directive	Time-limit for transposition	Date of application
93/98/EEC	1 July 1995 (Articles 1 to 11)	19 November 1993 (Article 12) 1 July 1997 at the latest as regards Article 2(1) (Article 10(5))
2001/29/EC	22 December 2002	

ANNEX II

CORRELATION TABLE

Directive 92/100/EEC	This Directive
Articles 1 to 9	Articles 1 to 9
Article 10(1) to (4)	Article 10(1) to (4)
Article 10(5)	—
Article 11	
Article 12	Article 11(1)
Article 13(1), first subparagraph	—
Article 13(1), second subparagraph	
Article 13(1), third subparagraph	Article 11(2)
Article 13(2)	—
—	Article 12
—	Article 13
Article 14	Article 14
—	Annex I
—	Annex II

After **Part I** insert:

PART IA

COMMISSION RECOMMENDATIONS

IA1. COMMISSION RECOMMENDATION

of May 18, 2005
**on collective cross-border management of copyright and related rights
for legitimate online music services**

(2005/737/EC)
([2005] O.J. L276/54)

THE COMMISSION OF THE EUROPEAN COMMUNITIES,

Having regard to the Treaty establishing the European Community, and in particular Article 211 thereof,

Whereas:

(1) In April 2004 the Commission adopted a Communication on the Management of Copyright and Related Rights in the Internal Market.

(2) The European Parliament, in its report of 15 January 2004,[1] stated that right-holders should be able to enjoy copyright and related rights protection wherever such rights are established, independent of national borders or modes of use during the whole term of their validity.

(3) The European Parliament further emphasised that any action by the Community in respect of the collective cross-border management of copyright and related rights should strengthen the confidence of artists, including writers and musicians, that the pan-European use of their creative works will be financially rewarded.[2]

(4) New technologies have led to the emergence of a new generation of commercial users that make use of musical works and other subject matter online. The provision of legitimate online music services requires management of a series of copyright and related rights.

(5) One category of those rights is the exclusive right of reproduction which covers all reproductions made in the process of online distribution of a musical work. Other categories of rights are the right of communication to the public of musical works, the right to equitable remuneration for the communication to the public of other subject matter and the exclusive right of making available a musical work or other subject matter.

(6) Pursuant to Directive 2001/29/EC of the European Parliament and of the Council of 22 May 2001 on the harmonisation of certain aspects of copy-

---

[1] A5-0478/2003.
[2] See recital 29.

right and related rights in the information society[3] and Council Directive 92/100/EEC of 19 November 1992 on rental right and lending right and on certain rights related to copyright in the field of intellectual property,[4] a licence is required for each of the rights in the online exploitation of musical works. These rights may be managed by collective rights managers that provide certain management services to right-holders as agents or by individual right-holders themselves.

(7) Licensing of online rights is often restricted by territory, and commercial users negotiate in each Member State with each of the respective collective rights managers for each right that is included in the online exploitation.

(8) In the era of online exploitation of musical works, however, commercial users need a licensing policy that corresponds to the ubiquity of the online environment and which is multi-territorial. It is therefore appropriate to provide for multi-territorial licensing in order to enhance greater legal certainty to commercial users in relation to their activity and to foster the development of legitimate online services, increasing, in turn, the revenue stream for right-holders.

(9) Freedom to provide collective management services across national borders entails that right-holders are able to freely choose the collective rights manager for the management of the rights necessary to operate legitimate online music services across the Community. That right implies the possibility to entrust or transfer all or a part of the online rights to another collective rights manager irrespective of the Member State of residence or the nationality of either the collective rights manager or the rights-holder.

(10) Fostering effective structures for cross-border management of rights should also ensure that collective rights managers achieve a higher level of rationalisation and transparency, with regard to compliance with competition rules, especially in the light of the requirements arising out of the digital environment.

(11) The relationship between right-holders and collective rights managers, whether based on contract or statutory membership rules, should include a minimum protection for right-holders with respect to all categories of rights that are necessary for the provision of legitimate online music services. There should be no difference in treatment of right-holders by rights managers on the basis of the Member State of residence or nationality.

(12) Royalties collected on behalf of right-holders should be distributed equitably and without discrimination on the grounds of residence, nationality, or category of rightholder. In particular, royalties collected on behalf of right-holders in Member States other than those in which the right-holders are resident or of which they are nationals should be distributed as effectively and efficiently as possible.

(13) Additional recommendations on accountability, rightholder representation in the decision-making bodies of collective rights managers and dispute resolution should ensure that collective rights managers achieve a higher level of rationalisation and transparency and that rightholders and commercial users can make informed choices. There should be no difference in treatment on the basis of category of membership in the collective

---

[3] [2001] O.J. L167/10.
[4] [1992] O.J. L346/61. Directive as amended by Directive 2001/29/EC.

rights management society: all right-holders, be they authors, composers, publishers, record producers, performers or others, should be treated equally.

(14) It is appropriate to continuously assess the development of the online music market,

HEREBY RECOMMENDS;

Definitions

1. For the purposes of this Recommendation the following definitions are applied:

(a) 'management of copyright and related rights for the provision of legitimate online music services at Community level' means the provision of the following services: the grant of licences to commercial users, the auditing and monitoring of rights, the enforcement of copyright and related rights, the collection of royalties and the distribution of royalties to rightholders;

(b) 'musical works' means any musical work or other protected subject matter;

(c) 'repertoire' means the catalogue of musical works which is administered by a collective rights manager;

(d) 'multi-territorial licence' means a licence which covers the territory of more than one Member state;

(e) 'collective rights manager' means any person providing the services set out in point (a) to several right-holders;

(f) 'online rights' means any of the following rights:

    (i) the exclusive right of reproduction that covers all reproductions provided for under Directive 2001/29/EC in the form of intangible copies, made in the process of online distribution of musical works;

    (ii) the right of communication to the public of a musical work, either in the form of a right to authorise or prohibit pursuant to Directive 2001/29/EC or a right to equitable remuneration in accordance with Directive 92/100/EEC, which includes webcasting, internet radio and simulcasting or near-on-demand services received either on a personal computer or on a mobile telephone;

    (iii) the exclusive right of making available a musical work pursuant to Directive 2001/29/EC, which includes on-demand or other interactive services;

(g) 'right-holder' means any natural or legal person that holds online rights;

(h) 'commercial user' means any person involved in the provision of online music services who needs a licence from right-holders in order to provide legitimate online music services;

(i) 'reciprocal representation agreement' means any bilateral agreement between collective rights managers whereby one collective rights manager grants to the other the right to represent its repertoire in the territory of the other.

General

2. Member States are invited to take the steps necessary to facilitate the growth of legitimate online services in the Community by promoting a regulatory environment which is best suited to the management, at Community level, of copyright and related rights for the provision of legitimate online music services.

The relationship between right-holders, collective rights managers and commercial users

3. Right-holders should have the right to entrust the management of any of the online rights necessary to operate legitimate online music services, on a territorial scope of their choice, to a collective rights manager of their choice, irrespective of the Member State of residence or the nationality of either the collective rights manager or the right-holder.

4. Collective rights managers should apply the utmost diligence in representing the interests of right-holders.

5. With respect to the licensing of online rights the relationship between right-holders and collective rights managers, whether based on contract or statutory membership rules, should, at least be governed by the following:

(a) right-holders should be able to determine the online rights to be entrusted for collective management;

(b) right-holders should be able to determine the territorial scope of the mandate of the collective rights managers;

(c) right-holders should, upon reasonable notice of their intention to do so, have the right to withdraw any of the online rights and transfer the multi territorial management of those rights to another collective rights manager, irrespective of the Member State of residence or the nationality of either the collective rights manager or the right-holder;

(d) where a right-holder has transferred the management of an online right to another collective rights manager, without prejudice to other forms of cooperation among rights managers, all collective rights managers concerned should ensure that those online rights are withdrawn from any existing reciprocal representation agreement concluded amongst them.

6. Collective rights managers should inform right-holders and commercial users of the repertoire they represent, any existing reciprocal representation agreements, the territorial scope of their mandates for that repertoire and the applicable tariffs.

7. Collective rights managers should give reasonable notice to each other and commercial users of changes in the repertoire they represent.

8. Commercial users should inform collective right managers of the different features of the services for which they want to acquire online rights.

9. Collective rights managers should grant commercial users licences on the basis of objective criteria and without any discrimination among users.

Equitable distribution and deductions

10. Collective rights managers should distribute royalties to all right-holders or category of right-holders they represent in an equitable manner.

11. Contracts and statutory membership rules governing the relationship between collective rights managers and rightholders for the management, at Community level, of musical works for online use should specify whether and to what extent, there will be deductions from the royalties to be distributed for purposes other than for the management services provided.

12. Upon payment of the royalties collective rights managers should specify vis-a-vis all the right-holders they represent, the deductions made for purposes other than for the management services provided.

Non-discrimination and representation

13. The relationship between collective rights managers and right-holders, whether based on contract or statutory membership rules should be based on the following principles:

(a) any category of right-holder is treated equally in relation to all elements of the management service provided;

(b) the representation of right-holders in the internal decision making process is fair and balanced.

Accountability

14. Collective rights managers should report regularly to all right-holders they represent, whether directly or under reciprocal representation agreements, on any licences granted, applicable tariffs and royalties collected and distributed.

Dispute settlement

15. Member States are invited to provide for effective dispute resolution mechanisms, in particular in relation to tariffs, licensing conditions, entrustment of online rights for management and withdrawal of online rights.

Follow-up

16. Member States and collective rights managers are invited to report, on a yearly basis, to the Commission on the measures they have taken in relation to this Recommendation and on the management, at Community level, of copyright and related rights for the provision of legitimate online music services.

17. The Commission intends to assess, on a continuous basis, the development of the online music sector and in the light of this Recommendation.

18. The Commission will to consider, on the basis of the assessment referred to in point 17, the need for further action at Community level.

Addressees

19. This Recommendation is addressed to the Member States and to all economic operators which are involved in the management of copyright and related rights within the Community.

Done at Brussels, 18 May 2005.

Index

All references in this index are to paragraph number